New Jersey Governor Brendan Byrne

New Jersey Governor Brendan Byrne

The Man Who Couldn't Be Bought

Donald Linky

FAIRLEIGH DICKINSON UNIVERSITY PRESS
Madison • Teaneck

Published by Fairleigh Dickinson University Press
Copublished by The Rowman & Littlefield Publishing Group, Inc.
4501 Forbes Boulevard, Suite 200, Lanham, Maryland 20706
www.rowman.com

16 Carlisle Street, London W1D 3BT, United Kingdom

British Library Cataloguing in Publication Information Available

Library of Congress Cataloging-in-Publication Data

Linky, Donald.
New Jersey Governor Brendan Byrne : the man who couldn't be bought / Donald Linky.
  pages cm
Includes bibliographical references and index.
ISBN 978-1-61147-742-9 (cloth : alk. paper)—ISBN 978-1-61147-743-6 (electronic)
1. Byrne, Brendan T., 1924- 2. Governors—New Jersey—Biography.
3. New Jersey—Politics and government—1951- I. Title.
F140.22.B97L56 2014
974.9'043092—dc23
[B]
                                                                    2014027171

Printed in the United States of America

To the memory of Susan Jane Byrne,
who knew sorrow, but much joy

Contents

Foreword

My friend and colleague in the Byrne Administration, Don Linky, does a remarkable job revealing so much of the background and life experiences of Brendan Byrne and describing the principal accomplishments of his two terms as governor. It is with some trepidation that I add my reflections on this gifted and complex man who served the State of New Jersey in many capacities over his singular career. Yet, having spent many hours thinking about and discussing with others what truly distinguished Brendan Byrne, and aided immeasurably by Don Linky's work, I find in these chapters some unifying threads about the man that deserve to be called out. In the interest of candor, I am an unabashed admirer of Brendan Byrne and his career and would never profess to be critical or even objective about him so consider my thoughts in that context.

Deeply embedded in the governor's Irish heritage is a sense of fatalism. Much of the history of his ancestors was shaped by others so it is perhaps understandable that notwithstanding his ambition and the example set by his family, he might concede that occasionally events outside his own control influenced his career, such as the post-Watergate political climate which bolstered the candidacies of honest, reform-minded politicians around the country and in New Jersey. Supplementing this fatalism was an extraordinary grounding in his outlook on life. I recall asking him one day, in the midst of several crises, how he remained so calm: he replied that on a return flight from a bombing mission over Europe when his survival was uncertain, he achieved a perspective about what was important in life that remained with him ever since. It is that balanced view of life and his somewhat limited ability to control it that explains, to me at least, his fearless tendency to draw lines in the sand on issues of great importance (the Pinelands, the rescue of the

Meadowlands Complex, and the revitalization of Atlantic City for example) and to dare the political establishment to cross it. It is a trait so uncommon in successful political leaders that it begs to be called out about Brendan Byrne. One may wonder whether there will ever be another governor who can boast of accomplishments as significant as his.

Combine that fatalism and "groundedness" with personal courage, deeply rooted respect for his family and their traditions, a keen and questioning intellect, and an acute sense of what is right and wrong and you achieve the moral and intellectual self-confidence that enabled Brendan to be such a gifted leader. Quite simply, I think, he just believed that when he was right on an issue and steadfastly advocated for it, others would eventually come along. And often, they did.

Brendan Byrne, as governor, was a modern progressive leader, deeply convinced that talented, principled, and well-meaning people of diverse backgrounds could, through government, achieve significant improvement in the quality of life. Only a man of such beliefs with a great sense of his own strengths would assemble such a diverse cabinet and staff of extremely talented and, for the 1970s, so many exemplary women, many with national reputations for excellence in their fields. These colleagues dramatically reformed environmental regulations, innovated health care, made government more open and responsive, saved the Pinelands, and improved public transportation to name just a handful of areas where his administration had a deep and sustaining impact.

Finally, it should be noted that aside from his unparalleled public accomplishments and his intellect, Brendan Byrne is a complex and perhaps enigmatic human being. While his keen mind might intimidate some, and his self-confidence can be mistaken for arrogance at times, neither reaction would be warranted. He is a gifted humorist and a very loyal friend. At his core, he is a devoted father who takes much pride in the accomplishments of his children and grandchildren. He speaks of his former wife, Jean, with affection and admiration and he revels in the success and ebullience of his current wife, Ruthi Zinn Byrne who has helped him settle into the life of an immensely admired, respected, and distinguished former governor.

He continues to be sought out for advice and counsel by his successors and so many of his friends and family. He has earned the tribute to his character and to his career that is comprehensively expressed in this book.

John J. Degnan

Introduction

"Some people think he was only the first of a long line of bastards to be New Jersey's governor," Brendan Byrne liked to say in referring to William Franklin, the last Royal governor of the New Jersey colony and the illegitimate son of Benjamin Franklin.

Nearly 200 years after the younger Franklin, who remained loyal to the Crown as his father became a leader of the rebellion, was arrested and imprisoned by angry colonists in the tumult leading to the Revolution, Brendan Byrne was elected in the state's largest landslide in 1973 as "the man who couldn't be bought." Although he escaped Governor Franklin's fate, within months after Byrne took office, the label of "bastard" was one of the few epithets not tossed his way. In the backlash to his advocacy of the state's first income tax, he was called "a dilettante," "an inept politician," and "an egotist." With less venom, others called him an "enigma," perplexed by his intentions. Dismissed as "one-term Byrne," few thought he would risk the humiliation of running for a second term. Yet he would engineer New Jersey's most dramatic political comeback, and leave office with a record compared to that of Woodrow Wilson, his most famous predecessor as New Jersey's governor.

To a remarkable degree, Brendan Byrne's personal story reflects a template of the American experience. After emigrating from Ireland in the middle of the nineteenth century, his grandparents faced poverty and discrimination in their new land. They struggled to support their families, accepting whatever work came their way, serving as gardeners and coachmen to the wealthy who lived above them in mansions on the top of the hill. Like many, some worked on factory assembly lines and raised their children in the cramped quarters of industrial cities subject, as the Byrnes came to know, to sudden disease and devastation.

In the twentieth century, a new generation succeeded in working their way up to careers as plumbers and accountants, policemen and firemen, sometimes joining through politics to help in finding jobs or establishing their own businesses. During the 1920s, Frank Byrne, son of a man who tended the horses and gardens of the wealthy, succeeded as an insurance salesman, began his own family, allowing his son Brendan and his siblings a brief taste of prosperity. But after the optimism of the decade spurred Frank to start a business of his own, his new venture and the family's upward path were brought to an abrupt halt by the Great Depression. Along with millions of others in the 1930s, the Byrnes were forced to make do with less—having meals without meat, lacking the pennies to go to the movies. Still a teenager uncertain of his abilities, Brendan Byrne would fight in World War II, finding that he could more than hold his own with his older peers, returning to civilian life with a new confidence and the means to better his life.

As he readily admitted, Byrne's life and career owed much to good luck. In his childhood, he overcame a potentially fatal illness. He survived bombing missions that suffered one of the highest casualty rates of the war. As a young lawyer, chance meetings gave him life-changing mentors in a governor and a state chief justice who helped guide his legal and political careers. The job he coveted of county prosecutor opened up only after two key politicians failed to agree on another choice. The unprecedented release by the FBI of transcripts of mobsters talking about the futility of corrupting the "boy scout" brought him to the attention of the press and public. Corruption scandals tainting state and federal Republican leaders coincidentally arose, making his personal profile as an incorruptible prosecutor and judge an ideal fit with a cynical public's desire for change. Perhaps most critically, as he neared the end of his turbulent first term, the inability of his opponents to unite allowed his nomination for a second term in an election in which a strong majority of voters in his own party rejected him.

Yet if luck played a part, Byrne also demonstrated the persistence and skill to seize an opportunity when it came by. In arguing his way into Harvard Law School, obtaining his appointment as prosecutor, seeing a narrow opening for reelection, pushing for his proposals on the income tax and the pinelands, he demonstrated a "gutsy" side that contrasted with, perhaps contradicted, his inherent shyness.

Byrne's election as governor in November 1973 occurred in a time of transition for the state and its politics. In 1947, New Jersey adopted a new constitution that, for the first time, gave its governor strong formal powers, indeed making the chief executive's authority perhaps the strongest of any state in vetoing legislation, making appointments, and managing the state government.

But despite the   ority, governors still worked within a
politi   ower and concerns. On major issues,
a   opposition or gaining support from
b   confront problems confronting the
s   tate budgets and workforces of any
                                   liticians and voters resisted raising
                                   explain the absence of a state-
                                   to psychological and spiritual
                                   'ego" and a "soul." The state's
                                   1 corruption, organized crime,
                                   cities—all had taken their toll.
                                   public esteem: (Woody Allen:
                                   d, not unlike certain parts of
                                   kes me want to die!").
                                   eels of the sudden surge in
                                   Petroleum Exporting Coun-
                                   ow that only exacerbated
                                   sector. Soon after taking
                                   ergy shortages, which at
                                   ...ories, stores, and schools,
                                   jobless rates not seen since the

                                   coupled with national and state
                                   not an easy fit as a politician or
                                   h came so naturally to his father
                                   oncern for engaging in the back-
                                   e state's politics. Some viewed
                                   nought his persona bordered on
arrogance, with his own Ivy League pedigree and those of his key confidants provoking distrust among large circles of street-schooled politicians. Critics targeted his propensity for travel, volleying with celebrities on tennis courts, and enjoying other perks of his office. Saying simply "that's the way I am," he rejected pleas by even his closest advisers to tailor his image as "hypocrisy," declining to play the role of what most expected of a governor. Apart from issues of style, his reforms in curtailing the barter in jobs, contracts, and other benefits, which had previously tainted his predecessors, eroded the rewards long viewed as the expected payback for loyalty of key politicians and supporters, further undermining his own base.

At other times Byrne would further perplex his supporters, stubbornly pressing for the politically volatile income tax only months after running for office saying there was no need for one in the "foreseeable future," sparking the backlash which nearly swept him from office. At the depth of his fall in approval, he would stubbornly strike out to pursue issues with little political payback like the Pinelands, then stretching his legal powers to get his way.

To be sure, after eight years in office, Byrne had not eliminated all the New Jersey jokes (some of which he liked to tell himself), but it would be hard to argue that he had not given people other things to talk about. On his watch, he had overseen development of the Meadowlands, approval of the income tax, preservation of the Pinelands, casino gambling in Atlantic City, creation of New Jersey Transit, opening of Liberty State Park, electoral and fiscal reforms, and a host of other initiatives. Byrne's long-term legacy continues to be debated. But judged by his own terms—that governors should be measured by the personal stamp they left on the state—even his harshest critics would find it difficult to argue that Brendan Byrne as governor did not make a difference in producing lasting change to New Jersey.

I confess to a certain amount of bias in undertaking this project. I worked in the Byrne administration, initially as an assistant counsel to the governor and, in his second term, was appointed to head the newly created governor's office of policy and planning. During the last six months of the administration, I served concurrently as counsel to the governor and director of policy and planning. After he left office, I assisted the Governor in teaching classes at Princeton and Rutgers universities. I continue to have pride in the accomplishments of the Byrne administration, although from time to time I differed on matters of policy or style. Nonetheless, readers should be aware that while I have strived for a certain level of objectivity, they should look elsewhere for a harsher narrative profiling the life of Brendan Byrne.

I also have made extensive use of resources and related research developed while I coordinated the Brendan T. Byrne Archive at the Eagleton Institute of Politics at Rutgers, now part of the program known as the Center on the American Governor. Much of the initial research for this book was conducted while I was at the Eagleton Institute, including overseeing the series of interviews of Byrne and his associates, conducting subject forums, and researching documents that serve as sources cited in the text of this book. Several Rutgers students assisted me in that project, particularly Melissa Jane Kronfeld and Michael Ford.

Sources for this book and additional research on Byrne's life and administration include the New Jersey State Archives, which hosts the collection of official government documents and other materials of his administration. The current director, Joseph Klett, and its former director, Karl Niederer, along with Bette Epstein and Joanne Nestor of the Archives staff, were helpful in identifying relevant materials in its collections. The Byrne Papers donated by Governor and Mrs. Ruthi Zinn Byrne to the Rutgers University Libraries hold materials and memorabilia on his life and career. Ronald Becker, head of Special Collections and University Archives, and his staff committed extensive time and resources in curating and cataloguing the Byrne collection, as well as assisting in the research for this book. David D'Onofrio drafted a timeline and guide to the Rutgers holdings. Seton Hall University's Monsignor William Noe Field Archives and Special Collections Center is the repository of The Brendan T. Byrne Collection comprised of selected personal and political papers and memorabilia from his political campaigns.

This book was written with the full cooperation of Governor Byrne, who sat for several interviews and provided input in editing the text. I have also benefited greatly from access to interviews of Byrne and others conducted for previous incarnations of this project conducted by Andrew Szanton and Barry Evenchick. Special appreciation is due to the contributions and enthusiasm of Arthur Vanderbilt III, a noted author and former law partner of and assistant counsel to the Governor, who offered helpful suggestions on themes, organization, and editing. Roger Labrie, an experienced editor, provided useful comments in reviewing and revising the text.

Harry Keyishian, Director of the Fairleigh Dickinson University Press and Emeritus Professor of English at Fairleigh Dickinson, offered the needed encouragement and input in the publication of this book. Kalman Goldstein, Fairleigh Dickinson Emeritus Professor of History, also reviewed the manuscript, making helpful suggestions along the way.

Others who reviewed earlier drafts of sections of the manuscript include Jerry Breslin, Barbara Byrne, Brendan T. Byrne, Jr., Michael Catania, Charles Carella, Kathryn Crotty, John Degnan, James Dugan, Barry Evenchick, Fariborz Fatemi, Michael Fedorko, Louis Gambaccini, Clifford Goldman, Martin Greenberg, Lewis Kaden, Joseph Katz, Jeffrey Laurenti, Richard Leone, Terry Moore, Robert Mulcahy III, Steven Perskie, Alan Rosenthal, Arthur Vanderbilt III, Jeffrey Warren, Richard Weinroth, James Zazzali, and Cliff Zukin.

Financial support for this book was largely made possible through the efforts of Ruthi Zinn Byrne, who also provided helpful direction and input in its drafting and publication. The Geraldine R. Dodge Foundation and its president, Christopher J. Daggett, also played a critical role in the evolution and coordination of the project.

While I greatly appreciate the valuable support and assistance of those who have aided this publication, any remaining errors in facts or judgment are entirely my own.

Donald Linky

Chapter 1

The Byrnes and the Brennans of Essex County

Beginnings

In 1887, diphtheria and typhus struck the factory city of Orange in Essex County, New Jersey. Within a single week, six of the nine children of Michael and Margaret "Maggie" Hearn Byrne died—one girl and five boys ranging from an infant to a 14-year-old—leaving three surviving boys aged 10, 7, and 4. When they lost their six children, Maggie and Michael had been married some twenty years; their wedding took place soon after they both emigrated separately from Ireland around the time of the U.S. Civil War. Maggie had come alone by sailing ship to America at age 15; Michael, then 24 years old, had arrived from Ireland with his two brothers.

In the year after she lost her six children, Maggie gave birth to her tenth and last child, Francis Aloysius, soon to be called "Frank." Frank later married Genevieve Brennan, the daughter of Patrick Brennan, another recent immigrant whose father was a stonemason in Ireland. After arriving in the country, Patrick joined the Navy and later worked in a hat factory in Orange, becoming a labor organizer and political activist. On April 1, 1924, Genevieve Brennan Byrne gave birth to Brendan Byrne, who some fifty years later was sworn in as the forty-seventh governor of the state of New Jersey. "My grandmother never spoke to me about the death of her children," Brendan reflected years later. "It was never mentioned, never talked about."[1]

The story of the Byrnes and the Brennans was one of many similar stories of the Irish who came to America. Although the wave of Irish emigration had begun before the American Revolution, it grew sharply through the nineteenth century. Between 1845 and 1852, a potato blight resulted in the Great Famine, with one million dying from starvation and another million leaving Ireland.[2]

1

When the Byrnes and the Brennans came to New Jersey, two million people born in Ireland were living in the United States, with many settling near New York and Boston, the ports where they entered the country. The surging demand for workers in America—to do the hard labor of building bridges, canals, and railroads—persuaded many Irish to escape the desperate conditions in their homeland. But for many of the new arrivals, life was not easy. "At times the New World seemed little better than the world they left behind," wrote one scholar. "The streets were not paved with gold. Indeed, as the rueful joke had it, they were not paved at all and it was the job of the Irish to pave them."[3] Immigrants were forced to take jobs that paid little and were often dangerous; a common expression heard among railroad workers was "an Irishman was buried under every tie."[4] To supplement the meager wages of their men, women worked as chamber maids, cooks, and caretakers of children.

The often unschooled Irish, most of whom were Catholics, competed with newly freed African slaves and other minorities for the available jobs at the bottom of the labor market.[5] During the Civil War, when President Lincoln freed the slaves in the Confederacy through signing the Emancipation Proclamation, Irish workers feared a wave of former slaves coming north would compete with them for jobs. In March of 1863, the nation's first draft had been instituted, which many newly arrived Irish resented as disproportionately targeting them for service.[6] The tension soon sparked clashes in northern cities; in June of that year, according to one historian, "draft officers visited Irish sections of Newark, only to be stoned by local women."[7] In the following month, after a suspiciously high proportion of Irish names were selected in the new draft, riots broke out in Manhattan, continuing for five days and resulting in eleven freed blacks being lynched on lampposts, with recent Irish immigrants prominent leaders of the mobs. "Some of the most vivid stories my grandmother told us," Brendan recalled many years later, "were of the sights of dead blacks hanging on the lampposts in Manhattan."[8]

Michael Byrne and Patrick Brennan each had found their way to the City of Orange in Essex County, a fast-growing industrial center on highlands first known as the "Newark Mountains" but later called the Watchung Mountains (in actuality, hills that do not exceed 500 feet in height).[9] Originally part of Newark, Orange evolved from the initial Watchung settlements of farmers, hunters, and trappers.[10] Soon, however, the highland rivers and streams were harnessed to open mills processing grain and cutting logs into timber, and later in the nineteenth century the energy would provide the power for heavier industry that offered thousands of jobs to the new immigrants.[11]

In 1860, a few years before the Byrnes and the Brennans came to New Jersey, the residents of what was then known as the village of Orange seceded from Newark, legally establishing the community as a separate municipality; a few years later—as would be the case with several other New Jersey towns—Orange itself fragmented as some of its own neighborhoods separated to incorporate themselves as the independent municipalities of South Orange, East Orange, and West Orange. The new municipal governments—sometimes founded as a result of disputes over spending and taxes to pay for the costs of establishing paid police, fire, and street departments—would become a major source of stable, better-paying jobs for Irish-Americans as they sought to move up the scale from lower-income work as laborers and factory workers.[12]

By the latter half of the nineteenth century, Orange had evolved into one of the nation's leading industrial towns, with its factories making shoes, boots, other leather goods, and most notably, hats. To house the influx of factory workers and their families, tightly packed multiple-family dwellings and tenements were built surrounding a small business district. The 1880 census shows Michael and Maggie Byrne living with their five children on Monroe Street in Orange.[13]

In 1888, the year after the six Byrne children died, Maggie gave birth to her tenth and last child, Frank, Brendan's father. Three months after Frank was born, the family moved to the less-populated West Orange, evidently to seek a healthier environment and distance themselves from the tragic loss they had suffered in Orange.[14]

In West Orange, the family lived in a two-story, four-bedroom home on the slope below Llewellyn Park, a gated enclave of homes in West Orange built in 1853 for the affluent as the first planned residential community in the nation. Llewellyn Park was landscaped in the style of New York's Central Park, featuring ornamental trees, shrubs, and flowers along winding paths and streams. In 1865, a glowing account in the *New York Times* described Llewellyn Park, then with twenty-five homes, as "once a rough, shaggy mountain side, now transformed into an enchanted sound, or fairy land."[15] In 1887, the year that Maggie and Michael Byrne lost their six children, Llewellyn Park gained its most prominent homeowner when Thomas Edison moved his family to a new twenty-nine-room home, near the laboratories that he also had relocated to West Orange, which at their peak employed 10,000 workers.[16] As Newark, Paterson, Jersey City and other cities became increasingly industrialized, the health benefits of living above the pollution drew residents to West Orange and the other highland towns on the Watchung Mountains. Many of the Byrne family's neighbors in West Orange included those employed in servicing the affluent Llewellyn Park homeowners, working at the Edison laboratories and offices or commuting to work in Orange or other nearby factory cities.

Perhaps with some exaggeration, Michael Byrne's occupation would be listed in published records as a "landscape architect" after the family moved to West Orange, but it appears in reality that he worked at various jobs serving the affluent Llewellyn Park homeowners as a gardener and liveryman tending their horses and stables. In the 1900 census, when he was 58 years old, Michael's occupation is listed as "coachman" and that of his younger brother Patrick, who lived next door with his family, as "gardener." The occupations of Michael and Maggie's three eldest sons—Michael Jr. (aged 25), William (20), and John (17)—are described, respectively, as "plumber," "bookkeeper," and "stenographer." Then 13 years old, Frank, Brendan's father, is the only child recorded by the census as a student still in school.[17]

Patrick Brennan, the father of Brendan Byrne's mother Genevieve, followed a somewhat different course. Soon after coming from Ireland to the United States as a laborer, Patrick joined the Navy and was honorably discharged in 1873.[18] In the same year, at age 28, Patrick married Anna Cullinane, also a recent immigrant from County Roscommon, at Saint John's Church in Orange. Patrick and Anna would have eight children, including their daughter Genevieve. At his confirmation in 1934 when he was 10 years old, the name of Genevieve's brother Thomas, who died earlier in the same year, was taken by Brendan Byrne as his middle name.

After his marriage to Anna, Patrick found work at a hatmaking factory in Orange. Known as "hat-maker to the world," Orange hosted at the industry's peak in the 1890s more than thirty hatmaking factories employing some 3,700 workers who made nearly five million hats annually. The industry's roots went back to the 1790s, when the first settlers began trapping beaver and muskrat, softening their pelts by soaking in the clear mountain water, later fashioning the pelts into hats and coats. Hemlock trees were tapped for tannic acid for the tanning of animal hides to produce leather that, in addition to hats, could be used to make shoes, saddles, bags, and other products.[19] While the jobs in the hatmaking factories were perhaps a step up from the hard labor that other immigrants accepted, they were nonetheless not without risk; chemicals, including mercury, used in processing pelts for hats were suspected causes of the widespread incidence of neurological and emotional problems in workers (arguably the origin of the expression "mad as a hatter").[20]

As their numbers increased, the political clout of Irish-Americans grew rapidly as they joined in labor unions and political organizations. Like many of the new Irish in America who found collective action to be a vehicle for advancement, Patrick Brennan pursued ties with his fellows in social, labor, and political organizations. He joined the Ancient Order of the Hibernians, the fraternal organization originally founded in the 1850s to protect Catholic churches from Protestant attacks; the Hibernians later became an important focus of Irish-American political activity. He was active in the nascent movement to organize factory workers as a member of the Hatters Local at his factory and as a founder of the Knights of Labor, which in several states pushed for adoption of the 8-hour work day and for a ban on child and convict labor. At the age of 50, Patrick was elected an Alderman of Orange, serving from 1899 to 1902; in 1904, he was appointed the Orange Commissioner of Tax Appeals.[21]

Patrick and Anna Brennan's daughter Genevieve met Michael and Maggie Byrne's son Frank at the Our Lady of the Valley Church in Orange. In addition to their common roots as members of the new generation of American-born Irish Catholics, their relationship was strengthened by their mutual interest in acting and singing, which they sometimes pursued by performing as leading man and lady in amateur local theater productions.

With fine black hair and classic features, Genevieve initially was cool to the attentions of Frank, a prematurely balding redhead whose family was a bit lower in social prominence than her own. Moreover, she was being courted by another local Irishman, Frank Codey, whose grandson Richard would also serve as New Jersey's governor.[22] Yet Frank's interest in acting and music, complemented by his fine voice and a characteristic persistence—a trait he later would pass on to his children—gradually brought the couple together. In one play in which the two co-starred, there was a scene in which Frank, in his role as the hero, was stabbed in the arm by the villain, with the wound tended to by Genevieve, who stemmed the bleeding by tying her hero's arm with her handkerchief. As was typical in such amateur productions, Genevieve had contributed one of her own handkerchiefs as a prop, offering Frank the opportunity after the play's final performance to show up at Genevieve's home to return the handkerchief. Making the most of the visit, Frank asked her out, initiating what would become a lifelong partnership of the leading man and leading lady.[23]

Frank and Genevieve Byrne would have five children: Thecla was the first to be born in 1914, followed by Francis Jr. (1917), Nancy (1919), Brendan—born on April first of 1924 in Orange Memorial Hospital in the City of Orange—and Muriel, the youngest, born in 1926. Along with their grandmother Maggie, Thecla and Francis Jr.—some 10 and 7 years older than Brendan—often served as surrogates for their parents in rearing Brendan and his younger sister Muriel.

The family lived in the same home that Maggie and Michael Byrne had moved to in 1888 after the death of their six children and in which Frank Byrne had been raised. Brendan's earliest memories were happy ones, even while he recognized that his and neighboring families were less well off than those living above them in Llewellyn Park. "My friends and I could see the good life," Brendan would later remember, "the wealthy life of a country squire, but just above us, just out of reach. There was no bitterness about that. It was just a fact."[24]

Over the years, as her focus turned to her children, Genevieve's passion for theater would ebb, but Frank's continued, even as he, too, had to bow to family and business demands and phase out his performing career. Many years later, Brendan recalled listening to his father in the home's cellar recite long passages or poems that he had memorized—a love of language that left a lasting impression on his young son: "I could hear my father down in the cellar delivering these lines with all the force and poetry of which he was capable, to an audience of no one at all, and I was touched by that. He really cared about the words."[25]

From his boyhood, Brendan followed his father's example, indeed often committing to memory several of his father's favorites such as the Irish patriot Robert Emmett's response in 1803 to the judge who sentenced him to be hanged, drawn and quartered:

> Let no man write my epitaph. No man can write my epitaph, for as no man who knows my motives and character dares now to vindicate them, let not prejudice or ignorance asperse them. Let them rest in obscurity and peace until other times and other men can do justice to them. When my country takes her place among the nations of the earth, then shall my character be vindicated, then may my epitaph be written.[26]

As a boy, Brendan also was fascinated by his grandmother Maggie's stories of her childhood in Ireland and her early years in America. He was struck by her still apparent bitterness, more than six decades after she left Ireland, at the treatment that the Irish had received at the hands of the English in their homeland and the discrimination they faced in their new nation. Brendan would take from his family's accounts of Irish history "a feeling of resentment—that we Irish just didn't belong, that we should know our place and accept our lot. It was this sense that pushed many Irish to work harder and join together to get ahead."[27]

Maggie made sure that Catholic teachings of humility were instilled in the children and that they attended church on Sundays and holidays. At Sunday dinner, Frank often quizzed the children on which gospel lesson had been the subject of the priest's sermon. The legacy of the sudden deaths of Michael and Maggie's six children, although it was not a topic discussed in the presence of Brendan and his siblings, also must have left a sense of fatalism, hope, and faith—that any of their problems could not approach the despair of that loss. At an early age, Brendan could remember hearing his father say that "any Byrnes who were alive and well should consider ourselves lucky."[28]

The family's Catholic faith had the strongest impact on Thecla, the oldest child, who served as a "second mother" to Brendan and his younger sister Muriel; as Brendan would remember, Thecla "reminded us that God loved everyone, rich or poor." For a time when he was six or seven, Brendan thought about becoming a priest, but he was troubled by some aspects of his Catholic upbringing. "I admired the strong sense of right and wrong of Catholic teaching," he later said. "But I found its application in real life sometimes overly simplistic." During the two years that he went to Catholic school, he recalled, "the nuns would rap me across the knuckles whenever I wrote with my left hand to correct my natural left-handedness. I just thought this was so rigid, based on their stubborn belief that 'right is better than left.'"[29] A more positive lesson from his religious upbringing that stayed with Brendan was a respect for the importance of moral thinking. "Whether it was a Catholic thing or just my nature," he later related, "I did sometimes have a real sense of guilt." In sixth grade, he was the only member of the class caught clowning around when his teacher left the room, earning a "D" in "deportment" for the quarter. "I really felt badly about that, and was ashamed when I brought my report card to my parents."[30]

The Byrnes' local Catholic Church—Our Lady of Lourdes—was within a mile's walk of their home, and the children were expected to be regulars at the confessions heard by Father Joe Connors on Saturday afternoons.[31] Brendan easily mastered the routine, confessing "Forgive me, Father, I lied to my mother this week" and triggering a typical penance from the priest: "Then say five 'Hail Mary's'—and make a perfect act of contrition." Reflecting on the process in his senior years, Brendan conceded that while "in one sense, it was a rather empty exercise," he still felt "there was always this sense that a powerful God was watching. Watching *everything*. When Father Connors told us to make a perfect act of contrition, he wasn't telling us to apologize to our victims, but to God."[32]

In addition to the more serious teachings of Father Connors, Brendan also was drawn to the priest's love of music. Father Joe penned several popular songs, some under his own name and others under the pseudonym "Pierre Norman." Years later, at a dinner with Frank Sinatra at Manhattan's "21" restaurant after the opening of one of Sinatra's films, Brendan learned that Sinatra himself had recorded Father Joe's songs.[33] On another occasion, when Byrne asked Joe DiMaggio whether he knew Father Connors and received an affirmative response, Byrne suspected that "Father Joe and Joe DiMaggio had done some carousing together."[34] After Father Joe was transferred to a church in another town, his close friends Tommy Dorsey and Glenn Miller both brought their famed bands to entertain to raise money for Father Joe's new church.[35]

Brendan's sister Thecla and brother Frank, who "were more Catholic than I was," attended Catholic schools in downtown Newark. While Brendan also was initially enrolled in a Catholic school about a mile from the Byrne home, for most of his first two school years he was often kept home due to illnesses. "I was a skinny, sickly kid and my mother stuck by me all the way," he recalled in his senior years. "When I had to have my appendix out, she stuck by me. When I was six, I got scarlet fever and she told me she could put me in the hospital or she'd nurse me herself at home if that's what I wanted." He chose to be cared for at home, learning only later that due to the possibility of contagion, "my mother had risked her life doing that." Perhaps in light of the memory of the Byrne family's tragic loss in 1887 of their six children, Genevieve Byrne was, as Brendan recalled, "very proud" that she and her young son successfully battled through his serious illnesses, and they formed a special bond. "To her, I was a little fighter and I could do no wrong. My father was always very nice to me, but there was something extra with my mother. She was my advocate." In the few conflicts between his parents, his mother took his side. "Sometimes my father would turn me down for a second piece of roast beef at Sunday lunch," Brendan recalled, "saying that I had had enough. But my mother would jump in and say, 'Oh, Frank, give him another piece.'"[36] By second grade, his parents decided to send him to the public school, Washington Street Elementary, which was only a block from home, and he would continue attending public schools in West Orange through high school.

From an early age, possibly due to his repeated illnesses that kept him out of school, Brendan also realized that he lacked the outgoing personality of both his father and brother, that "I was shy with people. It was something I never outgrew." But in contrast to his shyness, he developed other lasting traits that that he would describe as "gutsy," a stubborn perseverance in competing, in challenging himself to achieve a goal.[37]

The first year that Brendan could clearly remember was 1928, when he celebrated his fourth birthday. "That was a very good year for America and a good year for my family," Brendan recalled. "The economy was booming. My father sold insurance for the Travelers Insurance Company. He commuted every day into New York City and came back in the evening. He was running the whole Travelers office that sold insurance in the Bronx." Indeed, Frank's business prominence was reflected in his inclusion in a book published in 1928 profiling leading figures in the Bronx, noting that he supervised 200 people in the Travelers office. Another article reported that "starting from scratch" he grew the business of the Bronx office to over $3 million.[38]

For a time, the family was able to enjoy the simple pleasures of prosperity. Frank bought his first car, the Oakland introduced by General Motors as a brand above its low-priced Chevrolet, but below its more upscale Buick. On occasion, Frank packed Brendan and the rest of the family into the car for drives to visit relatives in the nearby city of Elizabeth, proudly showing off both his children and his automobile. In the summer, Frank took the family on occasional excursions to the Jersey Shore, sometimes venturing for stays as far as the Wildwoods with an occasional side trip to Atlantic City. But to

Brendan, trips to the beach had an uncomfortable drawback. "In those days," he explained, "bathing suits were only made of wool. I was allergic to wool and my skin always broke out in a rash."[39]

In the summer of 1928, his parents splurged and shared with two other families the rental of a summer home on the Jersey Shore in the upscale town of Deal. One of the other families was that of Henry O'Neill, an actor who had become a close friend of Frank Byrne since they had first met in amateur theater productions and who later had roles in several movies. Brendan enjoyed the daily walks to the beach, and the games he and his siblings played with the children of the other families. Yet that idyllic seaside stay would be, in the adult Brendan's memory, "the last summer we were rich. My father was doing so well, and the national economy was doing so well that he decided to strike out on his own, start his own business—in 1929."[40]

Frank Byrne's unlucky timing in setting up his own firm to sell insurance before the October 1929 stock market crash that ushered in the Great Depression meant that the family, along with millions of others, would suddenly have very little money. Frank struggled to keep his business afloat, but it ultimately failed about a year after the market crashed. Later, he took a job as an agent in Newark selling insurance for the Colonial Life Insurance Company and kept working to sell insurance through the Depression. He kept up appearances, as well as his dignity, by dressing in a business suit and continuing his daily routine of going to his Newark office, even when it became obvious that on most days he found little or no business to conduct. Often, after returning home and having dinner with the family, he worked into the evening, making cold calls to potential clients, a routine that was never easy in good times and, during the Depression, frequently resulted in the humiliation of the rejections overheard by his youngest son. "My father had a set routine when he phoned to sell insurance," Brendan later remembered, "and when the call ended quickly, I knew he hadn't made a sale."[41]

The family's finances, as Brendan later recalled, "got hit about as hard as you can get hit." No longer would there be luxuries like a summer at the shore; the children would be forced to share and go without, often pushing clothes and shoes far beyond their useful life. "We lived by the saying, 'Use it up. Wear it out. Make it do. Or do without,'" Brendan remembered. Thecla, his eldest sister, used her strong faith as a guide for her younger siblings. "She helped and supported us, but she also drove home the principles of making do, and not complaining. We all hung together."[42] But the pain of doing without could not be completely removed from the lives of the Byrne children. "You could get a special ticket to the Wednesday discount movie at the playground for only three cents," Brendan recalled, "but I'll never forget the feeling of not having the three cents and having to tell my friends I couldn't go with them. I knew not to ask my parents for it."

At times, Frank Byrne was forced to swallow his pride. He borrowed from his mother, who had a little money left from a bequest from her late husband; from his better-off brother, Willie, who was able to keep a job through the Depression working at an insurance agency in New York; and from his brother-in-law, Tom. Willie also had a soft side when it came to the children. "He would come to Sunday lunch at our house and give all of his nieces and nephews a quarter, and I'd take that quarter and go out and buy some candy," Brendan recalled. "For a few days, I'd have some spearmint leaves or coated licorice."[43]

Reflecting some eight decades later on the tough times of the Depression, Brendan said he "learned a two-part lesson—about the importance of having money and the even greater value of a strong family that pulls together in hard times. My parents didn't complain, and they didn't let us complain either."[44] Despite their own diminished circumstances, Frank and Genevieve Byrne would point to images of bread lines and the homeless, extremes of poverty that the Byrnes did not approach. While the Byrnes no longer could afford to eat meat during the week, they had new appreciation for the hot dogs for dinner on Saturday night and, on Sundays, a platter of roast beef for lunch and ham sandwiches for dinner. It was not difficult to find examples of those whose lot was far worse than that of the Byrnes. "People all around West Orange and all over the country were struggling," Brendan remembered. "My parents expected their children to smile through the pain."[45]

In 1932, when he was eight years old, Brendan gained his first political hero with the election of Franklin D. Roosevelt as president. "Roosevelt made an enormous impression on me, and on everyone who lived in America at that time," Brendan would recall. "Proud men were selling apples on the street, but there was Roosevelt, in the newspapers, on the radio, almost like a father, explaining his goals, announcing new programs, taking pleasure in goading the do-nothing Republicans, but always positive in his vision of what a united country could achieve."[46]

The Byrne family, so fond of the spoken word, relished listening to Roosevelt's talks broadcast over the radio. "I loved President Roosevelt's speaking voice," Brendan recounted. "It was dignified and patrician but never stuffy. He had a lot of humor and a love of politics, a love of life."[47] Apart from Roosevelt's comforting talks, Brendan also saw more practical signs of the President's New Deal Programs, as some of his family's friends and neighbors got jobs in projects in West Orange funded by the Civilian Conservation Corps and the Works Progress Administration.

In addition to Roosevelt's talks, the Byrnes also enjoyed listening to programs on the radio, particularly the Sunday night NBC-Radio broadcasts of *The Jack Benny Show* and *The Fred Allen Show*. Brendan marveled at

Benny's impeccable sense of timing, of "milking the long pause," a device that the adult Brendan would copy for his own lighter talks at public events. One of Brendan's favorites was the skit in which—after carefully crafting over his long career the image of a tightwad—Benny was confronted in a mock hold-up by an armed thief who demanded, "Your money or your life!" followed by a long silence finally broken by Benny's shout: "I'm thinking, I'm thinking!"[48]

The Byrnes also followed the news on the radio. Perhaps the most widely reported and debated event of Brendan's childhood was the kidnaping on March 1, 1932, of Charles Augustus Lindbergh, Jr., the twenty-month-old son of the famous aviator and Anne Morrow Lindbergh, from the nursery on the second floor of the Lindbergh's house near Hopewell, some 60 miles southwest of the Byrne's home in West Orange. After an investigation and the payment of a ransom in which both Lindbergh and Norman Schwarzkopf, the head of the New Jersey State Police, were actively involved, the baby's body was discovered in the woods some 4 miles from the Lindbergh home on May 12. The ensuing "trial of the century" was prosecuted by New Jersey Attorney General David Wilentz, who in 1935 won a still-controversial conviction of Bruno Richard Hauptmann, leading to Hauptmann's execution in the electric chair at Trenton State Prison on April 3, 1936. "My mother never thought Hauptmann could pull off the kidnaping on his own," Brendan recalled years later. "A lot of other people, both then and now, agreed with her."[49]

Brendan would later assert that "I've wanted to be a lawyer since I was 12 years old." Curiously, however, he could not pin down whether there was a specific person or event—such as Hauptmann's execution, which, in fact, took place two days after Brendan's twelfth birthday—that triggered his interest. At about the same time, Brendan also targeted Harvard Law School as his school of choice, but again could not recall how he came to know of Harvard. "Somehow, I learned that Harvard was the best law school and that the best students went there," he said years later. "If it was the best, that's where I wanted to go."[50]

Another prominent news item that the Byrnes followed closely was the fire that consumed the ocean liner *Morro Castle* on September 8, 1934, and which ultimately led to the ship drifting ashore on the beach near the Convention Hall in Asbury Park on the Jersey Shore. Some 134 of the 539 passengers and crew died of burns, smoke inhalation, or other injuries. Frank Byrne packed up Brendan and the rest of the family to go see the scorched wreck, joining thousands of others. The excursion provided Brendan's brother Frank—a budding doctor—a chance to practice his medical skills; after a woman walking on the jetty rocks at the shoreline tripped and sprained her ankle, Frank went to her aid by fashioning an impromptu wrap and bandage. Like the

Lindbergh kidnaping, the *Morro Castle* fire would continue to spark debate for decades over how it had occurred and who was to blame.[51]

Brendan committed most of his attention and energy to what became a lifelong fascination with sports, both as a participant and a fan. Brendan's height, which as a teenager reached nearly 6 feet, led to his playing in pick-up basketball games, but his favorite sport was, and would remain, baseball. After overcoming his early health problems, he played baseball and football with a local team called the Rangers. His teammates included friends who would grow up to be priests, like the Hourihan brothers, as well as the occasional tomboy like Sylvia Levine, the daughter of a local storeowner. Brendan also played hundreds of informal games on the field just below Llewellyn Park on Nanny Goat Hill, with its infield littered with rocks. Usually playing first base, Brendan was particularly adept at using his considerable speed to catch foul balls. But the overgrown area past the foul line also was where Thomas Edison was growing goldenrod plants for his experiments in developing artificial rubber (in collaboration with Henry Ford and the tire magnate Harvey Firestone). After a series of incursions into Edison's goldenrod, Brendan and the other boys were warned by Edison's guards to stop trampling the inventor's plants.[52]

When Frank Byrne returned home in the evening, he often played ball with his sons and their friends. At times, they ran afoul of "a crotchety old grouch named Mr. Beetle" who lived on one side of the Byrne home. Their neighbor had various complaints, including the scraggly Byrne lawn resulting from the many games played on it. Frank Byrne would dismiss Beetle's concern by curtly informing him, "We're not raising grass; we're raising children." But when baseballs hit by Brendan started landing in Mr. Beetle's prized rose bushes, Frank asked his son to change from his natural left-handed stance to hitting right-handed; as a right-handed batter, Brendan's "home runs" landed on the other side of the Byrne home, where a friendlier family, the Underwoods, were much more tolerant of the incoming baseballs. The forced shift to being a right-handed batter cut short what Brendan felt could have been a budding career in the majors. "I was never the hitter that I'd been batting lefty," he remembered some eight decades later, "So I have to say it was Mr. Beetle and his rose bushes that ruined my hopes of one day playing for the St. Louis Cardinals."[53]

Most residents of West Orange, located some 20 miles from Times Square, divided their loyalties among the New York teams—the Yankees, Giants, and Dodgers. But Brendan picked up on his father's affection for the famed Saint Louis Cardinals "Gashouse Gang" and its fiery player-manager, Frankie Frisch. A New York native known as "the Fordham Flash," Frisch was one of the few college graduates of his time to play in the major leagues. In 1934, with Frisch at second base, Johnny "Pepper" Martin at third, Leo "the Lip" Durocher at shortstop, and Joe "Ducky" Medwick in the outfield, the Cardinals won twenty of their last twenty-five games to just catch the New York Giants in the pennant race, and then went on to win the World Series over the Detroit Tigers.[54]

The team's star pitcher was Jerome Hanna "Dizzy" Dean, who won thirty games that season (the last National League pitcher to do so); his brother Paul (labeled "Daffy" by the press) contributed nineteen more wins. The Dean brothers would account for two wins each of the four victories making the Cardinals the 1934 Series champions. When the Cardinals came to town to play the Giants that season, Frank Byrne took Brendan to the Polo Grounds on the day that Dizzy Dean was pitching against the Giants ace, Carl Hubbell. Dean beat Hubbell 8-3, a memory that stuck in the 10-year-old Brendan's mind; nearly eighty years later, he recalled "I went home very happy."[55] Brendan also enjoyed the swagger of Dean, an Arkansas native who shrewdly used his country-bumpkin image to draw attention to himself and his value to the team. One of Dean's more lasting quotes—"It ain't braggin' if you done it"—would later be inserted by the adult Byrne in his own talks.[56]

Like other Irishmen of his generation, Frank Byrne turned to politics as a vehicle for advancement and to expand the circle of his friends and associates. Politics came naturally to the gregarious and articulate Frank Byrne; indeed, it was a comfortable extension of the skills he had exhibited as an actor and singer. To his more withdrawn son Brendan, the ease with which his father worked with political colleagues and interacted with constituents was a trait he greatly admired, but when he launched his own political career many years later, would never quite master. "Dad just enjoyed people," Brendan remembered. "He got a kick out of sitting down with a guy and finding a solution to a problem." Brendan also recognized that his brother Frank shared their father's comfort with people: "when Frank took me to a party at someone's house, I was the one who wanted to leave early and Frank would want to stay longer. I just couldn't reach out to people the way my father and brother could."[57]

At the age of 22, Frank was appointed West Orange tax assessor, initiating a public career in which, for over fifty years, he would serve in several appointed and elected positions, aided by the growing political clout of Irish-Americans in the Democratic Party. From the 1930s through the 1960s, the political and ethnic makeup of West Orange was roughly similar to that of many other towns in northeastern New Jersey. In West Orange, one voting ward was dominated by those better-off families who lived "up on the hill" where Llewellyn Park stood—primarily Protestant, with some residents even descended from the early colonial settlers from Britain, Sweden, and Germany. Over the years, however, those families had been joined by newer Catholic immigrants from Ireland and Italy, as well as by Jews dispersed from Europe, with the respective groups typically settling near each other in discrete neighborhoods at the bottom of the hill. Election tickets for office increasingly became balanced as the old-line WASPs were forced to share power with candidates from the Irish, Italian, and Jewish constituencies. From time to time, one ethnic group might be ascendant, but it was always an evolving balance that demanded compromise and respect.

In 1938, Frank was elected to the West Orange Town Commission, the municipal governing body. By law, town elections were nonpartisan, without party labels identifying each candidate, but in reality Frank's election swung majority control of the Commission from the Republicans to the Democrats. He served on the Commission for fourteen years, including as the public safety director supervising the police and fire departments, and as chair of the West Orange Zoning Board of Adjustment. In 1940, Frank was elected as an alternate delegate at the Democratic National Convention pledged to President Roosevelt's nomination for reelection, and in that year's general election Frank was the Democratic nominee for Essex County Clerk, losing in an election in which Democrat Charles Edison, Thomas Edson's son, was elected governor of New Jersey. In 1952, Governor Alfred Driscoll, a Republican, appointed Frank to the Essex County Tax Board, the body overseeing property tax assessments and appeals, and he was subsequently reappointed by Democratic Governors Robert Meyner and Richard Hughes, serving as the Board president for three terms until his retirement in 1970.[58]

During his promising early career with Travelers Insurance, Frank's political contacts must have facilitated his success in selling insurance; later, during the Depression, as his own insurance business suffered, the small income he made from public positions was increasingly important for meeting the family's basic needs. As the economy contracted and private sector jobs became scarce, the remaining government jobs became increasingly prized for stability and security. Brendan's Uncle Joe, one of his mother's brothers, was able to keep his job as the head of operations at the Orange Post Office, the highest nonpolitical position at the facility.

One lesson that the father was able to pass to his son was an uncompromising stance on honesty and integrity in politics. "Dad was honest, and he expected those he dealt with to be honest also," Brendan later recounted. But Frank Byrne's principles sometimes placed him at odds with the highly tolerant political culture of his day, which featured many examples of politicians who had chosen another path. Years later, Brendan as governor would sum up the life of perhaps New Jersey's most famed political boss: "The mayor of Jersey City, Boss Frank Hague, had been born poor and honest but, through unstinting hard work, had overcome those handicaps."[59] One of the few times that Frank Byrne lost an election, for the West Orange municipal committee, was when he publicly called out the mayor for having the town spend $20,000 to control flooding, work that benefited the mayor's own property. When the mayor demanded an apology, Brendan recounted that his father replied, "I'll apologize when you return the money."[60]

Of the local Irishmen that Frank Byrne worked with in politics, perhaps the most significant was Ben Degnan, the mayor of West Orange from the late 1930s to the late 1940s. For most of that time, Frank Byrne, in his capacity as the town's public safety director, appointed Jim Degnan, the mayor's brother, as the municipal court judge. While Ben Degnan usually was an ally of Frank Byrne's in local and county politics, the two Democrats occasionally differed over policy or appointments. Many years later, Judge Degnan's son John, who would play a significant role in Brendan Byrne's political history, recalled the part that politics played in integrating Irish-Americans into the larger society. "Like most immigrant groups, like many of them," Degnan said in an interview, "politics was a way up and out for the Irish Catholic community in Essex County. They did it for two reasons. They broke out of the stereotypical buckets they were put in. And they also did it in my experience based on a real perception that they could influence the lives of people they cared about. So some of it was self-interest and some of it was true generosity."[61]

Like their move up the economic ladder, the Irish had to struggle for a role in government. "It was a rough and tumble politics," Degnan continued. "They wrested control of West Orange . . . from what I would call the traditional WASP control. And began to establish themselves as the power base. So there was a Moran and a Quinn and a Degnan and a Byrne on the town commission. And they did some patronage. They provided jobs, personal assistance, basically helped people in a personal way."[62]

Despite the tight family finances and his own early health issues, Brendan enjoyed life in West Orange. His parents, grandmother, and siblings were good talkers, and there were enough visits from other relatives, neighbors, friends, and Frank's political and business associates to keep the Byrne home a lively hub of conversation, jokes, and gossip. "Our home was always an active place with people coming and going," Brendan later recalled. "On Sundays, neighbors or relatives would visit and bring cakes and candy or we would go to their homes."[63] Within the household, Brendan's grandmother Maggie could be an intimidating presence, sometimes asserting her will and opinions against her more reserved daughter-in-law Genevieve. On Sundays after church, Maggie acted as the hostess, welcoming the relatives, neighbors, and friends who regularly dropped in for talk and food. In fending off requests for recipes of her favorite dishes, such as her prized blueberry cake, she would, as Brendan recalled, boast in her Irish brogue that the ingredients were not important since the secret was in "it's the ways it's cooked."[64]

Brendan never quite shed his innate shyness, but he was a good listener and learned to appreciate a good story and a good joke, lessons he later put to effective use in his public life. Brendan's Uncle Willie, known for his fondness for drink, was the butt of most family jokes; throughout their lives, Brendan and his brother Frank would exchange "Uncle Willie" jokes, trying to top each other. One story had a drunken Uncle Willie stumbling along the sidewalk, only to bump into and knock over a man coming out of an antique shop carrying a grandfather clock. To the man's angry complaint, "Why don't you look where you're going!" Uncle Willie slurred a response, "Why don't you wear a watch like everybody else!"[65]

Looking back, Brendan fondly recalled the simple pleasures offered by his home town. "I liked West Orange. A lot of things about it were appealing to a kid like me. It was just a great little town. It was on a human scale. At least half the places I needed to go in town I could walk to." One of those places was the store of Isidore Levine, whose daughter Sylvia was the tomboy who often joined in the sports played by Brendan and his friends. "In his store," he continued. "Mr. Levine had penny candy and an ice box with drinks in it. For a nickel, I used to buy a chocolate soda that was wonderfully cold. And men came into the store and bought cigars and stood around talking about Franklin Roosevelt, and the New Deal the President was bringing to America."[66]

Despite his interest in sports and his own self-assessment that he was "all grown up, big and strong," in reality Brendan was a scrawny 150 pounds throughout high school as he grew near to his adult height of six feet. At one point, he clashed with his mother when, in a clandestine move in the kitchen to fatten him up, he caught her trying to slip a raw egg into his chocolate milk. Although his thin build posed some risk, he nonetheless tested his mother's patience by making the West Orange High football team in his sophomore year in 1939, where his comparative height made him an asset as a pass-catching end. Brendan's speed also was put to good use; while he did not try out for the track team, in informal races he was able to beat the team's best sprinters. (West Orange High did not have a baseball team, despite Frank Byrne's plea to the principal that one be formed so that Brendan could play.)

At football practice on September 1, 1939, Brendan heard, over a radio in the locker room, the news that soon would shape his life following high school: the invasion by the Germans of Poland, which marked the opening of World War II. "It was a war," Brendan immediately recognized, "I would be fighting in before long."[67]

Later in the season, playing in a game against Eastside High of Paterson, he bent down to catch a low pass and smashed his face into the knee of Eastside's star player, a black kid named Larry Doby. The collision broke Brendan's nose. Doby went on to become a baseball star, beginning with the Negro National League's Newark Eagles for four seasons, leading them to a championship in 1946, before becoming the first black player in the American League as an outfielder and seven-time all-star for the Cleveland Indians.[68] Apart from that collision in the football game, Doby and Byrne had no further contact in their youth, but they would reconnect in later years.

A high school friend with whom Brendan would maintain a lifelong relationship was Jim Sheeran, his classmate at West Orange High. In his senior year, Sheeran quarterbacked West Orange's football team to its first and only state title by defeating Larry Doby's Eastside Paterson High. A few years later, Sheeran would become a celebrated hero of World War II. On D-Day, he parachuted into Normandy with the 101st Airborne Division and, after being captured by the Nazis, orchestrated an escape from his prisoner-of-war train bound for Germany and subsequently fought with the French underground resistance forces. (After the war, Sheeran was elected West Orange's mayor at the age of 35, and later rejoined his high school classmate as the commissioner of the Department of Insurance in Governor Byrne's Cabinet.)[69]

To help the family's finances when he was in high school, Brendan took a job in a shoe store in Orange, a job that kept him from playing high school football after his sophomore year. He made only fifty cents an hour, but the commissions were good. On Saturdays, he worked from nine in the morning until the store's closing at nine at night, sometimes coming home with $65, which he felt "was a lot of money for a teenager to make in one day." Brendan also acquired skills he could put to good use in other contexts. "At first, I wasted a lot of time trying to sell shoes to customers who just weren't ready to buy," he later recounted. "Soon I learned that you had to focus your time on the ones who were serious, and I became a really good salesman with customers who would come back specifically to see me." Indeed, Brendan's success at selling shoes at one point led his father to suggest that, rather than going to college, his son consider opening his own shoe store. Although he wouldn't pursue a career as a shopkeeper, the savings from his time as a shoe salesman would help to pay for college and law school, supplementing his wartime military benefits.[70]

Brendan later attributed the lifelong attention that he gave to the care of his shoes—which he would often continue as governor by leaning under his desk to shine his shoes during meetings—to his job of selling them. "You learn when you work in a shoe store," he recalled, "that no one's going to take your advice about shoes unless your own shoes look sharp." Earlier, he had worked as a locker boy at the well-known Goldman Hotel in West Orange, where his brother was a lifeguard, and Brendan "got a couple a bucks a week but also got to swim." Many years later, he recalled with a smile that one of the things he learned at Goldman's was "how to get yelled at in Yiddish."[71]

"During that time, none of my sisters," Brendan later recalled, "were expected to go to college, but they all worked to help out the family." His sister Thecla worked as a secretary in a real estate firm and Nancy as an aide in a hospital emergency room. His younger sister Muriel would work from 1947 to 1954 as an assistant to Bob Smith, who would become one of the best-known personalities of the early days of television. She started with Smith when he hosted a local New York radio show, where she selected the records he would play on the air, and stayed with him through his rise to become one of the first stars of television as "Buffalo Bob" of the pioneering *Howdy Doody Show*, the most popular children's television show of its time. Muriel's duties included the coveted responsibility of overseeing the selection and coaching of children for the show's "Peanut Gallery," the on-stage audience of children interacting with Buffalo Bob, Howdy, Clarabell and the show's other characters and puppets. Bob Keeshan, the actor who played Clarabell the clown and later went on to even more fame as Captain Kangaroo in the children's television program broadcast for some thirty years, became a good friend of Brendan's. They would go on double dates and years later, despite his conservative leanings, Keeshan would campaign for Brendan's election as governor.[72]

The need to work and make money limited the time Brendan could spend on other interests outside school, and his lingering shyness contributed to his being "scared to death of girls." Indeed, his apparent hostility led to his being labeled "a woman hater" in the high school yearbook. While he thought the charge was an exaggeration, and, in fact, he dated occasionally, he later recalled viewing girls as a "temptation" that could distract him from his single-minded focus on becoming a lawyer. "I was afraid," he confided many years later, "a lovely woman was going to come along and lure me into a marriage that would divert me from Harvard Law School, and my dream of becoming a trial lawyer."[73]

When Brendan did risk female companionship, he typically took his dates to the movies and, when they both felt like extending the evening, to Pals Cabin, the restaurant (founded in 1932 as a clapboard cabin selling hot dogs for a dime) that would remain his longtime favorite. "By 8 p.m. Saturday," he later reminisced with obvious feeling, "Pals already had the Sunday papers, and you could order something, and sit there quietly with your girl, reading the papers. A very warm, comfortable place, classy without being fancy, and I loved it there."[74] Frank Byrne also gave a boost to Brendan's ability to impress his dates by securing tickets—probably through an insurance client—to the radio taping at a Manhattan studio of *The Fred Allen Show*, the program hosted by the popular comedian. Using the tickets to take dates into the City to sit in the audience, Brendan was intrigued by how the show was prepared for broadcast. "I was especially interested in the mechanics of how the show was produced," he later remembered, "the things that you wouldn't know about when you listened on the radio. I watched how the actors picked up their cues and how the sound effects were integrated into the script."[75]

Brendan's dating life also was helped when his father was named in 1938, after his election to the municipal governing body, as the public safety commissioner overseeing the West Orange police and fire departments. In that role, one of Frank's responsibilities was inspecting the Llewellyn Theater on Main Street—the best theater in town. Knowing his son's interest in the movies, Frank Byrne delegated the duty to Brendan. It was an assignment that Brendan undertook very seriously, indeed sometimes three times a week, taking full advantage of the free admission afforded in his quasi-official capacity.[76] He routinely saved each of the movie programs that theaters then handed out, assembling a prized collection that he kept in his bedroom and regularly added to through his graduation from high school.[77]

In addition to eating at Pals, Brendan sometimes traveled, accompanied by his brother Frank, by streetcar or walked the two miles to Orange to eat spaghetti or pizza (somewhat rare at the time) at the Italian restaurant owned by Tony "Two-Ton" Galento, the colorful heavyweight boxer later known for his famous (and ultimately incorrect) boast before his 1939 championship fight with Joe Louis that he would "moida the bum."[78] The trips to Galento's with Frank were at the urging of their parents, who hoped that the hearty Italian fare might put weight on their skinny younger son. "Frank wasn't crazy about his little brother tagging along," Brendan recalled, "until he realized that I only ate half the spaghetti on my plate, and he could have the rest."[79]

Brendan's parents came to watch some of his football games, but he was puzzled by their relatively low-key attitude at the outcomes. "In sports I wanted to be the hero, to win the championships," Brendan would recall, "and my parents didn't get caught up in any of that. That was totally foreign to me as a boy; I needed to win. I *burned* to win."[80] His love of competing, of testing himself against others to achieve a goal, was a trait that he would carry into later life. But it was not until his adult years, particularly after he entered public life, that Brendan understood the wisdom of his parents' example that winning wasn't the most important thing in life. "I realize as I look back," he would reflect, "that another gift my parents gave me was the idea that you play these sports and games hard, you give it your all, but the final scores ultimately don't make a whole lot of difference. When I got older that was quite helpful. You can't live or die by the final score. You do your best, and then let it go."[81]

As the worst years of the Depression passed, Frank Byrne's insurance sales improved somewhat, but the family never returned to the level of prosperity it had previously enjoyed. Frank later was named president of a newly formed bank, the West Orange Savings and Loan Association, but the title was primarily honorific, with the founders of the bank recruiting Frank largely for his contacts within the Irish Catholic community.

In high school, Brendan began to leave behind the somewhat withdrawn personality of his childhood. Gradually, he was assuming the self-described "shy, but gutsy" character that would persist into adulthood, typically seizing opportunities and stubbornly persevering until he achieved his goals. His deep voice led to his frequent selection as the master of ceremonies for events in the school auditorium and his wit led to a growing popularity among his classmates. In his senior year, after declining requests that he run for class president in prior years, he was elected president of the class and president of the debate team. Reflecting later on his interest in debate, Brendan said "I just wanted to perform"—perhaps an echo of his parents' fondness for the stage and his own desire to become a trial lawyer. In preparation for some of his debates, Brendan visited Frank Kingdon, the president of the University of Newark and the father of one of his high school classmates. Kingdon took a special interest in his debate preparation, discussing the topics and giving him reading materials he felt might be helpful.[82]

The positive reaction of his classmates to his sense of humor was not shared by his high school principal, who was concerned that—with only above-average grades—Brendan was not taking a serious enough approach to his studies and was failing to make the most of his intelligence. The principal was, according to Brendan, "one of those men who have absolutely no sense of humor themselves, and consequently dislike seeing it in others. They've been left out of the joke and they react by trying to prevent people from being amusing."[83]

One example Brendan later recalled was, during a debate against another school, he argued against the proposition that a voter referendum be required before the nation could go to war. "Can you imagine," he asked the audience, "that if Hitler invaded, President Roosevelt would have to say, 'We're waiting for the vote from Jersey City.'" The principal told Brendan firmly that "this lighthearted approach was inappropriate for the serious nature" of the proposition.[84]

But despite the principal's efforts to keep his wit in check, Brendan learned that his own love of humor was shared by most others and could be a useful political tool. His clashes with the principal over his use of humor "actually helped my election as senior class president," Brendan recalled. "So many of my classmates thought that the principal had been unfair to me that I was elected. I learned an important life lesson: stick to your guns and trust your sense of humor."[85]

With money remaining tight within the Byrne household and the looming prospect of military service, it appeared highly unlikely that Brendan could achieve his goal of attending college, going to law school and becoming a lawyer. "My father told me he wouldn't have much money to pay for me to go to college," Brendan remembered. "He still wasn't making very much, and my older brother Frank was going to medical school and Dad was doing his best to help with his tuition." His brother's medical education could be financed only with help from other relatives, and Brendan would look only at colleges he could afford with his own savings and any earnings from part-time work he could find after he enrolled. Brendan's need to focus on how he could pay for his education also led to a lifestyle choice: believing that he might have a chance at a college track scholarship as a sprinter, he decided to avoid cigarettes, and later alcohol, paths that he would follow throughout his adult life.[86]

In his senior year at West Orange High, Brendan was at home on Sunday, December 7, 1941. "Everyone else in the house but me," he recalled, "was listening to a football game. I was listening to a dramatization of a Greek play, while shining my shoes. Suddenly, the play was interrupted with the announcement of Pearl Harbor. I thought, 'Well, here we go. I'm going to have to fight in this war.'"[87]

After graduating from high school in June 1942, Brendan worked briefly as a busboy at the Berkeley-Carteret Hotel in Asbury Park, the leading hotel in the shore resort, while sleeping in a bed at the local YMCA. But the job and his stay was brief. "The waitresses were supposed to share their tips," he remembered, "but they stiffed us busboys. After a couple weeks, I quit."[88]

In September, anticipating that he would soon be drafted, Brendan enrolled at Seton Hall College in South Orange, which had been founded in 1856, shortly after establishment of the Archdiocese of Newark, to support the growing Catholic population of northern New Jersey. "Seton Hall was nearby," Brendan later recalled in explaining his decision. "It only cost four dollars a credit, and because it let guys like me, who expected to be drafted at any time, to take one course at a time for 4 to 6 hours a day, . . . we could get a few full course credits even if we were drafted very soon."[89]

As he expected, Brendan was drafted in March 1943 before completing his freshman year at Seton Hall. "I knew it was coming," Brendan later reflected, "but when you open that envelope, you know you're going to war."[90]

Chapter 2

The War

"I Was Lucky"

At the time Brendan was drafted in March 1943, the draftees were allowed to choose either the Army or Navy for their service, and Brendan initially intended to join the Navy. After thinking it over, however, he decided to join the Army, where, as a recent high school graduate, he thought he would be better suited, rather than competing with the higher numbers of college men in the Navy.[1] His brother Frank, who had recently completed his medical education, had already enlisted in the Navy and would later see combat in the Pacific.

After a brief stop in Fort Dix for an assignment, Brendan was sent to Fort Knox in Kentucky to commence training as a tank driver. But he immediately disliked the prospect of spending the rest of the war fighting in the cramped quarters of a tank. "Driving a tank was not my cup of tea," he later admitted. "If I'm going to risk my life, let me at least have a little comfort."[2] When he saw a bulletin board notice that the U.S. Army Air Corps was looking for cadets, he applied, but failed the physical exam on account of high blood pressure. Brendan then asked his brother Frank, who was waiting for his orders on his Navy assignment, to send him some pills to lower his blood pressure, but the pills had not arrived by the next week, when he had to retake the exam. "I go down and take the exam," he remembered, "and I'm so calm, knowing I'm going to flunk it, that I passed it."[3]

Brendan then took another exam for the flight training school, where "the top scores on the exam became pilots, the ones near the top became navigators, and those with average scores became bombardiers."[4] He barely passed the part of the test for becoming a pilot (scoring five out of ten), but his strong performance on the section for navigation (nine out of ten) led to his being assigned to train to become a navigator, who were most needed at the time. Although "disappointed" that he would not be a pilot, he felt that as a navigator he would fill a need. After preflight training for ten weeks at a state college in Oklahoma, he was sent to Ellington Field in Texas for flight training as a navigator.[5]

Conceding that he was "basically lazy," Brendan got through training by cutting some corners. "I hated the routine stuff," he later recalled, "like learning to march. I was a terrible at marching."[6] Flight training for navigators included celestial navigation, which required selecting three stars and measuring through triangulation the angle to the visible horizon to fix one's position. At first Brendan had difficulty learning the "tricky" system and tried to cheat a bit by getting "the same leg every night, so that all I had to do was memorize the stars at one particular time."[7] Soon, however, his scheme was discovered, and he was forced to learn enough so "I could at least get through the course." At the end of his training, he had mastered enough celestial navigation to use it (the sole time he would employ it during his entire service) to guide a B-17 bomber from Gander, Newfoundland, across the Atlantic to the Azores Islands and then over to Italy in the summer of 1944.

At the end of July 1944, Brendan was deployed to the 98th Bomb Group of the Fifteenth Air Force at a base just outside Foggia, along the Adriatic coast in southeastern Italy. Initially assigned to the 342nd Bomb Squadron, within a couple of days he was transferred to the 414th, which had run out of navigators. As he unpacked his gear in his tent, he received a grim hint about the reason for the navigator shortage in the 414th when an enlisted man welcomed him with, "I hope you have better luck than the last two guys who slept in that bed."[8]

On Brendan's first combat mission, he again had reason to regret his failure to be more conscientious during his training in Texas. "I didn't know what I was doing," he recalled, "absolutely didn't know what I was doing. . . . The guy who debriefed me knew that I didn't know what I was doing."[9] Yet that first mission "served me well" since he quickly recognized "that's no way to fight a war" and immediately focused on learning what he needed to know. He later became the youngest squadron leader in his bomb group, in charge of seven (and occasionally nine) of its twenty-eight planes. Near the end of his tour, on his last five or six missions, he would be the leader of the entire twenty-eight-plane group and navigator of the bomber carrying the general in charge of the group, "who doesn't like me to begin with, since I'm a young kid."

Even as a group leader, Brendan's navigation skills sometimes were tested. On one noncombat flight of only 80 miles, his plane was transporting the commanding general. Such short trips posed special challenges for a navigator because they did not allow much time to reset a misguided course, and suddenly Brendan realized that he was lost. "In a panic," he recalled, he pushed the button to advise the pilot of his predicament, only to first hear,

"Okay, I see it," thus learning to his relief that he had been saved by the pilot's coming upon their destination entirely "by accident."[10]

Brendan was the navigator on the ten-man crew of B-17 "Flying Fortresses," which were first developed by Boeing in the 1930s. B-17s would drop more bombs than any other U.S. aircraft in World War II, accounting for nearly half of the 1.5 million metric tons dropped by the United States on Germany and its occupied territories. The plane was armed with nine machine guns and carried a 4,000-pound bomb load; fully loaded, it could fly at 150 to 250 miles per hour at 30,000 feet, with a flight range of up to 1,800 miles.[11] Despite the impression given by novels and movies that airmen on bombers were a close-knit bunch who grew attached to their planes throughout their tours of duty, Brendan's experience was different. "I flew with a lot of guys on several B-17s," he recalled. "From mission to mission, the crews and the planes varied depending on who was available and which planes were ready to fly."[12]

B-17s were celebrated for their ability to withstand hits and continue flying, sometimes returning to their base with one, two, or even three of their four engines knocked out and with huge holes in their fuselage. Indeed, earlier in the war, one of the B-17s in Brendan's squadron had been the inspiration for *Comin' In on a Wing and a Prayer*, the best-selling song of 1943, based on an actual mission in North Africa during which the bomber was rammed and badly damaged by a German fighter but managed to limp home, where upon landing, its fuselage split in two.[13] B-17 crews generally preferred their rugged plane to the larger B-24, contending that their bomber was more stable, both in formation flying and when missing an engine and that its electrical systems were less vulnerable to damage than the hydraulics of the B-24.[14]

Brendan and his fellow airmen were billeted in four-man tents with wooden cots and a single light bulb. An orderly room and mess hall were located at one end of the rows of tents, which were set up in an olive grove.[15] Once in a while, good-natured fights broke out in which the men flung the abundant olives at each other. In order to minimize potential casualties from a German attack, the tents were situated 1 to 2 miles from the airfields, with the crews shuttled back and forth by truck. British airmen also shared the Foggia base, and seemed "to have access to a little more liquor than we did," Brendan remembered, which may have fueled the bawdy songs that he enjoyed hearing them sing.[16]

A typical schedule for Brendan would include an evening briefing for squadron leaders, each of whom was responsible for seven planes, on the following day's mission and the target's location and expected defenses. The leaders were ordered to keep the briefing confidential, but after returning to his tent, Brendan recalled, "the others would look closely at my face to see if they could pick up any clues on how tough the mission might be."[17]

Shortly after dawn on the following morning, the entire crew was given a more general briefing, usually on the extent of anticipated opposition from antiaircraft installations, and the crew members were then taken by trucks or jeeps to board their planes. Following completion on the ground of preflight checks, the crews waited for a green flare from the tower and then took off in rapid succession at thirty-second intervals. The planes normally were in the air by eight o'clock in the morning, gathering in formation, with three groups of eighteen planes making up a combat wing. The wing then searched for a signal from the radio beacon that would guide it to take its place with the other wings forming the strike force. Once over the Adriatic, the bomber crews test-fired their guns. At 10,000 feet, the crew donned their oxygen masks as they ascended to their normal altitudes of 25,000 to 30,000 feet. On some missions, they had fighter escorts for the first part of the flight, but due to their shorter range the fighters normally would peel off and depart before the bombers reached their targets. Sometimes, the bombers were forced to rely only on instruments as they flew through thick cloud cover that could extend to 23,000 feet.[18]

As the navigator, Brendan sat in the nose compartment on the port (or left) side, behind a shelf-like desk holding his charts and instruments. He also operated two guns on the right side of the nose to ward off possible fighter attacks, although by the summer of 1944 the Luftwaffe's fighter squadrons had incurred such heavy losses that they were not a significant threat to the Allied bombers based in Italy. Windows were located along each side of the fuselage, and an astrodome in the cockpit aided in determining the relationship of the stars to the earth. To the front of Brendan was the bombardier; positioned over an aiming instrument, the bombardier controlled the handle that opened the bomb bay and the switch that released the bombs over the target.[19]

Navigators like Brendan were responsible for setting a course to keep the bombers stable for the final run over the target. The navigator would then give up control of the plane to the bombardier, who employed the highly classified Norden bombsight to calculate the bomb's trajectory based on current flight conditions, and then adjust the flight path through the autopilot to compensate for changes in wind speed or direction.[20] "When the bombardier controls the airplane," according to Brendan, "you don't move, you don't dive, and you're a sitting duck. You've got to take what's coming at you. During that six or eight minutes or whatever it is, it's very tense." As soon as the bomb load was dropped, "we would break the tension by shouting, sometimes all at once, 'Let's get the hell out of here!'"[21]

In addition to the enemy defenses, the bomber crews also had to endure the harsh cold of flying at altitudes above 20,000 feet in unheated planes. To provide some protection against temperatures that could drop to

60 degrees below zero, the crew wore electrically heated suits and heavy gloves. But, as one historian put it, with so little heat in the B-17, "most of the crew shivered and shook in their alpaca coats and pants and sheepskin flying boots."[22] When forced to take off their gloves, such as to look at maps or to eat on long flights, the bitter cold sometimes caused their hands to instantly freeze to any metal they touched. Over the course of several flights where he exposed his left hand to the cold, Brendan got frostbite, which long after the war kept him from taking up skiing and on very cold days would reappear, turning his hand white.[23]

Brendan's bomber group was occasionally escorted by P-51 fighters flown by the Tuskegee airmen, the first African-American aviators in the U.S. military. Sixty years later, he still remembered their keen sense of humor, recalling verbatim one of their exchanges he overheard on his radio:

"Backstop Six to Backstop Leader, come down and help me out. There's a Messerschmitt on my tail," followed by the immediate response: "Backstop Leader to Backstop Six, help yourself, man. You're drawing flying pay."[24]

Several of Brendan's early missions were part of the "oil campaign" waged to deny the Nazis the crucial petroleum supplies needed not only for gasoline and oil for their tanks, planes, and other vehicles, but also for producing chemicals for bombs, artillery shells, and bullets.[25] Almost wholly lacking in its own petroleum reserves, Germany was highly dependent on oil supplies and refineries outside its borders. When Hitler invaded Poland in 1939, Germany was importing some 70 percent of its liquid fuel and had only a two to three month reserve of aviation fuel and gasoline.[26]

Recognizing their oil vulnerability, the Nazis under Minister of Armaments and Production Albert Speer launched a crash program to produce synthetic oil.[27] As Allied ground forces succeeded in seizing oil fields, refineries, and pipelines in formerly Nazi-controlled countries, the dependence on synthetic oil became crucial for Germany's ability to continue the war.

Bomber attacks on Nazi petroleum resources had begun in 1943, while Brendan was still in training in Texas. The first phase of the assault concentrated on the oil fields and refineries in Romania, which supplied an estimated 60 percent of the refined oil necessary for the German war effort. On August 1, the U.S. Army Air Force suffered the worst loss in its history on a single mission in "Operation Tidal Wave," attempting to bomb the heavily defended Romanian oil refineries at Ploesti. On what was later called "Black Sunday," 53 aircraft and 660 crewmen were lost in the poorly planned assault launched from airfields in Libya, nearly a 1,000 miles from the target, as the bombers encountered stiff resistance from Nazi fighter planes and by flak shot from ground installations.[28]

Following the early long-range missions from Libya, the Air Force had much greater success when it moved to airfields in Italy in October 1943. The Italian airfields had been seized by the British Army from the Luftwaffe, which had taken control from the Italians after Italy signed an armistice ceasing hostilities with the Allies the previous month. A few weeks after the British took control of the Italian airfields, the Americans established the new Fifteenth Air Force, in which Brendan would serve. Its fighters and bombers were largely taken from the previously established Twelfth Air Force in North Africa and, to a more limited extent, from the Eighth Air Force based in England. One of the Fifteenth's primary objectives was to bomb Nazi-held industrial facilities in Europe and to support the Allied ground invasion of southern France from the airfields in Italy, which had more favorable weather conditions than what the Eighth Air Force experienced at its bases in England.[29]

The creation of the Fifteenth sparked perhaps inevitable jealousy and rivalry among the American flyers. "The heroism of the crews of the Fifteenth Air Force," one historian noted, "received only backpage coverage in the American press. The Eighth, the darling of news reporters from the big papers stationed in London, captured the headlines."[30] An article assessing the reasons for the media's preference for covering the Eighth over the Fifteenth cited this unattributed quote: "If you were a war correspondent, would you rather sip scotch in a London hotel or swig vino in a tent at Foggia?"[31] Thus, it was understandable that some of the Fifteenth airmen would sing, to the melody of "As Time Goes By":

> *It's still the same old story*
> *The Eighth gets all the glory,*
> *While we go out to die.*
> *The fundamental things apply.*
> *As flak goes by.*[32]

In April 1944, General Dwight D. Eisenhower, the supreme Allied commander, ordered the Fifteenth Air Force to escalate bombing of the Ploesti refineries and the synthetic oil plants. In a massive assault by over 330 bombers, Ploesti suffered extensive damage, severely reducing its capacity for conventional petroleum production. By the spring of 1944, synthetic fuel plants were producing nearly all of Germany's aviation gasoline and 85 percent of its high-grade motor fuel.[33] In June, the American bombers also attacked the railway networks in southeastern Europe in support of the Soviet army's advance in Romania. At the time Brendan arrived in Italy in July 1944, the Fifteenth was in the final stage of its assault on Ploesti, which would be overrun by the Soviet army at the end of August.[34] As the Nazis lost control of Ploesti and other sources of conventional oil and gasoline supplies, Byrne's first missions would focus on the synthetic petroleum plants and the support of ground forces advancing toward Germany.

Flak was the deadliest threat to Allied bomber crews, and the stress of flying missions through skies pock-marked by exploding metal exacted a high toll on airmen. By the end of the war, Nazi flak gunners had downed some 5,400 planes, compared with 4,300 shot down by fighters; flak accounted for over 70 percent of the wounds suffered by the crews of the Eighth Air Force. But the severe mental impact of flak was much more difficult to measure. "Flak was insidious; it reduced men to a state of complete helplessness—passive stress, Air Force physicians called it," one historian wrote. "[I]t was a devastatingly effective psychological weapon, designed to unnerve the aircrews and impair bombing accuracy."[35]

As the bombers approached their targets, the crews put on their flak jackets, which were waistcoats made of reinforced cotton with steel plates sewn into the fabric; the jackets could weigh up to thirty pounds and were too bulky to wear for the entire flight. Flak that penetrated the fuselage usually was deflected by the jackets, but occasionally metal fragments ripped through to cut or scratch skin. In an attempt to confuse the radar used by Nazi flak gunners, the bombers dropped chaff (or what crews called "tinsel" for its resemblance to Christmas tree decoration), comprised of thousands of strips of aluminum tape. When asked many years later whether the tactic was successful, Brendan replied with a smile, "Well, those of us who survived thought it was."[36] After the war, Brendan said that every time he saw a fireworks display he was reminded of flying through flak. "The sky would be filled with black puffs of smoke. There wasn't any way to avoid flak. When it came close, the plane would shake, we'd be jerked in our seats and you just prayed that the next one wouldn't be a direct hit."

Although flak often hit his planes, none of Brendan's crews experienced major injuries.[37] Brendan and others in his crews often came back bleeding from minor flak wounds—which technically qualified for being awarded the Purple Heart—but none of his crewmen applied for the medal because "we thought that was a disservice to the guys who got hurt badly."[38]

The bombers were most vulnerable on their return trip to base if they had lost an engine or had suffered other damage that forced them to drop out of formation. On three or four missions, Brendan's crews struggled to return to base alone after losing one or two engines. In those "really scary" situations, he recalled, the skills of navigators were tested as they calculated whether they had enough fuel to reach base without ditching in the Adriatic. "Once, we were so close to going down," he recalled, "I had my hand on the door ready to jump out, but somehow we made it back."[39]

Even though his own crews escaped death and serious injuries, Brendan was still affected by losses of other airmen based at Foggia. He had become friendly with a person named Kirsch, whose family owned a furniture store in Newark. Brendan and Kirsch had jointly started saving from their pay until they had enough money to hire local labor to build a brick hut to upgrade the quality of their lodging from their drafty tents. Whenever Brendan would see Kirsch, he good-naturedly asked how much he had managed to sock away in their mutual building fund. The project abruptly ended, however, when Kirsch was killed when his bomber was shot down. When he returned from the war, Brendan avoided entering the Kirsch store in Newark even though he often passed by it, saying "I was afraid that if I went in to see the family, it would just make them feel worse, seeing that I survived, but not their son."[40]

Casualty rates among bomber crews were among the highest of all the military units in World War II. Over the course of the war, the average B-17 crewman had only a one-in-four chance of actually completing his tour of duty, and 46,500 of the 250,000 airmen who flew on B-17s were either killed or wounded. In 1944, the year of Brendan's service in Italy, one-third of B-17 crews did not survive. Of the total 12,731 B-17s built through 1945, nearly a third were lost in combat. The Fifteenth Air Force lost 1,850 bombers on operations by its fifteen bombardment groups.[41]

Along with many other airmen, Brendan felt that while the odds of being killed or wounded were obviously high, somehow he would be one of those who would be spared. "I mean you worried," he recalled, "but you didn't worry too much, and I'm talking for me now. I think I handled it pretty well. Some guys didn't. I wound up, with my limited skills, as the group leader and the reason for that was that I kept my calm."[42] Yet Brendan also recognized that ultimately his fate would not be determined by either his calm demeanor or his ability as a navigator. "Don't let anybody ever tell you that it's all skill up there," he said. "You have to be lucky to get out of combat alive, and I was lucky."[43]

Despite his own ability to cope with the stress of combat, Brendan didn't feel superior to those who broke down under pressure, concluding that they were simply of a different makeup, "that there were some guys that just can't take it." Nor did he have empathy for General George S. Patton, who was reprimanded by Eisenhower for slapping soldiers suffering from "battle fatigue" and accusing them of cowardice. "I think," Brendan said later, "he was asking people to do what, in some cases, they just weren't able to do. Those of us who were able to summon the courage to do it, it was within us. It wasn't within some of these guys."[44]

One of Brendan's missions would be profiled in *The War*, the public television documentary on World War II broadcast in 2007 and directed by Ken Burns. As their B-17 was approaching its target, the bombardier on Brendan's plane passed out after losing his oxygen, which occasionally happened because of a crimped or detached hose. Noticing that the bombardier was slumped over, Brendan quickly undid his own seat belt and rushed to the other man's side to revive him. After reattaching the bombardier's oxygen and pulling him out of his seat, Brendan took his place and dropped the bomb load over the target. Neither he nor the bombardier knew each other's name until years after the war. As Brendan recounted, "Out of the blue, I got this call and the guy on the other end asked me a series of questions pinning down where and when I had served, finally saying, 'you're the guy who saved my life.'"[45]

Each mission had a primary target as well as one or two alternate targets in case the primary target could not be hit, usually due to cloud cover or other weather issues. Crews were instructed never to return to their base with their bombs; if none of the targets could be reached, they were directed to drop their payloads on populated areas. On one mission, Brendan rebelled against the order to hit the nearest populated area, choosing instead to chart a course to bomb a rail line in the woods. "I think I almost got court-martialed for that," he later recalled, "but I just didn't see any purpose in dropping them on people." On his return to the base, he was reprimanded, but received no further discipline.[46]

Brendan flew most days, but when the weather scrubbed a mission, the crews typically went into the town of Foggia, where there was an officers' club. (According to one account, upon the opening of the Foggia officers' club, three B-17s were sent to Rome, returning "loaded with ladies of easy virtue.")[47] On one visit to the club, Brendan met Madeleine Carroll, who had been a popular movie star before volunteering to serve as a Red Cross nurse, and who, at Byrne's request, kindly wrapped a present for him to send home to his mother.

There was local food that provided a break from what was served at the base canteens. On one occasion, after being frustrated when discovering that no restaurant in Foggia made pizza, which he had come to enjoy at home, he asked around and a local family came forward, offering to bake him one in their own home kitchen. "It was a big mistake," Brendan remembered. "I really got sick from that pizza."[48]

Seamier options to mix with local girls were also available, but Brendan said that "most of us were fairly scared"—a fear reinforced when one of his crew contracted venereal disease. He also kept in mind his goal of going to law school, a path he did not want to complicate by having to deal with any unintended Italian pregnancies. In the middle of his six-month tour, his crew was given a week's break in Rome, which he spent mostly pursuing what would become two lifelong passions: devouring chocolate candy and attending opera. One day he made a visit to the Vatican and even met the Pope; after telling the Pope that he was a Seton Hall student, he received what he assumed was a stock response, "Oh, that's a fine school."[49]

Brendan's fondness for chocolate became obvious to his fellow airmen when he regularly turned down the jigger of whiskey offered to the crews on their return from a mission, trading the drink instead for any available chocolate. His mother also sent him monthly packages of chocolates. On the day after he opened the first shipment, he found that rats had partially eaten the pieces and threw out the entire box; the next month, he cut around the parts nibbled by the rats and ate the remainder; by the third month, he recalled, he said "the hell with it, whatever was left from the rats, I would eat."[50]

Several of Brendan's missions targeted the heavily defended Nazi industrial complex in Blechhammer, then located in Germany less than 20 miles from the Polish border (and which was returned to Poland after the war to be known as Blachownia Slaska). Typically, the round-trip flight time to Blechhammer from the base at Foggia was seven to eight hours. Nicknamed "Black Hammer" by the Americans, the site was first established in June 1942 as a detention camp for Jews who were used as forced labor to construct a synthetic oil plant. Subsequently, an adjacent refinery and chemical plant were built, along with facilities to support mining and the repair and maintenance of railway equipment. The plant complex also produced nitrogen and ammonia, essential for making explosives and ammunition. At its peak under the Nazis, nearly 50,000 prisoners, including about 2,000 British soldiers mostly captured in North Africa, provided workers for the various facilities. Twenty-five flak batteries defended the area, with many manned by students as young as 15 years old.[51]

Blechhammer was the most dangerous target Brendan would bomb.[52] His composure was most tested during one specific run on the complex. "I remember one mission where, instead of going over as a diamond, we went over as a straight [horizontal] line, and my plane was on the right wing of the straight line, and there were two lines ahead of us. And the first wave that went over, the plane on the right side got knocked out. The second wave goes over, and the plane on the right side gets knocked out. I'm the third wave. That's as scared as I have ever been."[53]

Bombing missions in September 1944 extensively damaged Blechhammer, and by late December the oil plant was destroyed. In January 1945, as Allied armies approached, some 10,000 prisoners in the labor and prisoner-of-war camps in the area were evacuated in a death march to other concentration camps, including Buchenwald; about 800 prisoners who were unable to walk any further or tried to escape were shot by SS guards.[54]

The oil war and the destruction of Blechhammer and the other synthetic oil plants proved to be a major factor leading to Germany's surrender. In the summer of 1943, a year before Brendan arrived in Italy, Nazi Field Marshal Erhard Milch had written: "The hydrogenation plants are our most vulnerable spots; with them stands and falls our entire ability to wage war. Not only will planes no longer fly, but tanks and submarines also will stop running if the hydrogenation plants should actually be attacked."[55]

While Brendan and the other airmen did not know of it at the time, Auschwitz, the infamous concentration camp in Poland just 45 miles from Blechhammer and 645 miles from Foggia, would become the focus of an intense and ongoing debate both during and after the war on whether it should have been bombed. By the time of Brendan's first missions in mid-1944, British and American intelligence had learned of the operations at the death camp, which was within easy reach of the Fifteenth Air Force. Allied political and military leaders, however, were divided on whether an air attack on Auschwitz would be effective in deterring executions or simply result in mass deaths of the prisoners.[56] Brendan later said that the larger issues of the war, and the strategy for how the Allies should conduct it, were of little concern to him and most of the crewmen he flew with: "All we wanted was to do our job, stay alive and go home. It was just that simple."[57]

In addition to Blechhammer, Brendan's missions included bombing runs on Athens, Salzburg, Vienna, Budapest, and Munich, as well as one mission to support the advance of ground forces in southern France. The mission to Athens, he recalled, "at first made us afraid that we might damage the classic temples and the other ruins, but when we were briefed I realized that we would be bombing targets on the outskirts of the city." The attacks on the other cities usually targeted railroad marshaling yards, seeking to destroy locomotives, freight cars, tracks, and other infrastructure. "Compared to Blechhammer," Brendan said, "we thought the runs on the cities were a lot easier since we didn't face as much flak." On the missions to Vienna and Budapest, with the Danube River flowing through both cities, the crews would sing, to the melody of the Blue Danube waltz, "we're on our way to bomb Vienna, boom- boom, boom- boom!" Commenting on the songs, jokes, and banter that often punctuated their bombing runs, Brendan later said: "You were under such pressure. We just did anything to ease the tension, to take our minds off what was going on."[58]

As the November 1944 election approached, Brendan was still only 20 years old—old enough to fight but not yet old enough to vote. He badly wanted to vote for President Roosevelt, whom he and his family so admired. He nearly fulfilled his wish when he persuaded one of his buddies, who had an absentee ballot but didn't care much about politics, to let him fill in the ballot. But when his buddy "saw that I'd voted for Roosevelt, he tore up the ballot in disgust."[59]

Brendan was proud that, as his skill as a navigator became known, he was often chosen by crewmen to guide their last missions before completing their tours—a tradition that allowed airmen to select those in whom they had the most confidence to ensure a safe final mission. On one of these flights, Brendan's plane lost two of its four engines after being hit by flak, forcing him to set a precise course over the Adriatic to get the bomber safely to base before it was out of fuel. After landing, the relieved crewman who had survived his tense final mission dramatically expressed his gratitude. "He stooped down," Brendan recalled, "and literally kissed my boots."[60]

In December 1944, as Brendan was nearing the completion of his tour of duty, Hitler launched his last counteroffensive in what the Allies would label the Battle of the Bulge. "When we learned in Italy of the attack," Brendan recalled years later, "I worried that those of us who were coming home would be ordered to stay longer in Europe."[61] But the initial success of the assault was blunted as Nazi tanks, trucks, and other vehicles rapidly ran short of fuel; out of gasoline, some German units abandoned their vehicles and surrendered—a victory that Brendan and the other bomber crewmen had helped secure through their destruction of the Nazi petroleum facilities.[62]

Upon completion of his fifty-mission tour in January 1945, and eager to return home, Brendan turned down the Army's offer of promotion to captain with higher pay if he agreed to fly only five more missions in Europe. After rejecting the potential promotion, he returned to the United States by ship on the U.S.S. *West Point*, after safely making it through the Straits of Gibraltar, a dangerous passage in which German submarines often targeted troop transports. In order to save space for provisions on the crowded ships, the troops were limited to two meals a day, a point that provoked much grumbling. On the way home, Brendan befriended a nurse who happened to be from Maplewood, only a few miles from his home in West Orange, who succeeded in sneaking him additional snacks to partly make up for the limited rations.[63]

Making port in Boston, he and the other disembarking troops were treated to a steak dinner on their first night home. As he waited in the long line, Brendan snuck out to seek a shop selling chocolates, later returning to reclaim his spot and rewarding those who had saved his place in line with samples from his haul of chocolates. From Boston, Brendan was ordered to Atlantic City, which had been largely taken over by the military as a center for housing and training troops embarking for Europe and, upon their return, as a way station for treating the wounded and reassigning returning soldiers to new posts throughout the country. With hundreds of other soldiers, Brendan stayed in the once-elegant Ritz Carleton, which, along with the city's other hotels and attractions, was on a steady path to the decline that he would address some three decades later as governor.

Brendan's initial orders were for him to be retrained in Texas as a bombardier, with the possibility of later being transferred for action in the Pacific. Along with other proud navigators, Brendan resented the directive to become a bombardier, considering it below their prior status. He and the others did their best to circumvent the Army's plan when, given a written test on their skills for their new assignment, they deliberately chose the wrong answers: "If we got one right," he recalled, "it was only because we didn't know the answer."[64]

The atomic bomb was dropped on the Japanese cities of Hiroshima and Nagasaki in August 1945, and the war ended on September 2 when the Japanese formally surrendered to General Douglas MacArthur on board the U.S.S. *Missouri* anchored in Tokyo Bay. With the prospect of a raucous and drunken celebration by the soldiers on the night of the Japanese surrender, Brendan was ordered to temporary duty as a military policeman, with his superior officers assuming that Byrne's well-known abstinence from alcohol would serve him in good stead in monitoring the carousing. While the night passed without major incidents, Brendan proudly kept his "MP" arm band as a souvenir of his one night of service as a policeman.[65]

Less than a week later, along with other soldiers who had seen the most combat, Brendan was discharged from active service, although he continued to serve in the Air Force Reserve after the war. Credited with an extraordinary fifty-one missions (with double credit for some of his thirty-five sorties due to their length), he was awarded the Distinguished Flying Cross and three Air Medals, and ultimately promoted to the rank of lieutenant.

Brendan had entered the military as a 19-year-old somewhat unsure of his ability to measure up to his seniors in age and rank; he came out at age 21 confident not only in his abilities but also in his capacity for leadership. Like many of his fellow soldiers in what later would be called "the greatest generation," after returning to civilian life Brendan rarely spoke of his experiences in the war. In contrast to many of his peers, he avoided joining veterans organizations where he felt conversations would understandably dwell on the past. "I just wanted to get on with my life," he explained years after the war. "I had done what I was asked to do, but it was time to move on with my education and becoming a lawyer."[66] To the later chagrin of his political advisers, he also resisted highlighting his military service during his campaigns for public office.

His brother Frank, who had seen combat in the Pacific, also returned to West Orange for a family reunion. "It was just so good to be back home," Brendan remembered, "and see lots of relatives, neighbors and friends."[67] The welcome home was dampened only when Brendan discovered that "while I was gone, my mother had thrown away my precious collection of movie programs."[68]

Chapter 3

Returning Home

"I've Always Wanted To Be a Lawyer"

After returning to civilian life, Brendan Byrne proceeded to pursue his boyhood goal of becoming a criminal trial lawyer by seeking admission to Harvard Law School. Although he had only the few undergraduate credits from his single semester at Seton Hall and only above-average high school grades, he boldly asked Harvard Law for admission without a college degree. "It was pure ego," he later conceded. "We were heroes and I was a decorated combat veteran. The fact that I didn't have a college degree seemed to me a minor detail, and I liked to argue." Although he didn't quite know how he had fixed on his goal of attending Harvard, he felt its prestige "would give me a veneer that I wasn't entitled to. It had a great reputation and was full of very smart people. That's where I wanted to be."[1]

But when he went up to Cambridge, his arguments for being admitted without an undergraduate degree failed, and to persuade Harvard's veterans' counselor, a professor named Warren Seavey, who advised Brendan that pursuing undergraduate work at Williams or Princeton would best set him on a path to admission. He chose Princeton, both because of its convenience and because it fortuitously had an upcoming admissions test and a semester starting in November. He could also rely on the G.I. Bill to pay his tuition—$600 a semester—along with a stipend for living expenses, thus avoiding putting a burden on his family, which was still struggling to pay for his brother Frank's medical education.[2] Brendan also had managed to save $4,000, some from his high school earnings selling shoes but mostly from his military pay and bonuses for his combat service.[3]

Despite his grades in high school, Brendan was admitted to Princeton after receiving an excellent score on his admissions test. He also was given one term of credit for his military service and for his time at Seton Hall, as

Princeton and most other colleges instituted special programs for returning veterans to expedite the completion of the requirements for them to obtain their degrees.

In the wake of the turmoil that had led to war, Brendan briefly was interested in studying international law, and he was admitted into Princeton's School of Public and International Affairs (later renamed the "Woodrow Wilson School of Public and International Affairs"), taking courses skewed toward his concentration in government and history. Brendan's favorite course, modern European history, was taught by Professor Walter P. "Buzzer" Hall (so nicknamed by students due to the buzz emitted by the professor's hearing aid). The highlight of Hall's course was his impassioned lecture on Giuseppe Garibaldi, the Italian independence fighter, which drew overflow crowds of students, faculty, and other visitors. To Brendan, the gist of Hall's message was that "history doesn't make men, men make history."[4]

Brendan went through the competitive three-week "bicker" interview process for selection for membership in one of Princeton's private dining clubs. Under the "ironbound" system used at the time, he was placed with two other classmates to go through the interviews at the various clubs, with the clubs required to accept or reject all or none of the three for membership. He and the other two students were accepted (extended a "bid") by the University Cottage Club, one of the four most selective clubs, which was profiled by its alumnus, F. Scott Fitzgerald, in *This Side of Paradise*, his novel published in 1920.[5] Brendan later reflected that he would not have been invited to join the Cottage Club except for the fact that "the other two guys drank and I didn't. I wouldn't have gotten into Cottage on my own." Despite the presumed benefits of forging friendships with others in the club that might be valuable in later life, Brendan was not an active member, only occasionally having his meals there and rarely attending its parties and receptions, preferring instead to eat at the track team's training table and socialize with his fellow teammates.[6]

At times, the mix at Princeton of returning war veterans and recent high school graduates led to occasional conflicts. One tradition allowed upperclassmen passing any freshman on McCosh Walk—the main path crossing the campus—to physically push the freshmen off the Walk; some of the grizzled veterans would have none of the high jinks and after some fought back, the custom was quickly suspended. On another occasion, a snowball barrage, which was launched against a dormitory housing veterans, abruptly ended when one of the former soldiers fired a shot from his service revolver over the heads of the attacking students.[7]

Brendan was a sprinter on the Princeton track team, running in the 100- and 220-yard dashes and the half-mile relay. "I was pretty fast," Brendan recalled years later, "but two other guys were close to Olympic caliber in the 100. I was more competitive in the 220."[8] His parents came to watch him run at a meet in Newark, where, after winning several qualifying heats, he lost in the finals. "So much had changed in my life since I was a small boy," he later reflected, "but not where sports were concerned, it seemed. I still couldn't win the highest prize with my parents watching." In another meet among Princeton, Penn, and Columbia, Penn and Columbia were neck and neck going into the meet's climactic last event, the half-mile relay in which Brendan anchored the Princeton team. If Princeton could beat Columbia in the event, Penn would win the meet, but the Columbia anchor running the leg against Brendan was a potential Olympian. "My teammates ran well and gave me a little lead," Brendan recalled, "and I ran my best race and barely held off the Columbia fellow. Suddenly, the Penn team came along and carried me off the track on their shoulders. That was my Princeton track career in a nutshell—promising but never completely satisfying."[9]

In 1946, Brendan's freshman year at Princeton, the University marked its 200th anniversary, with a year-long series of celebratory events featuring visits and talks by President Harry Truman, General Dwight Eisenhower, former President Herbert Hoover, and other leaders. Brendan invited his uncle, Joe Brennan, to visit him for the closing anniversary program, and took his uncle to lunch at Lahiere's Restaurant, the town's best-known, and most expensive, restaurant. "Uncle Joe insisted on picking up the check," Brendan recalled years later, "but when I saw that he had only left a dime as a tip, I waited until he had turned his back to leave a little extra on the table."[10]

Brendan also volunteered to help the student drama group, Theater Intime, resume its operations after their suspension during the war. His primary role was not acting, but in helping it to reorganize its operations after the war. After finding some old unused postcards found in the basement of its theater, he returned the cards to the post office for reimbursement, raising enough funds by to support its first postwar meetings to plan its programs and recruit its actors and administrative staff.[11]

After his first year at Princeton, Brendan sent his grades up to Warren Seavey in Cambridge, asking, "Now can I come to Harvard Law School?" but Seavey replied, "No, but those are pretty good grades." With characteristic persistence, Brendan would continue to pester Seavey. "Every semester at Princeton," he later recalled, "I sent Warren Seavey my grades. The next time I sent them, he said 'If you keep those grades for one more semester, then we'll look at you.' He didn't exactly promise I'd get in, but he hinted at it pretty strongly."[12]

When he again received good grades for the next semester, Brendan decided to head up to Harvard, intending to give the grades personally to Seavey, only to discover that Seavey was no longer the veterans' counselor; moreover, the admissions officer he was directed to see, as he later said, "seemed distinctly skeptical about admitting me." But in a stroke of good fortune or crafty planning, this time Brendan happened to bring along his five-year-old nephew, whose parents were then living near Cambridge. "If the fellow from Harvard Law School assumed this was my son," Brendan admitted years later. "I didn't do anything to correct that impression. I thought having a little boy would make me look a little more mature, and with this mouth to feed, help explain my impatience to get my legal education underway." The nephew's presence may have helped to change the admissions officer's mind; Brendan subsequently accepted as a student in the class that entered Harvard Law in September 1947. Brendan later learned from Ted Stevens, a Harvard classmate who later became the longtime U.S. Senator from Alaska, that a similar misperception of his being a young father had also helped gain his own admission.[13]

Brendan actually left Princeton without qualifying for his degree: he had not completed enough credits and had not submitted a senior thesis. Following his first year at Harvard, at the suggestion of Princeton's dean of students, Brendan returned to Princeton in the summer of 1947, took additional courses for the needed credits and completed his thesis, "Proportional Representation in Municipal Government," a study of how municipalities created districts to promote representation on their governing bodies by different ethnic or geographic constituencies. He would receive his bachelor's degree as a member of the Class of 1949.

Brendan used his remaining two years of credit under the G.I. Bill to pay for his first two years at Harvard Law. Now enrolled at the school he had targeted since he was 12 years old, Brendan became a more focused student. In those days, Harvard flunked out a significant percentage of students (giving rise to the probable apocryphal quote attributed to a dean addressing a new class: "Look to your left, look to your right, because one of you won't be here by the end of the year").[14] "So you were always worried about that," Brendan later reflected about the possibility of flunking out, "and this was what I was going to do the rest of my life to make a living, and I didn't want to take a risk. So I really studied hard."[15]

Although he intended to be a trial lawyer and recognized that Harvard "really wasn't set up to train criminal lawyers who wanted to work in a courtroom," Brendan found jurisprudence—the sometimes ethereal study of the philosophy of law—to be one of his favorite courses: "I liked the thought of thinking through what the law really is. I mean, most of the other courses have a mechanical aspect to them. But the course in jurisprudence, you're trying to think of what's right and what's wrong with the law."[16]

In his off-hours, Brendan played basketball on pick-up teams with his law school friends, usually coming off the bench in a sixth-man substitute role on teams that were sometimes talented enough to beat the Harvard varsity. On one occasion, however, in a game against an extremely weak opponent, John Keto, Brendan's roommate and later lifelong friend, orchestrated the other players to continuously feed the ball to Brendan until he had scored 100 points. Another one of Brendan's teammates was married to a professional model, who was able to secure freelance assignments, when male models were needed, for her husband, Brendan, Keto and others to model clothes at events sponsored by Filene's, the well-known Boston department store.[17]

On one of his visits home from Harvard, Brendan managed to persuade Joseph Weintraub, a prominent New Jersey lawyer, to allow him to work at his Newark law firm as an unpaid law clerk during school breaks in his final year in law school. At the time, one of the requirements for admission to the New Jersey bar was serving for nine months as a clerk to a judge or a lawyer. Getting the job was not easy. Brendan first asked the West Orange municipal attorney, who was a friend of his father, to call Weintraub in his behalf. As Brendan later told the story, when he subsequently phoned Weintraub, he was asked what law school he had graduated from. When Brendan told him he still had a year to go, Weintraub brusquely replied, "I don't want you," to which Brendan responded, "But you don't understand. I'm willing to work for nothing." Weintraub then responded, "No, *you* don't understand. I don't want you," ending the exchange. Nonetheless, a few days later, Weintraub called Brendan to say, "If you're really willing to work for nothing, come on in." The conversation, as Brendan put it, "forged a life-long friendship" in which Weintraub, in his later roles as counsel to Governor Robert Meyner and as chief justice of the New Jersey Supreme Court, would be, aside from Brendan's parents, "the greatest influence in my life, the best mentor and guide I ever had."[18]

Although Brendan had mostly kept his distance from girls during his years in high school, the military, and college, while in law school he began what he would describe as his "first really serious relationship." The woman, who also lived in West Orange, was a high school classmate of his sister Muriel named Beryl Anfindsen. "A Scandinavian blonde," Brendan described her years later. She was a "knockout who turned men's heads as she walked by." On first seeing Beryl with Brendan, his Harvard classmate Ted Stevens said simply: "Wow!" Beryl was also intelligent and would receive a master's degree from New York University, but Brendan felt "something was missing," and her occasional unpredictability was perceived as "flighty" by some in his family, suggesting that she was not the sort of match they were seeking for their son. Brendan continued to date Beryl through law school, but the couple eventually drifted apart after his graduation in 1950.[19]

Muriel was also the matchmaker for his next serious romance with her good friend Jean Featherly. Jean's family also lived in West Orange; her father worked as an accountant for Thomas Edison in analyzing costs and determining pricing for products and her mother was a patent librarian for a local firm that manufactured calculating machines. Jean had graduated from West Orange High School two years after Brendan, but the two had had few contacts while in school. A Bucknell College graduate with a master's degree in education from New York University, Jean was an elementary school teacher. "She was the best-looking girl in her class," Brendan later recounted, "and we shared interests in theater and music, particularly opera." For a time, Jean served as vice president of the West Orange Republican Club, but the couple generally avoided talking about politics on their dates.[20]

A more serious problem, however, was that she was not Catholic and made it clear that she did not want to raise children outside her own Presbyterian faith. While conceding that he was not as strong a Catholic as his sister Thecla or brother Frank, Brendan nonetheless was committed to raising his children as Catholics, and so he and Jean reluctantly broke off their relationship. But after they had both begun dating others, to his surprise Jean called and said, "Brendan, I'll do it. I'll raise our children as Catholics if you want."[21] Deeply affected by what he knew was an extremely difficult decision on her part, Brendan responded by proposing marriage and they were wed at the Saint Joseph's Church on June 27, 1953, when Brendan was 29 and Jean was 27 years old. "Money was tight for the wedding," Brendan recalled, "and we invited only family and close friends. But I persuaded Jean to invite one of my friends from Princeton who was then living in Florida, telling her 'he'll never come.' He came."[22] After a honeymoon in Florida, the couple, after living for the first few months of their marriage in the home of Jean's parents, moved to an apartment in West Orange.

As was then required, Jean gave up teaching when she became pregnant with their first child, who was born in June 1954 and named Brendan Thomas Byrne, Jr., and soon called "Tom." Tom would be followed by six siblings: Susan (1956), Nancy (1957), Timothy (1961), Mary Anne (1963), Barbara (1967), and William (1969). Mary Anne was born with Down syndrome and would spend her life in institutions or group homes. Jean assumed the bulk of the child-rearing duties, and enjoyed sewing to make clothes for the girls and cooking the family favorites, often steak and pork chops. She also played the piano, and for a time gave lessons to her daughter Susan. The family enjoyed traveling and took short trips to visit local relatives or into Manhattan on Sunday outings to shows or restaurants. Later, particularly when Brendan was Essex County prosecutor, Jean or the children would accompany him to meetings of the National District Attorneys Association in such locations as Los Angeles, Las Vegas, New Orleans, and Phoenix.

As an adult, Tom recalled that his father was typically home for family dinners and often came to school events, calling him a "pretty normal father." Sports were an interest tying the family together. "We used to go to Yankee Stadium," Tom continued, "he'd take us there, take me and friends there for birthdays and just other games. He was a big baseball fan. We'd play sports out in the yard."[23] The Byrnes erected a basketball backboard at the end of their dead-end street in West Orange, which became a popular gathering spot for the children of the neighborhood. Yet like many fathers of his generation, Byrne would winsomely reflect after his children were grown and raising their own families, "I was preoccupied with my career, I probably didn't spend as much time with them as I should have. But Jean was a wonderful mother, she was always there for the kids whenever they had a problem or needed anything"[24]

Following his graduation from Harvard Law and admission to the New Jersey bar in February 1951, Byrne was finally able to launch the career he had mapped out with single-minded focus since he was a boy—working as a lawyer. He first rejoined the Weintraub firm as a junior lawyer, recognizing that the job was temporary because the firm could only afford to pay a nominal salary and his own goal of moving on to a situation where he could get more courtroom experience. "It was only peanuts—maybe $25-a-week—but it still meant a lot to me," Byrne reflected years later. "I had value to Joe Weintraub."[25]

Working under Weintraub, Byrne continued his education as a lawyer, particularly given the older lawyer's concern for language. "He would always tinker with what you wrote," Byrne recalled, "and often he'd tear it apart. One time I wrote a veto message for him about the governance of the town of Absecon, and he tore that veto message completely apart. But that was Joe, and I admired him for how much he cared about being precise with words."

Byrne also admired Weintraub's broad range of interests outside the law, interests that he often probed from a lawyer's perspective. "Joe was very well-read," Brendan recounted. "You could ask him a question about anything, and that great intellect would start working. He'd analyze the issue, break down the question, arrive at the core of the issue, and then address it with impeccable logic." Weintraub's integrity would be a lifelong model for Byrne. "Joe Weintraub had what I think all moral people need," Byrne would later say, "and certainly all public figures, and that's an internal compass—something which guides him in making decisions, something independent of transient things like popularity."[26] Many years after Weintraub's death, while speaking to a forum of hundreds of attorneys, judges, and academics, Byrne related a conversation with Weintraub: "I went to him when I was governor, and I said, 'You know, I have an old friend of the family, a friend of my father, who has a son who he wants me to put on the bench.' And Weintraub said, 'Well, does he have the qualifications?' I said, 'He's an old friend.' And Weintraub says, 'If he wants you to do something like that, he's not a friend.'"[27]

After several months with Weintraub, Byrne learned that John McGeehan, Jr., an older attorney who at this late stage in his career primarily practiced with only a sole associate, had an opening in his office. Weintraub advised Byrne that working with McGeehan would be a valuable learning experience while he waited for potential other opportunities. Particularly celebrated for his dramatic presence and commanding voice in the courtroom, McGeehan had been known, according to Byrne, as "the best trial lawyer of New Jersey"—a hard-nosed model for his own legal career. But Byrne recognized that by the time he went to work for McGeehan in the early 1950s, the older lawyer was "slightly past his peak," and it took a while to adjust to his work habits. "If he wasn't trying a case," Byrne remembered, "he often didn't come into the office until three p.m. His friends knew not to call him at the office before lunch. But he'd work five solid hours, until 8 p.m., and then go home."

Byrne respected McGeehan's oratorical ability both inside and outside the courtroom, but in his senior years there was an occasional slip-up. One of Byrne's favorite stories was about McGeehan's speech at a dinner honoring a Monsignor Conroy. Conroy was a close friend of a Monsignor McNulty, and McGeehan knew both men well. After reciting Monsignor Conroy's many qualities, McGeehan concluded his talk with a typical dramatic flourish: "If I had to ask just one person to plead my case before the throne of Saint Peter, I would want no one but Monsignor McNulty." When the audience went silent at McGeehan's gaffe in paying tribute to the wrong monsignor, the lawyer's skills quickly kicked in as he smoothly recovered, "And failing that, I'd want Monsignor Conroy."

Byrne learned to take heed of the older lawyer's experience and advice. "I was a young man full of beans, and sometimes I needed a little constructive criticism," he conceded. "John would give it to me. Never in an ugly way, never a putdown. The feeling was: 'I'm older than you, and I've seen more of the world. Take it from me, you ought to do it this way.'"

On one occasion, while he was trying a case, Byrne called McGeehan for help in the middle of the trial. "Mr. McGeehan, I just found out the witness I have to cross-examine this afternoon is a minister," Byrne recalled asking. "'How the heck do you cross-examine a minister?' John McGeehan gave me one of those wonderful pauses and then said, 'Well, Brendan, it isn't as if he were a priest.'"[28]

One of McGeehan's best-known clients was Abner "Longy" Zwillman, a mobster who had begun as a bootlegger during Prohibition. Working under the famed Meyer Lansky, Zwillman later became a major figure on his own, "the Al Capone of New Jersey" controlling illegal numbers and other gambling rackets. He was reputedly a key figure in the murder in 1935 of the mobster "Dutch" Schultz, who was shot in the Palace Chop House, a Newark restaurant. Zwillman's colorful career also included a romance with the movie star Jean Harlow and the hidden financing of a buyout of Columbia Pictures. Zwillman lived in a large house in West Orange located only a few blocks from the Byrne home, and Byrne previously had heard occasional news of Zwillman and his family through his girlfriend, Beryl Anfindsen, whose brother was a close friend of Zwillman's stepson. "Most people in West Orange had heard the stories about Zwillman," Byrne later recalled. "But you never knew how many of them were true."[29]

While McGeehan generally handled Zwillman's various legal problems on his own, he once asked Brendan to deliver a package of papers to the Zwillman home. "I knocked at the door," Brendan recalled years later, "but no one came to let me in. I figured they were suspicious about who I was, so I drove home, phoned McGeehan and he called Zwillman. I drove back, they let me in and took the papers." When Zwillman came to McGeehan's office, Byrne sometimes greeted him, recalling him as "a big man. I was struck mostly by the size of his hands. They were just huge."[30]

During his three years at McGeehan's firm, Byrne worked to refine his basic skills as a lawyer, interviewing clients, writing briefs, appearing for motions, and performing the other tasks of a young lawyer. In one case, in which he represented a woman who had been injured while riding in a taxi, he proudly recalled years later obtaining a settlement of $5,000 from the taxi company, a considerable increase from the offer of $500 that the company had previously extended when the woman was represented by another lawyer. Byrne enjoyed his time with McGeehan, but much of the work involved handling civil matters. "I wanted to be in the courtroom trying criminal cases," he later reflected. "That was always my goal as a lawyer."[31]

Byrne received his chance when he received a call from David Satz, then a deputy state attorney general who later became the U.S. Attorney for New Jersey. Byrne had first met Satz during the 1953 gubernatorial campaign of Robert Meyner, when both were among a group of young Democratic lawyers campaigning for Meyner. In his call to Byrne, Satz offered him an appointment as a deputy attorney general temporarily assigned to the Passaic County prosecutor's office. The office, which the state attorney general had taken over pending the appointment of a new prosecutor, had a growing backlog of cases, and the attorney general had been directed to hire new lawyers to reduce the delays in scheduling trials.

Byrne resigned from McGeehan's firm to take the job. "John tried to talk me out of it," Byrne later reflected, "and I agreed to stay a little longer to help him clear up as many cases as I could before I left. But I was eager to get started with the prosecutor job."[32] While in Passaic County, Byrne relished the busy trial schedule and was even allowed at the age of 31 to try two murder cases, a responsibility usually reserved for attorneys with much more experience.

In one case, the defendant, who had reputed mob connections, was on vacation with his wife staying at a rental apartment at the Jersey Shore, but had left her alone for the day when he went to the Monmouth Park Racetrack. During the husband's absence, his wife struck up a conversation in a bar with a male acquaintance and, assuming that her husband would remain at the shore overnight, she and the man drove up to the home in Clifton that the wife shared with her husband. The husband unexpectedly came home to get an extra shirt, entered the bedroom, and found the two sleeping in the nude in his marital bed. Startled awake, the wife's lover fled the home, as Brendan recalled, "running stark naked into the street."[33] Later that night, the police were called and they found the wife's body, dressed only in a bathrobe, lying in the rear yard, with two bullet holes in her head. On the next day, the husband, who had returned to the apartment at the shore, was arrested and charged with his wife's murder.

At the trial, the state's case presented by Byrne was largely circumstantial: no gun was found and the wife's lover, who as he rushed out of the bedroom had only gotten a quick glimpse of the husband, had run from the home before the shooting and had not heard any shots from the street. The attorney for the defendant argued that the evidence failed to establish that his client was at the scene, and ended his summation to the jury, saying "it's a rainy day and the grass will soon be green. I ask that you acquit my client to allow him to walk outside again on that green grass on a beautiful spring day." John Farmer, then a young reporter for the *Newark Evening News* covering the trial and later communications director for Byrne as governor, recalled: "I thought Brendan was going to lose the case, but he gave a great summation."[34] In his own summation, Byrne repeated his adversary's comments about the green grass, but noted that, as a result of the defendant, "the body of his wife lies under that green grass today." The defendant was convicted of second-degree murder and sentenced to twenty-five to thirty years in prison.[35]

In the other murder case tried by Byrne, the defendant shot his wife as she was standing in front of a tavern in Passaic while he was seated in his car parked on the opposite side of the street. After the shooting, the defendant picked up his wife and took her to the hospital, but she died shortly after arrival. Following his arrest at the hospital, the husband gave a statement to the police admitting that he raised the gun to "scare" his wife, but claimed that its firing was accidental when his finger slipped on the trigger. Testimony at the trial disclosed that the wife was an alcoholic; had engaged in a series of affairs; and had previously been convicted of child neglect for leaving her three children alone in their apartment while she was out drinking, resulting in two of the children suffering severe burns when a fire broke out. On the night of the shooting, the couple had an argument and, after the wife left the apartment, the husband later tracked her down, finding her standing on the sidewalk before the tavern where the shooting took place. The defendant was convicted of second-degree murder and sentenced to thirty years in prison.[36]

Byrne's stay in Passaic County was relatively brief. After a year prosecuting cases, he would move on to connect once again with Joseph Weintraub.

Chapter 4

The Public Career Begins

After his stay in Passaic County prosecuting criminal cases as a deputy attorney general, in 1955 Byrne was reunited with Joseph Weintraub as an assistant counsel to Governor Robert Meyner. Elected in 1953, Meyner was the first Democrat to win the office since 1940, and had appointed Weintraub to the position of counsel to the governor. When Weintraub offered him a job as an assistant counsel, Byrne briefly hesitated before accepting. "I really enjoyed trying cases," he later reflected, "and that's what I wanted to do as a career. But I couldn't turn down the chance to work with Weintraub again."[1]

Along with other young Democratic lawyers, Byrne had been a volunteer in the Meyner campaign, usually speaking at local events, but had not played a significant role. His only direct contact with the candidate came when Meyner forgot his raincoat at a campaign stop, and Byrne was dispatched to drive to catch up with Meyner at his next event to return the coat. "He thanked me," Byrne recounted, "but that was the only time I talked to him during the campaign."[2]

Meyner's election came as a bit of a fluke. A World War II veteran and well-known trial lawyer, Meyner had been elected in 1947 to the state senate representing Warren County, but after a single term had been defeated in 1951 for reelection. Despite the loss, he won the Democratic gubernatorial nomination in 1953, a victory aided by a split in the powerful Hudson County organization. Former Hudson County boss and longtime Jersey City Mayor Frank Hague supported Elmer Wene, the Democratic gubernatorial nominee in 1949 and a former Congressman and state senator from South Jersey, while Hague's one-time protégé and the then Jersey City mayor, John V. Kenny, threw his support to Meyner in a successful effort to block both Wene's nomination and Hague's attempt at a political comeback. Carrying only three of the twenty-one counties in the primary election, Meyner won by less than 1,700 votes, aided substantially by the 30,000-vote plurality produced in Hudson County by John Kenny. In the general election, Meyner was elected over Republican Paul L. Troast, head of a major construction firm and a former chairman of the New Jersey Turnpike Authority, after it was disclosed that Troast had written to New York Governor Thomas E. Dewey urging clemency for a convicted labor racketeer then in a New York prison. As governor, Meyner quickly became popular for his efforts to limit spending and uncover corruption.[3] A handsome 45-year-old bachelor with silver hair who later was described by the *Saturday Evening Post* as "The Glamorous Governor of New Jersey," Meyner also soon gained national media attention as an emerging Democratic leader.[4]

Meyner and Weintraub had first met when they both served on a commission investigating labor corruption in the northern New Jersey ports. A position initially established by Governor Alfred Driscoll in 1947, the governor's counsel aided in developing the governor's legislative and policy initiatives, as well as in reviewing legal documents and matters presented for the governor's approval.[5] "In the Meyner days," Byrne later reflected, "there were only about four or five of us in the whole office. There was me. There was a press secretary. There was a policy guy and a couple of other people. . . . But there were only four or five of us. So there was no way of talking about organization and structure. We all did our thing."[6] As an assistant counsel, Byrne gained exposure to the workings of the State House—drafting legislation, reviewing extraditions, pardons, and other legal documents requiring the governor's approval, writing speeches, and meeting with lobbyists and interest group representatives. He frequently met with members of the legislature, when they were still without their own staff and largely dependent on the governor and the executive agencies for information on the bills pending before them. "We would have a meeting of the Democratic legislators," Byrne later recalled. "And I or somebody else would sit and tell them what the administration's position was on the bills that were coming in out there. They had no independent research."[7]

In November 1956, Weintraub resigned as counsel to the governor upon his appointment by the governor as an associate justice on the state Supreme Court to the seat previously held by William Brennan, who resigned after his nomination by President Dwight Eisenhower and confirmation by the U.S. Senate as a justice of the U.S. Supreme Court. Following the death of New Jersey Chief Justice Arthur Vanderbilt in June 1957 from a heart attack, Meyner named Weintraub to succeed Vanderbilt as Chief Justice.

When Weintraub left Governor Meyner's staff to become a judge, Byrne continued to develop his own independent ties with the governor. In 1956, Robert Burkhardt, who had served as Meyner's campaign director and was a seasoned Democratic activist, left as Meyner's executive secretary to join the presidential campaign of former Illinois Governor Adlai Stevenson, and the Governor surprisingly asked Byrne to succeed him, albeit with "acting" before the title in the event Burkhardt decided to return.[8] Despite the relationship that Byrne had developed with Meyner, he lacked the political pedigree and contacts of Burkhardt, whom Byrne later described as "a political pro who was recognized throughout the country." When Burkhardt recommended to Meyner that Byrne's promotion be rewarded with a $500 raise to his $7,000 salary, the Governor vetoed the hike. "Meyner was known as a tightwad," Byrne recalled years later, "not only with the state government's money, but especially with his own. I think he liked having that image."[9]

Yet the position allowed Byrne to gain his own visibility as the state's most powerful officials and politicians needed to go through Byrne as executive secretary to convey messages to the governor or to seek appointments to see him. According to Martin Greenberg, who became an assistant counsel to Meyner after Byrne succeeded Burkhardt, another aspect of the executive secretary job was to review the merits of job seekers and potential appointees to government boards and commissions. "I think he was more of a conduit between people who were recommending people to the governor and the governor's need for people." Greenberg later remembered. "And Brendan would kind of screen them and make recommendations as to who he thought would best fit the bill, whether that bill was 80% political or 92% talent or whatever."[10] As time went on, Byrne was able to establish his own network of relationships; "for the first time," he later recalled, "people began to see me as a comer in politics, a possible Congressman or something like that."[11] Yet Byrne's rapid rise also provoked jealously among some veteran politicians. "There was resentment toward me," he later explained, "in becoming one of Meyner's palace guard, particularly since I hadn't worked my way up the political ranks."[12]

As he would in later jobs, Byrne forged strong personal ties with those he worked with, ties that would endure through the years. Greenberg, for example, would later follow Byrne to the Essex County prosecutor's office and become his law partner and political adviser. Having grown up in Newark's largely Jewish Weequahic neighborhood (later the subject of the early novels of his high school classmate Phillip Roth), just a few miles down in the valley from the West Orange home of the Byrnes, Greenberg's first contact with the young Catholic Irishman Brendan Byrne, left him taken aback. "He was a gentile person that I had not ever been exposed to," Greenberg later recounted. "He was from a different world." Yet beyond their differences in faith and upbringing, Greenberg recognized Byrne's special qualities. "Brendan was a piece of work," he would recall fondly. "He was a very impressive young man. . . . Brendan was different. . . . Liberal, caring, bright, good looking . . . I never met anybody like Brendan Byrne."[13]

Along with other lawyers working in the State House who lived in Essex County, Greenberg took advantage of Meyner's decision to allocate to Byrne one of the two state cars assigned to the governor's office; they shared the driving back and forth to Trenton. Apart from relishing the banter in the car usually spiced by Byrne's sharp wit, Greenberg said he, Byrne, and others working for Meyner shared more serious goals: "We were liberal Democrats, and we were impressed with Bob Meyner and we wanted to help him. We liked what Bob Meyner did, so we were all on the same page."[14]

In his role as executive secretary, Byrne also gained political experience by taking an active role in Meyner's successful 1957 reelection campaign, in which Meyner defeated state senator Malcolm S. Forbes, publisher of *Forbes* magazine, by 203,000 votes, thus becoming the first governor in the history of the state to be elected to a second four-year term.[15] Meyner's reelection enhanced his prominence as an emerging national figure, with *TIME* magazine in 1958 including him in a cover story profiling six potential contenders for the 1960 Democratic presidential nomination.[16]

Byrne developed a strong personal relationship with the Governor. "We had lunch together nearly every day in his office," he recalled. "Meyner often would go off on little kicks. Someone would mention hot dogs, for example, and he'd have hot dogs for lunch every day for over a week. Then he'd start on something else to eat." But on one occasion, Byrne ran afoul of Meyner's distaste for change. "There was no place in the governor's office," Byrne later recalled, "to hang the coats of people who came in for meetings, and coats and hats would be strewn all over. Without telling Meyner, I brought in coat racks. When he saw them, he hollered at me and told me to get rid of them."[17]

Indirectly, Byrne played a small role in Meyner's courtship of Helen Stevenson, a distant cousin of Adlai Stevenson, the Democratic presidential nominee in 1952 and 1956. During Stevenson's 1956 presidential campaign, Meyner spoke at Oberlin College in Ohio, where Helen's father, William Stevenson, was president.[18] After being introduced to Helen at the Oberlin event, Meyner phoned Byrne to ask that he get tickets for a future performance of *My Fair Lady*, then the most popular Broadway musical. Byrne called David Wilentz, the former state attorney general, who was able to use his contacts to secure the hard-to-get tickets. "Meyner took Helen to the show on one of her next trips east," Brendan recalled years later. "I think that was one of their first real dates, but I didn't know how serious their relationship would become." They were married in 1957, and shortly after returning from their honeymoon, would move into Morven, the historic home in Princeton that former Governor Walter Edge had previously purchased as his own residence and had subsequently donated to the state to serve as the official residence of the governor.[19]

Initially, Byrne was a bit wary of the Governor's new wife: "I was afraid she would disrupt the close relationship I had with Meyner. She also did little things that annoyed me, like changing the soap in the tennis house at Morven to a 'sissy' soap." Over time, however, as Byrne recalled, "she became one of my closest friends and supporters." Byrne later encouraged Helen Meyner to run for Congress in 1972 and she in turn would urge him to enter the gubernatorial race the following year.[20] Byrne's wife Jean also became friends with Helen and the Meyners got the Byrnes to start playing tennis regularly. Despite having played on and off as a boy, Byrne had developed no special love of the game until the Governor repeatedly drafted him to play, and he and Jean grew to share the Meyners' fondness for it. "Jean didn't like politics," Byrne recalled, "but she liked tennis, and got pretty good at it."

Byrne admired Meyner's honesty and his stance against corruption. "He was a very decent guy," Byrne said long after Meyner's death, "who tried to do the right thing, to fight for principle." One episode that Byrne cited as illustrating Meyner's political courage was his nomination of former Superior Court Judge John Bigelow to the Rutgers University Board of Governors. Republicans in the state senate attempted to block the appointment because, as an attorney, Bigelow had once represented—at the request of the state Bar Association—a Newark school teacher who had taken the Fifth Amendment.[21] Despite the controversy over Bigelow's nomination—it even received television coverage, highly unusual for the time—Meyner stood behind the nomination, which was confirmed by the state senate only after, as one reporter wrote, "one of the most violent legislative storms in the state's history."[22] As Byrne later reflected, "I think it was Meyner's greatest moment. It was at the height of McCarthyism, and people like Malcolm Forbes in the Senate weren't standing up for Bigelow, but Meyner's sense of decency and fair play wouldn't allow this man's good name to be dragged through the mud."[23]

Even with his overall admiration for Meyner, Byrne nonetheless felt that on broader issues Meyner "respected public opinion too much," as Byrne put it, "waiting for the mail to come in" before taking a position. One of Byrne's daily tasks was to sort through the incoming mail, select the letters he thought Meyner should read himself, and prepare a summary and count of the views expressed by all writers on issues then being debated. "He strongly favored whatever was currently popular with the voters of New Jersey," Byrne reflected. "He was mildly in favor of what was mildly popular. And he was dead set against what the people of New Jersey were dead set against." This didn't fit with Byrne's own idea of how a governor should lead. "I've always thought a governor has to do more than that," he later said. "He's got to be able to get out front on an issue, take the heat for an unpopular stand, and explain to the voters why he's doing what he is. A politician should respect public opinion—but never too much."[24]

Another weakness Byrne recognized was the governor's failure in public talks to convey a sense of humor. "Privately, Meyner could be funny," Byrne later reflected, "but when he spoke to a group he just couldn't master how to tell a joke." When Meyner emerged as a national figure in the Democratic Party, efforts were made to improve his timing and delivery of jokes and anecdotes. On a national speaking tour designed to boost Meyner's visibility, Byrne and others close to Meyner did their best to insert humorous asides to lighten his talks, but Meyner's wooden delivery proved to be an insurmountable hurdle. "He just couldn't handle it," Byrne later recalled, "he couldn't tell a joke."[25] But Byrne held his opinions on Meyner's weaknesses to himself. By the end of Meyner's second term, he had become, in Byrne's words, "sort of a father figure to me."[26]

After his inauguration for a second term, the Governor asked Byrne what he wanted to do next. "I've always been a lawyer," Byrne replied. "I'd love to be prosecutor of Essex County." But according to Byrne, Meyner told him, "I probably can't do that for you."[27] Joe Katz, then a reporter for the *Newark Evening News* and later a key staff member for Governor Richard Hughes, succinctly summarized the political stakes surrounding the post: "In addition to providing a valuable source of patronage—assistants, investigators, detectives and office personnel—a friendly prosecutor's office is considered a valuable asset by the prosecutor's political party. In political circles, an unfriendly prosecutor is viewed as a source of worry, harassment and trouble with his direction of the grand jury and his investigative powers."[28]

Meyner was delaying making a nomination while the two leading Essex Democrats—State Senator Donal Fox and Essex Democratic Chair Dennis Carey—tried to reach an agreement on recommending a candidate for appointment. Fox, a former assistant Essex County prosecutor, had expressed interest in the job for himself, but it became clear that Meyner would not nominate him due to concerns over the potential loss of Fox's Senate seat to a Republican. Carey supported another lawyer who had been active in supporting the county political organization. As Meyner waited for Fox and Carey to get together on a choice, he suggested to Byrne that he instead consider heading the state motor vehicles agency, a position that Meyner told Byrne could provide statewide visibility in the event Byrne eventually decided to seek elected office. "I really wasn't interested in the motor vehicles job," Byrne reflected years later. "I wanted to get back to being a courtroom lawyer."[29]

Fox and Carey had been at odds following Fox's unsuccessful attempt, along with Newark Mayor Leo Carlin, to depose Carey as county chair. Carey had survived as county chair after Meyner stated that he would remain neutral in the fight, but feelings among the three Democrats remained strained. "I just wasn't part of Carey's team," Byrne later explained. "I don't think it was personal."[30]

Carey's opposition was understandable. As Martin Greenberg explained years later, Byrne "was a young guy who came from a Harvard and Princeton background, and who wore white bucks which he would clean every day in our office by hand. But this is not the guy, the kind of guy, that a county chairman would be comfortable with. . . . So you don't want a stranger in that office, and he viewed Brendan as a stranger."[31] Appointment of a prosecutor also was viewed as a measure of the county chairman's political clout; "unlike some other county bosses," Byrne later reflected, "I think Dennis Carey was an honest guy, but it was important to him that others recognized his power and his ability to influence who got important positions." In any event, Carey continued to strongly oppose Byrne's nomination, indeed reportedly saying to one of his confidants, as disclosed at the time to Byrne, that "Brendan Byrne will become prosecutor over my dead body."[32]

In February 1959, Meyner and Byrne were flying back from Washington together on a National Guard plane after attending the annual Congressional reception sponsored by the state chamber of commerce when Meyner informed Byrne that he would appoint him on an interim basis—an appointment that did not require confirmation by the state senate—as deputy attorney general in charge of the Essex County Prosecutor's Office.[33]

Byrne made two further requests of Meyner. "I wanted a trusted friend who was then the deputy state treasurer to come with me to Newark as my chief deputy prosecutor, but I knew I could only persuade him to come if Meyner agreed to appoint him later as a judge," he later recounted. "I also wanted Meyner to direct that a state trooper be assigned to the prosecutor's office, where I wanted him to be seated in uniform just outside the door to my office to give a signal to the politicians and the mobsters of the type of operation I intended to run. Meyner agreed to both of my requests, and that was really a great help to me."[34]

Even in his interim status as Essex County Prosecutor, Byrne took aggressive steps to reshape the office, partly as a result of calling Chief Justice Weintraub for advice, who told him that he should "clean house." He fired most of the remaining lawyers, and recruited replacements without strong political ties. Governor Meyner also followed through on Byrne's request that a state trooper be assigned to the office; Clinton Pagano, the trooper who received the assignment, would many years later be named by Byrne to head the State Police. The prosecutor's staff had twelve detectives, who were civil service employees, and an equal number of investigators, who were considered not covered by civil service protections, such as subject to being fired without cause. Soon after coming to Newark, a former Essex County Democratic chairman, whose wife also was a prominent activist in the party, came to see Byrne to ask that the new prosecutor not fire an investigator who was one of his relatives. "As he was sitting there with me," Byrne recounted later, "I phoned the investigator at home. It was the middle of the morning, and he still hadn't come in to work. I think I made the point that he wasn't worth keeping and fired him and most of the others."[35]

Dennis Carey would continue to create problems for Byrne, usually on his requests to increase the budget to support an expansion of the legal staff and to allow replacement of outmoded equipment and weapons for its detectives and investigators. "When I went to Newark," Byrne recalled, "I tried to be extremely polite to him, and would always call him 'Mr. Carey.' As a courtesy, I told anyone I hired to phone and introduce themselves to him. We never became close, but he knew that I had the support of Meyner, Weintraub and Judge Alex Waugh, the assignment judge in Essex. He had to tolerate me."[36]

After Byrne had served for a few months as interim prosecutor, at the end of May Meyner submitted Byrne's nomination as prosecutor to the Senate despite Carey's continued opposition. Meyner's decision came after Senator Fox had a new clash with Carey when the county chairman objected to Meyner's appointment of one of Fox's friends to the board of the New York Port Authority. When Fox found out that Carey was holding up his friend's appointment, he met with Meyner and succeeded in getting the Governor to agree to submit the nomination; on his way out of Meyner's office, according to the account related by Meyner to Byrne, Fox told Meyner, "And if you want to send Brendan's nomination as prosecutor up at the same time, go ahead."[37]

Meyner's decision to make Byrne's appointment permanent also may have been due to his anger with Carey, Hudson County's John Kenny, and other Democratic bosses when they rejected his request that their legislative delegations support his veto of a bill to expand a college scholarship program. "It was no coincidence," according to a later account, "that the day his [Meyner's] veto was overridden in the Assembly, he appointed his former aide, Brendan Byrne, to the post of prosecutor of Essex County."[38]

Following his confirmation by the Senate, Byrne took the oath as Essex County Prosecutor in July 1959 at the age of 34. In those days, prosecutors served only part-time and thus were allowed to continue in private legal practice or other nongovernmental posts to supplement their salaries, which in Byrne's case was $12,000 when he was appointed. Byrne fulfilled a pledge to serve full-time as the prosecutor for his first year, but later accepted private sector positions as a partner in what would become the law firm of Teltser, Byrne and Greenberg in East Orange; as chairman of the Intercontinental Life Insurance Company that he cofounded in 1965; and as a director of the Broad National Bank of Newark.[39] The prosecutor's staff usually numbered ten to twelve attorneys whose pay began at $8,000 but, like their boss, were able to supplement their public salaries by income from private legal practice or other positions that did not conflict with their roles as prosecutors.

One of Byrne's youngest hires was James Zazzali, who had just completed a clerkship with Superior Court Judge Lawrence Whipple (later to become chief judge of the U.S. District Court for New Jersey). Zazzali's older brother Andrew had previously joined Byrne's staff, but Jim, who intended to go to work in his father's firm in representing the labor movement, had little interest in criminal law; he nonetheless had agreed to the interview at the urging of Judge Whipple, who suggested that the prosecutor's office offered an opportunity to learn basic trial skills regardless of what area of practice a young lawyer eventually pursued. In his meeting with Byrne, Zazzali (later to become Byrne's attorney general and subsequently chief justice of the state supreme court) was taken aback at the Prosecutor's behavior. "For the entire fifteen minute interview," Zazzali recalled, "he was seated behind his desk shining his shoes, shining his loafers, never once looking up . . . I don't think I ever made eye contact with him until the end of the interview. And then he finally looked up and said, 'O.K., you're hired. But it will be a risk.'" Reflecting on Byrne's off-putting manner many years later, Zazzali said, "I was annoyed, but others told me that this was Brendan's unique style of 'motivating' new assistants."[40]

Soon after coming to Newark, Byrne met with Joseph Weldon, the Newark police director under Mayor Leo Carlin. When Byrne mentioned how extensive illegal gambling was in the city, Weldon replied, "I hope you'll do something about it," thus making it clear to Byrne that the police did not consider enforcement of gambling laws a priority for themselves.[41] Somewhat later, Byrne received a call from then Congressman Hugh Addonizio, who requested that he meet Byrne in the prosecutor's office. At their meeting, Addonizio asked Byrne to downgrade a gambling charge against one of his political supporters. Byrne rejected Addonizio's request, and Addonizio responded, "But you did one of these before for [state Senator] Donal Fox," provoking Byrne's angry retort, "Look, if you can show that I did anything like this for Donal Fox, I'll not only downgrade the charge against your guy, I'll have it dismissed."[42] In 1962, Addonizio was elected mayor of Newark, defeating Mayor Carlin; FBI files released years later disclosed that leading mobsters helped fund the Addonizio campaign, with a member of the Genovese crime family recorded on a wiretap saying about the new mayor: "He'll give us the city."[43] As mayor, Addonizio and his police director, Dominick Spina, would continue to have a prickly relationship with Prosecutor Byrne.

Byrne received another sign of the extent that gambling was accepted when his office was informed that a reporter at the *Newark Evening News*, then the dominant newspaper in New Jersey, was running a bookmaking operation out of the newsroom that had expanded to take bets from hundreds of customers. Rather than raiding the newsroom, Byrne decided to visit the newspaper's executive editor to advise him of what was going on and request that he shut down the bookmaking before Byrne was forced to act. But instead of gratitude for the tip, the editor, as Byrne later recalled, "gave me a lecture, telling me there would be no time for any such operation. Now get out of the building." Byrne left, waited a week to see if the bookmaking was shut down and, when it wasn't, raided the newsroom and arrested the book-maker. "I thought the editor owed me an apology," Byrne reflected later, "but I never got one. But then I'm sure the editor felt: 'The *Newark News* is never wrong.'"[44]

Byrne's primary initiatives were targeting organized crime and illegal gambling on the "retail" level, which he felt were often linked since profits from local bookmakers, numbers runners, and gambling in social clubs were passed up the ladder to fund higher level mobsters. His view of how critical the lowest gambling ranks were to supporting the organized crime hierarchy was also shared by Chief Justice Weintraub who, empowered by the significant administrative authority the chief justice had been given under the 1947 state constitution, ordered that a single judge in each county hear all gambling cases and that stiff jail sentences be given to bookmakers and numbers runners.[45]

After Addonizio's election in 1962, Byrne and his staff quickly came to realize that the Newark police could not be trusted when a series of planned joint raids against gambling establishments were undercut when the targets apparently were tipped off in advance of the operations. The prosecutor's office then began keeping its plans from the police, undertaking raids with the aid of state police, an action that strained relations with the Newark police and city officials. Byrne also began undercover surveillance of Dominick Spina, the Newark police director whom Addonizio had appointed after his election, suspecting him of mob connections.

In addition to prosecutions, Byrne also used grand jury investigations to highlight specific issues and the need for potential reforms.[46] In April 1965, the Essex County Grand Jury released a report charging the police department with a failure to enforce gambling laws. "We have a lack of full confidence in the Newark Police Department's enthusiasm for a crackdown on the underworld," the grand jury reported. "Nowhere has our attention been focused on any policy statement by the Police Department vigorously attacking organized crime."[47] This presentment was followed by another in December 1965, in which the Grand Jury again harshly criticized the lack of gambling enforcement by the Newark police. Spina publicly denounced the findings as "vicious," and challenged Prosecutor Byrne to show him the organized gambling in Newark. Within forty-eight hours, the Prosecutor's Office raided two apartments in Newark and charged fifteen people with operating a lottery.[48]

The connection between organized crime and gambling, which was the basis of much of Byrne's strategy as prosecutor, also wasn't apparent to most of the public. "This wasn't always popular with a lot of people who didn't see anything particularly wrong with a little gambling," Byrne would later admit, "and who thought it gave guys in corner stores or barber shops a way to make a little extra money."[49]

One of those guys making a little extra money was Frank Byrne's longtime fishmonger. After the man was charged with bookmaking, Byrne was asked by his father to drop the case. "Brendan, you arrested the man where I buy my fish," Byrne recalled his father's plea, going on to say he was "a good guy" who always greeted him warmly by name when he came to shop, "Where am I going to get fish?" But the son replied, "I'm sorry Dad. If they're guilty, we arrest them." Following that rebuff, Frank would say to the friends who came to him hoping to influence his son to go easy on a relative or friend, "I can't help you. I can't even get Brendan to go easy on my fish man."[50]

Byrne's first step against organized crime was to create the "Charlie Squad" (so called because the three lawyers assigned to it were named "Charlie"). The "Charlie Squad" was headed by Charles Carella, whom Byrne had first met at Saint Joseph's Catholic Church in West Orange, where Carella was the catechism teacher for Byrne's oldest son, Tom.[51] Some actions taken by the "Charlie Squad" were intended simply to harass their targets. "We encouraged informants through publicity," Carella said in a later interview. "We would have stakeouts. We would follow criminals that were known organized crime participants and we would put them under surveillance. We would obtain search warrants and we would find areas in the county where there were some form of organized, illegal gambling."[52]

Byrne's focus on organized crime came at a time of renewed public attention to mob activities. In November 1957, less than two years before Byrne became prosecutor, a meeting of national crime leaders at a farm in the rural town of Apalachin in upstate New York had been raided by police, who had become suspicious over the unusual number of high-priced, out-of-state cars parked on the country road. Among the sixty arrested were Vito Genovese, "the Boss of All Bosses," who had assumed the leadership of the New York mob following the assassination of Albert Anastasia a few weeks before the Apalachin meeting, and Jerry Catena, a native of South Orange and a soldier in the Genovese crime family. Genovese had reportedly called the meeting to confirm his role as the family's boss as well as to approve Carlo Gambino as boss of his own family.[53]

Early in his tenure as prosecutor, on February 27, 1959, Byrne had to deal with the death of the prominent mobster "Longy" Zwillman, whom Byrne had first met when Zwillman was a client of the McGeehan law firm.[54] Zwillman was found hung in an apparent suicide in the basement of his West

Orange home; his death occurred shortly before he was to testify before the U.S. Senate committee investigating organized crime chaired by Arkansas Senator John McClellan. After the police entered Zwillman's home, Byrne received a call from the medical examiner at the scene, who asked, "Is it all right if we cut him down now?" Byrne later recalled. "When he asked me that, I got a clear picture of what they were looking at in the cellar."[55] Although Byrne accepted the conclusion of the police and the medical examiner that Zwillman had hung himself, rumors surrounding the death would persist. Some accounts alleged that the hanging was a disguised assassination or a forced suicide engineered by the mob in fear that Zwillman had agreed to cooperate with the McClellan committee and federal law enforcement agencies.[56]

In October 1963, national attention was again focused on the structure of organized crime by the televised testimony before Congress of Joseph Valachi, who was the first mobster to publicly acknowledge the existence of the Mafia, or what he said was commonly called "Cosa Nostra," or "Our Thing". Valachi's cooperation with the government began when—as he was serving a drug trafficking sentence in a federal prison—he came to believe that Vito Genovese had ordered his murder, suspecting that he had become an informer. Valachi then killed a fellow inmate, mistakenly believing that he was the designated hit man. After Valachi agreed to cooperate with the government, he was transferred for greater security to the Army stockade at Fort Monmouth in New Jersey, where federal agents interrogated him prior to his public testimony before Congress.[57]

Following Valachi's congressional appearance, Byrne received permission to question him to obtain possible information relating to organized crime activities in Essex County. In his testimony, Valachi had identified, among others, Jerry Catena, Ruggiero "Richie the Boot" Boiardo, and his son, Anthony "Tony Boy" Boiardo as key Essex County figures in the Vito Genovese mob family.[58] At their meeting, Byrne recalled, Valachi appeared "uncomfortable" as he fidgeted in his constraints: "he kept stretching his arms and moving in his chair, he looked like he was trying to get some exercise."[59] When Byrne showed Valachi photos of crime figures and asked whether he could confirm that they were linked to Mafia operations, Valachi repeatedly replied, "Would it help you if I said they were?" Believing that Valachi was simply fishing to determine what information would best further his own interests, Byrne ended the interrogation. "I just didn't think he was credible," Byrne recounted years later. "I had the feeling he'd say anything he thought would get him better treatment."[60]

As Byrne neared the end of his five-year term as prosecutor in 1964, Mayor Addonizio and other politicians stepped up pressure on Democratic Governor Richard Hughes, who had succeeded Meyner in 1962, to appoint another prosecutor to replace Byrne. Byrne's public criticism of the city's law enforcement efforts under Police Director Spina and his strained relationship with Addonizio had made removing Byrne a political priority of the mayor.[61] According to a conversation recorded by the FBI, mobster Angelo "Gyp" DeCarlo claimed that Jersey City Mayor John Kenny also was trying to persuade Governor Hughes to nominate Byrne as a judge as a way of removing him as prosecutor. At one point, when Byrne's name came up, DeCarlo snapped, "Well, the hell with him. He's gonna be out of there soon."[62]

In fact, Hughes offered Byrne the post of director of the Alcoholic Beverage Commission, making the case that Alfred Driscoll had effectively used that position to gain public recognition that eventually contributed to his election as governor in 1946. Hughes also followed up by having Bob Burkhardt, who preceded Byrne as Governor Meyner's executive secretary, and others contact Byrne to recommend that he take the Alcoholic Beverage Commission job. But Hughes could not afford to alienate Byrne by pushing too hard for him to give up the job of prosecutor. "Governor Hughes faced a far greater political risk if he did not re-appoint Brendan," Jim Zazzali later reflected, "who was so greatly respected by the press and the public."[63]

Finally, after the repeated suggestions by Hughes and others that he leave the prosecutor's office, an exasperated Byrne told Hughes, "I'll resign right now if that's what you want." But Hughes quickly said "No, no, no," and reassured Byrne that he would not force him out as prosecutor.[64] And, despite the political risk of crossing key Democrats, Hughes did reappoint him, as Byrne later put it, "very courageously" to a second five-year term in July 1964.[65]

While the bulk of the prosecutions Byrne would bring were aimed at the lower ranks of bookmakers and numbers runners, he also harassed some of the higher-ups, including "Richie the Boot" and his son "Tony Boy" Boiardo.[66] The senior Boiardo had assumed control of mob activities in North Jersey after the 1959 "suicide" of Longy Zwillman, with whom he previously had divided crime profits in an uneasy alliance for many years.[67] "When I was prosecutor," Byrne later said, "Richie was in his 70s and had delegated most day-to-day operations to his son, but we still seized any chance we could to let him know that we were watching him." In the summer of 1966, after three teenaged trespassers were shot at on the Boiardo property, Byrne obtained a search warrant and dispatched a team of investigators and police who seized three shotguns in the Boiardo home.[68] Byrne called Boiardo and nineteen other witnesses to testify before a grand jury, but none of Boiardo's crew broke ranks to give information that would support an indictment.[69] In September 1967, Boiardo gained national attention when *Life* magazine began publishing a two-part series on organized crime based on information from FBI files. One of the articles profiled Boiardo's twenty-nine-room ornate mansion in Livingston (described by *Life* as in a style that "might be called Transylvania traditional"), and cited allegations that it had been the site for disposal of bodies from various murders, with some victims barbecued or incinerated in a furnace in the backyard.[70] In April 1969, Richie Boiardo was convicted of conspiracy to violate gambling laws and sentenced to up to three years in a state prison.

Boiardo's son "Tony Boy" had a tougher time. In the spring of 1968, Byrne subpoenaed the younger Boiardo to testify before a grand jury in connection with his alleged involvement in a shooting at a nightclub in Newark, but Boiardo delayed his appearance by fleeing to Florida. A bartender at the club who was expected to be Byrne's star witness in placing Tony Boy at the club disappeared, with suspicions that Tony Boy's father, "Richie the Boot," had orchestrated the bartender's murder to protect his son.[71] After refusing to answer Byrne's questions before the grand jury, Tony Boy was convicted of contempt and served two months in jail. In 1969, after Byrne had resigned as prosecutor, Boiardo was indicted, along with Mayor Addonizio and other Newark municipal officials, on federal charges including extortion and conspiracy, with the federal case based on some of the evidence previously presented to an Essex County grand jury by Byrne.[72] Addonizio was convicted and served over five years in a federal prison, but in July 1970, Boiardo's trial ended in a mistrial after he suffered an apparent heart attack; he subsequently was able to avoid being retried on the basis of poor health.[73]

Byrne and Tony Boy would have one final encounter. After Byrne had resigned as prosecutor and been confirmed as president of the Public Utilities Commission (PUC) in January 1968, he was exiting the steam room at the old Goldman's Hotel in West Orange, where he had worked as a locker boy while in junior high school. On his way out to shower, he met Boiardo entering for his own steam bath, both men stark naked. "Do you remember who I am?" Byrne asked. Grabbing his head in both hands, Boiardo exclaimed, "Oh my god, do I remember who you are!"[74]

Concurrently with Byrne's investigations, the FBI was conducting its own probe of organized crime in northern New Jersey. Although Byrne met regularly with FBI agents, he was never informed that—without judicial authorization—the FBI had bugged various places frequented by leading mobsters Sam "the Plumber" deCalvacante and Angelo "Gyp" DeCarlo, recording their conversations with other associates.[75] The eavesdropping by the FBI was conducted to develop intelligence on the structure of the mob network and its operations, not with the intent to compile evidence for any specific prosecution, which in fact would be excluded at any trial since the bugs had been planted without warrants. In 1970, however, after Byrne had resigned as prosecutor, the FBI transcripts of the conversations were released by federal prosecutors during the trial of DeCarlo and three others on extortion charges in response to a motion by defense attorneys for the disclosure of information relating to surveillance of their clients.[76]

In the conversations, the mobsters boasted of their ties with various public officials whom they claimed to have paid for favors and influence, including Newark Mayor Addonizio and Police Director Spina. DeCarlo was recorded as urging other mob associates to give money to then Congressman Addonizio for his 1962 mayoral campaign against Newark Mayor Leo Carlin, describing Addonizio as "a good bet."[77] DeCarlo also worked to keep potential opponents who might split Addonizio's support in Newark's Italian neighborhoods from filing as candidates. In one conversation, a DeCarlo underling claimed to have threatened Nicholas Caputo, the Essex County Clerk: "I'm gonna break your legs for you if you file. I'm warning you now. I'll be the guy to break your legs."[78]

But the references to Brendan Byrne in the FBI recordings, according to a press account, "make clear that the mob had no use for him. . . . The transcripts show that Byrne tried to do a job and was disliked for it."[79] He was called an "S.O.B.," a "Boy Scout," "no damn good" and "obnoxious." One mobster concluded that "trying to buy him only makes it worse."[80] The *New York Post* headlined its article on the transcript's comments relating to Byrne, "The Man the Mob Couldn't Bribe," a label that in slightly tailored form soon would reappear in another context.[81]

As the transcripts of FBI bugging operations indicated, the mob did recognize Byrne as a problem, but the risk of violence wasn't something that overly worried him. "Common sense tells you it's going to make things very hard on organized crime all over the state if the county prosecutor is gunned down by the mob," he later commented, "because the next county prosecutor will be under enormous pressure to get tough with organized crime. The media will be investigating a lot of things which organized crime would not like to see investigated. So when organized crime goes after prosecutors and politicians, it's usually not with a gun but with a bag of money. They try to buy you."[82]

Still, Byrne later recalled that while he and Jean were hosting a New Year's Eve party at home, he received a call from the State Police advising that a wiretap had detected some mobsters talking on a phone at a Friendly's ice cream parlor saying "someone was going to 'get Brendan Byrne.'" Although he called the local police to request that they run a patrol car by his house every few minutes, which they did for the rest of the evening, "the party went on." Byrne also relied on his wartime experience. "If I hadn't worried much in World War II about my B-17 getting shot syndrome," he concluded. "I wasn't going to worry much about mob reprisals. I guess I thought death was unlikely, and I didn't want to give the bad guys the satisfaction of making me worry about it."[83]

On July 12, 1967, two white Newark policemen arrested a black cab driver for improperly passing their patrol car. The cab driver was taken to a police precinct across from a large public housing project, whose residents could see the cab driver being dragged by the police into the precinct. A rumor spread that he had been killed while in police custody, when in fact he had been taken to a local hospital. Over the following six days, the incident escalated into riots with widespread arson and looting.[84]

When the violence overwhelmed the Newark police, who became a special target of the rioters, Newark Mayor Hugh Addonizio asked Governor Hughes for additional support. Hughes arrived in Newark at 4:30 in the morning on July 15 to assess the situation. He later stopped at Byrne's office, where his first request upon seeing Byrne was "Can I have an aspirin?"[85] The Governor initially took a hard stance against the rioters, declaring "This is a criminal insurrection by people who say they hate the white man but who really hate America."[86] He then ordered the State Police and later the National Guard to patrol the city's streets to curtail widespread looting and the burning of stores. The initial harsh response by the state authorities, however, only increased the tension. It was only when the Governor—on the advice of his commissioner of Community Affairs, Paul Ylvislaker, and Raymond Brown, a well-known black Newark attorney who also was a colonel in the National Guard—softened his tone and agreed to meet with representatives of the community to discuss the underlying political and social issues that the violence eased and the situation was brought under control. "After the first day or two," Byrne would later recall, "Hughes was superb. He demonstrated the right mix of toughness and compassion in calming things down. Addonizio hardly performed at all."[87] By the time order was restored, 26 people were dead and 725 were injured, with over $10 million in property losses.[88]

As prosecutor, Byrne oversaw the processing of nearly 1,500 arrests during the Newark riots. "A major problem," Byrne later recalled, "was simply coping with the paperwork. We didn't have enough secretaries to type the complaints and other forms necessary to process those who had been arrested."[89] Some 700 people subsequently were indicted by grand juries, but charges against all but 200 were downgraded by Byrne to nonindictable offenses, largely due to relatively small monetary amounts involved in the looting of stores. He requested and received additional support from the state attorney general, who designated lawyers on his staff to go to Newark to assist Byrne in prosecuting the cases. Despite warnings that the trials of those arrested would be disrupted by demonstrations, they proceeded without incident the following September.[90]

The stress of the situation provoked one of Byrne's few outbursts of temper. In the midst of the riots, he received a notice from Chief Justice Weintraub advising that a brief on an appeal pending before the Supreme Court was overdue. On the Saturday of the riots, Byrne phoned Barry Evenchick, the chief of his appellate section, who was at home, and berated him for the brief being late. Evenchick remembered that he was "truly shaken" by Byrne's "genuine temper tantrum," but quickly realized that Byrne's outburst was serving as "the relief valve for the pressure building up" from the riots. Evenchick promptly remedied the oversight, and the two men resumed their warm professional relationship and lifelong friendship.[91]

Subsequent federal and state investigations found that underlying causes leading to the Newark riots were the minority community's longstanding resentment of its lack of political representation, its distrust of public officials and the police, and the failure to alleviate persistent high levels of crime and poverty.[92] The state commission appointed by Governor Hughes was chaired by Robert D. Lilley, president of the New Jersey Bell Telephone Company (and later of AT&T), and included among its members former Governors Driscoll and Meyner. Its staff was headed by Sanford "Sandy" Jaffe, previously one of Byrne's assistant prosecutors who later had become a special assistant to U.S. Attorney General Robert Kennedy. The Lilley Commission's report cited as one of the causes of the disorders "a widespread belief that Newark's government is corrupt," quoting a source that those doing business in the city felt that "'everything at city hall is for sale.'" The report also found a widespread lack of confidence by the minority community in the integrity of the Newark police, stating that "no effective action has been taken to follow up" on the findings of connections between organized crime and police corruption that had been included in presentments by four Essex County grand juries convened by Prosecutor Byrne.[93]

During his nine years as prosecutor, Byrne also made decisions to seek the death penalty in cases in which seventeen people were ultimately sentenced to the electric chair. Many years later, Byrne told an audience that he was troubled by how arbitrary the decision to impose the death penalty could be. "I was prosecutor—sworn to uphold the constitution—it was me who decided which cases would be exposed to the death penalty," Byrne said. "And I think that that's shocking. It was me." In another example, he cited a case where he as prosecutor withdrew a recommendation for the death penalty because the attorney for the defendant was having a nervous breakdown. "And that man did not go, was not sentenced to the electric chair," Byrne recalled, "and not because of the evaluation of the case, but because his lawyer was having a nervous breakdown. That's how arbitrary it can be."[94]

Despite his misgivings about the death penalty, "I had a rule that if you killed a cop," Byrne later related, "that you were going to be exposed to the death penalty. . . . The reason I had that policy is because I felt if you kill a police officer, you ought to be exposed to whatever the extreme penalty was in New Jersey. And if you asked for anything less, the police community felt let down."[95] Byrne made it a policy to personally try all prosecutions involving the killing of police officers. In one trial in which the defendant was charged with killing a policeman, Byrne incorporated in his own closing remarks to the jury excerpts from the summation delivered in 1830 by U.S. Senator Daniel Webster in prosecuting a murder of a prominent resident of Salem, Massachusetts. Drawing from Webster's summation, Byrne recited, "What is innocence? How stained with blood, how reckless in crime, how deep in depravity can it be, and yet remain innocence?"[96]

Because murder convictions by statute were all granted automatic appeal to the state Supreme Court, Byrne appeared frequently before that Court and his mentor, Chief Justice Weintraub. Indeed, Byrne believed that while he was prosecutor he made more appearances before the Supreme Court than any other New Jersey lawyer.[97]

In addition to trying the cases of accused cop killers—and unlike many if not most prosecutors who focus on administering the work load of their offices—Byrne regularly handled other trials on his own. "He tried cases," Charlie Carella would later say. "He was very interested in what was going before the grand jury. And he was very, very proactive as a prosecutor. . . . As a prosecutor his interest wasn't really to grab headlines. It was really to do a job that had to be done to see that everything was done fairly and openly."[98] Jim Zazzali recalled that Byrne "knew precisely what was going on. You did your job, you were fine. He had very, very high standards. You never wanted to let him down. . . . His presence kept you on your toes."[99]

Morale among Byrne's prosecutorial staff was high, and his relative youth helped build open relationships within the office. "You could go and talk with him and go over the case with him," Carella continued. "We were young guys. We were not 50 years behind or 20 years behind. We were contemporaries with BT."[100] Justin Walder, another assistant prosecutor for Byrne who later founded one of New Jersey's most prominent law firms, jokingly recalled many years later that he believed his own hiring by Byrne was "an attempt to improve the office softball team."[101] Another lawyer hired by Byrne for his staff was June Strelecki, whom Byrne had first met when she interned for the Passaic County prosecutor's office while Byrne was assigned there as a deputy attorney general. Strelecki was one of the first female graduates of Harvard Law School, and female attorneys still were only grudgingly accepted. Years later, Byrne recalled that some months after Strelecki was hired, he advised his chief of detectives that another woman would be joining the office as an assistant prosecutor, and the chief's immediate response was "But we already have a girl!" Reflecting on the chief's reaction, Byrne continued, "That was the common attitude among men in those days. Women might have a role, but it was an awfully small one."[102] Most of the lawyers met for lunch on Fridays at Vesuvio's, a Newark restaurant, and some also socialized together during evenings and weekends with their families and friends. Some of those he hired for his staff would play key roles under Byrne as governor, and years later those who worked with him would fondly recall the experience as one of the highlights of their professional careers.

Barry Evenchick said that when he joined the staff in 1965 he felt the office had gained "the reputation as one of the best law enforcement offices in the country."[103] Justin Walder said he learned important lessons while working under Byrne. "Brendan was just a wonderful boss and mentor, showing the rest of us not only to be good at winning cases but also to be honest and ethical."[104] Long before prosecutors were required to provide the defense with evidence that might help the defendant's case, Walder said Byrne directed him to do so in a double homicide case because it was the "just and right thing to do."[105] On another occasion, when Andrew Zazzali was trying a robbery case, he determined that in a previous case a mistaken identification had led to a defendant's conviction. Zazzali suggested to Byrne that they move to vacate the conviction, a recommendation that Byrne accepted. One of the earliest members of the Byrne prosecutorial team, Zazzali later became First Assistant Essex County Prosecutor.[106]

Byrne served as prosecutor during the years that the U.S. Supreme Court under Chief Justice Earl Warren was expanding the protections of the rights of criminal defendants. These included guaranteeing the right to counsel during police interrogations; to warn defendants that they may decline to be questioned; and to exclude the use of evidence seized in unreasonable searches in state courts (extending the protection previously applicable in federal prosecutions).[107]

One of the early applications of the exclusionary rule to state prosecutions arose in 1960 when detectives assigned to "the Charlie Squad" on Byrne's staff raided an apartment in Orange after obtaining a search warrant, with the two occupants later indicted on bookmaking charges based on the betting records and other evidence seized in the raid. The lower court granted the defendants' motion to suppress the evidence, finding that the detective's affidavit submitted to justify the search set forth "mere conclusions rather than facts."[108]

Byrne personally argued the appeal before the state Supreme Court, contending that the affidavit was sufficient and, even if it failed to detail specific facts, the evidence should not have been suppressed without a showing that the detective engaged in improper conduct or otherwise demonstrated bad faith. In an opinion written by Justice Nathan Jacobs, a unanimous court rejected both contentions and held that it was now bound by the U.S. Supreme Court's decision in *Mapp v. Ohio* to extend the exclusionary rule to state prosecutions. In a brief concurring opinion, Chief Justice Weintraub agreed with the decision, but stated that he believed the facts of the case did not require reaching the issue of whether good faith by police could under some circumstances be considered as an exception to the exclusionary rule articulated under *Mapp*.[109]

In other opinions, Weintraub was more openly critical of the U.S. Supreme Court's setting of new national standards in criminal law. Reflecting long after Weintraub's death on the Chief Justice's perspective on criminal law, Byrne said that Weintraub saw the issue more in terms of what "ninety-nine would have to give up to assure the rights of one." To Byrne, Weintraub was "more of a law and order man" who felt there was a strong obligation of the courts to preserve a stable society, which may have been shaped by Weintraub's urban roots growing up in Orange and his attending high school in Newark.[110] "I generally agreed with Weintraub's view that state courts were better suited to develop flexible rules of criminal procedure than a single national rule," Byrne said years later. "At least in New Jersey, I trusted how the courts had responded over time to balance the interest of the state with the rights of criminal defendants."[111]

Byrne was active in both the state and national organizations of prosecutors, serving as president of the County Prosecutors Association of New Jersey and vice president of the National District Attorneys Association. He frequently brought his wife Jean and one of their children on trips to meetings of the national organization, sometimes extending their stays for longer visits to nearby sites. At a meeting in New Orleans, he introduced a resolution for the group to endorse abolition of the death penalty, but found no support.

Shortly before he left office as prosecutor in 1968, he proposed resolutions to the state prosecutors' association asking its endorsement of a study of legalized gambling and reduction of the penalties for marijuana possession. By the time the resolutions came before the group, Byrne was no longer prosecutor, but he nonetheless traveled to the meeting in Atlantic City to argue for their adoption. The resolutions were overwhelmingly defeated, with only Essex County, now headed by Joseph Lordi, Byrne's successor as the county's prosecutor, casting an affirmative vote for the gambling study and all counties rejecting the review of marijuana sentences.

"I loved being a prosecutor," Byrne said years later. "You were on the side of the angels, putting bad guys away and making it safer for the rest of us. And I thought I was pretty good at it."[112] But after the Democrats lost control of the state senate in the November 1967 election, Byrne recognized that it was unlikely he could be confirmed for a third term as prosecutor and that it was time to move on. In December, just weeks before Republicans would take control of the Senate in the next month, Governor Hughes appointed Byrne as president of the Public Utilities Commission, the quasi-autonomous agency headed by a three-person bipartisan board that oversaw the operations, finances and rates of electric, gas, and water utilities. His appointment ran into last-minute delays when the Democratic senator from Essex County initially declined to endorse Byrne's nomination, but after Hughes threatened to call the Senate into special session to act on the nomination of Byrne and others, the senator reconsidered and Byrne was confirmed for the PUC position. On the same day, Joseph Lordi, Byrne's former deputy in the prosecutor's office who subsequently had become the director of the Alcoholic Beverage Commission, was also confirmed to succeed Byrne as Essex County prosecutor.[113]

The Public Utilities position made Byrne a member of Hughes Cabinet. While at that time the post, like that of county prosecutor, was considered to be part-time, allowing concurrent employment in the private sector, as a practical matter the PUC would take up much less of Byrne's time than the prosecutor's job did, providing him greater opportunity to build his private practice in the law firm in which he was a partner with his old friend Marty Greenberg. Before he accepted Hughes's offer, Byrne faced a mild complaint from his young son Tim, who did not want to give up the prosecutorial perk of having the flashing red light and siren on the family car, but Byrne overruled the objection.[114] A further benefit to the PUC post was that it would broaden his statewide exposure beyond that which he had received as Essex County prosecutor. The PUC's actions in setting rates, investigating rail and bus accidents and other matters often brought it media coverage throughout the state.

Most gubernatorial appointees to the utilities commission knew little about the complex issues relating to utility finance and operations and the setting of rates for consumers. Byrne was no exception. Upon announcement of his appointment, he was asked about his experience on electric and gas matters. Conceding that his background was largely in law enforcement, he nonetheless quipped, "but I did send 17 people to the electric chair."[115] To better grasp the mechanics of the industry, he enrolled in two courses specifically designed for utility regulators: a brief session in New York and a more intense two-week program in Colorado. A few weeks after joining the PUC, Byrne recruited Barry Evenchick, who had headed the appellate section on his prosecutor's staff, to come to the PUC as his administrative assistant. Evenchick, who like Byrne had no prior experience with utility matters, said he was amazed how, "like a duck to water," Byrne mastered the complexities of rate-setting and other utility issues.[116] Byrne characteristically attempted to puncture the pomposity of some of those coming before the PUC. At one meeting with executives of a railroad company, Evenchick recalled that the executives seated around a conference table introduced themselves as "B. Smith," "J. Jones," and so on, only to have Byrne, after sitting through the parroted introductions, say, 'O.K, let's do it again, and this time tell us your full names."[117]

The three-member board, which was mandated by law to be bipartisan, included William Ozzard, a Republican veteran of the legislature who, after succeeding to the state senate seat in Somerset County formerly held by Malcolm Forbes, had been elected Senate president in 1963. After resigning from the Senate, Ozzard had been appointed by Governor Hughes as the Republican commissioner on the PUC in 1967. At the first public meeting presided over by Byrne, Ozzard attempted to raise a point that Byrne viewed as blatantly political and Byrne quickly cut him off, stating that Ozzard should have reserved the issue for the confidential off-the-record conference of board members then allowed prior to public meetings. Following that brief confrontation, "Ozzard and I would later get along fine," Byrne later recalled. "eventually becoming good friends."[118] From the start, Byrne had a warm relationship with the third member of the PUC board, Anthony Grossi, a former Democratic state senator from Passaic County whom Byrne had known since the time he was assigned as a deputy attorney general to the Passaic County prosecutor's office. Grossi later became a trusted political adviser to Byrne, helping to line up support in Passaic County, and after his inauguration as governor, Byrne named Grossi as the new PUC president to succeed Ozzard.

The PUC was viewed in those days as having a relatively cozy, informal relationship with the companies it regulated. Byrne sought to counter this perception by ending some of the commission's more casual practices in reaching decisions, such as when the Board approved utility requests solely on the basis of information submitted by the utility. "When I first started at the PUC," Byrne later recounted, "the staff would come in to see me on a rate request or something, and they'd ask, 'how do you want to decide it?' implying that they would draft the decision any way I wanted regardless of the facts. I didn't think that was the way we should make decisions." To insure a more objective review, he established an adversarial process similar to a trial, opening formal dockets for matters and notifying potential opponents who might wish to be heard, such as advocates for consumer or other interests, thus forcing the utilities to justify proposed actions.[119] Bolstered by subsequent court decisions and legislation, the basic practices established unilaterally by Byrne would endure as the standard in future years.

One episode during his commission tenure brought Byrne into his first contact with Louis Gambaccini, then heading the Port Authority Trans-Hudson (PATH) rapid transit system of the Port of New York Authority (later renamed the Port Authority of New York and New Jersey) who some ten years later would become Byrne's transportation commissioner. When Byrne sought to have the PUC investigate the causes of an accident on the Authority's PATH line, Austin Tobin, the powerful and imperious Authority executive director, rejected Byrne's contention that the New Jersey agency could assert jurisdiction over the bistate authority. As Gambaccini later recalled, when Tobin told Byrne that he and the Authority were not subject to the PUC's jurisdiction, Byrne curtly replied, "Then don't come," sparking what Gambaccini described as "nose-to-nose conflict" with "two Irishmen going at it." Eventually, recognizing that Byrne would likely win any legal action to enforce a subpoena, Tobin backed down, agreeing voluntarily to participate in the PUC probe while expressly denying any legal obligation by the Authority to subject itself to PUC oversight.[120]

One of the tasks entrusted to the PUC under Byrne was to investigate the deaths of two bystanders who had jumped on the railroad tracks in Elizabeth on June 8, 1968, to see the funeral train carrying the casket of Senator Robert F. Kennedy as it came from New York on its way to Washington and his subsequent burial at Arlington National Cemetery. The onlookers were killed by another train passing north in the other direction. The trip from New York to Washington, normally about four hours, took twice as long.[121]

In 1969, former Governor Meyner announced his candidacy for a third term as governor after being out of office for eight years. Byrne's name had been mentioned as a potential candidate, but he promptly dismissed any speculation that he would run. He played a minor role in the Meyner campaign against his Republican opponent, Congressman William Cahill, speaking as a surrogate on Meyner's behalf and helping to raise funds. Initially, Byrne was highly optimistic about Meyner's chances. "I thought," Byrne later recalled, "that Bob Meyner's moderate record would get Republican backing and that possibly he could run as the nominee of both parties. I was very wrong."[122]

As Meyner's campaign got underway, however, Byrne privately concluded, along with other Democrats, that Meyner had "lost it," that his campaign organization and his personal style no longer were up to the task. To Byrne, his political mentor often appeared distracted and rambling.[123] Just after the June primary, Byrne attended a debate between Meyner and Cahill sponsored by the state Chamber of Commerce. "Meyner started first," Byrne said, "and gave a civics-type lecture talking about what each of the state departments did and so forth. Cahill then followed with a fiery talk, shouting 'There's nothing wrong with this state that appointing twenty-one strong county prosecutors can't solve!' It was clear who won."[124] Joe Katz, the former *Newark News* reporter and key media and political adviser to both Meyner and Hughes, recalled his own frustration with Meyner's campaign: "That was a trying time," Katz remembered in an interview some forty years later. "Meyner became very eccentric. He was getting older and he wouldn't want to have any strategy meetings. He was on all these company boards and he'd get paid a couple hundred bucks for going to a meeting. He'd rather go to a board meeting, even in the middle of his campaign . . . because he liked the couple hundred bucks, though he now was a wealthy man."[125]

Nationally, Democrats were seeking to recover from their divisive 1968 national convention in Chicago that had been disrupted by riots and sharp conflicts over the Johnson Administration's policy on the Vietnam War. In New Jersey, the more liberal Democrats, many of whom were antiwar activists, had come together in a loose group named the New Democratic Coalition chaired by Dan Gaby, who would later become a valued member of Byrne's 1973 campaign. Most in the group were not pleased with the return of Meyner, whom they viewed as the representative of the party's old guard they were seeking to replace.[126]

Meyner's campaign was also undercut by his strained political relations in Hudson County, whose Democratic organization had endorsed its State Senator, William Kelly, in the Democratic primary election. Some of the county's political leaders still held a grudge over Meyner's stubborn refusal at the 1960 Democratic National Convention to release the state's delegates from supporting his favorite son candidacy so they could vote for John F. Kennedy. Meyner had also declined to support the emerging movement by reformers in Hudson to challenge the County's traditional boss-dominated politics. "The times had changed," Joe Katz recounted, "and I tried to get him to go into Hudson County, and denounce [County boss John V.] Kenny, and run against him and the bosses. . . . He wouldn't do it."[127] Given the divisions among the Democrats and Meyner's indifferent campaigning, Cahill won a decisive victory in which he swept twenty of the state's twenty-one counties and won by a half million votes over Meyner.

During his first year in office in 1970, Governor Cahill appointed Brendan Byrne as a judge of the Superior Court. The appointment was consistent with the tradition prevailing since the adoption of the 1947 constitution that appointments by governors would maintain a judiciary balanced between each party.[128] Following his confirmation by the state senate, Judge Byrne was again working under one of his first bosses as a lawyer, Joseph Weintraub, who was now chief justice of the New Jersey Supreme Court. Byrne was first assigned to the Law Division, sitting at the Essex County court house in Newark where he had spent so much time as prosecutor.

Soon after his swearing in as a judge in 1970, Byrne was mentioned in press reports as a potential candidate for the U.S. Senate, after Senator Harrison Williams became the subject of controversy when he gave a speech in Atlantic City during which he repeatedly slurred his words. ("The party bosses in New Jersey said they were going to dump him because he would be defeated by any Republican," the staff director of the Senate Labor Committee recalled in an interview years later.)[129] But Williams was able to salvage his political career after publicly admitting to being an alcoholic and undergoing a rehabilitation treatment program. While some Hudson County Democrats in fact mounted a challenge to Williams in the June 1970 primary election, their candidate, then state Senator Frank Guarini, was decisively beaten by a nearly two-to-one margin.[130]

Judge Byrne gained wide media attention for his 1971 decision holding the state's death penalty statute unconstitutional—an action for which he was privately chastised by Chief Justice Weintraub. Byrne's ruling in *State v. White* held that New Jersey's death penalty law, enacted in 1893, violated the rights under the U.S. Constitution against self-incrimination and to a jury trial because it allowed defendants in capital murder cases to escape the death penalty by pleading guilty or no defense, thus avoiding the jury trial required for imposing a death sentence.[131] In his opinion, Byrne explained that the effect of the law was to coerce defendants to plead guilty by waiving their right to a jury trial, and cited *United States v. Jackson*, a U.S. Supreme Court decision holding the federal kidnaping law unconstitutional on similar grounds.[132]

After his decision was released, as Byrne later retold the story, Weintraub called him and said: "Brendan, you're a trial judge. The constitutionality of the death penalty is not something you should rule on. Leave that to an appellate court." When Byrne protested that he was simply following what he felt was a precedent from the U.S. Supreme Court, the Chief Justice brought him up short, pointing out that the decision had only recently been issued and was only three sentences long, leaving considerable ambiguity over its impact. Without thinking, Byrne persisted in the exchange, saying "Well, how long does a U.S. Supreme Court opinion have to be in effect before I'm obliged to follow it?" While Byrne thought he had made a valid point, he immediately regretted his flippant response, belatedly realizing that it lacked the respectful tone he owed to the mentor whom he so greatly admired.[133]

In 1972, Byrne was appointed by Weintraub as assignment judge to manage the docket of cases and assign judges to specific cases in Morris, Sussex, and Warren Counties, presiding from the county court house in Morristown. In addition to his administrative duties, Byrne continued to preside over trials, "more than normal for an assignment judge," according to August Lembo, his last law clerk, and took actions to expedite the handling of cases on the trial calendar. On one day, for example, as Byrne was leaving for home, Lembo recalled that Byrne asked him how many motions were scheduled for the next day and Lembo replied, "well x number of summary judgment motions, 2 of which were slam-dunks, y number or discovery motions, number of . . ." At that point, Byrne cut him off: "I just asked how many motions." To Lembo, the lesson he learned was, "Just answer the question—don't waste time responding to unasked questions."[134]

In Byrne's last year on the bench, Lembo also recalled that when a "little old lady" was asked during the pretrial interview of potential jurors what she did for a living, she said, "Oh Judge, I do absolutely nothing." Judge Byrne promptly responded: "Mrs. Smith, I don't think there is enough room in this court for both of us."[135] Although Byrne tried before the trial began, as he later put it, "to entertain" the jurors to ease any anxiety, "once the jury was in place, it was serious business." As a lawyer, Byrne had disliked "judges who got in your way by interrupting, trying to dominate the trial," and on the bench he avoided intervening whenever possible, preferring "to just let the lawyers try their cases."[136]

During slow periods, Byrne at times sought to lighten the solemnity of his court room. When the court was not in session, he participated in informal stickball games with court attendants using wadded paper as a ball. Michael Critchley was then employed as a security guard in Byrne's court room while working his way through law school (he later became an assistant governor's counsel to Byrne and subsequently one of the state's most prominent criminal and white-collar defense attorneys). Critchley recounted that during one game, an attorney unfamiliar with Byrne arrived for a scheduled conference with the judge, asked where he could find Byrne and was told, "He's the one at bat." On other occasions during hearings on motions, Byrne would sometimes startle the attorneys before him by interrupting their arguments, then addressing the uniformed Critchley with his holstered gun: "Mr. Critchley, what do you think of this?" and Critchley would respond with his own analysis of the merits of the respective legal positions.[137]

In the fall of 1972, Judge Byrne's name appeared in newspaper articles as a potential nominee by Governor Cahill to fill one of two vacancies on the seven-member New Jersey Supreme Court. During his two terms ending in January 1962, Governor Meyner had appointed eight justices to the Supreme Court, and by the time Cahill took office in 1970 a majority of the Meyner appointees were nearing the mandatory retirement age of 70. By tradition, the makeup of the seven-member court included no more than four members of a single political party, and Byrne, then 48 years old, was one of the Democrats identified as a potential nominee. Cahill delayed announcing his choices for the seats until the following spring, when he was facing a difficult primary election for re-nomination that he would lose to Charles Sandman. After the election, Cahill appointed his counsel, Pierre "Pete" Garven, and Mark Sullivan, a Democratic Superior Court appellate judge, to the court.[138] "I was disappointed," Byrne recalled, "but you can't expect an appointment to the Supreme Court. I hadn't been a judge for very long and was still very young, so I wasn't at all surprised."[139] Two weeks after Cahill named Garven and Sullivan, Chief Justice Weintraub announced that he would retire, later deciding to make his retirement effective at the beginning of September 1973 prior to the commencement of the court's annual term.

Byrne later said that he was prepared to continue on the bench until he was ready to retire, but it's questionable whether, over the long term, his interests and personality would have been a good fit for a lengthy judicial tenure at a level below that of the state Supreme Court. Given his admiration of the legal career of Joseph Weintraub, his role model, and the fact that he had previously been mentioned as a potential appointee to New Jersey's highest court, Byrne's ego also might have prodded him eventually to resign as a judge if it appeared that he would remain on the Superior Court for the rest of his judicial career. As a prosecutor and judge, he chafed at the complex rules that he felt had gotten in the way of determining the simple issue of whether an accused was innocent or guilty. Moreover, his impatience was difficult to mesh with the protracted posturing of attorneys and the delays in reaching a result. "Judge Byrne enjoyed being a judge," Gus Lembo later reflected, "but he missed the action and the give and take of being a trial attorney."[140]

So it was perhaps not surprising that when an unusual series of events lined up to offer an opportunity to explore a return to the more activist world of politics, Judge Byrne was willing to listen.

Chapter 5

The 1973 Election

"The Man Who Couldn't Be Bought"

Judge Byrne's decision to resign from the bench and enter the 1973 gubernatorial race came, as he later put it, "by accident." Over the years since he first entered public life, Byrne's friends and political associates had urged him to seek elected office, including the governorship in the 1969 election in which Cahill defeated former Governor Meyner and in the following year the election for a U.S. Senate seat when Democratic Senator Harrison Williams faced a challenge to his nomination for reelection. Those who had previously encouraged Byrne to become a candidate included Archibald Alexander, a former state treasurer under Governor Meyner who served as undersecretary of the Army in the Truman Administration, and Anthony Grossi, the former Passaic county Democratic state senator and county party chairman who had served with Byrne on the Public Utilities Commission. Byrne had listened to their arguments but ultimately decided not to run and, after becoming a judge in 1970, expected to spend the rest of his career on the bench. "I enjoyed being a judge," Byrne later said. "I wasn't looking to give it up for politics."[1]

Byrne respected the record that Republican William Cahill had compiled as governor during his first years in office, particularly his plan to develop the Meadowlands sports complex, his environmental initiatives and his courage in proposing tax reform, including an income tax to fund increased school aid to the most distressed cities. "I thought Bill Cahill had been a good governor," Byrne said years later "and really didn't think he could be beaten. Even more, if he could be beaten, I wasn't sure that I was the one who wanted to beat him."[2]

But more than a year before the 1973 election in which Cahill was expected to seek a second term, Byrne was again approached to consider running for governor, both by those who had been his personal advocates and others who were unimpressed with the Democrats expected to enter the campaign. Party activists Alexander and Grossi again urged Byrne to run, and they were joined by Don Lan, a Democratic leader in Union County; Stephen Adubato, the leader of the North Ward Educational and Cultural Center in Newark; Dan Gaby, the leader of Democrats opposing the Vietnam War who in 1972 had unsuccessfully sought the Democratic nomination for U.S. Senate; and Joel Jacobson, a former leader of the Congress of Industrial Unions and the United Auto Workers union in New Jersey. Byrne was reluctant, later saying "I had no serious quarrel with Bill Cahill's policies." And Cahill still seemed likely to defeat any Democrat in the general election; in a meeting with a few friends in late 1972, Byrne recalled that the consensus of the group was that Cahill "could not be beaten in '73, so there was no use looking any further at it."[3]

Governor Cahill's political position, however, had begun to erode within his own Republican Party. His moderate record, including his support of a sales tax increase and a new income tax, placed him at odds with more conservative Republicans, who traditionally had strong influence in primary elections determining the party's candidates. Coupled with his pugnacious style, Cahill's policy positions had led to sharp divisions among Republican legislators and county chairmen. In July 1972, he suffered a stinging defeat and angered legislators in his own party when he insisted that his income tax proposal be brought to a recorded public vote by the full Assembly, despite knowing that it would fail. The measure was rejected fifty-two to twenty-three, with only nine of thirty-nine Republicans supporting the governor.

Cahill's reputation for honesty as a former FBI agent and deputy state attorney general, which was a key theme of his 1969 gubernatorial campaign, also was tarnished by the conviction in October 1972 of Paul Sherwin, his Secretary of State and perhaps closest political adviser, on charges that he tried to fix a $600,000 state highway contract for a contractor who then kicked back $10,000 to Republican fundraisers close to Cahill.[4] In the month after Sherwin's conviction, Cahill suffered yet another political rebuke when the Senate rejected his nomination of Commissioner of Education Carl Marburger to a second term. Initially appointed by Governor Hughes, Marburger had gained Cahill's confidence, but had sparked controversy for his support of school integration by proposing realignment of urban and suburban school district boundaries; the plan provoked sharp opposition from suburban legislators and the powerful New Jersey Education Association.[5]

During the December 1972 judicial holiday break, Byrne reconsidered his prior decision not to become a candidate in 1973. Years later, perhaps in jest, he remarked that his interest in running piqued when, as he arrived to play tennis at an indoor court and parked his car, "I looked at the car next to me and it said 'DeRose for Governor' and I thought to myself, I can do better."[6] Byrne felt that, objectively, his own experience—staff member to one governor, a cabinet member for another, and prosecutor and judge—stacked up well against Ralph DeRose, a state senator from Byrne's home base of Essex County who was backed by its county chairman Harry Lerner, and the other Democrats either running or often mentioned as possible candidates.

None of the other leading Democrats—Morris County Assemblywoman Ann Klein, Middlesex County Senator Edward Crabiel, Bergen County Congressman Henry Helstoski, and Mercer County Senator Richard Coffee—had demonstrated that they could broaden their support much beyond their county bases. But for Byrne to enter the race at this point, less than six months before the June 5, 1973, primary election, would be extremely difficult, given that other Democratic candidates had been organizing their campaigns for some months and, as a sitting judge, Byrne was barred from engaging in any public political activity. At one point, after his name continued to appear in newspaper articles as a potential candidate, Byrne phoned Chief Justice Weintraub to seek advice on whether he should take action to avoid any ethical issues but, according to Byrne, "Weintraub said to me 'don't flatter yourself,' and that I should wait until I knew what I would do." But a Byrne candidacy still seemed highly unlikely. In late December 1972, Camden County Democratic Chairman James Joyce, who had been urged by some Camden Democrats to persuade Byrne to become a candidate, told Byrne that "it's too late" to put together a campaign.[7]

As the 1973 election year began, despite his political setbacks, Governor Cahill was still favored to win the reelection, largely because his prospective Democratic opponents had limited statewide support. "For several months," a newspaper article published at the end of January concluded, "many of New Jersey's leading Democrats have expressed despair at the chances of defeating Governor Cahill, partly because of the governor's own political strength and partly because of a dearth of opponents with impressive political credentials."[8]

In an attempt to narrow the Democratic field, State Democratic Chairman Salvatore Bontempo appointed a committee of ten county chairmen to screen the potential candidates and invite them for interviews. Ann Klein, a former president of the League of Women Voters, rejected the invitation, stating that the process smacked of an attempt by the party bosses to supplant the choice of voters in an open primary election. In fact, according to a newspaper account, Bontempo's unstated objective—in alliance with Lerner of Essex and Joyce of Camden—was to marshal support for DeRose, but at the end of January a meeting of the special committee of county chairmen broke up in disarray, failing to endorse DeRose or any of the others. Following the meeting's collapse, the *New York Times* reported that "an influential group of young New Jersey Democrats, apparently dissatisfied with the present field of candidates for their party's nomination for Governor, were reported

attempting to persuade Superior Court Judge Brendan T. Byrne to enter the
June primary."[9]

After the failed effort for DeRose, Union County Democratic leaders
Chris Dietz and Don Lan again asked Byrne to become a candidate with the
county's support. "Don Lan had told me," Byrne recounted, "if you want to
run, let us know by Valentine's Day . . . and we'll give you the line in Union
county. I had called him and told him I didn't think I wanted to do it."[10] Joel
Jacobson, the labor official, also offered to run himself as a "stalking horse"
candidate in the primary to reserve a place for Byrne on the ballot if the judge
needed additional time to decide on entering the race.[11]

Byrne's appeal as a candidate to the Democratic activists was based not on
any stand he had taken on issues, but rather on his career profile as a judge
and former prosecutor. Byrne's reputation for integrity had been enhanced
by media coverage of transcripts of FBI surveillance tapes that recorded
conversations of Mafia figures in the early 1960s. Publicly disclosed by
the government during mob trials, the transcripts reported the boasts of crime
leaders of their ability to influence New Jersey government officials. In one
of the tapes, however, Simone de Cavalcante, more popularly known as "Sam
the Plumber," was recorded as saying, "But there's one guy, this prosecutor
Byrne that we can't buy."[12] With the aid of the FBI tapes, the Democrats
pushing Byrne to run felt that his reputation for integrity would contrast
with the Republican scandals surrounding President Nixon resulting from
the Watergate burglary and the controversies relating to Governor Cahill's
advisers, and that his law enforcement and judicial background would be
received positively by voters weary of soaring crime rates. The de Cavalcante
quote gave the prospective Byrne campaign the ideal slogan that fit the public
mood: "the man who couldn't be bought."

To the extent that Byrne had any political network of his own, it was
largely due to the personal and professional relationships he had previously
developed during his career. Martin Greenberg had first met Byrne when they
both served as assistant counsels to Governor Meyner, sharing drives from
their homes in Essex County to and from Trenton. Greenberg later joined
Byrne's prosecutorial staff in Essex County, and the two men subsequently
became partners in private law practice. Greenberg had been active in Essex
County politics, and in fact would be elected to the state senate in the 1973
election, ironically running with the support of the Essex County Democratic
Committee chaired by Harry Lerner to fill the Senate seat of the district previously represented by Senator DeRose, who did not seek reelection in order
to run for governor.

Another confidant who had served under Byrne as an assistant prosecutor was James Zazzali, who had developed strong relationships in the labor
movement after he joined the law firm founded by his father. Byrne also

reached out to David Waters, who had worked on the staff of the PUC under Byrne, and then founded a politically active law firm. Kenneth McPherson, one of the partners in the law firm, had strong Hudson County political contacts and in fact had been nominated in 1969—the same year that Byrne was confirmed for his second term as Essex prosecutor—by Governor Hughes to be the Hudson prosecutor.[13] McPherson would work closely with Byrne in securing support in Hudson and throughout the state.

Byrne also could call on many of the elected officials and political leaders he had come to know during his time as the gatekeeper for Governor Meyner. One of the key figures he had first met while on Meyner's staff was David Wilentz, the powerful Middlesex County Democratic leader and former state attorney general and prosecutor in the Lindbergh baby kidnapping and murder trial. Although Wilentz tacitly backed the candidacy of Middlesex Senator Edward Crabiel, when Judge Byrne asked for his advice, he would respond, according to Byrne, "Just keep doing what you're doing," a somewhat Delphic pronouncement that Byrne interpreted as encouraging him to continue his outreach to explore a potential candidacy.[14]

Some in Byrne's family doubted the wisdom of his entering the race. His father, who was in failing health and would pass away in the summer of 1973 at age 86, recommended against a run, suggesting that appointment to the state Supreme Court would offer more prestige and security.[15] His wife Jean also was reluctant. When they married in 1953, she had not foreseen that her husband would enter politics. "I was a teacher. He was a lawyer," she said in an interview years later. "So I thought that's the way it was going to go."[16] But as her husband's name began appearing in the press as a potential candidate for the U.S. Senate or governor in the early 1970s, she recognized that a more public life might be in the family's future. "Now, did I see something coming?" she later reflected, "Well, maybe I was pushing it out of my head because I didn't want to see it. But I would go to the local grocery store, and they'd say, 'Mrs. Byrne, your husband's going to be governor some day.'"[17]

As Byrne came closer to making his decision to run in 1973, Mrs. Byrne expressed her concerns about the impact on the family, particularly since their daughter Mary Ann, born with Down syndrome, required costly institutional care. Also, their son Tom was the first of the seven children to attend college (as a freshman at Princeton), and college tuitions for the younger children would soon place additional claims on the family's finances. Jean also worried about the intrusion on the family's privacy and wasn't comfortable dealing with the public life forced on a candidate's spouse. "People who got to know her really loved her," Byrne would later say, "and she loved them. But Jean felt overwhelmed in a crowd of people. Strangers were off-putting, at best. She'd never wanted to be a Governor's wife, and when we'd married I hadn't had any idea that elective politics was in my future."[18]

As the campaign season began in earnest leading to the primary election in June, Byrne's name continued to be raised in conversations among political insiders, a rather ominous specter to the announced candidates. One of those candidates, state Senator Coffee, met with Byrne, advising the judge that he was confident of the coalition backing his own candidacy and would not consider withdrawing. But Coffee's support, like that of the others in the race, was narrowly focused on his home county of Mercer, and Byrne remained unconvinced that Coffee or any of his rivals had yet demonstrated the ability to pull away and win in the crowded field.[19]

The final lineup for the primary election also remained uncertain when one of the strongest potential candidates, Congressman Henry Helstoski of Bergen County, who had come in third behind former Governor Meyner in the 1969 Democratic gubernatorial primary, announced that he would "reconsider" his prior decision not to run.[20] Byrne previously had phoned Michael "Jerry" Breslin, who had been elected Democratic chairman in Bergen, to explore whether the county organization could support a Byrne candidacy, but was told that Bergen would defer making an endorsement until Helstoski decided whether he would run.

Yet, despite the hypothetical attractiveness of Byrne as a candidate, any campaign faced steep practical hurdles. As a judge, he was unable to actively plan, organize, or raise money for a campaign. Moreover, he had no political base or wealthy supporters and had never run for elected office. The Democratic leadership in Essex, his home county, was already pledged to back Senator DeRose. As Ken McPherson put it, "the scenario would be coming off the bench . . . with absolutely no political organization, nothing other than his reputation, running for governor. And, you know, a great story, but still the practicality of it was he had no troops."[21]

While Judge Byrne was mulling his options, his mother Genevieve died on April 1, her son's forty-ninth birthday. During her funeral, the priest comforted the mourners by noting that her two sons had reached the "pinnacle" of their professions as a judge and a doctor. "I went up to her casket and whispered," Byrne later recalled "'not yet, Mom, not yet.'"[22]

On April 3, two days after his mother's death, Byrne's mentor Chief Justice Joseph Weintraub delivered a decision that would have a major impact on Byrne and the governors who would succeed him into the next century. In a unanimous opinion by the New Jersey Supreme Court written by the Chief Justice, the Court issued the first of its decisions in the *Robinson v. Cahill* litigation holding that the State's heavy reliance on the local property tax for funding public education violated the state Constitution; it set a deadline of December 31, 1974, for the governor and legislature to enact a new, more equalized funding system to take effect no later than July 1, 1975.[23]

Given Byrne's lack of a political base and limited time to put together a campaign, the support of powerful Democratic county committees and their leaders would be essential to winning the nomination in the primary election. In 1973, the county committees and their chairmen, while perhaps not quite as influential in selecting gubernatorial candidates as in earlier elections, could provide money, workers and, most significantly, the ballot "line," the preferred position at the top of the list of candidates signifying the organization's choice. In primary elections that typically drew low turnouts of registered voters, the ability of county organizations to rely on their network of loyalists—many of them holding government jobs or contracts or receiving other favors—to produce votes often was the crucial factor in determining the nominee. Byrne's promised support from Union County leaders was encouraging, but in itself did not provide a sufficient base to launch a campaign without a larger county also aligning behind Byrne.

Hudson County's Democratic organization had remained uncommitted to any of the announced contenders, and Byrne resolved that he would not enter the race unless he could secure Hudson's support. After years of leadership by Jersey City's powerful and often corrupt mayors Frank Hague, John V. Kenny, and Thomas J. Whelan, a reform movement had assumed control in Hudson headed by, as Byrne later described it, a "triumvirate" of Democrats—Harrison Mayor Frank Rodgers, Bayonne Mayor Francis Fitzpatrick, and Jersey City Mayor Paul Jordan. Rogers and Fitzpatrick had long clashed with the Jersey City bosses and had joined forces with political newcomer Jordan, a physician who had first been elected in 1971 at age 30 as a reform candidate in a special election following Mayor Thomas J. Whelan's conviction for extortion and conspiracy in a kickback scheme in the award of contracts.[24] With the support of the reformers, Fitzpatrick was elected chair of the county Democratic organization in 1972, the year before the gubernatorial election.[25] Byrne reached out directly to Rodgers, who knew his father, and was encouraged to enter the race. In approaching Jordan, Byrne contacted intermediaries he knew, especially Bernard Hartnett, a Jersey City lawyer who was one of Jordan's advisers, and received positive feedback from Hartnett that Jordan also would be receptive to a Byrne candidacy.

A key protégé of Fitzpatrick's was James Dugan who, after serving in the Korean War where he had had been severely wounded as a Marine lieutenant leading his platoon's charge against an entrenched Chinese position, returned to New Jersey to become a lawyer, later working with Fitzpatrick to restructure Bayonne's form of government, and subsequently appointed as director of the City's a law department. After a single term in the state Assembly, Dugan was elected to the state senate in 1969, serving with his Senate colleagues—and announced 1973 gubernatorial candidates—DeRose, Coffee, and Crabiel. In assessing the potential Democratic field, Dugan had come to believe that Byrne—with his "photogenic looks," military record, and career as a prosecutor and judge—was the best chance for the Democrats in the November election, a contest which he and most other Democratic operatives still believed would be an uphill race to unseat incumbent Governor Cahill. Without Byrne's knowledge, Dugan also had contacted Bergen Democratic chair Breslin to explore a possible alliance between Bergen and Hudson Democrats to support Byrne, but Breslin advised him that his county could not act until Congressman Helstoski made a final decision on whether he would be a candidate.[26]

Despite the encouraging signs of support for Byrne from some Hudson Democrats, Mayor Fitzpatrick proved to be a much tougher sell. Like some of the older Hudson Democrats who remained influential, Fitzpatrick still harbored resentment toward former Governor Meyner, the man who had been so important to launching Byrne's public career. Meyner, whose own nomination in 1953 was aided by key support from Hudson boss John V. Kenny, had declined to back the emerging reform movement in Hudson to challenge the County's traditional boss-dominated politics. Fitzpatrick also never forgave Meyner for his refusal to release the New Jersey delegates at the 1960 Democratic National Convention from their support of Meyner's favorite-son presidential candidacy in order to free them to vote for the nomination of John F. Kennedy, whom Rodgers and many Irish-American Catholic Democrats were eagerly lining up to back for the presidency. But Byrne's past close association with Meyner made Fitzpatrick suspicious that, like Meyner, Byrne might lack the flexibility of a pragmatic politician.[27]

Ironically, Byrne himself, who had left Meyner's staff to become the Essex County prosecutor in the year before the 1960 presidential campaign, viewed Kennedy as a political hero. "It was hard to describe everything that John Kennedy meant to me," he later said. "For all of us who were Irish, and interested in politics, he was the Irishman who became President of the United States and broke down the final barrier. He was smart as hell, quick with a quip, never stuffy. . . . He cared about doing the right thing, but would never boast about it." Byrne also saw similarity between the Kennedy family lineup and that of his own. He viewed himself as the sickly, more withdrawn younger brother to his more outgoing older brother Frank, somewhat akin to the role within the Kennedy family that John had first assumed in relation to his older brother Joseph Jr.—the vigorous, confident first-born son killed in action in World War II.[28]

Byrne indeed had gone out of his way before the 1960 Convention to meet Kennedy at an appearance in Essex County and later—using press credentials for the "Hobo News" seized during a raid on a seller of pornographic materials by his prosecutor's staff—snuck into a Kennedy press conference restricted to "Press Only." Indirectly, Byrne also was drawn into the Kennedy campaign's effort to have Meyner drop his candidacy when he received a phone call from Joseph DeGuglielmo, the former mayor of Cambridge, Massachusetts, whose wife was a native of West Orange. During his first weeks at Harvard Law School, Byrne had stayed with the DeGuglielmos at their home in Cambridge, and DeGuglielmo called to ask him to intervene with Meyner. "He was a Kennedy insider," Byrne later recounted, "and asked me if I could help persuade Meyner to drop out. I told him that it was useless. Meyner had his mind made up."[29]

On the day before Meyner left for the Convention, he phoned his former aide to ask what he thought of his prospects. "I told him," Byrne reflected years later, "that I thought Kennedy would be nominated on the first ballot. Meyner quickly ended the conversation, it was not what he wanted to hear."[30]

Assessing Meyner's motives years after his death, Byrne said that Meyner's strategy depended on Kennedy failing to get the nomination on the first ballot at the Democratic National Convention. "If there was a second ballot," Byrne later explained, "Meyner thought that the delegates pledged to Kennedy on the first ballot would look for someone else to support. He thought he had a commitment that Pennsylvania's delegation would swing its votes to him and then other states would follow." As the alphabetical roll of the states was called on the first ballot, the New Jersey delegation's 41 votes were cast for Meyner, but the Governor's strategy failed when, at the end of the tally, Wyoming's 15 votes secured Kennedy's nomination. As the boisterous celebration erupted on the Convention floor of Kennedy's victory, Meyner's belated attempt to change New Jersey's vote never was officially recorded when he vainly sought recognition from the chair, but spoke into a dead microphone.[31]

Many years later, Byrne reflected that Meyner's long-shot campaign for the presidency was "delusional," but noted that "delusions are an occupational hazard in politics, where egos are large, the public is fickle and there's never a script. . . . Bob Meyner came down with 'presidentialitis' and, as [Democratic Arizona Congressman and 1976 presidential candidate] Mo Udall used to say, the only cure for presidentialitis is embalming fluid."[32]

When Fitzpatrick refused to take Byrne's calls as the April 26 filing deadline for candidates approached, the judge sought help from Ken McPherson, who met with the mayor. Fitzpatrick initially was dismissive, saying "He's got to be like Meyner," and showing McPherson a photo he had of Meyner and Byrne playing tennis together. Although he had never met Meyner, McPherson did his best to persuade Fitzpatrick that Byrne was different from Meyner, finally succeeding in getting Fitzpatrick to agree to meet with Byrne in the mayor's office on April 23, three days before the filing deadline.

But the meeting did not go well. According to Dugan, the two "just did not hit it off," partly because their respective "expectations" differed: Byrne assumed that he was there to be, as Dugan put it, "anointed" by

Fitzpatrick as Hudson's choice; in contrast, Dugan felt that Fitzpatrick was still holding back, wanting to use the meeting to discover "what was behind all this attractive persona that Brendan had." Prior to the meeting, Byrne had been warned that Fitzpatrick likely would seek Byrne's pledge to support rebuilding and restoration to service of a railroad bridge connecting Bayonne with Staten Island, which shipping concerns had cited as a hindrance to larger ships entering and departing New York harbor.

Before seeing Fitzpatrick, Byrne had phoned contacts at the Public Utilities Commission, who advised him that the bridge undermined the competitiveness of the port as increasingly larger ships were built, and Byrne resolved that he could not make any commitment to restore the bridge to service. But in their meeting, Fitzpatrick pressured him to the point that Byrne concluded that the bridge's reconstruction was a quid-pro-quo for Hudson's endorsement. Finally, Byrne bristled and rose from his chair; as he turned to leave, he told Fitzpatrick: "Good luck with Ed Crabiel."[33] After Byrne departed, Fitzpatrick said to McPherson, "He's just like Meyner."[34] Years later, Byrne reflected, "I think I could walk out on Fitzpatrick because being governor wasn't the most important thing to me, especially if I had to agree to political deals to be elected. I could be happy being a judge."[35]

Yet McPherson and Dugan declined to give up. "Don't let him leave town," Dugan told McPherson, suggesting that McPherson take Byrne to dinner at a local restaurant while Dugan attempted to ease the tensions with Fitzpatrick that had led to the abrupt end of the earlier meeting at City Hall. Dugan then went over to Fitzpatrick's home and reviewed with him the options for Hudson in the coming election, including "sitting it out" without endorsing anyone in the primary or backing a candidate other than Byrne. "At that point, I didn't think the Republican Party would be so stupid as to reject Bill Cahill, who had been a really good governor," Dugan later said. "I told Fitzpatrick that I didn't think the other candidates had the background of Brendan or the potential to expand their support beyond their own counties. I felt we needed a candidate who would have a chance against Cahill, and Brendan was the strongest choice." McPherson also phoned the mayor from the restaurant, making what he termed a "sales pitch" to reinforce Dugan's argument that Byrne was the "best shot" for the Democrats. Hudson County's support of Byrne, McPherson suggested, would help elect a governor of whom the state could be proud and that Hudson's role could help rehabilitate its long-standing tarnished image, "with the history of corruption all of a sudden lifted into the good guy category . . . by backing this man of great integrity."[36]

Later in the evening, Dugan phoned McPherson at the restaurant and told him to bring Byrne to Fitzpatrick's home, where the two resumed their talk, watching a pouring rain while sitting on the mayor's front porch. At the end, Fitzpatrick said, "You're our candidate," to which Byrne immediately asked,

"What does that mean?" Fitzpatrick assured him that it meant that Byrne would have the important "line" with his name at the top on the ballot indicating the organization's support and the two men shook hands. Byrne headed home to tell his wife Jean. When Byrne returned home to West Orange, he advised his wife Jean of what had gone on and that he was entering the race for governor. With some reluctance, she went along with her husband's desire to run, "if that's what you really want to do."[37]

Byrne would never know what changed Fitzpatrick's mind, whether it was McPherson's principled argument that the county's Democrats should align with the former prosecutor and judge to demonstrate that the new reformers were cut from a different cloth than the Hague–Kenny heritage, or whether it was based more on ego, with Fitzpatrick assuming the mantle of the new Hudson statewide king-maker. As Byrne recounted decades later, "I'm told that a lot of people said to him, 'Every other leader in Hudson County has made a governor and this is your chance.'"[38]

The next morning, Byrne phoned Chief Justice Weintraub. Earlier in the month, after he had delivered the Court's landmark ruling in *Robinson v. Cahill*, Weintraub had announced that he planned to retire at the end of the 1973 calendar year. According to Byrne, Weintraub took the call, saying "Well, Brendan, I guess I know why you're calling," and Byrne replied, "Well, unless you can talk me out of it, I plan to resign as a judge at noon and run for governor." Weintraub not only said that he would not discourage him, but also that "if I had known you were going to run, I wouldn't have announced I was retiring."[39]

After ending the conversation with Weintraub, Byrne hurriedly cleared the remaining matters he had before him as a judge. He directed his law clerk, August Lembo, to call the attorneys in a pending case to ask if they wanted to have him deliver an oral decision before he resigned or to have the case retried before a new judge. Both sides agreed to have Byrne decide the case, and came to his courtroom to hear his decision, in which he ruled against the client represented by attorney Stewart Pollock, who would later become Byrne's governor's counsel and whom he subsequently appointed to the state Supreme Court. "Look, I ruled against you," Byrne told Pollock from the bench, "but I've never seen a case tried better," a comment which Pollock later said he found "small consolation" for losing the case. Pollock continued the story: "as I was leaving the courthouse, who should be walking down the steps alongside me but Judge Byrne, and he had this batch of papers in his hand. And I turned to him, I said, 'Judge, you know I'm going to have to appeal this.' He said, 'I understand that.' And I said, 'Well, look. There's no hard feelings. Let me wish you the best of everything.' And what he had in his hand was this petition to run for governor. And he held it up and said, 'I don't know how this is going to turn out,' and the rest is history."[40]

Byrne also took a call from lobbyist Joe Katz, the former veteran reporter and staff member for Governor Hughes, who had heard from Bergen Democratic activist Jerry Breslin that Byrne had received the backing of the Hudson organization. "I knew he was gonna run," Katz remembered. "I called him up and said, 'I think you should come down to the state house and get on the steps down here. You've got the whole press here, rather than doing something in Newark or anywhere like that, and announce that . . . you're resigning from the bench and announce your candidacy.' . . . He said, 'What'll I say?' I said, 'I've written you a statement.' I had written a pretty good statement, and I read it to him on the phone, and he liked it, and I got it up to him. He came down, and he read it."[41]

On April 24, two days before filing the deadline, Byrne traveled to Trenton accompanied by McPherson, Dugan, Lan, and Breslin to deliver his letter of resignation as a judge to Governor Cahill and, immediately after, declare his candidacy to the media waiting in the hall outside the Governor's office. On the night before, Dugan had phoned his own press contacts to advise that there would be an important announcement. Although the Bergen organization still was waiting for Helstoski to decide on whether he would enter the race, Breslin attended at Dugan's suggestion to signal his personal support for Byrne. When he arrived at the State House, Byrne first went to speak to the Governor in an awkward meeting. "I handed in my resignation to Bill Cahill," Byrne related years later. "He looks a little upset, and I said, 'Governor, you have to run against somebody.'"[42] One reporter recalled that the scene in the State House had a certain dramatic flair: "It was like the Second Coming, if you will. The press was all over the place, waiting for him to come, in anticipation of this great announcement. . . . It was almost like it was choreographed, but I don't think it was. And I think the press at that time was hungry for a new candidate."[43]

After leaving Cahill's private office, Byrne announced that he would be a candidate for governor, saying in part that he was running because "an administration that must contend almost daily with corruption by its own can have little time for anything else." He also stated that his decision to resign as a judge was "a difficult step . . . cutting short a judicial career that has been personally satisfying," but that he had received over 200 phone calls in the last few days urging him to run.[44] One press account of Byrne's announcement described him as "a soft-spoken, 49-year old man with an Ivy League demeanor . . . regarded by virtually every Democratic leader in the state as the only Democratic candidate with the potential to 'turn on' the party and exploit his image of being strong on law enforcement in a year when corruption in government appears to be the major issue."[45]

Following Byrne's announcement, the Democratic organizations in Hudson, Union, and Bergen counties proceeded to put in place the practical mechanics to launch the campaign, circulating petitions for signatures by the required number of voters to get his name on the ballot. Byrne reached out to his closest associates to solicit help, particularly those from his prosecutor's staff. He asked Jim Zazzali, then in private practice, to draft a summary of his record as prosecutor for use in the coming campaign; other former aides, including Barry Evenchick, Angelo "Buddy" Bianchi, and June Strelecki soon served as surrogate speakers or as organizers of events to mobilize specific groups and constituencies.

Byrne's sudden resignation as a judge also required other pragmatic steps to allow him to campaign. "Brendan needed some income and a place to meet with people and take calls," Martin Greenberg later recalled, "so I and the other partners in our law firm asked him to re-join the firm while he campaigned."[46]

The announcement of Byrne's candidacy was followed by key support from Senator Coffee, despite his earlier assertion to Byrne of confidence in his own campaign. Meeting with Byrne, Coffee indicated his interest in being appointed as the state Democratic chairman, but was told that Byrne already had committed to support Dugan for the post if he won the nomination. Coffee then endorsed Byrne and was named chairman of Byrne's campaign.[47] In the next week, Senator Edward Crabiel initially resisted dropping out after Byrne's announcement; "Ed Crabiel's wife really thought he should be governor," Byrne recalled, "and it took a few days before he decided to drop out and endorse me."[48] Byrne's remaining primary opponents included Assemblywoman Ann Klein of Morris County, endorsed by women's groups and more liberal leaders, and state Senator Ralph DeRose of Essex County, running with the support of the Democratic organization in Byrne's home county and viewed as aligned with more conservative factions.

When Byrne entered the race, Martin Greenberg, Byrne's former law partner, found himself in what he later described as a "highly uncomfortable" position in that he had accepted—when he believed Byrne would remain a judge—the invitation of Essex Democratic chair Harry Lerner to become the organization candidate to succeed DeRose in the Senate, running in a primary election in which Byrne was now opposing DeRose for the gubernatorial nomination. "Harry Lerner was a real gentleman. I offered to drop out of the election, but he simply asked that I not actively campaign for Brendan against DeRose," Greenberg later recounted. "I also went to see DeRose, who was a neighbor of mine, to suggest that he end his primary campaign, back Brendan and I would give up the Senate nomination to allow Ralph to run for his Senate seat. But he told me, 'We're going to beat him.'"[49]

Both Coffee and Crabiel brought important support from their respective campaign organizations to compensate for Byrne's lack of his own political operatives. Coffee's political team included Richard Leone, who had already become a seasoned veteran in New Jersey policy and political circles since interrupting his doctoral studies at Princeton to become an aide to Governor Hughes and who later worked in the presidential campaigns of Senator Robert Kennedy in 1968 and Senator Edmund Muskie in 1972.[50] Then in his early thirties, Leone was named as Byrne's campaign manager. Leone brought with him Lewis Kaden, who would work closely with him on strategy and issues. After his graduation from Harvard Law School, Kaden had become a member of Senator Kennedy's staff, later working on the 1968 Kennedy presidential campaign until the Senator's assassination on the night he won the California primary. In 1970, Kaden himself had run as an anti-Vietnam War candidate in the Democratic primary challenging incumbent Congressman Edward Patten in a largely Middlesex County district. Orin Kramer, who had previously directed a high-profile investigation in New York of nursing home abuse and had come to the attention of Leone, worked as Kaden's deputy on developing and briefing the candidate on issues for campaign appearances, interviews, and debates.[51]

Another transplant from the Coffee campaign was Fariborz Fatemi, who had met Leone when they both worked in the 1968 Robert Kennedy presidential campaign. Fatemi was a seasoned veteran of other Democratic campaigns, starting with that of John Kennedy in 1960 and then continuing with Lyndon Johnson in 1964, Hubert Humphrey in 1968, and George McGovern in 1972. Fatemi became the campaign's trip director, traveling with Byrne and coordinating scheduling, advance planning, and press contacts. Fatemi had learned from the highly professional Kennedy campaign operations the basics of advance work: researching and visiting sites of scheduled events; preparing briefings of the expected activity, and profiles of key participants; physically guiding the candidate to the proper location; and identifying the principals for the candidate to greet or recognize in his remarks at each appearance.

From Crabiel's campaign came Jerry Fitzgerald English, who had served a single year of an unexpired term in the state senate representing a Union County–based district in 1971; run unsuccessfully for Congress against Republican incumbent Matthew Rinaldo in 1972; and later served as counsel to the state senate when Crabiel was the Democratic leader. After Crabiel dropped out, she joined Byrne's campaign to head outreach to citizens' groups.

For Byrne, the transition from judge to gubernatorial candidate was not easy. "You have to understand," Fatemi recalled many years later, "that as a judge, Brendan had a relatively leisurely schedule where he typically could leave the courthouse at four in the afternoon, then perhaps fit in a tennis game before heading home for dinner with the family and then going to bed before 10." Fatemi recognized that the new lifestyle wasn't an easy fit for the ex-judge. "It was a radical change for him to have to shift to the daily grind of a campaign, forced to do things he'd never done before and didn't really enjoy, like the parades, the dinners and all the other things you have to do."[52]

The campaign also impacted Byrne's children. Years later, Byrne recalled that he thought "the kids got a kick out of it," but that the youngest ones initially had difficulty understanding how their lives had changed. His son Billy was four years old at the time, Byrne remembered, and "had some trouble adjusting . . . because he had been raised in a quiet life of a judge's kid." As the campaign got underway, Byrne continued, "Now all of a sudden . . . there's people at my doorstep starting at breakfast. And then milling around the house, and the house is no longer what this four-year-old kid's expecting." Tom, his oldest child then a freshman at Princeton and a reporter for *The Daily Princetonian*, encountered a different problem. He had, as Byrne remembered, "written an article saying that it was too late for me to get into the race. And they were upset that he didn't have a scoop on the story when I did get in."[53] Tom later worked in the campaign to coordinate youth groups. The extended family also offered support. "I was really pleased when so many relatives called," Byrne later recounted, "to ask how they could help. We had lots of cousins and nieces and nephews at the campaign headquarters stuffing envelopes and working at other campaign chores. The campaign really brought the family together."[54]

On the weekend following Byrne's announcement, Leone and Coffee convened a briefing session with Democratic legislators to give the new candidate an overview of the major issues he would have to deal with during the campaign. "They did not have any great confidence in me as a candidate when I first came in," Byrne recalled in a later interview. "I had no political experience. I had been a judge. I was not, you know, up to date on all of the issues."[55] Some who participated in the meeting with Byrne were already staunch supporters of his candidacy, but others, like Atlantic County's young Assemblyman Steven Perskie, who had endorsed Coffee, and Bergen County Assemblyman Albert Burstein, who was uncommitted, had little if any knowledge of Byrne's policy views, particularly on the crucial issue of financing public education. Perskie and Burstein had been among the Democratic legislators who had supported Cahill's fiscal program that included an income tax to increase state school aid, and were particularly eager to explore Byrne's position as a candidate. On the most important issue affecting his Atlantic County district, the legalization of casino gambling in Atlantic City, Perskie was surprised to learn that the former prosecutor and judge had publicly testified in support of gambling for the city.[56]

In fact, Byrne's primary campaign focused primarily on making his background as a judge and prosecutor better known to voters. "We had an unknown candidate, completely unknown," Dick Leone reflected years later.

"Just insiders had heard of Brendan Byrne." By stressing Byrne's law enforcement experience and branding him as "the man who couldn't be bought" adapted from the FBI transcripts of the mob conversations, the campaign found a theme that was readily picked up. "The media defined Byrne as the prosecutor who couldn't be bought," Leone continued. "We immediately had an anecdote in people's mind to identify him as someone who could confront the biggest problem in the state—corruption. And it wasn't just somebody promising to do it, it was somebody with a relevant record, who actually had gone after people."[57] To reinforce the anticorruption theme, Byrne's campaign proposed a series of election reforms, including providing limited state financing of gubernatorial election campaigns; imposing ceilings on the amounts private contributors could give and candidates could spend; and making it easier to register to vote.[58]

Some of the more seasoned Democratic politicians questioned where Byrne stood at a time when the party was sharply split between its more conservative and liberal wings. After their initial fundraising efforts were disappointing, Alan Sagner, a wealthy developer and liberal Democratic activist, was brought into the campaign by Martin Greenberg to head fundraising, but Sagner found resistance to his early attempts to solicit support for Byrne from mainstream Democratic leaders. One of those initially cool to a Byrne candidacy was Congressman Peter Rodino, a native of Newark who in the following year gained national prominence as chairman of the House Judiciary Committee that presided over the impeachment proceedings against President Nixon. Rodino "liked Brendan," Sagner said in a later interview, "but felt he was surrounded by too many lefties." To counter the impression, Sagner hosted a barbecue at his home in Livingston, where Rodino apparently was reassured of Byrne's moderate leanings through discussions with the candidate and with Sagner, Leone and Kaden, his most prominent "lefties."[59]

Byrne's campaign skills in his first run for elected office also raised concerns. "I wasn't a backslapper or a bon vivant," Byrne later said in assessing his failings as a campaigner. "I wasn't a political animal." He went on to identify the qualities—ironically those that his father and brother naturally possessed—that he lacked: "Natural-born politicians walk with a spring in their step, and they can make their face light up in a smile any time they want. But I walked with a kind of shuffle, and I can't smile unless I'm happy. I look around and try to get comfortable but I don't pretend to be delighted if I'm not. I wouldn't know how."[60] Years later, one reporter wrote of Byrne's curious inability to take advantage of his natural physical qualities: "Tall and handsome, born to look statesmanlike, Brendan Byrne nevertheless lacks presence. He shuffles, sort of ambles, never in a hurry, never looking like he's quite happy to be where he is."[61] Jerry English, who accompanied the candidate to events with citizens' groups, also wasn't impressed by Byrne's early campaign style: "He would, first of all, fumble around. Look basically terrified most of the time. Couldn't remember anyone's name and would talk in this mumbly way about not too much."[62]

James Florio, who in 1973 was running for his third term in the Assembly representing a Camden County district, met candidate Byrne for the first time when the county organization endorsed his candidacy and invited the former judge to speak to, as Florio remembered, a "couple hundred" active Democrats. Like many, Florio knew little about the candidate other than that some county leaders thought he was "squeaky clean" and would be a stronger candidate than the other choices in the primary. Introduced by the county chairman as "our guy," "our candidate," Byrne was dressed, as Florio later recalled, in "a seersucker blue and white suit, red argyle socks and white bucks. . . . During the whole course of the presentation, Brendan looked at his shoes, didn't project to the audience very well . . . and mumbled a lot." When Byrne finished his talk, Florio sensed the reaction of the audience was "who is this guy, where did he come from?" and that the event was "sort of an underwhelming introduction" to Brendan Byrne.[63]

Years later in separate interviews, Dick Leone and Daniel O'Hern, then mayor of Red Bank (and in Byrne's second term his environmental commissioner, counsel, and appointee to the state Supreme Court), both labeled Byrne's stump performance in the 1973 campaign as "terrible," citing his reluctance to engage in the customary glad-handing with politicians and voters and his tendency to mumble.[64] Byrne's speaking style, as he himself later described it, was the "oratorical equivalent of a blocked punt."[65] At the outset of the campaign, a speech coach was hired to help Byrne enunciate more clearly and to make his points more forcefully, but after a few days, the apparently frustrated coach quit, telling Byrne's campaign aides, "Save your money."[66] Orin Kramer, the campaign's issues director, later pointed to Byrne's laid-back preparation for campaign appearances, recalling that prior to a New York television interview, he refused to rehearse responses to expected questions, finally cutting off Kramer's briefing so he could catch a quick nap on a sofa at the television studio.[67]

Byrne also rebelled at the regimen of the campaign, sometimes retreating into a funk. His characteristic impatience and his lifelong early-to-bed schedule were not easy to mesh with the typical screw-ups and delays. Recalling Byrne's frustrations with the campaign, Dick Leone said, "He hated it . . . He was sick of it. He would sit in a room and he would say, 'I can't do this anymore, this is horrible, I hate this.'"[68] Lacking the technology that later evolved, the logistics of arranging campaign appearances occasionally broke down. "In an era when there were no cell phones, no texting, no laptops, and no email," Fatemi related years later, "communication was face-to-face, land lines or any other methods that we devised."[69] One accommodation to Byrne's distaste for late evenings that the campaign staff reluctantly accepted was to avoid the normal practice of having the candidate sit through dinner before giving his remarks. "I told the staff," Byrne later recalled, "that if we had an early morning event, I'd do that but not to schedule anything late at night on the same day." With some difficulty, Byrne's scheduling and advance staff would advise the candidate's hosts that the appearance would be a "meet-and-greet" and "speak and leave," with Byrne leaving before dinner was served and before other speakers were heard. "He wanted to go to bed at 8 or 8:30 or something like that," Jerry English remembered, "and it would be our job to go into whatever hall and explain to whoever was running the event that the Governor-to-be wanted to speak first."[70] When the event could not be so structured, "we had a very upset candidate to deal with," his trip director Fatemi remembered, and after a series of scheduling problems, emotions came to a head. "I walked out," Fatemi said, "telling him he does not need me." The split, however, was brief. "After a day or so of cooling off," Fatemi continued, "we were back together and it was campaigning as usual."[71]

Byrne also wasn't comfortable with the drinking so frequently a sign of fellowship at political events, but on occasion the staff did its best to cloud his image as a non-drinker. At a summer barbecue sponsored by a carpenters union, Fatemi remembered taking a bottle of beer, pouring half of it out, and handing it over for the teetotaling candidate to hold while whispering in his ear, "just pretend." In highlighting Byrne's background, the campaign also, as Fatemi put it, "tried to play up the Seton Hall and downplay the Princeton and Harvard." They sought out venues and situations offering opportunities for photographs depicting him bowling at local alleys, visiting firehouses and police stations, and attending church.[72] At events attracting ethnic constituencies, they gave him a few phrases in the relevant native language; before a Latin American group, he greeted the gathering, as one reporter wrote, "in Berlitz Spanish thick with the accents of Mr. Byrne's native West Orange."[73]

Yet even with the rough patches in Byrne's style, he gradually adjusted to the demands of the campaign. "All in all, despite the occasional flare-up," Fatemi later said, "he worked hard, he did fine, he did what he had to do." Fundraising chairman Alan Sagner also concurred with Fatemi's assessment of Byrne's effort: "He worked hard. He took the time to answer people. He accepted all the impossible assignments. Going to 18 different meetings in one day, going out of his way to meet somebody who I thought was a potentially large contributor, to go talk to him."[74]

Meanwhile, as Byrne tried to hone his political skills, Ann Klein was running a hard-hitting campaign on issues, coming out forcefully for an income tax, urging expanded support of social services for the poor and seniors and criticizing Byrne and Ralph DeRose for their alliances with the old-line political bosses. When Byrne entered the race, Klein said, many Democrats had expected that he would be "a forceful leader," but his campaign performance had demonstrated that he "does not know the issues" and had given only a "blurry image" to voters on what policies he would pursue if elected.[75] DeRose took a similar tack, contending that Byrne "deals in generalities" without detailing specific positions.[76]

Reflecting in later years on what he described his own "cautious" strategy, Byrne conceded that "we thought with Hudson County we had the primary won. And so we did not do a very aggressive campaign. . . . It turned out that Ann Klein started coming up, because the liberal part of the party that pays attention was a little bit disappointed with me."[77] A few days before the election, a *Star-Ledger* reporter wrote that "Byrne has had trouble establishing himself as an effective spokesman on the issues."[78] In its profile of Byrne, the *New York Times* reported that Byrne offered "no program" for tax reform other than "regaining the confidence of the people that they will get one dollar's worth of service for one dollar's worth of taxes," and an editorial before the election criticized him for being "disturbingly vague."[79]

While Byrne was running without the formal support of the Essex County Democratic organization, he nonetheless felt he would cut into the DeRose vote from the county. "People still recalled the job I had done as county prosecutor, and I had made a lot of contacts when I ran the grand juries." he reflected. "Some voters also remembered my father and other people from our family. I also had support from Mayor Gibson and Steve Adubato in Newark, so I was confident of doing fairly well in Essex."[80] Apart from his support in Hudson and Essex, Byrne also relied on the promises from the county organizations in Union, Bergen, Middlesex, and Mercer to turn out the vote on election day, but the outcome still seemed uncertain. Three weeks before the June primary, an Eagleton Institute poll found a virtual dead heat between Byrne and Klein, with 14 percent for Byrne and 13 percent for Klein, and DeRose trailing badly at 3 percent.[81]

Among the Republicans, Governor Cahill's principal opponent was Congressman Charles Sandman from Cape May, a conservative who would become one of President Nixon's most vocal defenders as the Watergate investigation unfolded. Sandman shared with Byrne the World War II experience of serving as a B-17 navigator. After his bomber was shot down over Czechoslovakia in 1944, he was captured by the Germans and spent seven months as a prisoner of war. He later built his political career in the narrow confines of the South Jersey shore, serving ten years in the state senate representing a Cape May County district before his election to Congress in 1966. He also had become a powerful political boss: "Charlie Sandman runs Cape May County," one journalist wrote during the 1973 campaign, "like Hughie Long ran Louisiana."[82]

The 1973 primary election was Sandman's third run for the Republican gubernatorial nomination; in his last race in 1969, he had lost to Cahill in the primary by a 39 percent to 36 percent margin. In 1973, Sandman attacked Cahill's moderate positions, particularly the Governor's support for an income tax that had divided Republicans in the legislature and influential county leaders. At the start of the primary campaign, most expected that the incumbent governor would turn back Sandman's challenge, but news of scandals implicating Cahill's associates soon undermined the Governor's reelection efforts. A few days before the primary filing deadline, two key Republican fundraisers were indicted on charges that they sought political contributions from a bank in return for a promise to steer state funds for deposit in the bank; just days later, Cahill's former Treasurer Joseph McCrane took the Fifth Amendment in declining to answer questions before a grand jury investigating his fundraising for Cahill's 1969 campaign. In the weeks leading up to the June 5 election, two separate federal indictments of McCrane and of Nelson Gross, the former Republican state chairman, were announced charging them with advising businessmen to conceal campaign contributions by listing them as tax-deductible business expenses (charges on which they were convicted in the following year).[83]

Raymond Bateman, then the state senate president, recounted years later that Cahill had met with him in November 1972. "I'm not going to run again," Bateman said Cahill confided to him. "Nobody knows this but my family and Paul Sherwin [his Secretary of State] and I want you to run." After Bateman discussed the potential campaign with his wife, he decided that he would run, but when over a month had passed during which he had not heard anything further from Cahill, Bateman reached out to the Governor. Cahill then told Bateman he had changed his mind, explaining that he had been told by his advisers: "I'm the only person that can beat Charlie Sandman in the primary." Bateman accepted Cahill's decision, but said Cahill ran an indifferent campaign, making only token appearances. "I spent the whole spring," Bateman recalled, "debating Charlie Sandman because Cahill never came out, he never showed." In Bateman's view, the stress that Cahill was under had taken its personal and political toll: "A lot of his friends were being indicted, the U.S. Attorney was after his good friends; every week somebody else was getting shot at by the U.S. Attorney, and it really preyed on him and it preyed on his wife and it got to the point he wouldn't even go out. . . . I don't remember one major campaign stop that he made in that primary."[84]

The same Eagleton Institute poll taken three weeks before the election that showed Byrne and Klein running even reported Sandman leading Cahill by 29 percent to 22 percent.[85] The poll also showed, however, that if Cahill were nominated, he would hold a small lead over both Byrne and Klein in voter preference for the November election, but that either Democrat would best Sandman.[86]

On election day, Byrne won comfortably with 195,000 votes, beating Klein with 115,000 and DeRose with 96,000. Speaking to his supporters gathered at the Holiday Inn in Newark on election night, Byrne said that "no candidate has ever run for statewide office in five weeks and won," and called for party unity in the fall campaign to "show a source of pride again in government and public life." Congressman Sandman also won a landslide 58 percent to 41 percent victory over the incumbent Cahill, with the Governor carrying only five of the twenty-one counties. Cahill became the first incumbent New Jersey governor to be denied renomination in his party's primary election.[87]

Despite the late start, the Byrne campaign was perhaps New Jersey's most professional campaign to that point, utilizing techniques in polling, voter targeting, and media strategy that would later become commonplace, but were still innovative in 1973. In the general election, Leone recruited David Garth, the pioneering media consultant who was later described as "the master of the sound bite," and was credited as a major factor in New York Mayor John Lindsay's uphill 1969 reelection victory, to develop the media strategy. Garth assigned Jeff Greenfield, another Kennedy staffer and campaign veteran, to write drafts for Byrne's major speeches.[88] Garth seized upon the label of Byrne as "the man who couldn't be bought" as the simple, direct message that he knew would connect to New Jersey voters weary of scandals in both Trenton and Washington.[89] He also taught Byrne the discipline of distilling his thoughts to fit the time and pacing constraints of broadcast media. "He never had me say anything I didn't believe in," Byrne said in recalling Garth's patience with his early struggles to express his views, "but he could shape the floundering comments I would make into a sharp, concise spot of precisely 29 and a half seconds long that told the voters what I stood for."[90]

Byrne's image as the "man who couldn't be bought" contrasted sharply with that of Sandman, whose rise to political power had prompted questions of integrity. He had prospered as a lawyer by receiving large fees as bond counsel for projects by the county and local governments and school districts within his sphere of influence, but which critics contended entailed little work to justify his high legal bills. Sandman's connections in the historically mob-influenced politics surrounding Atlantic City also came to light, ironically, from another of the same series of FBI wiretaps conducted during the 1960s that led to Byrne's label as "the man who couldn't be bought." In one tape, Herman "Stumpy" Orman, the owner of an Atlantic City hotel and a major Sandman fundraiser, was identified by a Mafia insider as "the main (Mob) guy in Atlantic City."[91] Paul "Skinny" D'Amato, the proprietor of the well-known 500 Club in Atlantic City, which was a popular meeting spot for mob figures also was linked to Sandman.[92]

Despite his questionable connections, Sandman had successfully cultivated a network of contacts within his party by the force of his genial personality. "Charlie was always well accepted by everybody, because he didn't hurt anybody," Frank McDermott, a Republican state Senator from Union County who directed Sandman's 1973 campaign, later put it. "He would always help you, and that's the way he portrayed himself, and he was always a jolly guy, you know. He could be accepted as one of the boys."[93]

Sandman's nomination was welcome news to the Byrne campaign. Senator Dugan, who after the primary election had been elected state Democratic chairman with Byrne's support, said that a "malaise" came over the state Republican Party "after they woke up and said what have we done to ourselves?"[94] With the Republicans turning to a right-wing candidate who was one of the rapidly dwindling defenders of the increasingly unpopular President Nixon, Democratic insiders were confident that the broader electorate in the general election would reject Sandman. As the Watergate scandal continued to unfold during the fall campaign, most of the Byrne forces expected that Sandman would be an easy target running as the candidate of a Republican Party still sharply divided after a bruising primary.[95]

Even with the overall confidence of Democrats in defeating Sandman, Byrne had to deal with divisions within his own campaign. The crucial endorsement by the Hudson organization in the primary had led to an uneasy alliance between the Byrne campaign staff and the county's politicians. Hudson's leaders apparently believed that Senator Dugan's position as the state Democratic chairman would bring them a strong role in setting Byrne's strategy, as well as influencing decisions on spending on consultants, advertising, and the like. Additional friction came from a perception by Hudson leaders that the Byrne campaign was dominated by the Coffee-Leone network from Mercer County, a county which the Hudson politicians viewed as significantly less important in Democratic voter turnout, and therefore deserving less clout, than their own. Tension developed to the point that Byrne called for a meeting with Dugan and Leone, where he firmly informed Dugan that "Dick's in charge." The rebuff, as Leone later recalled, left Dugan "stunned" and even surprised Leone, who had not been given any advance notice by Byrne of how the candidate intended to resolve the budding power battle for management of the campaign.[96]

But the Republican side was saddled with even more sharper internal conflicts. Moderate Republicans largely stayed aloof from or provided only token backing of their gubernatorial nominee's general election campaign. Cahill gave tacit support to Sandman, but made no campaign appearances for him and the state's other senior Republican, U.S. Senator Clifford P. Case, withheld his endorsement. "Frankly, Cahill knew I was going to win," Byrne recounted years later, "and Cahill wasn't a bit disappointed. Not that I won but that Sandman lost."[97] The incumbent administration also publicly announced that it anticipated having a $200 million surplus at the end of the state's fiscal year, a disclosure that eased pressure on Byrne to adopt a firm position on whether a broad new tax would be needed.[98] The announcement of the projected surplus "fueled speculation," according to one journalist, "that Republican Cahill wouldn't mind seeing Democrat Byrne beat Republican Sandman."[99]

With the divisions among the Republicans, Sandman's campaign also had difficulty in fundraising. Sandman kept promising that his campaign would launch a television and radio advertising "blitz" toward election day, but it failed to materialize. Byrne's campaign raised nearly $1.5 million, with the Democrats outspending the Republicans by a three-to-one margin. In the last week of October, Sandman attempted to make an issue of the spending disparity: "Make no mistake about it, Byrne is ahead. He's bought the election."[100]

Although a profile of the general election campaign published in *New York Magazine* said Byrne was "as stiff on the stump as he is in person," by most accounts Sandman did not match up well in the several debates and joint appearances of the two candidates.[101] "Nobody liked Sandman, nobody liked his policies," Byrne would say years later. "And he was not, in the public view, he was not a nice guy. I didn't mind public appearances with Sandman because people didn't like him."[102] Sandman's record as an extreme conservative was easily attacked; as Byrne recalled, he "once voted in the legislature against having hot and cold water for migrant workers." On another occasion, when asked about his position on federal proposals to allow oil and gas drilling off the New Jersey coast, Sandman neglected to recognize that he was running for statewide support by responding "we don't want offshore drilling at Cape May, if you are going to do offshore drilling, do it in Monmouth County where they don't care about clean beaches."[103]

To a great extent, the final weeks of the fall campaign were overshadowed by events outside the state. On October 6, the "Yom Kippur War" broke out when Egyptian and Syrian forces crossed ceasefire lines to attack positions which in the Sinai Peninsula and Golan Heights which had been captured by Israel in 1967. Hostilities continued into the last week of October, and would lead to the oil embargo that created fuel shortages and spikes in energy prices throughout the nation. On October 20, in the "Saturday Night Massacre," President Nixon ordered Attorney General Elliott Richardson to fire Watergate Prosecutor Archibald Cox, leading to the resignations by Richardson and his Deputy Attorney General William Ruckelshaus in protest of Nixon's action. The uproar over the incident heightened national attention on the

Watergate cover-up, further undermining Nixon's support and tainting those Republicans, including Sandman, who continued to defend the President.

Apart from the issue of corruption that had led to the Democrats selecting Byrne as their nominee, the major subject in the election was whether the state should enact an income tax in response to the *Robinson v. Cahill* decision. Some Democrats, particularly those legislators who had voted for the 1972 Cahill tax program, felt that Byrne should come out forthrightly to endorse an income tax to meet the Supreme Court's mandate. Others, however, cautioned against taking such a political risk, arguing that it would be more prudent to wait until the new governor had access to the State government's resources and was able to build broader public support before putting forth a specific plan. Still not confident that Byrne's election was assured, some veteran Democratic leaders, including David Wilentz of Middlesex and Harry Lerner of Essex, met with the candidate to urge him to either come out against an income tax or hedge on the issue, advice that Leone felt reflected their outdated political instincts based on the traditional fear among New Jersey politicians of the danger of supporting any statewide tax.[104]

Byrne himself was wary of the political history of the tax issue. "The income tax in New Jersey had been a hysterical issue over the years," he related in an interview years later. "In the old days, when the *Newark News* was the dominant newspaper in New Jersey, the *Newark News* would write editorials about the income tax and how bad it was and anybody that proposed it, and Hughes proposed it, . . . got killed. So it was an issue to stay away from."[105] In fact, during the first weeks of the campaign, Byrne hedged on how he would meet the State's responsibility to increase its support of school funding pursuant to the *Robinson* decision. He said that the state tax system needed "restructuring," primarily to relieve local taxpayers of the burden of high property taxes to finance public schools but, as the *New York Times* reported, he "avoided any statement indicating any support for an income tax."[106]

Sandman strongly opposed any income tax, saying "I haven't found anyone who's mad because we don't have one."[107] In an interview more than thirty years after the 1973 campaign, Sandman's campaign manager Frank McDermott said he believed New Jersey voters at the time remained so opposed to an income tax that a firm stand by Byrne in favor of the tax could have swung the election to the Republicans.[108] A magazine profile of the campaign published three weeks before the election also reported that in private polls Sandman was only ten points behind Byrne and was "killing" Byrne on the tax issue.[109]

At a debate with Sandman on October 15 at Seton Hall University, Byrne attacked Sandman's own alternative fiscal plan that called for the federal government to assume a greater share of state welfare costs and allowing

New Jersey and other states to receive revenues paid by their residents in federal excise taxes on alcohol and tobacco. Byrne contended that the Sandman proposal would result in steep increases in federal taxes.[110] In an appearance before the New Jersey School Boards Association on October 26, Byrne called generally for "financial reform" that would guarantee each child in public schools throughout the State the same level of financial support for their education and pointed to the Cahill Administration's anticipated surplus as the primary vehicle to fund the increase in State school aid. He also stated, "I have said loud and clear that I don't think we need an income tax in the foreseeable future," but he later said that what he really meant was "We don't need an income tax to balance the budget."[111]

Whatever his intention, Byrne surprised and dismayed some in his camp who saw the income tax as the only viable option to reduce the state's reliance on the local property tax as the primary funding source for public education. Albert Burstein, the Bergen County assemblyman who had become a leader of the Democratic legislators pushing for a broad-based tax and educational financing reform, said that he "cringed" when he heard reports of the "foreseeable future" comment by Byrne because it was "contrary to everything" that he and other Democrats who had studied the issue had come to believe.[112] Many years later, Leone said that he felt Byrne's off-the-cuff remark may have been a result of the prior meeting of Byrne with David Wilentz, Harry Lerner, and the other veteran pols who urged the candidate to oppose or waffle on the need for the tax; to Leone, the "foreseeable future" comment may have been an attempt, perhaps subliminal, by Byrne to take a position that would not directly go against their advice. "Most people were confident," Leone recalled, "but there were people, including Brendan Byrne, who started to get nervous at the end. He was encountering some resistance to his message, . . . some criticism of the fact that he hadn't been strong enough in swearing that he would never support an income tax."[113]

As the campaign wound down, Byrne renewed his use of the "foreseeable future" remark. The *New York Times* reported that two separate joint appearances on New York television stations two days before the election reflected the "bitterness" of the contest. Byrne's demeanor toward Sandman was described as "icily hostile" and Sandman's as "smilingly sarcastic," the Republican candidate mocking the "foreseeable future" remark, asking "with a chuckle, whether the foreseeable future might not mean the second week after inauguration."[114]

Few issues other than the income tax gained much attention during the campaign. Byrne's speeches and messages focused on the obvious strengths and issues that had led to his entering the race—his personal reputation for integrity as "the man who couldn't be bought" in the wake of the federal Watergate and state corruption scandals and his proposals for campaign fundraising, election reforms, and stronger controls over the award of government contracts. To the extent that he raised any new issues on his own, they tended to be subjects that he had dealt with in his prior public roles, such as repeating the call he had made as head of the Public Utilities Commission for a state takeover of public transit and, as he had when he was a prosecutor, calling for an overhaul of the state's archaic criminal code, including repealing laws against social gambling, setting forth more specific guidelines for sentencing, and allowing judges to order restitution to victims.

With polls showing 70 percent of New Jersey voters favoring restoration of the death penalty, Sandman attempted to exploit their differences: "It's very simple. I'm for the death penalty and Byrne's against it."[115] Sandman took a somewhat divergent position on Byrne's law enforcement record. Early in the campaign, he suggested that he would create a new office of a special prosecutor to fight corruption, and that he would appoint someone "of the caliber of Brendan Byrne" to the post.[116] Later, however, he questioned Byrne's record as prosecutor, saying that credit for attacking corruption in Newark was more properly attributed to efforts by U.S. Attorney Herbert J. Stern, a Nixon appointee. "When was Newark any more corrupt than in the 10 years he was Prosecutor?" Sandman charged in a debate with Byrne at Seton Hall University. "Newark was cleaned up, but it was cleaned up not by Byrne but by Stern."[117]

Late in the campaign, Byrne became concerned over the impact among his fellow Catholics over his differences with Sandman relating to abortion, which had become the focus of national debate following the issuance in the previous January of the landmark *Roe v. Wade* decision of United Sates Supreme Court. Also a Catholic, Sandman was a sponsor in the Congress of a proposed amendment to the federal Constitution prohibiting abortion and had endorsed the call by New Jersey Catholic leaders for a similar amendment to the state constitution. In an interview years later, Byrne summarized his abortion position as "I was personally opposed to it, but that I respected a woman's right to choose. That's the position a lot of Catholic politicians take and the Church is totally against that position." On October 10, the day after Byrne visited the campus of Saint Peter's College, its president, Father Victor Yanitelli, wrote a "Dear Brendan" letter in which he thanked him for the visit but said that in his remarks on abortion "you have communicated a sense of 'hedging.'"[118] On the Sunday before the election, "there were two million leaflets distributed," Byrne recalled, "at every Catholic Church in the state telling people not to vote for me. I worried about that."[119] And on election day, additional brochures were handed out to voters on their way to the polls with a photo of a dead fetus and calling for the rejection of Byrne: "He supports abortion. He feels that it is an individual's right to kill the unborn."[120]

Yet neither the abortion issue nor any of Sandman's other charges took hold, and the Republican campaign could not repair the damage that had tainted the party throughout the country. As one press account put it, "the seemingly endless round of controversy surrounding the Nixon administration, has prompted many candidates to drop the word 'Republican' from their campaign billboards and brochures and to run almost as independents."[121] Following the "Saturday night massacre" on October 20, the New Jersey election was seen as an early test of voter reaction to the President's firing of Special Prosecutor Cox and the resignations of Attorney General Richardson and Deputy Attorney General Ruckelshaus. In an appearance in Bergen County about a week before the election, former Nixon Treasury Secretary John Connally said that he understood why some Republicans were hiding their party label and that the New Jersey election would be seen as a referendum on the Watergate scandal.[122]

Byrne held a twenty-point lead over Sandman in the last Eagleton Institute poll of prospective voters taken before the election, with 43 percent to 23 percent expressing their preference for the Democrat, but with one-third of the respondents still undecided.[123] Polls closer to the election by both NBC and CBS television stations each reported Byrne increasing his lead to over thirty points.[124]

The New York Times endorsed Byrne's election in an editorial on October 24:

For any New Jersey resident with even a casual concern about the staggering problems that beset his state, the obvious choice for Governor is Brendan T. Byrne. Judge Byrne, a Democrat, has impressive qualifications for Governor apart from the integrity conceded even by political opponents; but in this election he will command the votes of concerned, public-spirited citizens of both parties almost by default. Representative Charles W. Sandman, Jr., the Republican candidate, has waged the most negative, demagogic, and fiscally irresponsible campaign in recent New Jersey history.

But the *Times* went on to mildly chastise Byrne's "cautious, middle-road campaign that liberal Democrats have reluctantly accepted in order to preserve freshly rebuilt party unity," an approach which it found to be "generally humane, pragmatic, and common sense, if frequently not so forthright as we would wish."[125]

On the day of the election, after voting and making a final campaign swing, Byrne returned to his home in West Orange and reviewed the victory speech Dick Leone had drafted for him. According to Leone, he then asked, "what should I say if I lose?" and Leone responded, "Brendan, if you lose you can say anything you want."[126] Byrne later related that he found the hours on election day after campaigning had ended as the most stressful: "The most nervous, I think, a political candidate gets is, like, from about 5:30 on election night until the polls close, because you're sort of helpless during that time. You know, the fate is in somebody else's hands."[127]

By the time Byrne arrived at the election night party, held at the former Goldman's Hotel in West Orange where he had worked as a locker boy, his victory was already known. "The networks called the election some ten minutes after the polls closed at eight o'clock," Byrne later recalled. "There wasn't any suspense. When I walked in, I asked 'did Marty win?' since I wanted to know if Marty Greenberg had won his race for the Senate." (Greenberg did win.) At the victory celebration, Byrne's brother Frank was quoted, "If people knew what a terrific guy my brother was, Sandman wouldn't have even got one vote!" In his own remarks, Byrne declared his determination "to restore faith in the political process," and that his "first obligation is to pursue the ideal of integrity in government."[128]

When all votes were counted, as the *Star-Ledger* reported, Byrne "swept to a landslide victory of monumental proportions, outstripping even the wildest predictions on his chances in the race."[129] Winning the largest plurality in the state's history, Byrne's tally of 1,397,613 votes more than doubled Sandman's total of 676,235 and accounted for some 68 percent of the total vote. His election also brought Democratic victories in many traditionally Republican legislative districts; according to one account, Democrats "piled up incredible margins winning districts that had never been carried before." Democrats swept to a three-to-one majority in the state senate and a five-to-one margin in the General Assembly, only the third time in a century that Democrats controlled both houses.[130]

At a press conference in the State House on the day after the election, Byrne attributed his victory to "a significant lack of public confidence" in the Nixon administration. Ray Bateman, who would oppose Byrne in the 1977 election, noted years later, "That was the first campaign in the United States after Watergate. First one. And we paid the price. No Republican was going to win that election. I wouldn't have won that election."[131] The Republican state chairman was more direct, saying the defeat "was a case of the word 'Republican' being repudiated and punished by the voters."[132] Another state Republican leader called it simply, "the worst political defeat ever suffered by any party here."[133]

Years later, Byrne added that he felt the Republican divisions within the state leading to Governor Cahill's defeat in the primary election also had been critical factors to his victory. "I'm not sure, even with his problems, I would have beaten Bill Cahill," he reflected, "but I was glad that I had beaten Sandman."[134]

Chapter 6

1973 Transition

"It Will All Be Uphill from Here"

In their first meeting after Byrne's election, Governor Cahill gave Governor-elect Byrne some prophetic advice. "Bill Cahill told me," Byrne later recalled, "You will never again be as popular as governor as you are today. It will all be uphill from here."[1]

Brendan Byrne had perhaps the most unusual transition to office of any New Jersey governor. Apart from the normal tasks of selecting a staff and cabinet and developing his first legislative proposals and other initiatives, before taking the oath of office Byrne was called on to make decisions which had significant consequences for his tenure as governor. He sanctioned the choice of a new chief justice; salvaged the floundering plan for the construction of Giants Stadium in the Meadowlands; and blocked the construction of a Turnpike extension through the pine forests of South Jersey. These decisions set the stage for major actions Byrne would later undertake as governor.

On November 8, 1973, the day after Byrne's election, Governor Cahill announced that he intended to nominate Richard J. Hughes as Chief Justice of the State Supreme Court. The appointment of the former Democratic governor, who had served as a Superior Court judge, was to fill the unexpected vacancy created by the sudden death from a stroke on October 19 of Pierre Garven, Cahill's former counsel, just seven weeks after Garven had been sworn in by Cahill to head the court following the retirement of Chief Justice Joseph Weintraub.[2]

The announcement was not a surprise to Byrne, who had been given advance notice by Cahill before the election. "Cahill calls me," as Byrne later told the story, "and says he wants to appoint the successor to . . . Garven. I said to Cahill—I'm not sure why Cahill thought he needed me, by the way, but he was convinced he couldn't get a justice confirmed without me. I'm just a candidate. I said to Cahill that I would okay his appointing a justice but not a chief justice. He comes back to me and he says, 'I got a chief justice that you can't refuse.' He gave me Hughes's name. Actually I ran the Hughes name by Weintraub and Weintraub came back on that and said, 'I think it's going to be all right.'"[3]

While Byrne had hoped that Cahill would leave the nomination open for him to make after his inauguration, the appointment of the popular former governor—who had appointed Byrne to a second term as prosecutor in the face of strong opposition and had later brought Byrne into his cabinet as president of the Public Utilities Commission—could not be opposed. From Byrne's inauguration in January 1974 until Hughes left the Court in 1979 when he reached the mandatory retirement age of 70, the Hughes Court would be a valuable ally in pursuing Byrne's key goals, particularly by pressing the Legislature to act on school finance reform and by delaying a decision on pending litigation that could have undercut Byrne's Pinelands preservation program.

After the 1973 election, Cahill sought the New Jersey legislature's approval of the agreement he and his representatives had negotiated with the New York Giants to build a stadium for the team which, along with a new racetrack, would constitute the core of the proposed New Jersey Sports Complex in the Meadowlands. Under the plan, revenues from the racetrack would be the primary source to finance the costs of construction and operation of both facilities.

Cahill had signed legislation in May 1971 establishing the New Jersey Sports & Exposition Authority to finance, build and manage the sports complex.[4] The idea of a sports complex had first been advanced by Joseph McCrane, Cahill's state treasurer and 1969 campaign finance director who previously had been the general manager of the Garden State Park racetrack in Cherry Hill, which was owned by his father-in-law, Eugene Mori.[5] In the following month, Cahill named David A. "Sonny" Werblin, who had been called "the world's greatest agent" by the show business newspaper *Variety* for his prominent career in Hollywood representing clients like Elizabeth Taylor, Frank Sinatra, Johnny Carson, and Ronald Reagan. Later, Werblin was one of the investment group which in 1963 purchased the New York Titans of the struggling American Football League and renamed the team as the New York Jets; as president of the Jets, he signed Joe Namath in January 1965 to a record $427,000 contract to quarterback the Jets, helping the AFL to survive until it announced in the following year that it would merge with the National Football League.[6]

Within two months after becoming chairman of the Authority, Werblin disclosed that he had reached an agreement with the New York Giants of the NFL for the team to relocate from Yankee Stadium to play at a newly-built

Giants Stadium in the Meadowlands. After borrowing $51 million from a consortium of New Jersey banks to start construction, the Authority held a groundbreaking in November 1972 to begin building the stadium and racetrack; as described by one journalist, the scene at the groundbreaking was not promising: "Huddled on an island of landfill trucked in for the occasion, Werblin and his shivering guests were surrounded by industrial litter—auto skeletons, oil drums, bedsprings—settling into a glutinous mire. Nearby, rats the size of cats nosed through mounds of garbage, and off in the windswept reeds, in tidal creeks tainted with chemical wastes, fish lay belly up in the pale winter light."[7] To finance completion of the project, the Authority announced plans for a $262 million bond issue, but in March 1973, New York Governor Nelson Rockefeller pushed through his legislature major changes in New York's racing laws, improving the competitive position of the New York tracks and undermining the prospects of any new track in New Jersey. According to Adrian "Bud" Foley, a prominent attorney on the Sports Authority board who served as its treasurer, "Within two weeks, the financial houses supporting our bond began dropping like flies. It was a brilliant ploy, and was indicative of Rockefeller's single-minded determination to stop us. So there we were, owing $51 million and with no visible means of support."[8] Just before the November 6 election, in a memorandum to the legislature, Governor Cahill condemned New York's obstructionist tactics, and sought to rally support for his faltering plan: "The pride, the prestige, the image—the very credibility of the State of New Jersey throughout the nation—are on the line."[9]

But with the help of a friend at a Wall Street investment firm, Werblin succeeded in securing underwriters for another proposed bond issue (increased to $280 million to account for inflation) to be offered in October 1973, the month before the November 1973 election in which Byrne would be elected governor. On the day that the Authority announced its new bond issue, however, Governor Rockefeller again intervened, disclosing plans for a new $275 million sports complex—including a racetrack and stadium—to be built on a platform over the railway yards in Sunnyside, Queens. "It was a complete hoax!" Foley was later quoted as saying. "They never had a feasibility study, never had a plan—nothing! But with that, we went down the drain again."[10]

Given the questions being raised about the financing and revenue projections of the Meadowlands project, the bond underwriters determined that, in order to make another bond issue marketable, the legislature would need to enact a "moral pledge" to repay the debt issued by the Authority in the event that revenues from racing and the new stadium fell short of projections.[11] Although the moral pledge would not carry the same legal commitments as a full faith and credit pledge of the state government, it would require the Authority to request an appropriation from the legislature to make up any shortfall in paying interest and principal on the bonds. In his last weeks in office, Governor Cahill had been unable to muster enough votes for passage of the "moral pledge" legislation. "The stadium was not popular," Byrne would later recall, "most people didn't think it was worth the cost, others were worried over traffic on game days and still others objected on environmental grounds. Some even thought that after it was built, it would just sink into the swamp."[12]

During his campaign for governor, Byrne had supported Cahill's goal of bringing the Giants to New Jersey, but had questioned whether the agreement with the Giants adequately protected the state's interests and whether the financing of the sports complex was viable. Congressman Sandman had been firmly opposed. "Neither of us really advocated building that stadium in the campaign of '73." Byrne later reflected. "If I had lost that election, Giants Stadium would never have been built. Sandman was not for it, he was from South Jersey, it was irrelevant to him and did not support it."[13] There also were concerns that Cahill's eagerness to lure the Giants had skewed the terms of the agreement to their benefit. "It was really a sweetheart deal for the Giants," Dick Leone later said, "and the financing was largely dependent on the race track being this huge cash cow. Racing revenue already was showing early signs of declining, and some of us were skeptical about the longer-term prospects of racing being able to subsidize the rest of the complex."[14]

Perhaps the major reason for Byrne to avoid helping Cahill save the sports complex was political. One of the most prominent opponents of the Cahill plan and the proposed race track was David Wilentz, the former state Attorney General and a powerful Democratic leader. Wilentz was the majority shareholder of the Monmouth Park Jockey Club, which owned and operated Monmouth Park Racetrack in Oceanport on the Jersey Shore; he feared that the new Meadowlands track operated by a state authority not subject to taxes or the need to return a profit would undermine Monmouth's competitive position.[15] "David Wilentz and the rest of the group [that owned Monmouth Park] were definitely afraid that the sports complex would draw from Monmouth Park," Byrne later reflected. "I had great admiration for David, and he did not want a sports complex built, nor did a lot of other people."[16]

While there were strong reasons for Byrne to let Cahill try to salvage the race track and stadium on his own, the idea of a sports complex made sense to the governor-elect. An avid sports fan who had previously owned interests in race horses, he agreed with Cahill's assessment that professional sports could help improve New Jersey's long-festering "image" problem, a concern which also contributed to his support of casino gambling in Atlantic City.

As governor-elect, Byrne was forced to decide if he wanted to help Cahill save the struggling project and endorse passage of the moral pledge legislation. "I remember Cahill calling me one day while I am governor-elect,"

Byrne later recalled, "and he said, 'I have to have this bill on the board [posted for a vote in the legislature] this afternoon. And if I don't, I am going to have a press conference and declare the deal dead.' And I said, 'Governor, you can do that if you want to. I wouldn't. You know, I think I can explore something which would be acceptable to me and to this administration if I had a little time.' And Cahill hung up and called me back later this afternoon and he said, 'I have decided not to post the bill.'"[17] After the conversation with Cahill, Byrne issued a statement saying he had declined Cahill's request to endorse the moral pledge legislation, but reserved "the right to explore alternatives for the next two weeks which might result in a more attractive package for our state."[18]

On November 27, Byrne met at the Princeton Club in Manhattan with Sonny Werblin and Bud Foley of the Sports Authority and Giants owner Wellington Mara and other Giants executives and lawyers. Byrne brought with him Lew Kaden, who would become the governor's counsel; Dick Leone, the incoming state treasurer; and Jim Zazzali, who had worked under Byrne in the Essex County prosecutor's office and who had prepared a briefing memo for Byrne on the proposed contract with the Giants. Byrne also relied on Clifford Goldman, who as the first executive director of the Hackensack Meadowlands Development Commission had been actively involved in the initial Cahill negotiations with the Giants and in the planning of the stadium's construction and who would soon join the incoming Byrne administration as Leone's deputy treasurer.[19] Years later, Byrne remembered Mara as "tough, a very nice guy, smooth, old fashioned Irishman, soft spoken, but do not try to get anything by him, and totally committed to the Giants."[20] Bargaining was "difficult," Byrne recalled. "The Giants assumed the arrangement they'd worked out with the Cahill Administration was a done deal. We felt it was too restrictive and gave the Giants too much control."[21]

After negotiating for a few hours, the two sides broke for lunch, with the contingents for the Giants and for Byrne going to separate rooms. Werblin went to eat with the Giants. "That signaled to me," Jim Zazzali recalled, "how much Werblin wanted to save his deal with the Giants, but it annoyed our side that he had not stayed with us."[22] After lunch, the two sides resumed negotiations, with Byrne presenting the changes that he wanted in the contract. "During those delicate talks," a *Star-Ledger* columnist later wrote, "when the Giants could easily have walked away from the table and back into the arms of then Mayor John Lindsay—and a renovated Yankee Stadium—Brendan Byrne played tough guy and took a gamble."[23] The Giants asked for twenty-four hours to review the revisions, and as Byrne later put it, "We got the deal. On our terms."[24]

The revised agreement retained state ownership of the stadium, with the Giants as a tenant, a change from the original Cahill deal in which the stadium would be built for the Giants by the state while the Giants would control its use. Among other things, the Giants agreed to allow the Authority to lease the stadium for other events, including football, soccer, and other sports, concerts, and special events; the Authority also was given the right to impose a ticket surcharge and higher parking fees in order to augment its revenues. The new contract increased the expected return to the Authority by five-fold, ultimately generating $20 million in net annual revenue, and in later years would allow the New York Jets to join the Giants in New Jersey.[25] A point that Byrne did not raise with the Giants was the team's dropping "New York" from its name. While the "NY" logo on the helmets was removed after the relocation to New Jersey, Byrne felt that Mara's strong identification with New York made it futile to ask for the change. "Wellington Mara would never have consented to be called the New Jersey Giants," Byrne later reflected, "maybe the Giants, but not the New Jersey Giants."[26]

After the Giants agreed to the revised terms, Byrne announced that he would support the pending moral pledge legislation to strengthen the marketability of the proposed bond issue. Byrne's decision to support the moral pledge placed the governor-elect in a difficult position with members of his own party. "Most of the Democrats in that Senate had been opposed to Cahill's original bill to create the Sports Authority in 1970," Jeffrey Laurenti, then an aide to Mercer County Senator Joseph Merlino, recalled, "and now they were obliged to eat crow and vote for the moral pledge behind the Authority bonds because the governor-elect of their Party had decided to support it."[27]

Cahill then summoned a group of key legislators to his office. According to one published account, after citing the efforts by Governor Rockefeller to undercut the sports complex, he told them, "That's what those bastards have done to us. New York is pushing us around again and that's why New Jersey is the way it is. Are we going to sit still for this?" After the bill passed the Senate by a 29 to 7 vote, Senator James Dugan, whom Byrne had named as chairman of the Democratic State Committee after the June 1973 primary, declared: "This legislature is finally telling Rockefeller that we're no longer simply going to be a dumping ground for New York. We're standing up to New York and telling it we're its equal!"[28] Even with Byrne's support, the moral pledge legislation barely passed in the Assembly, with 42 votes for and 27 against (one more than the minimum needed for passage).[29] Governor Cahill signed the legislation on December 4, the day after the Assembly vote.[30]

Despite the approval of the "moral pledge" and the improved revenue prospects for the Authority, the financing for the project was still at risk. As the Authority made another attempt to sell bonds, an Italian bank which previously had agreed to buy $50 million reneged on its commitment, reportedly under pressure from the Chase Manhattan Bank, which was chaired by Governor Rockefeller's brother David. Other potential investors also backed out. After his inauguration on January 15, 1974, Byrne was compelled to convene a meeting of leading executives of New Jersey–based firms—including major banks and the Prudential Insurance Company—and urged them to demonstrate their commitment to the state by buying the Authority's bonds.[31] Prudential agreed to provide to the $50 million needed to replace the funding from the Italian bank, guaranteeing that the bond issue would succeed. "Prudential's commitment was the most important," Byrne later recalled. "When they decided to buy the bonds, they gave us credibility to get the rest of the financing."[32]

Once the Authority's initial financing was in place, construction was expedited, and the track and the stadium opened on schedule for the fall 1976 racing and football seasons. The track proved to be a great financial success: the betting handle during its first harness season surpassed all expectations, and the following year's inaugural four-month thoroughbred meeting set records for attendance and revenues.[33] The Sports Authority soon was able to return its profits to the state Treasury. In 1976, the Treasury refinanced the "moral pledge" bonds by selling lower interest general obligation bonds, with the savings from the lower interest on the new bonds sufficient to largely finance the costs of construction of the new indoor arena that opened in 1981.

While Byrne went along with Cahill's selection of Richard Hughes as chief justice and rescued the Giants Stadium project, the governor and the governor-elect found themselves in opposition on at least one issue: the attempt by the outgoing administration, along with the Republican leadership controlling both houses of the legislature and the New Jersey Turnpike Authority, to expedite the construction of a spur from the New Jersey Turnpike across the state to Toms River in Ocean County.

In 1972, Governor Cahill had signed legislation authorizing the construction of a 36-mile-long, four-lane toll expressway from the New Jersey Turnpike in South Brunswick to the Garden State Parkway in Toms River. The new link—which the legislation named the "Alfred E. Driscoll Expressway" in honor of the governor who had built the mainline New Jersey Turnpike and whom Cahill had named as chair of the Turnpike Authority—was to provide a high-speed corridor for central and southern New Jersey, and serve as the only controlled-access route to the southeast part of the state fully open to trucks. Scheduled for completion by 1976, the road was projected to carry approximately 40,000 vehicles per day, with the improved access expected to encourage residential, commercial, and industrial growth along its corridor.[34]

During his 1973 gubernatorial campaign, Byrne had opposed the project as wasteful spending, also contending that it would lead to overdevelopment in

Ocean County and require cutting through substantial forests in the Pinelands. He also questioned whether earlier traffic and revenue assumptions used in planning the road were outdated, given the sharp reductions in traffic volumes resulting from steep increases in gasoline prices from the Arab oil embargo, thus undermining the argument that the road was needed to ease congestion on other highways.

After Byrne's election, however, the Turnpike Authority, with the support of Cahill and the Republican majorities in the legislature, attempted to speed construction of the Expressway before Byrne and the Democrats assumed control of the state government in January. The Authority rejected Byrne's objections and asserted that because the Expressway had been previously authorized by Governor Cahill and the legislature and bonds already had been issued for its financing, "it had no legal recourse" except to proceed with construction.[35]

Less than three weeks after Byrne's election, the Authority awarded the first construction contract for the Expressway despite legal challenges from environmental and civic groups.[36] This further provoked Byrne, who had recently learned that construction of the spur might result in toll hikes of 80 percent on the mainline Turnpike. In a letter to Driscoll and the other Authority commissioners, Byrne laid out his reasons for opposing the road, writing that "construction costs were excessive in terms of benefits provided," and that local governments in Ocean County, then the fastest-growing county in the nation, "would find it difficult to supply adequate supporting services for a greater population density and commercial growth."[37]

Byrne then met with Driscoll and the other commissioners and secured their agreement to postpone plans to award additional contracts for construction until there could be further evaluation of the potential financial loss to the Authority if the road was not built.[38] Contentious negotiations with the Authority continued into Byrne's first term; in February 1975, as Driscoll's five-year term as a commissioner on the Authority was expiring, there were press reports that Byrne was considering not reappointing him to a new term.[39] The next month, Driscoll died unexpectedly of a heart attack, and at his widow's request, Byrne did not attend the funeral.[40] "I was surprised he took our differences over the Turnpike spur so personally," Byrne said in reflecting years later on the clash with Driscoll. "He had appointed my father to the state tax board and I was grateful for that."[41] One week after Driscoll's death, the Turnpike Authority officially dropped its plans for the Alfred E. Driscoll Expressway.[42]

As with any newly elected governor, particularly one succeeding an incumbent of the opposing political party, Byrne's election victory was immediately followed by the inevitable jockeying for jobs by those pushing their own merits and marshaling support from others for their selection. Much of the time during his transition involved, as he later recalled, "talking to a lot of people, evaluating candidates for different jobs, trying to figure out how to structure the government, figure out aside from Cabinet officers, who else we wanted in government." In an interview two weeks before he took office, Byrne noted his resistance to the lobbying for jobs. "I think a lot of people realize that I resent being pressured into an appointment," he said. "One man had every major figure in the country, or at least every major Democratic figure, and I got word back to him that, merely aside from being impressed with the signatures on the letters, I think that I react negatively to that kind of pressure."[43]

Some of those Byrne appointed to key posts came with ideas, personalities, or other baggage that were difficult for the more traditional political bosses to accept. "He was his own person," Byrne's counsel Lew Kaden said later. "They should have known that since they had known him for some years. . . . He was determined to set a different tone and a different quality in his judgment in the people he assembled into the government. And so the whole administration, if you look at the cabinet, if you look at the governor's staff, he was going to pick the people he thought were the right people in those positions even if they were unpredictable."[44]

Like most newly elected political executives, Byrne first turned to those who had been closest to him during the campaign. Dick Leone, the campaign manager and State House veteran who had served on the staff of Governor Hughes, was named head of the transition and later state treasurer. "Because, I think, somehow he helped project the image," Byrne said years later, "that this was an administration that had a lot of integrity and wasn't for sale, and wasn't peopled by anybody who was interested in other than good government."[45] Lew Kaden, his campaign policy adviser, was named "special counsel" to the Governor, with the word "special" added to reflect the fact that Kaden, a lawyer who had practiced in New York, at that point was not a member of the New Jersey bar.[46]

Byrne's selections of Leone and Kaden, both just past 30 years of age and like Byrne with Ivy League pedigrees, would be greeted with suspicion by some of the traditional Trenton insiders and party leaders. "I think it was pretty jarring to them," Kaden later said, "to wake up after the election and confront the fact that the people, two of the people he was putting in the most important positions in his administration were these two 31-, 32-year-olds who were identified as—whatever else they were, smart or not—they were not from the party establishment."[47] Byrne's earlier decision to resolve the conflict between Leone and Hudson County Senator James Dugan in his gubernatorial campaign by firmly telling Dugan that Leone was "in charge" had signaled the Hudson County political establishment; his choices of Leone and Kaden reinforced the message to other veteran bosses that they too would need to go through the young policy wonks. Byrne himself later said that he had to balance the "two factions" that had helped him to become governor: "One was the Dick Leone, or the egg-headed faction, if you will. And the other was the Hudson County practical politics faction. . . . And so there were times when I had to make the choice between Dugan and Dick Leone. And mostly, I came down on the side of Dick Leone because it was a, kind of, reform movement that I had envisioned. Dugan never forgave me."[48]

Leone's staff would include as deputy treasurer Clifford Goldman, his roommate at the Woodrow Wilson School at Princeton, who would succeed Leone as state treasurer in Byrne's second term. Goldman had first joined state government in the Hughes Administration as an aide to Paul Ylvislaker, the commissioner of the Department of Community Affairs, and later was named as the first executive director of the Hackensack Meadowlands Development Commission, a position he held on an acting basis into the first two years of the Cahill Administration. David Beale, the Treasury executive director, was a Harvard Law graduate whom Leone had met in Democratic presidential campaigns. Orin Kramer, who had developed issues and briefed Byrne for campaign appearances, also joined Leone's staff as an aide, later working as a liaison overseeing fiscal and management issues such as the financing and management of the Meadowlands sports complex. Late in Byrne's first year in office, Kaden hired John Degnan, a Harvard Law graduate like himself, as an assistant counsel. Degnan's family had worked for many years with Byrne's father in West Orange politics, and Degnan would soon develop his own close relationship with Byrne, later becoming his executive secretary and counsel and, in the second term, attorney general. One of the other assistant counsels was Michael Critchley, who had worked for Judge Byrne as a security officer in his Morristown court room while attending law school.

In comparison to the time when Byrne had worked for Meyner with only a handful of other staffers, the governor's office had a similar organizational structure, but had expanded in size with new positions created to handle scheduling; appointments to boards and authorities; and political and constituent outreach. A state office in Washington created under Governor Cahill monitored federal actions and served as a liaison to the state's Congressional delegation. Additional assistants to the counsel and the press secretary brought the size of staff in Byrne's first term to range around twenty professionals.

To be sure, Byrne brought aides into the governor's office with more traditional political experience. Don Lan, who had been one of the first to urge Byrne to enter the race with the support of the Union County Democratic organization, was appointed executive secretary to the governor, the loosely defined gatekeeper post that Byrne himself had held under Governor Meyner that primarily oversaw the governor's schedule and travel arrangements and frequently served as a liaison to state and local political leaders.

Jerry Fitzgerald English, who during the campaign had been a liaison to citizens' groups and had previously served a portion of an unexpired term in the state Senate, was named to the newly created post of legislative counsel. English's new role occasionally sparked controversy, with some critics contending that it bred confusion in communicating the administration's priorities. But Byrne viewed her outgoing personality as helpful in contacts with those legislators who did not take to the brusque styles of Kaden and Leone. "To put it simply," an unidentified Byrne colleague was quoted in the *New York Times*, "Jerry might not make policy, but she can make policy work. She gets along with everyone, she makes people feel good."[49] English later brought to her staff Robert Torricelli, a young Rutgers graduate from Bergen County who had worked in the first Byrne campaign and would assume a more prominent role when the Governor sought reelection.

Byrne also brought to Trenton Charlie Carella, who had headed the "Charlie Squad" organized crime unit that Byrne created when he was Essex County prosecutor. Carella initially was appointed executive director of the state lottery, which had been created under Governor Cahill; "Charlie and I knew how to run a lottery," Byrne said in recalling their experience in Essex County, "and thought we could use some of the lessons we learned in the illegal games to make more money for state-run games."[50] In Byrne's second year in office, the lottery became the first in the nation to introduce "pickit" and "scratchcard" games, significantly expanding its sales. Carella would move to the governor's office in 1976 as Byrne's executive secretary, succeeding Don Lan.

Herb Wolfe, the campaign press secretary, was appointed as the director of public information. Wolfe, a former reporter for the *Trenton Times*, would later resign from Byrne's staff to return to the newspaper as executive editor.[51] The state's office in Washington, which had been established in the Cahill Administration to monitor federal actions affecting New Jersey, was headed by Marilyn Berry. She and her staff worked closely with the state's Congressional delegation and regularly advised state agencies on federal legislation, regulatory issues, grants and other actions that might be relevant to their operations.

Dorothy Ann Seltzer, known as "Dottie," was officially Byrne's secretary, but had one of the closest relationships with him of anyone on the staff. The two had first worked together on Governor Meyner's staff in the 1950s, and she became Byrne's secretary when he succeeded Robert Burkhardt as Meyner's executive secretary. Seltzer also had worked for Governor Hughes; after Byrne was elected governor, she often would point out, to Byrne's mild annoyance, that "Dick Hughes would have done it this way."[52] Seltzer's long relationship with Byrne, and knowledge by insiders that she would not hesitate to speak candidly on any subject with Byrne, led to her being used as a conduit to convey bad news or sensitive information that others were reluctant to raise with him on their own. As Harold Hodes, later Byrne's chief of staff, recalled: "She was his secretary, she was the gatekeeper, she was an individual who wasn't afraid to say what she thought. She was a person that you would go to for guidance and would be able to read his moods. She was invaluable, . . . she controlled that gate and she had his trust and she was just a unique individual."[53]

In assembling his cabinet, Byrne's first task was "to figure out how many cabinet officers were in the administration," as he later said, bringing himself up to date on the changes that had occurred since he served in the cabinet of Governor Hughes. An early message he sought to convey was "a willingness to keep anybody from the Cahill administration, who would be appropriate to keep. . . . I wanted the message to be that I'm not trying to get rid of Cahill people just because they're Republican."[54] William Marfuggi, Cahill's state treasurer, declined Byrne's invitation to continue, but Banking Commissioner Richard Schaub stayed for over a year into the new administration. Byrne also had been intending to reappoint another Cahill cabinet officer, but withheld an offer when Cahill advised against his retention.[55]

The governor-elect made Ed Crabiel, who had ended his own campaign to endorse Byrne, his first cabinet appointee, naming him secretary of state, the post that in past administrations generally had gone to key political operatives. Its last two occupants, however, Paul Sherwin in the Cahill Administration and Robert Burkhardt in the Hughes Administration, each had been convicted of participating in illegal kickback schemes. Crabiel was expected to be a key liaison to the legislature, where he had been well-liked as the Senate Democratic minority leader and known as "Steady Eddie."[56]

For his attorney general, Byrne initially attempted to persuade Nicholas Katzenbach, the former U.S. attorney general and then corporate counsel for IBM, to take the job. Lew Kaden, who was sent by the governor-elect to see whether Katzenbach was interested, later recalled that "Katzenbach said he was flattered but it didn't take him long to say that wasn't part of his life plan." Despite the failed effort, Kaden felt it reflected Byrne's willingness to depart from the traditional circles of those brought into the state government; "to me all of that showed that Byrne was trying to send a different signal and make a different statement about the composition of the team that he was assembling."[57]

Byrne also offered the attorney general's post to Herbert Stern, a Republican who had served as the United States Attorney for New Jersey and who was widely reported as a probable nominee by President Nixon as a judge on the federal District Court. Stern declined the offer, however, and subsequently was nominated and confirmed for the federal judgeship. Nonetheless, extending the offer to Stern, as the *New York Times* reported, "indicated to some politicians here that . . . [Byrne] was absolutely determined to fight political corruption in a state that has a notorious reputation for politicians on the take; or that he was a canny politician or both things."[58]

After Katzenbach and Stern declined to become Attorney General, Byrne selected William F. Hyland, a former speaker of the General Assembly who had preceded Byrne as president of the Public Utilities Commission and later chaired the State Commission of Investigation. Hyland had been considered a leading contender for the Democratic gubernatorial nomination in 1961, but reportedly was bypassed for Richard Hughes by political bosses, who thought Hyland, at 5 feet 6 inches in height, was too short to impress voters in campaign appearances or on television.[59]

Ann Klein, who had finished second to Byrne in the 1973 Democratic primary, was named commissioner of what was then the Department of Institutions and Agencies. At that time, "I&A" was the state's largest—and most unwieldy—department, overseeing a range of welfare, family and child protection services as well as the operation of state prisons, mental hospitals, and other facilities.

There was substantial opposition to Klein being offered the job. "We had a small meeting to discuss her heading the department," Dick Leone recounted. "She didn't really have relevant experience, there were concerns that she wouldn't be a team player, that she'd cause us trouble. But I said, 'Don't we want someone in that job who will cause trouble?' She turned out to be fine."[60] Byrne later recalled that, while there briefly was discussion of Klein as a possible transportation commissioner, he felt that she was "a natural" to head I&A, given her advocacy of increased support of social service programs during the campaign. "We were concerned, however, whether Ann could manage such a huge department," Byrne later reflected, "so we made sure that she had a strong staff to help with administering its operations." Robert Mulcahy, a former mayor of Mendham who had supported Klein's gubernatorial campaign, was later named as a deputy commissioner. Byrne restructured the department in 1976, spinning off prisons and correctional facilities into a new Department of Corrections headed by Mulcahy, with Klein as commissioner of the renamed Department of Human Services. After his reelection in 1977, the governor brought Mulcahy to the State House in the newly created position of chief of staff to the governor.[61]

In a somewhat convoluted process, Alan Sagner, Byrne's campaign finance director and a wealthy real estate developer, was chosen as commissioner of transportation. After the 1973 election, Byrne asked Sagner whether he was interested in joining the administration, and Sagner, who was chairman of the board of Newark Beth Israel Hospital, asked that he be appointed commissioner of the Department of Health.

Byrne agreed to Sagner's request, but a few days later he called back to say, "Al, between now and January, you have a lot of work to do." When Sagner asked, "What do you mean?" Byrne replied, "The commissioner of health has to have an M.D. degree." Byrne then asked what else he would like. "I thought about it," Sagner later related, "and I remembered the treasurer was usually the heavy hitter in the state government, so I said to him the next time 'How about treasurer?' He said, 'Dick Leone has that job. Pick something else.' I hadn't the faintest idea. I didn't really know that much about state government." Sagner asked Byrne for some time to respond, and called Joe Katz, then a lobbyist and former aide to Governor Hughes, who "was one of the few people I knew in Trenton who knew their way around." According to Sagner, Katz said, "'Take transportation. It's important. It's going to be important.' So I said to Brendan, 'How about transportation?' He said, 'Yes.' And that's how I got to be commissioner of transportation."[62]

Sagner brought to Trenton, as his then aide Timothy Carden later related, "a developer's mentality, which means his attention span was very short, which was both an asset and a liability but you wouldn't have a meeting that Alan Sagner sat through that would last longer than an hour. . . . I think we probably got more done in the course of a day as a result of that."[63] Byrne would appoint Sagner to the board of the Port Authority of New York and New Jersey, where he would be the point person in the Governor's frequent clashes with the Authority in his efforts to expand its role in mass transit, and would become, after he resigned from the cabinet in 1977, chair of the Authority's board through Byrne's second term.

Byrne's most controversial cabinet appointment was Fred Burke, the commissioner of the Department of Education. "We looked all over the country for an education commissioner," Lew Kaden later said. "Education was going to be a central issue, including education finance, and we found Fred Burke in Rhode Island, where he was the state commissioner, and he came to New Jersey."[64] During three years as Rhode Island's education commissioner, Burke had overseen the state's assumption of responsibility for full funding of public schools with money raised from the state's first income tax, a task similar to that which he was expected to face in New Jersey as a result of the state Supreme Court's decision in *Robinson v. Cahill* declaring that the state's heavy reliance on the property tax to finance public education was unconstitutional.

Throughout Byrne's two terms, Burke would be a target of criticism by the New Jersey Education Association, the powerful 85,000-member teachers' union, as well as by principals and other administrators, school boards, legislators, and a variety of other education interests and constituencies.

Byrne later reflected that Burke had "some good ideas," but that he "looked a little pugnacious and was an easy target for people who hated, either, the education program or the way he was administrator or the amount of red tape."[65]

James Sheeran, Byrne's classmate at West Orange High School who had chaired the "Republicans for Byrne" group in the 1973 campaign, was the first Republican appointed to Byrne's cabinet, as commissioner of the Department of Insurance.[66] Sheeran had been the quarterback of the West Orange High team that won the school's only state championship in 1941. Perhaps the most combative member of Byrne's cabinet, he was a hero of World War II, having parachuted into Normandy on D-Day; been captured by the Nazis; and escaped from his prisoner of war train; after which he fought in the underground with the French resistance before rejoining U.S. forces to fight in the Battle of the Bulge. Following the war, he attended law school under the G.I. Bill, worked as a special agent for the FBI, and was elected as West Orange's youngest mayor at the age of 35. As commissioner, Sheeran often clashed with the state's major insurers over their traditional approaches in setting premiums, such as their charging much higher rates for motorists in the larger cities.[67]

Some weeks after taking office, Byrne named David Bardin to head the Department of Environmental Protection (DEP), replacing Richard Sullivan, who had been appointed by Governor Cahill when the Department was established in 1970. "Dick Sullivan was a pioneer in the environmental movement," Byrne later recalled, "and had worked hard in developing the laws that the DEP enforced."[68] But during the 1973 primary election campaign, Byrne had described Sullivan as "well motivated, but he's bogged down to a point where the administration is at a standstill in so far as the environment is concerned."[69] Despite his support within the environmental community, Sullivan had been criticized for management problems within the DEP, which had grown rapidly since it was created in 1970.[70] Just days after Byrne was sworn in, Sullivan resigned when he was unable to obtain assurances from Byrne that he would continue as commissioner.

Bardin was then a Washington-based lawyer who earlier had worked as assistant to the Attorney General of Israel, dealing with public utilities and environmental law, and later as a lawyer and consultant in Jerusalem and Washington. He had been recommended to Byrne by Attorney General Hyland, who had come to know Bardin from legal work in Washington. Bardin was a colorful character, well over six feet tall with a full beard. An Orthodox Jew, he typically wore sandals to work, and was known for occasional outbursts, throwing pencils at staff who displeased, as he put it, "your commissioner." Betty Wilson, who joined the DEP as an assistant commissioner after losing her Assembly seat from a Union County district in the 1975 election, recalled: "He was a workaholic. . . . He was probably the smartest person

I ever worked for. He was brilliant. He was exceedingly difficult for people and I learned quickly that . . . when he would get into his . . . tirades, the way to shut it down was to yell back at him or to push back in some way."[71] Bardin relished a good political fight, and eagerly signed on to the governor's goal to protect the Pinelands, which Byrne had already signaled prior to taking office when he blocked the proposed Driscoll Expressway.[72]

Joanne Finley, appointed commissioner of the Department of Health, had been the head of the health department of the city of New Haven and also a lecturer in the public health program at Yale, which had published papers on new approaches to controlling soaring health care costs and insurance premiums. In Byrne's first term, Finley would aggressively implement programs to cut hospital costs, using the legislative authority for state review of hospital rate-setting and hospital construction and major equipment purchases enacted in the Cahill administration, but which had led to the routine approval of most hospital requests.

Patricia Sheehan became commissioner of the Department of Community Affairs, the department which acted as a liaison to county and municipal governments, particularly with regard to housing and community development. A former mayor of New Brunswick and government relations executive with Johnson & Johnson, Sheehan would work with groups in that city when Byrne pushed for completion of Route 18 over the Raritan River, a project Johnson & Johnson considered as crucial to its decision to stay in New Brunswick and build a new global headquarters. Sheehan would later clash with the Treasury and the governor's office over a plan to dissolve the department and reallocate its various programs, indeed even successfully lobbying against the proposal to protect the continued existence of the department.

Byrne appointed Joseph Hoffman, who had directed field operations for the gubernatorial campaign, to head the Department of Labor and Industry, the principal liaison to organized labor and the business community. He did so, however, only after recognizing that the appointment of Joel Jacobson, "one of my dearest friends and solid supporters" who wanted the job, "would have clearly divided the labor movement."[73] Jacobson was a veteran of the former Congress of Industrial Organizations and headed the state CIO when it merged in 1961 with the American Federation of Labor, becoming executive vice president of the consolidated state AFL-CIO. But despite the merger, rivalry between factions of the former industrial and craft movements in New Jersey had continued, and Byrne knew that naming Jacobson to head the state department would spark renewed conflicts. He accordingly appointed Hoffman, a lawyer who had worked for AT&T and had served as first assistant state attorney general in the Hughes Administration. Hoffman had wanted to be Byrne's attorney general, but early in the transition, he was given a signal that he would not get that job when he was assigned to draft a transition report on the Department of Law and Public Safety, which was headed by the attorney general. "We had a rule that if you were assigned to review a department during the transition," Dick Leone recounted, "you wouldn't get a job there, so he knew he wouldn't get to be attorney general."[74] After a series of conflicts with Byrne, Hoffman eventually resigned under pressure in 1976 and became a candidate challenging Byrne in the 1977 Democratic gubernatorial primary election.[75]

Following his decision to appoint Hoffman, Byrne had to persuade Jacobson to become a commissioner on the Public Utilities Commission, which Byrne said "at first, he didn't want to do." In 1975, his second year in office, Byrne named Jacobson to succeed Anthony Grossi as the PUC president, and in 1977, after Byrne restructured the PUC and other state energy programs into the newly created Department of Energy, he named Jacobson as commissioner of the new department.

Under New Jersey's constitution, the governor has only indirect authority over the appointment of the secretary of agriculture, whose nomination is initiated by the State Board of Agriculture subject to the governor's approval and confirmation by the state Senate.[76] When Byrne was elected, the incumbent secretary, Philip Alampi, had served in the post since 1956, when his nomination was approved by Governor Meyner. Alampi previously had become known by farm interests as a host of agricultural news shows broadcast by New York City radio and television stations. "Phil Alampi was the best showman that the state has ever had," Byrne later said. "He certainly was a good spokesman for the farm industry and for the state."[77] Alampi forged strong relationships using his public relations skills, often distributing fruits and vegetables to the legislature, the governor's staff, and the press in the State House, as well as hosting farm tours for state and local officials and the media. Under Byrne, Alampi would focus on efforts to slow the loss of the state's farmland, including implementing a pilot project to purchase development rights to retain land in agricultural uses that later led to legislation establishing a permanent program that acquired or preserved thousands of farm acres.[78]

Like the Secretary of Agriculture, the Chancellor of Higher Education was nominated by a board—the Board of Higher Education—subject to the governor's approval to head the Department of Higher Education. (The Department and the chancellor's position were abolished in 1994 during the administration of Governor Christine Todd Whitman). In 1967, when the Department was created during the Hughes Administration, Ralph Dungan, a former special assistant to President Kennedy and later U.S. ambassador to Chile under President Johnson, was appointed as the chancellor. During his tenure, Dungan oversaw the expansion of the county and state college system. During the 1973 campaign, at a meeting of the New Jersey College Presidents

Association, Byrne had outlined his views when asked what he expected of the state's higher education system. "I remember telling them that I had seven kids," he recalled, "and each one of them had different capabilities, and that I wanted a higher education program in New Jersey which would recognize the individuality of each one of my kids and provide an education consistent with bringing out the best of each of those kids. And from that little capsule, I think, I got my message across."[79]

Another significant change Byrne oversaw was the replacement of David B. Kelly, the superintendent of the State Police, who had held the position since 1965. Kelly's tenure had seen significant modernization of the force, but he also had been sharply criticized for alleged overly aggressive tactics of troopers during the Newark riots and in arresting civil rights protestors. The troopers' union also had charged that Kelly was autocratic in imposing discipline and awarding promotions. To the surprise of many, Byrne declined to waive for Kelly the normal age 55 retirement rule for the State Police, and directed that a search committee chaired by Attorney General Hyland provide recommendations on Kelly's successor. When the committee gave him the names of its three recommended candidates, Byrne learned that Clinton Pagano, then a State Police captain who early in his career as a trooper had been assigned to Byrne in the Essex County prosecutor's office, had not been included on the recommended candidate list "because his name was Italian." Reacting to what he felt was the arbitrary rejection of Pagano, Byrne overruled the committee and appointed Pagano to the position, a post he would hold through Byrne's time in office.[80]

For the most part, despite the conflict over the Driscoll Expressway, the incoming Byrne team found the Cahill cabinet and staff and the Republican legislative leadership extremely helpful during the transition. Cahill and the lame-duck Republican legislative leaders enacted legislation for a salary increase for the incoming governor to $65,000 and for his cabinet ranging from $41,000 to $43,000, and cooperated in other areas.[81] "Not only did they keep open the jobs and positions we wanted," Dick Leone recalled, "but in one case they appointed a prosecutor to fill a slot so we wouldn't be able to fulfill our promise to someone we promised it to but didn't want to give it to."[82] Given Cahill's loss in the primary in June, there had been an unusually long period for the outgoing administration to prepare for the transition and to draft extensive briefings on issues and other matters for the Byrne team. Cahill's counsel, Richard DeKorte, developed a close relationship with Dick Leone and Lew Kaden, with DeKorte agreeing to stay on after Byrne's inauguration to head a new state energy office.

At a meeting during the transition, Cahill and DeKorte informed Leone that the State government now faced a substantial deficit, a sharp reversal from the $200 million surplus that had been projected during the election campaign. As Leone later recalled, Cahill and DeKorte "both started laughing uproariously" and then explained that the deficit had not been disclosed since they "thought it would help Sandman if it got out" and that "the only person who wanted Sandman to lose more than we did was Cahill."[83] The shortfall in meeting the state government's revenue projections—in part a reflection of the national economic downturn following the October 1973 Arab oil embargo—greatly complicated the task of finding the additional funds to increase school aid needed to comply with the *Robinson* decision, as well as severely limiting the options of the new administration in undertaking any new programs or projects.

Before his inauguration, Byrne met with neighboring public officials, including separately with Pennsylvania Governor Milton Shapp and New York Governor Nelson Rockefeller. The meeting with Shapp dealt primarily with the environment, transportation, and the application of Pennsylvania income and employment taxes on New Jersey commuters. While Byrne and Shapp would find mutual interests on most issues, they later differed on the proposed construction of the Tocks Island Dam on the Delaware River, which Shapp strongly supported.[84]

Rockefeller was then completing his fourth and final term as governor, and a year later was appointed vice president by President Gerald Ford to fill the vacancy created by the resignation of Spiro Agnew. In welcoming Byrne, Rockefeller commented on how Byrne's sweeping election victory had also brought in strong Democratic majorities in the legislature, but then offered a lesson from his own experience. "Rockefeller told me," Byrne later recalled, "that he had the toughest time with his legislature when he had the largest Republican majorities. It was something I'd later remember when I ran into my own problems."[85]

Some ten days before Byrne's inauguration, there was an early sign that—despite his sweeping election victory at the top of the ticket helping the Democrats gain strong majority control in both houses of the legislature (Senate: twenty-nine Democrats, nineteen Republicans, one Independent; General Assembly: sixty-six Democrats, fourteen Republicans)—his ability to assert his influence in the state senate would be limited.[86] On January 4, in a private caucus prior to the new legislature taking office, the incoming senate Democrats rejected Byrne's request to abolish the practice of "senatorial courtesy," which allowed a single senator to secretly block gubernatorial appointments of persons from their home district. The tradition allowed senators, and often their respective county bosses, to assert leverage over governors, not only on the specific appointment but also on unrelated matters. "The vote represented a defeat for Governor-elect Brendan T. Byrne," one reporter wrote, "who opposes the custom and had urged the new Democratic majority to reject it."

The vote tally on the issue was not made public, but Senator Dugan, whom Byrne had selected as state Democratic chairman, opposed the repeal, telling the press with apparent satisfaction that the vote "was not even close."[87]

Byrne's influence in the election of the Democratic leadership was limited, but he did indicate his preference for Senator Frank "Pat" Dodd from Essex County, who was elected by his fellow Democrats as the Senate president. Matthew Feldman of Bergen County, who had just been elected to his first term in the Senate, was elected as Senate Majority Leader. In the General Assembly, S. Howard Woodson, Jr., a minister from Trenton, was chosen as its Speaker, the first African American in the nation to become the presiding officer of a house of a state legislature. Hudson County's influence with Byrne also was demonstrated in the selection of Joseph LeFante as the Assembly Majority Leader, with LeFante's victory over the highly-respected Albert Burstein of Bergen attributed to intervention by aides to Byrne.[88] In 1976, LeFante became Speaker when Byrne appointed Woodson to his cabinet as commissioner of the Department of Civil Service.

As he completed the final days of his transition, Brendan Byrne was better prepared—on paper at least—to become the state's chief executive than any other governor in New Jersey's history. He had served as a lawyer and top aide to one governor and as a cabinet officer to another. Unlike his predecessors, Byrne knew the mechanics of New Jersey government. He understood the respective roles and responsibilities of a governor's staff and cabinet, as well as the potential for occasional friction as they sought to define the scope of their turf. From both within and outside the State House, he had seen how prior governors had organized their administrations and handled day-to-day relationships with the legislature, local officials, politicians, and key interest groups and constituencies. While he had not served in an elected office, he had gained an early education in street politics from his father's years in local government and also had sat side by side with legislators in the days when they relied heavily on guidance from the governor's staff. But even with his experience and knowledge, he would soon recognize that his time in office as New Jersey's chief executive would not be easy.

"I knew what the job was, and thought we had put together a good team," Byrne reflected years later on his transition to office. "You never can plan for everything that comes up, but I thought we had done our best to be ready."[89]

Chapter 7

The First Term

"If You Win One, You're Great. If You Don't, You're Not"

"You look funny in formal clothes," Brendan Byrne explained as the reason that he ordered the top hats and tails of his predecessors' inaugurals be replaced by business attire at his own ceremony. "I mean, you look at pictures from Bob Meyner's and Dick Hughes's inaugural, they look silly."[1]

Byrne was inaugurated on January 14, 1974—the 47th governor of New Jersey since its first state constitution was adopted by its provincial congress on July 2, 1776, two days before the signing of the Declaration of Independence in Philadelphia. Like most of the former colonies that resisted Royal governors who had enforced the unpopular policies of the Crown and Parliament, New Jersey's first state constitution provided that the legislature—the popular body that had led opposition to British rule—would be vested with primary authority to spend, make appointments, and conduct most government functions. Governors were elected by the legislature to a single-year term; given no veto over legislation; and performed few other duties apart from heading the state militia.[2] In 1844, the state's second constitution marginally increased the governor's powers, making the office subject to popular election, lengthening the term of office from one to three years (albeit prohibiting a second successive term), and providing a veto that could be overridden by a simple majority of the legislature. In the twentieth century, as it became clear that a growing state government and new demands for services had outpaced the structure of its government, New Jersey adopted in 1947 a new constitution that, for the first time, gave the governor extensive powers. Under the new charter, he had sole authority to appoint state officials, judges, and prosecutors; veto or propose amendments to legislation; propose the state budget; "line item" veto specific appropriations; and manage the executive departments.[3] As former Governor and Chief Justice Richard J. Hughes wrote, the new constitution established "a strong governor, probably the strongest in the nation."[4]

Byrne was the fifth governor to be sworn in under the 1947 Constitution, following Governors Alfred Driscoll, Robert Meyner, Richard Hughes, and William Cahill. Despite the enhanced constitutional power of the office, New Jersey's strong home rule tradition still imposed practical constraints on the exercise of authority; on important issues and appointments, as Byrne had earlier experienced in his own career, governors often were forced to consult with, and sometimes defer to, the wishes of leading county and local party bosses.[5] When Byrne took the oath in January 1974, the failures of his two immediate predecessors, Governors Cahill and Hughes, to secure enough support from bosses within their own parties to enact their fiscal reform programs including an income tax illustrated the continuing localism of the state's politics.

Byrne had attended the inaugurals for both Meyner and Hughes, and accordingly was familiar with the formalities of the day. "I don't recall," he said years later, "being particularly nervous or excited. Most of the preparation involved just rehearsing my speech and getting the kids ready. I just wanted to get the day over with and get started on the job."[6] On the night before the inaugural, the Byrne family stayed at a hotel a few hundred yards from the State House, along with some fifty other relatives and friends. A newspaper reported that Jean Byrne's first task in the morning was to knock on the door of her teenaged daughters Susan and Nancy, loudly announcing "You know that we have to be absolutely on time!"[7]

Later in the morning, a mass was celebrated at Saint Mary's Cathedral, a few blocks from the State House. Father Cronan Tyms, a priest and lawyer who had worked on Prosecutor Byrne's staff, officiated at the service, along with Bishop George Ahr of the Trenton Diocese and three other priests who were Byrne's cousins as attendants. A few days before, when Byrne was advised that the Diocese had declined his request that his wife Jean's Presbyterian minister also be allowed to participate, Byrne had threatened to cancel the mass, but the Church backed down and the minister was permitted to read from the scriptures. As Byrne entered the Cathedral, "I noticed that Dick Hughes [who had been sworn in as chief justice by Governor Cahill in the prior month] was sitting in a pew at the rear," he later recalled. "I took his arm and ushered him to sit near me at the front."[8]

Following the mass, Byrne and his family proceeded to the State House, where they were greeted by Governor Cahill and talked briefly in his office, with the group then joining in a procession escorted by the National Guard and the State Police to the War Memorial Auditorium located a short distance away, in which an audience of some 2,000 was seated.[9]

At noon, the inaugural ceremony began with Hughes administering the oath to Byrne as Mrs. Byrne held the Bible, a Bible that Byrne later inscribed and gave to his sister Thecla. The ceremony continued with Governor Cahill handing Byrne the Great Seal of New Jersey, the symbol of the transfer of power. After taking the oath, Byrne noted in his address, "This is the first time a judge who is a former governor swore in a governor who was a former judge." He also recalled the similar ceremony at the inaugural of Governor Hughes in 1961, when the secretary of state solemnly announced the handing over of the "Great Steal of New Jersey."[10]

Byrne focused his inaugural address on two issues: the public cynicism that prevailed as a result of the Watergate scandal and the need to respond to the *Robinson v. Cahill* decision. He pledged to run an honest and account-able government "by using the powers of public policy to keep our state's government and our leaders honest," and called for legislation—the first of its kind by any state—to provide public financing of gubernatorial campaigns. He also proposed stricter controls on political contributions, expansion of public participation in elections by allowing voter registration by post card, and creation of a new state department—the public advocate—to represent the public interest.[11]

On education, he announced that he would call the legislature into special session in the late spring "to meet the mandate of the Constitution and make a thorough and efficient education for our children a reality." While not pro-posing a specific course of action on how to reduce reliance on the property tax to fund public education, he expressed support of the basic rationale used by the Court in *Robinson*, saying "to chart a young child's future on the basis of family wealth or neighborhood affluence, is to impose an unequal burden that mocks the deepest faith of our American system: the faith that ability, not nobility of birth or income, is the test of how well a citizen will achieve in his life."[12]

Following the conclusion of the inaugural ceremony, Byrne and the family greeted a long line of family, supporters, and members of the public. During the afternoon, Byrne visited the Shiloh Baptist Church in Trenton, whose minister was Howard S. Woodson, the newly elected Speaker of the General Assembly, and which was holding a program marking the birthday on that date of the Reverend Martin Luther King, Jr. In his remarks to the congre-gation, Byrne pledged that as governor he would seek to have New Jersey declare King's birthday as a state holiday. In the evening, the Byrnes attended the inaugural ball, where the new governor ("I'm a terrible dancer," he later confessed) attempted to keep his time on the dance floor to a minimum.

Despite the large issues he identified in his address and the planning he had done during his transition, upon taking office Byrne was confronted, like many new governors, with a crisis that he had not anticipated. Pub-lic protests, coupled with occasional violence, had erupted as a result of the shortages of gasoline from the embargo of oil exports imposed in the previous October by the members of the Organization of Petroleum Exporting Countries (OPEC). Motorists were frustrated by the closing of service stations and hours-long waiting lines at the gasoline stations still with gas to sell. On February 5, the new governor issued his first executive order declaring an energy emergency and establishing a new state energy office to coordinate responses by state agencies.[13] To reduce the lines at the gas stations, Byrne later directed that all motorists buy gas only on odd or even dates as designated by the last number on their license plates. The system had first been employed in Oregon, but New Jersey became the initial heavily urbanized state to test the approach. "We weren't the first to come up with the odd-even idea," Byrne later reflected, "but we got good press when our lines got shorter and places like New York still had long waits. The *New York Daily News* ran an editorial praising us and criticizing [New York Governor] Malcolm Wilson for not taking our lead."[14] The success of the system gained national attention, with other states and cities quickly adopting the plan. Within the state, the new governor's actions gained wide support; a Rutgers-Eagleton Poll taken a few weeks later reported an extraordinary 83 percent of respondents approving of Byrne's handling of the energy crisis.[15]

The short-term impact of the lines at the gasoline stations was handled effectively, but the effects of the OPEC embargo contributed to the long-term decline in New Jersey's economy that continued for much of Byrne's time as governor. From 1974 to 1975, Byrne's first year in office, the state's unemployment rate spiked from 6.3 percent to 10.5 percent, peaking at a post-Depression record of 10.7 percent in November 1976, a year before Byrne would face voters for reelection. In 1974, the national inflation rate rose by 11 percent, leading to sharply reduced spending by consumers and resulting drops in government revenues. Even prior to the oil crisis, the Northeast and New Jersey had begun to see the long-term loss of investment and industrial jobs to other regions with lower costs of labor, real estate, and energy. "The boom of the 1960s ultimately succumbed to the 'troubled '70s,'" two Rutgers professors later wrote. "It was also an era of energy shocks, of a surging Sunbelt that was capturing increased shares of America's economic and demographic growth, and of an unprecedented reversal in manufacturing."[16] Blue-collar workers, traditionally an important base of the state's Democratic Party, were particularly hard hit as manufacturers relocated to states or countries with lower energy, labor, and real estate costs.[17]

But before confronting economic issues, the new administration turned to meeting the governor's campaign pledges to increase public confidence in government in the wake of the Watergate break-in and the indictments of those close to Governor Cahill. "Byrne was an ideal candidate in those circumstances," his counsel Lew Kaden said in recalling the prevailing cynicism of the time, "and some of his most visible early proposals [that] went to that issue were campaign finance reform, voter registration reform, the creation of a public advocate. Those are all things he talked about during the campaign and moved forward on in the first weeks of the administration."[18] Making it easier to register to vote was a personal goal for Byrne. "People forget how difficult it was to register," he later reflected. "As a young lawyer, I used to lug those heavy registration books door-to-door to get people signed up to register."[19] A separate bill to require advance public notice and access to state agency hearings and meetings—the so-called Sunshine Act—was later introduced and enacted by the legislature.[20]

Soon after taking office, Byrne directed that his cabinet, staff, and other high state officials disclose their assets and income, later expanding the mandate through an executive order requiring that the statements include employment, assets, and business interests of their spouses and be filed under oath subject to criminal prosecutions for any false information.[21] The Treasury mandated public bidding for most state contracts and services, and Treasurer Leone appointed Earl Josephson, a *Trenton Times* reporter known for his knowledge of the state government and research in uncovering waste, to head the state division handling purchases, the award of contracts for services and dispositions of real estate and other property, the programs most prone to possible kickbacks and corruption. In departing from the traditional ways of dispensing jobs and patronage, the new Byrne team took away many of the accepted tools used to reward political supporters, contributing to the Governor's later problems with key legislators and county and local political leaders. At times, some Byrne insiders thought the effort went too far. On one occasion, Alan Sagner, Byrne's newly appointed transportation commissioner and former campaign finance director, recalled that early in the administration he took a call from a contributor to Byrne's campaign who had tried to meet with Treasurer Leone that, according to the contributor, Leone "wouldn't see me because he heard I gave a big contribution." Sagner went on to say, "I had to call Dick and tell him, 'This guy is okay. The fact that he gave a contribution shouldn't bar him from seeing you. You could judge after whether what he wants is right.' But Dick was correct almost to an extreme."[22]

To be sure, the image that Byrne wished to convey through his appointments and policies in his first weeks in office would be muddied by news reports in the month after his inauguration that Edward Crabiel, his secretary of state, was the subject of a state grand jury investigation for possible bid-rigging years before Byrne's election when he headed a major highway construction firm. The Crabiel controversy was a major distraction from the focus on honest and open government that the administration had emphasized as it took control of the government.

While Byrne dealt with the issues and controversies in his first weeks in office, there also were practical matters for the new governor and his family to address as they relocated from West Orange. Brendan and Jean Byrne were already familiar with Morven, the governor's official residence in Princeton, from Byrne's time on Governor Meyner's staff.[23] After Byrne's election, Governor and Mrs. Cahill also hosted the Byrnes for dinner at Morven to discuss the condition of the house and possible repairs and improvements.

First built in the 1750s by Richard Stockton, a signer of the Declaration of Independence, on land originally acquired in 1701 from William Penn by Stockton's grandfather, Morven was donated to the state in 1954 by former Governor Walter Edge for use either as the governor's residence or as a museum.[24] The home's colonial dimensions, however, were ill-suited to serve as an official residence, particularly for a family with as many young children as the Byrnes.

At the time of Byrne's inauguration, the Byrnes had four children in West Orange public schools: Susan (age 17); Nancy (16); Tim (12); and Barbara (6). Bill, the youngest at four years, was in pre-school. Tom, then aged 19, was in his sophomore year at Princeton and lived on campus, but regularly visited Morven on Sundays after he attended nearby church services, also taking the opportunity to bring his dirty laundry from the week for washing. Mrs. Byrne delayed moving to Morven with the children until March, when she completed arranging the various transfers to public schools in Princeton. For a time until the rest of the family relocated to Princeton, Byrne himself stayed at Morven during busier weekdays and on weekends commuted to the family home in West Orange. When the remaining Byrnes left West Orange, they rented their home to one of Byrne's former partners in his law firm.[25]

Years later, Jean Byrne would reflect on Morven's deficiencies, including its lack of a playroom and other space that the children had enjoyed in West Orange. "It irritates me," she said in an interview, "that people would refer to it as a mansion. It was not. . . . To me, it was just a big old, drafty, inconvenient house."[26] The home also demonstrated its age and apparent indifferent maintenance since it had come under state ownership twenty years earlier; on one occasion, the bedroom ceiling of Byrne's daughter Nancy collapsed, fortunately while she was away.[27]

Another problem was the loss of privacy. The State Police shared Morven's cramped space, with troopers from its Executive Protection Service posted to screen visitors at the door, answer the phone, drive the governor and family members, and provide security for the home and its grounds. To stretch the available space within the main house, the State Police used the former slave quarters, a small, separate structure just behind the residence, to allow off-duty troopers to rest or sleep overnight between shifts. "We tried to give the family," recalled Michael Fedorko, a trooper who began as Byrne's driver and later headed the security unit, "as much privacy as possible. We wouldn't, for example, enter the interior of the residence unless requested, normally talking with those inside only over the intercom."[28] But the inevitable comings and goings of people forced changes in the previous routines the family had followed; in a newspaper article published soon after the family's move to Morven, Susan Byrne said she no longer came downstairs without first putting on a bathrobe, a practice she never observed in West Orange.[29]

Security concerns also occasionally constrained the family. When the Byrnes first moved to Morven, the home and its grounds were open to the busy street some fifty yards in front of the house. The open access soon became a concern; on one day, an inpatient from a nearby psychiatric center was apprehended by a trooper scaling the fire escape to enter an upstairs window where family bedrooms were located. More frequently, curious or confused visitors appeared uninvited at the front door, sometimes asking to see the governor. Protestors frequently paraded on the sidewalk in front of the house, often holding picket signs displaying their complaints or causes. After several incidents, the State Police recommended that to improve security an iron picket fence and gate be installed to enclose the property. On one occasion, the new gate proved a frustration to the Byrnes' daughter Nancy: she drove up to the closed gate, asked over the intercom for the trooper to open it, but after he repeatedly failed to recognize her voice, shouted "Just open the f---ing gate!"[30]

Mrs. Byrne, who had kept house and cooked in West Orange largely on her own, was pleased with one aspect of the new residence: a housekeeper and a married couple who cooked for the family and guests. "It's terrific," Mrs. Byrne said in referring to the cooks in an interview shortly after their move, ". . . they make fresh bread daily and make the most delectable desserts. At home we never had desserts, except maybe ice cream." On weekends, when there were no guests or functions, the family generally dispensed with staff, with Jean Byrne preferring to cook herself. "Jean wanted to control the house," Byrne later explained. "When she could avoid it, she didn't want help to interfere with the family's privacy."[31]

Morven's dual status as a museum, with its paintings, colonial furnishings, and public tours scheduled one day a week, also wasn't designed for an active and athletic family. Among the prized furniture at Morven was a highboy thought to be a gift to the Stockton family from George Washington. While Brendan and Jean Byrne were uncertain if the alleged history of the highboy was in fact true, they nonetheless cautioned the children to avoid damaging it given its possible tie to Washington. As Byrne later related the story, one Sunday morning in church, he gave four-year-old Billy a quarter for the collection plate, and Billy asked whose profile was on the coin:

"George Washington," I whispered.
"Who?" asked Billy.
"George Washington . . . You know, the guy who gave
us the furniture for the living room."[32]

Another antique, a formal eighteenth-century Regency dining room table
at which Washington and nine other presidents had dined, also had its
limitations. It could comfortably seat only about twenty guests, forcing most
entertaining within the house to be restricted to informal buffets with guests
standing or seated at smaller tables temporarily set up in other rooms.[33]

On occasion, indoor family sports took their toll. "Billy and I used to play
stick ball in that main hall," Byrne remembered, "it was a good place to
play stick ball and he would be the New York Yankees and I would be the
St. Louis Cardinals."[34] Over time, however, the passing of footballs back and
forth in the hall resulted in "a few crystals missing from the chandeliers,"
Byrne later confessed.

From time to time, Byrne would seek opinions from Billy or the other
children on matters of state. When he showed the children alternative designs
under consideration for a new state license plate, "Barbie suggested that
we include the state logo," he remembered, "and we added that to the new
plates." But he rejected Billy's idea, after Byrne showed him a new undershirt
made of bulletproof material that the State Police had given him, that "I put
it on and we try it out."[35]

The family brought with them their dog "Kipper" (somewhat modified
spelling resulting from his being adopted on the Jewish holy day of Yom
Kippur); when Kipper died, he was succeeded by a Labrador retriever named
"Yankee" (adopted on the fourth of July). "Yankee learned that he could
open the storm door in front of the trooper's desk by jumping up to hit the
door latch," Michael Fedorko recalled, "and let himself out."[36] Roaming into
downtown Princeton on his own, Yankee frequently was rewarded with treats
from the local merchants. Byrne later contrasted how the focus of press coverage had changed over the years since he had worked for Governor Meyner:
"When Governor Meyner got a dog, the press took pictures and wrote articles
about how nice it was that the Governor had gotten a new dog. When we
got Yankee, they went down to the borough hall to see if we had gotten a
license."[37]

Byrne had no typical day at Morven, but did try to follow a few routines.
He rose at dawn to take a quick swim in the heated pool, usually swimming
nude (a practice he said Governor Meyner also had followed in the Morven
pool). His morning swims continued through the winter; on one frigid day,
he recalled "my wet footprints immediately froze on the stone patio." After
his swim, Byrne worked at Morven for a few hours before proceeding to

the State House in Trenton, reading the morning newspapers, and reviewing briefing memos prepared by his staff providing background on the meetings and other events scheduled for the rest of the day. When members of Byrne's cabinet and legislators learned of his early morning schedule, some would phone or ask to see him at Morven before his more hectic calendar in Trenton would intrude later in the day. On many Mondays, Byrne scheduled meetings of his key staff at Morven, sometimes during warm weather sitting around the pool. Taking advantage of Morven's seclusion from the press corps and other State House observers, Byrne also held more sensitive meetings at the house, usually interviewing, for example, prospective appointees as judges and prosecutors at the home to maintain confidentiality.[38]

As the Byrnes settled into their new home in Princeton, in May the administration secured its first legislative victory with the approval of public financing of gubernatorial general election campaigns, the first such program in the United States.[39] Financing campaigns with public funds would allow future candidates to be somewhat less dependent for support on the county party organizations—the traditional power base of New Jersey politics. Perhaps with considerable exaggeration, one scholarly account concluded: "Individual candidates' appeal, television and money replaced the county organizations as the driving forces in gubernatorial politics."[40]

In the same month he approved the campaign financing legislation, Byrne followed through on another campaign pledge by signing a bill to create the nation's first public advocate, a state department authorized to receive and resolve citizen complaints against government and to take legal actions "in the public interest," even if that entailed suing the state government of which it was a part. Byrne had been thinking about the concept since his time as head of the Public Utilities Commission, where by law attorneys were designated to represent the public interest in hearings on rates and other consumer matters. Byrne wasn't satisfied about how the system had worked at the PUC, but "I thought there were other areas that public representation was necessary—in insurance cases, in banking cases and so forth. . . . The genesis of the idea was mine."[41] Consumer advocate Ralph Nader hailed the creation of the New Jersey public advocate as "a measure that could represent a philosophic as well as a practical turning point in the citizens' struggle to control governmental decisions."[42]

To head the Department, the governor named Stanley Van Ness, who had previously been the public defender in the Cahill administration after serving as counsel and assistant counsel to Governor Hughes—the first African American to be a lawyer on a governor's staff. "The original response was negative to creating the Public Advocate," Byrne recalled years later.[43] "The people in the government resented Stanley, and every once in a while he went a little too far."[44] On one occasion, for example, a lawsuit (filed by a private attorney retained by the advocate) named not only the Department of Institutions and Agencies as a defendant, but also sought damages to be paid personally by Ann Klein, its commissioner—a situation that Klein vigorously brought to the attention of both Van Ness and the governor during a Cabinet meeting.[45] During the Byrne years, the public advocate instituted legal actions or joined litigation filed by other plaintiffs that resulted in court decisions to expand public access to beaches; invalidate local zoning practices restricting the development of affordable housing; suspend funding of nursing homes failing to meet state standards; and improve conditions in State mental institutions. In one case, the advocate sued the Boy Scouts of America after four members of a troop in Toms River, all disabled by muscular dystrophy, were denied promotion to Eagle Scout since they could not earn merit badges in swimming and life-saving; the suit later resulted in the Boy Scouts National Council changing its guidelines to allow physically handicapped scouts to meet alternative requirements.[46]

Despite the success of his first months in office resulting from his successful handling of the gasoline crisis and enactment of his election and government reform program, Byrne's popularity fell sharply when he announced his support for an income tax to meet the increased school aid required to comply with the *Robinson v. Cahill* decision. The Assembly passed the bill by a 41-38 vote on July 15—the minimum needed for approval—but after it became clear in private caucuses that it lacked the majority for passage, the Senate did not post the bill for a floor vote.[47] Given the large Democratic majorities in both houses of the legislature, Byrne's failure to get his own party to enact the measure provoked sharp criticism of his leadership.[48]

A week after the rebuff on the tax bill in the Senate, Secretary of State Crabiel was indicted by a state grand jury on charges that he had conspired, years long before he joined the Byrne cabinet, to fix bids on highway construction projects when he headed one of the state's largest highway contractors.[49] Byrne asked that he resign, but under the state constitution the secretary of state could only be removed for cause and Crabiel refused to quit voluntarily. Byrne then restricted Crabiel's role to only those ceremonial duties required by law, and Crabiel eventually took an eight-month leave of absence to fight the corruption charges (which in the next year were dismissed by a judge on the ground that the statute of limitations had tolled on the allegations that were the basis of the indictment).[50] The charges also effectively removed Crabiel, the former Democratic leader in the Senate, from the key position he had been expected to play as a liaison between the administration and the legislature. "Ed could have been very helpful," Byrne later recounted, "when we ran into problems with the legislature. We really didn't have anybody else like him."[51]

Byrne encountered opposition on other fronts. In the same week as the indictment of Crabiel, Charles Marciante, the president of the state AFL-CIO, organized a "march for jobs" that brought 18,000 union members to Trenton chanting "we want work!"—one of the largest protests in the capital's history. The demonstration took place shortly after Byrne announced that he would not support construction "at this time" of the Tocks Island Dam at the Delaware Water Gap at New Jersey's northwest boundary. Labor and development interests aggressively lobbied for the Tocks Island project as a stimulus for construction jobs in the state's struggling economy, expansion of the state's reservoir capacity, supply of cheaper energy through hydroelectric power and flood-control benefits to prevent losses similar to those of the Delaware River flood in 1955 that caused millions of dollars in property damage in Trenton and other riverfront towns.[52] Environmental interests opposed its construction, arguing that the river's natural flow should not be blocked. In referring to the mood of the demonstrators he brought to Trenton, Marciante said, "They were not cordial. They were chanting the governor's name and asking him to come out, and it was sort of reverberating off the building. It was a little chilling." A newspaper account continued to describe the scene: "When Gov. Brendan Byrne addressed them and blamed the lack of jobs on President Richard Nixon, the workers booed him."[53]

Years later, Byrne said that his decision not to build the dam was "a close call. [Democratic Congressman] Frank Thompson was strongly for building the dam, and I respected his judgment. I just thought that the dam and lake would take a very large amount of land and that we should try other options. After I left office when we had bad droughts, I wondered whether I made the right decision."[54] The Tocks Island dam was only the first of a series of clashes with Marciante, who had backed Ralph DeRose over Byrne in the 1973 Democratic primary and later opposed Byrne's proposed income tax and his policies to divert funds from highway construction to mass transit and to impose new controls on land-use development. "Marciante didn't like me," Byrne reflected. "We just didn't get along."[55]

Following the embarrassments of the failure on the tax proposal and the Crabiel indictment and the protests over the faltering economy, an analysis by a veteran *New York Times* reporter concluded that "Gov. Byrne's Democratic administration in Trenton is in deep political trouble," continuing that "the prospects for Mr. Byrne are gloomy."[56] By November, an Eagleton Institute Poll reported that only 34 percent of respondents rated Byrne's performance as either "excellent" or "good," a steep drop from the 56 percent that gave him positive marks in the survey taken in the previous May.[57]

As the Governor completed his first year in office, Byrne's fall in popularity since his promising early start led to a series of assessments of what had gone wrong. "Brendan had grown up in the heart of the Democratic Party," his counsel Lew Kaden later reflected, "but he wasn't temperamentally or culturally part of it—of the party in its old structure of powerful county leaders and party discipline. . . . He had gone to Princeton and Harvard Law School, but that wasn't the world that they were most comfortable with, and . . . there was always a tension in how independent minded he was, which reflected in the people he had around him as well as his own predispositions. So it was just a complicated relationship. It was that way from the start."[58]

Beyond the policy differences that they had with the new governor, critics of Byrne targeted his personality and style of governing. "It is not possible to consider the issues confronting the administration," a prominent national journalist wrote in an extensive profile of Byrne published in June 1975, "without considering the 'issue' of Byrne's personality." The piece went on to suggest that he lacked the personal touch, greeting most people with the same "'Hey. How are you doing?' or 'Nice to see you.'" Byrne's toughness also was questioned: "He treats friends and enemies the same," an anonymous Byrne aide was quoted. "He doesn't punish people. He conveys the sense he is a punching bag." A cabinet officer, also unidentified, was reported as saying, "He lacks passion."[59] In the administration's second year in office, Dick Leone reflected on the uneven start, "We had an exciting beginning, a period of rather widespread reform. That was a happier time. . . . But after things stalled on the tax issue last July, things became difficult."[60]

Some Trenton insiders found Byrne's self-described "shy but gutsy" persona tough to figure out. Those accustomed to the more outgoing, direct styles of his predecessors Bill Cahill, known for in-your-face confrontations, and Dick Hughes, the affable negotiator, struggled to decipher Byrne's leanings. His judge-like demeanor, often hearing out those before him without interacting and occasionally leaning down under his desk to shine his shoes, gave few clues to his intentions. One criticism reported by the press was that the former judge "continues to respond to people and their concerns as if he still wore his Superior Court robes," listening to arguments presented to him but rarely indicating how he would decide. Jerry English, his legislative counsel, defended his deliberative style: "And that's not bad. He does have the temperament of a judge. What is considered indecisiveness by others is actually a very probing manner. I would term it an insistence on a sound, factual approach, not indecisiveness."[61]

Years later, Jim Florio recounted that while in Congress he brought to Trenton a delegation of labor leaders to see Byrne to ask for his support for building a new Veterans Administration hospital in Camden. Florio recalled that, as the "big, gruff" union leaders gave presentations during the meeting to the Governor on the benefits of building the hospital, "the Governor appeared to be more engaged in filling his fountain pen." As the angry group left Byrne's office, Florio said he "heard some words that day I haven't heard since," but that he attempted to persuade them that the Governor in fact had been listening and "he was paying attention," even when he "appears to be unfocused."[62]

Some critics attacked Byrne's travels, his trips on foreign trade missions, to other states for conferences and, for shorter distances, his frequent use of the State Police helicopter. His helicopter trips became a frequent complaint, particularly during a time of the energy shortages that had led to sharp spikes in gasoline prices. "I just thought it was more efficient to take the copter," Byrne later explained. "It saved a lot of time when I had a full schedule of stops around the state."[63] Perhaps the most damaging image was that taken by a photographer of Byrne, at a national governors conference in New Orleans, sunning himself in a lounge chair by the hotel pool in a tight bathing suit—a photo widely reproduced in the state's newspapers. "We were supposed to have the afternoon off," Byrne later explained, "but one of the governors asked that we continue to meet and we wound up having only an hour free without a session. Most of the governors went to the bar, but I went to the pool and someone took that picture." Others focused on his mixing with celebrities, playing tennis and golf, and engaging in other leisure activities they found incongruous with his role in dealing with the serious issues facing the state.

Senator Dugan, Byrne's choice as chairman of the state Democrats after Dugan helped secure Hudson's support in the Democratic primary, called Byrne's administration a "shambles," attributing much of the blame to advisers he labeled "arrogant and ignorant." A newspaper reporter quoting Dugan's comments continued, "While he did not identify his targets, it is assumed that he was referring to State Treasurer Richard C. Leone and Lewis B. Kaden, the Governor's chief counsel."[64] Years later, Thomas Kean, the Assembly Republican leader, offered a softer view of Leone and Kaden's relations with some legislators: after noting the diversity in backgrounds and education among legislators, Kean noted that Leone and Kaden "did not suffer fools gladly."[65]

Byrne himself pointed to the simple fact that he had failed to deliver on his most visible program. "If I had gotten tax reform," he reflected, "all of the negative you hear would be positive. This is a very empirical business. If you win one, you're great. If you don't, you're not."[66]

Although much of Byrne's first term would be dominated, and at times overwhelmed, by the legislative battle over financing the public schools, his administration would take action on a number of other fronts.

On the same day that the union workers demonstrated in front of the State House, the legislature approved a bill drafted by the administration to establish the Economic Development Authority (EDA)—a quasi-autonomous agency structurally placed within the then Department of Labor and Industry authorized to issue tax-free bonds to lower financing costs for new and expanded private-sector industrial and commercial projects.[67] The EDA would evolve to become the primary state entity for economic development support and financing, and in later years would add an array of other financing, business assistance, and job training programs to its initial services. Later, the EDA model was widely replicated by other states.[68] "The EDA was an innovative idea in the 70s," Byrne reflected many years later, "but over time most states enacted their own programs. It became less effective, and states got into bidding wars among themselves to keep big employers or persuade them to move."[69] To complement the EDA, Byrne created new units to target specific economic sectors, such as technology and the entertainment industry.[70]

Byrne's most visible initiatives to spur the state's economy were the development of the Meadowlands and the Sports Complex; the revitalization of Atlantic City through the introduction of casino gambling; and the restoration of the Hudson waterfront with the opening of Liberty State Park in Jersey City. Byrne's intervention as governor-elect first salvaged the plan conceived by Cahill for the Meadowlands Racetrack and Giants Stadium and the new administration oversaw the construction of both facilities; after the track and stadium opened in 1977, a *Sports Illustrated* article reviewing the tortured history of the new complex was headlined the "Miracle In The Meadows," and continued, "What used to be one of the outstanding garbage dumps of our time has become a gold mine of a sports center—and more nuggets are on the way. . . ."[71] Subsequently, Byrne would proceed to place his own stamp on the complex with the construction of the new Meadowlands arena. Beyond the impact in jobs and spending, Byrne viewed these high-profile projects as "making it easier to develop pride in New Jersey. It took people's minds off the turnpike and the oil refineries. It got them talking about something else in New Jersey."[72]

Another measure approved by Byrne restructured the process by which the state evaluated proposed bond issues and capital spending for projects like highways, water supply, and other infrastructure. In the November 1975 mid-term election, voters rejected referenda seeking approval of bond issues for water supply resources and transportation. "When the bond issues went down," Byrne later explained, "I thought we had to have a broader consensus, and bipartisan support, to convince voters of the need for future bond issues."[73] Byrne then appointed a temporary commission headed by Donald MacNaughton, the chief executive of Prudential Insurance, to review the reasons for the rejections, evaluate the state's capital needs, and propose changes to the planning and approval process. Byrne followed up the MacNaughton Commission recommendations by submitting legislation that created the New Jersey Capital Budgeting and Planning Commission—a permanent commission with both public and private members to recommend action on future state capital budgets and bond issues prior to consideration by the legislature and the voters.[74] At Byrne's request, former Governor Cahill agreed to chair the commission. "I thought Bill Cahill was a great choice," Byrne later said. "With a former Republican governor heading it, the commission was given a high stature and a bi-partisan profile. Bill did a great job, and we had a lot more success after the commission was established in getting bond issues approved."[75] Perhaps the largest capital spending program of Byrne's first term was one that brought support from both labor and environmental leaders. Over $1 billion was spent in building or expanding sewage treatment plants—much of it funded by federal grants and targeted with much of the money to end sewage discharges into the ocean.[76]

Byrne also took steps to expedite the processing of permits by the Department of Environmental Protection, which developers had criticized for delays that increased the costs of construction. "The one criticism I think every governor has heard when running for election," Byrne remarked long after leaving office, "is that you can't get things done in New Jersey."[77] Following his inauguration, Byrne charged Commissioner Bardin with meeting a ninety-day timetable for the processing of permits for private development, a deadline strongly opposed by leading environmental groups.[78]

One of Byrne's principal themes was promoting investment in the cities, often by directing that state grants and financing assistance for economic development, transportation, housing, and other programs be targeted to areas with high unemployment or other measures of distress.[79] His actions included prohibiting the leasing of state offices outside Trenton, Newark, Paterson, and Camden, and directing the EDA and the Housing Finance Authority to target their financing and mortgage assistance programs to urban areas.[80] The Treasury developed an innovative "municipal qualified bond program"—later widely adopted as a model by other states—to enhance municipal bond credit ratings by diverting state aid due to cities, towns, or school districts to meet bond payments in the event the local government faced potential default. The prospect that the state would step in to reallocate aid reduced interest rates, saving cities and towns millions of dollars in debt service during a period when local government borrowing costs had spiked as a result of New York City's highly publicized fiscal problems.[81]

With mixed success, Byrne also intervened in private-sector investment and siting decisions to support the cities. In New Brunswick, the state worked with Johnson & Johnson to complete the long-delayed extension of State Route 18 across the Raritan River to ease congestion in the center of the city, which the company viewed as crucial to its "tentative decision" to remain in the city and construct a new global headquarters.[82] Patricia Sheehan, who had been appointed by Byrne as commissioner of the Department of Community Affairs after serving as mayor of New Brunswick and community affairs executive for Johnson & Johnson, had advised Byrne of the road's importance. "Pat came to me and said that J&J would move out," Byrne later recounted, "if the road wasn't finished. I knew we couldn't let a company like that move out of the state."[83] Over the protests of environmental groups, historic preservationists and some Rutgers University faculty and students, in July 1977 he signed the permit authorizing the project's construction, thus ending, as the *New York Times* reported, "one of the longest disputes over highway construction in the state's history."[84] During the following months, the state EDA worked with J&J and the newly established New Brunswick Development Corporation to implement the downtown redevelopment plan, including construction of the company's new global headquarters, a Hyatt hotel, and conference center and an office building.[85]

Redevelopment of the Hudson waterfront also emerged as a major urban initiative. Cleanup of the waterfront had long been discussed, but local interests had been unable to make progress until David Bardin, the commissioner of Department of Environmental Protection, received Byrne's approval to make the development of what became Liberty State Park a major state priority by clearing and restoring 1,100 acres of garbage-strewn former industrial land in Jersey City just a few hundred yards from the Statue of Liberty and Ellis Island.[86] The state opened the Park on Flag Day, June 14 of 1976. Three weeks later, the Park served as the focal point of New Jersey's celebration of the nation's bicentennial on July 4, hosting thousands of visitors drawn to the fireworks and other events in New York Harbor. Liberty Park soon became the state's most visited park, adding such facilities as the Liberty Science Center which, at Byrne's urging, was relocated to the Park from its original proposed site on Interstate 80 in western Essex County.[87] "Reclaiming the Hudson waterfront had been talked about for years," Byrne later reflected, "but nothing had been done. David Bardin deserves great credit for showing what you could accomplish. It really was the first step toward wider redevelopment of the Hudson waterfront."[88]

When Byrne took office, the federal government was planning to open the Mid-Atlantic offshore waters to allow exploration and potential drilling for oil and gas. In testimony before Congressional committees and in other forums, Byrne called for more control by the states over offshore drilling and stronger safeguards to protect against possible spills that might impact the State's tourist industry.[89] "I just didn't feel that offshore drilling was worth the risk to the shore and our tourist economy," Byrne recalled in a later interview, "but some labor leaders and others pushing for development thought it would produce new investment and jobs when our economy was in bad shape. When I ran for reelection, my position on offshore drilling was another issue that created problems for me with some labor leaders."[90] During the controversy over drilling in the Mid-Atlantic, Byrne appeared on a national television program with Governor Edwin Edwards of Louisiana, who promoted the economic benefits from offshore drilling that had come to his state. "After I was on TV with Edwards," Byrne later recalled, "I think I received more positive mail from New Jersey than anything else I did."[91]

As part of New Jersey's own efforts to protect against damages from spills, Byrne proposed legislation to tax oil and chemical companies on the transfer of hazardous substances within the State to create a fund to compensate for potential losses. Over the objections of the petrochemical industry led by its attorney Robert Wilentz, a former legislator and the son of the powerful Democratic leader David Wilentz, Byrne successfully pushed his bill through the legislature, signing it into law on January 6, 1977, as the Spill Compensation and Control Act. The $25 million fund established by the legislation provided compensation for and cleanup costs and other public and private losses resulting from spills, and soon would be expanded to include paying for the cleanup of toxic landfills and groundwater pollution.[92] The Spill Compensation legislation was the most comprehensive program of its type and became the model for the federal Superfund bill sponsored by then Congressman James Florio and signed by President Jimmy Carter in 1980.[93] In conjunction with the federal Superfund which it had spawned, the state compensation fund became the major financing source for the subsequent cleanup of oil and chemical spills and toxic landfills throughout the state long after Byrne had left office.

Byrne took office during the early recognition of links from toxic pollution to adverse impacts on health. In 1973, the year Byrne was first elected governor, a National Cancer Institute study reported that New Jersey had the highest incidence of cancer in the nation, with nineteen of the state's twenty-one counties ranking in the top 10 percent of all counties in the nation in cancer death rates.[94] After the report's release, journalists labeled the corridor between New York and Philadelphia as "Cancer Alley," and analysts largely attributed the high cancer rate to New Jersey's then-$4 billion chemical industry. "If you know where the chemical industry is," Glenn Paulson, an assistant commissioner in the state Department of Environmental Protection, said at the time, "you know where the cancer hotspots are."[95] Although the sweeping conclusions and methodology of the National Cancer Institute study would later be discredited, after Byrne's election its findings, coupled with growing national concerns over environmental health issues, generated support for cleaning up toxic landfills and tightening controls over air, water, and ground pollution. Disclosures of a series of highly publicized local environmental health problems also heightened public awareness.[96]

In response to these and other controversies, Byrne's established a cabinet-level Committee on Cancer Control, and signed a series of new laws to deal with health risks from toxic chemicals. These included mandating "worker and community right-to-know" disclosures requiring companies to publish inventories of toxic chemicals stored at their facilities; creating a system to inventory the production and to track the shipping of toxic substances; setting standards on the discharge of carcinogenic chemicals into the atmosphere; strengthening penalties for illegal dumping; and giving citizens the right to sue to enforce compliance with environmental laws and regulations.[97]

On broader healthcare issues, as Byrne took office the New Jersey healthcare system was experiencing rapid inflation as hospitals, physicians, and other providers passed on costs of what critics claimed were protracted hospital stays, excessive testing and other unnecessary services, with much of the costs passed on to the federal Medicare program. During the Cahill administration, the state enacted legislation to require state approval of construction and expansion of healthcare facilities, as well as the setting of treatment rates charged to patients and insurers. But the implementation of the new controls had been co-opted by the hospital industry's influence with state regulators, resulting in a routine rubber-stamping of hospital requests and, as one health analyst wrote, an "almost total erasure of a forward looking law that might have brought great public benefits."[98] Once sworn in as Byrne's new Commissioner of Health, Joanne Finley aggressively rejected or reduced hospital applications for rate increases and spending on new construction or major equipment, using the legislative authority previously enacted under Governor Cahill. Finley's stance provoked several lawsuits by the state hospital association and individual hospitals challenging the state's action.[99]

Given his background as lawyer, prosecutor, and judge, Byrne took special interest in those he nominated to be judges and prosecutors. "I often would ask Joe Weintraub for his opinion on potential appointments," Byrne later said, "and asked Alex Waugh, who I'd worked closely with when I was prosecutor and he was the Essex County assignment judge, and Jerry English, my legislative counsel, to vet the candidates with other judges and lawyers who knew them before I interviewed them myself."[100]

In the governor's first term, his Attorney General, William Hyland represented the state in the landmark "right-to-die" case involving 21-year-old Karen Ann Quinlan. Quinlan had lapsed into a coma after drinking alcohol and taking tranquilizers and was placed on a respirator when she was unable to breathe on her own; after months passed without any sign that she would regain consciousness, her father went to court for an order authorizing doctors to disconnect her respirator so she might die. Representing the state in

the trial court, after declaring that the case had "greater potential for affecting the lives of people on into the future than almost anything else," Hyland
successfully opposed the request, arguing that it would contravene New
Jersey's long-standing definition of death as the "cessation of vital signs" and
result in a new standard based on "brain death." On appeal, the New Jersey
Supreme Court in March 1976 issued its landmark "right to die" decision, ruling that Mr. Quinlan or another guardian appointed to protect his daughter's
interests could seek an order to remove artificial life support provided such
action was shown to be consistent with the wishes of the terminally ill person.
"I had confidence in Bill Hyland and the courts," Byrne said in reflecting on
the *Quinlan* case years later. "Like everyone else, I followed how the case
proceeded, but avoided discussing it with Hyland or publicly commenting.
Personally, I agreed with the Supreme Court's decision."[101] The *Quinlan* case
provoked a national debate on the definition of death and led to New Jersey
and several other states, through legislation or judicial decisions, further clari-
fying their own definitions and standards for determining death.[102]

A case of a very different sort than *Quinlan* pushed Byrne into a role
combining his experience as prosecutor and judge when, during his first
year as governor in 1974, he was petitioned to grant a pardon to the former
professional boxer Rubin "Hurricane" Carter and his companion, John Artis.
The two men had been convicted and sentenced to life terms in 1967 for the
murder of three white men shot in a Paterson bar; the bar shootings were
thought to be racially motivated retaliation for the fatal shooting only hours
earlier of a black man elsewhere in the city. Shortly after Byrne took office,
two witnesses who had testified at the trial recanted their identifications of
Carter and Artis as being at the murder scene, claiming that they had been
pressured by the police to implicate them. The story gained national attention through articles in the *New York Times*; the publication of Carter's
autobiography; a song, *Hurricane,* written and sung by Bob Dylan protesting
the conviction; and demonstrations in Trenton, featuring such celebrities as
Muhammad Ali.[103]

In addition to filing motions for a new trial, the supporters of Carter and
Artis filed a petition with governor requesting that he grant executive clemency through issuance of a pardon or commutation of sentence. "I met with
[the actress] Ellen Burstyn and some others protesting the convictions," Byrne
recalled years later, "but most of them really didn't have much knowledge of
the facts of the case."[104] Byrne asked Eldridge Hawkins, a black assemblyman from Essex County, to investigate the case and prepare a report which
concluded that Carter and Artis were at the scene, but further confused the
situation by disclosing new evidence and identifying a potential new witness
who did not testify at the trial. Before Byrne acted on the clemency petition,
the New Jersey Supreme Court unanimously vacated the original convictions

and ordered a retrial, holding that during the 1967 trial the prosecution had not disclosed to the defendants a tape recording of an interview of witness providing information favorable to the defendants' case.[105] Although the legal events freed Byrne from making a decision on the clemency petitions, he remained skeptical of the claims of innocence. "It was clear that they had lied about not being at the bar. I also had worked in the Passaic prosecutor's office and knew some of the people who were still there, including Burrell Humphries, the prosecutor. I was confident in their judgement."[106]

When Byrne took office, the Department of Institutions and Agencies, the state's largest department known in Trenton as "I&A," had responsibility for a wide range of social service and correctional programs, including managing mental hospitals, state prisons, and juvenile facilities. With a daughter born with Down syndrome, Byrne had special concerns for the disabled requiring care in state institutions. As the department's commissioner, Ann Klein frequently would visit the facilities and speak with residents. "Ann spent a lot of time going to the institutions," Bob Mulcahy, then one of her deputy commissioners, later recalled, "reaching out to the people in the institutions to let them know that she cared and she cared a lot. And sometimes, we had to rein her in a little bit because we just didn't have the capacity to do the things that she would have liked to have done at that time."[107] Klein was also a forceful advocate for increased funds to support her facilities and programs. "Ann was always the most aggressive cabinet member arguing for more money," Byrne later recounted. "I admired her for that and tried to help out when we had any extra money."[108] Under Klein, the department implemented a long-term policy to transfer residents from the large state hospitals to smaller facilities and group homes. Although supported by mental health professionals, the controversial program ran into substantial local opposition as the state attempted to find suitable locations for the smaller treatment facilities to house patients. "And we went about doing it," Mulcahy said later, "even though we knew that there were not sufficient facilities, halfway houses and other places to care for these people, believing that they were better off on their own than locked up the way they were in these institutions."[109]

In 1976, the legislature approved Byrne's plan to spin off the correctional programs into a new department, the Department of Corrections headed by Mulcahy as commissioner, with the former "I&A" renamed as the Department of Human Services.[110] Before the restructuring that made him a commissioner, Mulcahy had received positive attention for his handling of two disturbances at the Trenton State Prison and would face another soon after his swearing in to head of the new department. "I think I was Commissioner ten days," Mulcahy later recalled, "when I came home with the kids from a high school football game and Terry [his wife] was at the door and said that 'Colonel Pagano called and there's a woman hostage in the sex offenders unit and they're sending a helicopter for you.' So I went down there and I called the Governor, he was going to a black tie affair and he said 'Bob I have confidence in that you'll be able to handle it, if you need me just call me.' And that's the way he was. If he gave you a job to do, he let you do it." At one point during the hostage crisis, "this State Police Captain walked up to me," Mulcahy continued, "and he said, and I remember these words very vividly, 'Commissioner we have a sharp shooter in position, how do you feel about taking the inmate's life?' And I walked down the hall and I remember these words, I said 'Dear God what am I doing?' And I turned around and came back and I said, 'No I don't want to do it if I don't have to.'" (The hostage was safely freed after the inmates agreed to surrender.)[111]

Byrne's first term confronted a variety of other issues and problems, but he himself recognized that he would be measured by meeting the challenge of the *Robinson v. Cahill* decision. "I knew that whatever else I did, I would be judged a failure if I couldn't deliver on tax reform and the income tax," he would later reflect. "I didn't want to fail."[112]

Chapter 8

The Income Tax and Financing the Public Schools

One day I was coming out of a restaurant, and a man came up to me and said, "Brendan Byrne, you are going to burn in Hell!"
I said, "Why"
He said "For the income tax!"
I thought that was going a bit far. I told the man, "I'm going to burn in hell—but not for the income tax."

—Brendan Byrne

During the Great Depression, as governments in New Jersey and elsewhere faced bankruptcy, and the need to deal with the surge in jobless and homeless citizens, Governor Harold Hoffman had tried to push through the legislature both an income tax and a state sales tax. Only the sales tax was narrowly approved, but the public outcry against the tax forced Hoffman to assent to its repeal within months of its enactment. In a dramatic gesture displaying his objection, Hoffman signed the bill repealing the tax in red ink, while predicting that it would result in an "unbalanced budget and maybe hungry people."[1] Hoffman's humiliation was cited as a lesson to later New Jersey politicians that proposing broad-based taxes would be tantamount to political suicide.

"It was considered a life or death issue," Brendan Byrne later reflected. "Bob Meyner wouldn't go near an income tax, and Dick Hughes and Bill Cahill had tried and failed. All politicians in New Jersey knew that history."[2]

In his first year in office in 1970, Governor Cahill had created the New Jersey Tax Policy Committee chaired by state Senator Harry Sears, with its forty prominent members, including former governors Driscoll and Hughes, other legislators, as well as business executives and interest group representatives.[3] Cahill introduced legislation to enact the core of the Committee's proposals for both an income tax and statewide property tax, along with eliminating various exemptions to the sales tax, but on July 17, 1972, the Assembly rejected the key bill for an income tax by an overwhelming fifty-two to twenty-three margin, 18 votes short of the 41 needed for passage. Cahill was further embarrassed by the extent of the opposition to his plan within his own party; only nine Republicans voted for the tax compared to fourteen Democrats. After the vote, Cahill told the press that the defeat meant "tax reform in New Jersey is dead."[4]

But in April 1973, less than a year after the defeat of Cahill's plan in the legislature and while Byrne was in the final weeks of deciding whether to become a candidate for governor, the New Jersey Supreme Court ruled in a unanimous opinion in the case of *Robinson v. Cahill*—which arose from a complaint filed in the state Superior Court on behalf of lead plaintiff Kenneth Robinson, a Jersey City high school student—that the state constitution required the state government to provide a "thorough and efficient system" of education to all pupils in the public schools. The landmark decision struck down New Jersey's traditional heavy reliance on local property taxes for funding public education, finding that disparities in local property tax revenue and the resulting levels of spending on education could not be sustained given the state's own obligation to insure a basic level of educational quality.[5] "Whether the State acts directly or imposes the role upon local government, the end product must be what the Constitution commands," Chief Justice Weintraub wrote. "A system of instruction in any district of the State which is not thorough and efficient falls short of the constitutional command. Whatever the reason for the violation, the obligation is the State's to rectify it."[6]

Although New Jersey was only one of several states with litigation challenging the reliance on local tax revenue in financing public education, its situation was, as one scholar wrote at the time, "far worse than that in most states in terms of state contributions to public education." Nationally, state governments had been providing some 40 percent of the total cost of operating public schools, whereas in New Jersey the state share averaged only about 28 percent. Disparities in spending per pupil among the poorest and wealthiest school districts—particularly exacerbated by the fiscal burdens in older cities caused by declining property tax bases along with high welfare, law enforcement and other urban costs—also were among the largest in the country.[7]

To allow time for legislative action, the Court deferred ruling, as the plaintiffs had requested, on the issue of whether it could impose its own remedy independently of the legislature, subsequently directing that a revised school financing system be enacted by the legislature and governor by December 31,

1974—less than a year after the legislators and governor elected in November 1973 would have completed a year of their terms.[8]

After the release of *Robinson*, "a few curmudgeons in the senate made intemperate remarks," one scholar wrote, "a resolution was introduced to impeach all of the court's justices, and there was desultory talk of deleting 'thorough and efficient' from the state constitution, yet no one mounted an assiduous effort to take on the court and reverse its decision."[9]

On April 3, 1973, the date of the *Robinson* decision's publication, Superior Court Judge Brendan Byrne did not give much thought to the impact of the ruling. Byrne's mother Genevieve had died on April 1, coincidentally her youngest son's forty-ninth birthday, and he still had not decided whether to step down from the bench to seek the gubernatorial nomination—a decision that Byrne would make some three weeks later.

Because Cahill had already demonstrated his support for the goals of *Robinson* during his failed attempt to enact a radical overhaul of school finance in 1972, it was reasonable to assume that—bolstered by the Court's ruling and a voter mandate from reelection—his second term might well have seen a renewed push for a comprehensive school financing program to reduce the dependence on the local property tax. Reacting to the *Robinson* decision, Cahill said that it "translated into reality the need for state tax reform."[10]

Two months after the *Robinson* decision, however, Cahill was defeated for the Republican gubernatorial nomination by Congressman Sandman in the party's primary. Cahill's loss effectively ended any movement on *Robinson* until the November election determined who would become governor in the following January. "Instead of forceful leadership from the governor's office toward the *Robinson* challenge," an academic analyst later noted, "policy developments were shelved and initiatives delayed by the lame-duck executive."[11]

During the first weeks of the general election campaign, Byrne hedged on how he proposed to meet the State's responsibility to increase its support of school funding. He said that the state tax system needed "restructuring," primarily to relieve local taxpayers of the burden of high property taxes to finance public schools, but as the *New York Times* reported, "avoided any statement indicating any support for an income tax."[12] Later in the campaign, Byrne stated that he saw no need for one in the "foreseeable future."[13]

Despite the later cynicism that greeted his decision as governor to propose an income tax, Byrne insisted that during the campaign and upon his election he still had not decided that an income tax was the only way to raise the additional school-aid revenue to meet the *Robinson* mandate.[14] "I still had an open mind on what we would have to do," Byrne reflected years later, "particularly since we weren't sure how much money was needed. There had been various proposals, such as for a statewide property tax, and I thought we needed to take a fresh look at all the options."[15] Cliff Goldman, who as deputy state treasurer became a key person developing Byrne's tax policy, took a sympathetic view of the political context of Byrne's remark: "You know, that's what people do in campaigns," Goldman later explained, "and they carefully word things. And I suppose in terms of to balance the State budget, . . . you could certainly have balanced the State budget without an income tax."[16] (In fact, the Byrne Administration produced balanced budgets in its first three fiscal years without an income tax.)

On January 8, 1974, a week before he left office, Cahill gave his final "state of the state" address to the legislature, criticizing it for the failure to enact tax reform. "No, we have no income tax," Cahill said. "We still have a tax structure in which our lowest income residents contribute over 19 percent of their income to support state and local governments while those in the $25,000-and-up income brackets pay but 5.4 percent of their income in support of state and local government. Is there a member of this Legislature who believes that to be just?"[17]

On January 14, Byrne delivered his Inaugural Address, announcing that he would call the legislature into special session in the late spring "to meet the mandate of the Constitution and make a thorough and efficient education for our children a reality."[18]

The revised budget outlook resulting from the sharp economic downturn triggered by the OPEC oil embargo complicated any attempt to increase school aid without resorting to a new tax source. In addition to its impact on state revenues, the soured economy made new state taxes, always difficult in New Jersey, a much harder political sell to taxpayers increasingly worried about their jobs and incomes.

Still other factors argued against another push for tax reform to increase school aid. While New Jerseyans had long supported spending for public schools, increasing concerns had been raised over the content and quality of education. Spending more money on urban schools was particularly suspect given their poor performance and the perception of corruption associated with some of the largest cities such as Newark, Camden, and Jersey City.[19] Assemblyman Burstein, the co-chair of the legislature's Joint Education Committee, later said that a major obstacle was "the belief that you're pouring money down a rat hole, when you're adding large funds into the . . . areas that were most in need of educational assistance. It was not simple to overcome that attitude."[20]

The Byrne transition team evaluated various fiscal plans for responding to the *Robinson* decision. As chair of the transition and the incoming state treasurer, Richard Leone was fully aware of the risks of launching another effort to enact a broad-based tax. In 1969, he had written his doctoral dissertation at Princeton University on the tortured history of tax reform in the state, having had firsthand experience on the governor's staff during the Hughes

Administration's two failed efforts to enact an income tax.[21] Governor Cahill's similar failure in 1972 had contributed to the erosion of his Republican political support when, knowing that he lacked the votes for approval, he nonetheless insisted on forcing a vote on the income tax in the Assembly.

During the transition, when Leone had asked his former Princeton roommate, Cliff Goldman, to join the administration as the deputy treasurer, Goldman recalled replying, "if I could work on the school finance tax reform issue, I would do it," explaining years later that he welcomed the "interesting, important" challenge posed by *Robinson*. Leone quickly granted the request.[22] Like Leone still in his early 30s, Goldman had no special background in school finance but was already a seasoned veteran of New Jersey government, having served in the Hughes administration as an aide to the commissioner of Community Affairs and as acting executive director of the new Hackensack Meadowlands Development Commission.

Byrne resisted creating another large task force of public officials and private citizens similar to the "blue ribbon" commission established by Cahill, preferring instead an internal group drawn from state departments to evaluate options and make recommendations that occasionally sought input from others outside the new administration. "These were the experts," Byrne later explained. "They knew what the issues were and what needed to be done."[23] Cliff Goldman agreed that there was little need to repeat the process undertaken by Cahill. "The Cahill commission," Goldman said later, "had put together the most comprehensive and stellar report on the topic. We also looked broader at tax reform, proposing the elimination of some taxes like the Business Personal Property Tax. This fairly enormous effort was done without outside discussion and with very little specific guidance because there was no time for it."[24]

Goldman's group did reach out to sympathetic legislators, some of whom shared the youth and Ivy League degrees of Byrne's key staff. Steven Perskie, a Columbia and Yale Law School graduate who had been elected to the Assembly in 1971 and had been named two years later at age 29 to chair the Assembly Taxation Committee, later recalled attending a meeting soon after Byrne's inauguration in the Treasurer's office with Leone, Goldman, Governor's Counsel Lew Kaden, and Assemblyman Gordon MacInnes, a member of Perskie's committee: "Leone was the oldest one in the room, he was 34. At 29, I was the youngest. I kept looking around and asking myself 'where are the grownups?'"[25]

Apart from seeking ways to raise additional revenue to comply with *Robinson*, another option for the legislature would be simply to do nothing, to defer to the Court to fashion its own remedy. In addition to Weintraub, three other justices of the seven who had concurred in his *Robinson* opinion had retired. It was unclear whether newly appointed Chief Justice Hughes and the other new justices would risk the Court's prestige by taking the extraordinary, and constitutionally questionable, steps of either mandating a reallocation of existing school aid or imposing new taxes. By avoiding any action, Byrne and the legislature could shield themselves from the political backlash caused by any vote to approve new taxes or to reduce the amount of state aid going to more affluent districts. John Degnan, who joined Byrne's staff as an assistant counsel during the administration's first year and soon became one of his closest advisers, later reflected: "The easiest way to deal with the tax would have been to blame the Supreme Court, but I think the Governor's respect for Joe Weintraub and for the Court just wouldn't let him do that, to take the typical political line in avoiding responsibility. It just wasn't in his gut to do things that way."[26]

A threshold question faced by the Goldman group was how ambitious the plan to comply with the *Robinson* decision should be. Increasing state aid to poorer school districts conceivably could be accomplished by modest hikes to rates of existing taxes, such as the sales, tobacco, or business levies. Yet this minimalist approach and its lower revenue goals—narrowly targeted to increase school aid to the poorer, mostly urban school districts—nonetheless would face a difficult political path in a legislature where the balance of power was skewed toward the interests of suburban constituents. The other extreme of totally replacing the local school property tax with an income tax also was quickly rejected as unrealistic by both the Goldman group and key legislators; it would require an income tax levy at rates higher than those in most if not all other states.

Partly based on principle and partly based on practical politics, other advocates argued that any new tax program should more broadly aim for more comprehensive reform, raising substantial additional revenues to reduce, but not replace, the traditional dependence on the local property tax. Without outlining any specific plan, the Democratic Party's 1973 campaign platform had vowed to reduce the regressive property tax, so some type of tax reform effort had been, in theory at least, a campaign commitment of Byrne.[27]

One of the several proposals advanced, either to substitute for or in combination with an income tax, was to establish a statewide property tax, which had been included in the 1972 Cahill tax program along with an income tax. Revenues from this new tax would be pooled with existing state aid funds and then distributed on a per-pupil basis to all districts, helping to reduce the sharp disparities in support of public education.[28] Ultimately, the statewide property tax was discarded in the face of opposition from local officials, who saw it as an incursion by the state on their traditional exclusive province of taxing real estate.

Another option that was considered but rejected was increasing the 5 percent rate of the existing sales tax, along with broadening its coverage to then-excluded items such as food, clothing, and professional services. If the rate were increased, however, projections indicated that the 5 percent rate would have to go to 9 percent within three years and, at that level, New Jersey retailers argued they would lose business to neighboring states; eliminating exemptions for basic items like food and clothing also would make the tax more regressive by imposing a heavier burden on lower-income consumers.

In reviewing options under consideration throughout the country and consulting experts at the Harvard School of Education, the Goldman group narrowed its focus to adapting "power equalization" to the New Jersey situation, using state aid to supplement local school tax revenues so that combined state and local sources would provide the same total income per pupil.

Ultimately, Byrne returned to the income tax as the preferred choice, despite the concerns of the more seasoned political bosses, who were proposing either ignoring the *Robinson* mandate, reducing spending on other budget items to increase school aid, or hiking existing taxes like the sales, cigarette, and business tax levies. But after the subsequent repeated failures to secure legislative approval of his tax reform package, critics would cite Byrne's decision not to attempt to build more public support as a factor contributing to the problems he later encountered in the legislature.[29] Leone later expressed regret that there had not been more distance between Byrne's "foreseeable future" remark in the campaign and his announcement that he was proposing an income tax: "The strategy we had agreed on was to slash the budget to come up with money to increase school aid, and then see if the reaction to the cuts would create support for alternatives like the income tax. But Brendan decided to just go ahead. To the public, it was just too abrupt a change to come out for a tax so soon after Brendan's remarks in the campaign."[30]

"The income tax just made the most sense," Byrne later explained. "We could have cobbled together some smaller taxes and gotten by for a while, but it wouldn't solve the long-term problem."[31] Lew Kaden, Byrne's counsel, recalled years later: "I think all the options, statewide property tax, different forms of consumption or sales tax, were studied, evaluated over and over again, but my recollection of the decision-making process was that he always came back to the basic conclusion that the fair way to do it was an income tax."[32]

Early in the 1974 legislative session, the legislature created a Joint Committee on the Public Schools co-chaired by Assemblyman Burstein, who had voted for the Cahill income tax, and Senator Stephen Wiley, a newly elected senator from Morris County who was a law partner of former Governor Meyner. Their committee assumed the task of defining what the "thorough and efficient" education vaguely described in the *Robinson v. Cahill* decision would specifically require in setting forth the state's responsibilities and resulting commitments in resources. Other legislators took the lead in securing the even more difficult majorities to pass the income tax, including Steve Perskie (Atlantic), Richard Van Wagner (Monmouth), Joseph LeFante (Hudson), and William Hamilton (Middlesex) on the Assembly side and Matthew "Matty" Feldman (Bergen) and Joe Merlino (Mercer) in the Senate.

On June 13, Governor Byrne addressed the special joint session of the legislature that he had called to deal with tax reform. As outlined in his speech and detailed in an accompanying report of the Goldman group, Byrne's proposal used *Robinson* as a justification for going beyond just revising school financing to enact a broad restructuring of the state's tax base. The Goldman report bluntly stated: "The only equitable way to raise the revenue needed for this program of educational reform and property tax relief is an income tax."[33] The program included a state income tax at rates from 1.8 to 8 percent to raise more than $1 billion annually in new state revenue; as one analyst later noted, the amount was "truly a mammoth recommendation for a government whose expenditures at the time were in the neighborhood of $2 1/2 billion."[34] When fully implemented, the revised funding formula would have boosted the state government's share of the total costs of public education from 30 percent to 50 percent by increasing state aid and by partially replacing local property tax revenues.

To provide tax relief to taxpayers whose property taxes exceeded a certain percentage of their income, a "circuit breaker" was proposed—an idea that subsequently evolved into the homestead rebate with direct payments to taxpayers. Another proposal recommended revising the state municipal aid formulas to take partial account of higher costs larger cities incurred for social services, housing, law enforcement, and other programs to serve lower-income populations that limited their ability to fund education even with a fairer school-aid formula.

In his address to the legislature, Byrne argued that "unlike past legislatures" that had considered tax reform, there no longer was any "realistic option for complete inaction" since that path "had been removed by the New Jersey Supreme Court." But the reaction to his speech, according to one press account, was "basically negative," with Byrne receiving a "chilly reception in the chamber."[35] Senate Republican Leader Alfred Beadleston declared that "The Governor's program does not have the chance of a snowball in hell," and continued that, as he observed his Democratic colleagues during Byrne's address, "they looked like they had been hit in the gut—they looked positively sick."[36] The failures of Governors Hughes and Cahill to enact an income tax understandably made legislators wary of endorsing Byrne's tax plan. Some feared that they would be taking the political risk, while it still seemed highly questionable whether ultimately any tax would be approved by majorities in both houses. Legislators carefully weighed the pros and cons of how the new funding system impacted different municipalities, with some school systems and taxpayers benefiting from the new state aid for schools and property tax relief while others might not.

The Byrne plan was soon followed by alternatives advanced by legislators in both parties, including creating a statewide property tax or boosting rates of existing taxes that Byrne had considered but rejected.[37] Some Democratic legislators proposed shifting more of the tax burden to the business sector by authorizing higher property tax rates for business property or increasing existing corporation income and business personal property taxes. Treasurer Leone promptly rejected these approaches, saying the effort to shift more of the tax burden to businesses was "good politics but bad economics."[38] The Republican minority suggested a half-cent increase in the sales tax in an effort to meet the minimum revenue needs to comply with the *Robinson* decision.[39]

Even if their overall district would gain under the new formulas, legislators might still hesitate in belief that the emotional backlash of voters to any new tax would supersede any rational fiscal arguments. Indeed, some legislators from urban districts that would significantly benefit from tax reform proved to be among the most difficult votes to secure. In some cases, Democratic county leaders threatened legislators that they would be taken off the ticket for re-nomination if they voted for the income tax. "You couldn't really bargain with people who saw themselves losing their seats if they voted for the income tax," Byrne reflected years later. As an example, Byrne recalled that long after he left office, he was at a dinner with Thomas Deverin, a Democratic assemblyman who had represented a district which would benefit as much as any district from a state income tax, but had voted against the tax. As they reminisced about the income tax battle, Deverin told Byrne, "Governor, they would've taken me off the ticket if I had voted for it."[40]

Despite the three-to-one majorities held by the Democrats in both houses of the legislature, nearly three-quarters of the new seats they had picked up in the previous November were in traditionally Republican suburban or rural areas, typically with larger proportions of more moderate or conservative voters than found in districts with higher shares of Democrats. "The difficulty in the Assembly," Lew Kaden later said, "was just getting over the hurdle of so many members of the Assembly thinking it would spell the death of their political career if they voted for the tax."[41] Some legislators from traditionally Democratic districts resisted voting for a tax that they felt would provoke blue-collar constituents struggling in the economic recession. Throughout the tax battle, the AFL-CIO under Charles Marciante consistently opposed any income tax or increase in the sales tax, thus increasing the political risks to Democratic legislators dependent on the support of organized labor.

Ironically, the large Democratic majority in the Assembly undermined the ability of the leadership to enforce discipline to get the 41 votes needed for passage. "What happens with large majorities," Byrne later reflected, "is nobody feels obligated to vote on any particular measure so you put a bill on the board and the guy who sees it as unpopular . . . will say, 'Well you've got 66 Democrats, you don't need me.' And so enough people say that, you don't have 41 votes. And that became a problem, especially on the income tax."[42] Betty Wilson, the Democratic Assembly Whip whose leadership post entailed lining up the reluctant final votes needed for passage, had a similar view: "there was such an abundance of Democrats a lot of people felt . . . you don't need me, you can get someone else, so that was always a challenge."[43]

In the last week of June, at the end of a series of joint public hearings held by the Senate and Assembly taxation committees, it appeared that relations between Democrats in the two houses had frayed; five assemblymen issued a statement criticizing Senate President Pat Dodd for deferring action on school funding reform until the Assembly had passed the income tax. Growing tension between the Assembly and the Senate leadership would continue to hamper the subsequent debate. The contrasting ideas for alternative revenue-raising measures had fragmented support for the Byrne package of bills, which according to one account "appear to be bogging down in legislative resistance and inertia."[44]

On July 15, the legislation authorizing the income tax was approved in the Assembly by a vote of 41 to 38, the minimum needed for passage in the eighty-member body. Republicans claimed that some of the final Assembly votes were secured through "deals" to steer more funds to specific districts of key legislators, a charge that the Byrne team denied while conceding that negotiations had redirected aid to towns, notably in Hudson, Essex, and Bergen counties, where legislators had withheld support for the tax. Richard Codey, then a 28-year-old Assemblyman representing the Essex County communities of the Byrne family's roots, later disclosed that he received a Saturday night visit to his home from Alan Sagner and phone calls from Essex Democratic chairman Harry Lerner and other influential Democrats lobbying for his support of the tax. When Codey came to Trenton for the scheduled vote, he met with Byrne and received assurances that the City of Orange would receive significantly more state aid in the revised package of taxes, and consequently agreed to vote for the tax. Similar agreements were reached with others who had wavered in their support.[45]

But when the Assembly bill was considered in the Senate, new objections and proposed alternatives surfaced. Some senators argued for additional studies beyond those of the Byrne task force and the respective legislative committees. Democratic Senator Raymond Garramone, who had been elected to his first term from an affluent Bergen County district in the 1973 Byrne landslide, emerged as a vocal opponent of the income tax, suggesting that additional time was needed for evaluating options and that the broad tax reform proposal be scaled down to increasing state aid to only those districts most deficient in performance. "The decision in the *Robinson* case should not serve as a vehicle for massive changes in the tax structure without the necessity being clearly studied and demonstrated," Garramone said. "We neither need nor desire a State income tax."[46]

Two of the most difficult senators to persuade were Frank "Pat" Dodd of Essex and Jim Dugan of Hudson, both of whom ostensibly owed political favors to Byrne. After his election, Byrne had expressed his preference for Dodd, then in his mid-30s, to be elected as Senate president rather than older Democrats. "I didn't know Pat Dodd well and he had backed Ralph DeRose over me in the Democratic primary," Byrne later said. "But I thought he'd be more energetic than other Democrats who were interested in leading the Senate."[47] Yet Dodd apparently attributed his election to head the Senate more to his own abilities in lining up the backing of his fellow Democrats than to the new governor's intervention. Dodd's claim on the position also was bolstered by his representation of the state's largest Democratic county, along with his seniority in years of service among the other prospective leadership candidates.[48]

Dugan's position was more nuanced. He had been a member of the Cahill tax study commission that recommended both an income tax and a statewide property tax in its 1972 report, and indeed said in a later interview that "all thinking people" knew that an income tax was inevitable. Dugan had been named as state Democratic chair with Byrne's support in recognition of the critical role Hudson had played in Byrne's securing the party's nomination; he had clashed, however, with Byrne's inner circle during the campaign, conflicts which continued after Byrne's inauguration in his prickly relationships with Treasurer Leone and Counsel Kaden. Among other conflicts, Dugan chafed at what he viewed as their dismissive attitude toward what he felt were legitimate requests by county leaders for patronage and other traditional political favors, along with what he described as their tendency to treat the legislature as an "appendage" unworthy of consultation in developing the administration's policy and political strategy. On the tax and the fiscal reform program, Dugan felt that Byrne's proposed legislative package, which included some twenty separate bills, was "too complicated" and that a simple surcharge on the federal income levy would have a better chance of passage in the Senate.[49]

Initially, Dodd did not indicate his own position on the Byrne program in the private internal discussion in the Democratic caucus but, after the meeting adjourned, he held a press conference where he firmly came out in opposition. Dugan publicly announced his support for the Byrne package, but then unveiled his own variation based on imposing a surcharge on the federal income tax, thus further complicating the choices.[50]

Although attempts were made to persuade wavering Senators to support
the governor's bill, Byrne generally avoided direct meetings with legislators
in order to avoid negotiations that might be interpreted as quid pro quo bargaining for a vote.[51] The Senate's consideration soon became embroiled in
debate over the alternatives: some wanted a statewide property or payroll tax
to either replace or complement the proposed income tax; others suggested
various ways to structure an income tax or to determine its rates and coverage; and still others rejected any new tax at all.[52] Without any agreement on
either the bill passed in the Assembly or another alternative, the Senate failed
to take a vote on any legislation.

After the Senate adjourned, Byrne held a press conference. "The Senate
has said . . . that they will not pass a package which includes an income tax,"
he said in reply to a question. "Now the ball, as the expression goes, is in the
hands of the Senate and now it is time to see what they will pass."[53] Byrne
continued to press for a compromise in the ensuing weeks and months, but
was unable to obtain the needed commitments to pass the tax in the Senate.[54]
Years later, Byrne reflected that accepting a mix of smaller revenue measures
without confronting the need for long-term tax reform would have been a
concession of defeat that was not within his nature. "It just wasn't me," he
said. "I wanted to get it done."[55]

At the beginning of December, as the *Robinson* deadline at the end of
the year approached, the press reported that Democrats had reached apparent agreement on a $700-million tax package that included a 5 percent
surcharge on the federal income tax; a one cent hike in the sales tax; and
a statewide property tax. The tentative agreement to accept the federal surcharge was described, according to the *New York Times*, "as a victory, of
sorts," for Senator Dugan, "who has managed to block many of Governor
Byrne's most significant proposals."[56] But other Senate Democrats rebelled;
as Jeffrey Laurenti, the aide to Senator Joseph Merlino recalled, "on the day
that Dugan unveiled the proposal, we went into immediate combat mode to
discredit it. Joe Merlino was very active on that."[57] And the Dugan plan ran
into further hurdles. "The Treasury analyzed the Senate plan in December,"
Cliff Goldman recalled, "and reported that its revenues were inadequate for
the increased spending and that compromising with it to end the political
aggravation would be a bad mistake, as it would require the Governor to propose another tax increase a few months later in his budget and would make
everyone, including the senators, look inept."[58]

On December 20, after emerging from a final caucus to seek an agreement
before the deadline of December 31 set in *Robinson*, Senate President Dodd
briefed the press on the impasse among the Democrats: "I don't know what
to tell you. We're hopelessly deadlocked." Responding to a question as to
whether he had considered keeping the Senate in session over the holidays,

Dodd described the tense atmosphere: "It would make no sense. Tempers are frayed, we are all very frustrated. We can hardly sit down in the same room together anymore. I have just spent the most disappointing day ever in my public life."[59]

Also on December 20, Republican Senator Raymond Bateman, a former Senate president and the author of the state's school funding formula that the Weintraub court had found unconstitutional, wrote a "Dear Dick" letter to Chief Justice Hughes, with whom Bateman had developed a close friendship while Hughes was governor despite their differences in party. Bateman urged that the Court exercise restraint in forcing the legislature and the administration to resolve the issue by the new year. "Realistically, I don't believe the present time deadline is fair to Governor Byrne and his legislature," Bateman wrote. "In no way can they build public understanding and confidence in a plan-by-shotgun. To force an educational plan that is not ready will undermine the system."[60]

The legislature returned from its holiday break on January 6, 1975, and the bill that had previously passed the Assembly was amended in a Senate committee to provide a 5.5 percent surcharge on the federal income tax. It was defeated, however, in a Senate floor vote, with 15 for passage and 24 against.[61]

After the first Byrne tax reform proposal failed to pass, Democrats in the legislature began to develop a more independent approach from the administration, conducting their own research and holding a series of public hearings across the state. "Although we had guidance from the governor's office," Assemblyman Burstein later recounted, "we had to place some focus on the legislative process at arm's length from the governor's office. . . . The relationship between the governor's office and the legislature, not only on education issues, but on other matters, began to take on a tension that probably militated against full cooperation."[62] To some extent, the conflicts reflected a feeling among some legislative leaders that Byrne's key deputies had failed to demonstrate sufficient deference and respect—either to the legislature as an institution or to them personally. "Personality clashes began to take place," Burstein remembered, "as issue by issue arose between the group around the governor—the governor's staff, the governor's counsel—in dealing with legislative leadership. But the one fault they that they had as a collective body was a disdain for the legislative leadership. And that was a mistake. That was a mistake."[63]

Meanwhile, soon after the *Robinson* deadline had passed, the Supreme Court solicited motions from the parties in the litigation on what action it should take. Byrne submitted a brief arguing for an injunction to halt the distribution of existing school aid under the current formula while the Senate—in asking for a delay in the Court acting on its own to enforce *Robinson*—also cautioned the justices against imposing any relief that would further interfere with its legislative prerogatives.

On January 23, the Court issued its opinion declaring that "it would be inequitable and, indeed, chaotic as to many school districts to effect financial changes for the 1975–76 school year at this late date and on such short notice."[64] A majority of the justices thus decided to allow more time for legislative action, permitting the existing school aid formula declared unconstitutional in 1973 to remain in place for another year. The decision brought a sharp dissent from Justice Morris Pashman, who wrote that "the period of time seemed more than ample" for the legislature to act since the first decision was issued, and that the failure of the Court to impose a remedy "at this late date is to become a party to the perpetuation of the very wrongs which the Court denounced two years ago."[65] The ruling also disappointed Byrne and others who hoped that the Court would give a clear signal of its intent to enforce the first *Robinson* decision. "Regardless of intent, many officials interpreted the year's delay as a sign of retreat and indecision," wrote one academic analyst. "The Hughes Court, they concluded, would temporize and retire when faced with difficult issues rather than push forthrightly ahead."[66]

The Court's decision reduced the pressure to raise new revenues to meet the looming major deficit in the state budget for the new fiscal year commencing in July 1975. Just days after the Court's ruling giving another year for a legislative response to *Robinson*, the governor unveiled what he called a "rock-bottom" state budget of $2.82 billion, representing only a 1.8 percent increase over the prior year at a time when the inflation rate was over 10 percent.

Nonetheless, Byrne said the new budget would demand "personal sacrifices" and hikes in tax revenues to compensate for a deficit of $487 million largely caused by the state's continuing economic slide. "We have reached a moment of reckoning," Byrne said in his message to the legislature in February 1975. "Our tax revenues will no longer support the current levels of state aid." Without the income tax or another source for substantial new revenue, Byrne warned he would have to cut $180 million in state school aid, forcing some municipalities to make up for the lost revenues by enacting property tax increases that would "drive some people from their homes."[67]

He also challenged the opponents of the income tax by pointing to the overall impact that the state's tax structure was having in shifting costs to local governments and to those taxpayers with limited means. "It is time we stopped pretending that the failure to enact an income tax has been a good thing—when that failure has meant massive increases in local property taxes over the last 10 years," he contended. "The legislature has won credit for avoiding an income tax, but the poor and the middle classes, the senior citizens, the retired and the unemployed pay the bill for that credit."[68]

Byrne then reaffirmed his support for his income tax proposal that the Assembly had passed in 1974. Nonetheless, opponents to his plan introduced an alternative revenue-raising package, including increases of one cent in the sales tax; two cents in the gasoline tax; and a 2 percent hike in the corporate income tax (which would have made New Jersey's corporate tax rate higher than that of New York and Pennsylvania.)[69] He then went on to outline other proposed reductions needed to balance the budget, including laying off state government employees and imposing a wage freeze; increasing college tuitions by 50 percent; and ending most commuter bus subsidies and reducing rail services by half, along with hiking fares for the remaining services by 55 percent.[70]

Rather than submit a budget with the prospective cuts he had detailed, Byrne submitted one for the fiscal year beginning on July 1 that assumed revenue levels that could only be attained with the passage of the income tax. He thereby tied the tax not only to the need to comply with the "T&E" mandate in *Robinson*, but also to funding the state's other operating programs in areas outside public education, such as subsidies for rail and bus commuters and aid to higher education.[71] In another effort to develop an acceptable compromise, Byrne suggested that he would support a 2 percent cut in the sales tax, reducing it from 5 to 3 percent, if the income tax was approved.[72]

The proposed budget brought expected opposition from affected constituencies—a reaction that the governor welcomed to build momentum for tax reform. On February 13, when he attempted to talk to 2,000 state employees demonstrating in front of the State House, he was shouted down by chants of "One term for Byrne, one term for Byrne" and cut short his comments after less than a minute and retreated inside the building. "Feelings were so strong," according to a newspaper account, "that Mr. Byrne had to run a gauntlet of abuse and catcalls along the main State House corridor as he made his way back to his office through lines of demonstrators."[73] Later, somewhat more temperate protests were heard from school boards, college students and commuters who would feel the brunt of the budget cutbacks.

For a time, it appeared that the strategy of linking the budget deficit with the need to fund the added school aid to comply with *Robinson* was helping to develop the needed support for the income tax. In March, Byrne stated that there was now a "strong consensus" among the Democratic leadership in both the Senate and the Assembly for an income tax. "I think we're closer to an income tax in New Jersey today," Byrne said, "than we have ever been." According to one press article published in March, "Democratic leaders report that there is a good chance that the Senate will reverse itself and pass an income tax next month."[74]

Prospects for passage were also strengthened when the Supreme Court signaled that it was reconsidering its decision of January to give the legislature additional time to fund the new school aid required under *Robinson*. The sharp criticism of the Court's decision apparently had an impact on Chief Justice Hughes and the other justices who had voted for the delay. On February 25, Byrne submitted another brief to the Court, asking that the deadline be moved up to July 1 and that, if the legislature still was unable to act, the Court order the redistribution of $600 million in existing school aid.[75] In opposition, the state Senate, through its counsel, David Goldberg, argued that the Court should stay out of the school aid issue because its resolution was "not judicial in nature."[76]

At the oral argument on March 18, Byrne became the only New Jersey governor to personally argue a case before the state Supreme Court. The hearing took place in the stately wood-paneled court room in which the Court had met for over a century, with the seven justices sitting on a raised platform before the attorneys arguing the respective sides and an audience of some 300. "I had looked forward to the oral argument," Byrne later recalled. "I had enjoyed arguing before the Court when I was Essex County prosecutor, and think I probably made more appearances before the Court during that time than any other lawyer."[77] After the justices entered, the Court's clerk announced the case and Byrne introduced himself. "I am here pro se [on my own behalf]," he began, "because I think I have a point of view and have a fundamental approach that governs my view of this court's function. . . . I urge the court not to let an unconstitutional system to prevail. I completely reject the idea that this court should back away from the decision that virtually no one disagrees with."[78]

To his surprise—and unlike the normal process at oral arguments during which attorneys generally are interrupted by questioning soon after they begin speaking—none of the justices asked Byrne a question during his twenty-minute presentation, apparently having previously agreed to demonstrate deference to his office and acknowledge the significance of his appearance. "I was disappointed that they didn't ask me questions," Byrne later said. "I always enjoyed the questioning when I had appeared before the Court, and had prepared for a couple days to respond to questions." After he concluded his argument, Byrne asked for, and received, permission to leave the court room, allowing his counsel Lew Kaden to remain to represent him in what would become a highly unusual all-day hearing.[79]

The Court issued its decision in May 1975. It ordered that, if the legislature failed to enact a new school aid formula, $300 million in state minimum support aid to school districts for the 1976–1977 school year be redistributed from more affluent districts to poorer districts. Dismissing objections that it was usurping the legislature's constitutional spending authority, the Court declared that it was simply redirecting money that had already been appropriated. Still, two justices dissented, arguing that the rationale of the majority opinion was based on a "diaphanous thread" that could lead to court-directed appropriations on other issues that would undermine the traditional separation of the branches.[80]

Although the order indicated a somewhat tougher stance by the Court than its prior ruling, it had little practical effect in increasing pressure for legislative action because redistribution of the minimal state aid that wealthier districts received would have relatively little impact on school budgets. The ruling also led some legislators to believe that the Court ultimately would impose its own solution to *Robinson*, thus allowing them to avoid any responsibility for voting for an unpopular new tax.

On Wednesday, June 18, 1975, Byrne addressed the special session of the legislature that he had called, declaring that with only twelve days left before the start of the fiscal year, "there was now a crisis in New Jersey" resulting from the Senate's failure to pass the income tax. The governor called again for approval of his tax program, noting that the state needed $412 million to meet his proposed budget and an additional $321 million to finance additional school aid. He criticized those in the legislature who opposed enacting any new revenue measures, stating that this would result in "drastic" and "irresponsible" cuts to "a budget that has already been stripped of fat." He rejected any proposed "patchwork of nuisance taxes" to fund the budget deficit alone and any attempt by the legislature "to walk away from the problem of funding the schools in the hopes that it will somehow be easier to deal with at another time."[81]

Before the vote, Byrne's threat to cut the budget if the tax was not approved had provoked sharp criticism. Senate Republican Minority Leader Alfred Beadleston derided it as "blackmail." Yet some of the most searing comments came from the governor's fellow Democrats. Senator Raymond Zane said of Byrne, "Does he expect me to get down on my knees and beg for mercy? Just let him try it." Senator Carmen Orechio predicted that "taxpayers by the busload will be down here demanding his resignation. The whole thing would blow up in his face." Senator Eugene Bedell branded the strategy as "scare tactics and hypocritical."[82] Bedell also charged that Byrne's aides Lewis Kaden and Jerry English had "offered everything under the sun" in return for his vote, a claim that Byrne asked Attorney General William Hyland to review to determine if it constituted criminal libel.

Despite the Court's order and the optimism that Senate leaders had expressed weeks before, the Senate again rejected the income tax. In a vote on June 27, seventeen senators voted for passage and twenty-one voted against, with ten Democrats joining ten Republicans and one independent in voting against the bill. Immediately after the vote, the Governor cut his proposed budget by $384 million through a line-item veto of the appropriations act—an action that he had previously warned he would be forced to take to meet his constitutional responsibility to certify that anticipated state expenditures did not exceed anticipated revenues.[83] Byrne directed his executive secretary Charles Carella to personally deliver the veto message to the Senate chamber escorted by state troopers; as they made their way to the rostrum, the troopers accidentally knocked a Senate aide to the floor, worsening an already tense situation over what senators called "strong-arm tactics on the part of the Governor's office." Senate President Dodd stated that he would refuse to talk to Byrne as a result of the disruption in the Senate.[84]

Summing up the chain of events that had led to Byrne's veto, the *New York Times* reported: "The legislative tax battle in New Jersey between Governor Byrne and the huge Democratic majorities in both houses of the legislature culminated early this morning in bitter recriminations, partisan divisiveness and impotence. . . . Relations that were never good between Mr. Byrne and the Democratic majorities have now degenerated to the point where political leaders here believe there is . . . little chance of any rapprochement between the Governor and the Legislators."[85]

But a few weeks later, tempers had cooled to the point where Byrne and the leadership could agree on a package of taxes to raise sufficient revenues to restore nearly $250 million of the $384 million in spending that had previously been vetoed.[86] In the rush to plug the budget hole, the package included an "unearned income tax" on income from dividends, interest, pensions, and other nonwage sources, which disproportionately impacted wealthier taxpayers. One press account described the acceptance of the tax package by Byrne as a "retreat," adding "the incentive for an income tax has been largely removed."[87]

When the legislature reconvened in the fall of 1975, it deferred renewing the divisive debate over the income tax. The Joint Education Committee turned to draft legislation to define the scope of the state's obligation to guarantee the "thorough and efficient" education that had been mandated, but not spelled out, in the first *Robinson* decision. By outlining the extent and potential cost of the state's responsibility, it was hoped that the legislature could then determine if the Court would find it acceptable as providing the level of educational opportunity set forth in *Robinson*.

Developed after extensive research and public hearings, the joint committee's bill, which the governor signed into law on September 29 as the Public School Education Act of 1975, was less ambitious than the original Byrne plan.[88] It increased the state share of school spending from 31 percent to 38 percent (compared with the 50 percent share projected in the Governor's 1974 proposal), and reduced the overall revenues to be raised by new taxes by $100 million. It also weakened the equalization guarantee of the Byrne bill, allowing wealthier districts to continue to outspend their less affluent peers. With some reluctance, the committee also accepted the Department of Education's argument, aggressively endorsed by the state teachers union, that the quality of school performance be judged only by a subjective state evaluation by the Department, rather than by more objective criteria, such as through teacher evaluations and student testing.[89]

The compromises accepted by the committee in hopes of broadening support in the legislature provoked a split with the school reform advocates who had brought the original lawsuit in *Robinson*. They argued that the reductions in state support and the weaker equalization effort would "ensure that spending in the poorest districts could never catch up to spending in the richest."[90] (It was an argument that, after Byrne had left office, the state Supreme Court endorsed in a new round of litigation under the title *Abbott v. Burke*.) In November, at the Supreme Court hearing held to consider the constitutionality of the new law, Byrne's legal team, including Attorney General Hyland and Counsel Kaden, asked the Court to find that the law did meet the "T&E" benchmark of *Robinson*.

The Court took nearly two months to issue its decision, signaling the divisions among the justices that were evident in the opinions released on January 30, 1976. The majority opinion was unsigned; four justices wrote their own opinions; two others concurred with only parts of the majority opinion; and one, Justice Pashman, dissented. The Court's majority found that the new school aid formula would be constitutional if the legislature enacted measures to fully fund it. It concluded that the Act sufficiently addressed previous disparities in per-pupil expenditures and that any need for modification would become apparent after implementation.[91] Chief Justice Hughes wrote in his own opinion of his "personal doubts" that the new funding plan satisfied the T&E mandate set forth in *Robinson*, but he nonetheless joined the majority, explaining that he did so out of respect for the separation of powers and to allow time for the new school financing system to be evaluated after it went into operation.[92]

Six weeks after the Supreme Court decision upholding the 'T&E" law, the Court heard five hours of arguments on what action it should take if the legislature failed to fund the new formula. Among the several interests represented before the Court, the state Senate contended that the Court should not interfere with the legislature's authority while others asked that the Court, on its own, impose a new tax. Byrne's counsel Lew Kaden argued that the Court should not tolerate any further delay in imposing its own remedy to enforce *Robinson*. Ultimately, in a decision released on May 13, 1976, the Court declared: "On and after July 1, 1976, every public officer, state, county, or municipal, is hereby enjoined from expending any funds for the support of any free public school."[93]

Meanwhile, after the Court's rather half-hearted approval in January of the new funding system, the legislature's attention returned to the divisive issue of how to raise the money to implement it. Because the Assembly was constitutionally specified as the house to originate all revenue measures, the Assembly Taxation Committee took the lead, reviewing components of the Byrne program introduced in 1974 and other proposals that had been independently introduced. Ultimately, it produced a package of fifteen separate pieces of legislation, including an income tax; homestead rebates to reduce property taxes; a state revenue–sharing program; state assumption of the costs of local tax benefits given senior citizens and veterans; and caps on spending increases by local governments and the state.[94]

To counter the perception that new tax revenue would fuel expansion of the state government, the package also proposed a referendum seeking voter approval to amend the state constitution to dedicate all new revenues either to reduce property taxes or to pay for the additional aid provided under the Public School Education Act of 1975. "In principle, I opposed dedicating funds for specific purposes," Byrne later reflected, "since dedication took away the flexibility to respond to changing needs. But I recognized that dedication of the new tax was the only way we could get it passed."[95] The original gross income tax proposed by the committee was projected to raise about $950 million in its first year, with slightly graduated rates ranging from 2 to 4 percent (compared to the rates of 1.5 to 8 percent of the 1974 Byrne plan).[96]

Significantly, the legislative package included two provisions would later have major political impacts. It provided that the income tax would expire on June 30, 1978, thereby ensuring that the November 1977 election for governor and the legislature would become a de facto referendum on the merits of continuing the tax. And it also provided for homestead rebates to be paid directly to property taxpayers, foregoing such indirect options as funneling the money through local governments or crediting property tax bills. The direct payment of rebates to taxpayers had been previously advocated by Treasurer Leone who, in earlier overruling a recommendation by his own staff and those in the Department of Community Affairs that the rebates be provided through a credit on property tax bills mailed by municipalities, had scrawled a response: "Can't we do it so the state sends the checks directly to the taxpayers. That move is crucial."[97]

After a long debate continuing into the early morning, the key components of the committee's package, including the income tax, were approved by the Assembly on March 15, 1976. Again, however, the Assembly tax plan ran into stiff opposition as it was considered by the Senate. Tax protesters began running newspaper ads listing home phone numbers of senators, with one member stating he had received 150 calls on the night before the tax vote, all but six in opposition to the tax.[98] Anti-tax demonstrations were held throughout the state, including on the sidewalk in front of the governor's residence in Princeton and at the State House in Trenton on days of scheduled committee hearings or votes on the tax. "There were always protestors at the State House," Deputy Treasurer Goldman recalled years later, "particularly an apparently nude woman in a barrel with a guy in a big stove pipe hat."[99]

By the time the Senate finally scheduled a floor vote on the income tax for June 17, the Assembly bill had been radically amended to provide a flat tax of 1.5 percent without any graduation—a rate projected to raise only enough tax revenue to meet the T&E benchmark without any other property tax relief. The amended bill was able to garner the bare majority of 21 votes to pass the Senate. "In essence, the only thing that remained," Assemblyman Van Wagner, a sponsor of the Assembly bill, later wrote, "was a flat-rate tax with none of the tax reform measures."[100]

To be sure, the Senate's passage of the bill on June 17 marked its first approval of any income tax measure, but its achievement had a short shelf life. The minimalist bill approved by the Senate angered pro-tax Assembly members, and a few days later they, aligned with opponents of any tax, decisively rejected the Senate's 1.5 percent flat tax by a resounding 77-2 vote.[101] A bipartisan conference committee was then appointed by the leadership of both houses to develop a compromise, but after three days of discussion this group failed to reach any consensus on how to bridge the gap between the Senate and Assembly.[102]

On June 28, Jonathan Goldstein, the U.S. Attorney for New Jersey, and the thirty-one-member Republican minority in the Assembly filed separate legal actions in the U.S. District Court seeking an order to vacate the state Supreme Court's injunction closing the schools as of July 1. The highly unusual move by the U.S. Attorney—intervening in an already pending lawsuit filed by the New Jersey School Boards Association—named the Governor, Treasurer Leone, and other state officials as defendants. In a statement to the press, Goldstein said that Byrne had "abdicated his responsibility," and "at the Governor's urging" the state Supreme Court had "by judicial fiat" closed the schools—an action he called "unconscionable."[103] In his brief, Goldstein stated that the complaint was filed in the name of the federal government to challenge "the right of any state to totally abandon its responsibilities in the crucial area of education," contending that there was a guarantee under the U.S. Constitution for every state to insure "that its citizens receive at least minimal education." Paul Tractenberg, the director of the Education Law Center at Rutgers Law School, which had filed briefs in support of the *Robinson* goals, branded Goldstein's intervention as "politically motivated" and asked the Court to dismiss the action for lack of jurisdiction, an argument echoed by Attorney General Hyland and Counsel Kaden in behalf of the state and the governor. The Assembly Republicans independently argued that the state Supreme Court's injunction usurped the legislature's constitutional authority over state appropriations.[104]

After the actions were filed, Chief Judge Lawrence Whipple of the federal district court in New Jersey ordered a hearing for June 30, the last day before the order closing the schools would go into effect at midnight. He also directed that the cases, along with those previously filed by local municipalities and school boards, be heard in a rare *en banc* hearing before all eleven district court judges.[105] "It was an enormously complex and celebrated case," Lew Kaden recalled years later, "in which we argued for virtually a full day in Newark and then the court caucused. . . . They came back from their caucus and Judge Whipple . . . read a one-paragraph denial [of Goldstein's motion seeking to vacate the state Supreme Court's order closing the schools] on behalf of nine of the judges and then Judge Lacey and Judge Stern read lengthy dissents which obviously had been prepared before the argument because not enough time had passed to draft them during the judges' caucus."[106] When news of the decision reached the State House at 4:30 in the afternoon, one newspaper reporter wrote that repeated shouts of "nine to two!" were heard as legislators, lobbyists, and others called out to each other news of the court's vote.[107] The Assembly, which constitutionally was required to initiate tax legislation, then went into session that would continue through the night, passing the midnight deadline set by the Supreme Court order closing the schools. As the negotiations between the Assembly and Senate Democratic leaders proceeded, tempers became frayed. At five o'clock in the morning, Senate Majority Leader Matthew Feldman issued what one newspaper reported as an "ultimatum" to his Assembly counterparts: "Either you take the 1.5 to 2.5 percent tax or we will go home."[108] At 7:30 a.m., without any resolution, the two houses adjourned.

In the absence of any action by the federal courts to intervene, the state Supreme Court's order closing the schools had gone into effect at midnight on June 30. After failing to find a compromise, the legislature resumed its attempts to reopen the schools, with the Assembly reconvening at 4:30 in the afternoon of July 1. The marathon sessions took place during a heat wave in legislative chambers then without air conditioning. "It was really unbearable in the chambers," Senator Ray Bateman later recalled, "Every time we could, we adjourned to take a break and run downstairs where it was cooler."[109] In a legislature that typically commuted to Trenton on two days each week, many legislators slept in their chairs as the sessions dragged on through the night and into the next morning. Although the Democratic leaders lacked the votes to pass the income tax, they forced votes—to demonstrate that alternative revenue measures also had limited support—on two bills to increase the sales tax, with only 30 votes recorded for a one-cent increase and 10 votes for a two-cent hike. The Assembly adjourned at 8:20 the next morning, with Republican Leader Thomas Kean telling the press, "We're just too tired to do anything right now."[110]

On the following afternoon, the Assembly reconvened, seeking to resolve the crisis through party caucuses and sessions that again lasted through the night. In the face of continued opposition in the Senate to the prior tax measure passed by the full Assembly, the Assembly Taxation Committee amended the bill, scaling it down to an income tax with rates ranging from 1 to 3 percent; a floor vote on the revised bill, however, received only 31 votes, ten short of passage.[111] To attract votes from legislators representing more affluent districts, amendments were then added to continue existing aid for busing and special education; retain state funding of teachers' pensions; and expand state aid to a large group of smaller cities and less affluent suburbs, somewhat weakening the initial goal of equalizing school spending throughout the state.

The Democratic leadership believed that it had commitments for 40 votes, just one short of passage, and brought the income tax bill up for a vote at 7:30 in the morning. With the electronic "board" in the chamber signifying by red and green lights who had recorded their votes, Democratic leaders focused their efforts on Assemblyman Vincent "Ozzie" Pellechia of Passaic County. Pellechia's local newspaper, the *Herald-News*, had long been a staunch opponent of any income tax, and its editorials against Pellechia's fellow Democratic assemblyman, Herbert Klein, had contributed to Klein's defeat in the November 1975 election. "The pressure on Pellechia was visible," one reporter wrote. "Beads of perspiration stood out on his forehead. His hands shook." Another account reported that a "white-faced" Pellechia "appeared ready to collapse."[112] But Pellechia ultimately held firm, "I can't do it. I can't do it," he pleaded as his fellow Democrats huddled around him. "I come from a district where I'm dead if I vote for this."[113] As the time for voting reached over an hour, Republicans loudly called for the Speaker to end the vote. Unable to resolve the impasse in which there were only 37 committed votes of the 41 needed for passage, the Assembly adjourned for the July 4 holiday weekend celebrating the nation's Bicentennial.

Before the Assembly returned to Trenton on the following Tuesday, Democratic leaders worked to craft a package to secure the remaining votes for passage. Among other revisions, the amounts for property tax relief and homestead rebates were increased; a commitment was made to convene a tax convention to evaluate the impact of the income tax after it went into operation; and increased state aid for school construction was pledged. When the income tax again came up for a vote by the full Assembly on July 7, it was approved by a 41 to 38 vote, with thirty-nine Democrats and two Republicans voting for passage.[114]

After the final vote was posted, Byrne entered the chamber appearing, as one reporter wrote, "tired, almost grim" and congratulated the Democratic leadership.[115] "Virtually every dollar raised by the Assembly program," Byrne later stated in a press release, "goes to property-tax relief. It does not add to government spending; it solely provides a fairer way to raise that money."[116] Soon after the Assembly completed action, at nine o'clock on that same evening, the Senate approved the tax by a twenty-two to eighteen margin, with Senator Wayne Dumont the only Republican supporting the measure.

About an hour after the Senate vote, at one minute after ten p.m., Byrne signed the bill into law in a hastily convened gathering in his office, distributing fifteen pens he used for his signature to the legislators who had played key roles in enacting the income tax.[117] "This is the toughest task that the Legislature has faced in the last century," Byrne said in signing the legislation making New Jersey the 43rd state in the nation with an income tax. "Although it's not a giant leap toward real true tax reform, it nevertheless is a significant contribution. Governors have been waiting a long time for this."[118]

After he signed the bill, Byrne read a letter that he said he was sending to the Supreme Court:

Dear Chief Justice Hughes and Associate Justices:

I have today signed into law Assembly Bill 1513, imposing a tax on personal income. The enactment of the bill provides sufficient funds for the full implementation of the Public Education Act of 1975, Chapter 212, Laws of 1975.

I respectfully request that the court withdraw the injunction issued in Robinson v. Cahill against expenditure of funds for free public schools on the basis that the Legislature has acted to fund in full Chapter 212, Laws of 1975, which this court has held to meet the requirements of the New Jersey Constitution. Withdrawal of the injunction will permit the regular operation of public education programs in the State of New Jersey under statutes that insure, as of this date, a thorough and efficient system of education for the people of New Jersey.

Very truly yours,
Brendan T. Byrne
Governor[119]

On the next day, the Court vacated its order imposing the injunction closing the schools.[120]

Without Byrne's decision to tie his political future to the implementation of *Robinson*, it is doubtful that the Court on its own could have withstood the growing public and legislative pressure to retreat from on its ruling as the September 1976 school year approached with the schools continuing to be shuttered. "Probably the most important reason that *Robinson* did not stimulate a legislative assault on the judiciary," one scholar concluded, "was that the lawmakers would have had to take on not only the justices, but also the governor."[121]

The signing of the income tax into law brought only a brief sense of relief for the governor. Most political analysts thought the protracted struggle had dealt a fatal blow to Byrne's prospects for reelection in the following year. An opinion piece published a few days after the tax became law had the tone of a political obituary: "Brendan T. Byrne, a former gubernatorial aide, prosecutor and judge now serving in his first elective office, is plainly not a political animal. He is uncomfortable in purely political situations and finds arm-twisting, cajolery and wheeling-dealing repugnant. It is simply not his style, and it has hurt his political standing in the state."[122] In the week after he signed the legislation, Byrne suffered another political embarrassment when he attended the Democratic National Convention in Manhattan, with the state delegation led by Senator Dugan rather than the incumbent governor.

But the ultimate verdict on the income tax would be political. "Inevitably, the sunset provision would turn the 1977 gubernatorial campaign into a referendum on the income tax," one commentator noted, "and the legislature would almost certainly allow the hard-won tax to die unless somebody won the governorship on a pro-income tax platform."[123] Byrne's decision to enter the race ensured that the debate on the tax would be waged on his terms. While he weighed whether to run, he issued the challenge that later became the theme of his campaign. "Show us a better way," he declared in his January 1977 annual message to the legislature. "It is not enough to say you are for tax reform, but not this tax reform. It is not enough to hint of a secret plan to be unveiled later or to promise that some fiscal magic will reveal itself in the months ahead."[124]

Chapter 9

Atlantic City

"Keep Your Filthy Hands Out of Atlantic City"

In August 1964, Brendan Byrne, then president of the Public Utilities Commission, took his 10-year-old son Tom with him to the Democratic National Convention in Atlantic City. "It was a disaster," Byrne summed up years later, "because Atlantic City's dirty little secret was broadcast to the world—that it had deteriorated to the point that it was an embarrassment. From then on, Atlantic City was no place to go."[1]

The City had succeeded in securing the Convention the year before by pledging a mere $600,000 to the Democratic National Committee in the era before the conventions were highly sought after by cities throughout the country. President Kennedy's preferred site for the convention had been San Francisco, but after the Republicans announced San Francisco as their own choice, the Democrats settled on Atlantic City. Following Kennedy's November 1963 assassination, President Johnson also reportedly tried, as William F. Buckley, Jr., wrote at the time, "to change the site of this weary scenario to another city, a city of greater class."[2]

City and state officials of both parties, led by powerful Atlantic County Republican Senator Frank S. Farley and Democratic Governor Richard Hughes, had joined forces to lobby for the Convention, hoping that the national attention it drew would revive interest in the fading resort. But the decision backfired badly. Governor Hughes himself contracted a case of food poisoning so severe that he was unable to attend the closing reception of the Convention with President Johnson, and then was hospitalized for ten days.[3] Ironically, the convention debacle had one positive result: it provoked new discussion of what could be done to revive the tawdry city. "It was a mistake, but it also brought it to a head," said Byrne. "As a catalyst for revival, it was a good thing."[4]

During the early years of New Jersey's colonial era, the island on which the town of Atlantic City would develop—known by the Lenni Lenape Native Americans as "absegami" or "little water," and later modified by Europeans to "Absecon"—was viewed as unfit for long-term settlement, largely due to its lack of a natural harbor, marshland teeming with mosquitoes, and sandy soil unsuitable for farming.[5] Even as late as 1850, when Cape May to the south had become one of the nation's premier summer resorts, Absecon Island still had only seven permanent dwellings—all but one owned by descendants of Jeremiah Leeds, the first white man to build a permanent structure on the island.[6]

Atlantic City's development was largely due to the vision and persistence of Jonathan Pitney, a young doctor who in 1820 relocated to Absecon Island from his native Morris County. Intrigued by the island's potential as a health resort but recognizing that access for visitors had to be improved, Pitney successfully lobbied the state legislature to obtain a railroad charter and raised money from investors to build the line crossing the state from Camden.[7] On July 5, 1854, the first train arrived, soon followed by the opening of the 600-room United States Hotel—the largest hotel in the nation. After the railroad's launch, the City rapidly developed with new homes, shops, taverns, and other businesses; its permanent population, estimated at 250 in the 1855 census, grew to over 13,000 in 1890.

Atlantic City was a new kind of resort. In contrast to Cape May to the south and Newport to the north which catered to the comfortably rich, the City's attractions would be of greatest appeal to the new urban middle class created by the industrial revolution. As one of Pitney's partners put it, the City would provide affordable, usually shorter term stays, for "workers in the close and debilitating shops of the city, whose limited means prevent a long absence from his calling, will find here the rest and recreation he cannot now obtain."[8] While Atlantic City gained a well-deserved reputation for its wholesome family appeal, its growth also was fueled by satisfying seamier interests, with its elected officials openly ignoring calls for enforcement of laws to restrict easy alcohol, gambling, and prostitution.[9] By the end of the nineteenth century, the City had become one of the nation's most popular resorts. Its boardwalk, first built in 1870 to keep hotel guests from tracking sand into hotel lobbies and railroad cars, soon was lined with amusements, shops, food stands, and restaurants.[10]

Starting in the 1880s, Atlantic County and Atlantic City entered a remarkable era in which three successive Republican bosses—Louis "the Commodore" Kuehnle, Enoch "Nucky" Johnson, and Frank "Hap" Farley—ruled for a period lasting some ninety years. To be sure, from time to time they were forced to beat back challenges from political rivals or reformers, but for the most part the political machine they built was among the most powerful—and most corrupt—of any in the nation.

Kuehnle, the first of the bosses, was the son of the owner of a hotel that became the favored meeting place for South Jersey Republicans. Known as "the Commodore" for his prominent role in the Atlantic City Yacht Club, Kuehnle used his social, business, and political connections to become a bank president and obtain both open and hidden interests in other businesses, with his income reportedly exceeding a million dollars a year. The scope of Kuehnle's power gained begrudging respect outside New Jersey; as an editorial in *The New York Sun* commented: "If you were to take all the power exercised by Boss Tweed, the Philadelphia gang, the Pittsburgh ring, Abe Ruef in San Francisco, and Tammany Hall, and concentrate it in one man, you still would fall a little short of Kuehnle's clutch on Atlantic City."[11]

Kuehnle's reign ended after Democrat Woodrow Wilson was elected governor in 1910—an election in which Kuehnle orchestrated massive vote frauds—with the City's vote for Wilson's Republican opponent exceeding the total number of registered voters.[12] After a county grand jury selected by the sheriff from the Republican machine's supporters refused to indict Kuehnle, Wilson's new administration empaneled a special state grand jury that charged Kuehnle, along with some two hundred others, on a variety of counts. At a trial personally prosecuted by the state attorney general before a state supreme court judge sent from Newark to preside, Kuehnle was convicted of fraud in the award of a contract to build a water main and sentenced to one year in prison at hard labor and fined $1,000.[13]

Following a brief power struggle, Kuehnle was succeeded by Enoch "Nucky" Johnson, who served as the County treasurer and Republican boss for a reign that would span the next thirty years.[14] Johnson's swashbuckling style—making his rounds in a chauffeur-driven powder blue Rolls Royce, wearing his trademark red carnation on the lapel of over a hundred custom-tailored suits and residing on an entire floor of one of the City's leading hotels to which he often brought his various lovers—was a comfortable fit with the City's own boisterous image in the Roaring 1920s. Johnson openly boasted of the City's appeals: "We have whisky, wine, women and slot machines," he conceded. "I won't deny it and I won't apologize for it. If the majority of the people didn't want them they wouldn't be profitable and they wouldn't exist. The fact that they do exist proves to me that the people want them."[15]

Prohibition, which became fully effective in January 1920 (while Woodrow Wilson was president), not only gave Atlantic City added stature as the place where "anything goes," but also gave Johnson the vehicle to build a network of relationships with national crime figures. By making Absecon Island one of the nation's leading entries for the illegal import of alcohol, Johnson advanced the interests of bootleggers and mobsters throughout the nation; according to some estimates, perhaps 40 percent of all alcohol smuggled into the country between 1926 and 1933 passed through Absecon Island. Local prosecutors and police not only failed to enforce federal laws, but on occasion actively interfered with or even arrested federal agents who attempted to arrest bootleggers or others involved in importing and selling alcohol.[16]

By 1925, the City had over 2,500 hotels and boarding houses able to accommodate 400,000 visitors; nearly one hundred trains arrived or departed daily during the summer; and five ocean piers on its boardwalk provided amusements, food, and entertainment. Over twenty theaters established the City as the "Second Broadway," the favored site for previews of shows prior to their openings in Manhattan.[17]

In 1929, the year that young Brendan Byrne recalled warmly as the height of his family's prosperity marked by their idyllic summer stay in Deal, some 80 miles to the north of Atlantic City, Nucky Johnson reached the peak of his power. As the host of the first known national gathering of organized crime leaders, a three-day meeting later known as the "Atlantic City Conference," which began on May 16, Johnson welcomed, among others, Al Capone, Charles "Lucky" Luciano, Frank Nitti, Vito Genovese, Benjamin "Bugsy" Siegel, Frank Costello, Meyer Lansky, Albert Anastasia, and Morris "Moe" Dalitz. Convened just three months after the Saint Valentine's Day Massacre in Chicago, in which seven members of the Bugs Moran gang were murdered in a hit widely believed to have been engineered by Capone, the meeting's agenda apparently included chastising Capone for the unwelcome publicity he had generated, as well as warning others to avoid similar violence bringing increased law enforcement attention.

But another topic of discussion was how the gangsters could maintain their profits after the anticipated, eventual repeal of Prohibition (which took effect in 1933), such as in increasing their returns from gambling. Those conversations may have sparked the interest years later of some of the attendees, such as Meyer Lansky, Bugsy Siegel, Lucky Luciano, and Moe Dalitz, in establishing and financing the first casinos in Las Vegas.[18]

One of the younger participants at the meeting was the 25-year-old Abner "Longy" Zwillman, who at the time was viewed as a bootlegging contact between Lucky Luciano based in Manhattan and Nucky Johnson. Between 1926 and 1933, according to reports in FBI files, Zwillman ran "a $50 million bootleg ring" facilitated by his own speed boat.[19] Following the repeal of Prohibition, Zwillman became known as the "Al Capone of New Jersey"; over twenty years after the Atlantic City meeting, as a young lawyer working for John McGeehan, Brendan Byrne dealt with Zwillman as one of McGeehan's clients and later, as Essex County prosecutor, Byrne oversaw the investigation of Zwillman's death by hanging in his home in West Orange.[20]

Less than two weeks after the mobsters ended their conference, Nucky Johnson proudly presided over the opening of the Atlantic City Convention Hall, built at a cost of $15 million which, upon its opening, was the largest and most advanced facility of its kind in the world.[21] But just months after these festivities, the City's prosperity, like the nation's as a whole, would be jolted by the Great Depression that followed the stock market crash of October 1929. Saddled with debt from the Hall and other ventures, the City government contemplated bankruptcy while hotels, amusements, and other attractions struggled to pay the debts they incurred during the boom years of expansion.[22] By the end of the 1930s, Atlantic City's per capita debt was higher than that of any other city in the country.[23]

Like his predecessor Kuehnle, Johnson was finally toppled by forces from outside the world he tightly controlled. A series of articles on Atlantic City vice, published in 1930 by William Randolph Hearst's *New York Evening Journal*, pointed to Johnson as the key figure in the city's corruption.[24] In 1936, after the Hearst media outlets continued to focus on the racketeering under Johnson, President Franklin Roosevelt sent the FBI to the City in hopes of repeating the successful income tax evasion prosecution that had sent Al Capone to prison in 1932. The FBI investigation, which encountered widespread local resistance from Johnson's supporters and those who feared retribution from the machine, continued for five years before prosecutors were able to strike a deal with one of Johnson's key associates to testify against him and dozens of others. After several incidents of jury tampering, Johnson was finally convicted of tax evasion in 1941 and served four years in prison.[25]

Following Nucky Johnson's conviction, Atlantic County's Senator Frank "Hap" Farley became the Republican boss, besting Atlantic City Mayor Thomas D. Taggart, Jr. in a brief struggle for leadership. As a young lawyer, Farley had been selected by Johnson to run for the Assembly in 1937, and was elected to the state Senate in 1940.[26] Farley, whose six foot height was somewhat lessened by a stooped gait from a chronic back condition, had gained his nickname "Hap" from the usual broad smile that creased his moon-like face.

With a less flamboyant style than Johnson, Hap Farley nonetheless emerged as one of New Jersey's most powerful legislators, playing leading roles in the building of the Garden State Parkway (derided as "Farley's Folly"), the Atlantic City Marina (now renamed the Frank S. Farley Marina), Richard Stockton State College, and the statewide community college system.[27] "His seniority, combined with his mastery of the legislative process, made him, for more than 25 years, an insurmountable reality with whom every governor had to contend when creating an agenda," wrote Judge Nelson Johnson in *Boardwalk Empire*, his chronicle of the City. "Farley dominated the senate so thoroughly that it was political suicide to oppose him. The governors either dealt with Hap or saw their programs frustrated."[28]

In his role as executive secretary to Governor Meyner, Brendan Byrne came to know Farley in the 1950s. "He was a man of his word," Byrne said years after Farley's death. "He could be trusted to get things done."[29] On one occasion, when Governor Meyner was out of the state, Byrne recalled that Farley, who was serving as acting governor in his capacity as Senate president, asked to have a bill passed by both houses of the legislature brought to him so he could sign it into law, stating that Meyner had verbally approved his request prior to his leaving the state. When the governor's counsel objected, seeking a more formal indication that Meyner had so approved, Byrne took it upon himself to bring the bill for Farley's signature. "If Hap Farley said he had Meyner's O.K.," Byrne later said, "you just knew it was true. That's the way he was."[30]

But Farley's efforts to steer state money to the County could not stem the larger trends leading to Atlantic City's decline. During World War II, the City's economy suffered as wartime quotas on gasoline, food, and other staples cut travel and leisure; the City did receive a brief infusion of federal money as the government took over the larger hotels to house soldiers before they departed for Europe and, after their return, as a staging area for treating the wounded and reassigning soldiers to new duty posts in the states (including B-17 navigator Brendan Byrne who spent a week after his return from Italy at the annex of the once plush Ritz Carleton Hotel in January 1945).[31] After the war, Atlantic City's appeal to tourists fell sharply in the face of growing competition from newer resorts in Florida and the West that had become more accessible by improved air service and new highways; the City's aging hotels and other attractions deteriorated as they failed to attract new investment.[32]

In 1950, the City gained unwelcome national notice when the U.S. Senate committee formed to investigate organized crime and chaired by Tennessee Democrat Estes Kefauver held highly publicized hearings in fourteen cities, including Atlantic City. At the conclusion of its investigation in 1951, the committee issued a report outlining the links between Atlantic County's political machine and racketeers. "This machine has two heads, one the political boss of Atlantic County and the other the rackets boss of Atlantic City," the report said. "The political head is Frank S. Farley, State Senator for Atlantic County at a salary of $3,000 a year, treasurer of Atlantic County at a salary of $6,000 a year, and chairman of the Atlantic County Republican Committee. . . . The rackets head is Herman 'Stumpy' Orman, owner of the Cosmopolitan Hotel, which has served for many years as a rendezvous for political figures and perhaps underworld characters as well."[33] Despite the harsh assessment of the Kefauver committee, Hap Farley would continue to play a leading role in local, state, and national politics for another twenty years.[34]

In 1957, Skinny D'Amato, the proprietor of the 500 Club, a night club with an illegal casino covertly controlled by Philadelphia Mafia boss Angelo Bruno, reportedly suggested that Atlantic City pursue legalized casino gaming, but there was no organized effort to gain the statewide support that would be needed to amend the state constitution to implement the idea.[35] Some good government and tourism advocates also called for legalization of gambling as a step toward reducing corruption and to attract visitors in the off-season months. In 1958, Mildred Fox, the president the Atlantic City Women's Chamber of Commerce, pointed out the prevalence of highly visible illegal gambling already existing, noting that "every little store that had newspapers in the front had gambling in the back," and proposed that "municipally-controlled games of chance" be considered to boost tourism.[36]

The embarrassment over the City's sorry condition, so apparent during the 1964 Democratic Convention, sparked new discussion about the potential of legalized gambling as a tool for redevelopment. As the 1960s drew to a close, with New Jersey facing difficult fiscal choices over an income tax or other measures to broaden the state's tax base, the potential of gaming as a new state and local revenue source—along with its promise for spurring development for Atlantic City and other areas—began to gain serious attention.

In 1968, during public hearings of a legislative committee, then Essex County Prosecutor Brendan Byrne was the only law enforcement official to support legalizing casino gaming, breaking ranks with those who argued that casinos would be impossible to police or keep from mob infiltration. Byrne would later say, "I had seen too much, as prosecutor of the futility of trying to enforce gambling laws and the temptation it was to corrupt law-enforcement officers . . . who didn't really believe that the laws were in the best interest of the state and who were therefore subject to the temptation of being paid to look the other way."[37] On another occasion, Byrne said, "I thought why not legalize it and make the state a partner in the gambling operation?"[38]

In December 1968, a dinner at the Sherburne Hotel, ostensibly a black-tie birthday party for Skinny D'Amato, brought together some twenty political, business, and underworld figures to discuss Atlantic City's future, including Hap Farley and John V. Kenny, the successor to Frank Hague as the political boss of Hudson County.[39] According to an account by businessman Vince Del Raso, one of D'Amato's friends, "We discussed how depressed Atlantic City had become and how gambling was the only thing that could save it. We all agreed to unite behind legalization."[40]

Unlike Kuehnle and Johnson, Hap Farley was never indicted, but he was again mentioned as a potential target of investigations that led to the convictions of two former Atlantic City mayors and other officials for bribery, extortion, and conspiracy.[41] Farley avoided taking a public position on casinos for Atlantic City, probably because of continuing questions about his own ties to underworld figures.[42] Publicly, he expressed indifference, saying only "Well, if the people want it, they can have it."[43] But he was widely viewed as behind the proposal in 1970 by his close friend, Senator Frank McDermott from

Union County, to get the legislature's approval for a referendum authorizing casino gambling on the New Jersey ballot, a proposal that was defeated in the Senate.[44]

The outlook for legalizing casinos had dimmed with the election in 1969 of William Cahill as governor, who strongly opposed casino gaming.[45] Cahill had begun his career as an FBI agent, and later, as a state deputy attorney general in the early 1950s, led an investigation into organized crime's influence in gambling in Bergen County.[46] Cahill's election also took place in the wake of renewed concerns over organized crime and its political connections; in December 1968, New Jersey Assistant Attorney General William J. Brennan III, the son of U.S. Supreme Court Justice William J. Brennan Jr., was quoted saying that members of the state legislature were "entirely too comfortable with organized crime."[47] Brennan declined to publicly identify the legislators, but a subsequent press report disclosed that Hap Farley was one of six members who were the subjects of Brennan's allegations.[48] But despite Cahill's antigambling stance, some of his fellow Republicans favored the prospect, in part as a means to avoid the political risks of supporting the governor's proposals for a state income tax as a new revenue source. Beyond Atlantic City and other aging shore resorts such as Long Branch and Asbury Park, there was interest in the northwest part of the state in Sussex County, where the Great Gorge ski resort had opened in 1965 and Hugh Hefner's Playboy Enterprises had later built a Playboy Club, hotel, and golf course, reportedly in anticipation that casino gambling would be approved.[49]

In the November 1971 legislative election, with a federal grand jury pursuing another investigation of Atlantic County Republicans and spurring rumors that Farley himself might be charged, the Democrats, ran on the slogan "it's time for a change." The Democratic ticket was put together by Patrick McGahn (usually called "Pat" or "Paddy"), an influential lawyer in county Democratic politics. Pat McGahn's brother, Dr. Joseph McGahn, an obstetrician who had been the first Democratic mayor of Absecon; opposed Farley for the Senate; two young lawyers ran for the Assembly seats: 27-year-old James Colasurdo and 26-year-old Steven Perskie, a Penn Law School and Yale alumnus who came from a well-known family that included a father and grandfather who served as state judges and an uncle who was elected to the Assembly from Cape May in 1963.[50]

Reflecting on the campaign years later, Perskie wrote in a memoir that at the end of the final debate with McGahn, Farley "wound up in a virtually incoherent rant . . . rattling off names (Richard Nixon, Dwight Eisenhower, etc.) of people with whom he was 'close friends' and, at one point, he waved his arms and yelled, 'I know these people.'" According to Perskie, he was "gasping in astonishment" at Farley's embarrassing performance, which made it apparent that "time and circumstance had caught up with him and, even after all of his accomplishments, by 1971 he had nothing else to offer. . . . It was simply devastating and, honestly very sad."[51] The Democrats won all three seats, ending Farley's thirty-four-year career in the legislature.[52]

The Democratic sweep allowed the new legislators, without the burden of Farley's questionable ties, to launch a push in the legislature for legalized gambling for Atlantic City. Once they took their seats in January 1972, McGahn and Perskie each introduced proposals for a referendum on casino gambling but, as Perskie later admitted, "Governor Cahill was publicly and unalterably opposed to the concept and we knew it would go nowhere."[53]

In the same year, a state commission created to review the issues and options regarding legalized gambling chaired by Republican Senator Wayne Dumont, whose members included prominent opponents of an income tax, recommended that a referendum be placed on the ballot to amend the state constitution of the to permit the legislature to authorize the operation of gambling in Atlantic City.[54]

Much of the debate on early casino gambling initiatives continued to focus on where it would be allowed. Atlantic City was always viewed as a primary site given its decline and need for new investment, but politicians and business interests in other areas argued that restricting casinos to Atlantic City would undercut their own resort economies or that they had equally pressing claims for revenue and redevelopment. Two years before the Dumont Commission's report, Republican Assemblyman Ralph Caputo of Essex County sponsored a proposal for casinos in both Atlantic City and Newark, which was struggling to recover from the 1967 riots.[55]

Weighing against the interests pushing for expanded legalized gambling was the concern that it would lead to greater influence by organized crime and the potential corruption of both state and local public officials. The Nevada gambling industry, legalized in 1931, expanded rapidly in the 1940s and 1950s with investment by organized crime syndicates, which exercised covert control of the casinos. Indeed, some of the leading figures in the development of Las Vegas, such as Bugsy Siegel, Lucky Luciano, and Moe Dalitz, had attended the 1929 Atlantic City conference hosted by Nucky Johnson.[56] When Byrne visited Las Vegas for conferences of the National District Attorneys Association when he was a prosecutor, he took precautions against booking a room in a hotel that might have ties to mob interests. "We met from time to time in Las Vegas," he later said. "And before I went, I would call the FBI and ask, 'Where does J. Edgar Hoover stay when he goes to Las Vegas?' And I would stay wherever he stayed."[57]

In April 1973, shortly after Byrne entered the race for governor, Steve Perskie was invited to participate in a briefing session for the new candidate with other legislators. Perskie, who would chair the Assembly taxation committee and work closely with Byrne on the income tax program, met Byrne for the first time at the session and was unaware of his views on legalized gambling, but took the opportunity during a break in the meeting to raise the issue of casinos privately with Byrne. At first, Byrne told Perskie that as a prosecutor he had publicly testified on legalized gambling in Atlantic City, with Perskie then assuming that he had opposed the idea. "He went through all that knowing full well that it was my certain expectation," Perskie later recounted, "that his testimony as prosecutor would have been negative and that he was leading me to believe that that was going to be his . . . position as a candidate for governor." Perskie said he "recognized at that point that my political career was over, and he let me stew with that for a couple of minutes," until Byrne let him in on the charade: "he told me that in fact he was the only law enforcement official . . . to have appeared before the Legislature in 1968 to have suggested that casino gambling could be effectively monitored in Atlantic City and that it would produce more benefit than not."[58]

Perskie would become an active Byrne supporter in the general election and later a valuable ally in Byrne's long struggle to enact tax reform.[59] "I would not have supported a [casino] bill if it weren't for Steve Perskie," Byrne later said. "If I didn't have the confidence in Steve Perskie, I don't think the bill would have gone anywhere."[60] But the issue of legalized gambling and Atlantic City's future did not play a major role in the 1973 campaign. The Democrats assumed that Sandman, from neighboring Cape May, would bring back the disaffected Atlantic County Republican voters who had turned against the Farley machine in 1971, and invested little in advertising or candidate appearances in the southern shore region. Toward the end of the campaign, however, Sandman charged that Byrne was too close to "hotel interests" and the Democrats rebutted the claim with a late advertising effort.[61]

Soon after Byrne took office in January 1974, his interest was sparked in exploring options for revitalizing Atlantic City when he visited the city to campaign for Lillian Bryant, who was running for county freeholder. Bryant was the daughter of Horace Bryant, the state's first African American cabinet member, whom Byrne had known when they both served in the Hughes Administration. "I started being supportive of Atlantic City when early on in my term. . . . I went down and spent a Sunday campaigning [for Bryant] in some of the bad neighborhoods of Atlantic City. And I said to myself, we got to do something."[62]

Casino proponents advanced various ideas on how to draft a casino gambling question to be placed before voters the following November. Again, the issues of who would own and operate the casinos, and where they would be allowed to locate, were the principal points of contention. Byrne preferred that the casinos be operated by the state government and restricted to Atlantic City, but opposition from other areas forced a compromise that would allow casinos throughout the state if voters in the affected municipalities and counties approved. A resolution to place a referendum on the ballot required a two-thirds majority in each house, and four Senators interested in allowing casinos in their districts were refusing to support an "Atlantic City only" referendum. "The bottom line at the end of day was that we were going to be successful in getting a proposal to amend the constitution out of the Legislature only . . . if it was not by its terms limited to Atlantic City," Steve Perskie recalled, "which caused the Governor some significant distress because his position all along had been, 'I'm for casinos in Atlantic City'."[63] Byrne reluctantly backed the agreement, which also included a commitment that the state government own and operate the casinos, but only on the basis that if the referendum was approved, casinos would be located only in Atlantic City for the first five years.[64]

Within his own administration, Byrne also faced dissenters on his support for casinos for Atlantic City. Both Attorney General William Hyland and Treasurer Dick Leone advised the governor they opposed the referendum and offered to resign from the cabinet if he so requested, but Byrne assured them that they could express their opposition and remain in the administration. "Dick Leone comes in to say," Byrne recalled years later, "'why do you want to be remembered as the guy that brought gambling into Atlantic City?' I told him that I thought as long as I was governor, I could keep organized crime out of the casinos and that the strong regulatory structure we established would be kept by future governors." Beyond the potential stimulus to Atlantic City's economy, Byrne also felt that the casino-hotels would "bring excitement to the state through hosting major events, entertainers and celebrities, helping to counter the state's image problem in the rest of the country."[65]

While the resolution passed in the legislature, by 57-21 in the Assembly and 24-14 in the Senate, public opposition soon coalesced against approval of the referendum.[66] A loose antigambling coalition under the label "No Dice" enlisted public officials, and religious and law enforcement leaders to speak out against the referendum. Assembly Minority Leader Thomas Kean spoke out firmly against the casino referendum: "The contention that the location of casinos in Atlantic City will bring about a return to the city's past glories is, in my view, a fantasy."[67] Others who would join to urge rejection of the referendum included religious leaders; law enforcement officials; and good government types worried about corruption and the state's image.[68]

Jonathan Goldstein, the U.S. Attorney for New Jersey who had secured convictions against two former Atlantic City mayors, two commissioners and four other city officials on extortion, bribery, and conspiracy charges, was perhaps the most vocal critic. "Now Atlantic City's governmental and business leaders who have permitted an omnipresent fabric of corruption in Atlantic City," Goldstein had declared, "who have allowed Atlantic City to deteriorate and have made few if any meaningful investments to rebuild that city, now want the state to entrust to it to legalized gambling."[69] Goldstein's opposition, according to two Rutgers scholars, "cemented the link between casinos and corruption in the minds of voters" and "was pivotal in turning the tide against the referendum."[70] On the Sunday before the election, 3,000 clergymen throughout the state asked their congregants to vote against the referendum.

Voters solidly rejected the casino question by a three-to-one margin, with only Hudson and Atlantic of the twenty-one counties recording majorities in favor. Some analysts attributed the loss to voter worries, particularly in more affluent suburbs in the northern part of the state, that the failure to restrict the potential locations of casinos could lead to their proliferation throughout the state. A newspaper article published a few days after the referendum reported that Governor Byrne appeared "relieved and happy" at the rejection by the voters and, according to the article, assumed that the issue of allowing casinos in the state was now "dead." Byrne also disclosed in the article that the question had lost among the voters in his own family, with his wife Jean and son Tom voting against the referendum.[71] "While I voted for the referendum," Byrne said years later, "I really wanted to limit casinos to Atlantic City only, and didn't care too much when that referendum went down."[72]

The defeat was a severe blow to gambling supporters, with the *New York Times* headlining its article, "Outlook for Atlantic City is Bleak, Gambling Setback Casts a Pall over Atlantic City."[73] But supporters soon regrouped, assessed the lessons learned from their mistakes and fashioned another referendum aimed at attracting wider support from regions and constituencies that did not support the 1974 proposal.

The 1976 referendum question placed on the ballot restricted casino gambling to Atlantic City alone; allowed private ownership under State regulation; and dedicated tax revenue raised by gaming to programs for the elderly and disabled. The prospect of privately owned casinos helped to generate financial contributions from potential operators; much of the money supported a more professional and better-organized statewide pro-casino advertising and public relations campaign managed by the Committee to Rebuild Atlantic City (CRAC), chaired by Mayor Joseph Lazarow.[74] At Byrne's suggestion, Steve Perskie also drafted a bill spelling out how the casinos would be regulated to give voters an outline of how the state government would oversee their operations. Unlike 1974, both local Democrats and Republicans reached out to former Senator Farley for help, who despite his 1971 defeat, retained strong ties to Republican leaders around the state. In a gesture of respect for his one-time foe, Perskie invited Farley to come to Trenton to be present on the Assembly floor, as Perskie put it, "for a bow" on the day that the body approved the resolution for the referendum, a courtesy which Farley told Perskie he greatly appreciated. Farley was particularly helpful in securing support from his old friend Bergen County Sheriff Joseph Job, who had been a leading opponent of the 1974 referendum.[75] The referendum won by a wide margin, approved by a 300,000-vote margin compared to the 400,000-vote defeat in 1974.

Another major factor in the approval of the second referendum was its being on the ballot during a presidential election year, which brought out more voters and diverted the attention of some 1974 casino opponents to national issues. "In '76 you had a presidential campaign," recalled Carl Zeitz, at the time an Associated Press reporter who later was appointed in 1980 by Byrne to the Casino Control Commission. "People who'd been part of that [anti-casino] committee were more interested in electing a president of one stripe or the other than they were in stopping casino gambling, and that's where their energy and focus went. And you had a million dollar campaign for it, but you also had an election in which the presidency appeared to be the more important question on the ballot."[76]

The enabling legislation that established the state's oversight of Atlantic City's legalized gaming, the Casino Control Act, was developed after extensive research by legislators and Byrne Administration officials, which included visits to Las Vegas, the Bahamas, and other gambling jurisdictions to discuss and assess their regulatory approaches. Stewart Pollock, the governor's counsel, recalled that when he accompanied Byrne on a visit to several Las Vegas casinos, an executive asked the governor what he wanted to do, and Byrne responded, "What I'd like to do is follow a dollar from the moment it's bet to the moment it gets in the bank." To Pollock, "it was just further proof to me that he had not only a grasp of the intellectual principles that you need to govern, but he also understood the nuts and bolts, because there's an awful lot of money that can fall off a table at a casino."[77] Byrne also traveled to London, with his group including Attorney General Degnan and Byrne's teenaged daughter Nancy. On a side trip to visit the villages of his family in Ireland, Byrne asked the car's driver "Where would I go if I wanted to buy a *Playboy* magazine in Ireland?" and received the immediate response: "Governor, you'd go straight to hell!"[78]

The Casino Control Act created a Casino Control Commission appointed by the governor to oversee licensing of the casinos, and a Division of Gaming Enforcement in the Department of Law and Public Safety to investigate applicants for licenses and present its findings to the Commission. Governor Byrne took an active personal role in shaping the legislation, naming himself as chair of the cabinet committee to oversee development of the legislative and regulatory framework for licensing casinos and visiting Las Vegas to discuss what New Jersey could learn from the Nevada experience.[79] Atlantic

County's legislative delegation, principally Senator McGahn and Assembly-man Perskie, along with the then freshman Essex County Assemblyman (and later Senate President and Governor) Richard Codey, who chaired a special committee, were the key legislators drafting the legislation. In an interview years later, Codey said that he spent six months "travelling around the world, learning about an industry I knew nothing about, talking to people, trying to do the right thing, trying to ward of this criticism that we're going to let the mob get involved, which never happened."[80]

Apart from keeping the casinos free from the mob, Byrne had strong personal views on what he wanted for a new Atlantic City, ideas that he conveyed to legislators and staff designated to draft the new law and the subsequent regulations defining the standards that a casino applicant would be required to meet. Dismissing calls from conservationists who wanted to preserve some of the City's quirkier structures, such as the Moorish-style dome atop the Chalfonte-Haddon Hall Hotel, Byrne wanted a newly built Atlantic City.[81] "Frankly, I didn't think there was much worth preserving," Byrne later reflected. "The hotels and most of the other buildings were in such bad shape that I thought it would be best to tear most things down and start with new construction."[82]

Byrne also explored the potential for attracting non-casino attractions and hotels to the City. "We met with major developers who we thought might have an interest, but got nowhere," Byrne later recalled. "The Disney people told us that a new theme park was impossible in a climate like New Jersey since their existing parks in California and Florida didn't make money until Thanksgiving." Byrne also approached well-known hotel chains. "The Marri-otts weren't interested," he said later, "since they were Mormons who opposed gambling on moral grounds." An approach to Kemmons Wilson, the founder of Holiday Inns, was more successful: "Steve Perskie and I . . . went down to Memphis and sat with their board, and I talked Kemmons Wilson into buying some property in Atlantic City and he did."[83] Perskie said that it was a tough sell. "This was company with its roots in Tennessee and a very conservative board uncomfortable about any association with gambling," he later related. "Brendan spoke about the tough state law and regulatory program that had been created, and I emphasized the changes in local government."[84]

Byrne resisted "patch and paint" proposals to fix up the old hotels, see-ing them as relatively cheap ways for developers to quickly reap the profits offered by the new law. He wanted gambling to be a subordinate tool for the City's overall revitalization, avoiding the pervasive presence of slot machines and other games in Nevada's airports, bars, and convenience stores and the signs and advertising that focused on gambling as the primary attraction for visitors. Ignoring a history closely tied to seamy pleasures, state, and local officials boasted that the new Atlantic City would be a return to the "family resort" of the City's past.

On June 2, 1977, just five days prior to his win with only 30 percent of the vote in the Democratic primary election in which he was running for reelection, Governor Byrne signed the Casino Control Act into law in front of the Atlantic City Convention Hall. Planning the event had sparked debate within the Byrne campaign staff, with some worrying that the still vigorous opposition to the enactment of the income tax might spark a protest at the governor's appearance on the boardwalk similar to the hostile reception he had received the previous fall at the opening of the Meadowlands racetrack. Those arguing for the public signing in front of the Convention Hall won out.

But the Governor's plan for the day ran into objections from Atlantic City Mayor Joseph Lazarow, who wanted to hold the signing ceremony in his City Hall office, thus highlighting his personal leadership in promoting casino gambling and diminishing the roles of Byrne and Assemblyman Steven Perskie. The event had become enmeshed in the split that had developed between Perskie and Senator Joseph McGahn and his brother Pat. Perskie had been recruited by Pat McGahn to join the Democratic legislative ticket that defeated Hap Farley and his running mates in 1971, but Perskie had subsequently rebelled against what he viewed as McGahn's overbearing manner in running the county Democratic organization and also had differed with Joe McGahn on policy issues, notably over Perskie's role as the lead sponsor of the Byrne income tax program. The division between Perskie and the McGahns had proceeded to the point that Perskie launched a successful challenge at the April 1977 Democratic county convention seeking the nomination to run for the Senate seat held by McGahn. Before the convention, recognizing that Perskie had secured the votes to guarantee his nomination, McGahn withdrew his name as a candidate.

"Mayor Lazarow was an ally of Pat's and also not a 'friend' of the Governor," Perskie later wrote, "so the normal protocols for arranging a suitable event that would include the local officials, community leaders, state legislators, and the Governor were made excruciatingly difficult."[85] Byrne's advance staff, led by his trip director Fariborz Fatemi, first phoned the mayor but Lazarow told him he opposed any boardwalk ceremony. The advance staff then traveled to the City, but after a contentious, late-night meeting the mayor still insisted on holding the ceremony in his office. At one point, according to Fatemi, Lazarow "even threatened to have our advance people arrested if they left their room in the hotel."[86] Meanwhile, despite Lazarow's opposition, Byrne's staff covertly went ahead to organize the parade by phoning Steve Perskie, who made arrangements for convertible cars, bagpipers, bands, and clowns.

The next morning, after Fatemi informed the Governor of the impasse, Byrne phoned Lazarow. "In a brief but very direct conversation," Fatemi recounted, "the Governor told the mayor he had a choice, either the mayor cooperated with the Governor's staff, or the bill signing would be in the Governor's Office and the mayor would not be invited." Byrne also demanded a prompt response from the mayor. After the Governor took Lazarow's subsequent call, he turned to Fatemi and said, "Go ahead, the mayor will cooperate."[87]

"This was an old-fashioned ticker tape parade," Fatemi recalled. "Overhead were the barge balloons, confetti falling and the cars were led by the bands, bagpipes, and dancers. The crowd jamming the boardwalk was huge. As the cars passed, the occupants threw souvenir Atlantic City dice to the crowd."[88] After driving down the boardwalk seated on the trunk of an open convertible with McGahn, Perskie and Lazarow for several blocks, the group stopped in front of the Convention Hall before a jubilant crowd estimated at some 5,000. Seated at the rostrum was a frail Hap Farley, hobbled by a series of heart attacks and his chronic back problem. Making his way to the microphone with the aid of a cane, Farley spoke briefly, saying he thanked "God for being good enough to let me witness this occasion." (He died three months later). Following remarks by McGahn, Lazarow and Perskie, Byrne was introduced by Perskie, and at the end of his speech shouted his widely reported warning: "I've said it before and I will repeat it again to organized crime: Keep your filthy hands off Atlantic City. Keep the hell out of our state!" He then signed the bill, stood, and waved it over his head to the cheering crowd.[89]

The Casino Control Act sought to keep New Jersey from repeating Nevada's history that allowed infiltration of mob interests in casino ownership and operations through establishing a rigorous licensing process for casino companies and their key executives and gaming employees. To pursue the goal of using gambling only as a tool to restore Atlantic City as a family resort, the law and its subsequent regulations imposed restrictions on the design, marketing, and operations by the casino-hotels, such as segregating the casinos from nongaming areas in the hotels; prohibiting advertising which emphasized gambling and sex; and limiting casino operations to eighteen hours per day. In order to prevent developers from building casino "boxes" that skimmed gambling profits alone, each casino-hotel was required to have a minimum of 500 rooms, as well as restaurants, shops, conference and meeting rooms, and other visitor amenities.[90]

Although the design of casino-hotel buildings was regulated in some detail, the Byrne Administration and the legislature failed to create a regional agency to oversee land-use planning and development. Byrne later cited this as the "biggest mistake" of his eight years in office: "[O]ne of my great regrets is that when I did gambling in Atlantic City I did not regionalize

Atlantic City for that purpose. We should have." Byrne added that "my overwhelming concern was to keep it clean, law enforcement. When it came to . . . the housing and the other development, I did not have the foresight that I should have had."[91] Byrne also dismissed the suggestion that opposition from defenders of local home rule could have blocked the establishment of a regional agency to oversee development. "I should have had the whole thing—they would have given me anything . . . I mean if I wanted to zone an adjacent municipality, they would have let me do it. I didn't see the need for it at that time. I thought casinos . . . [were] something we could solve just by good law enforcement."[92]

His reluctance also may have been due in part to concern for the political survival of Steve Perskie, who had become a valuable ally in the bitter fight over the income tax and whose leadership in Atlantic County Byrne viewed as important in maintaining public confidence in the integrity of casino operations. Perskie had narrowly won reelection to the Assembly in 1975; in 1977, he defeated Senator McGahn for the Democratic Senate nomination, also withstanding McGahn's attempt to retain his seat by running as an independent in the general election.[93] Republicans took back one of the seats they lost in 1977 with the election to the Assembly of Atlantic County freeholder William Gormley, who would later succeed to Perskie's Senate seat in 1982 and serve until resigning in 2007. In a panel discussion in 2007, Perskie said, "It's always been my sense that the reason that he [Byrne] didn't push it [a regional agency] is because he was concerned about the political impact on me, and I have always felt a little bad about that because on the merits I think . . . it would have enabled us to attack quicker and more comprehensively some of the problems that have dogged us for the generation since then."[94]

While no regional agency was established, the state did take steps to evaluate larger planning issues in more informal ways. A cabinet committee on Atlantic City met regularly to coordinate the actions of various departments dealing with the environment, transportation, housing, and economic development.[95] But without any formal power over local agencies, the cabinet committee's recommendations had little impact.

With the benefit of hindsight, some of the initial planning decisions were questioned. Requiring the casino-hotels to include restaurants, shops, and other amenities, for example, was cited as hampering the City's broader development beyond the casino-hotels. "[R]estaurants that expected to get some spillover from the casinos were sadly disappointed when virtually no casino customers ventured away from the casinos to eat," one analyst wrote. "Some of the city's most venerable restaurants—Kent's, Hackney's, Starns, Carson's—all closed soon after casinos were introduced."[96] The surge in real estate values after the referendum also made it extremely costly to acquire land or develop property within the City, eventually leading to a shift of investment in new housing, retail shops and eating establishments to suburban areas, a pattern that might have been slowed had the state or county taken more aggressive steps to implement regional strategies to focus growth within the City.

Resorts International, a company whose origins derived from its founding as the Mary Carter Paint Company until it converted its business in the 1960s to real estate development and casino operation in the Bahamas, was the first casino-hotel developer to seek approval in Atlantic City.[97] Resorts sought to get a jump on potential competitors by proposing to renovate the old Chalfonte-Haddon Hall hotel, reducing its 1,000 rooms to a 566-room resort with the required casino, restaurant, shopping, and meeting space. Renovation of the existing property would allow the new casino-hotel to open at least a year before its competitors, as well as saving on construction costs required for a newly built facility.

The strategy received a cool reception from state and local leaders, including the Governor, because most had hoped that casino development would revitalize the City through new resorts, rather than the "patch and paint" approach for existing properties proposed by Resorts. The protracted investigations by the attorney general's staff of the applications of casino developers also brought increasing criticism of the delays in getting decisions that would allow Resorts and additional casinos to open. In January 1978, Byrne brought the heads of the relevant agencies together in a meeting at his office to ascertain the status of the investigation on the Resorts application. After being advised that the probe might continue for some months, he ordered that a plan be developed to allow casinos to open before the completion of the investigations.[98] "There was quite a bit of pressure to get these casinos open," recalled former Senator Gormley, who was then a freshman assemblyman. "It soon became apparent that the casino would be ready long before the investigation was over, so we had to amend the Casino Control Act to provide for temporary licenses."[99] The temporary licenses allowed casinos to open while the investigations and licensing process continued; should a casino later be rejected for permanent licensing, it would be forced to sell its facility to other potential operators.

The licensing proceedings for Resorts were slowed by the investigation by the Division of Gaming Enforcement, a unit in the Department of Law and Public Safety created by the Casino Control Act. "First of all, the climate was this," John Degnan, Byrne's attorney general, later recounted. "The governor had made the strongest possible statements about ensuring that the regulatory apparatus around casinos would be pristinely honest. That the kind of people we licensed would be without blemish, certainly without any remote connection to organized crime. And he had a lot vested in that." But Degnan was aware that the Resorts application was "difficult," and his Division recommended rejecting the application on the basis of prior operations in the Bahamas, where it allegedly had used consultants with questionable associations and where it had regularly made cash contributions to government officials (albeit not illegal under Bahamian law).[100]

Degnan later said that as speculation continued over both the timetable and the ultimate decision by the Casino Control Commission on the Resorts application, Byrne's only direction to him was to complete the process as soon as possible. "And the Governor, several times, said to me," Degnan recalled. "'You know, look John, just get it decided. The best result would be you give them a license. The next best result would be you oppose the license. But just get it decided.'" Degnan then said he "put a lot of pressure" on those doing the investigation to expedite their work, "But I was never told by the Governor one way or the other how to come out on it."[101]

On the morning of May 26, 1978, crowds waited in long lines to get into the Resorts casino as it opened under its temporary license. Before cutting a ceremonial ribbon allowing gamblers to enter the casino, Byrne gave a brief welcome to those in line: "My father told me never to bet on anything except Notre Dame and the New York Yankees. For those of you not willing to take my father's advice, this casino is now open."[102] For the first seventy-two-hour Memorial Day weekend, police estimated that 350,000 people came into the city, with two-hour waiting times to enter the casino. Over its first year, when it operated without competition from other casinos, Resorts outperformed even the most optimistic projections, returning a profit of over $50 million, more than paying back its entire construction cost.[103]

Shortly before Christmas of 1978, with Resorts still operating under its temporary license and awaiting action on its permanent license application, Joel Sterns, the lawyer for Resorts in its licensing proceedings and a longtime friend of Byrne dating from the years that Sterns served as counsel to Governor Hughes, phoned Robert Mulcahy, Byrne's chief-of-staff. According to the memo Mulcahy dictated summarizing the conversation, Sterns told him that the financing for the next two prospective casinos proposed by Caesar's World and the Golden Nugget had "fallen through" and that "a state of 'near Hysteria' was developing in Atlantic City." Sterns went on to suggest that the Governor appoint a retired supreme court justice or other prominent figure to review and evaluate the attorney general's findings on potential licensees, implying that this would avoid "some embarrassment" when Resorts and other applicants were licensed by the Commission over the attorney general's objections.[104]

Ultimately, the Commission granted a permanent license to Resorts, rejecting the contentions, among others, that James Crosby, the company's chief executive, had criminal ties and that the company had bribed officials

in the Bahamas. In approving the permanent license over the objections of
Attorney General Degnan, the Commission supported its decision by finding
that Resorts had operated its new Atlantic City casino under its temporary
license in compliance with the state's regulations.[105]

Degnan also opposed the subsequent licensing of Caesars World and Bally
Corporation on somewhat similar grounds that in past operations the principals of the companies had direct or indirect ties to criminal or otherwise questionable associates.[106] In licensing Caesars, the Commission conditioned its
approval on its founders, the brothers Clifford and Stuart Perlman, severing
their ties with the company.[107] Similarly, Bally's was licensed after William
O'Donnell, its founder and chief executive, resigned from the company and
sold his stock holdings after the Commission found that he had past ties to
underworld figures.[108] "The outcomes were disappointing to me," Degnan
later said. "They were a compromise result. And I think they diluted somewhat the promise of the proponents of casino gaming that we would have a
system that produced only pristine operators."[109]

While he did not intervene on the decision with Degnan, Byrne later
said that he respected how the Perlmans had built Caesars into a successful
company and understood how they might have been pressured in Las Vegas
to associate with the individuals who later resulted in their exclusion from
New Jersey. "At that time," he recalled, "it was difficult for anyone operating
in Las Vegas to avoid relationships with some figures you probably wouldn't
want to deal with, but you couldn't get things done without them. That
was the reality of the Nevada casino business."[110] Despite his experience in
New Jersey, Clifford Perlman would maintain friendly contacts with Byrne
long after the Governor had left office.[111]

In February 1980, the good feeling generated by the success of the first
casinos was jolted by the Abscam scandal, in which FBI agents posing as the
henchmen of a fictitious Arab sheik interested in potential investment opportunities in the United States, including real estate. Atlantic City wasn't the
original focus of the sting, but became embroiled when Camden Mayor and
New Jersey state Senator Angelo Errichetti reportedly told undercover agents
that, in exchange for $400,000, he could help the sheik secure land in Atlantic
City, build a casino, and get a gaming license. Errichetti claimed that he could
deliver three of five Casino Control Commission votes with the aid of a suggested $100,000 bribe for Vice Chairman Kenneth MacDonald. According to
Errichetti's unsubstantiated allegations, MacDonald "controlled" Commission executive director Joseph Lordi, whom Byrne had appointed and who
had succeeded Byrne as Essex County prosecutor.[112]

MacDonald, a former Republican mayor who had owned a car dealer-
ship, had been appointed by Byrne on the basis of recommendations from
Republican legislators, but otherwise had no personal or political ties to

the Governor. "While I didn't have any previous relationship with Mac-Donald, I had appointed him and was shocked by the charges. Abscam cast doubt on the promises I had made that we could have casinos in Atlantic City without corruption." MacDonald was indicted by a federal grand jury, but died before his trial. Byrne took some comfort from reassurances he received from Justin Walder, MacDonald's lawyer who had been one of Byrne's assistant prosecutors in Essex County. "Justin assured me," Byrne later recalled, "that MacDonald was innocent."[113] Robert Del Tufo, the U.S. attorney for New Jersey who previously had been the top deputy to Byrne's Attorney General William Hyland, concurred in Walder's assessment, later testifying before Congress that MacDonald should never have been charged (by his colleagues in New York at the U.S. attorney's office in Brooklyn).[114] Abscam later led to several federal bribery and conspiracy convictions, including for U.S. Senator Harrison Williams and Errichetti as well as veteran Congressman Frank Thompson from Mercer County.[115]

In response to Abscam, Byrne requested resignations from all Casino Control Commission board members and executive director Lordi and proposed restructuring the legislation establishing the Commission. Byrne's plan provoked a temporary split in his longtime friendship with Lordi, who publicly criticized the reforms, contending that they were based on "vague innuendos and suspicions concerning the integrity of the Casino Control Commission" not based on "established facts." Despite Lordi's lack of support, Byrne succeeded in developing and signing legislation to restructure the commission, changing it from a part-time to a full-time body focused solely on its regulatory role; prohibiting the issuance of temporary casino licenses; and imposing strict rules to prevent the Commission and its staff from discussing nonregulatory issues like development and investment. Prior to Abscam, there had been consideration within the administration of broadening the Commission's powers to enable it to take on some of the tasks of the regional development agency that was not created after the referendum was approved in 1976, but the scandal resulted in the new commission narrowly focused on licensing and oversight of casino operations.[116]

By the time Byrne left office in January 1982, the casino industry had resumed its growth, with seven casinos in operation. But the strict regulatory standards put in place by Byrne both before and after Abscam were later cited as adversely impacting the industry's longer term position after he left office, particularly as New Jersey's success sparked competition from nearby states. Barring casino industry executives from contributing to political campaigns or seeking office themselves was later cited as a factor in the poor quality of candidates for local office, as well as repeated episodes of corruption among municipal officials. New Jersey's lengthy and rigorous licensing process also may have chilled recruitment and retention of the most talented executives from other gaming jurisdictions; one Atlantic City casino chief executive, comparing the business and social standing of the industry and its executives in Nevada and New Jersey, later complained, "It's very hard to get people to come here when you treat us like crooks."[117] In a televised interview of Steve Wynn, then operating the Golden Nugget in Atlantic City, the journalist Bill Moyers asked Wynn, "How does it feel to be tolerated for your money, but despised for your presence?"[118]

Wynn, one of the industry's most innovative leaders, opened the Golden Nugget as Atlantic City's sixth casino-hotel in 1980, but sold the hotel to Bally's in 1987, using much of the proceeds to build The Mirage in Las Vegas, considered the first of the themed casino resorts that revitalized Las Vegas and that soon dominated the global industry.[119] Byrne's longtime close friend and law partner Martin Greenberg, who after resigning his seat in the state Senate had served as Wynn's attorney and president of the Atlantic City property, later put it: "Steve is brilliant, he's a genius, but New Jersey made it difficult for him from the start. He told me it was a mistake to come into the state and wanted to go back to Vegas. He didn't really like New Jersey. . . . They made his life difficult. The process by which you get licensed is difficult and in part I'm responsible for that [in his past role as the chair of the Senate Judiciary committee which drafted the legislation imposing the strict licensing standards]."[120]

In an article published in 2008 on Wynn's exit from New Jersey, David Schwartz, director of the Center for Gaming Research at the University of Nevada at Las Vegas and an Atlantic City native, speculated, "It's intriguing to wonder what would have happened if Steve Wynn had not become disenchanted with New Jersey regulators. If he had been given a freer hand here, it's a good guess that an 'Atlantic City Mirage' would have triggered a similar building boom by the shore. If that had happened, perhaps Atlantic City, not Las Vegas, would be the nation's leading casino destination today."[121]

Subsequent governors understandably looked to undertake their own initiatives in areas that were not so closely identified with Brendan Byrne.[122] The heritage of corruption in the City also resurfaced when the municipal government was shaken by a series of scandals, which led to convictions of Mayors Michael Matthews and James Usry and other City officials.[123] Criticism also continued over the lack of broader development beyond the casino-hotels. Competition among the casinos, and their desire to keep gamblers within their own hotels, hampered efforts to secure cooperation in promoting non-gaming projects that might broaden the City's appeal.[124] Yet despite the feuds and scandals, the overall Atlantic City casino industry continued to prosper after Governor Byrne left office in January 1982, accounting at its peak, some two decades later, for over 40,000 jobs and $6 billion in construction and related investment. In July 2003, The Borgata, perhaps the casino-hotel closest to Brendan Byrne's vision of a new Atlantic City, opened as the first property to rival the themed properties in Las Vegas. Initially conceived by Steve Wynn before he lost control of his company to MGM Grand, The Borgata quickly became the City's highest-grossing property and sparked investment by other Atlantic City hotels as they expanded and renovated to compete with the new mega-resort. Perhaps more significantly, the optimism sparked by The Borgata and the expansions of other hotels brought additional investment estimated at $1 billion in new retail and noncasino projects, heralding the long-awaited renewal of the City's commercial center. But the optimism sparked by the opening of The Borgata would soon fade.

Ironically, the success of the Atlantic City model sowed the seeds of its eventual decline. "Other states saw that New Jersey was able to keep organized crime out of the casinos, and that undercut a lot of opposition." Byrne later reflected. "Our laws and regulations became a model throughout the country."[125] As neighboring Connecticut, Delaware, Pennsylvania, and New York entered the casino business, competition cut into Atlantic City's market.[126]

In 2005, Atlantic City's gambling revenue reached a record $5.9 billion, but subsequently sharp declines in visitors, revenues and profits took hold, with the industry's financial position eroded further by excessive debt and capacity from overexpansion which took place just before the onset of the national economic recession that began in 2007. Visitors were increasingly drawn to new competitors in nearby states.[127] After Pennsylvania licensed its first casinos in 2006, new casinos opened in and near Philadelphia—the visitor market first targeted by Jonathan Pitney in 1850—particularly undercut Atlantic City's position, with Pennsylvania overtaking Atlantic City in 2012 to become the second-largest casino market in the nation behind Nevada. In 2014, following a series of casino-hotel bankruptcies and sales at distressed prices, four of the twelve Atlantic City casino-hotels closed after experiencing steep losses and failing to find buyers, highlighted by the Revel casino which, after being built at a cost of $2.4 billion, operated for just two years before shutting down.[128]

Looking back on the Atlantic City experience with casinos, Steve Perskie reflected: "Atlantic City certainly is a disappointment if you consider what it could have been. But compared with what it was before, it's been a success. Gambling brought jobs to people who had none before or allowed others a leg up into the middle class. Bank tellers became casino dealers and some later worked their way into management. The uplift in their lives has been staggering."[129]

Byrne had a somewhat tougher, but similar take. "Atlantic City had a 25-year free pass and didn't do anything with that," he reflected as the City struggled to stem its decline. "Maybe I should have been more forceful in pushing for some type of regional body like we had in the Meadowlands. I wish that more had been done to broaden its appeal beyond the casino-hotels. With all its problems, you have to remember what it was like before casinos. Without legal gambling, things would have been much worse."[130]

Chapter 10

The Reelection

"One-term Byrne"

Brendan Byrne's sense of relief and accomplishment following his signing into law of the income tax bill in July 1976 was quickly supplanted by the harsh realization of the cost that the protracted struggle had exacted on his political standing. Byrne had hoped to resolve the school funding issue within the first six months of his administration. In fact, it took an additional two years, and soon he would have to decide whether to seek reelection in 1977.

Doubts over Byrne's political future had been raised for some time. Early on, his critics, adapting the highly publicized "O.T.B." acronym used by New York State to promote its "Off-Track Betting" program, had branded him as "One-Term Byrne." On January 11, 1976, only half way into his term and some six months before the income tax was enacted, the *Star-Ledger* reported that Democratic Senator John "Jack" Fay of Middlesex County had suggested that other Democrats—including Attorney General William Hyland—consider challenging Byrne for the nomination in the June 1977 party primary. Hyland wrote Fay the next day, stating that he was not interested in running, but rumors persisted that Byrne could face opposition for the nomination.[1] Some two months before the income tax bill was passed, his own comments suggested he had reservations about running; in an article headlined "Brendan says one term may be enough," Byrne said that while he "enjoyed the challenges" of being governor, "I don't know if that's the criteria for deciding to run again."[2]

Personal considerations also argued for Byrne retiring from public life. Unlike most lawyers turned politicians, he had less reluctance to return to practicing law, the career he had pursued since boyhood and thoroughly enjoyed. In his mid-50s, he also was at the peak of his earning capacity. Of his seven children, only his eldest son Tom had completed college, and years of tuition bills for the younger children still were to be paid. His wife

197

Jean had never warmed to her public role; she bristled at the intrusion on the privacy of the family and was not comfortable in the cramped quarters of their temporary home at Morven so often the site for meetings or events.[3]

In the weeks after the enactment of the tax and school reform program, Byrne faced a political embarrassment when he failed to be elected as chair of the New Jersey delegation to the Democratic National Convention that would meet in mid-July in New York City. Senator Dugan of Hudson County, whom Byrne had selected after the 1973 election to chair the state Democratic committee, had become a frequent antagonist of the Governor during the conflict over tax policy and also in his role as chair of the Senate Judiciary Committee over nominees for judicial and prosecutorial appointments had differed with the administration.

In 1975, as the presidential election in the following year approached, Byrne's first choice for the Democratic nomination was former Vice President Hubert H. Humphrey. Byrne met with Humphrey, telling him that he thought he could help secure support from other Democratic governors, but "Humphrey told me he 'wasn't up to it'" and did not intend to run. Byrne then became an early supporter of Georgia Governor Jimmy Carter, perhaps the first incumbent Democratic governor to express a preference for Carter's nomination. "After I was elected governor in 1973," Byrne later recalled. "I wrote to all the Democratic governors asking for advice, and Carter was the only one to respond. I appreciated that, and admired what he and other southern governors had done in their states on civil rights and economic development."[4] Before Carter announced his candidacy, Byrne had hosted a reception for Carter to introduce him to leading New Jersey Democrats.

In the months before the July 1976 Democratic convention, Dugan had organized a slate of uncommitted delegates, which was viewed as an attempt to block Carter's nomination. In the June primary election, the Dugan slate won the majority of the seats in the New Jersey delegation, and Dugan was elected as its chair. But as Carter secured primary wins and delegate commitments in other states, it became clear that he would be the nominee. While Carter's nomination on the first ballot somewhat vindicated Byrne's political judgment, his secondary role in the delegation—relegated to sit only as an ordinary delegate—underscored how weak his political position in his own party within the state had become.[5]

Then, in September, the governor suffered another embarrassment when he and his wife Jean rode in a horse-drawn carriage making a ceremonial circuit at the opening of the Meadowlands Racetrack. With unfortunate timing, the event also occurred during the same week in which the first withholding from paychecks for the new state income tax had taken effect. The crowd gave a harsh greeting to the Byrnes. "People were ready to kill me," Byrne recounted years later. "I mean, we really felt we might be in some physical danger."[6]

As he watched Governor and Mrs. Byrne round the track, John Degnan recalled the scene: "Not only was the reaction boos, it was almost violent, and it was people spitting at him. People tried to hit them with placards and by the time the two of them got back up to the suite after they had gone down Jean was extremely upset and I thought he was shaken himself." Degnan, who had urged Byrne to do the circuit of the track to emphasize his role in salvaging the floundering Meadowlands project after his 1973 election, said that, given the crowd's reaction, "I wondered whether I'd have a job in the morning."[7]

Referring to the hostile Meadowlands reception in a *Star-Ledger* interview a few weeks later, Jean Byrne admitted that she had been "very upset," and that the "booing got to me and really shook me." She went on to disclose her frustration at the public's failure to recognize that the income tax was "the right thing to do for our state" and that her husband "had the courage to do it." Noting that "people voted for him in 1973 because they did not want your run-of-the-mill politician," she continued, "now that they've got the Governor who really cares about people, who is not your run-of-the mill politician, they don't know what to do with him."[8] Over a year later, after the November 1977 election, she revealed in another interview that she had urged her husband not to seek reelection: "I was pushing more for him to drop out, not that I didn't believe in him. But I told him, 'Brendan, listen, we tried it our way and the people don't like our way, so why knock ourselves out? We could go out with our dignity still intact.'"[9]

Byrne's political vulnerability found its way into the fall presidential campaign between Carter and President Gerald Ford, as Republican strategists tried to tie Carter to the unpopular New Jersey governor. "The people of New Jersey have already heard four sides of the tax issue—two from Governor Carter and two from Governor Byrne." President Ford said on October 13 at a Republican campaign reception in Union. "You know firsthand how risky it is when a candidate says one thing about taxes on the campaign trail and then does something else when he gets into office. . . ."[10] About a week before the November election, Carter canceled a campaign appearance in New Jersey, with one press report attributing the decision to the Ford campaign's success in associating Byrne with Carter. "Mr. Byrne's personal popularity has plummeted to its low point, as evidenced by polls and the heckling he receives," the account concluded, "and this has encouraged President Ford's campaign staff to attack the New Jersey Governor by name and then try to link him with Mr. Carter."[11] Carter's failure to carry New Jersey in the November election muted the benefits Byrne gained from his early support for the candidacy of the president-elect.

Despite the major roles played by the state Supreme Court in ordering the closing of the schools and the legislature in taking the lead in crafting the final income tax and school reform bills, in the public's mind the income tax was primarily the doing of Brendan Byrne. An Eagleton Poll taken in October 1976 reported that 52 percent of New Jerseyans surveyed cited Byrne as "most responsible" for the income tax, well over twice the proportion attributing primary responsibility to the legislature (19 percent) and more than three times the percentage naming the Court (16 percent). And it was clear that being held "most responsible" for the income tax was not a positive association; in the same poll, 63 percent of the respondents said they disapproved of the new tax, double the 31 percent who said they supported the levy.[12]

Another embarrassment surfaced at the end of November when the *Trenton Times* published an editorial headlined "Governor should say it: 'I do not choose to run.'" The executive editor of *The Times*, Herbert Wolfe, had taken a two-year leave of absence when working as a reporter for the newspaper to be press secretary for Byrne's 1973 campaign; after Byrne's inauguration, Wolfe was appointed as the Governor's first press secretary, later returning as the newspaper's executive editor in 1975. Conceding that "he's a decent man who has taken some enlightened stands and made some good appointments," the editorial nonetheless went on to assert that "he lacks the qualities of leadership a governor needs to be effective. He has little visible support among the public, in the Legislature and in his own party." By delaying a decision, the piece argued, "he prevents good potential candidates from gearing up to enter next spring's Democratic primary." Among the candidates the writer suggested had "excellent credentials" to succeed Byrne but who otherwise would decline "out of a sense of propriety" from challenging the Governor were three members of his cabinet—Attorney General Hyland, Public Advocate Stanley Van Ness and Corrections Commissioner Robert Mulcahy—and two Democratic legislative leaders, Albert Burstein and William Hamilton.[13]

Byrne was on a trade mission to Asia when the editorial was published, but the criticism provoked his wife Jean. "I thought, this is really nasty, and it just got me," she recalled many years later. "So I wrote, got out my yellow legal pad, and I wrote a letter to the editor."[14] As published by the *Times*, Mrs. Byrne's letter began, "Aside from Governor Byrne's refusal to sacrifice principle for political expediency and his real distaste for conducting government in that manner, I think his basic trouble is that he has told the truth to the politicians and the people of the state regarding the problems that face us, and the truth is somewhat unpleasant." After pointing out that "not one penny" of the income tax was used for state spending and that her husband's administration had kept total spending over his first three years to an increase of less than 10 percent, much below the average of his predecessors, she challenged his critics. "The problem is there," her letter concluded. "It will not go away. What is their answer?"[15]

After Carter's inauguration, inquiries were made of the new administration relating to the potential appointment of Byrne as an ambassador. The appointment would offer Byrne a somewhat graceful exit from the state, as well as possibly sparing Carter the expected embarrassment of Democrats losing one of only two gubernatorial elections held in 1977, his first year in the White House. "I probably would have accepted going to Ireland as an ambassador," Byrne would later say, "but when they said only New Zealand was available I wasn't interested. If I had taken that, it would have looked like I was looking for any way out, that I was running away."[16]

When Byrne and some of his key advisers traveled to Washington for Jimmy Carter's inauguration in January, John Degnan took the opportunity to visit Peter Hart, Carter's pollster, who had been commissioned by a New Jersey labor union to conduct a poll of New Jersey voters. "Peter Hart told me," Degnan recalled, "that he had never before in his public career seen a public official less likely to get re-elected. He had 22% [of Democrats] under the most favorable circumstances. And Hart said there was not a chance in the world that this guy could get reelected." But when Degnan returned to Trenton and reluctantly summarized Hart's findings to Byrne, he surprisingly heard Byrne systematically raise points where he felt Hart had overlooked potentially more positive issues to target for any campaign.[17]

Somewhat more positive findings for Byrne could be found in surveys that reported—once voters were informed of the impact of the full package of reforms enacted with the income tax—they had a much more favorable view of the Byrne program. The Eagleton Poll taken in October 1976, for example, which reported a two-to-one margin of respondents disapproving of the income tax, also found that, when they were advised of the entire program (including increased school aid, property tax relief, homestead rebates, and caps on spending increases), the approval rating rose significantly, with 54 percent approving to 38 percent disapproving.[18]

In December, at a Byrne family gathering at Morven, the conversation turned to whether the Governor would seek reelection. His older brother Frank, whom Brendan had always viewed as a more natural politician than himself, challenged him to enter the race to demonstrate that, win or lose, he had the courage to defend himself and his policies to the skeptical press and public.

As Byrne mulled whether to seek reelection, other Democrats began exploring their own potential candidacies. On January 2, 1977, the *New York Times* noted that Byrne's political decline had brought about the unusual prospect of several fellow Democrats challenging their incumbent governor for the party nomination. "The prize, the governorship, seems attainable, because the incumbent, Brendan T. Byrne, does not appear to have a firm grip on his job, his party's loyalty or the public's affection."[19] But as the primary election field to oppose Byrne took shape, no candidate appeared able to break out of the pack. Joseph Hoffman, Byrne's former cabinet officer who had been replaced in August 1976 when it became apparent that he was planning to enter the primary, said, "At this point, everyone has support a quarter of an inch thick."[20]

Congressman Florio, who commissioned his own poll, met with Byrne to share its rather negative assessment of the Governor's prospects. The Washington-based firm that conducted Florio's poll summarized its findings starkly: "Governor Byrne is in trouble." The summary went on to conclude that Byrne "might be able to squeak through a multiple candidate primary race, but he would have virtually insurmountable problems against any reasonable GOP candidate in November." Yet, according to the analysis, the "most striking figure" of the survey relating to Byrne was that "31% of these Democratic voters say that they *would not support him under any circumstances*" [emphasis in original].[21] Of the other potential Democratic candidates, the poll found that Florio and Mayor Paul Jordan of Jersey City had roughly equal support, but that Florio had a more secure base and more potential to expand it outside his home county of Camden.[22]

In an interview years later, in what he cited as illustrating "the cleverness of Brendan Byrne," Florio recounted that he approached Byrne when there was "a lot of speculation that he would not even run" given his low standing in the polls, and advised Byrne he would not enter the primary if the Governor decided to run. But if Byrne chose not to seek another term, Florio told Byrne that he believed he had a good chance with his South Jersey base to win the nomination in a multi-candidate field, given that the several North Jersey candidates would likely split the votes among themselves. According to Florio, Byrne "led me on, saying 'I don't know, I don't think so, who knows, whatever, whatever.' And they keep on doing that right up to the very end."[23] As the filing deadline for candidates approached without a clear answer from Byrne, Florio finally filed as a candidate. "I later found out," Florio continued, "that the goal was to get me into the race because that would have that many more people in and you . . . wouldn't have to have as big a margin to prevail."[24] There was, according to Florio, "a conscious effort on their part . . . encouraging me to run without really telling me so."[25]

While much of the public criticism of Byrne focused on his advocacy of the income tax and his credibility after stating in the campaign that he did not see a need for one in the "foreseeable future," an undercurrent of the election was a reaction to his stubborn refusal to comply with the politically correct behavior and gestures many expected in a governor. His propensity for travel, for tennis, for mixing with celebrities, and for enjoying other perks of his office often grated with his critics, as well as members of the press and the public. At times, Byrne tried to deflate the criticism with humor. At the annual "roast" of the state's politicians held by the State House Correspondents Club, Byrne addressed recent newspaper accounts that his daughter Susan, then a student at Georgetown University, was involved in an accident while driving a state government car in Washington, DC. Referring to the mishap, Byrne said to the audience of over a thousand members of the state political, business, and media establishment, "You know, a lot of people say I use the state helicopter too much. But what's a guy to do when his daughter's got the car? He's got to use the helicopter!" He received a standing ovation.

Some of Byrne's closest friends were concerned about the personal toll the criticism was having on Byrne and his family, along with what appeared to be, if he sought reelection, a likely stinging rejection at the polls. Barry Evenchick, who had previously worked under Byrne as an assistant prosecutor and as his aide at the Public Utilities Commission, said years later that "as a friend, it was sad for me to see him encountering this sort of flak" and that "had he asked me if he should run again, I'm not sure I would have said 'yes' only out of concern that he might have suffered what I thought would be a humiliating defeat."[26] At a meeting at Morven as Byrne was pondering whether to run, Robert Wilentz, the former legislator who had helped develop issue positions during Byrne's 1973 campaign and his transition, lingered after others at the meeting had left and asked to speak privately with the governor. Wilentz was "very uncomfortable and apologetic," according to Byrne's later account, "but he told me frankly that he did not believe there was any chance I could win and that he hoped I would avoid embarrassment by staying out of the race."[27]

The 1977 campaign got an early start soon after the new year. When former Assembly Speaker Thomas Kean announced his candidacy on January 13, Kean targeted the income tax as his principal issue, pledging that if elected, he would allow the tax to expire as scheduled at the end of June 1978. "Brendan Byrne promised no income tax," Kean said during the press conference announcing his candidacy, "and then imposed one of the most unfair and unjustified taxes in New Jersey history. Never again must any candidate ever simplify the tax issue."[28] Kean declined to say how he would make up for the loss of revenue from the income tax, but he implicitly criticized Byrne's tactics in failing to seek broader public input in the tax debate, declaring that he would solicit such participation by holding either a tax convention or creating a broad-based study commission.[29] By taking an aggressive position against the tax, Kean pushed Senator Ray Bateman, his principal rival for the Republican nomination, to a similar stance. "He took a very tough anti-tax position in the primary," Bateman later recalled, "and forced me . . . to do the same thing or I probably wouldn't have sustained myself for the primary."[30]

In February, Byrne convened a dinner meeting of advisers and friends at the Princeton Club in Manhattan. The group included the pollster Peter Hart, David Garth, Dick Leone, Lew Kaden, Charlie Carella, Henry Luther, Alan Sagner, Jerry English, and John Degnan. "David Garth presented and Peter Hart presented the polling results," Lew Kaden recalled in an interview, "and basically said they didn't see a critical path to success and the governor's favorable rating was in the single digits. It was below ten I think at the time."[31] The political professionals, as Byrne recalled many years later, "all told me I couldn't win, that there was no way I could win. There was enough of an unmovable negative that I couldn't overcome."[32] Most around the table expressed their views that he shouldn't run, "Hart told me," Byrne remembered, "that my chances weren't getting better, and that there just didn't seem to be any hope of convincing people that the income tax was the right thing to do."[33] Yet Degnan nonetheless argued that Byrne should seek reelection. "I thought he deserved to go down fighting," Degnan said in a later interview. "It sounds kind of hokey but he had done the right thing, he had stood up for what he believed in and in the way I grew up you don't run away from that fight, you fight it to the end and I thought there was a remote chance that he could win."[34] At some point, Byrne turned to Leone and asked if he thought he could win; "I told him yes," Leone later recalled, "but it would be like steering a big ocean liner into a narrow berth. Everything would have to go just right."[35]

Many years later, Byrne reflected that even during the course of his political fall, he remained remarkably calm. "In all the time I was in politics, I don't think I ever lost a night's sleep. I mean, I would have a hectic day, I would hear a poll that showed I was way behind, and I would go to sleep, and so be it." Some of those closest to him, including his long-time secretary Dottie Seltzer, his counsel Daniel O'Hern, and his Attorney General Jim Zazzali, later speculated that Byrne's demeanor during periods of high tension as governor may have been due to his wartime combat experience, but Byrne himself had a somewhat less prosaic explanation. "You control as much as you can," he said years later. "You know, the fate is in somebody else's hands."[36]

As the meeting neared a close, "David Garth said that his advice was that I not run," Byrne recalled, "but if I was not going to take his advice, I shouldn't announce that I was going to run until very late. Those polls would be old polls and people would think that I had something else up my sleeve."[37] Byrne's oldest son Tom attended the meeting and on the drive home he recalled that his father asked his opinion. "Look, right now you're so unpopular that every county in this state is going to have their own horse in the race," Tom remembered as his response. "You're the only one with a profile. The vote is going to break down as pro-Byrne versus anti-Byrne vote. And as long as the anti-Byrne vote is whacked up in enough different ways, you'll win the primary."[38] While Byrne made no decision on that day, he would later point to the meeting, and particularly to Degnan's arguments, as pushing him to defend his record and seek a second term.[39]

In early April, with Byrne still not having made any public announcement of his candidacy, Ann Klein, who had run against Byrne in the 1973 primary and then joined his cabinet as Byrne's commissioner of the Department of Institutions and Agencies, met with Byrne to share the findings of the most recent poll she had commissioned to explore her own potential chances in the primary. The poll reported Byrne's low overall standing in approval ratings, but also, as Byrne remembered, "that people were starting to move back to me."[40] Years later, John Degnan recounted that "the poll showed that Ann could win the primary and is more likely to win the primary than Brendan Byrne but it also showed that under a certain set of circumstances Brendan could win the primary." Degnan then went on to note his appreciation for Klein's unselfish gesture: "What did Ann do with that poll? She sat down with Brendan and told him the results. That was an enormously generous thing to do, and if she hadn't told him, . . . he wouldn't have had any real polling data that suggested he could win."[41]

David Garth, who had advised Byrne against running, reluctantly agreed to help again, but only by shielding himself from too direct an identification with Byrne; he created a new company named "Shooting Star Productions" in an attempt to cloak his role with what he viewed as likely to be a losing effort. Garth also insisted that Byrne admit publicly that he made a mistake in his first campaign with the widely reported comment that the state would not need an income tax "in the foreseeable future." Byrne initially resisted, arguing that his comment was taken out of context and was in fact accurate given the available information at the time on the state's fiscal situation. Yet Garth contended that Byrne's effort to parse his comment was too nuanced to communicate to the average voter, and Byrne agreed to stop defending the comment and admit that it had been a mistake.

Taking Garth's advice, Byrne waited until shortly before the deadline to file as a candidate in the primary. On April 25, he spoke at the opening of his campaign headquarters in South Brunswick. "We're here to launch a fight," Byrne said. "We won't have anything to apologize for, we won't duck any issue. Make no mistake about it, New Jersey is a better place today than when I walked into the governor's office in 1974."[42]

Henry Luther, Byrne's former executive secretary, agreed to become the campaign manager, but Dick Leone, who had earlier resigned as state treasurer, also later returned to help with the campaign's strategy. Byrne later described Luther as "the smartest political operative, I think, I've ever seen."[43] Fariborz Fatemi, the 1973 campaign veteran who would again direct the advance team in 1977, later said Luther "was the glue that kept the campaign together. He met with the staff, county chairmen, mayors and anyone else who needed something or had a problem and worked it out. Everyone liked Henry."[44]

Dick Coffee, the staff director of the Assembly Democrats, assumed a major role in developing political strategy. Jeffrey Laurenti, a Trenton native who was a legislative aide to state Senator Joseph Merlino, became the principal issues adviser and speechwriter. Bob Torricelli, then an aide to Jerry English, also took a leave to work full-time as the deputy campaign director focusing on operations and logistics. Later in the campaign, Harold Hodes, one of the most significant new additions, would take a leave from his staff position under Newark Mayor Kenneth Gibson to accompany Byrne on campaign stops and serve as a liaison with local politicians.

Hodes recalled that once Leone came back to the campaign, he ran a tough ship. "Moody, tough, knowledgeable, respectful, but at the same time a hard master," Hodes said of Leone, "but you learn and you see things and understand why. You went to a staff meeting with Dick Leone every morning and his assignment to you was to make sure that you knew what was going on in the state before you came to the meeting. So you would have to read the newspapers, well we didn't have, you know, telecommunications then and if you didn't know the newspapers, he would ask you to leave the room."[45]

Garth produced the most effective television commercial of the campaign. In the spot, Byrne directly faced the camera and declared, "Four years ago, I said New Jersey didn't need an income tax. And that was wrong." He then went on to outline the reasons for his change in position and challenge his opponents to come up with a better alternative. "The minute we shot the commercial," Byrne remembered, "Dave Garth came running out of his little control booth, and said, that's all we're going to do. We're going with this one."[46] Jeff Laurenti, his issues adviser, recalled years later, "It was the only televised ad that Byrne aired in the primary. And Garth did not acknowledge paternity until the results were in on the night of the primary."[47] The commercial would be aired repeatedly through both the primary and general election campaigns.

Byrne's political luck, combined with considerable skill in sizing up his prospects in a field of multiple opponents, again played a major role in the June 6 primary election. None of the challengers was able to emerge as a frontrunner or to persuade any of the others to drop out of the race to consolidate the anti-Byrne forces. Bob Mulcahy, who would become Byrne's chief of staff in the second term, later reflected: "It gets down to personal egos . . . and they all think that they can be elected and they all want the shot and they're unwilling to get together for what may in their view be the common good and I think this is what happened here. They all thought they had a shot and in reality none of them did."[48]

Byrne's strongest potential opponent, Jersey City Mayor Paul Jordan, who had decided not to run for reelection in Jersey City in order to seek the gubernatorial nomination, saw his campaign collapse when his slate of candidates in the mayoral and council elections held in May was defeated by a rival faction headed by Thomas F. X. Smith, who was elected mayor. Three weeks before the June gubernatorial primary election, Jordan withdrew from the race and endorsed Byrne for the nomination. Smith also fielded slates of legislative candidates in the June primary election which defeated the Jordan-aligned incumbents in two of the three Hudson districts, including most notably Senator Dugan, the state Democratic chairman. Smith endorsed Ralph DeRose over Byrne in the primary, but after a vigorous effort by the Byrne campaign to persuade Smith of the benefits of the tax program and the Governor's plans for new urban initiatives, he later became an aggressive spokesman for Byrne in the general election campaign.[49]

Congressman Robert Roe, chairman of the House Public Works and Transportation Committee, was unable to expand his base beyond Passaic County and, to a limited degree, split his organized labor support with Joseph Hoffman, Byrne's former cabinet officer who had been forced out of the administration in 1976. Former Senator DeRose was unable to broaden his support beyond Essex County, where Byrne also was expected to run strongly, particularly after securing the endorsement of Newark Mayor Ken Gibson. "Gibson was committed to Byrne," Gibson's aide Harold Hodes recalled, "because of what Byrne did, that he felt that standing up for the income tax is a courageous thing to do."[50]

On the night of the primary election, Byrne recalled that he was at Morven watching television reports of the early returns. "Nothing looked certain," he recalled later. "Campaign aides were getting reports, TV was being cautious, and tension was running pretty high." His eight-year-old son Billy then walked into the room to ask when they would know the election result, and his father replied that the returns would be in by ten o'clock. "Good," was the son's response. "Then I can watch the end of the Yankee game."[51]

When the returns were reported, Byrne had won comfortably, albeit with only 30.3 percent of the vote, trailed by Congressman Roe (23.16 percent); Senator De Rose (17.26 percent); Congressman Florio (15.15 percent); and Joseph Hoffman (10.16 percent). The combination of Byrne's strategy, and the failure of other candidates to drop their campaigns in favor of uniting behind one of Byrne's stronger opponents, allowed him to win in the large field. "If it had been one on one," Jim Florio reflected years later, "Governor Byrne versus Congressman Roe, probably Congressman Roe would have won . . . One on seven, he was able to win."[52] Byrne himself concurred with Florio's assessment. "Bob Roe was the strongest challenger," he said in a later interview, "and if I had decided not to run, I probably would have endorsed him. He would have had the best chance to win."[53] Despite the victory, the reality was that seven out of ten Democrats had voted against the incumbent governor of their own party, a rather ominous sign for Byrne's ability to unite the party behind him for the fall general election campaign. (Until 2006, Byrne's percentage of the vote would rank as a national record for the lowest in a primary election of any incumbent governor seeking reelection.)[54]

Senator Raymond Bateman, with 54.7 percent of the vote, easily defeated former Assembly Speaker Thomas Kean (36.1 percent) for the Republican nomination. On the day after the election, Byrne phoned Bateman to congratulate him. "I also told him," Byrne later recalled, "that if he ever felt our campaign was doing anything unfair, he should call me personally so we could talk it over between ourselves."[55]

When Bateman entered the race, he had not expected Byrne to be his opponent. Given the Governor's low standing in the polls, he had assumed that Paul Jordan, the Jersey City mayor, would utilize the Hudson County organization's support to win the nomination over the other candidates from smaller counties. When Jordan's campaign collapsed after his own slate of candidates in the municipal election was defeated, Bateman was further surprised when the anti-Byrne candidates failed to coalesce around the strongest challenger to the Governor. "None of them got together," Bateman later recalled. "If any two of them had gotten together, they'd have won."[56]

"We were elated and yet depressed," John Degnan recalled as the mood of the inner campaign circle on primary election night when they met at a diner around 3 a.m. for breakfast. "And, you know, there weren't many of us around the table who really believed we could win in November. And yet we were going into this long summer fight for it, every bit as committed and zealous. But the elation was tempered by a realistic realization that when you win by that margin it doesn't bode well for the November election. And we all liked and respected Ray Bateman, by the way."[57] Bateman had many Democratic friends, notably including Chief Justice and former Governor Hughes. Hughes and other Democrats had admired his moderate positions and his past leadership in sponsoring the existing school aid formula that increased state school aid for the most distressed cities; supporting the Cahill tax reform program; and in expanding the state's higher education system.[58] Unlike the right-wing Charlie Sandman in 1973, Bateman's record was viewed by the Byrne insiders as much more in line with the independent and moderate voters who ultimately would decide the election.

Another sign that the prospect of reelection still appeared dim after Byrne's primary victory was confirmed on election night was that President Carter failed to phone to offer Byrne congratulations and support. "Bert Lance, Jimmy Carter's budget director, phoned and we had a short conversation," Byrne later recalled. "But I interpreted the fact that the President asked Lance to call and didn't phone himself as a signal that the White House didn't think I had much of a chance in November. I knew they thought I would lose."[59]

The pessimism of Byrne's campaign staff was matched by optimism in the Bateman camp. Holding a ten-point lead over Byrne in polls taken in August, Bateman chose to continue his long practice of spending much of the month in Maine. Bateman's absence was exploited by the Democrats as Byrne made frequent visits to greet voters on the Jersey Shore, at county fairs, festivals and campaign at other events attracting large crowds. "I think Ray's decision to take his usual break in Maine was a big mistake," Fariborz Fatemi later reflected. "While Ray was away, the Governor received excellent coverage in local newspapers of his talking casually with voters and defending his record."[60]

Byrne also made effective use of his status as the sitting governor, signing bills in public settings, awarding grants to hospitals and schools, and otherwise participating in a wide variety of events throughout the state. When he did campaign in the summer, Bateman quickly learned of the difficulty of running against an incumbent, later citing as an example a visit he made during the summer to the popular Sussex County horse show. "I went up there on a Thursday," he recalled, "at seven o'clock in the morning, had a breakfast meeting with a lot of people, shook hands all day long, all day long. Left there about seven o'clock that night, totally wiped out but very satisfied. The next morning Brendan gets in a state helicopter, flies up to the Sussex horse show and signs a bill making the horse the New Jersey state animal. Now, who won that battle?"[61]

The summer of 1977 also was an opportunity for Byrne to engage in a bit of gallows humor during one of his weekly Saturday morning tennis groups at Morven. "The guys rarely spoke of the upcoming election," Byrne later remembered. "Sorta like not mentioning rope in the home of a man who has been hanged. This one Saturday we had split sets and had got to 6-all in the third set. Naturally, someone asked if we should play a tiebreaker. 'Play it out,' I said. 'We have the court until January.'"[62] The home of one of his frequent tennis partners, Peter Benchley, the author of the best-selling novel *Jaws,* was within walking distance of Morven; when Benchley began installing his own tennis court, Byrne took that as a signal that "Peter didn't think he'd be playing at Morven much longer."[63]

There also were tangible signs during the election year that the state was moving ahead in other areas. Just before the primary election, Byrne traveled to Atlantic City to sign the legislation establishing the regulatory program that would lead to the licensing of the first casinos, gaining national media attention through his challenge to mobsters: "Keep your filthy hands out of Atlantic City, keep the hell out of our state!"[64] In the Meadowlands, despite the hostile reception he had received in the previous fall at the opening of the new Racetrack, construction began on the new indoor arena, placing Byrne's own stamp on the Sports Complex and helping to demonstrate benefits in jobs and related investment to construction unions and development interests. The New York Cosmos of the North American Soccer League also played their inaugural season at Giants Stadium with their star Pelé, the most famous soccer player of his time, setting attendance records for soccer in North America and demonstrating a payback for Byrne's renegotiation of the agreement with the Giants to allow the Sports Authority to lease the stadium to other teams.

In September, Bateman released his long-awaited alternative to the Byrne income tax program. The plan was developed with William Simon, a New Jersey native who had served as Secretary of the Treasury in the Nixon Administration. Bateman's plan called for allowing the income tax to expire on June 30, 1978, enacting a series of increases of existing nuisance taxes and, if necessary, increasing the state sales tax by 1 percent. In the words of one analyst, the "Bateman-Simon" plan was "a hodgepodge of one-time savings, rosy economic projections, and unconvincing stopgaps."[65]

Clifford Goldman, who had become acting state treasurer after Leone's resignation the year before, later recounted how he had prepared to respond to the Republican program: "By 1977, I had accumulated three years' worth of Republican ideas about state finance from budget hearings and press accounts. I kept a handwritten list of some 30 or 40 ideas, each with a brief response of dismissal. When Bateman held his press conference to release his plan, someone in attendance called me with it and I handed my secretary my list with instructions to type up numbers 1, 4, 7, 14, 17, 23 (the actual numbers conforming to the Bateman plan). Within 15 minutes, we had the material to destroy the Bateman plan in a coherent presentation, which was used in that day's press conference."[66]

Following the release of the Republican plan, Goldman briefed Byrne on the response he would make at a State House press conference. Before Byrne left his private office to meet the press waiting outside, he told his secretary, Dottie Seltzer, "I think I'm going to call this plan by the initials," but according to Byrne she objected, saying, "Don't do that. That's not dignified." Byrne then said he decided "to take her advice, and not use it, but somebody asked the question at the end of the press conference who gave me an opportunity to say, 'This plan is going to become known by its initials.'" Immediately following his response, Byrne walked out of the press conference. "That was the most dramatic way to do it," he continued, "and that was the headline in the next day's paper. And the media picked that up, and it completely discredited the Bateman/Simon B.S. Plan."[67] Even Ray Bateman understood the popularity with the media of the shorthand label, reflecting in an interview years later: "A 'B.S.' plan attracted the press; they liked that. You can't blame 'em for that. If I'd been writing, I'd have found that quite fun to write about."[68]

For the remainder of the campaign, Byrne continued to attack Bateman's plan, consistently placing him on the defensive. "You just could tell that Ray himself didn't believe his own plan," Dick Leone later said. "He was an honest, decent guy who knew as much as anyone about the state government and knew that the plan didn't add up."[69] When the Democratic majorities in the legislature added a provision to the income tax legislation that the tax would "sunset" or lapse in 1978, the maneuver increased pressure on the Republicans to explain how they would make up the lost revenue if the income tax were repealed. Goldman's point-by-point rebuttal of the facts and assumptions of the Bateman-Simon plan also persuaded the majority of the press covering the campaign and their editors. "The press reaction to the Bateman plan and Byrne's response to it," Jeffrey Laurenti, Byrne's issues director, later said "was arguably the turning point in the public's reappraisal of the tax program. With rare unanimity, the state's newspapers expressed skepticism or outright scorn for the Bateman plan. We quickly aired TV ads quoting the torrent of editorials demolishing it."[70] At the first debate between the candidates following the plan's release, Bateman gave an unresponsive answer when asked by the moderator how he would replace the revenues from the income tax. The format of the debate called for Byrne to have sixty seconds to respond, but he quickly said, "I'll cede my sixty seconds if Senator Bateman will really answer that question." A flustered Bateman then meandered for another sixty seconds. "It was a disaster for Bateman," said John Degnan, "and it was read that way by the press and it was a brilliant tactic by Byrne."[71]

Reflecting years later on the impact of the Bateman-Simon plan on the election, both Byrne and Bateman concluded that it was a political "mistake" that the Republican could have avoided. "I think Ray was too honest and responsible," Byrne later said, "to go through the campaign without coming up with an alternative to the money raised by the income tax. But it probably was a political mistake. He could have simply said something like 'trust us, we'll come up with something after we can get in there and look closer at the numbers.'"[72] Bateman himself would agree that he could have tried to defer coming up with an alternative to the new income tax revenue. "I could have said," he told an interviewer, "I have to see what the composition of the legislature that gets elected in this election to see what I might be able to do with the next legislature, without taking a specific position. I felt obligated to take a specific position because in June I said I was gonna."[73]

At about the same time Bateman released his plan, the Treasury Department sent out the first rebate checks under the then new property tax relief program, accompanied by a letter signed by Byrne explaining the background of the tax reform program and its provision for tax relief. The Republicans filed a complaint with the state election commission charging that the Treasury had misused public funds for political purposes by enclosing the explanation with the rebate checks. "I was deposed," Treasurer Goldman later recalled, "and said that the explanation was included to forestall setting up an expensive phone bank to answer phone calls from recipients of the checks who would not otherwise know what the check was for."[74] The commission apparently accepted Goldman's argument and rejected the Republican complaint that the expenses for the Byrne letter with the rebate mailing should be borne by the Democratic campaign.

The Byrne campaign also targeted those constituencies that particularly benefited from the tax and school reform program, including commuters employed in New York and Philadelphia; senior citizens; veterans; tenants; and lower-income residents. The outreach included carefully planned appearances at train stations, senior-citizen communities and other locations around the state intended to highlight how the new system aided individual constituencies, providing positive images of Byrne interacting with prospective voters.[75] "We had a series of town-specific flyers for drops and mailings in all the larger cities and townships," Jeff Laurenti recounted, "that noted exactly what the average homeowner and renter had saved in property tax over what they paid in income tax."[76]

The educational effort gradually succeeded in persuading once skeptical voters that the Byrne tax program was perhaps worthy of support. "Once the program went into effect," Treasurer Goldman reflected, "it proved to be beneficial for most people and was almost imperceptible to those who did not benefit financially—just as it was planned. Property taxes went down in 1977 despite high inflation. Rebates went out. Withholding was miniscule for most people. Refunds were made punctually. In short, the emotionally charged income tax monster turned out to be a puff of wind."[77]

In contrast to the often mumbled, disjointed speaking style displayed in his 1973 campaign, as a candidate in 1977 Byrne spoke clearly and forcefully. One of his most important joint appearances with Bateman was before the convention of the state AFL-CIO, whose President, Charles Marciante, had long been an antagonist of both Byrne and his tax program. "There were thousands of people there, it was a wild, wild scene," Bateman later recalled. "Brendan Byrne could make a lousy, lousy speech, but that day he made a great speech, well-organized, snappy and punchy. . . . Charlie Marciante was the emcee and he was for me. . . . After Brendan had finished, to wild applause, Marciante was walking by me and he put his hand on my shoulder and said, 'You better be good, you bastard.'"[78] Byrne himself later said that it was "the best speech of my life. . . . When I got finished with that speech, they gave me a standing ovation. There was no way then that Charlie Marciante, as powerful as he was, could get the endorsement for Bateman."[79] Byrne received 63 percent of the delegates' votes—some six thousand short of the two-thirds needed for a formal endorsement—but his supporters justifiably claimed that the majority vote and enthusiastic reception he had received was a "moral victory" indicating that an "overwhelming majority of organized labor backs him for re-election."[80]

At one point, the Republican campaign sought to exploit a controversy relating to Joseph Lordi, whom Byrne had appointed to head the staff of the Casino Control Commission and who had previously served as chief deputy to Byrne when he was Essex County prosecutor and later succeeded him as prosecutor. During the campaign, the report of a State Police investigation of Lordi was mailed to the Bateman campaign, which gave it to the state Republican chairman for release to the press. (It was later determined that two State Police lieutenants had leaked the report to the Republicans without authorization.) The report implied that Lordi might have organized crime connections, based on rather flimsy evidence that he had frequented a Newark bar known as a mob hangout and that his brother, a lawyer, had once represented the brother of Gerardo Catena, the reputed Mafia leader.[81] But the attempt to taint Byrne with the so-called "Lordi scandal" backfired; many Italian Americans, resenting what they saw as a witch hunt based on Lordi's ancestry, turned out in high numbers to vote for Byrne.[82]

By mid-October, some internal polls showed that Byrne had pulled to within five points of Bateman and others showed the race nearly even. Byrne also was encouraged when U.S. Senator Joseph Biden of Delaware called to advise that he had been informed of a privately sponsored poll that had included a survey of the New Jersey gubernatorial race, and flatly predicted: "Brendan, you're going to win! You're eight points ahead!"[83] By the third week of October, a *New York Times*/CBS poll reported that the race was neck-and-neck, each with 43 percent of the vote. As the news improved, at one point Byrne said to Leone, "You think we're going to win, don't you?" and Leone responded, "Yes, but don't tell a soul."[84] A few weeks before the election, Byrne held a meeting of his cabinet; Robert Mulcahy, the corrections commissioner who soon would become Byrne's chief of staff in the second term, recalled years later that the Governor confidently told the group, "We're going to win and I don't want you to worry about it, just do your job and do your job well."[85] The final Eagleton Poll, taken in the last week of October through November 1, reported that Byrne had an eight-point lead, 44 percent to 36 percent.

But on election day of November 8, a new worry gripped Byrne's campaign team A severe rainstorm hit the northern part of the state, resulting in flooding that disrupted bus and rail transit out of Manhattan and made some polling places inaccessible, including in heavily Democratic Hudson County and other areas with high levels of commuters working in New York. Commuters who worked in New York (as well as Pennsylvania) were expected to be strong pro-Byrne voters, as Byrne later explained, since they "didn't have to pay the state income tax in New Jersey, because they got a credit from the New York state income tax. So it was a free ride for them."[86] Assessing the results of the election years later, Ray Bateman also pointed to the benefits to commuters from Byrne's tax program as a significant factor in his defeat. "If you look at the election results, you'll see it, towns like Ridgewood, Bernardsville, my Bernardsville, I used to win five to one, I just barely carried because there were rich homeowners or wealthy homeowners who were commuters who had no new tax because they were paying the same—they were paying a higher tax in New York actually and who got 500 bucks to boot. They weren't about to trade that in for me."[87]

Byrne phoned New York City Mayor Abe Beame, requesting that that the mayor issue a public statement urging employers to allow their employees to leave work early due to the storm and the transit problems. "Abe told me that he had just done so," Byrne recounted, "not to help me, but because it was the smart thing to do given the weather and the flooding blocking the trains and buses."[88]

"There was actually a debate going on in Morven that day," Degnan remembered, "about whether we could petition the Supreme Court to keep the polls open for a couple of hours later that day to ensure the people got the right to vote."[89] Late in the afternoon, Dick Coffee and Dick Leone requested that an executive order be prepared for Byrne to sign, unilaterally ordering extension of the voting hours on the basis of the weather emergency. Ultimately, neither action was taken.

Bateman had his own story about campaigning on the rainy election day. "Brendan and I campaigned together on election day, which was pouring rain. We went to two or three different places, you know, he'd be there or I'd be there. I went home about two o'clock in the afternoon because it was just absolutely a downpour for 48 hours." As Bateman continued the account, after he arrived home, "I sat down and my wife gave me my martini . . . and right at the top of my pile of stuff in the kitchen . . . was a letter, a 'Dear Homeowner' letter from Brendan saying that 'We're happy that you got your homestead rebate and your next rebate will be in March of next year.' The treasury department had sent one of those to everybody in the state of New Jersey, every homeowner." In Bateman's mind, when he read the letter, he knew "when all the bullshit is done, that was the election."[90]

Byrne crushed Bateman, winning 54.5 percent to 40.9 percent. "I think we were astonished by the margin on election night," Bob Mulcahy recalled, "and I can remember driving to the campaign headquarters . . . and turning on

CBS before we even got there and them declaring that Brendan was the winner. I mean it almost took some of the celebration out of it because by the time you got there, which was maybe a half hour or forty-five minutes after the polls closed . . . it was all over."[91] At the victory party at a restaurant in West Orange, Byrne first paid tribute to his opponent, saying "Ray Bateman didn't lose anything in this great campaign that he waged. He still has the respect of the people of New Jersey." Continuing his remarks to the boisterous crowd, he shouted, "I haven't found anyone in this room tonight who admits to calling me 'One-Term Byrne!'"

All of the Byrne family, including Byrne's siblings and cousins, had pitched in to help on the campaign. Yet Jean Byrne didn't realize how the pressure of the race had affected her own children until, after the election night celebration in West Orange, she returned to Morven and put her ten-year-old daughter Barbara to bed at one a.m.: "I was putting Barbara to bed, and she said to me that finally she could go to sleep without feeling nervous."[92]

Within a week of the election, Byrne and Bateman were back to playing squash together. "I'm sure Ray felt the voters of New Jersey could have made a better choice in that election," Byrne later said, "but he didn't hold the election results against me, and we kept our friendship."[93]

Chapter 11

The Second Term

On the night before Brendan Byrne's inauguration for his second term as governor on January 18, 1978, two unanticipated events upset the careful planning that had taken place over the previous weeks since his reelection: a snowstorm swept through the state and his seven-year old son Billy broke his arm sliding down the bannister at Morven. Billy Byrne's arm was easily dealt with through a cast, but the storm proved to be a more difficult hurdle. Roads throughout the state were covered with snow and ice, preventing some invitees to the inaugural ceremonies from making the trip. After some discussion, the events went off as scheduled, again beginning with a mass and a chilly procession from the State House to the nearby War Memorial where Byrne took the oath of office.

In his second Inaugural Address, Byrne began by wryly noting his surprising reelection victory: "For constitutional and electoral reasons, few New Jersey governors have delivered a second inaugural address. For several years, there was little fear that I would disturb that tradition." He then went on to take credit for a first term "not of symbols but of substance." Among the accomplishments he cited were maintaining an honest and open government; enacting tax reform; imposing caps on government spending; developing the Meadowlands sports complex; approving casino gambling in Atlantic City; and strengthening environmental controls.

When he entered office four years earlier, he noted, the state "was not held in high regard by our fellow Americans," but since then it had begun overcoming its image of "a people without an identity, . . . a state without an ego." He expressed hope that—freed of the "horizon of crisis" over tax reform that had so dominated the public policy agenda for so many years—the state would be able to turn to new initiatives, including targeting resources

217

to areas in greatest need and preserving its natural resources and undeveloped regions.[1]

An unintended consequence of Byrne's message was that it angered his predecessor, Bill Cahill, who was in the audience. "Bill was upset," Byrne later explained, "that I contrasted our progress with the past, and took that as a slap at his administration. I really didn't mean that, but told him I was sorry he felt that way. It took some time before we were on good terms again."[2]

With the sharp conflicts over the income tax and school reform program behind him, Byrne's second term would be one of the most productive in the state's history. A new staff helped improve communication and relationships with the legislature and its leaders. In contrast to his first term, the Democratic legislative leaders installed after his reelection had been key allies of Byrne during the tax battle and generally worked cooperatively with him and his staff to achieve his second-term goals.

Byrne's election victory contributed to a brief uptick in his popularity. At the beginning of his second term, his approval rating reached 45 percent—the highest since a survey taken in May 1974, four months after his first inauguration, after he had successfully dealt with the gasoline crisis and unveiled his reforms to combat corruption and increase government accountability.[3] But after Byrne's endorsement of the income tax as part of his school financing reform package, he would never again be as popular during his time as governor. "With Brendan Byrne," wrote Cliff Zukin, a Rutgers professor and director of its Eagleton Poll, "people formed their opinions based on the major, salient conflict of his administration—his handling of the income tax controversy."[4]

One of those counseling a new course was Jean Byrne: "I told him I think he has been too nice a guy in office. I said this time, 'Brendan, you've got to get tough.'"[5] To be sure, Byrne demonstrated a new aggressiveness—indeed on occasion a strategy of confrontation—in his relations with the legislature on the more difficult issues. "New Jersey's 1947 constitution gave the governor substantial power," reflected Rutgers professor Alan Rosenthal, a noted national expert on state legislatures, "but Byrne pushed that power to the limit, and perhaps beyond, to get his way."[6]

Soon after the election, Byrne tried to persuade Ray Bateman, his Republican opponent, to join the administration. Author of the school funding formula that the state Supreme Court had found unconstitutional in *Robinson v. Cahill*, Bateman had long advocated increasing state aid to distressed school districts and had also played a leading role in the expansion of the state college system during the Hughes and Cahill administrations. "I thought if Ray came into the cabinet," Byrne recounted, "it would have been a clear signal of my commitment to running a bi-partisan administration and getting a highly respected guy. I'm sorry he didn't accept."[7]

In another gesture indicating that he was seeking to bridge partisan divisions, Byrne appointed Thomas Kean, whom Bateman had defeated in the 1977 Republican gubernatorial primary election, as a commissioner on the New Jersey Highway Authority, the quasi-independent agency operating the Garden State Parkway. The appointment allowed Kean to continue in a public role after he left the legislature following the 1977 election, in which he did not run for reelection to his Assembly seat. "I know that a lot of Democrats probably weren't happy with Brendan for appointing me," Kean later recounted, "These appointments usually went to political supporters or contributors and Democrats knew I might be a future candidate for office." But Byrne told Kean that he thought it was a good idea for someone from each party serve on the boards of the major authorities to monitor any questionable actions. "I thought that made a lot of sense," Kean continued, "and it was a practice that I later followed when I was governor. Brendan told me to call him personally if I ever saw anything that I thought the authority was doing wrong."[8]

Byrne first reorganized the staff in the governor's office, creating the new position of chief of staff at the head of a more hierarchical structure. "We had been criticized during the first term," Byrne later reflected, "that sometimes it was difficult to determine who was speaking for me. I'm not sure that was true, but thought that designating a chief of staff would make it clear who was in charge, someone recognized as able to speak for me."[9]

Under the new organization, the governor's counsel, the director of communications and the director of policy and planning (also a newly created position) reported to the chief of staff. Byrne named Robert Mulcahy, who in the first term had been named the commissioner of the Department of Corrections, as chief of staff, and Mulcahy quickly became a key confidante with whom Byrne discussed major appointments and initiatives.

"When the Governor asked me to become chief-of-staff," Mulcahy recalled years later, "he told me he wanted to create and manage a staff structure with more central control. We developed a list of priority projects designating who on the staff and within the departments was accountable for their implementation. We also told the cabinet that they and their staff should not go to legislators to push their own agenda without our approval, which had been an occasional problem in the first term."

Byrne asked Mulcahy to put together the other key staff, and he asked Harold Hodes, who had taken a leave from his position as an aide to Newark Mayor Kenneth Gibson to join the Byrne reelection campaign, to serve as his deputy chief of staff. Stewart Pollock, the Republican lawyer who had lost the last case decided by Judge Byrne before he resigned to enter the 1973 gubernatorial race, was named counsel to the governor. "I thought Harold would give us someone who knew politics in urban areas," Mulcahy later reflected, "and having Stew, as a Republican, was a message to Republicans that we were reaching out for their support." Midway into the following year, Pollock was nominated by Byrne and confirmed as a justice on the state Supreme Court. The new office of policy and planning was headed by Donald Linky, who had been an assistant counsel in the first term; the office focused on coordinating the administration's policy initiatives and on longer term planning and development issues, such as those involved in the Meadowlands, the Pinelands, and Atlantic City.[10] Another second-term addition to the staff was Edward "Ted" Hoff, a recent graduate of Georgetown University who initially worked as an aide to Mulcahy, frequently accompanying Byrne on trips outside the State House and ultimately named as the governor's liaison to the cabinet. (On a trip with Byrne to a conference of the National Governors Association, Hoff was introduced to Bill Clinton. Years later, as a faculty member at Harvard Business School, Hoff would follow up the brief contact, being named as the Massachusetts finance chair for Clinton's two presidential campaigns.)

Another goal of the second term was to avoid the strained relations with the legislature and others that at times had marked Byrne's initial four years in office. "The Governor gave me and Harold his credit card to use," Mulcahy recounted, "and we would frequently go to Lorenzo's [a popular Trenton restaurant and tavern] to socialize and buy drinks for legislators, including the Republicans, to get to know them on a more personal level." Beyond the purely social interaction, the outreach also provided insight into the political realities faced by individual legislators. "You had to find out how far they could go in their districts on a specific issue," Hodes later said. "If you understood what concerns they and their constituents had, you knew what they could and couldn't do in voting on bills we were pushing."[11]

A few months into Byrne's second term, the new legislative strategy was tested when the Democratic leadership in the Assembly advised that they lacked the votes to pass one of Byrne's personal priorities—a bill establishing a new process for executive departments to propose and adopt regulations and to resolve disputes relating to departmental decisions by creating a more objective process presided over by administrative law judges. Mulcahy and Hodes reached out to James Hurley, the Republican Minority Leader, to ask whether any Republicans would vote for the measure. After receiving a negative response, they suggested that if Hurley could identify any bill which the Republicans wished to pass with Democratic support, perhaps a compromise could be reached. Of the three bills that Hurley proposed, one was acceptable to Mulcahy and Hodes, and Hurley agreed that he would line up the needed Republican votes to assure passage of the administrative procedure legislation. "We'd do this from time to time," Mulcahy later recalled. "As long as we weren't giving in on an issue of principle or trading votes for a job or a contract, we'd negotiate to reach agreements that allowed us to get things done. It was never a quid-pro-quo, but legislators knew that if they were helpful to us we'd try to help them out when we could." On occasion, Mulcahy and Hodes stretched the limits of the discretion they had been granted. "Once, we agreed to add $5 million for rural towns," Mulcahy remembered, "in order to get enough votes to pass a bill supported by the governor to provide aid to urban areas. At first, he didn't want to go along with the additional money, and it took quite a while for us to persuade him to back us up."[12]

Among other legislative accomplishments in his second term, Byrne signed into law the landmark Pinelands Protection Act; restructured the state's commuter bus and rail services through the creation of New Jersey Transit; and enacted a wide-ranging revision of the state's criminal laws. "I wanted to shake things up," Byrne later reflected. "I wanted to make a difference."[13] Ray Bateman, the governor's 1977 Republican opponent and a past Senate president, was quoted: "I never saw more executive control of the legislature. The legislature has done everything he has wanted it to do. Quite frankly, I'm not sure whether to ascribe this to executive strength or to legislative weakness."[14]

To some, the hard lessons that Byrne learned in his difficult first term led to a different approach after his reelection. "I think that to some extent Brendan was feeling his way during his first term," Thomas Kean said years later. "By his second term, he had mastered the tools of the governor, and he was much more successful in getting legislation passed." Kean also felt that, perhaps due to the added confidence of Byrne's surprise victory, he appeared more relaxed, giving the public a picture of the warmth and wit that he had previously displayed only to insiders. "Brendan always has had a wonderful sense of humor," Kean said in a later interview, "but I don't think he showed it very often to the public in his first term. After he was re-elected, you saw it come out more frequently."[15] Reflecting on his second-term legislative record, Byrne later attributed its successful enactment to a mix of factors. "Much of the bitterness surrounding the income tax was behind us, and my re-election restored the political capital I had largely exhausted in the first term. But a lot of the credit goes to people like Bob Mulcahy and Harold Hodes, who earned the trust of the legislature and worked hard with the cabinet and the rest of the staff to get our bills passed."[16]

To some degree, Byrne continued to pursue in his second term the issues of his first four years in office. One of the first chores of the new legislature was to repeal the sunset provision that would have had the income tax expire as of July 1978—recognition that Byrne's reelection had been an implicit referendum on continuing the tax and the rest of the property tax reform program. But debate continued throughout Byrne's second term, and long after he left office, on whether the reforms made a difference in improving education in the poorer cities and whether the state's oversight role in ensuring a "thorough and efficient" education in all school districts had simply created a bureaucracy in the Department of Education that imposed excessive reporting requirements on school administrators and teachers.

Atlantic City also continued as a major second-term priority to which Byrne devote much of his time. A few months into his second term, he presided over the opening of the first casino; by the time he left office, seven casino-hotels were in operation. But the success of Byrne's Atlantic City initiative was later called into question by the Abscam scandal, forcing him to restructure the Casino Control Commission that had been created by the 1977 legislation. In the Meadowlands, in his last year in office, Byrne greatly expanded the types of events that could use the Sports Complex when the new sports and entertainment arena opened. But the backlash to the decision to attach Byrne's name to the facility would, in the view of many, undermine the achievement, contributing to the decline in his popularity as he left office.

In his first term, Byrne had raised the issue of preservation of the Pinelands and taken the initial steps to restrain development by rejecting a pro-development proposed master plan and initiating regulatory measures to protect the region's water resources. While he raised the issue as he campaigned for reelection, his second term would see the assertion of his executive power to force legislative action to establish a long-term program that radically changed the course of development in the southern region of the state.

There also were signs that key initiatives of his first term were bringing positive results. In the first year that the income tax was in effect, property tax rates declined in over half of the municipalities in the state.[17] According to a *New York Times* account published shortly before Byrne was sworn in for his second term, the new tax structure, along with other targeted measures, such as incentives for building urban industrial projects and renovating housing, had "brightened job prospects in cities almost accustomed to overwhelming unemployment;" jobless rates, according to the article, had dropped "by 2 percentage points or more in every major city in the state since mid-1976."[18]

Byrne's second term also saw decisions to retain or change those holding key cabinet positions. When William Hyland resigned as attorney general after Byrne's reelection, John Degnan told the Governor of his interest in being appointed as Hyland's successor. One of the few in Byrne's inner circle who had urged that he stand for reelection, Degnan had served as the governor's executive secretary and, beginning in March 1977, as counsel to the governor while assuming a major role in the reelection campaign. But

Byrne rebuffed Degnan's initial approach about becoming attorney general. "He told me I was too young," Degnan recalled years later. "I was 33. I was enormously disappointed, but I understood him."[19]

Degnan's interest had parallels to Byrne's own efforts to persuade Governor Meyner that he be named Essex County prosecutor. As Byrne had done with Meyner, Degnan persisted in making his case, and the governor continued to reach out to others for their opinions, including his wife Jean. As Mrs. Byrne recalled, when her husband asked, "What do you think?" she also thought back to Meyner's appointing her husband as prosecutor: "I loved John, but he was only 32 [actually 33] years old. But Brendan was only 34 years old when he became prosecutor, so it didn't seem outlandish to me."[20]

At some point, Degnan learned that Byrne had scheduled a press conference to announce Hyland's successor, and on the night before the announcement received a call at home from a state trooper asking that he stop, on his way to the State House in the morning, to see the Governor at Morven.[21] When he arrived on the next morning, both the Governor and Mrs. Byrne were waiting to see him. "And I'll always remember the words," Degnan recounted years later. "Brendan said, 'Jean and I would like to ask you to be attorney general in the second term.' For which I've always been grateful to Jean. I think she was the deciding vote."[22] Degnan recognized that, in the eyes of the public and the press, "I wasn't qualified. . . . I was seen as a Brendan Byrne protégé partisan devotee. But he had just won this incredible election. And he had the power to pick somebody who wasn't qualified."[23]

As attorney general, Degnan would oversee the investigations relating to the licensing of the first Atlantic City casinos and defend before the state Supreme Court Byrne's controversial executive order imposing a building moratorium in the Pinelands. Degnan also would deregulate the alcoholic beverage industry, abolishing price controls and restraints on competition that had artificially inflated consumer prices. When the industry challenged his action, Degnan personally argued the case before the state Supreme Court, which upheld his deregulation plan.[24] "A bottle of J and B scotch," Degnan said years later, "was probably sold for two dollars or two and a half dollars less at the end of my term than it was at the beginning."[25] The attorney general was less successful in his attempt to deregulate the retail price of milk, as dairy farmers and other agricultural interests were able to block action in the legislature.[26] In response to a surge in violent crime in the City of Trenton, Degnan also created a State Police task force to undertake street patrols and support local law enforcement.

Degnan also would help Byrne realize his long-time goal of reforming the state's archaic penal code. "The state still had laws on the books," Byrne later recalled, "that made it a crime to serve as a second in a duel, to commit adultery and to hold a poker game among friends. People also could get long sentences for minor crimes. It just didn't make any sense, and after my years as a lawyer, prosecutor and judge, I wanted to get this changed."[27]

The proposed revision of the penal code also became enmeshed with Byrne's opposition to restoring the death penalty, with some legislators attempting to include the death penalty in the legislation to rewrite the code.[28] The most controversial proposed changes related to sexual behavior; during the bill's consideration in the Senate, protesters in the gallery denounced legislators with cries of "perverts" and "sodomites."[29] When he signed the bill passed by the legislature on August 29, 1979, Byrne said the revisions made New Jersey's criminal laws "the most modern in the country." The new code eliminated crimes like social gambling; reduced penalties for offenses like marijuana use; allowed judges to dismiss minor offenses; established a new scheme for classifying sentences by the seriousness of the offense; gave prosecutors the right to appeal sentences they felt were too lenient; and authorized judges to order offenders to make restitution to their victims.[30]

In 1981, Degnan resigned as attorney general to launch his own campaign for governor and Byrne appointed James Zazzali as Degnan's successor. Zazzali had worked under Byrne in the Essex County Prosecutor's office, had played an active role in his campaigns by lining up labor support, and after helping Byrne renegotiate the lease for Giants Stadium, had been named counsel to the Sports Authority. As attorney general, Zazzali formed a task force to strengthen enforcement of the state's labor laws, particularly to combat the proliferation of sweatshops in the apparel industry. He also recommended increasing the state's drinking age from 18 to 21 (which was enacted in the next year); strengthened enforcement of solid waste disposal regulations; and chaired the interdepartmental "superfund" committee evaluating the most efficient means of compensating losses from toxic waste dumping.[31]

Byrne's most controversial decision in forming his second-term cabinet was whether to retain Fred Burke as the commissioner of the Department of Education. Burke had been the target of sharp criticism during Byrne's first term, particularly from Robert Braun, the education reporter for the *Star-Ledger.* "Robert Braun's campaign to rid the state of Fred Burke," one account said, "went on for years."[32] Many school administrators, teachers, and education analysts also contended that the department under Burke had imposed excessive administrative burdens and paperwork in the state's oversight of local school systems as part of the school reform program.[33] Recognizing these concerns, in his annual message to the legislature after the inauguration for his second term, Byrne directed that the Department of Education "reduce the inordinate amount of paperwork generated by the T & E process, and to confine the system to its absolute, basic requirements."[34] In the second term, some of the reporting and paperwork requirements were eased on local school districts, particularly on those demonstrating consistently high levels of meeting performance benchmarks.[35] While Byrne considered replacing Burke, he ultimately decided to reject the calls to appoint a new commissioner. "Fred had an almost impossible job," Byrne later reflected. "He had his faults, but it was an enormous task to implement the new law and its regulations. I thought a lot of the attacks on him were just unfair."[36]

Another decision debated among Byrne's advisers was whether to continue Joanne Finley as the health commissioner, despite substantial criticism during Byrne's first term of both Finley's policies and her sometimes abrasive style. In the first term, Finley's sharp cuts of requested hospital rate increases had provoked lawsuits challenging the state's action by the state hospital association and individual hospitals. Largely due to Finley's aggressive stance, some hospital industry leaders had strongly opposed Byrne's reelection.[37] But Byrne rejected calls to replace Finley, concluding that much of the opposition was due to her forceful personality, as well as the sexism of her critics. "Joanne could be difficult," Byrne recalled, "but I think a lot of the criticism was based on her being an assertive woman when that still wasn't common or accepted, particularly by a lot of men. Joanne was way ahead of her time in trying new ways to reduce the steep increases in health care costs."[38]

After her reappointment as commissioner, Finley instituted an approach to reimbursing hospitals and physicians for treatment services that gained national attention. The system—"Diagnosis Related Groups" (soon commonly called "D.R.G.'s")—was developed at Yale University where Finley had lectured before coming to New Jersey. The DRG system reimbursed hospitals by classes of diagnosis, thus paying a fixed amount for a patient's admission for "appendicitis" regardless of the length of stay or the number of individual services. By departing from the prevailing practice of reimbursing hospitals for each day of a patient's stay and paying for each physician visit and other services, proponents of the reform argued that it would be more cost-efficient, reducing excessive testing and extended hospital stays.[39] New Jersey's experiment was supported by federal Medicare officials, who gave the state waivers from existing federal rules and provided supplemental funding for the program; the DRG model later was adopted as the reimbursement system for the national Medicare program. By 1982, when Byrne left office, the DRG system had been phased in to apply to all New Jersey hospitals.[40]

A few months into his second term, Byrne persuaded Louis Gambaccini, the head of the Port Authority's PATH rail service, to take a leave from the Authority to be commissioner of the state Department of Transportation. After becoming commissioner, Gambaccini oversaw significant decisions on completing the state's remaining segments of the interstate highway system, notably deciding to complete Interstate 287 and not to build the unfinished segment of Interstate 95. He also successfully pursued Byrne's plan to have the state assume operation of commuter bus and rail services through the creation of New Jersey Transit, and secured approval of a $3 billion capital spending program for highways and transit, including a $475 million bond issue approved by the voters in a November 1979 referendum.[41]

Daniel O'Hern, the mayor of Red Bank and a former law clerk to U.S. Supreme Court Justice William Brennan, joined the cabinet as commissioner of the Department of Environmental Protection. In 1979, O'Hern moved to the governor's office, succeeding Stewart Pollock as Byrne's counsel after Pollock was confirmed as a justice of the state Supreme Court. "When I appointed Dan O'Hern as counsel," Byrne later remembered, "he told Stew Pollock that he would be 'overwhelmed' as chief lawyer for the Governor, but Stew told him, 'Don't worry Dan, the Governor knows more law than any of us.'"[42]

Jerry English, Byrne's legislative counsel, then took O'Hern's place as the DEP commissioner for the remainder of the second term. Under both O'Hern and English, the DEP continued to provide support for Byrne's Pinelands preservation program; the expansion of the state's efforts to identify and control discharges of potential carcinogenic substances; the cleanup of hazardous waste sites; and the implementation of a comprehensive water supply and water quality program. In April 1980, a massive fire broke out at the tank farm in Elizabeth containing 40,000 drums of chemical wastes formerly operated by the Chemical Control Corp., which the state had forced into receivership in 1979; the fire would burn for fifteen hours—one of the more spectacular illustrations of the state's legacy of toxic chemical disposal. In 1981, a state grand jury indicted three of the company's former principals on charges of polluting state waters.[43]

At the Department of Human Services, which was the new name of the former Department of Institutions and Agencies after it had been restructured in the first term by spinning off its correctional responsibilities into the newly created Department of Corrections, Ann Klein continued as commissioner until she resigned in March 1981 to campaign for the Democratic gubernatorial nomination. Timothy Carden, the governor's cabinet secretary who previously served in the first term as an aide to transportation commissioner Alan Sagner, succeeded Klein. Byrne's second term continued the effort to reduce the number of residents in large state institutions housing those with mental or physical disabilities, seeking to establish smaller community-based group homes and other facilities. After the state began receiving revenues from taxes on casinos in Byrne's second term, the funds helped support a range of new or expanded programs aiding seniors and the disabled, including discounts on pharmaceutical drugs, utility rates and public transit.

For the Department of Higher Education, which oversaw the state college system, T. Edward "Ted" Hollander, a nationally respected administrator who had been the second-ranking official in the New York State higher education agency, succeeded Ralph Dungan as the chancellor of the department in 1977, the year Byrne ran for reelection. Hollander would continue to head the Department for the following thirteen years, serving through the Kean administration until he resigned in Governor Florio's first year in office in 1990. Hollander's initiatives included revising the state's enrollment-based system for financing higher education to one that rewarded outstanding programs at each institution, part of an overall effort to improve the quality of the system after a period of rapid expansion in enrollments. In 1979, Hollander's proposal for a $95 million bond issue to finance new college capital construction projects was rejected by the voters in a referendum, a failure he later called the "major disappointment" of his tenure.[44]

Byrne also brought into the cabinet Angelo "Buddy" Bianchi, one of his former assistant prosecutors in the Essex County prosecutor's office, as commissioner of banking. Bianchi later would be named chair of the state ethics commission and elected president and chairman of the board of the national organization of state bank supervisors.

In the first months of his second term, Byrne faced a difficult political problem when Dick Leone, his former state treasurer and campaign manager, ran in the June 1978 Democratic primary for the U.S. Senate nomination against Bill Bradley, the former Princeton and New York Knicks basketball star. The popular and well-known Bradley had secured significant backing from many of those who had been key supporters of Byrne's own campaigns. "It's very tough to run against a celebrity like Bill Bradley," Byrne later said, "who was known across the country and can easily raise money and attract media attention to their campaign. I knew Dick would have an uphill race, but I had to support him given how loyal he had been to me."[45] Leone initially had decided not to run, but made a relatively late decision in December 1977 to enter the race, retaining David Garth, with whom he worked closely in Byrne's two campaigns, to direct his media. Leone also was encouraged to run by key Byrne insiders, who resented what they felt was Bradley's lack of visible support for the administration's prior policy initiatives, particularly in the income tax battle.[46]

Leone had early success in establishing himself as the most credible of two other candidates competing for the liberal vote against Bradley— Congressman Andrew Maguire and State Senator Alex Menza. Leone had hoped that Byrne, fresh from his own victory, would be helpful with both fundraising and organization support, particularly in Hudson County, where Leone's campaign projected he needed a 20,000-vote plurality to have a chance statewide against Bradley. But as Bradley's campaign benefited from appearances and support from such celebrities as Robert Redford and Jack Nicholson, Leone's early momentum soon stalled.[47]

In his later memoir, Bradley expressed his respect for Leone and his belief that the campaign was conducted on a high level, but attributed his victory, despite his lack of political experience, to his greater name recognition and fundraising advantages, including his own ability to contribute his personal funds for the campaign. "Leone couldn't parlay," Bradley wrote, "Byrne's support into contributions," noting that "Byrne rarely made fundraising calls."[48] Jersey City Mayor Tommy Smith, a former college basketball star himself who had played in a single game for the Knicks in 1951, issued a somewhat half-hearted endorsement of Leone despite his enthusiastic campaigning for Byrne in the 1977 general election: "I'm for Brendan Byrne, and if he's for Leone . . . I'm for Leone." But Smith failed to secure for Leone the county organization "line," the top ballot position signifying the organization's support. Bradley carried twenty of the twenty-one counties, defeating Leone by a more than two-to-one margin. Leone managed to outpoll Bradley in Hudson, but by a mere 1,600 votes.[49] Looking back on the campaign, Leone reflected years later, "The best thing Brendan Byrne could have done for me was to have convinced me not to run."[50]

In a much lighter episode, in June 1979 Tommy Smith recruited Byrne to "fight" Muhammad Ali, who had announced only days before that he was retiring as heavyweight champion, in an exhibition boxing match benefiting a Jersey City hospital. Byrne learned that Smith had trained intensively for his own match with Ali, including losing twenty pounds, running daily through the streets and engaging in sparring matches. "I was worried that the Mayor would really hit Ali and get him worked up," Byrne later recalled, "so I insisted that I fight first." Byrne later said that Ali had orchestrated the action: "he whispered to me 'throw a right,' but when I said, 'I'm a lefty', he repeated 'throw a right' and I did and he went down."[51] In the match against Byrne, one observer reported that Ali "stumbled and flopped into three knockdowns," and the match was declared a draw. Smith following, much more vigorous match with Ali, was announced as a decision for the Mayor.[52]

Byrne's aggressive assertion of gubernatorial power was perhaps most visible in his response to emergencies. "When there's an emergency," Byrne later reflected, "the public expects its government to act quickly and decisively. You have to make decisions without going through the normal delays of the bureaucracy and the legislature. I enjoyed that freedom."[53] In his first term, Byrne occasionally had been frustrated by the slow reaction of the state's emergency services which were administered by the state office of civil defense—the World War II era agency that loosely coordinated county civil defense services that were highly dependent on volunteers. In his second term, he restructured the state's emergency services programs under the State Police, which he felt were better able to respond promptly to his orders and marshal needed resources and personnel.[54]

Byrne exercised executive powers in a variety of natural disasters and other emergencies. In addition to his imposition of the odd-even license plate gasoline fill-up program soon after he first took office, in subsequent energy shortages Byrne ordered mandatory controls on temperature settings in homes and businesses and during droughts set mandatory restrictions on water use. In his first term, responding to an equipment failure at Trenton's water filtration plant on the Delaware River which cut off water supplies to some 200,000 homeowners and businesses, he issued an executive order to build an emergency pipeline system to connect the Elizabethtown Water Company system at Princeton with Trenton in Trenton, easing a crisis that ended when the plant was restored to service after nine days.[55]

Byrne faced his most publicized emergency when a partial meltdown occurred in a reactor at the Three Mile Island nuclear power plant near Harrisburg, Pennsylvania, at four o'clock in the morning on Wednesday, March 28, 1979. Some 75 miles west of the New Jersey border, the plant was owned and operated by General Public Utilities (GPU), headquartered in New Jersey at Morristown; GPU was the parent company of two public utilities, Jersey Central Power and Light Company in New Jersey, and Metropolitan Edison in Pennsylvania. Pennsylvania authorities notified federal officials at the Nuclear Regulatory Commission of the accident, and the next day Byrne phoned Pennsylvania Governor Richard Thornburgh for an update of the situation.

The meltdown, which resulted from a mechanical breakdown and a failure of plant workers to recognize the nature of the problem, released radioactive gases and iodine into the environment and would become the worst accident in U.S. commercial nuclear power plant history.[56] "At first, we weren't getting good information from the plant management about just what had happened and how serious the risk was," Byrne recalled years later. "It was only when the federal officials took charge that it became clearer what was going on."[57]

Initially, there were several unanswered questions concerning the potential danger of radiation carried by the prevailing winds to New Jersey. "The question was where was that cloud going to move, and what were the risks associated with that cloud?" recalled Tim Carden, then Byrne's cabinet secretary. "We knew that weather generally moves from west to east, but how quickly and when? With what degree of dissolution? No one knew."[58]

Byrne received periodic briefings from Harold Denton, the Nuclear Regulatory Commission official whom President Carter appointed as his personal representative to coordinate the federal responses at the Three Mile Island site. Radiation levels spiked on the third day of the accident, and

Pennsylvania Governor Thornburgh recommended the evacuation of pregnant women and the closing of schools in the region near the plant.

Throughout the emergency, Byrne worked closely with Clinton Pagano,
the superintendent of the New Jersey State Police whom he had designated
as the state's emergency services coordinator. Pagano ordered two State
Police helicopters carrying radiation monitoring equipment to fly to Three
Mile Island; set up monitors along the Pennsylvania-New Jersey border; and
coordinated planning for possible evacuation of areas that might be in the
path of wind-borne radiation.[59]

On Saturday, March 31, Byrne convened a meeting of his staff, emergency response officials, and representatives from the departments of health,
environmental protection and transportation, along with Professor Frank
von Hipple, a Princeton physicist and nuclear expert who provided technical
advice.[60] Meeting continuously through the weekend, the group began planning for potential emergency evacuations. "It was scary," Byrne recalled.
"We were most concerned over having to evacuate the barrier islands at the
shore that may have been in the path of any radioactive cloud blown by the
winds. It would have been very difficult to get so many people off the islands
with only one bridge, and we weren't certain whether we'd have gridlock and
panic as people rushed to get off the islands."[61]

Another urgent need was to identify sources of potassium iodide—a drug
capable of preventing radioactive iodine from lodging in the thyroid and other
glands in the body. At the time of the accident, no pharmaceutical or chemical company had medical-grade potassium iodide available in glass vials in
the quantities needed for distribution. Byrne ordered Joanne Finley, the state
health commissioner, to oversee contacts with glass companies to determine
whether the vast number of vials for the potassium iodide could be located
and distributed to the suppliers.[62]

As the threat of wind-borne radiation eased, Byrne reassured the public
that air monitors were reporting normal readings. In the weeks that followed,
he met with Governor Thornburgh, federal officials and GPU executives to
discuss the decontamination of the damaged plant and how to allocate its substantial cleanup costs, which over several years would total some $1 billion.
In New Jersey, 650,000 Jersey Central Power and Light Company customers
would be forced to pay $30 million a month to replace the electric power
previously supplied by the TMI reactor until Byrne was able to persuade the
utility consortium providing the power to lower its price.[63]

Byrne had a complex relationship with Georgia Governor and then
President Jimmy Carter, whom he initially admired as one of the progressive
southern governors seeking to bring more tolerant racial attitudes to their
states. In the fall of 1975, Byrne had hosted Carter at a reception at Morven

during the early stages of Carter's presidential campaign to introduce him to New Jersey Democrats, and later he became one of the first governors to endorse Carter in the 1976 presidential election. But Byrne was unable to secure a Carter victory in New Jersey in either the state's presidential primary or in the general election against President Gerald Ford. After his inauguration in January 1977, Carter failed to respond to Byrne's interest in a potential appointment as ambassador to Ireland and gave only limited support to Byrne's uphill reelection campaign, apparently accepting advice that he should keep his distance from what was widely viewed as a losing effort. Conversely, after Byrne had won his surprising victory in 1977 but Carter's own performance ratings in public surveys steadily declined, Byrne's decision to associate so closely with the President largely precluded any subsequent national political role for Byrne.

Following Byrne's reelection, Carter called on Byrne for specific assignments. Staff from New Jersey's Washington office under its director, Marilyn Berry Thompson, worked with Carter's domestic policy aides to develop a new community development program, but Carter later dropped the proposal when, according to Byrne, "he told us he didn't have the money."[64] Byrne was somewhat more successful in getting Carter's support for various programs to alleviate the adverse impact on the Northeast of the sharp spike in energy prices by the OPEC cartel of oil-producing countries. Much of this effort was occurred after Byrne was elected in 1978 as chairman of the Coalition of Northeastern Governors, the organization of seven states established in 1976 to encourage regional cooperation and lobby for increased federal support for programs and projects of special importance to the region. Byrne named his Chief-of-Staff Mulcahy to the CONEG board, and Mulcahy worked with state's Washington office director Thompson to establish CONEG as an effective force, particularly in lobbying for such programs as funding low-income homeowner energy assistance, public transit, housing and other infrastructure investment.[65]

In July 1979, Byrne and seven other governors were invited by President Carter to a "domestic summit" retreat with the President and key members of his staff and cabinet at Camp David. The meeting was hastily put together after Carter had canceled a scheduled address to the nation following the announcement of a steep oil price increase by the OPEC oil producers' cartel, which led to sharp declines in the President's approval ratings. Without further information from the White House on the purpose of the meeting, which ended up lasting ten days, rumors began to circulate about the topics to be discussed at the meeting and the condition of the President, including speculation about whether he intended to resign.[66]

"After I arrived," Byrne would recall many years later, "Carter himself welcomed me and took me to my cabin, which he said was the same cabin that Israeli Prime Minister Yitzhak Rabin stayed in during the negotiations with the Palestinian leader Yasser Arafat." But at a later point, Byrne decided to tell Carter of his concerns about the speculation over the nature of the meeting and Carter's plans. "I advised the President and his staff," Byrne recounted, "that I thought they really should leave Camp David and go back to Washington. I felt the rumors were getting out of hand, and he needed to show that he was back in charge at the White House." Later in the day, Byrne continued, "the President told me and a few other governors that he and his staff had discussed what I had said among themselves, but they had decided to stay." (Byrne was more successful in having several photos he took while at Camp David published by *Newsweek* magazine in return for a contribution the magazine made at Byrne's request to Seton Hall University.)[67]

Following the Camp David session, Carter delivered a televised speech to the nation (later dubbed by the press as his "malaise" speech) that was widely criticized for implying that the nation's problems were due more to the public's failure to accept necessary sacrifices than to his own lack of leadership.[68] Later, Carter appointed Byrne to chair a citizens committee to lobby for legislation imposing a windfall profits tax on oil companies, which the president signed at a White House ceremony at which Byrne spoke in April 1980.[69]

Byrne actively campaigned for Carter's reelection in 1980. One indirect contribution he made to Carter was the President's appropriation of Byrne's quip during his 1977 campaign that he knew his prospects were turning around "when people started waving at me with all five fingers."[70] But the Republican ticket of Ronald Reagan and George H. W. Bush soundly defeated Carter, with the President taking only six states and losing New Jersey with only 38 percent of the vote. Recognizing that the Reagan victory would bring a sharp change in federal policies, Byrne successfully pushed to get two major environmental measures completed before Carter left office. In December, Carter signed the federal "Superfund" law, sponsored by Congressman Florio, which was modeled on the New Jersey Spill Compensation and Control Act that Byrne had proposed and signed into law in 1976.[71] The Superfund and the Spill Act would later provide the bulk of the hundreds of millions of dollars to fund the cleanup of the state's toxic waste sites. Byrne's staff also rushed to have Cecil Andrus, Carter's Secretary of the Interior, approve the state's plan for protection of the Pinelands, securing Andrus's signature in the final week before he and President Carter left office.[72]

Byrne was invited to the White House for a final visit before Carter's departure. In his role as chairman of the Democratic Governors Association, he presented a set of golf clubs to Carter in behalf of the Association—a set that Byrne later learned Carter gave away to his son. "The President thanked me," Byrne later reflected, "and I told him that I appreciated the help he and his administration had provided to New Jersey. It was a bit sad."[73]

Reagan's first year in office in 1981 overlapped Byrne's last year as governor, and Byrne's role as chair of the Democratic Governors Association resulted in his speaking out in behalf of his peers to criticize the sharp cuts in the federal budget the new administration imposed affecting the states, particularly in programs for public transit, welfare, and housing that heavily impacted New Jersey. Despite their policy and political conflicts, Byrne's position as chair of the Association also resulted in invitations to events at the Reagan White House and the two Irishmen, both of whom relished telling stories and jokes, got along well personally. Byrne also was able to fulfill one goal he was unable to achieve under Carter: playing on the White House tennis court. While Carter was in office, Byrne had mentioned his interest to the President, but Carter—who was famously known to personally approve those allowed to use the court—failed to follow up. Byrne later learned that Carter had taken tennis lessons from Frank Brennan, a coach who had worked with Billie Jean King and other professionals and who had seen Byrne play at a celebrity tournament. According to the account related to Byrne, Carter had asked Brennan, "Can I beat him?" to which Brennan reportedly replied, "I don't think so"; whatever the reason, Carter never invited Byrne for tennis before he left office. At an event at the White House after Reagan's inauguration, Byrne told the story to Reagan. "President Reagan immediately called in an aide to say," Byrne later recounted, "that the next time Governor Byrne is in Washington, make sure he uses the tennis court. Only then did it happen." In public talks, Byrne enjoyed repeating the story, topping it off by pausing and then dryly telling his audience, "That's why Reagan served two terms."[74]

By the time he completed his eight years in office in January 1982, Brendan Byrne had appointed five of the seven justices on the state Supreme Court, including the chief justice. Three of his five appointees were serving as counsel to the governor when they were nominated to the Court. The justices named by Byrne would comprise a majority on the Court through the succeeding administrations of both Governors Thomas Kean and James Florio into 1996, when Governor Christine Todd Whitman was in her second year in office. Byrne's last appointee would serve until retiring in May 2000, some eighteen years after Byrne completed his second term.[75]

In 1975, Byrne made his first appointment to the Court in naming Sidney Schreiber, a former Superior Court judge. In 1977, the year he ran for reelection, Byrne named Alan Handler, who had succeeded Lewis Kaden as his counsel the previous year when Kaden resigned to return to private legal practice. At the beginning of Byrne's second term, Stewart Pollock, who had replaced Handler as Byrne's counsel, was in turn nominated and confirmed as a justice in June 1979. Reflecting years later on his relationship with Byrne, Pollock recalled: "When he [Byrne] first asked me to work for him,

I thought he might have forgotten that I was a Republican, so I reminded him. He paused for a moment and said, 'I can stand it if you can.'"[76] In Byrne's last year in office in 1981, he nominated Daniel O'Hern, who had replaced Pollock as counsel after previously serving in Byrne's second-term cabinet as environmental commissioner, as his final appointee to the Court.

When Chief Justice Richard Hughes reached the mandatory retirement age of 70, in August 1979 Byrne named Robert Wilentz as Hughes's successor. Wilentz was a former two-term Democratic Middlesex County assemblyman who had left the legislature before Byrne took office in 1974 to return to private practice at the prominent law firm founded by his father, David Wilentz, the former state attorney general who had prosecuted Bruno Hauptmann at the 1935 trial for the kidnaping and death of the Lindbergh baby. Robert Wilentz had advised Byrne against running for reelection in 1977, believing that he should avoid the embarrassment of what Wilentz felt would be Byrne's rejection by the voters.[77] As an attorney, Wilentz also had represented the petroleum industry in opposing one of Byrne's signature legislative achievements, the Spill Compensation and Control Act of 1976 that established a tax on the transfer of petrochemicals to create a compensation fund for losses from spills or other discharges.[78] But Byrne had long admired Wilentz's legal skills, and also believed he would bring administrative talent to the position of chief justice during a time when the lower courts faced substantial backlogs in processing trials and appeals. "I thought he had one of the best legal minds in the state," Byrne reflected. "But unlike a lot of smart lawyers, I also felt he had experience in running the large Wilentz law firm that would help with the administration of the courts, which is a big part of the chief justice's responsibilities. I thought Bob Wilentz would do a good job."[79]

The appointment initially faced objections from David Wilentz, who told Byrne that he was concerned about the impact on his law firm of the loss of his son. Jerry English, Byrne's legislative counsel and environmental commissioner, who had first met David Wilentz when she worked as an aide to Middlesex County Senator Edward Crabiel, recalled years later that Wilentz (whom she described as "a short, slight man . . . always chewing on an old cigar hanging out of the side of his mouth") was inordinately concerned—despite its apparent success—over the business side of his law firm, worrying whether "they were going to make enough money to keep the doors open."[80] But Byrne ultimately was able to convince Wilentz to go along with his son's appointment. "David and I talked," Byrne later reflected, "and he finally said, 'Well, all right, as long as it's for *chief* justice.'"[81]

Wilentz would serve as chief justice in the first of the series of rulings in the *Abbott v. Burke* litigation that was initiated by a trial court complaint filed in 1981 during Byrne's last year in office, naming Byrne's education commissioner and other state officials as defendants. Over the course of the protracted *Abbott* litigation, the Court expanded the precedent set by the 1973 *Robinson* decision defining the state's role in school finance and oversight. Among other rulings, the Court held that the legislation enacted in 1976 by Byrne and the legislature revising the formula for allocating state school aid was unconstitutional, finding that spending disparities between wealthy suburban school districts and poor urban districts had increased, and accordingly ordered that the legislature enact further measures to reduce the differences in spending levels.[82]

Yet after all the appointments and decisions he made in his second term, and indeed over his eight years as governor, Byrne would leave office convinced that his most lasting legacy was the accomplishment he achieved largely by his own initiative—the preservation of the Pinelands.

Family Parents Siblings
The Byrne family shown while vacationing in the oceanfront town of Deal, New Jersey, in the summer of 1929. The stay at the shore was, as Byrne later recounted, "the last summer we were rich," as Francis Byrne's insurance firm later failed in the aftermath of the stock market crash of October 1929 and the resulting Great Depression. Pictured surrounding Francis and Genevieve Byrne are their children (from left) Muriel, Thecla, Nancy, Francis Jr. and Brendan (at five years old). Papers of Brendan T. Byrne, Special Collections and University Archives, Rutgers University Libraries.

Family Air Corps 1943
In a photo taken with his parents and siblings shortly before Brendan entered military service in 1943, shown (standing from left) are Arthur Zoubek, his wife Thecla Byrne Zoubek, Nancy Byrne, Edith Byrne, her husband Francis Byrne, Jr. and (seated from left) Francis Byrne, Sr., Muriel Byrne, Brendan, and Genevieve Byrne. Papers of Brendan T. Byrne, Special Collections and University Archives, Rutgers University Libraries.

Aircrew
Brendan shown with three fellow airmen after they completed training in Texas and
stopped briefly at the Byrne home in West Orange before flying for deployment at their
base in in Italy. Shown kneeling with his arm around Brendan is Ray Nolan; standing
(from left) are Arthur Hayes and Alex Boris. Papers of Brendan T. Byrne, Special
Collections and University Archives, Rutgers University Libraries.

Princeton Track
Brendan shown practicing for the mile relay as a member of the Princeton University track team. The photo was taken at Princeton's Palmer Stadium by Jim Lebenthal, Brendan's classmate at Princeton, and later chairman of Lebenthal & Co., the prominent Wall Street tax-exempt bond investment firm. Courtesy Jim Lebenthal, reprinted with permission.

Pros Charles Squad

Essex County Prosecutor Byrne shown with the "Charlie Squad," the unit he created to focus on organized crime. Charles Carella, the chief of the unit, 4 stands at left next to Byrne, along with assistant prosecutors Charles Acocella (leaning) and Charles Dughi. Papers of Brendan T. Byrne, Special Collections and University Archives, Rutgers University Libraries.

Victory Celebration

Victory celebration on night of June 4, 1973, when Byrne won the Democratic gubernatorial nomination in the primary election, with wife Jean and son Tom seen at right. Papers of Brendan T. Byrne, Special Collections and University Archives, Rutgers University Libraries.

Family Move
The Byrne family in the living room of their West Orange home shortly before he was inaugurated for his first term as governor in January 1974. From left are Nancy (age 16); Billy (4); Tim (12); Barbara (6); wife Jean; Susan (17); and Tom (Brendan Jr. 19). Photo credit Bill Stahl, Jr., New York Daily News, reprinted with permission.

77 Election Debate

Senator Raymond Bateman, the Republican nominee in the 1977 general election, with Byrne during a debate sponsored by the New Jersey State Chamber of Commerce in Newark. Papers of Brendan T. Byrne, Special Collections and University Archives, Rutgers University Libraries.

Carter Byrne Kids

President Jimmy Carter with Byrne and children (from left) Billy; Tim; Susan; Barbara; Nancy; and wife Jean (over Byrne's shoulder) in photo taken on steps of White House during the 1977 re-election campaign year. White House Photograph, Papers of Brendan T. Byrne, Special Collections and University Archives, Rutgers University Libraries. White House Photograph, Papers of Brendan T. Byrne, Special Collections and University Archives, Rutgers University Libraries.

NEW JERSEY ELECTION SPECIAL

DAILY ⊙ NEWS

Partly sunny today.
Mid-60s. Cloudy
tomorrow, mid-60s.
Details page 95

Vol. 59. No. 117 — New York, Wednesday, November 9, 1977 — Price: 20 cents

BYRNE WINS!

Routs Bateman by 3-2 Margin; Democrats Keep Legislature

Bond Issues Pass Easily

Koch Takes New York's Mayor's Race

*Stories begin on page 2;
Other pictures in centerfold*

Rain scarcely dampens enthusiasm of Gov. Byrne at West Orange poll. UPI photo

Daily News 1977

*New York Daily News front page on Wednesday, November 9, 1977, featuring Byrne's
election victory on the previous day over his Republican opponent Raymond Bateman.
Courtesy of New York Daily News.*

Three 'Brendan Byrnes' in front of the Brendan Byrne Arena in the Meadowlands: Brendan T. ("Tom") Byrne, Jr., Brendan T. Byrne, III, and Brendan T. Byrne. Papers of Brendan T. Byrne, Special Collections and University Archives, Rutgers University Libraries.

Clintons

Brendan and Ruthi Zinn Byrne with President Bill Clinton and First Lady Hillary Clinton in visit to the White House. White House Photograph.

Star-Ledger

Star-Ledger editorial cartoon by Bill Canfield published shortly before Byrne completed his second term in January 1982 indicating his impressive record of accomplishments among the state's governors. Papers of Brendan T. Byrne, Special Collections and University Archives, Rutgers University Libraries.

Jim McGreevey

Governor James McGreevey shown at the ceremony in the Pinelands on July 24, 2002 in which the Governor announced that he had signed an executive order re-naming the former Lebanon State Forest as the Brendan T. Byrne State Forest, comprising over 37,000 acres and more than 25 miles of marked trails. McGreevey stated that he had taken the action to recognize Byrne's efforts in the enactment of the Pinelands Preservation Act in 1979, providing the framework for protection of the resources in the 1.1 million acre Pinelands region. The Byrne Forest is also the site of Whitesbog Village, once an active 19th and 20th-century cranberry and blueberry producing community founded in the 1870s by Joseph J. White. Photo credit Michael Zinn, reprinted with permission.

Byrne Unveiling Statue
Byrne shown on October 3, 2013, at the ceremony during which a bronze statue of
him was unveiled on the plaza in front of the Essex County Courthouse in Newark,
where Byrne once served as Essex County prosecutor and a Superior Court judge. Also
pictured are (from left) former Governor James Florio, Governor Chris Byrne biography
images and captions. 10 Christie, Ruthi Zinn Byrne and former Governor James
McGreevey. Photo credit Betsy Michel, reprinted with permission.

The extended Byrne family gathered for celebration of his 90th birthday (left to right): Floor – Grandchildren Luke Stefan, Jack Stefan, Alexandra Byrne. Front – Nancy Byrne Reinhart, Scarlett Byrne, Barbara Moakler Byrne, Governor Byrne, Ruthi Zinn Byrne, Brendan Thomas (Tom) Byrne, Jr. Standing – Peter Reinhart, Tim Byrne, Meaghan Byrne, Bill Byrne, Saiya Stefan (held by Barbara Byrne Stefan), Erin Byrne, Kelly Byrne, Jill Munro Byrne, Brendan Byrne III. Photo credit: Meaghan Byrne, reprinted with permission.

Chapter 12

The Pinelands

"It Was on No Political Party's Agenda"

> *I always said that one of the things I am proud of is that I don't think that*
> *there is any other piece of legislation, during my time as governor, which*
> *is unique in the sense that it would not have been passed if I didn't take an*
> *interest in it. The Pinelands was on nobody's particular political agenda.*
> *It was on no political party's agenda.*
>
> —*Brendan T. Byrne, at "The Pinelands Protection Act: A Discussion*
> *by Participants in the Process," Rutgers University, October 15, 1987*

Preservation of the Pinelands was Brendan Byrne's most enduring achievement as governor. It radically changed the pattern of land use in New Jersey, placing the central core of the southern half of the state—one-fifth of New Jersey's total land area—under protection to escape the suburban sprawl that covered much of the northern part of the state.

But apart from its significance as public policy, the Pinelands effort reflected Byrne's view on how a governor's performance should be measured. To Byrne, much of what any governor accomplished probably would have come to pass at some point. Even the income tax, so linked to Byrne in the public mind, was to him inevitable; if he failed to push it through on his watch, he felt that sooner or later the pressure of fiscal and political reality would see its enactment by one of his successors.

Preservation of the Pinelands was different. As he put it, the Pinelands "was on nobody's particular political agenda," and he believed, with good reason, that its protection never would have happened without him. The Pinelands also sparked Byrne's love of a challenge, proving that he could succeed against high odds to use the power of his office to accomplish a personal goal—one that would permanently change the future of New Jersey. The preservation of the Pinelands simply fit with Brendan Byrne's idea of how a governor should lead.

The Pinelands is comprised of pine oak forests, streams and rivers, spacious farms, crossroad hamlets, and small towns stretching across the southern part of the state. It also contains a vast underground reservoir of over 17 trillion gallons of pure water, enough to cover the entire state to a depth of 10 feet. Much of the land is unsuitable for common farm crops, contributing to the region commonly labeled as the "Pine Barrens," but the high water tables and acidic soil are excellent for growing cranberries and blueberries, with New Jersey's production ranking among the leading states.[1]

In the nation's early years, the Pinelands was a place where a few fortunes were made from lumber, bog iron, and glass, but where most residents struggled to make a living through farming, hunting, or handwork.[2] Glassmaking, which began in 1739 by taking advantage of the high quality of the sand and the abundance of wood as fuel for furnaces, was the most successful industry; by 1909, T.C. Wheaton and Company employed 2,000 workers, with Wheaton and a few large companies operating into the twenty-first century.[3] But as the state's major roads and railroads bypassed the area, the region was—as the "Pine Barrens" label implied—generally considered a wasteland of little interest to outsiders.

Like most New Jerseyans, Byrne had little knowledge of the pines during his years living in West Orange. Apart from the bus trip Brendan Byrne took to Fort Dix after being inducted into the Army in 1943, his first memory of the pine forests was a drive he took to the shore a few years later with his first serious girlfriend, Beryl Anfindsen. On their way, Byrne was surprised by the miles of pine trees lining the road, the meandering streams and, most of all, the sense of isolation. Years later, he recalled his first impression of the Pinelands as being "incredibly romantic," but quickly added with a smile, "but Beryl and I didn't stop in the woods."[4]

It wasn't until 1974, his first year as governor, that he read *The Pine Barrens*, a book by John McPhee published in 1968 adapted from articles he previously wrote as a staff writer for *The New Yorker*.[5] Byrne had become acquainted with McPhee's father and older brother during his college days at Princeton, where John's father, Dr. Harry McPhee, was the physician for the Princeton football team, and Roemer McPhee, John's brother, was Brendan's classmate. After his inauguration in 1974, Byrne met John McPhee when he was brought by Bill Dwyer, a reporter and columnist for the *Trenton Times* newspaper, to fill a spot in a tennis doubles group hosted by Byrne at Morven, the governor's residence in Princeton.[6] "When I read John's book, I understood for the first time why the Pine Barrens is unique," Byrne later recalled.

"The book showed how special it is—the people, the sandy roads, the forests, the streams. Yet toward the end of the book, Byrne had been struck by McPhee's pessimism over the region's future. McPhee noted the relatively weak political support for conservation proposals and complexity of getting "all the big and little powers that would have to work together to accomplish anything on a major scale in the pines," finally concluding "it would appear that the Pine Barrens are not very likely to be the subject of dramatic decrees or act of legislation. They seem to be headed slowly toward extinction." When John would come to Morven to play tennis," Byrne later said, "once in a while I would kid him that I would prove he was wrong in predicting that the Pine Barrens would be lost."[7]

John McPhee had grown up in Princeton and later graduated from the university, but like Byrne, for much of his early life he knew little of the pine forests, even though their outer edges were less than an hour's drive from his Princeton home. While working as a staff writer for *The New Yorker*, he became intrigued by a friend's colorful stories (some of which he later found to be untrue) of the people he had met in the region. After gaining the approval of William Shawn, the magazine's long-time editor, McPhee spent "about eight months driving down from Princeton day after day, or taking a sleeping bag and a small tent" to research the *New Yorker* articles that led in the following year to his book *The Pine Barrens*.[8]

Byrne was most taken by McPhee's sympathetic view of the lifestyle and character of "the Pineys," the forest residents he had met and interviewed. Long the subject of rumor and suspicion, the Pineys were sometimes viewed as hermits pursuing lifestyles bordering on depravity. Some tales claimed that the pine forests sheltered supernatural beings, including the "Jersey Devil," the legendary horned creature purportedly born to a local woman.[9] In 1913, following publication of dubious research suggesting that incidents of incest, intermarriage, and child abuse were prevalent among several Pinelands families, New Jersey Governor James T. Fielder traveled to the forests to investigate, later reporting that he was "shocked" by what he had found.[10] "Evidently these people are a serious menace to the State of New Jersey," Fielder said after completing his tour. "They are inbred and lawless and lead scandalous lives 'til they have become a race of imbeciles, criminals and defectives. . . . The state must segregate them, that is certain. I think it may be necessary to sterilize some of them."[11] No action was taken on Fielder's warning, but his cautions—along with the questionable genetic studies—for many years made outsiders wary of the people in the forests.

When Byrne read McPhee's book, he was impressed by how "John didn't find the Pineys he met to be lazy or degenerate, but described their way of life with respect."[12] One of Byrne's favorite stories in the book was McPhee's account of his talks with Fred Brown, who lived in an isolated cabin without

electricity or running water in the midst of abandoned cars and other discards.
McPhee wrote of a framed poem that Brown had hanging on a wall:

> *God hath not promised*
> *Sun without rain*
> *Joy without sorrow*
> *Peace without pain*[13]

"I always have had a love of words," Byrne later said, "but the poem that
John repeated in his book from Brown's cabin touched me. In its few lines,
it brought back much of what I had experienced in my childhood and the
war."[14]

Soon after Governor Fielder gave his warning of the "imbeciles, criminals
and defectives," the expansive, largely unsettled area drew the interest of
the military as it mobilized for World War I. The federal government built
Camp Dix—a training and staging ground for soldiers—and later, to the east,
Camp Kendrick—a proving ground for testing poison gas and defensive measures.[15] After the war, Camp Kendrick was taken over by the Navy, renamed
the Lakehurst Naval Air Station, and became its center for airship development. Most famously, on May 6, 1937, Lakehurst was the site of the disaster
in which the German passenger airship Hindenburg burst into flames as it
was about to land after crossing the Atlantic, resulting in thirty-six deaths.
In 1941, an air force base was built as part of what was now called Fort Dix,
and after the end of World War II, it was reopened in 1948 as the McGuire
Air Force Base. Yet, for most of the first half of the twentieth century, the
Pinelands and its residents generally were left alone.[16]

As the areas on the fringes of the Pinelands experienced rapid suburban
growth in the 1950s and 1960s, the Pinelands—situated between the rapidly
developing suburbs in the Delaware River Valley and the Atlantic shore—
began to be targeted for development because of its relatively cheap land and
new roads making it more accessible, such as the Garden State Parkway on
the eastern edge.[17] Major housing subdivisions and planned retirement communities were built, with developers marketing the comparatively low-cost
housing to both young families and retirees.[18] From 1950 to 1960, population
in the Pinelands grew by 36 percent, more than twice the rate of growth of
the state as a whole, and Ocean County's increase of 93 percent ranked it as
the nation's fastest growing county.[19]

In 1960, Burlington and Ocean Counties created the Pinelands Regional
Planning Board, which some four years later released a report, "The
New Jersey Pinelands Region," outlining four options for developing the
Pinelands, including a "jetport-new city"—an airport the size of Kennedy,
Newark, and LaGuardia airports combined, with an adjacent "garden city"

of 250,000 people.[20] The proposed Pinelands jetport followed the rejection by Governor Richard Hughes of a prior plan advanced by the New York Port Authority to build a new airport in Morris County's Great Swamp, a project that sparked opposition from environmentalists and homeowners in the surrounding affluent suburbs.[21] After the Great Swamp site became politically unacceptable, Governor Hughes and others advocating a new airport shifted their support to the Pinelands as a location to serve both New York and Philadelphia.[22] "Many New Jersey state and local government officials have contended," according to a press account, "that the pinelands would be the ideal site for a jetport, that high-speed rail transport could be set up to the metropolitan area and that the site is one of the few that has not run into concerted local protests."[23] Years later, Brendan Byrne reflected on the pro-growth sentiment of the times: "Everyone assumed in those days that, just as a child grows over time and needs more room, so does a town—and a region," Byrne said. "Growth was a natural thing and a good thing, and politicians thought their job was to smoothly lay the groundwork for sustained growth."[24]

But spurred in part by the 1968 publication of McPhee's *The Pine Barrens* and expanding interest in conserving open space, concerns were raised over the potential Pinelands jetport and the associated development it was expected to spur.[25] In the 1969 gubernatorial election, the Republican candidate, Congressman William Cahill from Camden County, who at one point had endorsed the idea of a jetport at the McGuire Air Force Base, changed his position to oppose any new jetport in New Jersey.[26] Cahill's victory over former Governor Meyner in the November election was seen as at least shelving, if not killing, the jetport idea during his time in office.[27]

Although Cahill's election in 1969 blocked the move for a jetport, he and his fellow Republicans in Trenton nonetheless enacted legislation in January 1972 establishing the Pinelands Environmental Council (PEC)—an agency to create a master plan for a 320,000-acre region in Burlington and Ocean counties (about a third of the area eventually protected under the program later approved by Governor Byrne). Skewed toward local control, fourteen of the fifteen PEC board members were named by the two counties; the sole state government representative was the commissioner of the DEP. The PEC's regulatory authority over development was restricted to delaying construction projects for ninety days; if it was unable to secure voluntary cooperation from the developer within the ninety-day period, the project was allowed to proceed.[28] One of the largest Pinelands landowners and cranberry farmers, J. Garfield DeMarco, was elected as the PEC chairman; he also chaired the Burlington County Republican Committee and was a long-time power in the county's politics. "We realize that we can't just tell a man he can't use his land, that he can't build anything there," DeMarco said soon after he was elected as the Council's chair. [29]

After his election in November 1973 as Cahill's successor, Brendan Byrne opposed the New Jersey Turnpike Authority's plan to build the "Alfred E. Driscoll Expressway" through sections of the Pinelands.[30] By blocking the Authority's attempts to award contracts for the Expressway's construction before he took office, Byrne prevented interests promoting development from organizing, and potentially undermining, his subsequent efforts to enact the landmark legislation he signed in 1979.[31]

In August 1975, during Byrne's second year in office, the PEC released its proposed master plan, "A Plan for the Pinelands." The plan allowed for development to accommodate 400,000 people, with zoning to permit homes to be built on lots as small as half an acre—a density that would have exceeded that in many suburban municipalities outside the area.[32]

After consulting with Byrne, David Bardin, the commissioner of the Department of Environmental Protection, wrote to DeMarco, declaring that "the proposed Plan fails, and fails dismally, to carry out the legislative mandate" and that it "essentially treats the Pinelands as ordinary land ripe for suburbanization." In an accompanying press release, Bardin publicly blasted the PEC's plan as a "land speculator's dream."[33] After the release of the plan, the Byrne administration cut off state funding for the PEC, thus forcing it to operate with limited funds from the two counties.[34] The plan provoked sharp criticism from both builders unhappy with any constraints on development and environmentalists opposing the scope of potential building. In light of the negative response, the PEC began to work on a new master plan but, according to a later account, many public officials and environmentalists concluded that the PEC had lost credibility and "that new and much different regulatory mechanisms would be needed to protect the Pine Barrens."[35]

In October 1975, Commissioner Bardin met with Nathaniel Reed, the Assistant Secretary for Fish, Wildlife and Parks in the Department of the Interior. The meeting apparently went well; in a memorandum to his key staff, Reed described Bardin as "interested and energetic" and directed that an internal task force be formed within the Department to prepare an options paper for a cooperative federal and state program to preserve the Pinelands.[36]

The resulting report released the following April, "The Pine Barrens: Concepts for Preservation," called for treating the Pinelands as an entire ecosystem and for the state to enact strong regulatory measures, including imposing a moratorium on development during the planning process before long-term land-use and water controls could be put in place. "Before the federal government would assume any role," according to one analyst, "it needed assurance that appropriate land and water policies would be developed and enforced by the state."[37] Although the Department of the Interior report lacked formal legislative or regulatory authority, it nonetheless provided an outline for state action to establish the necessary legal controls.

After he signed the income tax into law in July 1976, Byrne turned to the Pinelands as a priority for the coming months—a path that few in his camp viewed as offering any benefit for repairing his political standing as he decided whether to run for reelection in 1977. "I remember that the Governor told us at one of our Monday morning breakfasts," John Degnan, then the governor's counsel and executive secretary, recalled, "that the Pinelands would be the next issue." Degnan conceded that he and others on Byrne's staff knew little about the Pinelands. "I had never heard of the Pinelands when I grew up [in West Orange]. And we all went out with books," Degnan continued. "Don [Linky] found a copy of John McPhee's book and we educated ourselves on what the Pine Barrens was. And we figured we were off on another war."[38] But the subtle attractions of the pines depicted in McPhee's book were not an easy sell. "[A]lthough the Pinelands are a treasured ecological and recreational resource," one author noted, "it lacks the star quality mountains, glaciers, lakes and rushing streams that are the stuff of Sierra Club posters and films."[39]

In the November 1976 election, New Jersey voters approved the referendum authorizing casino gambling in Atlantic City, which was expected to spur housing and other development in the Pinelands. Other building impacts were projected from the Nixon Administration's plans to allow offshore drilling for oil and gas off the New Jersey coast, potentially leading to landside storage tanks and pipelines crossing the Pinelands to refineries in Philadelphia. "The threats are becoming stronger," David Moore, the executive director of the New Jersey Conservation Foundation, said in assessing the potential impact on the Pinelands. "Land speculators hope major oil companies will be interested in development. Casino gambling could generate pressure for a transportation corridor from Philadelphia to Atlantic City."[40] During a period when the state's unemployment rate reached the highest levels since the Great Depression, the prospect of removing so much land from potential development soon antagonized statewide development interests and construction unions.

On November 19, Byrne met at the State House with Democratic legislators, mayors, and other officials to review the options for legislation or other action to restrict Pinelands development. Participants included a Democratic freeholder and a mayor who both had lost their seats in the recent election; in a newspaper article assessing the election results, PEC chairman Garfield DeMarco cited their defeats and Republican victories in Burlington and Ocean counties as indicating that "the people approved of the council's plans" and that voters "prefer local control."[41] According to the briefing memo prepared for Byrne prior to the meeting, Senator John Russo from Ocean County felt that "there is no chance for passing such legislation" and recommended against its introduction. Another attendee, however, Mayor

Floyd West of Bass River, urged Byrne to support a strong Pinelands preservation effort.[42]

In the following month, Byrne convened a conference on the future of the Pinelands at the Woodrow Wilson School at Princeton University, where he had been a student some thirty years earlier. The conference was largely an attempt by Byrne's staff to demonstrate outreach to the various interests before unveiling any specific legislative proposals, thus hopefully avoiding the criticism that had followed his tax reform proposals in 1974. The attendees were an invited mix of public officials, interest group representatives, environmentalists, academics, the media, and others, including DeMarco and a few other notable Byrne critics. In his opening remarks, Byrne made clear his intention to push for a strong preservation program, saying "the piecemeal development which now threatens the integrity of the Pine Barrens must be stopped."[43] Yet given his low standing in the polls and the still unanswered question of whether he would seek reelection in the following year, many of his opponents probably assumed that it was doubtful that any Byrne initiative on the Pinelands would survive past the 1977 election.

In January 1977, a few weeks after the Princeton conference, Byrne again declared his intention to take action to preserve the Pinelands in his Annual Message to the Legislature. Shortly after his message, the DEP issued new water quality standards to sharply reduce discharges of effluents into the Pinelands aquifer. The new regulations provoked a strong response from local officials, landowners and builders, including claims, according to one scholar, that the restrictions "amounted to a taking of land without compensation, that they would destroy the value of land, cause erosion of home rule and erode local tax bases."[44]

On May 28, 1977, just days before he won the Democratic gubernatorial primary over seven opponents, Governor Byrne issued an executive order establishing the "Pinelands Review Committee (PRC)," a body comprised of designated state cabinet officers and private persons appointed by the Governor.[45] Unlike the PEC, the PRC had members from outside the Pinelands region, including environmental advocates and academics. Byrne named Craig Yates, a Burlington County businessman and the brother of Democratic Assemblyman Charles Yates, to chair the committee. Among other things, the committee was directed to delineate the geographic boundaries of the Pinelands and develop a plan within one year that would have as its primary goals "the preservation of the unique environmental resources of the Pinelands" and the "discouragement of scattered and piecemeal development in open space areas."[46] During Byrne's 1977 reelection campaign, despite misgivings of Democrats in the region who feared that his advocacy of preserving the Pinelands would hurt the Party's legislative and local candidates in the November election, Byrne continued to argue for strong measures to control development.

Byrne's initial inclination was to avoid the delay inherent in creating another commission, but reluctantly accepted the advice that he had limits to his power. "I called [DEP Commissioner] David Bardin into my office." Byrne remembered years later. "I said to David, 'Do not issue any more permits to build in the Pinelands.' I just said it. And he came back a few months later and he said, 'I'm having trouble with the law on this, you know, I'm not giving permits and they're threatening to sue me and I don't know that I got a good defense.'" The attorney general's lawyers, according to Bardin, had concluded that he lacked legal authority to deny permit applications without any legislative basis to do so.[47] Byrne fully recognized the impact on private landowners of restricting development. "I really wanted to buy all that land," he would later say, "but the State of New Jersey didn't have a fraction of the money we'd need to buy it. Some people donated land, piecemeal, to the State of New Jersey. But there was a limit to how much land we could acquire that way."[48]

But securing legislative support for Pinelands preservation would be an uphill trek. Legislators representing districts with municipalities that might be included within the scope of any proposed legislation—along with the vast majority of county freeholders, mayors and other local officials—objected to the intrusion on their traditional home rule authority over land use.

Meanwhile, the attention that Byrne had focused on the Pinelands helped to spark action in the U.S. Congress. In March 1977, a week after he announced he would enter the Democratic gubernatorial primary in which he would oppose Byrne for the nomination, Congressman James Florio introduced a bill to authorize the creation of "greenline parks" and specified that 970,000 acres in the Pinelands would become the first such park, with $50 million authorized in federal money to purchase land.[49] Competing with Florio's proposal was a bill jointly sponsored by Republican Congressman Edwin B. Forsythe and Democratic Congressman William J. Hughes, whose districts included several Pinelands municipalities, that would give counties and local governments much stronger control, an approach that Florio criticized for relying too heavily on "uncoordinated counties and municipalities" and for failing "to provide for area-wide planning."[50]

A third bill introduced jointly in the Senate by Republican Clifford P. Case and Democrat Harrison A. Williams Jr., incorporated elements of the House bills and also included input from Governor Byrne's Washington office, which served as liaison between the Administration and the state's Congressional delegation. Just over a year after Byrne's reelection, the Case-Williams bill was added as an amendment to the National Parks and Recreation Act of 1978 that President Jimmy Carter signed on November 11, 1978. As enacted, the legislation authorized the creation of "national reserves" to preserve areas that were, according to Senator Case, "too big, too complex, too valuable, and too interwoven with the fabric of existing communities" for traditional preservation in national and state parks. The Pinelands was expressly designated as the first "national reserve planning area," with the state given two years to form a commission and develop a pinelands conservation plan to be submitted for approval by the Department of the Interior to qualify for federal land acquisition funds. On December 10, Secretary of the Interior Cecil Andrus wrote to Byrne, formally requesting that the Governor create the commission authorized by the legislation for the Pinelands National Reserve.[51]

Late amendments to the Case-Williams bill specified that the Pinelands planning body was to be composed of fifteen members: seven members appointed by the governor; another seven appointed by the relevant counties; and one member—a potential swing vote in the event of a split between the appointees of the governor and the counties—designated by the U.S. Secretary of the Interior.[52]

To some on the governor's staff, the federal legislation was seen as complicating, indeed undermining, the administration's efforts for state legislation. By fixing the composition of the planning entity with an equal number of gubernatorial and county appointees, the federal appointee, who could become a crucial deciding vote, could align with county representatives when a conservative Administration controlled the White House. Indeed, this would in fact occur after the November 1980 election in which Ronald Reagan defeated Jimmy Carter, when Reagan appointed a Secretary of the Interior who was widely viewed as opposed to land conservation and environmental protection.[53]

On February 8, 1979, Governor Byrne signed Executive Order 71 establishing the Pinelands Planning Commission as a successor body to the PRC and directing it to prepare the plan required by the federal National Parks and Recreation Act.[54] Most importantly, the order also imposed an eighteen-month moratorium on the approval by state agencies of pending applications for development, an unprecedented exercise of gubernatorial power that provoked strong protests from Pinelands legislators, local officials, and development interests.[55] The executive order adopted a map of the Pinelands that covered 1.1 million acres in seven counties (compared to the 320,000 acres in Burlington and Ocean counties subject to the oversight of the PEC) published in September 1978 by the Rutgers Center for Coastal and Environmental Studies under a contract for the National Park Service.[56] Based primarily on identifying common vegetation and water resources characteristics, the Rutgers map was prepared without consideration of the political impacts of a regulatory program restricting development in the proposed region.[57] Nonetheless, the Rutgers map provided an objective, albeit expansive, outline delineating the area proposed for planning and regulation.

On the day after Byrne signed the executive order, the New Jersey Builders Association filed a lawsuit challenging its constitutionality, claiming
that Byrne's action had exceeded the governor's executive powers, usurped
the authority of the legislature and would produce substantial adverse economic impacts. In a legal brief submitted a few weeks after Byrne issued
the order, the Association contended: "Virtually all construction has been
halted. . . . The results have been chaotic and catastrophic. Builders are going
out of business, construction workers are out of work and persons who have
invested everything in land are facing bankruptcy."[58] Recognizing the importance of the issue, the state Supreme Court agreed to hear the Association's
appeal of a lower court's refusal to issue an injunction to halt the enforcement
of the moratorium and scheduled oral arguments for May 8.[59]

Upon signing the executive order, Byrne also announced that legislation
to establish the permanent commission with power to regulate development
would be introduced with his support by two Democrats, Senate President
Joseph Merlino of Mercer County and Senator Charles Yates of Burlington
County. Less than a week after Byrne signed the order, on February 13, 1979,
Merlino and Yates introduced Senate Bill 3091, titled "The Pinelands Protection Act." Merlino had been the Senate majority leader from 1976 to 1977
when he and Yates were valuable Byrne allies in the income tax fight; Yates,
who was elected to the Senate in 1977, was the brother of Craig Yates, whom
Byrne had named as chair of his PRC. In personality and style, Merlino and
Yates were a study in contrasts. Merlino was a lawyer brash cigar-smoking,
a native of Trenton's Chambersburg Italian neighborhood known for occasional aggressive tactics in leading the Senate (asked to comment on a female
senator who had leaked to the press details of confidential discussions in the
Democratic caucus, Merlino said: "If she were a man, I'd have punched her
in the mouth"); Yates was a courtly, intellectual millionaire whose father
had founded one of the first companies to supply copper foil components for
computers. Although Merlino's legislative district was centered on Trenton,
he believed restrictions on suburban development were not only crucial to
maintain open space, but also were essential to slow the suburban sprawl that
had undermined the economies and tax revenues of older cities like Trenton.[60] "We have to save the pinelands," declared Merlino upon filing his bill,
"before they are paved over with shopping centers and parking lots, lined
with fast food stands and crowded with half acre lots."[61]

Byrne had made clear to his staff and relevant cabinet officers that his goal
was to preserve the Pinelands, but otherwise he did not involve himself in
the specifics of how to design the legislation. The bill was drafted primarily by Michael Catania, the aide assigned to environmental legislation from
the nonpartisan Office of Legislative Services, with input from an informal
group including Merlino's staff, the governor's office, and the Departments

of Environmental Protection and Community Affairs.[62] Like Byrne's executive order, the proposed legislation also incorporated the map by Rutgers in drawing the boundaries of the Pinelands, which over the years had never been delineated.

The wide geographic coverage proposed in the bill as introduced by Merlino and Yates, in the view of some staff members, could be a useful starting point for later negotiations to gain votes for the bill to secure its passage, possibly allowing the area to be narrowed, perhaps to the central core defined as the "preservation area" in the legislation.[63] Restricting the scope of the regulatory controls to the preservation area would be a primary goal of the legislation's opponents, but it was a deal which in fact never came to pass. "It was probably just miscommunication that we, on the substantive side, never told those doing the lobbying that we didn't think we needed all that land which allowed all that area to be included in the final bill," recounted the Governor's policy director Donald Linky. "I thought we had a lot to give up in the way of negotiation, at that point, that we never, in fact, did give up."[64]

Another late drafting decision was to insert specific goals in the proposed law. Rather than give the Commission freedom to adopt any plan, the legislation included language directing that such objectives as land conservation, preservation of water quality, and concentration of development in existing towns be priorities of any plan. By including specific guidelines in the legislation, future commissions would need to comply with its paramount goals or face potential legal actions to overturn decisions in conflict with the legislation's expressed intent.[65]

Other key provisions of the Merlino-Yates bill granted the Pinelands Commission regulatory power to enforce its master plan; required that the seven counties and fifty-two municipalities within its boundaries revise local master plans and ordinances to comply with the Commission's plan; and authorized the commission to approve or reject applications for local and county development approvals until it was determined that the local master plans and ordinances were in compliance. The proposed legislation also gave the state a right of first refusal before landowners could sell their land, and abolished the PEC.

Byrne's order and the Merlino-Yates bill sparked stiff opposition. On one point, there was agreement: "Proponents and opponents," the *New York Times* reported, "assert it [the executive order] is unprecedented in the 50 states."[66] "In the setting of the times," Bergen County Assemblyman Albert Burstein reflected years later, "when you consider you were dealing with about twenty percent of the land mass of the state of New Jersey, to set that aside as being restricted with respect to future development was a major, major achievement."[67]

Newspaper editorials generally favored the moratorium and the legislation to establish a permanent preservation program. The *Trenton Times* wrote that "development in the Pinelands should be strictly controlled and limited by a federal-state-local partnership for the long-term benefit of the state as a whole." The *Star Ledger* endorsed a growth policy that preserved "farmlands, Pinelands, future parklands and protects critical natural resources." *The Record* declared that "if a choice has to be made between orchids and asphalt, we'll take the Pine Barrens over the pine barons any day." The *Asbury Park Press* wrote that "Scatter shot development that threatened the ecology of the Pinelands required the 18-month moratorium that Gov. Byrne imposed by executive order." The *Press of Atlantic City* stated, "whether you agree with Byrne's plan or not, it has at least started the ball rolling in an area that has been the victim of procrastinators for too long."[68]

Soon after the Merlino-Yates bill was introduced, Senate Majority Leader John Russo of Ocean County, the second-ranking Democrat to Merlino in the Senate leadership, introduced his own bill to limit any regulatory program to the inner core of the Pinelands and require state reimbursement to local governments of any lost property tax revenues resulting from land acquisition. Russo's bill was promptly endorsed by the Ocean County board of freeholders and the Pinelands Mayors Coalition, a newly formed organization comprised of mayors of 54 municipalities.[69]

Publicly, Byrne defended the moratorium—which went far beyond the requirement in the federal legislation that the state institute "interim protection of the area" during the planning process—as necessary to protect against the further loss of open space while the long-term plan was in preparation. But perhaps more important was the unstated political strategy: placing intense pressure on the reluctant legislature to establish a permanent commission with extensive power to override municipal land-use planning and zoning decisions. Without Byrne's unilateral executive action to halt most construction, it seems highly unlikely that any political coalition could have mustered the votes to force final action on the legislation.

In addition to filing its lawsuit against the governor's executive order, the Builders Association mounted an attack on the Merlino-Yates bill in the legislature. It hired the lobbying firm of Joseph Katz—ironically, a close Byrne friend and political confidante who had drafted the April 1973 announcement of his candidacy—to coordinate efforts to kill or weaken the bill. Katz demonstrated the extraordinary geographic scope of the proposed regulatory program by reproducing a map with an outline of the potential region and superimposing it on North Jersey, thus seeking to impress legislators from that region with the extent of the Byrne plan. "I couldn't blame Joe for his bogus map; he was a gun for hire, making a living, and the bogus map was a clever idea," Byrne later said. "But the fact was that the Pinelands were not in North Jersey; they were in the southern part of our state—and they needed protection."[70]

With a few exceptions, farmers and agricultural interest groups also lined up against any mandated state development controls. "When I did the Pinelands," Byrne later reflected, "the farmers were totally against it for pretty good reasons. I mean, putting their farms under the Pinelands restrictions affected the property value of the farm and frankly their ability to borrow money." Byrne understood the difficult position in which he had placed Phil Alampi, his Secretary of Agriculture: "Phil had to walk the fine line between my determination to save the Pinelands and the farmers' outrage that I was interfering with their private property. I knew privately he was on their side, but publicly he did the best job he could to explain what we were trying to do."[71]

Most South Jersey legislators opposed the Merlino-Yates bill. Protesting Byrne's action at a public hearing held on the bill in the Pinelands, Gloucester County's Democratic Assemblyman Kenneth Gewertz said: "He's got more people mad than I've ever seen in my 20 years in government," and was "cheered and applauded," according to a newspaper account, when he announced that he would seek to impeach Byrne. Outside the hearing, protestors carried caskets in a mock funeral for the region's economy, and a picket sign read, "Property owners and taxpayers should have the same rights as trees and frogs." Democratic Senator Steven Perskie of Atlantic County, who had been a key supporter of Byrne on the income tax and was grateful for Byrne's leadership in securing approval of casino gambling in Atlantic City, predicted that the bill would pass only if it included compromises to eliminate or weaken its regulation of land use in the outer areas facing development pressure with the onset of casino gambling.[72]

In fact, a Gannett News Service poll, taken soon after Byrne signed his executive order and the Merlino-Yates bill was introduced, reported that across the state, the public was divided. Statewide, 49 percent believed the state should control the future of the Pinelands, while 34 percent felt that local governments should remain in control. In Camden, Burlington, and Gloucester counties, 50 percent favored state control and 41 percent local; in Atlantic, Cape May, and Cumberland counties, 41 percent favored state control and 39 percent favored home rule.[73]

For each of the opposing sides, there were reasons to take action on the Governor's proposed legislation rather than wait for the New Jersey Supreme Court to issue a decision in the lawsuit challenging the governor's authority to order the moratorium. Opponents of the legislation feared that a court decision upholding the executive order would set a precedent by which Byrne or future governors could halt construction in other areas of the state. On the other side, supporters of Byrne's action feared that a court decision holding the executive order unconstitutional would undercut the preservation effort and shift the momentum in the legislature to those who sought to weaken or kill the bill.[74]

As the date neared for the oral arguments before the state Supreme Court, there were serious doubts whether Byrne's moratorium would be upheld. "I think it's fair to say that everyone in the attorney general's office," Attorney General Degnan later said, "with the possible exception of [First Assistant Attorney General] Mike Cole, believed that the executive order was unconstitutional." According to Degnan, Byrne never asked for a formal legal opinion on the executive order. "There was some very strong discussion," Degnan continued, "in the Governor's office—Dan O'Hern and I and Don [Linky] and other people—on whether we had a chance of passing what I used to call the 'ha, ha test,' in sustaining the constitutionality of the executive order."[75]

Byrne himself was uncertain over the legal outcome. "At the time I used it," Byrne later recalled, "there was considerable doubt whether I had the right to issue so broad an order." Shortly before the scheduled argument, he received a phone call from Chief Justice Hughes. Byrne knew that the unusual outreach by Hughes stretched the traditional rules applying to the separation between the branches of government. "It's not really appropriate for the chief justice to discuss pending cases with the governor," Byrne later said, "but Richard and I knew each other well, and he had a little talk with me, and told me he didn't want to have to decide this case, and I should find a way to strike a deal with the legislature." Byrne also recognized how extraordinary the situation had become. "I think it's the only time that the head of one . . . branch of government," he continued, "actually called upon another branch of government and said, 'Can't you get something done with the third branch of government [the legislature] so the second branch of government [the judiciary] doesn't have to rule on what the first branch of government [the executive] did?"[76]

At the time, Degnan was unaware of the Chief Justice's contact with the Governor, but he knew of Byrne's grasp of the Court's internal decision-making. "Sometimes he had a unique insight into the Court," Degnan later said, "and I really never asked how he acquired it. Whether it was just his legal ability or he had a pipeline, I don't know."[77]

Despite his misgivings about the legal merits of the executive order, at the Governor's insistence, Degnan agreed to argue the Builders Association case personally before the Supreme Court, an appearance that Byrne believed "would convey to the Court the special importance of the bill from the executive point of view." Still, Degnan was pessimistic about the reception he would receive from the Court, saying "I clearly expected to have my head handed to me." But to his surprise, the tone of the questioning by the justices quickly set him at ease: "I have never seen such a one-sided oral argument against the home builders. The Court was making it loud and clear that it was not as troubled with the constitutionality of the executive order as we were."[78] News of the Court's positive reaction promptly spread to opponents of the moratorium. "The likelihood that the Court might affirm the extraordinary exercise of executive power," Degnan noted, "brought some additional pressure on the people whom you couldn't convince on the merits that the bill might be a better way than the executive order."[79]

The Merlino-Yates bill was reported out of the committee chaired by Senator Dodd without significant amendments on May 10, 1979, and went before the full Senate on May 21. The critical test of the sentiment within the Senate was the vote on Senator Russo's motion to send the bill back to committee in order to restrict the moratorium to the inner core, which would effectively kill the bill.

After intense lobbying by the interests on each side, Russo's motion was defeated by a vote of 17 to 12, with 11 senators absent or not voting. The full Senate then approved the bill by a vote of 33 to 2, with only Senator Russo and James Cafiero, a Cape May Republican, voting against. The wide margin suggested that many Senators, after the Russo motion was defeated, did not want to be on record opposing the Governor on an issue on which he felt so strongly and which might anger voters in their own districts, including those in primarily Republican upscale suburbs, who were becoming increasingly concerned with environmental issues and the loss of open space. Camden Democrat Joseph Maressa, for example, whose district included parts of the Pinelands, called the legislation "absurd" but ultimately voted in favor.[80]

The Assembly scheduled a vote on the Senate-passed bill for Thursday, June 21. As the Assembly vote neared, much stronger opposition than in the Senate was anticipated, particularly after Congressman William Hughes turned against the bill and Democratic Assembly opponents from South Jersey were able to build alliances with members from North Jersey who ordinarily would have been expected to vote for approval. "I received a call on Friday in the week before the vote from Dick Coffee, the director of the Assembly Democrats," Bob Mulcahy, Byrne's chief of staff, later recounted, "who told me that there were enough votes to send the bill back to committee for amendments, which we knew would effectively kill the bill. Assemblyman Donald Stewart, chairman of the Agriculture and Environment Committee, was able to "mend fences with key northern legislators on some of the things he had done before," recalled Harold Hodes, the Governor's deputy chief of staff.

Over the weekend, Mulcahy and Hodes called some of those members to ask that they stay home or at least away from the State House when the vote to recommit was called. "We promised that we would arrange transportation so that, after the vote on the motion to send the bill back to committee was defeated, to give us time by calling a long recess to get them back to the State House to vote for the bill's passage."[81] As Byrne later explained, the strategy was a clever ploy by the opposition forces. "Nobody wanted to be on record as against the bill protecting the Pinelands," Byrne recalled. "What the opponents wanted to do was to vote to send the bill back to committee, using the excuse 'I want a better bill.' But most of the people who said they wanted a 'better bill' really didn't want any bill at all."[82]

On the following Monday morning after Mulcahy and Hodes had made their calls over the weekend, Chief Justice Hughes phoned Mulcahy, asking that he come see him in his chambers to discuss routine "personnel matters" relating to the judiciary. At the end of the meeting, Hughes inquired about the prospects for the Pinelands bill, and Mulcahy advised that the administration hoped it would be passed later in the week by the Assembly. "When I told him that," Mulcahy later recalled, "he replied, 'Good, that will make Justice [Morris] Pashman's job a lot easier.'" To Mulcahy, the comment indicated that the Court was having difficulty in forming a majority in support of the constitutionality of Byrne's executive order.[83]

On the morning of the vote on June 21, Hodes became particularly concerned when Assemblyman Raymond Lesniak of Union County who, in Hodes's words, "in those days was Mr. Environment," informed him that "we couldn't count on his vote" and that he intended to vote to return the bill to committee. Lesniak apparently had been persuaded to return a favor from earlier in the legislative session when Assemblyman Stewart had allowed a controversial bill supported by Lesniak to advance to a vote. When Byrne was informed of Lesniak's defection, "the Governor," according to Hodes, "started to get really antsy."[84]

As the members of the Assembly began to arrive in Trenton for the scheduled vote, Byrne met with some of the Democrats opposed to the legislation who had been elected with him in 1977. He stressed that, despite their fears over a voter backlash to restricting development in the Pinelands, the election results had shown that there was substantial public support for preservation. "The other thing is everybody knew where Byrne stood in '77," Hodes later recalled, saying that Byrne told the group, "I carried your districts. I won your districts. And this is what the people in your district want. And you are only here because of the developers and whatever else."[85]

Recognizing that the outcome of a vote was in doubt, Byrne's staff discussed potential compromises to ensure enough votes for passage. Late in the afternoon, some fifty people crowded into a room on the second floor of the State House review amendments that might persuade reluctant South Jersey Democrats to end their opposition to the bill. "Everybody wanted to see a map," Hodes recalled of the scene. "People would come in with their magic markers with different scenarios, saying 'take this out,' 'put this in,' 'split towns up.' It was crazy."[86] Michael Catania, the legislative committee aide who had drafted much of the bill, described the process: "And [Assemblymen] Marty Herman and John Paul Doyle are negotiating their hearts out trying to get the area cut down, trying to get the Commission's powers reduced. We are going back and forth. Harold [Hodes] is saying, 'What are we doing? What sections are we changing?' So finally, after about an hour of haranguing, Harold looks up and says, 'Look, I can get the Republican votes a hell of a lot cheaper. We don't need this grief. Do what you have to do. Let's go.'"[87]

Byrne left the State House for his residence at Morven, telling Hodes to keep him informed about the evening's debate. On his way out the door, he turned to state firmly, "And I want this bill"; according to Hodes, it was "the first time that he ever told me that he wanted something as bad as he wanted it." Before he left, Byrne also had scrawled a note for Mulcahy and Hodes: "If the P bill passes, call it," meaning that the bill should be brought to the governor's office immediately after the vote, thereby removing the legislation from the custody of the legislature to prevent any final maneuver to recall the bill for reconsideration.[88]

As the Assembly debate began that evening on the bill, Assistant Democratic Majority Leader John Paul Doyle, Senator Russo's running mate who had broken a century of Republican control in Ocean County in winning the 1973 election, led opposition to the bill.[89] Other assemblymen attempted to filibuster the bill by repeatedly questioning the Assembly sponsor, Gerald Stockman, a dialogue that ended only when, after two hours, Stockman refused to answer any more questions.[90] At two o'clock in the morning, the motion to return the bill to committee was defeated by a vote of 35 to 31, with fourteen members absent or not voting. After the motion was defeated, Mulcahy and Hodes hurriedly made arrangements to bring the members who had agreed to stay away from the State House back from their homes or other locations, a task complicated by the fact that many gas stations were closed by the shortages resulting from the Arab oil embargo. "We used the State Police," Mulcahy recalled, "to either pick up the members and drive them to Trenton or check with them to make sure they had enough gas to drive on their own. I had asked Mike Rowe, the operations director in the governor's office, to insure that we had a plan to get each of them back for the vote."[91]

Finally, after seven hours of debate, at around three o'clock in the morning of June 22, the bill was approved by a 48-16 vote.[92] As in the Senate, the tally of votes for the bill was inflated by some Democrats who had earlier withheld support, but voted for it once it became apparent that it would pass. Looking back many years later on the harried efforts to line up votes, Hodes would say, perhaps jokingly, "there's an extension on the Garden State Parkway, there's cardiac surgery in Perth Amboy, and there might be an extension of the Parkway down in South Jersey" as a result of the meetings he had throughout the night with the holdouts he persuaded to vote for the bill's passage.[93]

On June 28, 1979, Governor Byrne signed the Pinelands Protection Act in a public ceremony in his State House office, flanked by Senator Merlino and First Lady Jean Byrne.[94] One press account described the event as "festive" and noted that Byrne's voice was "cracking with emotion." He began to read the excerpt from John McPhee's book expressing skepticism that the Pinelands "are not very likely to be the subject of dramatic decrees or legislation" and were "headed slowly toward extinction," noting that he had taken McPhee's words as a "challenge" in his fight for preservation. When his eyes teared up, Byrne asked Senator Merlino to take over in reading the quote. After Merlino finished, Byrne went on to say, "I think this bill, 100 years from now, will be the most significant bill I have signed."[95]

The legislature was in session on the day the bill was signed, and Harold Hodes arranged for pine cones and pine needles to be placed on the desk of each legislator who had opposed the bill. "I just wanted to show them that the battle was over," Hodes later explained, "and it was time to move on."[96]

Enactment of the legislation made moot the pending case before the Supreme Court. By promptly dismissing the appeal by the New Jersey Builders Association, the court thus avoided a decision on the constitutionality of the executive order imposing the construction moratorium.[97] Byrne later speculated that the call he had received from Chief Justice "indicated that he was having trouble lining up the votes to sustain the executive order, and it probably would have been held unconstitutional."[98]

After the bill became law, Byrne proceeded to appoint the members of the Pinelands Commission. Perhaps his most significant choice was that of the chairman, Franklin Parker III, a Republican Morris County resident who previously had been active in the effort to save the Great Swamp in North Jersey from the proposed jetport in the 1960s. A partner in a prominent New York City law firm, Parker had been suggested to Byrne by Laurence Rockefeller, a dedicated conservationist from the Rockefeller family whom Byrne had met through their positions as board members of Princeton University. "Frank's calming presence," Byrne later reflected, "made it hard for our opponents to argue that the conservation of our state's resources was a radical plan being rammed down their throat by a pack of raving liberal Democrats."[99] Parker would continue as chair for nearly ten years, with his courtly, nonpartisan demeanor praised as a key factor in avoiding sharp conflicts among the commissioners as they developed and implemented the master plan. Just before Byrne signed the new law and announced his appointees as commissioners, Byrne declared that he was naming Terrence "Terry" Moore as the first executive director of the commission—ignoring a provision in the legislation he was about to sign stating that the executive director was to be appointed by the commissioners (and in fact the prospective commissioners privately had agreed on another person for the position).[100]

Candace Ashmun, another original commission appointee of Byrne's who had headed the Association of New Jersey Environmental Commissions, recalled years later that at the commission's first meeting, Parker declared, "There's not going to be any occasions where we have 'we' against 'them.'" Despite the concerns that the even split in the number of members appointed by the governor and the counties, mandated by the federal legislation, would lead to voting blocs pitting the counties against the state, Ashmun said that in fact "it never happened that way, I guess primarily because the Chairman didn't want it that way. There's never been an occasion when all the Governor's people voted one way and all the county people voted another way."[101]

The commission began its work without any direct state appropriation, and was forced to put together a package of funding from diverse public and private sources.[102] Serving on the unpaid board of the commission required a high level of personal commitment. Commissioners participated in frequent meetings, hearings, and other events during the design of the Pinelands plan; members like Parker who were employed in full-time private positions also were required to travel well over two hours back and forth to evening meetings that could run past midnight.

The Pinelands Commission took eighteen months to complete its Comprehensive Management Plan. The plan prohibited nearly all development in the inner core "preservation area" of approximately 350,000 acres, but allowed limited development in the surrounding 700,000-acre "protection area." Specific sections where development had already occurred were designated as "growth areas" where more intensive development would be allowed. In the face of criticism that the schedule specified in the legislation gave insufficient time for review of the issues in the outer "protection area," the Governor agreed to a compromise whereby the preservation area plan would be adopted as scheduled, but the approval of the plan for the outer protection area, where there was considerably more controversy over the extent of proposed development constraints, would be extended by an additional six months.[103]

After the release of the draft plan for public comment on June 6, 1980, an article in the *New York Times* stated that the plan "is as unusual as the Pinelands themselves. It is the first effort in the United States to coordinate Federal, state and local government funds, agencies and regulations to protect an area without acquiring all of it outright."[104] Following the draft plan's publication, opponents in the state legislature moved to reconsider or delay the program, but Senate President Merlino effectively blocked any vote in the Senate.[105]

On August 8, 1980, the Pinelands Commission voted 11 to 4 to approve the preservation area portion of the master plan, which went into effect in the following month. Despite the initial concern that the commission's composition would lead to splits between the gubernatorial and county appointees, three of the county representatives joined the seven gubernatorial appointees and the federal representative in voting to approve the plan. The final plan, including the outer protection area, was approved on November 21, 1980, by a vote of 11 to 3 (with one abstention from the Cumberland County appointee) and became effective in January 1981.[106]

The Pinelands Protection Act called for the plan adopted by the commission and the governor to be submitted for approval to the Secretary of the U.S. Department of the Interior in order to establish the Pinelands National Reserve authorized under federal legislation.[107] Following the defeat of President Carter by Ronald Reagan in the November 1980 election, Byrne had directed his staff to expedite the commission's approval to allow the state to seek federal approval of the plan from the outgoing Carter Administration before Reagan's inauguration in January 1981, in the expectation that Reagan's new Secretary of the Interior would be less sympathetic to the preservation goals of the plan.

The federal legislation did not require the state to submit the plan for federal review until November 1981, but the plan was forwarded a full year before the legal deadline to allow the Department of the Interior to complete a required environmental impact statement. Under an unusually tight schedule, the impact statement was released in December with an endorsement of the master plan.[108] In the closing days of the Carter Administration, Byrne's staff in Trenton and Washington worked closely with the Interior officials, particularly Robert W. McIntosh in its Philadelphia regional office, who, as Terry Moore later recalled, "walked the plan through the Interior approval process right into the Secretary's office for signature."[109] Secretary of the Interior Cecil D. Andrus approved the plan on January 16—four days before he and President Carter left office.[110]

Despite the federal approval of the preservation plan, local builders, officials, and interest groups continued their efforts to block or delay implementation of the plan. Litigation would continue to challenge the validity of the plan, with developers arguing that its restrictions on building exceeded the authority provided under the legislation or that its development restrictions amounted to unconstitutional takings of property without compensation, contentions that were not rejected by the courts until after Byrne had left office.[111] Congressmen Forsythe and Hughes issued a joint statement opposing the plan on the ground that "the restrictions called for in the Forest Region go beyond the original intent of the federal laws," and they both objected to a pending application by the state for the first federal appropriation of eight million dollars for acquisition of land in the preservation area.[112]

In the summer of 1981, Byrne's last year in office, Senator Perskie, who had worked closely with Byrne on both casino gambling and the income tax, made the most serious attempt to weaken the Act. Amendments proposed by Perskie would have limited the commission's oversight authority to developments of over two hundred housing units; made its powers in the Protection Area only "advisory"; and required a two-thirds vote of the commission to uphold a denial of a project application. "I don't want anyone to think that we're backing away from the goals of restricting development," Perskie said in explaining his bill to amend the Act, "The goal here is to try and make it work."[113]

Perskie further announced that he believed he had support within the governor's staff to recommend the proposed changes to the Governor, who was attending a conference in the Soviet Union. "I don't have a written contract," he said. "I have the benefit of six and a half months of an exchange of views and discussions and what I consider a mutual respect of intentions. Both sides know we are committed to the same goals." An effort was made to push the bill through the legislature on an expedited basis, but that was blocked when objections from environmentalists and others persuaded legislators not to bring the bill up for a vote.[114]

Reaction to the bill was mixed. Congressmen Forsythe and Hughes backed the bill, indicating that they would remove their hold on the federal appropriation for acquisition of land if the bill was approved. But Carol Barrett, spokeswoman for the Sierra Club, declared, "They're really decimating the plan. They haven't got the public welfare in mind at all with this thing." Most newspaper editorials also criticized the Perskie amendments. The *New York Times* wrote that the Pinelands Commission's master plan was "a reasonable compromise and deserves a chance. . . . Mr. Perskie's bill might well demolish that chance." Only the *Press of Atlantic City,* Perskie's home district paper, expressed mild support, declaring that "the Perskie measure contains a little of the good things designed to keep both sides happy, and a little of the bad things that make both sides angry."[115]

The governor's office had an internal debate over the Perskie bill following Byrne's return from his trade mission.[116] On July 7, Byrne said he would accept the bill only if the Pinelands Commission supported it; on the next day, the commissioners voted against it. The Governor's Office then issued a one-sentence press release that read:

Governor Byrne announced today he has informed Sen. Steven Perskie (D-Atlantic) he cannot support S-3335, which would amend the Pinelands Protection Act.

Perskie responded by declaring that "I consider that this is a serious breach of faith, both personally and politically." He added, "It just shows that if enough misinformed people scream loudly enough, they can destroy a credible and worthwhile idea." Congressman Hughes said the governor "has responded to a very limited, special interest group."[117]

In the face of Byrne's opposition, Perskie's bill was never voted on by the Senate. Reflecting years later on the conflict, Pinelands Commission Chairman Franklin Parker said that if Byrne not intervened to defeat Perskie's bill, "we might not have any Pinelands protection today."[118]

After Byrne left office in January 1982, Perskie renewed his effort with Thomas Kean, Byrne's successor. Soon after his inauguration, Kean recalled at a forum years later, Perskie came to see him and said, "now you're Governor the first bill we're going to send you is a repeal of the Pinelands Law." Perskie claimed, Kean remembered, that he had commitments from an "overwhelming number of votes in both houses and . . . a letter from the Reagan Administration guy, [U.S. Secretary of the Interior] James Watt, . . . and two or three New Jersey Congressmen." Kean said he replied, "It's not what I'm going to do. I'm in favor of the Pinelands law," and that Perskie told him, "We may be able to give you your first override [of a veto]." Kean said he responded: "Go ahead." Kean's firm stance blocked any attempt by Perskie to repeal the Pinelands legislation. Kean also resisted a subsequent effort by Republican Senator William Gormley (who was elected in 1982 to Perskie's Senate seat after Kean named Perskie as a Superior Court judge) to abolish the commission and transfer its regulatory authority to the DEP.[119]

The Pinelands legislation and the management program would gain wide attention outside New Jersey as a model for preservation efforts.[120] Speaking at a Rutgers conference that brought Byrne, Merlino, Parker, Moore, and other key actors together some eight years after the Pinelands legislation was enacted, Terry Moore cited the New Jersey program as "a land use measure that is now being borrowed for lots of other areas of the country. . . . If you go to other states in this nation, you will find the Pinelands concept—which was [Governor Byrne's] concept in New Jersey, not being duplicated in toto, but very large pieces of the Act are being applied to other states. . . . The Pinelands plan is the most classic growth management plan in existence."[121]

The Pinelands initiative benefited by the unusually long tenure of the core appointees that Byrne had named to the Commission's board and staff, thus giving the program a rare continuity of some of its key actors. Franklin Parker continued as chair for ten years, and Terry Moore, the first executive director, served for twenty years. Candace Ashmun, one of Byrne's original appointees to the board, served for more than thirty years. Michael Catania later became a deputy commissioner of the DEP and executive director of The Nature Conservancy of New Jersey, a group that raised private funding to buy large tracts in the Pinelands.

Local opposition, so intense during the legislative battle, gradually eased as the commission board and staff reached out to county and municipal officials to discuss how the plan's policies would work in practice, and what changes in local plans would be needed to comply with the comprehensive plan. A few mayors, such as Floyd West of Bass River, had long supported Byrne's vision for their region, while others would come on board over time. "I think one of the most exciting things for me," Candace Ashmun said after she had gone through the early years of bringing local plans into conformance, "has been working with the local officials and seeing them change from people who said, 'We won't walk into the office, we won't come near you.' These same people, those same planning people and those same mayors, came in and worked with us very closely and it was extremely rewarding."[122] Ultimately, all the Pinelands counties and municipalities would bring their master plans and zoning into conformance with the Comprehensive Management Plan.

While there have been controversies, for the most part the Pinelands program has achieved its goal of preserving the region's unique resources. "In the face of many obstacles," the author of a national study of land-use initiatives concluded, "the Pinelands program not only has endured, but has prospered. It has weathered many legislative, administrative and legal storms—many gentle, others quite threatening."[123] A study released in 2013 by researchers at Rutgers and Rowan Universities found that the Pinelands plan "has functioned well at channeling the development into the designated growth areas" while sharply curtailing construction in the more protected preservation areas.[124]

Preserving the Pinelands required that Byrne resort to an extraordinary, and legally questionable, use of the tools of his office to force his will upon a reluctant legislature, an assertion of executive power with few if any precedents in the history of the governor of New Jersey, or indeed of any state. "Byrne's personal commitment," scholars later wrote, "went well beyond short-term political opportunism; indeed, he viewed Pinelands protection not simply as a legislative victory, but as a legacy for New Jersey."[125]

Some three decades after Byrne left office, Terry Moore reflected: "There is the very important direction in the Pinelands Act that the Commission identify and protect 'the essential character' of the pinelands environment. We spent a lot of time during the planning process on that issue. I have always said since that the true 'essential character' of the New Jersey Pinelands environment was Brendan T. Byrne."[126]

In his senior years, Byrne would have time to reflect on how the Pinelands initiative provided insight on his perspective of public leadership. "I thought back to the conversations I'd had with some of my most talented aides who'd told me: 'Governor, this is totally impractical. It will force us to squander all our political capital and leave us barely able to govern.'"

As a sometimes reluctant politician, Byrne nonetheless recognized the pragmatism of their advice:

You'll always have staff people who will say 'You-have-to-do-this, because governors always do' or 'You can't do that, because governors never do.' And sometimes they're right. But sometimes the things the staff tell you that you 'have to do' you don't actually have to do; and sometimes the things they say you 'can't do'—actually, you can. But staff people are going to let you know when you're departing from the conventional wisdom on an issue. That's *their* job. And sometimes you have to depart from conventional wisdom to lead. That's *your* job.[127]

Chapter 13

Public Transportation and the Creation of New Jersey Transit

Brendan Byrne's mother Genevieve never learned to drive a car. For most of her daily tasks, she could easily walk from the Byrne home just off Main Street in West Orange to visit neighbors, to shop or do other errands. For more ambitious excursions, she could take Brendan and her other children on the trolley, which had first connected the towns on the Watchung Mountains to the valley below during the Civil War. By trolley, the Byrnes could easily visit Newark, where they could lunch in the then upscale cafeterias of major department stores like Bamberger's or Hahnes. "It always bothered me," Brendan Byrne reflected years later, "that when I was a kid, New Jersey had a better transit system than we did when I was an adult. It was something I wanted to change."[1]

The trolley that Byrne used in his childhood was part of the sprawling streetcar network that crisscrossed most of northern New Jersey, operated by the Public Service Coordinated Transport System, a unit of the state's largest electric and gas utility, later to become the Public Service Electric and Gas Company.[2] Public Service initially entered public transit when electricity was the source of power for the streetcar system, but after electric trolleys were supplanted by gasoline-powered buses, continued its transit role as the state's largest bus operator.[3]

From the mid-1830s through the Civil War, the railroad became a major force fueling the New Jersey economy, as well as an often corrupt influence in the state's politics. Chartered in 1830 by the state legislature with the state receiving stock in the company, The Camden and Amboy Railroad Company secured a monopoly over the lucrative corridor crossing the state from New York City to Philadelphia and, as past state Assembly Speaker Alan Karcher wrote in his book reviewing the state's political history, was "immune from criticism by the governors and the legislatures, despite charging higher rates than any other railroad in America."[4] With much of the state government's budget funded from stock dividends or duties on passengers and freight from the Camden and Amboy, New Jersey was derided as the "state of Camden and Amboy"[5]

During Brendan's childhood in the 1920s and 1930s, the extensive streetcar network in New Jersey was gradually converted into bus lines that initially used hybrid vehicles that ran either under electric wires as trolley buses or as regular buses powered by diesel gasoline. To the sickly young Brendan Byrne, however, trips on the gasoline-powered bus often made him nauseous, sometimes forcing his mother to quickly abandon the bus for the trolley, a ride apparently more comforting to Brendan's stomach.[6]

The trolley and bus network had easy and frequent connections to rail stations linking to stops throughout the state and nation. West Orange, which in the middle of the nineteenth century had pioneered the prototype of the modern suburban community with the building of the upscale homes in Llewellyn Park, increasingly saw its residents commuting by rail to jobs in Manhattan and nearby cities in New Jersey. Arguably, the City of Orange was the nation's "first railroad suburb," with many of its residents commuting daily by train to and from their jobs.[7]

During Brendan's boyhood, rail transportation continued as the dominant mode of interstate transit and shipping; after the end of World War II, however, the northeastern railroads increasingly found their position eroded from competition by highway and air travel. The growth of the federal and state highway system commenced in the 1950s by the Eisenhower Administration further undermined the viability of railroads, which were saddled with high fixed costs, including property taxes on their extensive real estate holdings, expensive labor contracts, and regulations that constrained their ability to pass higher costs on to their customers. Railroads contended that they were increasingly at a disadvantage to highways in competing for passengers and freight, and threatened to curtail or terminate money-losing commuter services. In the 1950s, when Brendan Byrne worked on the staff of Governor Meyner, New Jersey begun subsidizing commuter rail service, but the economic position of the railroads continued to erode.

In 1962, the first year of the Hughes Administration, an agreement was reached whereby the New York Port of Authority (subsequently renamed the Port Authority of New York and New Jersey) assumed operation of the rail service of the former Hudson & Manhattan Railroad between New York and New Jersey in return for the rights to build the World Trade Center on land occupied by H&M's Hudson Terminal in Lower Manhattan. The Authority then undertook a major rehabilitation of the H&M, subsequently operating the commuter service through its own subsidiary, the PATH system, which provided links between Newark, Jersey City, Hoboken and other New Jersey stops and Manhattan. Despite the Authority's early reluctance to risk its financial standing by taking on the inevitable deficits of public transit service, the new PATH system was widely praised for its new cars, stations, and the efficiency of its operations. A significant condition of the agreement for the construction of the World Trade Center and the creation of PATH, however, was the addition of a covenant to bonds issued by the Authority that restricted its future support of money-losing transit operations beyond the original PATH system.[8]

In 1966, Governor Hughes unsuccessfully proposed that the excess profits from the New Jersey Turnpike be used to prop up the money-losing commuter rail services.[9] The once-robust Pennsylvania Railroad, which had assumed the interstate corridor service first run by the Camden and Amboy and at its peak had 250,000 employees and a budget larger than the federal government, merged in 1968 with its rival, the New York Central Railroad, to form the Penn Central Company (renamed in the following year as the Penn Central Transportation Company.) Shortly after the merger, Richard Leone, then an aide to Governor Hughes and later Byrne's campaign manager and state treasurer, recalled a meeting he attended in the governor's office with Hughes and Stuart Saunders, the new chief executive of the Penn Central when, to Leone's surprise, Hughes interjected to advise Saunders, "Well Stu, the memo Dick Leone prepared for me before this meeting says we ought to let you go bankrupt." Within two years after the merger, the Penn Central declared bankruptcy, the largest bankruptcy to that point in the nation's history.[10]

In 1968, the same year of the merger creating the Penn Central, Brendan Byrne's official involvement in public transportation began when he was appointed by Governor Hughes as president of the Public Utilities Commission. By law, the PUC regulated safety of bus and rail operations and its president was designated as a member of the Commuter Operating Agency (COA), the state entity created in 1966 to negotiate and administer contracts with rail and bus operators that received state subsidies.[11] The subsidy program kept the services operating, but the carriers had little incentive to invest in new equipment or to improve service. "Railroads are strictly running passenger service on an available loss concept," Byrne told the press while inspecting the site of a collision in Newark between a freight and passenger train that injured 94 persons. "They'll run it if the state picks up the loss. There is no motivation for the railroads to minimize losses and there is always the suspicion railroads are loading in other losses to the passenger operation. . . . Government gives them the money now to administer it. With that money, the state should do the job itself and administer the railroads."[12] In his campaign for governor in 1973, Byrne again called for a state takeover of commuter bus and rail services. He also sharply criticized the Port Authority for failing to expand its transit operations.[13]

When Byrne took office as governor in January 1974, the bus and rail system was near collapse. Soon after arriving in Trenton, he and Alan Sagner, his first transportation commissioner, faced an immediate crisis when Transport of New Jersey, the state's largest bus operator and a subsidiary of the Public Service Electric and Gas Company, for the first time sought a subsidy from the state. "The state didn't operate the buses," Sagner recounted in a later interview. "Private contractors operated them and the state provided a subsidy and ordered them to provide the service. We were out of money to do it. We were $30 million short of what we needed."[14] In his first weeks as commissioner, Sagner also displayed his lack of government experience when, speaking "off the top of my head" in an appearance before the state chamber of commerce in Newark, he suggested that a two-cent gasoline tax increase could raise the needed funds. His offhand suggestion of a gas tax increase—when the governor and the legislature were struggling over passing a broad-based tax to finance the increased school aid to comply with the *Robinson v. Cahill* decision—resulted in Sagner receiving, as he recalled, "a very cold reception by the administration and leadership." Over time, however, Sagner, who said he was used to "being your own boss in the building business," learned the rules of government and politics. The deficit was dealt with by shifting some of other budget items to reduce its impact.[15]

In 1975, separate issues came together at the same time to create another crisis in commuter rail and bus operations. In February, Penn Central threatened to end its rail service if it did not receive a 25 percent fare increase in northern New Jersey, and at the end of the month the governor was forced to sign a bill to provide $25 million in emergency aid. A few months later, the situation worsened when the legislature failed to pass another income tax proposal; to balance the budget, Byrne vetoed specific spending items, including slashing bus and rail subsidies from $100 million to $23 million.[16] When the legislature restored only some of the cuts, at the end of the year, rail and bus fares went up by an average of 35 percent, with cutbacks in service including the closing of selected rail lines and stations. In announcing the reductions, Commissioner Sagner said the fare hikes and service cuts "go against everything this administration and this department has fought for."[17]

In 1976, Byrne and Sagner proposed legislation to establish an Agency for Public Transit, which would replace the COA in administering the state's subsidy program and, in the event it could not reach agreements with private operators to maintain service, be authorized to assume operation on its own. "The bill was vehemently opposed by Jack Gilhooley, the president of Transport of New Jersey," Martin Robins, then the policy chief of the Department of Transportation, later recalled. "He saw it as a step toward a state takeover of TNJ and argued that other publicly operated systems had led to higher operating losses and poorer service." In the face of the opposition from TNJ and other smaller bus lines, the bill did not receive a vote in either house of the legislature.[18]

Like other New Jersey governors, Byrne at times had a contentious relationship with the Port Authority of New York and New Jersey. In the month after he took office, Byrne came into conflict with the Authority over a proposed fare increase on its PATH rail system from thirty to fifty cents. This would be only the first of a series of clashes with the Authority, and at various points Byrne would seek to enforce his views relating to the Authority's management or operations by vetoing the minutes of the Authority's board meetings, effectively preventing it from approving major actions.

To improve communication of his positions to the Authority, Byrne also appointed Sagner to the Authority's board of commissioners, the first commissioner of the state department to serve. At his first meeting, Sagner informed the board that Byrne opposed the increase, saying it was "ill-timed" in light of the energy crisis that followed the OPEC oil embargo imposed in the previous October and that the governor believed the PATH operating deficit should be subsidized by toll revenues from the Authority's bridges and tunnels. After the Authority's board withdrew the fare hike, one commissioner explained the reversal by saying, "Fundamentally, Governor Byrne doesn't want the fare increase, and he's the boss. It took us about a tenth of a second to decide."[19]

Shortly after he vetoed the PATH fare increase, Byrne introduced legislation, which was later enacted in both New Jersey and New York, to repeal the covenants in bonds issued by the Port Authority in 1962, when it took over the bankrupt Hudson & Manhattan Railroad and converted it to the PATH system, restricting the Authority from undertaking future transit operations that would operate at a deficit.[20] Byrne also questioned whether William Ronan, the Authority's chairman, had "the capacity to continue" in his position.[21] With the covenants ostensibly no longer preventing additional transit investments, both states received commitments from the Authority to provide $250 million for new projects for rail service from Manhattan to Kennedy Airport and for extending the PATH system to Newark Airport and Plainfield in Union County. But the repeal promptly was challenged by the holders of the bonds that included the covenant; in 1977, the U.S. Supreme Court ruled that the retroactive repeal by the two states was an unconstitutional violation of the contract clause, effectively terminating both proposed rail projects in the two states.[22]

After his reelection in 1977, Byrne made restructuring of the state's public transit services a major priority of his second term. "Since my time at the Public Utilities Commission," he later recounted, "I thought it just didn't make any sense for the state to spend money to keep the trains and buses running without having more control over their operation. In my first term, we had struggled to keep the system going. After I was re-elected, I wanted to overhaul and make major changes."

When Byrne persuaded Lou Gambaccini to join the administration in May 1978 as commissioner of transportation, Byrne told Gambaccini that abolishing the state's existing subsidy program was his most important goal. "I told Lou." Byrne later recalled, "We needed some way for the state to end the subsidies and operate the commuter trains and buses on our own. He didn't need a lot of convincing, and I think the challenge of creating a new system was a big reason that he agreed to take the job."[23] With his long career at the Port Authority, Gambaccini easily bought into Byrne's plan to establish a public authority as the preferred way for the state to assume its new role in transit. "From my point of view," Gambaccini said, "creation of a mass transit authority is a no-lose situation. We're now the butt of criticism from angry commuters, but we can't do anything to effect a change because we don't have an authority."[24]

Soon after he became commissioner, Gambaccini began to explore potential support for legislation to establish what would become New Jersey Transit. Most of the opposition, Gambaccini later recalled, was based on the argument "that government can't do anything right, so why should we go from private to public."[25] A somewhat typical criticism came from Senator James Wallwork of Essex County: "If the state Department of Transportation couldn't correct this with the power of a bus subsidy, how could we expect them to operate the bus system itself?"[26]

More focused opposition also came from Jack Gilhooley, the president of Transport of New Jersey, the subsidiary of Public Service Electric and Gas which was by far the largest bus operator in the state, carrying over half of the 650,000 passengers riding buses each day. Although TNJ was losing an estimated $30 million each year, Gambaccini recognized that Gilhooley was seeking to protect his own position and that of others working under him. Both men had sometimes engaged in contentious negotiations over the level of the state subsidy which TNJ had received since 1974; indeed, years later Gambaccini recalled that during some of their heated exchanges Gilhooley "would turn beet red and I would worry about his having a heart attack or a stroke."[27] In December, Gambaccini himself was angered when Gilhooley had TNJ pay for a special advertising section in the *Star-Ledger* "excoriating the state government," Gambaccini remembered, "for not giving enough subsidy to TNJ and I was furious that he would be spending state money to publicly lambaste the subsidy program."[28]

Perhaps the turning point in the relationship with Gilhooley came when Gambaccini rejected TNJ's subsidy application to include in its payment pension liabilities incurred by the company for employees who had retired years before the state began to subsidize TNJ in 1974.[29] "Gilhooley knew that without the subsidy money to help pay the large pension liability for the past employees," Martin Robins later recounted, "the principals at Public Service would abandon him." Sitting in on a meeting of Gambaccini with Gilhooley, Robins recalled that Gilhooley "started pounding the table and got red in his face, but he got nowhere with Lou. Soon after that meeting, we heard that the Public Service leadership had muzzled Gilhooley, that they would not oppose our legislation and that they were prepared to sell TNJ to the state."[30]

Gambaccini then ordered his staff to expedite completion of the remaining work needed prior to introducing the legislation to create the new transit agency. "So I accelerated everything several months ahead of schedule," he recalled in a later interview "and said, 'Look. We can't let this continue. You're gonna have to work harder, faster, rap up some of the draft legislation and approved studies and so forth.'"[31] In January 1979, Gambaccini's staff published its report on the problems with the bus subsidy program, which it subtitled "The Horror Story." Its findings specifically rebutted the contentions of TNJ's Gilhooley that the company was an efficient operator. "On two-thirds of the comparisons with other systems," the report stated, "TNJ's performance is not better or preferable to the performance of the other carrier." It also pointed out that while nationally the number of bus passengers had increased since 1970, New Jersey's ridership had fallen by 41 percent during the same period. In the 1970s, the state also had become the major buyer of new buses for the private firms, with over 1,600 new buses purchased with the aid of federal grants and leased to the companies at one dollar per year.[32]

On January 25, 1979, Byrne and Gambaccini publicly announced plans to create a state authority to take over the state's major commuter rail and bus operations. A month later, the bill was introduced in the state senate by its principal sponsor Senator Frank Herbert, a Bergen County Democrat.[33] "Frank Herbert was the chair of the transportation committee," Byrne later recalled. "He also was excellent in rounding up votes and at times he'd ask me to help with a particular legislator. He deserves a lot of credit for getting the bill passed."[34]

As introduced, the bill created a "New Jersey Transit Corporation" within the Department of Transportation to "acquire, operate and contract for transportation service in the public interest," but stated that the corporation should operate independently from the department. Its management would be overseen by a seven-member board, including the commissioner of transportation as chairman, representatives of the state treasurer and the governor's office and four members from the public appointed by the governor.[35] Senator Herbert was able to get the bill passed in the Senate with 23 votes, two more than needed.

Securing Republican support in the Assembly was viewed as crucial since several Democrats were expected to vote against the bill as a result of pressure from labor unions, privately owned bus operators, and other interests. Hudson County Democrats were a special problem since independent bus lines in the county feared competition from a new state agency able to operate without the taxes and other overhead that they incurred. Separate legislation protecting the interests of the independent bus lines was introduced as an alternative to the bill being developed by Gambaccini and his staff. Additional political opposition came, according to Gambaccini, from Hudson County Democrats who were "holding hostage the legislation to Governor Byrne's appointment of a political hack to a judgeship." Gambaccini knew that Byrne would not give in to the demand and told him, "You're absolutely right. As much as I want the bill you can't give ground on that."[36]

Harold Hodes, Byrne's deputy chief of staff approached Bergen County Republican Assemblyman W. Cary Edwards (later Governor Kean's counsel and attorney general) as one Republican who might be persuaded to support the bill. In a later interview, Edwards recalled that "Hodes came to me and a bunch of other Republicans when they were trying to put the NJ Transit bill together. And Lou Gambaccini . . . lived in my district in Ridgewood. And they asked me if I would support the bill. I went and knocked on Lou's door in Ridgewood one Saturday morning and spent eight hours with him going through the formation of NJ Transit and the pros and cons with him."[37] Edwards was convinced by Gambaccini's arguments, saying it was "very obvious when I got through looking at it," and also was impressed by Gambaccini's professional manner and presentation. "I liked Lou," he continued. "I thought he was an honest and forthright guy, and he gave me good information that proved to be absolutely accurate. I then went together to try to put together 8 or 10 votes in the Assembly because the Hudson County delegation was trying to hold up the governor."[38]

Still, even with the Republican support lined up by Edwards, the legislature stalled in taking up the bill, and Byrne threatened to suspend the entire subsidy program if the bill was not passed. "Byrne was gutsy as hell to a point that I thought he was dangerous," Gambaccini recalled. "He set a deadline after which there'd be no transportation service in the state. I said, 'You know, knowing you, I know you mean you'll do it but you're crazy. You can't do that.'" But after years of reflection, Gambaccini decided Byrne was right. "That was what it took to get the legislature to act. . . . Otherwise they would have continued to procrastinate and not ever bite the bullet. And so that really got the whole legislature focused."[39]

Like the Pinelands legislation, the passage of the bill remained doubtful on the day that the Assembly had scheduled its final vote. Negotiations to secure wavering legislators proceeded through the morning and afternoon;

just before a dinner break, Speaker Christopher Jackman advised Chief-of-Staff Mulcahy and Hodes that he did not have the votes and had given up any hope of passage. "We took Chris across the river to an Italian restaurant in Pennsylvania," Mulcahy later recalled, "and we encouraged him as he drank three Scotch sours. It seemed to give him some new energy, and we went back to the State House to try to round up the last votes we needed."[40] After the Assembly reconvened following their dinner break, debate on the transit bill ran well past midnight. "It was our strategy to keep the debate going all night," Mulcahy explained. "We needed the time to round up our votes, to wear down those who were still resisting." Martin Robins later remembered the efforts to secure the final votes. "There was incredible tension. We really weren't sure whether we had the votes to pass the bill." At two o'clock in the morning, the final vote recorded 43 in favor and 25 against, two more than needed for passage. Byrne signed the legislation on the following day, July 17, 1979.[41]

When Gambaccini agreed to accept Byrne's request that he become commissioner, he received a commitment that he would not be required to get involved in any political activity or be forced to hire staff for political reasons. For the most part, the arrangement also stayed in place with the organization and staffing of New Jersey Transit. "When I created NJ Transit," Gambaccini later recounted, "Governor Byrne every now and then would ask me if I would interview somebody but he was careful to say, 'It's your decision.' Every now and then he would also bug me and say, 'Just because they're political doesn't mean they're necessarily incompetent.' And I'd say, 'I agree with you.' And in one or two cases . . . I did go along with selection from that source. But he was very careful and lived up to the commitment not to push me or force me to take anybody."[42]

With somewhat more difficulty, Gambaccini also received Byrne's approval to exempt the new transit agency from the civil service laws and regulations relating to hiring, compensation and management that pertained to all other state employees. In so doing, New Jersey Transit would have much more flexibility in recruiting and paying new employees, as well as avoiding giving preference on the basis of seniority in promotion and layoff decisions. "When NJ Transit was set up," Gambaccini recalled, "I did prevail on him and it was an uphill argument but he finally relented to let me create the non-union staff outside of the civil service and my argument to him was, and this is directly a result of my experience. At a point I said, 'Are you sure you want to commit this early because you may want to weigh the political consequences.' He said, 'No. I'm satisfied.'"[43]

Shortly after, Gambaccini opened negotiations to purchase Transport of New Jersey, which centered on the $75 million price that TNJ's parent company, Public Service Electric and Gas, initially set for the acquisition, as well as its attempt to have the state assume $93 million of its unfunded pension liabilities, a substantial portion of which was incurred well before the state and TNJ had entered into any subsidy contracts. In February 1979, Attorney General John Degnan recruited Alan Lowenstein, founding partner of one of the state's largest law firms, to represent the Department of Transportation in the negotiations as its special counsel, an assignment that Lowenstein later described as "the most important and complex transaction of my professional career."[44]

The negotiations began in October 1979 and continued for six months. In addition to his frequent contacts with Degnan and Gambaccini, Lowenstein also periodically briefed Byrne. "I remember meeting alone with him on one sunny morning," Lowenstein wrote in a later memoir, "as we sat beside the pool at Morven. . . . The governor urged me to be fair but tough in my negotiations with Public Service and assured me of his support." Lowenstein ultimately persuaded Public Service that it could assume the pension liability without any state contribution after the tax lawyers in his firm concluded that the company could get significant tax benefits through purchase of a group annuity to guarantee the pension obligations.[45]

There remained, however, a substantial difference in the price that Public Service set for TNJ's assets compared to what the state was prepared to pay. In February 1980, after Public Service had requested $75 million, Byrne met with Robert Smith, the chief executive of Public Service, in an attempt to bring the deal to a close. Soon after the meeting, "the Governor insisted," according to Lowenstein, "that the matter be resolved or an announcement made that there would be no agreement." In April, an agreement was reached, after some TNJ real estate holdings were removed from the acquisition, in which New Jersey Transit purchased TNJ for $33 million. Some $28 million of the purchase price was provided by the Port Authority, which bought the TNJ buses, terminals, stations, and other assets and leased them back to the state at no cost. The final cost to the state treasury was just over $5 million.[46]

In announcing the acquisition of TNJ, Byrne said that for the first time in the state's history "the major provider of bus service will be a truly public transit system—owned and operated by a public agency, directly accountable to the public."[47] After Byrne left office, New Jersey Transit would also acquire the commuter rail operations of Conrail and ultimately would become the nation's largest statewide public transportation system.[48]

Also in 1979, the administration turned to putting in place the largest capital investment transportation program in the state's history—the $3 billion Transpac program. Transpac was a combination of commitments from the state and the Port Authority, which pledged $120 million to purchase buses for the state's use, which would trigger an additional $480 million in federal government matching funds. The state government's contribution to the package was primarily to come from a $475 million bond issue to be put before the voters in a referendum in the November 1979 election.[49] After negotiations with the diverse highway and transit interest groups, the proceeds from the proposed bond issue were to be allocated with $245 million for highways; $150 million for public transit; and $80 million in state aid for county and local roads. Gambaccini recalled when he first briefed Chris Jackman, the colorful speaker of the general assembly known for his plaid sport jackets and unmistakable Hudson County accent, on the size of the package, Jackman "was off the wall crazy saying, 'Billions? Are you talking billions? Are you nuts?'"[50]

Three previous transportation bond issues had been defeated by the state's voters in 1974 and 1975. "We concluded that one of the reasons past bond issues failed," Gambaccini later said, "was that the environmentalists and highway builders were at war and the promises of the past were never delivered. Our response was: 'that was then; this is now.' We would not overpromise."[51] Gambaccini then gathered support from the diverse transportation interests for the new proposal, including creation of a "blue ribbon" committee of prominent citizens to raise private funds for an advertising campaign and media tours to see crumbling bridges and roads in need of repair.

Most of the proposed package was dedicated to rehabilitate the state's aging system, including the repair of highways and roads and the purchase of new buses to replace the aging fleet, goals which were intended to reassure voters that the state was not investing in expensive new projects. "Our road and public transportation programs will continue to deteriorate," Byrne said in launching the public campaign to support the bond issue's approval, "while the cost of making these repairs will continue to escalate as time passes"[52] Byrne, Gambaccini, and members of the "blue ribbon" committee made appearances around the state and met with editorial boards to promote approval of the referendum. George Warrington, then an aide to Gambaccini who later in his career would become president of AMTRAK and executive director of New Jersey Transit, coordinated the outreach program, meeting with local officials and interest group representatives.

The bond issue was approved by the voters by a surprisingly wide margin, with 747,272 votes in favor and 638,758 votes against.[53] The proceeds would later help support implementation of the long-term transportation master plan that Gambaccini had prepared.

In Byrne's last year in office, Gambaccini received Byrne's permission to explore support in the legislature for increasing the state gasoline tax by five cents to create a dedicated fund for transportation projects. Byrne withheld his own endorsement of the proposal until he could see if Gambaccini would be able to secure enough backing. "I was generally against dedicating revenue from taxes to specific purposes," Byrne said years later, "because I thought it didn't give legislatures and governors the flexibility to shift money to meet different needs over time. But if Lou could have gotten enough support, the added money would have been a big help later when the state ran out of money for both highways and transit."[54] The idea for a dedicated gas tax would remain, as Gambaccini later reflected, "the single largest undone job" he had as commissioner. In July 1981, some six months before Byrne completed his second term, he announced his resignation to return to the Port Authority as its director of administration.[55]

"I was proud of what we were accomplished in restructuring and modernizing public transportation," Byrne later reflected. "I think we did a good job."[56]

Chapter 14

The 1981 Election and Leaving Office

"A Sense of What's Important"

Entering his final full year in office in 1981, Byrne had already accomplished much of the legislative and administrative agenda he had set for himself and the state.

He had secured the enactment of a state tax and school financing reform program including an income tax that had eluded his two predecessors. He had succeeded, largely on his own, in putting Pinelands preservation to the top of the state's public policy priorities, reshaping the future pattern of development in the southern part of the state. He had brought casino gambling to Atlantic City, stimulating billions of dollars in new investment, creating thousands of jobs in the decayed resort and dedicating tax revenues from gambling to programs for senior citizens and people with disabilities. He had rescued the Sports Complex and the Meadowlands development plan, which when he left office was hailed in the press as "the most successful sports and entertainment complex in the nation."[1] He had overhauled the state's archaic criminal laws and despite strong pressure, refused to sign bills restoring the death penalty. He had instituted key reforms in government accountability and the electoral process, creating the first state public advocate, requiring financial disclosures of state officials, providing public financing for gubernatorial campaigns, easing voter registration, and directing that government meetings be open to the press and the public.

Significantly, as one reporter wrote, he "ran a scandal-free administration for eight years in a state legendary for corruption," including transforming "the state Treasurer's office from a nexus of political scandal into an agency known nationally for its professionalism and innovative money management."[2]

To John Degnan, Byrne's attorney general, counsel, and executive secretary, Byrne's most valuable contribution was in the quality of the people he put to work and the ideas they put in place: "Good people come to work for a governor in large part because they are excited by his vision and they trust his integrity, and Governor Byrne's ability to put those kind of people together. New Jersey was a thought leader in state governments in the nation. . . . It was cutting-edge public policy and that . . . I think was the hallmark Byrne accomplishment."[3] Bob Mulcahy, Byrne's chief of staff, had a similar view: "Brendan demanded absolute integrity," he recalled years later, "and he had no patience for anyone who couldn't meet his own high standard. Then he let us do our jobs."[4]

Perhaps the most significant remaining issue on Byrne's agenda was his proposal to reform automobile insurance and lower premium rates that were the highest of any state in the nation. Byrne had sought unsuccessfully to restrict the ability to sue for minor injuries suffered in auto accidents in order to make policies more affordable, but faced stiff opposition from groups representing trial lawyers. With many lawyers among its members, the legislature failed to take action.

Of his goal to help the largest cities, Byrne felt his record was mixed— years later he said he was disappointed that he had been unable to "create another Baltimore."[5] Nonetheless, his income tax and restructuring of school aid constituted the single largest redistribution of tax resources to distressed cities in the state's history. Beyond the income tax and school reforms, Byrne had targeted most other programs in housing, economic development, transportation, and environmental infrastructure to benefit urban areas and discourage suburban sprawl. He commenced the redevelopment of the Hudson River waterfront and Atlantic City; supported affordable housing in the suburbs; and halted the dispersal of state offices outside Trenton and the larger cities. In his final year in office, Byrne proposed the state's first capital program to provide grants for urban redevelopment through the $85 million Community Development Bond Act, which after he left office, would provide the seed money for construction of such projects as the New Jersey Performing Arts Center in Newark and the Liberty Science Center in Jersey City.[6] He also proposed new tax incentives for urban investment, which later were adopted through passage of the state enterprise zone program during the Kean administration.

Yet Byrne's final year in office was not lacking in, the "tumult, crisis and controversy" as one reporter put it, that had marked his previous seven years. In July of 1981, Byrne presided over the opening of the new Meadowlands arena, with the first of six concerts by Bruce Springsteen. In September, the New Jersey Nets professional basketball team, which had played its previous four seasons at Rutgers University, relocated to the arena. The financing of the arena had been significantly aided when state Treasury officials refinanced outstanding state bond issues, including the "moral pledge" bonds used to finance the race track and stadium, saving millions of dollars in interest payments, much of which was then used to support the construction of the arena.[7]

But the new arena had already contributed to a sharp drop in Byrne's popularity. In. November 1980, the board of the Sports Authority—all of whose members were appointed by Byrne or were members of his cabinet—announced that it was naming the new arena then under construction as the "Brendan Byrne Arena," a decision that provoked immediate criticism. Initially, the board had also intended to name the racetrack after former Governor Cahill, but Cahill declined the recognition, thus leaving Byrne as the sole governor to be honored. Even within his inner political circle, there were dissenters on the wisdom of the name choice. Michael "Jerry" Breslin, the Bergen County Democratic chairman whom Byrne had appointed to the Sports Authority board and who chaired the construction committee for the arena, recounted later that he raised concerns when the idea was first floated at a board meeting: "That poor guy was crucified with the income tax. He doesn't need another thing like this, to name the arena after him. John Degnan hits me and he says, 'Jerry, you're a friend of his.' I said, 'Yeah, I am a friend of his. That's why I'm talking like this. I don't want to see the guy crucified again. I don't know how he lived through that income tax thing.'"[8]

In the following months, the decision to put Byrne's name on the arena sparked increasing controversy. One poll, taken in October 1981, reported that only 7 percent of respondents supported naming the arena for Byrne; 48 percent thought that the name should be changed; and 42 percent said it did not much matter one way or another.[9] Politicians in Bergen County, where the arena was located, started a petition drive for a referendum asking voters to endorse a name change to Veterans Memorial Arena; the referendum was blocked when the New Jersey Supreme Court held that placing the question before county voters was not authorized by statute.[10] Byrne did his best to make light of the controversy, telling one audience, "I just got back from Rome. . . . They got this big coliseum in Rome, and I think I talked them into naming it for me."[11] But the criticism continued throughout his final year. In an editorial positively evaluating his overall record, the *New York Times* nonetheless wrote that Byrne displayed "offensive vanity in having his name put on the new Meadowlands arena in five foot letters."[12]

One defender of Byrne's name remaining on the arena was Richard Codey, then a Democratic assemblyman and later Senate president and governor. In an opinion piece published in the *New York Times*, Codey wrote that naming the arena after Byrne "is merely giving public recognition to the fact that Mr. Byrne has consistently believed in the entire Sports Complex," noting that when Byrne became governor "there was no stadium, no race track, no arena," but only "two large holes in the ground and the vigorous opposition of the New York financial community." Codey argued that the success of Byrne's efforts justified the honor: "Today, New Jersey boasts some of the finest professional sports facilities in the world. We didn't get from 'there' to 'here' by luck; we got it by leadership, and Brendan Byrne provided just that in this case."[13]

Jean Byrne also spoke out, telling a newspaper reporter: "At this time, at the end of my husband's administration, instead of recognizing his 26 years of public service—eight of them in elective office—and recognizing how he spearheaded the successful Meadowlands Sports Complex, why is there such a furor over the naming of the Brendan Byrne Arena? Would this happen if it were a crummy arena—a bomb—and not making money?"[14]

Byrne rejected the calls to remove his name from the arena. "I thought it was appropriate to recognize," Byrne later reflected, "that the Sports Complex would not have existed without Bill Cahill and me. When Cahill decided not to have his name on the track, the critics all focused on my name on the arena."[15]

In the month after the arena opened, Byrne presided over another milestone for the Sports Complex with the first running at the Meadowlands Racetrack of the famed Hambletonian race for 3-year-old trotters. First run in 1926 in New York State but held since 1957 at the state fairgrounds in DuQuoin, Illinois, the Hambletonian was known as "the Kentucky Derby" of trotting. In September 1979, Byrne and Bob Mulcahy, the head of the Sports Authority and his former chief of staff, had led a small group in a clandestine trip to DuQuoin to present a proposal to the Hambletonian Society, the sponsors of the race, for relocating the race to the Meadowlands, competing with proposals presented by the governors of Illinois and New York "Jim Thompson, who was the Illinois governor," Byrne later recalled, "really was angry that we took the race from the state." According to Mulcahy, the antipathy in DuQuoin toward the New Jersey contingent was reflected by the management of the hotel in which they were staying, which "refused to let us eat in their restaurant." The successful bid by New Jersey pledged significant expansion of the Hambletonian's purse, promotion, and visibility, aided by the New York–New Jersey media market, and included several related events, receptions and family attractions in the days leading to the race. "We wanted to establish the national stature of the Meadowlands up as a racing venue," Byrne later said. "By getting the Hambletonian to come to New Jersey, we were able to do that soon after the track opened."[16]

As Byrne left office in January 1982, one journalist wrote that the arena name issue illustrated Byrne's characteristic resistance to being swayed by public opinion: "But letting the arena be named after himself was such a typically *Byrne* thing to do. It gave people the perfect opening to jump on him again, instead of recognizing his accomplishments as he left office."[17] Despite criticizing the action during his 1981 gubernatorial campaign, his successor, Thomas Kean, allowed the Byrne name to remain and in fact, appointed Byrne to the board of the Sports Authority in 1983.

With some reluctance, Byrne found himself drawn into the June 1981 Democratic gubernatorial primary election campaign. Byrne's former opponents in the 1977 primary, Congressmen Jim Florio and Bob Roe, were again seeking the nomination and were viewed as favorites because of their prior exposure to the statewide electorate and their existing political and fundraising networks. The large field in each party's primaries—eight Republicans and thirteen Democrats—was partly a result of Byrne-instigated reforms that, for the first time, provided public matching funds for primary candidates and also prohibited county party organizations from awarding the ballot "line" to their preferred candidates.[18] In signing the "open primary" law, Byrne said it would insure each candidate "a fair shot" at the party nominations and, coupled with public financing, would reduce the influence of wealthy contributors and political bosses.[19]

On the Democratic side, the candidates included several Byrne supporters to whom he owed varying degrees of loyalty. John Degnan, whose family had worked alongside Byrne's father in West Orange political circles, had become perhaps the governor's closest adviser after he had urged him to seek reelection in 1977. After that election, the governor had appointed him attorney general.

But there were others in the field who had demonstrated their own loyalty to Byrne. Don Lan had been one of the first to urge Byrne to resign as a judge to run for governor in 1973, later becoming his first executive secretary and, in the second term, his secretary of state. State Senate President Joseph Merlino had worked to implement the Governor's initiatives, particularly in sponsoring the Pinelands protection legislation and also had played a key role in the battle over the income tax. Similarly, Assembly Democratic Majority Leader William Hamilton had been a key Byrne ally in developing the school and tax reform legislation. Ann Klein, Byrne's 1973 primary election opponent, had been a valued member of the Byrne cabinet. Newark Mayor Kenneth Gibson had been a loyal political supporter, producing a strong turnout for Byrne in the 1977 primary and general elections and allowing his key aide Harold Hodes to join Byrne's reelection campaign. Jersey City Mayor Thomas Smith had been an effective campaigner for Byrne in the general election.

Degnan persisted in seeking Byrne's endorsement, but he also received rather pragmatic advice on his prospects. "The governor did not encourage me to run," Degnan remembered. "He openly questioned whether I could win.

He did not promise to endorse me." Byrne also asked Degnan whether he was prepared for a rough campaign. "John, you've been treated for three and a half years as attorney general," Degnan recalled as Byrne's warning. "It's going to be different when you're a candidate. You're not going to be an attorney general. You're just going to be another candidate. And are you up for that? Can you make the transition quickly enough?" If he still decided to run, according to Degnan, Byrne advised that "I should resign as attorney general because he didn't think I could run as attorney general." Degnan took the advice and resigned as attorney general in March 1981, before announcing that he would be a candidate in the June primary.[20]

After announcing his candidacy, Degnan continued to argue his case to Byrne, as he had previously done to persuade Byrne to name him attorney general. "I wasn't going to let him off the hook that way," Degnan said when he could not get a clear answer from the governor on an endorsement. As Degnan lagged in the polls, his campaign advisers, who included Byrne's past consultant David Garth, counseled that Byrne's support might help in the primary, but would probably ensure his defeat in the general election. "John came to me and said he was losing," Byrne recalled years later. "He told me he wasn't sure that he could win even with my support, but still hoped that I would endorse him. I decided he would be the best candidate to carry on what we had tried to do during my time in office."[21] Byrne agreed to make a commercial announcing his support. The impact of the endorsement, however, was muted somewhat when Byrne was quoted saying that he would be willing to make commercials for some others in the race, "but nobody has asked me." As an example, he said, "I have said good things about a number of candidates in the past and will continue to. . . . If Ann Klein asked me to say good things about her service as Human Services Commissioner, I would be happy to do so."[22]

Nonetheless, Degnan appreciated the support, knowing that it had been a difficult decision for the Governor. "And he's never said this to me," Degnan would say years later, "but I think he knew it wasn't going to make the difference, but in the end he was maybe paying me back for my loyalty. When he did it, he made enemies of a couple of important people in his life, other candidates, and I think that pained him and probably he did pay a price for that."[23] With his popularity weakened over the controversy surrounding the naming of the Byrne Arena, criticism of his foreign travel and other complaints over both his policies and personality, Byrne's support was a mixed blessing: "One thing I learned through my polling," Degnan would recall, "was that not everybody who loved Brendan Byrne loved John Degnan, but everybody who hated Brendan Byrne hated me."[24]

After he endorsed Degnan, Byrne attempted to narrow the field in an effort interpreted by one press account as intended to head off a Florio victory.[25]

He met with Don Lan, whom Byrne thought "was just spoiling it" for Degnan to ask that Lan withdraw from the race. Lan rejected Byrne's request in their meeting, but he would later fold his campaign and endorse Florio for the nomination. "I wouldn't have been governor without Don Lan, and Don was bitter," Byrne reflected. "It wasn't until many years later that we renewed our friendship." Byrne also asked Jersey City Mayor Tommy Smith to withdraw in a meeting at one of Byrne's favorite places on the Jersey Shore, Max's restaurant in Long Branch known for its hot dogs. "Tommy was absolutely convinced," Byrne later remembered, "that he would win. I got nowhere with him." A similar approach to Newark Mayor Kenneth Gibson also failed. Byrne did not ask Ann Klein to withdraw, later saying: "I knew it would be futile to ask Ann to drop out. She had a mind of her own. From her first campaign against me, I knew she really wanted to be the state's first woman governor."[26]

Congressman Florio won the primary relatively comfortably, by ten points over his closest challenger, Congressman Roe. Degnan finished fifth with 10 percent, also trailing Mayor Gibson (15 percent) and Senator Merlino (11 percent). Former Assembly Speaker Thomas Kean won the Republican nomination with 30 percent of the vote, ten points ahead of his closest challenger, Paterson Mayor Lawrence "Pat" Kramer.

In their fall campaign, Kean and the Republicans argued that it was "time for a change" after eight years of Democratic control of the executive and legislative branches, and made Byrne's performance one of their themes in attacking Florio. In a poll taken at the beginning of the campaign in September, Byrne's approval ratings had fallen, with 73 percent of respondents rating his performance as "poor' or "fair" and 23 percent as "excellent" or "good."[27] Asked in one debate to cite an example of how he differed with Florio, Kean said, "We disagree about the Byrne administration. He's happy with it, I'm not."[28]

On another occasion, Kean said he would ask the Sports Authority to reconsider its decision to name the Meadowlands arena after Byrne; the Republican national and state committees ran commercials showing the Governor signing a bill with the controversial arena bearing his name pictured behind him.[29] One Kean commercial charged that Florio was "just a carbon copy of Brendan Byrne."[30] Kean's attacks on Byrne, as Kean's biographer Alvin Felzenberg later wrote, presented a "dilemma" for Florio: "If the Democrat agreed with any of Kean's criticisms, he risked antagonizing Democratic activists, donors and a state administration upon which he relied for expert knowledge and assistance. If he defended Byrne's record, he stood to inherit all the retiring governor's critics."[31] Florio tried to avoid taking either extreme, but pointed to issues on which he differed with Byrne, such as his support of the death penalty.[32] Florio also attempted to divert voter attention to the impact that the Reagan Administration's sharp cutbacks in federal aid to state and local governments was having on New Jersey's economy.[33]

On the election night of November 3, 1981, Byrne was at Morven, expecting a relatively uneventful evening watching television to learn who would be his successor. But as the returns came in, it became increasingly evident that the election would be very close. After most counties had reported substantial percentages of their votes, Byrne became concerned that Camden County, the home base of Congressman Florio, had not reported any returns. Whatever the reason for the delay, Byrne worried that public confidence in the outcome of the election could be undermined by suspicions that Camden was delaying its reporting until it could be determined how many votes from the county would be needed for Florio to beat Kean.[34]

Without waiting for legal advice or a formal request from the Kean campaign, Byrne ordered the State Police to impound the Camden County voting machines in anticipation of an expected request for a recount. "Some people said I didn't have authority to impound the voting machines," Byrne would later say, "and maybe by the letter of the law, I didn't. But it was the right thing to do. If I didn't act, voters would have lost confidence in the integrity of the count and the results of the election."[35] At the end of the night, with the Camden machines in the custody of the State Police, the tally showed Kean holding a slim lead of less than 1 percent of the total cast, a result that the Democrats promptly challenged by asking for a recount.[36]

Republican officials initially were concerned that the recount would be overseen by Byrne's outgoing Democratic administration, but they were quickly reassured when Attorney General James Zazzali assigned assistant attorney general Michael Cole, who was widely respected for his professionalism and integrity (and who in fact was later named by Kean as his governor's counsel), to oversee the recount.[37] The lack of a clear result had an inevitable impact on the two candidates. "You are at it night and day," Kean later said, "seven days a week for eight months. Every fiber of your being tells you it's over and then you have to start all over again." Florio later told the *Star-Ledger*: "It was not the most pleasant experience in the world. I assumed I was going to win, then had reconciled myself to waiting."[38] During the weeks of post-election uncertainty over who would be declared the winner, Byrne ordered that both candidates be treated as potential governors, directing that each be given state office space for their transition, security protection by the State Police, and briefings for their transition staffs on pending issues by state officials.

At the end of November, the results of the recount were announced: Kean had won by 1,797 votes. Florio conceded the election in a phone call to Kean and then visited the State House to advise Byrne that he was abandoning any further efforts to contest the election.[39] "I was disappointed," Byrne later reflected, "that a Democrat wouldn't be my successor, but I knew that Tom Kean would do what he thought was best for the state."[40]

With Kean certified as the governor-elect, Byrne began a series of meetings with the incoming governor and his key staff. Kean decided to adopt the restructured organization of the governor's staff that Byrne had instituted at the beginning of his second term: naming Lewis Thurston, a veteran legislative staffer, as his chief of staff; W. Cary Edwards, a Bergen County assemblyman, as his counsel; and Gary Stein, an attorney whom Kean had first met when they both served in the National Guard, as the director of policy and planning.

Despite the harsh rhetoric Kean had used in his campaign to attack Byrne and his administration, the two men worked easily together during the transition. After Kean had lost the 1977 gubernatorial primary election to Ray Bateman, Byrne had appointed him as a commissioner on the New Jersey Highway Authority, and the two men's respect for each other, and their understanding of the realities of politics, allowed them to quickly move forward. "I realized that you have to say things in campaigns to get elected," Byrne later reflected. "I never took what Tom said personally."[41] Dick Leone, Byrne's campaign manager and state treasurer said years later, "I never remember Brendan holding a grudge. He was really remarkable in that. It's very rare in politics."[42] Kean's biographer later wrote that "the easy rapport Kean enjoyed with Byrne made for a smooth transition."[43] During the transition, Byrne consulted Kean on major decisions and appointments; pushed salary increases for Kean's incoming cabinet through the legislature to aid recruitment for the new administration; and appointed Jon Hanson, Kean's chief fundraiser, to the board of the Sports Authority.

In his final weeks in office, Byrne and his family began preparing for his life as a former governor. At Christmas, Governor and Mrs. Byrne hosted the extended family at a final holiday dinner at Morven. After dinner, while preparing to leave, two cousins were embarrassed when their toddler erupted in a tantrum, but Byrne quickly reassured them: "That's also the way they're going to have to drag me out of here—kicking and screaming!" The Byrnes also held a series of receptions at Morven to thank staff, political supporters, and friends. Jean Byrne undertook the tasks of packing up and looking for a new home in Princeton. "We liked living in Princeton," Byrne later reflected, "and the younger kids were still in school."[44]

But Byrne also had official business to tend to. He dealt with a flurry of activity by the lame-duck legislature as it rushed to pass bills to present to Byrne before he left office. Some Democrats feared that a new Republican governor might be more difficult to persuade to sign their pet bills; other legislators, either retiring or defeated in the November election, made final

attempts to revive measures they had long pushed and hoped to get enacted in
the session's closing days. During the last week of the lame-duck legislative
session, Byrne signed ninety bills into law and allowed another ninety-six
passed bills to die by declining to approve them. After the final legislative
session on January 11, 1982, when the legislature remained in session until
just before midnight, the staff in Byrne's counsel's office worked through
the night and into the next morning to prepare the memos on each bill for
Byrne to review on the following day—his final opportunity to take action
on measures passed by the outgoing legislature.[45] "The bills were spread
out," Byrne later recalled, "covering the dining room table and the floor at
Morven. When I signed a bill, another one would be given to me. It was like
an assembly line."[46]

In leaving office, Byrne also attempted to help those who had worked for
or otherwise supported him with their own futures. He contacted potential
employers and wrote reference letters for staff in his own office and the state
departments. He appointed judges and others—usually with Governor-elect
Kean's concurrence—to posts on authorities and commissions. One controversial appointment that Kean opposed was Byrne's naming of his old
friend Joel Jacobson, the labor leader who had offered in 1973 to stand in as
a candidate in his behalf until Judge Byrne made up his mind about running
for governor, to the Casino Control Commission. Overriding opposition from
both Senate Democrats and Republicans, Byrne secured Jacobson's confirmation by the Senate for a five-year term on the commission.[47]

On January 12, Byrne delivered his last annual message to the legislature,
addressing the newly sworn members who would serve under his successor
to be inaugurated a week later. He criticized the "irrational and counter-
productive" policies of the Reagan administration to cut education and social
programs and defended the place of government. "To the degree that we
deny government its proper role, we reduce our chances of ever managing
our problems and elevating the life of our people." He also called for further
efforts to enact a more progressive tax structure and to continue the progress
he declared the state had made on the other problems he had confronted. At
the end of his speech, one newspaper reported, "tears filled his eyes and his
voice sputtered" as he struggled to complete his final sentence: "Whatever
history's verdict, my family and I shall always be grateful to the people of
New Jersey for the honor and opportunity you have given me."[48]

On his last day in office, January 19, 1982, Byrne engaged in one final act
of political drama. Since his conviction in May 1981 for taking bribes in the
FBI's undercover Abscam sting, U.S. Senator Harrison Williams had been
facing expulsion from the Senate. Leading Democrats had tried to persuade
Williams to resign so that Byrne could appoint a Democrat to his seat before
Thomas Kean was inaugurated. In an editorial published over a month before

Byrne left office, the *New York Times* speculated on Williams's refusal to quit: "The Senator seems convinced that outgoing Gov. Brendan Byrne is part of a conspiracy to drive him from office and, though he, like the Senator, is a Democrat, must be prevented from making the appointment."[49] Years later, responding to the report, Byrne said: "I don't think there was any conspiracy to push Pete Williams out, but it was clear that he was going to lose his seat. Democrats both in Washington and the state wanted to make sure that the party kept that seat."[50]

As influential party leaders worked to convince Williams to step down even as Kean was about to be sworn in, Byrne brought with him to Kean's inauguration a letter designating an appointment for the Senate vacancy in the event Williams changed his mind at the last minute. In order to keep his selection from being known to even his closest aides, Byrne had separate letters prepared designating six different individuals for the appointment. Some twenty years later, Byrne disclosed that his choice was former Senate President Joseph Merlino.[51] "Joe Merlino fought hard for things I believed in like preserving the Pinelands, increasing aid to the older cities and reforming our tax structure. I thought he would be a strong, feisty senator."[52] But Williams did not resign his U.S. Senate seat until the following March 11, just before the Senate was scheduled to vote to expel him. Governor Kean then appointed investment banker and Somerset County Republican Chairman Nicholas Brady to fill the vacancy on an interim basis until the next election in November 1982, in which Democrat Frank Lautenberg defeated Republican Congresswoman Millicent Fenwick.

Before leaving his State House office to attend the inauguration of his successor, Byrne repeated a gesture of good will that Bill Cahill had extended to him—he left a bottle of champagne on his desk with a note wishing Tom Kean success and good luck.

During his final weeks in office, Byrne's tenure as governor received much media attention and analysis. For the most part, his record received highly positive reviews in editorials and profiles. A *Bergen Record* editorial praised Byrne's "towering achievements, they'll be mountains on the historical landscape of the state."[53] Yet even with his substantial record, some still puzzled over how Byrne had pulled it off. Many of the state's political insiders still viewed Byrne as an enigma: "the man who after eight years as governor they still couldn't understand," wrote a veteran State House reporter in an extensive profile of Byrne published as he left office. "Stubbornly, Byrne refused to act the way the public would have like him to," she continued. "Hypocrisy, he called it. Just as stubbornly, he fought for programs he wanted. And more often than not, he got them."[54] Another reporter, describing Byrne as a "strange paradox," continued: "His record of success has drawn praise even

from his political detractors, but in the public's eye, his personal manner
has overshadowed his achievements." Noting that Byrne had consistently
"refused to play to the audience," the profile concluded: "The voters were
to be reckoned with when it counted. But throughout he has played to
history. . . . His reputation will rise in the years ahead, when the speeches are
forgotten and the deeds remain."[55]

To those who had the often difficult job of defending his unique style to
the public, Byrne's resistance to tailoring his image often brought frustration,
but also left him with grudging respect. Robert Comstock, Byrne's communications director from 1975 to 1977 during the battle over the income tax
and his subsequent reelection campaign, reflected: "He didn't care about the
criticism of his travel, his playing in tennis tournaments and such. He'd say
the hell with it. Those are not bedrock things. He feels he can be an excellent
governor and play in tennis tournaments that take him away from the office
on Wednesdays. He's interested in more substantial things. His attitude is,
'That's the way I am.'" John Farmer, who held the same communications
position as Comstock during most of Byrne's final year in office and was a
past national editor of the *Philadelphia Bulletin,* said: "His style mocks his
accomplishments. It suggests that he holds the office in less regard than the
public holds it. The same kind of ceremony that Byrne regards as hypocrisy,
the public puts great store by. . . . The amazing thing is that he was able to
accomplish what he did in spite of that attitude."[56]

Byrne himself would later reflect that he believed his eight years in office
had seen New Jersey change "more than in any other eight-year period in its
history." In assessing his performance, he continued: "I had compromised at
times, when compromise was in order. But I had never been afraid to draw a
line in the sand—to stake my career, and even my reputation, on unpopular
positions that I knew were right for New Jersey. Maybe I have a better sense
of proportion than a lot of people. I have a sense of what's important."[57]

Chapter 15

Return to Private Life

"The Elder Statesman of New Jersey"

After eight years as governor, Byrne later admitted, he could afford to buy the new family home in Princeton only by borrowing money from trust funds established for his children. But the house was particularly welcomed by Mrs. Byrne for the added space and the new sense of privacy it provided, with four of her seven children, then ranging in age from 12 to 27, still living at home. "It is very similar to the home we enjoyed in West Orange before the election of November 1973," Mrs. Byrne said at the time. "When I saw the five bedrooms, I said, 'This is it.'"[1] The home also included a tennis court and a pool, amenities that the Byrnes had enjoyed at Morven.

For six months, with the aid of state funds provided to outgoing governors, Byrne had an office in downtown Princeton staffed by his long-time secretary Dottie Seltzer where he dealt with matters relating to his time in office. He was the first governor in New Jersey history to order that all papers during his time in office be accessible to the public at the State Archives in Trenton, and he later donated personal papers, campaign materials, photos, and memorabilia to Seton Hall and Rutgers Universities.

Another task funded by the state government was to select an artist and pose for his official portrait to be hung in the State House with those of his predecessors as governors. Byrne recalled that well before he had run for governor, at the invitation of his close friend Maria Jeritza, the former star soprano of the Metropolitan Opera, he had attended a party in Manhattan at the Metropolitan Club in Manhattan dedicating a portrait of the club's president. The artist, Everett Raymond Kinstler, attended the ceremony. Impressed with Kinstler's work, after he left office Byrne sought him out to paint his portrait, learning only later that Kinstler was one of the nation's premier portrait artists, who also painted the official White House portraits of Presidents Ford and Reagan.

In public talks, Byrne occasionally commented on his return to private life. "I first realized I wasn't governor anymore," he quipped, "when I got in the back seat of the car, and it didn't go anywhere."[2]

Byrne also continued his warm relationship with Governor Kean. Kean had first heard of Byrne through his brother Robert, who headed the family-controlled Elizabethtown Water Company, and had come to know Byrne when he was president of the Public Utilities Commission that had regulatory authority over the company. "My brother Bob told me then," Thomas Kean later recalled, "that he thought Brendan might be a future governor." During Byrne's first term, Kean, who served as Speaker of the Assembly in the Cahill administration, was one of the fourteen Assembly Republicans who survived the 1973 Democratic landslide and was elected as the minority leader. "During the battle over the income tax," Kean remembered later, "people were so angry that I had to sneak up through the basement in the State House to see Brendan in order to avoid the protesters."[3]

Kean also appreciated Byrne's role in ensuring the accuracy of the recount following the November 1981 election, and the assistance provided in the post-election transition. After his inauguration, he continued to reach out to Byrne. "When I first became governor, I would call on Brendan a lot," Kean later reflected. "I had a lot of problems with the Democratic leaders in the legislature, and he gave me really good advice on how to deal with them. Once in a while, he'd also suggest going to other Democrats in the legislature or on the outside who might be of help when I was having trouble with the leaders."[4] In an interview, Kean told a reporter, "We'd get away from the State House, usually prior to a tennis game, and I'd ask him very frankly things that you can only ask people who have had the same job before you."[5]

As governor, Kean also borrowed a tactic Byrne had employed: aggressive use of the executive order to pressure the legislature to take action on one of his key priorities. In 1987, when legislation he supported to protect freshwater wetlands stalled in the legislature, Kean issued an executive order placing an eighteen-month moratorium on development adjacent to over 320,000 acres of freshwater wetlands.[6] Kean's order, like Byrne's moratorium on development in the Pinelands, was challenged by a lawsuit, but the state Supreme Court refused to delay its enforcement, which generated pressure for the legislature's approval of legislation that Kean signed into law on July 1, 1987.[7] "Brendan's executive order with the Pinelands," Kean reflected years later, "was a model for me. He showed how a governor can use the tools of the office to get things done."

Byrne had great respect for the contributions of the Kean family to New Jersey in the years since its ancestor William Livingston was elected as New Jersey's first state governor in 1776, just weeks after the colony declared its independence. "The Kean family has been one of the most prominent in the state's history," Byrne later said. "And everyone likes Tom Kean. He shares my view that you could differ in politics, but still remain friends. We may be members of a vanishing breed."[8]

In the months before he left office, Byrne understandably thought, "What do I do next?" At one point, Senator Bill Bradley suggested that he consider running for the Senate for the seat formerly held by Harrison Williams, but Byrne quickly dismissed the idea, responding, "Bill, I don't want to move to Washington. It's not where I want to live and I can't see myself shuttling back and forth to New Jersey." Byrne later reflected on other differences in the executive and legislative roles: "I had fun as governor. You could get things done. It's a lot tougher getting much accomplished when you're one of a hundred senators."[9]

Byrne seriously considered an offer by a major university to head a new public policy center, but he ultimately decided to return to private legal practice. "The university position was interesting," he said, "but I really needed to make money. After so many years in public service, I couldn't afford to take a job like that. It wouldn't be fair to the family."[10] He became a partner in the law firm headed by Charles Carella, the former head of the "Charlie Squad" organized crime unit that Byrne had created as prosecutor. Carella had later joined Byrne in Trenton as state lottery director and as executive secretary. The Essex County office of the firm, which was renamed following Byrne's joining as a partner with his name, at Byrne's insistence, listed behind that of Carella, gave Byrne a base to renew contacts with old friends, as well as for visiting some of his boyhood haunts, such as the Pals Cabin restaurant, where he had taken his high school dates to read the Sunday papers.[11] One of his most frequent lunch companions was Barry Evenchick, his close friend since their days together in the Essex County prosecutor's office and later at the PUC. Evenchick, a partner in the nearby law firm founded by Justin Walder, another of Byrne's former assistant prosecutors, also organized reunions of Byrne's prosecutor's staff and, separately, of his gubernatorial cabinet, staff, and other close family and friends.

"I knew that part of my role at the firm would be to try to bring in new clients," Byrne later said, "but I wasn't sure if I would be good at that. I did my best, but it wasn't something I enjoyed doing as a lawyer. I just wanted to help clients solve problems."[12] In his first years after his return to private practice, Byrne occasionally agreed to represent clients in trials or appear to argue appeals on their behalf. "I still enjoyed being a lawyer," Byrne later said, "and didn't want to simply sit back and never go back to court."[13]

He represented a major petroleum supplier in a federal court trial in Camden that lasted for three months in the early 1990s. According to the complaint filed against Byrne's client by a company operating rapid motor vehicle lubrication centers, the supplier had attempted to destroy the plaintiff's business after negotiations between the two companies failed to reach an agreement for the supplier to acquire the plaintiff's business. "I interviewed their key witness on a Sunday," Byrne recalled, "and he testified in court the next day, completely changing his story from one day to the next." Despite his best efforts to impeach the witness, repeatedly pointing out the conflicts in the accounts by the witness, Byrne lost the case, but on appeal much of the judgment against the client was greatly modified.[14]

One client that came to the firm was Alitalia Airlines, then the national airline of Italy. Byrne had first met the chief executive of Alitalia in 1978 at a reception at the U.S. ambassador's residence in Vatican City when Byrne was a member of the official delegation appointed by President Carter to attend the investiture of Pope John Paul I. After he left office, Byrne was surprised to be contacted by Alitalia management to represent them on legal matters in the United States. Some of the legal work related to Alitalia's operations at Kennedy International Airport; its relations with the Port Authority of New York and New Jersey; and customer service and baggage problems. One of the younger lawyers assigned to Alitalia was Gus Lembo, Byrne's last judicial clerk before he resigned to run for governor and who would later be an assistant counsel to Byrne after his election. A benefit of representing Alitalia was the periodic trips Byrne would take, usually accompanied by Lembo and Carella, to the Alitalia headquarters in Rome to brief executives on the status of legal matters they were handling for the airline. The better Roman restaurants, however, did not fit with Byrne's dinner and sleep schedule; "I usually ate at Chinese restaurants in Rome," he later explained, "because they were the only ones open early enough to get to bed by ten. The Italian places didn't open until nine."[15]

Another corporate client was the ice cream maker and retailer Carvel Corporation founded in 1929 by Tom Carvel and based in Westchester County in New York. "I first met Tom Carvel in George Steinbrenner's box at a Yankees game on opening day," Byrne recalled. "We hit it off, especially because we both loved music. I think Tom knew every word in Gilbert and Sullivan operettas. After we met, he asked me to help with his legal work."

Much of the work for Carvel focused on litigation pertaining to contracts and relations with franchise owners and operators. Carvel was one of the first national firms to use the franchise concept, and Tom Carvel frequently took steps to prevent franchises from substituting lower-quality ice cream or ingredients. On one occasion, Byrne recalled years later with obvious satisfaction, he cross-examined a franchisee's expert witness in a dispute over the concentration of butter-fat in pistachio ice cream used by the franchisee; when questioned by the franchisee's lawyer, the expert contended that the analysis conducted by Carvel of the franchise's ice cream that found that it did not meet the required butter fat content was not significant since additional butter fat was provided by the pistachio nuts in the ice cream. "So it's your testimony that the butter fat content was provided by the pistachios included in the ice cream," Byrne remembered asking the expert. After receiving an affirmative response, Byrne pursued the line of questioning until the expert himself realized that he had been trapped, finally conceding on the stand, as Byrne pointed out, "that Carvel pistachio ice cream contains no nuts."[16]

But Byrne and the mercurial Tom Carvel sometimes clashed. Carvel was known as a micro-manager, and he often tried to intervene in the legal cases being handled by Byrne. "He kept firing me," Byrne recalled, "because I wouldn't go along with his suggestions to 'tell the judge this' or 'tell the judge that,' most of which would have hurt our case. Usually, he'd see I was right and then re-hire me." In another trial, after Byrne had advised the judge that Carvel was unable to come to court because he was "frail," an energetic looking Carvel unexpectedly arrived in the courtroom later in the day—to Byrne's considerable embarrassment. For the most part, however, the two men got along, as Byrne recalled, "at least after he checked the time I had billed him against the hours that his own in-house counsel had reported for his own work and found that my time was lower than the other lawyer, a very rare occurrence. When he found out I wasn't over-billing, he trusted me."[17]

Apart from working on Carvel's legal matters, Byrne was drafted by Tom Carvel for a singing role in one of Carvel's well-known "America's Freshest Ice Cream" commercials; the commercials featured, as one media analyst later put it, Tom Carvel's "extremely unpolished and often unrehearsed voice-overs that put his voice, at once phlegmy and gravelly, and his disastrous diction, on display."[18] Byrne recorded his commercial at the in-house studio Carvel had built in his corporate headquarters, singing repeated takes of the Carvel jingle, "we make fresh ice cream every day at Carvel, America's freshest ice cream, every day at Carvel . . ." Years later, Byrne reflected that apparently his singing voice didn't make the cut, even given the homespun standards set by Tom Carvel himself. "I don't think they ever used it," he recalled. "I guess I just couldn't get it right."[19]

Byrne became a board member of the Carvel charitable foundation that provided grants to arts, education, and other causes in New York and New Jersey, including such personal interests of the Byrnes as the Paper Mill Playhouse, the Shakespeare Theatre at Drew University and the Juvenile Diabetes Foundation.[20]

He also was active in founding, along with former North Carolina Governor James Hunt, the State Capital Law Firm Group, a national network of law firms with special interests in state and local government issues and legal developments.[21] The network was originally intended to identify law firms in each state capital that had experience in legislative and regulatory matters, but would eventually expand, under the name SCG Legal, to refer other types of legal work and to comprise over 145 law firms with more than 11,500 attorneys in offices around the world.[22] Byrne hosted in New Jersey one of the annual conferences held by SCG Legal that brought together lawyers from the various states to review recent legal developments and foster networking. A major case that Byrne brought to the law firm was representing Dupont and Merck in the defense of their patent Coumadin—the blockbuster drug combating blood clots—in their battle against generic competition.

Byrne maintained his interest in the New Jersey legal profession, serving as a member of the editorial board of the *New Jersey Law Journal,* a weekly newspaper reporting on significant news relating to law firms, as well as publishing judicial opinions, laws, and regulations. The editorial board, comprised of prominent attorneys and retired judges, met each week to discuss recent legal issues, with its members writing editorials expressing opinions on court decisions, potential statutory changes and other legal reforms. One year, Byrne was given the *Law Journal*'s award for the quality and brevity of his editorials. Some of the points Byrne raised in his editorials criticized the excessive complexity, delays, and costs of contemporary legal practice that had evolved since the time when he was a young lawyer, prosecutor, and judge. "I think the lawyers of today might be a little better at procedure than we were many years ago," he would reflect. "But what's been lost is a lot of humility and common sense."[23]

He served on several corporate boards. In addition to joining the board of the Elizabethtown Water Company, Byrne became a director of Prudential Insurance, New Jersey Bell Telephone, the discount retail chain Jamesway Corporation, industrial equipment manufacturer Ingersoll Rand Inc., leather fabricator Seton Leather Company, and real estate developer Mack-Cali Realty Corporation.[24] After joining the Prudential board, he was asked to help recruit as a director Paul Volcker, his Princeton classmate who later chaired the Federal Reserve. "I didn't know Paul well when we were at Princeton," Byrne later said. "But after I was elected governor he used to seek me out at alumni reunions, I think primarily because he knew I had a state police trooper who could drive us around. In any event, while I doubt I had much to do with it, he eventually agreed to join the Prudential board."[25] Years later, in reflecting generally on his service as a corporate board member, Byrne said, "I should have had those experiences before I became governor, because you get a great insight into corporate government . . . I did learn a lot."[26]

In his last year as governor, Byrne had taught a seminar in state politics and policy development at his alma mater, the Woodrow Wilson School of Public and International Affairs at Princeton. The class frequently met at Morven, with Byrne occasionally bringing in guests, including former Governor and Chief Justice Richard Hughes and Byrne's campaign media adviser David Garth. After leaving office, Byrne continued to teach seminars and lecture at Rutgers, Drew, and Monmouth universities. At the invitation of Michael Dukakis, the former Massachusetts governor, Byrne returned to Harvard as a guest lecturer for Dukakis's class at the John F. Kennedy School of Government. For several years, Dukakis used a case study focused on decision options confronted by Byrne and his staff on the siting of a foreign trade center in New Jersey.[27]

Byrne continued his interest in sports. In May 1982, at the request of John McMullen, a New Jersey native and longtime resident of Montclair, he became a minority partner, with Goldman Sachs chairman John Whitehead, in the purchase of the Colorado Rockies National Hockey League franchise for $8.5 million, with the team then relocating to the Byrne Arena in the Meadowlands for the 1982–1983 season. (At the time, McMullen also owned the Houston Astros major league baseball team and previously had been a limited partner in the ownership of the New York Yankees, famously saying, "There is nothing more limited than being a limited partner of George Steinbrenner".)[28]

Byrne had never been a hockey fan, conceding that "I didn't know what a blue line was when John contacted me about buying the Rockies."[29] Following the team's renaming as the "New Jersey Devils" and objections on religious grounds by critics to the new name, Byrne defended the selection: "Do they object to Duke University calling its teams Blue Devils, or to Arizona State being called the Sun Devils?" Would they complain less if we called them Ice Devils?"[30] Although having only a small ownership interest in the team, at McMullen's suggestion Byrne represented the Devils at the National Hockey League ownership meetings held at sites around the country. "I enjoyed going to the league's meetings," Byrne recalled years later. "It gave me an inside look at how the league and the teams were run. I learned a lot about the business of sports, particularly the importance of television to the bottom line of both the league and the teams."[31]

Just a few months after the purchase of the hockey team, in November 1982, the press reported—following a vote by major league baseball team owners that rejected offering a new contract to incumbent baseball commissioner Bowie Kuhn—that Byrne was one of a few suggested as a potential new commissioner.[32] "I don't think I ever was a serious candidate," he later reflected, "but I was told that John McMullen, George Steinbrenner and perhaps one or two other owners had mentioned me as a possible choice." The appointment did not come to pass. "I would have loved to have been commissioner," Byrne said. "I've always loved the game and being commissioner would have been challenging, as well as a lot of fun."[33]

In 1983, Byrne was nominated as a board member of the Sports Authority by Governor Kean, with Kean perhaps returning the favor Byrne had extended when he appointed Kean to the board of the state Highway Authority. Byrne first warned Kean that his confirmation in the Senate might face trouble since membership on the Sports Authority board was a coveted political plum. Kean brushed off his predecessor's concern, saying, "Well, let's see," and Byrne was easily confirmed. After the nomination was confirmed by the state Senate, Byrne sold most of his shares in the Devils back to McMullen at a nominal profit and gave the rest to his son Tom. Once on the board, Byrne again worked closely with Bob Mulcahy, his former chief of staff, in reviewing the Authority's operations. Occasionally, he also played peacemaker, such as when the relationship between the Devils and the Authority began to sour over disputes on the terms of the lease for the Arena. "On one day," Byrne remembered, "I had to physically separate John McMullen and Jon Hanson [the Authority chairman named by Governor Kean] when they got into a shouting match. I pushed both of them into a closet and told them not to come out until they worked it out."[34] In 1987, the Kean administration and the Sports Authority proposed a $185 million bond issue to build a baseball stadium for a potential major league team (widely expected to be the Yankees), but the referendum to authorize the bonds was soundly rejected by the state's voters.[35] "I never believed that George Steinbrenner would move the Yankees out of New York," Byrne later said. "When I was governor, George would occasionally talk about coming to New Jersey, but I always thought he was just using us as leverage to get things from New York."[36]

After Christine Todd Whitman was elected governor in November 1993, Byrne and the other Sports Authority members came into conflict with the governor-elect, who had asked the outgoing Florio administration not to make or extend appointments before she took office. Byrne nonetheless successfully pushed for a two-year extension of Bob Mulcahy's contract as president of the Authority at a $175,000 annual salary, an action that Florio declined to veto during his final weeks in office. Defending the action to retain Mulcahy, Byrne later said, "The governor-elect had a right to make that selection, but I think we also had an obligation to send a message that we operated the authority as a private business." When Whitman was elected, Byrne's term on the Authority had expired and he was serving in a holdover status. "She phoned me on the morning after she was inaugurated," Byrne later recalled, "and told me she was appointing someone in my place. I told her I understood, and appreciated her courtesy in calling me."[37]

In 1996, the Sports Authority under Whitman entered a contract to sell the naming rights of the Arena to Continental Airlines for $1.3 million a year, thus removing Byrne's name. In what he later described as "one of the most difficult conversations of my life," Bob Mulcahy informed Byrne of the decision.[38] One of the harshest critics of the name change was Byrne's son Tom, who at the time was chairman of the Democratic State Committee: "It is one more manifestation of the mean-spiritedness coming out of the Republicans in general today. I think a number of Democrats and Republicans have gone to the Governor and suggested that it is unseemly and not a classy thing to do, but she is determined to do it anyway."[39] (In 2007, when Continental did not renew its contract in 2007, the Izod clothing firm became the arena's title sponsor.) Years later, after Whitman left office and had established her own government relations firm, she asked Byrne to lunch, they discussed the past friction and repaired their relationship.

In 1986, Byrne was an interested observer when Robert Wilentz, whom he had appointed chief justice of the state Supreme Court in 1979, was coming up for reappointment to a second term by Governor Kean. Under the state constitution, judges appointed to the Supreme and Superior courts are appointed for an initial seven-year term, and, if reappointed and confirmed by the Senate to a second term, are granted tenure until reaching the mandatory retirement age of 70. But Wilentz's reappointment to the court became highly controversial. His opponents attacked the court's decisions on such issues as school funding and affordable housing, as well as questioning his status as a New Jersey resident due to his protracted stays at an apartment he owned in Manhattan. Wilentz explained his stays in Manhattan as needed to be close to his wife while she received cancer treatments at a New York hospital.

"I did not get involved in the fight over Bob Wilentz's reappointment," Byrne later reflected, "but I admired Tom Kean's courage in standing up against many in his own party. If Tom hadn't backed Wilentz and his reappointment wasn't confirmed, it would have been a serious blow to the independence of the Court."[40] Wilentz was confirmed by a 21 to 19 vote—the minimum needed for his confirmation for a new term. Wilentz went on to serve as chief justice for seventeen years—the longest tenure of a chief justice since the adoption of the 1947 state constitution—until he resigned in July 1996, some three weeks before he died from cancer.[41]

Byrne's marriage to Jean Byrne ended in divorce in 1993. "We had a brief try with counseling," Byrne said, "but it was too late to save the marriage. Some part of me still loved Jean—but the marriage was over. We had grown too far apart and couldn't bridge our differences. She is a wonderful lady and a great mother."[42] In the following year, Byrne married Ruthi Zinn, who headed her own public relations firm and was also divorced. "I'd first noticed her around 1976," Byrne said, "She was a whiz at public relations, very energetic, attractive and great at networking." The two had first met when Zinn was executive director of a group formed to change the government charter of Essex County to establish a county executive as the chief administrator of all county agencies. "She organized the campaign," Byrne said, "raised a lot of the money for it, and convinced 68,000 people to sign a petition that the change was needed."[43] After one meeting that the charter change advocates had with the Governor, Byrne came over to Zinn, and they chatted briefly.[44]

Zinn also was member of the board of the League of Women Voters, and the two saw each other casually at large events for the next ten years or so, later beginning dating. As Zinn later recounted, "There was a very strong attraction and although we tried several times to separate, we finally decided to commit to each other." As a couple, they shared an interest in the theater—attending dramatic and musical productions on Broadway and in New Jersey—and in travel and literature.[45]

Their wedding was held on August 20, 1994, in the restaurant at the Byrne Arena in the Meadowlands, with the ceremony performed by a state judge whom Byrne had appointed, who also was the father of the daughter-in-law of the new Mrs. Byrne. They honeymooned on a cruise to Alaska—a reunion of Byrne's Harvard Law School class hosted by Byrne's Harvard classmate Ted Stevens, then a U.S. Senator from Alaska.[46] Over the years, Stevens and Byrne had spoken at several Harvard alumni reunion dinners together, frequently trying to outdo each other with their jokes.[47] The couple lived in Mrs. Byrne's home in Short Hills in Essex County, a few miles from the offices of the Carella Byrne law firm.

With her public relations background, Ruthi Byrne encouraged her new husband to speak at or participate in a wide variety of events, media interviews, and other forums. "I wanted to keep him in the public eye," she later said, "I think he loved the attention. He also became more outgoing, like going around shaking hands of people at public events and even when we were eating alone in restaurants, which I was told he generally tried to avoid doing when he was governor."[48] After Tom Kean completed his two terms as governor in 1991 and became president of Drew University, she arranged a series of joint appearances for the two former governors. "Ruthi kept us very busy," Kean later recalled, "we spoke at a lot of dinners, conferences and other events discussing issues and politics."[49]

After Byrne and Kean had appeared together several times on New Jersey public television exchanging views on politics and public issues, Ruthi Byrne suggested to the editors of the *Star-Ledger* that they consider publishing a similar colloquy; subsequently, "The Kean-Byrne Dialogue" would appear weekly in the newspaper and on its online site. In 1997, *The Washington Monthly* magazine, in granting the column its Journalism Award, wrote:

"In monthly 'conversations,' the political adversaries and long-time friends take on pressing issues with the unusual perspective of commentators with experience. . . . Whatever the subject, careful thought and an insider's knowledge make for original, provoking columns."[50] "Tom and I have different perspectives on government," Byrne said. "I'm usually for government taking a more active role in solving problems and he's more cautious. But we agree on a lot of things, like the need for government to protect the environment and to help support the arts."[51]

One of the few sharp differences Byrne could recall with Kean was on a proposed bond issue submitted for voter approval in November 2012 to finance higher education construction and renovation projects. The two former governors were asked to co-chair the campaign to support the bond issue, but Byrne declined. "I said I'd happily support the spending," Byrne explained, "if you could tell me how the debt was going to be paid off. It was a good cause, but when the state is asked to borrow, taxpayers should know where the money is coming from to pay the debt."[52] But even when they disagreed, the dialogue between Byrne and Kean displayed a warmth and respect more common to their times, when politicians could differ and remain friends. Carl Golden, who had served as Kean's press secretary, commented on the relationship of the two men: "There is a very deep affection. They have become the elder statesmen of New Jersey politics—not their party, but New Jersey politics as both of them would like to see it practiced. That is, with vigor, but with not such a partisan edge and coarseness to it."[53]

A *New York Times* article discussing their relationship also pointed out the contrasts of the two former governors: "To be sure, their approaches are vastly different, which widens their appeal. Mr. Kean has never given a political interview in his home; Mr. Byrne has never had an unlisted telephone number. When asked to be interviewed, Mr. Kean chose his office at Drew University; Mr. Byrne arranged lunch at a Chinese restaurant that featured live jazz. Mr. Kean was alone; Mr. Byrne arrived with his wife, Ruthi, and invited nearly as many people as he ran into along the way to join them, debriefing guests about the best selections on the menu."[54]

Soon after their marriage, when they both were in Washington, D.C., Byrne phoned the White House at four p.m. to ask if he and Ruthi could come visit President Clinton, whom he had first met through meetings of the National Governors Association after Clinton was elected to his first two-year term as Arkansas governor in 1978, the first year of Byrne's second term. "Any chance the President can say hello to me and meet my new wife?" Byrne remembered asking, "I get a call back and they say, 'Come over here at 5:45.'" On their way to the White House, Byrne predicted to Ruthi, "When I introduce you to the President, he's going to say, 'Let me tell you about the time Brendan and I had lunch at a Chinese restaurant.'"

As Byrne had predicted, after they arrived at the White House and were ushered to the Oval Office, "I meet the President, introduce him to Ruthi, and he says, 'Let me tell you about the time your husband and I had lunch at the Chinese restaurant.' And he remembered what street that Chinese restaurant was on. I never did." The Chinese restaurant lunch, Byrne later explained, took place in Washington after Clinton had been defeated for reelection in 1980 to a second term as governor of Arkansas; at the lunch, Clinton asked Byrne, who was then chairman of the Democratic Governors Association, to support Clinton's attempt to be elected chairman of the Democratic National Committee. But after Byrne made several calls in Clinton's behalf to members of the committee and other influential Democrats, Clinton "withdrew without telling me," Byrne recalled, "and I called him and I gave him hell." Despite their brief conflict, the two men subsequently mended fences. Byrne enthusiastically supported Clinton's later political comeback that led to his election as president in 1992, and following their first impromptu visit to the President, the Byrnes attended many White House receptions during Clinton's presidency.[55] In 2008, when Hillary Clinton launched her own presidential campaign, both Brendan and Ruthi Byrne supported her candidacy, helping to raise funds.

Another president that Byrne encountered after leaving office was Richard Nixon, whom Byrne happened to see when they were both dining at the 21 Club, the Manhattan restaurant. "I went up to Nixon," Byrne recalled, "and told him that there had been four presidents during the eight years I was governor, but that he was the only one that I hadn't gotten to know. He gave me his card, I called his office and we scheduled a lunch." Byrne prepared for their lunch by reading a few biographies of Nixon so that he knew the details of Nixon's childhood and his early career. "When we met for lunch, it was mostly small talk about our families and sports, not much about politics. I carefully avoided raising anything controversial like Watergate, which in fact was a major reason I was first elected governor. I thought he was very gracious in agreeing to see me."[56]

As a former governor, Byrne frequently was asked to lend his name to or participate in a diverse range of fundraising efforts. One of the favorite causes of both Brendan and Ruthi Byrne was the Paper Mill Playhouse in Millburn, the theater on the site of a mill built in 1795. The theater's productions had begun in 1938, and Byrne recalled seeing Gilbert and Sullivan operettas there while still in high school. In January 1980, when Byrne was governor, the Playhouse stage and auditorium were destroyed in a fire. "Most people thought the Playhouse would never re-open after it was destroyed by the fire, but the state and a lot of private supporters raised enough money to get it rebuilt."[57]

In 2007, however, the Playhouse faced another crisis threatening its survival, resulting from a sharp decline in support due to the economic recession and continuing competition from the New Jersey Performing Arts Center in Newark. After announcing that without additional funds it would be forced to close, the theater formed a new fundraising group. Ruthi Byrne, who had previously been named as a trustee on the Playhouse governing board, was among those asked to lead the campaign, which succeeded in rescuing the theater from closing. She persuaded her husband and former Governor Kean to sponsor an annual "Byrne/Kean Arts Advocate Award," which was a highlight of the Playhouse's gala 75th anniversary celebration in 2013.[58] "Tom and I even performed," Byrne later recalled. "With top hats and canes, we did a little soft-shoe dance to the tune of 'Tea for Two'. It was fun. The audience really seemed to enjoy it."[59]

Another cause that the Byrnes supported was research on the treatment and potential cure of juvenile diabetes after their grandson Danny Zinn was diagnosed with the disease. "We're a close family and what happens to one of us, happens to all of us," Ruthi Byrne said in speaking of the time the family was informed of the diagnosis. "There were 15 family members in the doctors' office at that first meeting to learn what to do. . . . It's a frustrating disease because there's been a lot of research but no cure." In 2012, the Byrnes were honored as the Family of the Year by the regional chapter of the Juvenile Diabetes Research Foundation for their efforts in expanding knowledge of and support for combating the disease.[60]

The Byrnes also raised funds to establish the Center on the American Governor at the Eagleton Institute of Politics at Rutgers, the only academic program in the nation focused on the study of the office of the governor in New Jersey and the other states. The Center's origins could be traced to Ruthi Byrne's attempts to clean the basement of their Short Hills home. "The basement," she related, "was full of Brendan's memorabilia, which I regularly sent him down to clean it out—things were getting moldy and deteriorating. He would spend time down there and then come up with some pictures in hand to show me, identify the subjects and tell me an anecdote, but the process clearly wasn't working. In mild desperation I instigated the formation of a foundation to raise money for preservation of this historical material." With the aid of the money raised privately and funds appropriated by the state, over $650,000 was raised; Rutgers President Richard McCormick, "then shipped his archivists down to our basement," Ruthi Byrne later said, "to sort and cart the stuff away." The Byrne memorabilia was catalogued for its own collection in the Rutgers library, and the Center was established to conduct conferences and interviews related to his time in office—a model later used for other New Jersey governors. "It turned out wonderfully well," Ruthi Byrne later reflected, "but the truth was I just wanted to clean out the basement."[61]

The former governor also occasionally took time to visit the forests and paddle the meandering rivers of the Pinelands. On one canoe trip with Carleton Montgomery, the head of the Pinelands Preservation Alliance, the leading nonprofit group monitoring issues affecting the region, their canoe started taking on water which, despite their best efforts, resulted in a swamping, leaving Byrne soaked for the rest of the outing wearing his typical tennis outfit. Their embarrassment, however, later was mined by Byrne for humor; speaking at the celebration of the twentieth anniversary of the Pinelands protection legislation, he quipped, "For some years I'd been a bit distracted from the Pinelands issue, but you know recently I've become more immersed in the Pinelands again."[62] On a more serious level, Byrne also spoke out on what he viewed as threats to his initiative; in December 2013, he joined with former Governors Kean, Florio and Whitman in opposing a proposed 22-mile natural gas pipeline though the Pinelands supported by the Christie administration—a project that only failed to proceed after a 7-7 tie vote of the Pinelands Commission.[63]

On July 24, 2002, at a modest ceremony, Governor McGreevey announced that the Lebanon State Forest in the Pinelands, the second largest forest in New Jersey, was being renamed the Brendan T. Byrne State Forest. "I'd be lying," Byrne said, "if I said I didn't get a kick out of that."[64] The new name, as stated by McGreevey's executive order, recognized Byrne's "bold steps . . . to protect and preserve the vast pine-oak forests, cedar swamps, and the extensive surface and ground water resources of New Jersey's Pinelands."[65] At the ceremony, Byrne again read the prediction from McPhee's book that the Pinelands was "headed slowly toward extinction"; as he had when he signed the legislation, Byrne once more turned to Joe Merlino, the former senator who had sponsored the legislation, to continue, giving the gruff politician from Trenton the opportunity to share the credit for what they had accomplished together.[66] Byrne had first come to know McGreevey early in his career when he was a staff member to the Assembly Democratic leadership, and had counseled him in later roles when he was elected to the legislature and as mayor of Woodbridge. In April 2004, McGreevey also hosted a celebration of Byrne's eightieth birthday attended by a few hundred of Byrne's family, friends and associates at Drumthwacket, the governor's official residence that Byrne had renovated for his successors. After McGreevey resigned later in that year following his disclosure that he was gay, both Brendan and Ruthi Byrne maintained close contact with him, often socializing with McGreevey and his partner, Mark O'Donnell.

Byrne also was cited for other achievements during his retirement from public life. In 2006, he returned to Atlantic City for the dedication of a plaque at the Convention Hall where in 1979 he had signed the legislation to allow the licensing of casinos. In 2011, he was inducted into the New Jersey Hall of Fame to mark his contributions to the state, sharing the honor that year with, among others, his friend, the crime novelist Mary Higgins Clark, singer Tony Bennett, actor John Travolta and lifestyle guru Martha Stewart. At the event honoring the inductees at the New Jersey Performing Arts Center, Byrne noted that the state had come a long way since it was so often a butt of jokes: "New Jersey pride has now become part of the state's culture, and we're happy to have it."[67]

The Byrnes usually took an annual trip to London, often attending theater almost daily over two-week stays. On one occasion, they also traveled to Ireland, visiting some of Byrne's relatives in one of the ancestral villages. In their 2010 London visit, when he was 85 years old, Byrne was mugged, punched in the face by a deranged man in the Waterloo railroad station as he and Mrs. Byrne were on their way to a matinee performance at the National Theater. The man, whose earlier odd behavior had aroused suspicions of the police posted at the station, was immediately subdued and arrested. An ambulance arrived and treated Byrne, but he refused to go to a hospital. "Some nut came out of the blue and punched me in the jaw," Byrne said by phone to a reporter. "I never fell down, like when I fought Muhammad Ali."[68]

Byrne continued to play a role in the state's politics, sometimes privately offering advice to budding politicians or potential candidates on their career moves or strategies. Among his children, Byrne's eldest son Tom was the most active in politics, serving as chair of the New Jersey Democratic State Committee in the 1990s. Tom later filed as a prospective candidate for the U.S. Senate race in 2000, but withdrew from the race in favor of eventual winner Jon Corzine, who subsequently was elected governor in 2005. His daughter Nancy served as the state tourism director. His son Tim became an attorney at a major Manhattan law firm specializing in financial industry regulation after earlier working as a staff lawyer at the Federal Reserve. His youngest daughter, Barbara, became a world champion lightweight rower; Byrne admitted to "tearing up" when he watched her receive a gold medal as a member of the four-oared U.S. team at the world championships in Brussels. His son Bill pursued a career in journalism and public relations. His oldest daughter Susan, who died in an accidental fall in 2006, was an accomplished professional photographer whose work had been published in national magazines.

More publicly, often through his *Star-Ledger* column with Tom Kean or at other forums, Byrne expressed opinions on issues and elections, sometimes with a characteristic independence. In the 2009 gubernatorial election, Byrne leaned toward endorsing the candidacy of Christopher Daggett, a past Republican and former environmental commissioner under Governor Kean

who was running as an independent against incumbent Democratic Governor
Jon Corzine and Republican Chris Christie. "I would have done it," Byrne
disclosed soon after Christie's inauguration, "but didn't because I did not
want to go out on that limb alone and could not convince Tom Kean to go
along with me." (Kean endorsed Christie.)[69] "Brendan wasn't publicly active,
remained behind the scenes," Ruthi Byrne later recounted, "but was very
much in favor of Daggett's candidacy. I was an active member of the Daggett
team, I got a fair amount of grief from Democratic party leaders because we
were not only not on the Corzine team, but working for Daggett."[70]

When Governor Christie ran for reelection in 2013, Byrne provoked many
Democrats when, noting that Barbara Buono, the likely Democratic nominee
to oppose Governor Christie's bid for reelection, was trailing badly in the
polls, he suggested she should consider withdrawing from the race, comparing her situation to his own. "I was way behind in 1977 and I was thinking,"
Byrne said in his column with Tom Kean, "if it gets worse, I'm going to
withdraw. It didn't get worse. As a matter fact, it got better. But at one point
I thought of dropping out in favor of a better-positioned candidate. I don't
know whether that consideration would appeal to Buono, but I would advise
she make that evaluation."[71] Buono was defeated by a 22-point margin by
Governor Christie, the highest since the record-setting plurality rolled up by
Governor Kean in 1985.

In October 2013, a seven-foot high bronze statue of Byrne was dedicated,
standing outside one of the entrances to the Essex County Courthouse in
Newark where he had served as a prosecutor and judge. Some five years
before, the plaza outside the Courthouse had been named after Byrne. The
ceremony at which the statue was unveiled brought together some two hundred from Byrne's family, friends, and others from his public and private life,
as well as four other New Jersey governors—Governor Chris Christie and
former Governors Tom Kean, Jim McGreevey and Jim Florio. Ruthi Byrne
welcomed the crowd, commenting on her relationship with Byrne: "It's been
a journey, a wonderful journey, it's been a blast." In his remarks, Byrne's
son Tom recalled the highly competitive family football games that preceded
their Thanksgiving dinners, games that usually were abruptly ended by his
father as soon as his side took the lead. He then predicted that the statue—
unlike the former Brendan Byrne Arena—would be a more lasting honor:
"When something looks like you, they can never change the name." After citing Byrne's model for integrity and the achievements in office that Byrne had
left as a legacy to the state, Governor Christie noted, "He has been a tough
act to follow." McGreevey praised Byrne for his World War II service as a
member of "the Greatest Generation;" Florio credited Byrne with preserving
the Pinelands. Kean said of his friendship with Byrne, "We argue and argue

and yet we're the best of friends. That's how government should be," and concluded, "New Jersey and Brendan Byrne, perfect together."[72]

On Byrne's ninetieth birthday—April 1, 2014—he was also the focus of a good-natured "roast" presided over by Governor Christie including comments by former Governors Kean, Florio, Whitman, DiFrancesco, McGreevey, and Codey. The event, arranged by his wife Ruthi to benefit educational programs of the New Jersey Performing Arts Center in Newark, featured mild jabs, mostly targeting Byrne's age (Governor McGreevey: "The pilot of Brendan's bomber in the war was Wilbur Wright."). Yet the talks quickly turned to recognition of Byrne's contributions to the state, with Governor Christie calling Byrne "a treasure" to New Jersey.[73]

The milestone ninetieth birthday also allowed Byrne the opportunity to reflect:

> I've had an interesting life. Some of the times weren't easy, like the depression and the war. But our family hung together, and I cherish the memories of growing up with my parents and my brother and my sisters, later raising my own family and helping New Jersey in the ways I could. It's been a full life, but I'm still pursuing my goal to become the only New Jersey governor to reach 100. After that, I intend to be buried in Jersey City so I can remain active in politics.[74]

Notes

CHAPTER 1

1. Brendan T. Byrne, interview with author, September 28, 2012. Much of the Byrne family history is from Barbara Moakler Byrne, e-mail to author, May 11, 2013.

2. See generally Peter Gray, *The Irish Famine*, New York: Henry N. Abrams, 1995.

3. Dermot Quinn, *The Irish in New Jersey: Four Centuries of American Life*, New Brunswick, NJ: Rutgers University Press, 2004, 66, 68.

4. The quote "an Irishman was buried under every tie" is cited in "Immigration," Library of Congress. Accessed May 26, 2012 at http://www.loc.gov/teachers/classroommaterials/presentationsandactivities/presentations/immigration/irish4.html

5. Hostility toward Catholics was also encouraged by suspicions about their loyalty because of their obedience to the Pope and their choice of sending their children to parochial, rather than public, schools. See generally Quinn, *The Irish in New Jersey*, 66–69.

6. See Leslie M. Harris, *In the Shadow of Slavery: African Americans in New York City, 1626–1863*, Chicago: University of Chicago Press, 2003, 278–88, excerpt reproduced at http://www.press.uchicago.edu/Misc/Chicago/317749.html. Accessed September 8, 2012.

7. Quinn, *The Irish in New Jersey*, 107.

8. Brendan T. Byrne, interview with author, September 28, 2012.

9. The relatively high ground of the Watchungs has been exploited for military purposes. During the Revolutionary War, General George Washington used the protection of the Watchungs to erect the first and second Middlebrook encampment. The high ground allowed him to monitor the area between Perth Amboy and New Brunswick, as well as to identify and disturb British movements between Manhattan and Philadelphia. See Mark Edward Lender, "The Cockpit Reconsidered: Revolutionary New Jersey as a Military Theater," in Maxine Lurie (ed.), *A New Jersey Anthology*,

New Brunswick, NJ: Rutgers University Press, 2010, 90–92. During the Cold War with the Soviet Union in the 1960s, the Watchungs also hosted Nike missile installations defending New York City from potential attacks. Virginia B. Troeger, *Berkeley Heights Revisited*, Charleston, SC: Arcadia, 2005, 74.

10. In 1780, the residents of the highlands voted to adopt the name "Orange," and in 1860 officially incorporated as a municipality, allowing creation of their own fire, police, street, and other town departments. See City of Orange Township Historical Overview, City of Orange Township. Accessed September 12, 2012 at http://www.ci.orange.nj.us/history_main.html

11. The City of Paterson became one of the nation's first industrial centers by harnessing power generated from the Great Falls of the Passaic River from water falling over the face of First Watchung Mountain. Marcia A. Dente, *Great Falls of Paterson*, Charleston, SC: Arcadia Publishing, 2010.

12. South Orange was organized on January 26, 1861; East Orange on March 4, 1863; and West Orange on March 14, 1863 (which also included the former municipality of Fairmount, another former section of Orange which previously had been established on March 11, 1862 as a separate municipality). For the history of the evolution of New Jersey's municipalities, see generally Alan Karcher, *New Jersey's Multiple Municipal Madness*, New Brunswick, NJ: Rutgers University Press, 1998.

13. Michael Byrne's brother Thomas and his wife Mary and their three children are listed in the census as living next door.

14. Barbara Moakler Byrne, e-mail to author, May 11, 2013.

15. The expanded account of Llewellyn Park in the *New York Times* included: "We have been visiting a piece of large-patterned workmanship, reminding us of the project of the ancient architect to carve Mount Athos into a statue of a king, holding a city in his right hand, and a basin of rivers in his left: we refer to the unique, beautiful, and romantic Llewellyn Park, at Orange, New Jersey—once a rough, shaggy mountain side, now transformed into an enchanted sound, or fairy land." The journalist also wrote that the community was worthy of wide replication: "We make these remarks on Llewellyn Park, not so much for praising a good thing already done, as for holding up a pattern for something like it that might be done elsewhere. It is a beautiful example which ought to find repetition in other quarters. Many towns and cities, both in New-England and other parts of the country, have surroundings which, if not in all respects equal to the slope of Orange Mountain, might, by equal skill and public spirit, be so beautified as to stand as a marvel to all who should contrast their old aspects with their new." "Llewellyn Park," *New York Times*, April 23, 1865.

16. Other Llewellyn Park residents over the years included abolitionist James Miller McKim, whose house contained secret chambers to hide escaped slaves traversing the Underground Railroad. Both the Merck pharmaceutical family and the Colgate toothpaste family also were homeowners. See "Llewellyn Park," Llewellyn Park Historical Society. Accessed July 25, 2012 at http://www.llewellynpark.com/History-of-Llewellyn-Park~101499~13266.htm. About half of Edison's nearly 1,100 patents were based on experiments conducted in West Orange, including his work with motion pictures and his improvements to the phonograph. See also

Thomas Alva Edison Papers, Mertz Library, New York Botanical Garden. Accessed September 12, 2012 at http://sciweb.nybg.org/science2/libr/finding_guide/edison2. ashtml

17. Twelfth Census of the United States, 1900, West Orange Town, NJ. US Census Bureau.

18. Thomas Brennan, Patrick's father, was a stone mason who worked in building the Saint Mark's Church in Orange, but later returned to Ireland.

19. One of the early hatmakers in Orange was Stephen Stetson; his son John, born in 1830 in Orange, would later establish his own factory in Philadelphia that would make the hat so identified with the Western frontier. See City of Orange Township Historical Overview, City of Orange Township. Accessed September 12, 2012 at http://www.ci.orange.nj.us/history_main.html; James P. Johnson, *New Jersey History of Ingenuity and Industry*, Northridge, CA: Windsor Publications, 1987, 140. For more information on the history of hatmaking in Orange, see Antoinette Martin, "Hat Factory Is a Focus of Redevelopment in Orange," *New York Times*, May 9, 2004.

20. As early as 1860, John Addison Freeman, a physician in Orange, authored a paper linking the use of the chemical mercuric nitrate in the "carroting" process in which the fur was separated from the pelt to the high rate of neurological problems of those employed in hatmaking. Others would dispute the research, however, linking mental issues and tremors to mercury poisoning. See Pat Ryan, "'Mad as a Hatter': The History of a Simile," *New York Times*, March 6, 2010.

21. Barbara Moakler Byrne, e-mail to author, May 11, 2013.

22. Many years later, Brendan speculated that the rivalry for his mother's affections may have subsequently led to Byrne family funeral arrangements consistently being directed to the West Orange funeral home owned by the Quinn family, a local competitor of the Codey-owned funeral home.

23. Brendan T. Byrne, interview with Andrew Szanton.

24. Ibid.

25. Ibid.

26. "Robert Emmett," Information about Ireland Site. Accessed July 14, 2012 at http://www.ireland-information.com/articles/robertemmet.htm

27. Ibid.

28. Brendan T. Byrne, interview with Andrew Szanton.

29. Ibid.

30. Brendan T. Byrne, interview with author, September 28, 2012.

31. Ibid.

32. Brendan T. Byrne, interview with Andrew Szanton.

33. Father Connor's best-known songs were "When I Take My Sugar to Tea" and "You Brought a New Kind of Love to Me"; in addition to Sinatra, his songs were recorded by Nat King Cole, Tommy Dorsey and several others. He also was the chaplain of the New Jersey State Police for twenty-four years, and the New Jersey State Guard (predecessor of the National Guard). See "Pierre Norman", IMDb.com. Accessed November 3, 2012 at http://www.imdb.com/name/nm0635604/bio

34. Brendan T. Byrne, interview with Andrew Szanton.

35. Brendan T. Byrne, interview with author, October 5, 2012.

36. Ibid.

37. Ibid.

38. Ibid.

39. Brendan T. Byrne, interview with author, September 28, 2012.

40. Ibid.

41. Ibid.

42. Ibid.

43. Brendan T. Byrne, interview with Andrew Szanton.

44. Ibid.

45. Ibid.

46. Ibid.

47. Ibid.

48. The recording of the Jack Benny "Your money or your life!" bit is accessible at YouTube at http://www.youtube.com/watch?v=-tVzdUczMT0

49. Brendan T. Byrne, interview with author, September 28, 2012.

50. Ibid.

51. See, e.g., Hal Burton, *The Morro Castle: Tragedy at Sea*, New York: Viking Press, 1973.

52. Brendan T. Byrne, interview with Andrew Szanton. Edison worked in collaboration with Henry Ford and Harvey Firestone in an attempt to develop artificial rubber to reduce the dependence on foreign sources of supply. Reynold M. Wik, *Henry Ford and Grass-Roots America*, Ann Arbor: University of Michigan Press, 1972, 145–46; see also Thomas Alva Edison Papers, Mertz Library, New York Botanical Garden. Accessed September 12, 2012 at http://sciweb.nybg.org/science2/libr/finding_guide/edison2.ashtml

53. Brendan T. Byrne, interview with Andrew Szanton.

54. See generally, John Heidenry, *The Gashouse Gang: How Dizzy Dean, Leo Durocher, Branch Rickey, Pepper Martin, and Their Colorful, Come-from-Behind Ball Club Won the World Series—and America's Heart—During the Great Depression*, New York: Public Affairs, 2007.

55. Brendan T. Byrne, interview with Andrew Szanton.

56. In his talks, Byrne would recount the tale, perhaps apocryphal, of Dean's being inserted in the 1934 World Series as a pinch runner and running to second; being hit square in the forehead by a throw; and the next day's newspaper headlined: "X-rays of Dizzy Dean's head showed nothing."

57. Brendan T. Byrne, interview with Andrew Szanton.

58. *Newark Sunday News*, November 23, 1970. In 1940, Frank was elected as an alternate delegate at the Democratic National Convention pledged to President Roosevelt's nomination for reelection, and in that year's general election Frank was the Democratic nominee for Essex County Clerk, losing in an election in which Democrat Charles Edison, Thomas Edson's son, was elected governor of New Jersey. Brendan T. Byrne, interview with author, September 28, 2012.

59. Brendan T. Byrne, interview with author, October 5, 2012.

60. Ibid.

61. John J. Degnan, interview for Center on the American Governor, Eagleton Institute of Politics, Rutgers University, Brendan T. Byrne Archive (hereafter cited as Rutgers-Eagleton Byrne Archive).

62. Ibid.

63. Brendan T. Byrne, interview with author, October 5, 2012.

64. Brendan T. Byrne, interview with author, July 23, 2013.

65. Ibid.

66. Brendan T. Byrne, interview with Andrew Szanton.

67. Ibid.

68. After Doby retired from baseball, he ran into financial difficulties through bad investments, and Byrne hired him when he was an Essex County prosecutor for a position as a community youth sports coordinator and when he was governor as the state lottery's celebrity conducting the daily lottery drawing. See also "Larry Doby," National Baseball Hall of Fame and Museum. Accessed May 26, 2012 at http://baseballhall.org/hof/doby-larry

69. In 2007, the French government awarded Sheeran its highest decoration, naming him as a Chevalier of the Order of the Legion of Honor. Sheeran's memoir of the war was published as *No Surrender: A World War II Memoir*, New York: Berkley Caliber, 2011; see also "James J. Sheeran," Obituary, *Trenton Times*, July 17, 2007. Accessed June 25, 2012 at http://obits.nj.com/obituaries/trenton/obituary.aspx?n=james-j-sheeran&pid=90869755

70. Brendan T. Byrne, interview with author, September 28, 2012.

71. Ibid. The Goldman Hotel was built in the 1930s, eventually expanding to become a large complex that included a nine-hole golf course. Somewhat similar to better-known hotels in New York's Catskill Mountains, the hotel also became popular for stays by Jewish families and as an occasional site for social events targeted to Jewish singles. After several subsequent changes in ownership, it was extensively renovated and its site is currently the Wilshire Grand Hotel. See Joseph Fagan, "Fertile Farmland that Became the Pleasant Valley," WestOrangeHistory.com. Accessed May 26, 2012 at http://www.westorangehistory.com/id94.html; Robert Weiner, "To 'land' a date, Jewish kids found the 'Dunams'," *New Jersey Jewish News*, December 16, 2009.

72. Brendan T. Byrne, interview with author, October 5, 2012.

73. Brendan T. Byrne, interview with Andrew Szanton.

74. Ibid. In 1937, Pals Cabin added a dining room, which for six months featured an 18-year-old piano player from Wisconsin named Wladziu Valentino Liberace, who earned $40 a week. Pals was also "a favorite haunt of Babe Ruth, who loved to chow down on its hot dogs after a round of golf at nearby Crestmont Country Club." Pete Genovese, "Legendary Pals Cabin in West Orange to close pending approval," *Star-Ledger*, March 21, 2013.

75. Brendan T. Byrne, interview with author, October 12, 2012.

76. Brendan T. Byrne, interview with Andrew Szanton.

77. In 1933, when Brendan was nine, the movie *Tugboat Annie* featured Wallace Beery and Marie Dressler playing a married couple who argued on how to operate a tugboat, with Beery's character repeatedly growling "Aw, now, come on, Annie"—a

phrase that Byrne would use over and over in later years "when I feel I'm being crowded on something."

78. Galento's nickname of "Two Ton" derived from the excuse he once gave his manager for nearly being late to a fight: "I had two tons of ice to deliver on my way here." Galento's aggressive style succeeded in getting him a 1939 title fight in Yankee Stadium with the great heavyweight champion Joe Louis, before which Galento famously predicted that he would "moida the bum." Although the heavy underdog Galento knocked Louis down, the champ would quickly get up from the canvas to win in the fourth round by a technical knockout over the badly bleeding challenger. Long after hanging up his gloves, Galento would insist to his restaurant patrons and all others that he would have beaten Louis if the referee hadn't prevented him from fighting "my kind of fight," namely a no-holds-barred street brawl. John F. McKenna, "Famous Ring Wars: Joe Louis vs. 'Two Ton' Tony Galento," BoxingNews. com, January 29, 2012. Accessed January 12, 2013 at http://www.boxingnews24. com/2012/01/famous-ring-wars-joe-louis-vs-%e2%80%9ctwo-ton%e2%80%9d-tony-galento/#D2PHGjTV14Vz8BZF.99

79. Brendan T. Byrne, interview with Andrew Szanton.

80. Ibid.

81. Brendan also avidly read the entire Baseball Joe series of books written by Lester Chadwick—e.g., *Baseball Joe at Yale*, *Baseball Joe in the Big League*, etc.— finding "every one of them was marvelous, as far as I was concerned, they kept me reading." Brendan T. Byrne, interview with Andrew Szanton.

82. The University of Newark was established in 1936 through a merger of the New Jersey Law School; Dana College; Newark Institute of Arts & Sciences; Seth Boyden School of Business, and Mercer Beasley School of Law. A decade later, legislation was enacted merging the University of Newark into Rutgers University as its Newark campus.

83. Brendan T. Byrne, interview with author, February 27, 2013.

84. Ibid.

85. Brendan T. Byrne, interview with Andrew Szanton.

86. Brendan T. Byrne, interview with author, June 21, 2012.

87. Ibid.

88. Ibid.

89. Ibid.

90. Byrne would donate to Seton Hall many of his personal papers and memorabilia. See Brendan Byrne Papers, Monsignor Field Archives & Special Collection Center, Seton Hall University. Accessed January 2, 2013 at http://academic.shu.edu/findingaids/mss0007.html#N10000

CHAPTER 2

1. Brendan T. Byrne, interview, Rutgers Oral History Archives-World War II, Korean War, Vietnam War, Cold War (hereafter cited as Rutgers World War II Oral History Archives), December 10, 2007, 13.

2. Brendan T. Byrne, interview with Andrew Szanton.

3. Brendan T. Byrne, interview, December 10, 2007, Rutgers World War II Oral History Archives, 13.

4. Brendan T. Byrne, interview with Andrew Szanton.

5. Brendan T. Byrne, interview, Rutgers World War II Oral History Archives, December 10, 2007, 13.

6. Brendan T. Byrne, interview with author, September 12, 2013.

7. Brendan T. Byrne, interview, Rutgers World War II Oral History Archives, December 10, 2007, 16.

8. Ibid. 15.

9. Ibid, 31.

10. Ibid, 19.

11. Donald L. Miller, *Masters of the Air*, New York: Simon & Schuster, 2006, 41.

12. Ibid.

13. The B-17 was the *All-American* piloted by Lt. Kendrick R. Bragg. The song was by Harold Adamson (lyrics) and Jimmie McHugh (music). Here's an excerpt from the song:

> *With just one motor gone*
> *We can still carry on*
> *Comin' in on a wing and a prayer*

Accessed February 22, 2013 from LyricsFreak.com at http://www.lyricsfreak. com/r/ry+cooder/comin+in+on+a+wing+and+a+prayer_20171102.html

14. Alan J. Levine, *The Strategic Bombing of Germany, 1940–1945*, Westport, CT: Praeger, 1992, 14–15.

15. Earlier in the war, tents would be protected from Nazi air attacks by camouflage paint and slit trenches dug next to them for the crews to escape to in the event of bombing or strafing from fighters. By the time Byrne arrived in Italy in the summer of 1944, however, the Luftwaffe had been so weakened that such assaults were no longer a risk. Brendan T. Byrne, interview with author, October 22, 2012.

16. Brendan T. Byrne, interview, Rutgers World War II Oral History Archives, 37.

17. Brendan T. Byrne, interview with author, October 22, 2012.

18. Miller, *Masters of the Air*, 84–85.

19. Ibid., 83–84.

20. The Norden bombsight was developed by Carl Norden, an engineer retained as a consultant by the U.S. Navy; it used an analog computer and gyroscope to keep the planes level on their bombing runs. During the war, it was considered highly secret, with crews cautioned against discussing its operation or allowing its inspection by unauthorized persons. Malcolm Gladwell: "The strange tale of the Norden bombsight," (video) TED Conferences July 2011. Accessed April 4, 2013 at http://www.ted.com/talks/malcolm_gladwell.html

21. Brendan T. Byrne, interview with author, October 22, 2012.

22. Miller, *Masters of the Air*, 85.

23. Brendan T. Byrne, interview with author, October 22, 2012.

24. Ibid.

25. Donald L. Caldwell, Richard Muller, *The Luftwaffe Over Germany: Defense of the Reich*, London: Greenhill, 2007, 190–222.

26. Miller, *Masters of the Air*, 312.

27. The process to produce synthetic oil treated coal with hydrogen under high pressure at high temperatures. It was developed by Friedrich Bergius, who was awarded the Nobel Prize in chemistry in 1932. See Friedrich Bergius, "Chemical reactions under high pressure," Nobel Lecture, May 21, 1932. Accessed January 2, 2013 at http://www.nobelprize.org/nobel_prizes/chemistry/laureates/1931/bergius-lecture.pdf

28. Miller, *Masters of the Air*, 186–92.

29. Albert F. Simpson, "Sicily and Southern Italy," in Wesley Frank Craven et al. (ed.), *The Army Air Forces in World War II*, 564–65. Accessed January 12, 2013 at http://www.ibiblio.org/hyperwar/AAF/II/AAF-II-16.html

30. Miller, *Masters of the Air*, 321.

31. Barrett Tillman, "The Forgotten Fifteenth," *Air Force Magazine*, September 2012. Vol. 95, no. 9. Accessed December 22, 2012 at http://www.airforcemag.com/MagazineArchive/Pages/2012/September%202012/0912fifteenth.aspx

32. Quoted in Miller, *Masters of the Air*, 321.

33. Ibid., 313.

34. Frederick A. Johnsen and Walter J. Boyne, *B-17 Flying Fortress: The Symbol of Second World War*, New York: McGraw-Hill, 2000, 195.

35. Ibid., 316–17.

36. Brendan T. Byrne, interview with author, September 28, 2012.

37. Johnsen and Boyne, *B-17 Flying Fortress: The Symbol of Second World War*, 34–35.

38. Brendan T. Byrne, interview with author, September 28, 2012.

39. Ibid.

40. Ibid.

41. B-17 casualty and loss statistics are from "B17 Flying Fortress," History Learning Site. Accessed January 13, 2013 at http://www.historylearningsite.co.uk/b17_flying_fortress.htm; "Life and Death Aboard a B-17, 1944," *New Yorker Magazine*, August 12, 1944. Accessed January 13, 2013 at EyeWitness to History, www.eyewitnesstohistory.com, http://www.eyewitnesstohistory.com/b17.htm; Gregory Fremont-Barnes, *American Bomber Crewman: 1941–45*, Oxford: Osprey, 2008, 56; Barrett Tillman, "The Forgotten Fifteenth," *Air Force Magazine*, September 2012, accessed January 22, 2013 at http://www.airforcemag.com/MagazineArchive/Pages/2012/September%202012/0912fifteenth.aspx

42. Brendan T. Byrne, interview, Rutgers World War II Oral History Archives, 18.

43. Brendan T. Byrne, interview with Andrew Szanton.

44. Ibid.

45. Ibid.

46. Brendan T. Byrne, interview, Rutgers World War II Oral History Archives, 30.

47. Henry Steele Commager, Donald L. Miller, *The Story of World War II*, New York: Simon & Schuster, rev. ed. 2002, 471.

48. Brendan T. Byrne, interview with author, October 4, 2012.

49. Ibid.

50. Ibid.

51. Duane L. Bohnstedt, "Blechhammer," 15th Air Force. Accessed February 12, 2013 at http://www.15thaf.org/55th_BW/460th_BG/Stories/PDFs/Blechhammer.pdf

52. Brendan T. Byrne, interview with author, November 22, 2012.

53. Brendan T. Byrne, interview for Rutgers-Eagleton Byrne Archive, August 28, 2006.

54. "Blechhammer," Fold3.com. Accessed February 23, 2013 at http://www.fold3.com/page/286060902_blechhammer/.

55. Field Marshal Erhard Milch quoted in Peter Becker, Ph.D., "The Role of Synthetic Fuel In World War II Germany," *Air University Review*, July–August 1981. Accessed December 10, 2012 at http://www.airpower.maxwell.af.mil/airchronicles/aureview/1981/jul-aug/becker.htm

56. Ibid., 322–25.

57. Brendan T. Byrne, interview with author, September 28, 2012.

58. Ibid.

59. Brendan T. Byrne, interview with Andrew Szanton.

60. Brendan T. Byrne, interview with author, July 29, 2013.

61. Ibid.

62. Miller, *Masters of the Air*, 372–73.

63. Brendan T. Byrne, interview with author, July 29, 2013.

64. Brendan T. Byrne, interview with author, October 5, 2012.

65. Ibid.

66. Ibid.

67. Ibid.

68. Brendan T. Byrne, interview with Andrew Szanton.

CHAPTER 3

1. Brendan T. Byrne, interview with author, October 5, 2012.

2. Ibid.

3. Brendan T. Byrne, interview for Rutgers-Eagleton Byrne Archive, August 28, 2006.

4. Brendan T. Byrne, interview with author, October 5, 2012; see also "Noted 'Buzzer' Hall Dies of Heart Attack," *Daily Princetonian*, May 4, 1962.

5. In brief profiles of the various clubs in *This Side of Paradise*, which as a student Fitzgerald began writing in the Cottage Club library, he described the Cottage members as "an impressive melange of brilliant adventurers and well-dressed philanderers." Interactive Media, 2013 (Google e-book), 47.

6. Brendan T. Byrne, interview with author, October 5, 2012.

7. Ibid.

8. Ibid.

9. Brendan T. Byrne, interview with Andrew Szanton.

10. Ibid.

11. William McCleery, "A Visit with New Jersey's 'Born-Again' Governor," *Princeton Alumni Weekly*, June 28, 1978.

12. Brendan T. Byrne, interview with Andrew Szanton.

13. Ibid.

14. George A. Thompson, "Look to your right, look to your left—one of them won't be here next year," (blog entry) at "The Bug Apple," BarryPopik.com. Accessed July 22, 2013 at http://www.barrypopik.com/index.php/new_york_city/ entry/look_to_your_right_look_to_your_left_one_of_them_wont_be_here_next_ year/

15. Brendan T. Byrne, interview with author, October 5, 2012.

16. Brendan T. Byrne, interview for Rutgers-Eagleton Byrne Archive, August 28, 2006.

17. Brendan T. Byrne, interview with author, October 5, 2012. Keto would later become an official with the Atomic Energy Commission.

18. Ibid.

19. Brendan T. Byrne, interview with Andrew Szanton.

20. Brendan T. Byrne, interview with author, October 5, 2012.

21. Ibid.

22. Brendan T. Byrne, interview with author, September 19, 2013.

23. Brendan T. Byrne, Jr., interview for Rutgers-Eagleton Byrne Archive, May 18, 2009.

24. Ibid.

25. Ibid.

26. Ibid.

27. Brendan T. Byrne, remarks at Conference on "New Jersey Governors and the State Supreme Court," New Jersey Law Center, May 8, 2008. Video accessed May 27, 2012 at http://governors.rutgers.edu/interview_forum/NJ_state-supreme-court. php

28. Brendan T. Byrne quotations relating to John McGeehan from interview with Andrew Szanton and interview with author, October 4, 2012.

29. Brendan T. Byrne, interview with author, October 5, 2012. For more information on Longy Zwillman, see Robert A. Rockaway, *But He was Good to His Mother: The Lives and Crimes of Jewish Gangsters*, Jerusalem: Gefen Publishing House, 2000, 30–39 and John Austin, *More of Hollywood's Unsolved Mysteries*, New York: Shapolsky Publishers, 1992, 170.

30. Brendan T. Byrne, interview with author, October 5, 2012.

31. Ibid.

32. Ibid.

33. Ibid.

34. John Farmer, Sr., interview with author; see also "Bucanis Escapes Death Sentence," *Herald-News*, June 25, 1955; *State v. Bucanis*, 26 NJ 47 (1958).

35. Brendan T. Byrne, interview with author, October 5, 2012.

36. *State v. Cerce*, 22 NJ 236 (1956).

CHAPTER 4

1. Brendan T. Byrne, interview with author, September 19, 2013.

2. Ibid.

3. In his first months in office, Meyner reported the discovery of accounting irregularities in the state unemployment insurance division and suspended its director, former Democratic Governor Harold G. Hoffman. When Hoffman died before the investigation had been completed, Meyner was accused of "killing" the former governor, but Meyner's action later was affirmed when, in a letter written shortly before his death, Hoffman admitted using $300,000 in state funds to cover his embezzlement from a bank of which he was president. William Lemmey, "Robert Baumle Meyner," in Michael J. Birkner, Donald Linky, and Peter Mickulas (eds.), The *Governors of New Jersey 1664–1964: Biographical Essays*, Trenton: NJ Historical Commission, 1982, 219.

4. Wayne King, "Robert B. Meyner Is Dead at 81; Flamboyant New Jersey Governor," *New York Times*, May 29, 1990.

5. During his gubernatorial campaign in 1946, Driscoll announced he would appoint' his own personal counsel when elected and ignore Attorney General Walter D. Van Riper, who had been appointed by Governor Walter Edge and was not required to resign under the state's then constitution adopted in 1844. See J. Joseph Gribbins, "Under the State House Dome," *Independent-Leader*, November 14, 1946. Accessed January 12, 2013 at http://archive.woodbridgelibrary.org/Archive/IndependentLeader/1946/1946-11-14/pg_0007.pdf. Weintraub and Brennan were members of the Class of 1924 at Barringer High School in Newark. For more background on their personal and professional connections, see Daniel J. O'Hern, "Brennan and Weintraub: Two Stars to Guide Us," *Rutgers Law Review* 45, 3 (Spring 1994), 1049. Accessed July 21, 2012 at http://njlegallib.rutgers.edu/weintraub/PDF/weintraub.1994.pdf

6. Brendan T. Byrne, interview for Rutgers-Eagleton Byrne Archive, August 7, 2006.

7. Ibid.

8. Burkhardt later worked in John F. Kennedy's 1960 presidential campaign; was named as executive director of Kennedy's inauguration; and appointed director of facilities for the U.S. Post Office. He returned to New Jersey to direct the 1961 gubernatorial campaign of Richard J. Hughes, and served as secretary of state in the Hughes cabinet, as well as chairman of the Democratic State Committee from 1962 to 1970. In 1972, he pled guilty to a federal charge of accepting $30,000 in bribes to fix a bridge construction contract in 1964, when he was serving as Secretary of State. Wolfgang Saxon, "Robert J. Burkhardt, 83, Leader Of New Jersey Democrats in 60's," *New York Times*, January 5, 2000.

9. Brendan T. Byrne, interview with author, September 19, 2013.

10. Martin L. Greenberg, interview for Rutgers-Eagleton Byrne Archive, June 6, 2006.

11. Brendan T. Byrne, interview with Andrew Szanton.

12. Brendan T. Byrne, interview with author, September 19, 2013.

13. Phillip Roth's work would include vivid chronicles of the neighborhood in books such as *Goodbye Columbus*. Martin L. Greenberg, interview for Rutgers-Eagleton Byrne Archive, June 6, 2006.

14. Ibid.

15. New Jersey's first constitution of 1776 set the governor's term at one year. Its second constitution of 1844 increased the length of the term to three years, but prohibited an incumbent from running in the succeeding election. The 1947 constitution allowed the governor to run successively for two four-year terms.

16. "Democratic Hopefuls," *TIME Magazine*, November 24, 1958.

17. Brendan T. Byrne, interview with author, September 19, 2013.

18. Helen Stevenson's father, a Rhodes Scholar and gold medal winner on the U.S. 1,600-meter sprint relay team at the 1924 Olympics, served as president of Oberlin College from 1946 to 1961, when he was appointed ambassador to the Philippines by President Kennedy. See also David M. Halbfinger, "Ex-Rep. Helen S. Meyner, 69; Born Into Democratic Politics," *New York Times*, November 3, 1997.

19. Byrne later recounted that Meyner's bachelor party, held at a private club in Manhattan, was upstaged when the guests realized that, coincidentally, Yankee star Mickey Mantle and the actress Julie London were at the bar. Brendan T. Byrne, interview with author, August 1, 2013.

20. Brendan T. Byrne, interview with Andrew Szanton.

21. See Sidney Hook, *Common Sense and the Fifth Amendment*, New York: Criterion Books, 1957, 126.

22. "Bitter Session Ends with Bigelow OK'd for Rutgers Board," Associated Press, August 11, 1956.

23. Brendan T. Byrne, interview with Andrew Szanton. Meyner had been a vocal opponent of U.S. Senator Joseph McCarthy's hunt for alleged Communist sympathizers in the federal government. In 1953, McCarthy began his investigation of the Camp Evans Signal Corps Laboratory at Fort Monmouth, where Julius Rosenberg, who was executed in that year after his conviction for providing nuclear secrets to the Soviets, had been employed during World War II. Over forty employees were suspended from their jobs without any hearing, based on accusations by unnamed persons forwarded to McCarthy's Congressional Committee. After interrogating the employees, McCarthy eventually gave up the investigation, with Meyner denouncing McCarthy's tactics as "a perversion of basic American principles." Quoted in Lemme, "Robert Baumle Meyner," in *The Governors of New Jersey 1664–1974: Biographical Essays,* 291.

24. Brendan T. Byrne, interview with Andrew Szanton.

25. Brendan T. Byrne, interview with author, October 5, 2012.

26. Ibid.

27. Ibid.

28. Joseph W. Katz, "Byrne Named for Essex Post," *Newark Evening News*, May 26, 1959.

29. Brendan T. Byrne, interview with author, October 5, 2012.

30. Ibid. The structure of New Jersey's political parties, and the significant role of county chairs, is reviewed in Maureen Moakley, "Political Parties," in Gerald

M. Pomper (ed.), *The Political State of New Jersey*, New Brunswick, NJ: Rutgers University Press, 1986, 58–61.

31. Martin L. Greenberg, interview for Rutgers-Eagleton Byrne Archive, June 6, 2006.

32. Brendan T. Byrne, interview with author, October 5, 2012.

33. Joseph W. Katz, "Byrne Named for Essex Post," *Newark Evening News*, May 26, 1959.

34. Brendan T. Byrne, interview with author, October 5, 2012.

35. Ibid. Byrne's action in firing the investigators was challenged in court, but ultimately upheld by the state Supreme Court in *Brennan v. Byrne*, 31 NJ 333 (1960).

36. Brendan Byrne, interview with author, October 5, 2012.

37. Brendan T. Byrne, interview with author, September 19, 2013.

38. Donald R. Raichle, *New Jersey's Union College: A History, 1933–1983*, Madison, NJ: Fairleigh Dickinson University Press, 1983, 156; Joseph W. Katz, "Byrne Named for Essex Post," *Newark News*, May 26, 1959.

39. Byrne's resigned as chairman of the insurance company in 1970, when he was appointed as a judge, but his role became a subordinate issue in his 1973 gubernatorial campaign after the company went bankrupt. Michael Kramer, "Byrne Is Ahead, But . . .," *New York Magazine*, October 15, 1973, 76.

40. James R. Zazzali, December 14, 2009, interview for Rutgers-Eagleton Byrne Archive.

Barry Evenchick, who would become one of Byrne's closest friends after being hired in 1964, described arriving on a Saturday at the Byrne home in West Orange for a scheduled interview but getting no response after ringing the bell at the front door. Assuming he had mistaken the date of the interview, Evenchick prepared to walk down the sidewalk and drive home, but then heard noise in the backyard, where Byrne and his son Tom were vigorously throwing a baseball back and forth. After reluctantly being drafted barehanded to join the game of catch, Evenchick later had his interview in the Byrne home in which they discussed his rowing on the Rutgers crew and one of Byrne's high school football teammates. On the way home, he realized that during the entire interview they had said nothing about legal topics. Barry H. Evenchick, interview for Rutgers-Eagleton Byrne Archive, November 29, 2006.

41. Brendan T. Byrne, interview with author, October 5, 2012.

42. Ibid.

43. Joe Blackwell, *Notorious New Jersey: 100 True Tales of Murders and Mobsters, Scandals and Scoundrels*, New Brunswick, NJ: Rutgers University Press, 2007, 205.

44. Brendan T. Byrne, interview with author, October 5, 2012.

45. New Jersey Supreme Court Justice Haydn Proctor, conversation with author, circa 1973.

46. After completing months of hearing witnesses and reviewing documents and other evidence, the grand juries would then issue public reports, or "presentments," summarizing the results of their investigation and recommending potential actions. Some of the findings of the presentments would include pointing to the collusion of Newark police in protecting gambling operations; recommending that state wiretap

and witness immunity laws be strengthened to enhance law enforcement tools against organized crime; and proposing that the state government undertake a study of whether legalizing gambling would undercut the revenues of the mob.

47. In addition, the Grand Jury criticized the appointment of Harry (Tip) Rosen as public relations man for the Police Department at a time when Mr. Rosen still held a part-time job in a firm owned by Gerardo Catena, "who had been widely reputed to be a syndicate leader in New Jersey." Quoted in Lilley Commission, 20. Accessed October 10, 2012 at http://slic.njstatelib.org/slic_files/digidocs/c5815/c58151968.pdf

48. Lilley Commission, 20. Accessed October 10, 2012 at http://slic.njstatelib.org/slic_files/digidocs/c5815/c58151968.pdf

49. Brendan T. Byrne, interview with author, October 5, 2012.

50. Ibid.

51. Charlie Carella's father-in-law, a Newark banker, was also a friend of Byrne's father. They would maintain a lifelong friendship and professional relationship. See Charles Carella, interview for Rutgers-Eagleton Byrne Archive, December 14, 2009.

52. Ibid.

53. Donald Ray Cressey, *Theft of a Nation: The Structure and Operations of Organized Crime in America*, New Brunswick, NJ: Transaction Publishing, 2008, 57–60, 145.

54. See Chapter 3.

55. Brendan T. Byrne, interview with author, October 5, 2012.

56. "Abner Zwillman," FBI Records, The Vault. Accessed October 5, 2012 at http://vault.fbi.gov/Abner%20Zwillman

57. See "Permanent Subcommittee on Investigations Historical Background," U.S. Senate, December 1, 2000. Accessed October 22, 2012 at http://www.hsgac.senate.gov/subcommittees/investigations/media/permanent-subcommittee-on-investigations-historical-background; Charles Grutzner, "Mafia Obtained Secret U.S. Data," *New York Times*, 1970.

58. Richard Linnett, *In the Godfather Garden: The Long Life and Times of Richie "the Boot" Boiardo*, New Brunswick, NJ: Rutgers University Press, 2013, 56.

59. Brendan T. Byrne, interview with author, October 5, 2012.

60. Ibid.

61. John B. Wefing, *The Life and Times of Richard Hughes: The Politics of Civility*, New Brunswick, NJ: Rutgers University Press, 2009, 120.

62. "Mob put up cash for favored candidates," *Star-Ledger*, January 7, 1970.

63. James R. Zazzali, e-mail to author, May 20, 2013.

64. Brendan T. Byrne, interview with author, October 5, 2012.

65. Sandor M. Polster, "The Man the Mob Couldn't Bribe," *New York Post*, January 8, 1970.

66. One of various explanations for Boiardo's nickname of "The Boot" was his alleged use of his boot to stomp on a prone victim's head propped up on a street curb. Linnett, *In the Godfather Garden*, 1.

67. Longy Zwillman and Richie Boiardo had originally based their criminal activities in Newark during Prohibition, with Zwillman's focused on the city's

predominantly Jewish third ward, and Boiardo's on the Italian neighborhoods of the first ward. When Boiardo began intruding into Zwillman's territory, a violent war between the two gangs broke out for several weeks, during which both Zwillman and Boiardo were targets of failed assassination attempts. They reached a truce in the fall of 1930, but less than two months later Boiardo barely escaped death when he was badly wounded in a shotgun attack, an assault which apparently was not related to his conflict with Zwillman. See Brad R. Tuttle, *How Newark Became Newark: The Rise, Fall, and Rebirth of an American City*, New Brunswick, NJ: Rutgers University Press, 2009, 102.

68. Gil Reavill, *Mafia Summit: J. Edgar Hoover, the Kennedy Brothers, and the Meeting That Unmasked the Mob*, New York: St. Martin's Press/Thomas Dunne Books, 2013, 83.

69. Linnett, *In the Godfather Garden*, 109–10.

70. Sandy Smith, "The Crime Cartel," *Life Magazine* 63, 9 (September 1, 1967); Richard Linnett, *In the Godfather Garden*, 109–10. Another writer described the Livingston home as "a bizarre, inordinately expensive mansion, a massive confection made of imported Italian brick and stone, with gargoyles and spindly ornamental chimney stacks protruding from the roofline." A marble statue of Boiardo depicted on horseback adorned the garden. Gil Reavill, *Mafia Summit: J. Edgar Hoover, the Kennedy Brothers, and the Meeting That Unmasked the Mob*, New York: St. Martin's Press/Thomas Dunne Books, 2013, 83.

71. Linnett, *In the Godfather Garden*, 98.

72. See *United States v. Addonizio et al*, 313 F.Supp. 486 (U.S. Dist. Court 1970); With some irony, after he resigned as prosecutor, Byrne would be hired as a private lawyer to represent one of those indicted with Addonizio and Spina, Newark Municipal Court Judge Anthony Giuliano, who had been charged with income tax evasion, extortion, and conspiracy. Before he went to trial, however, Giuliano died after suffering a heart attack and, on the day following Giuliano's death, Byrne obtained a dismissal of the charges so that his funeral could be held without the cloud of the indictment, telling the court, "I would have much preferred to have come before this court to clear Judge Giuliano's name in life than in death." "Giuliano Charges Canceled," *Newark Evening News*, February 5, 1970.

73. Linnett, *In the Godfather Garden*, 135.

74. Brendan T. Byrne, interview with author, September 28, 2012.

75. "Excerpts From FBI Transcripts of Tapes Released at the De Carlo Trial," *New York Times*, January 7, 1970. Charles Grutzner, "Mafia Obtained Secret U.S. Data," *New York Times*, January 20, 1970.

76. The tapes were produced at the 1970 trial in response to a pretrial motion by DeCavalcante's lawyer requesting the results of any electronic surveillance of his client. The prosecution was required to disclose any tapes or transcripts under recent rulings of the U.S. Supreme Court, but previously the government had followed a policy of dropping major cases rather than reveal the content of its eavesdropping. Beginning with the DeCalvacante case, however, the government surprisingly complied, producing some 2,000 pages of DeCavalcante's conversations. See Paul Hoffman, *Tiger In The Court*, Chicago: Playboy Press, 1974.

77. "Newark election in 1962: A discussion on the mob's help to Addonizio," *Star-Ledger*, January 7, 1970.

78. Ibid.

79. Audrey A. Fecht, "Brendan T. Byrne: Name in The News," *Newark Evening News*, January 9, 1970.

80. Ibid.

81. Sandor M. Polster, "The Man the Mob Couldn't Bribe," *New York Post*, January 8, 1970.

82. Brendan T. Byrne, interview with Andrew Szanton.

83. Brendan T. Byrne, interview with author, October 5, 2012.

84. See generally "The Newark and Detroit Riots of 1967," Department of Sociology and Anthropology, University College-Newark, Rutgers University. Accessed June 2, 2012 at http://www.67riots.rutgers.edu/index.htm

85. Brendan T. Byrne, interview with author, August 6, 2012.

86. Homer Bigart, "Newark Riot Deaths at 21 as Negro Sniping Widens; Hughes May Seek U.S. Aid," *New York Times*, July 17, 1967. For a discussion of Governor Hughes and the Newark riots, see Wefing, 168–76.

87. Brendan T. Byrne, interview with author, August 6, 2012.

88. See generally "The Newark and Detroit Riots of 1967," Department of Sociology and Anthropology, University College-Newark, Rutgers University. Accessed June 2, 2012 at http://www.67riots.rutgers.edu/index.htm

89. Brendan T. Byrne, interview with author, August 1, 2013.

90. Walter H. Waggoner, "Courtrooms Calm as Trials Start for 27 Indicted in Newark Riots," *New York Times*, September 26, 1967.

91. Brendan T. Byrne, interview with Andrew Szanton.

92. See "Report for Action," Governor's Select Commission on Civil Disorder, State of New Jersey, February 1968. Accessed May 26, 2012 at http://blog.nj.com/ledgernewark/2007/06/report_for_action.html

93. Ibid. Grand Jury presentments cited by the Commission had been released in 1961, 1964 and two in 1965.

94. Byrne quotes on death penalty from "Commentary", New Jerseyans for an Alternative to the Death Penalty (NJADP). Accessed May 24, 2012 at http://www.njadorg/comment. Ibid.

95. Commentary, NJADP. Accessed March 4, 2011 at http://www.njadorg/comment

96. Daniel Webster, Select Speeches of Daniel Webster, 1817–1845. Webster summation in trial of Frank Knapp for the murder of Captain Joseph White. Accessed January 3, 2013 at Project Gutenberg, http://infomotions.com/etexts/gutenberg/dirs/etext05/7sweb10.htm

97. Brendan T. Byrne, interview with author, September 28, 2012.

98. Charles Carella, interview for Rutgers-Eagleton Byrne Archive, December 14, 2009.

99. James R. Zazzali, interview for Rutgers-Eagleton Byrne Archive, December 14, 2009.

100. Charles Carella, interview for Rutgers-Eagleton Byrne Archive, December 14, 2009.

101. Justin Walder, interview with author, September 22, 2012.

102. Strelecki was the first woman to prosecute a murder trial in New Jersey, and later would serve as state motor vehicles director and be appointed by Byrne as a Superior Court judge. Brendan T. Byrne, interview with author, September 28, 2012; "Hon. June Strelecki," (obituary), *Star-Ledger*, March 12, 2013.

103. Barry H. Evenchick, interview for Rutgers-Eagleton Byrne Archive, November 29, 2006.

104. Justin Walder, interview with author, September 22, 2012.

105. See *State v. Funicello*, 49 N.J. 553 (1967).

106. "Byrne reveals state sent wrong man to prison," *Star-Ledger*, February 11, 1965.

107. See *Escobedo v. Illinois*, 378 U.S. 478 (1964); *Miranda v. Arizona,* 384 U.S. 436 (1966); and *Mapp v. Ohio*, 367 U.S. 643 (1961) for the key Warren Court decisions expanding constitutional protections of those arrested on criminal charges.

108. *State v. Macri,* 72 N.J. Super. 511, 516 (Law Div. 1962).

109. *State v. Macri*, 39 N.J. 250 (1963). Weintraub, C.J. (concurring), 39 N.J. at 266–67. See also John B. Wefing, "Search and Seizure-New Jersey Supreme Court v. United States Supreme Court," *Seton Hall Law Review* 7 (1975–1976), 771. Daniel O'Hern, who later would be appointed by Byrne as a justice on the New Jersey Supreme Court after serving the Governor as counsel and commissioner of environmental protection, wrote that after reviewing a series of Weintraub opinions on the Warren Court's criminal law decisions, "I have found his attitude towards the United State Supreme Court little short of scornful." Daniel J. O'Hern, "Brennan and Weintraub: Two Stars to Guide Us," *Rutgers Law Review* 46 (Spring 1994), 1049.

110. Ibid., 1049, 1053.

111. Brendan T. Byrne, interview with author, September 28, 2012. Weintraub had been a classmate of Supreme Court Justice William Brennan at Barringer High School in Newark, would find little to justify the federal dictates to local police and state courts on criminal procedure. "The citizen looks to the State judiciary for fair and effective prosecution of violators of the criminal law," Weintraub wrote in 1972. "Yet, although the State Supreme Court is thus charged with the responsibility for that result, its power to lay down the rules has been shifted to the Federal Supreme Court by a run of its decisions over the past 12 years or so. Those decisions were not at all compelled by 'my copy' of the Constitution or its history." *State v. Funicello*, 60 N.J. 60, 70 (1972), Weintraub, C.J. (concurring). In another opinion, Weintraub wrote pointedly that the "nation's high court had omitted from its decisions a forgotten right, the right of protection from criminals." *State v. Davis*, 50 N.J. 16, (1967), *cert* denied, 389 U.S. 1054 (1968).

112. Brendan T. Byrne, interview with author, September 28, 2012.

113. Connie Cedrone, "Byrne and Lordi win confirmation by lame-ducks," *Star-Ledger*, January 10, 1968.

114. Brendan T. Byrne, interview with author, September 28, 2012.

115. Ibid.

116. Barry H. Evenchick, interview for Rutgers-Eagleton Byrne Archive, November 29, 2006.

117. Another legacy from his days as prosecutor would be ensuring that the PUC fielded a competitive staff team for sports; Evenchick remembers his struggles to keep up on the basketball court in a game against the New Jersey Bell Telephone team, which was laced with young, athletic recruits from its hundreds of linemen. Barry H. Evenchick, interview for Rutgers-Eagleton Byrne Archive, October 31, 2007.

118. Brendan T. Byrne, interview with author, October 5, 2012. Ozzard would later, after resigning from the PUC, be an unsuccessful candidate in the 1969 Republican gubernatorial primary election in which William Cahill won the nomination. After his inauguration, Governor Cahill re-appointed Ozzard to the PUC, where he served as president until resigning in 1973. After his own inauguration in January 1974, Byrne would name Grossi as the PUC president.

119. Brendan T. Byrne, interview with author, October 5, 2012.

120. Louis J. Gambaccini, interview for Rutgers-Eagleton Byrne Archive, February 7, 2006.

121. William Madden, "The PUC sees the train film . . . and shudders," *Star-Ledger*, June 27, 1968.

122. Brendan T. Byrne, interview with author, October 5, 2012.

123. Brendan T. Byrne, interview with author, November 21, 2012.

124. Ibid.

125. Joseph Katz, interview for Rutgers World War II Oral History Archives, November 18, 1995. Accessed January 3, 2013 at http://oralhistory.rutgers.edu/donors/30-interviewees/interview-html-text/487-katz-joseph-part-2

126. Charles Stile, "Seeds for liberal era take root from a defeat," *The Record*, July 26, 2009. Accessed January 22, 2013 at http://www.northjersey.com/news/politics/political_stile/Stile_Seeds_for_liberal_era_take_root_from_a_defeat.html?page=all Gaby and others from the Coalition, such as Richard Leone and Gordon MacInnes, later would form a key component of the campaign team that Byrne would hastily put together when he entered the 1973 race.

127. Joseph Katz, interview, Rutgers World War II Oral History Archives, November 18, 1995.

128. The Superior Court is comprised of three divisions: the Law and Chancery Divisions function as trial courts for criminal and civil matters, with appeals of decisions heard by the Appellate Division, whose decisions are subject to review by the state Supreme Court.

129. Stewart McClure, interview for U.S. Senate Historical Office Oral History Project, May 3, 1983, 248–50. Accessed September 11, 2012 at http://www.senate.gov/artandhistory/history/resources/pdf/McClure8.pdf

130. "Frank Guarini," PolitickerNJ.com, May 19, 2010. Accessed October 25, 2012 at http://www.politickernj.com/tags/frank-guarini#ixzz2AKNApIZ5

131. *State v. White*, 116 NJ Super. 416 (Law Div. 1971); see also "Jersey Judge Bars Penalty of Death," *New York Times*, October 13, 1971.

132. *U.S. v. Jackson,* 390 U.S. 570 (1968); *Funicello v. New Jersey*, 403 U.S. 948 (1971). See also Daniel J. O'Hern, "Brennan and Weintraub: Two Stars to Guide Us," *Rutgers Law Review* 46, 3 (Spring 1994), 1049, 1053. Accessed January 12, 2013 at http://njlegallib.rutgers.edu/weintraub/PDF/weintraub.1994.pdf

133. Brendan T. Byrne, interview with Andrew Szanton.

134. August Lembo, e-mail to author, December 9, 2012.

135. Ibid.

136. Brendan T. Byrne, interview with author, September 9, 2013.

137. Brendan T. Byrne, interview with author, November 21, 2012; see also Robert Rudolph, *The Boys from New Jersey: How the Mob Beat the Feds*, New Brunswick, NJ: Rutgers University Press, 1995, 92.

138. "Paul Sherwin," PolitickerNJ.com, February 19, 2009. Accessed October 25, 2012 at http://www.politickernj.com/tags/paul-sherwin#ixzz2AK7ayypa

139. Brendan T. Byrne, interview with author, August 1, 2013.

140. August Lembo, e-mail to author, December 9, 2012.

CHAPTER 5

1. Brendan T. Byrne, interview with author, October 5, 2012.

2. Ibid.

3. Brendan T. Byrne, interview with author, September 28, 2012; Brendan T. Byrne, interview for Center on the American Governor, Eagleton Institute of Politics, Rutgers University, Brendan T. Byrne Archive (hereafter cited as Rutgers-Eagleton Byrne Archive) April 4, 2006.

4. "Paul Sherwin," PolitickerNJ.com, February 19, 2009. Accessed October 25, 2012 at http://www.politickernj.com/tags/paul-sherwin

5. Ronald Sullivan, "Jersey Rejects Education Chief," *New York Times*, November 17, 1972; "Fight Over Marburger Poses a Threat to Cahill," *New York Times*, November 5, 1972.

6. Jeffrey Kanige, "Brendan Byrne on Brendan Byrne," *New Jersey Reporter*, June 1988, 8.

7. Brendan T. Byrne, interview with author, November 21, 2012.

8. "Insurgent Democrats Reported Urging Byrne to Enter Primary," *New York Times*, January 31, 1973.

9. Ibid.

10. Brendan T. Byrne, interview for Rutgers-Eagleton Byrne Archive, April 4, 2006.

11. Brendan T. Byrne, interview with author, October 5, 2012.

12. Audrey Fecht, "Brendan T. Byrne: Name in the News," *Newark News*, January 11, 1970.

13. Ken McPherson's nomination as Hudson County prosecutor stalled in the state Senate; however, as Republicans deferred a vote on his confirmation until after the November election, hoping that a Republican governor would be elected, which in fact came to pass with the election of William Cahill, who after taking office nominated a Republican as Hudson's prosecutor. Kenneth D. McPherson, interview for Rutgers-Eagleton Byrne Archive, September 22, 2006.

14. Brendan T. Byrne, interview with author, September 28, 2012.

15. Ibid.

16. Jean Byrne, interview for Rutgers-Eagleton Byrne Archive, January 30, 2013.

17. Ibid.

18. Brendan T. Byrne, interview with Andrew Szanton.

19. Brendan T. Byrne, interview with author, September 28, 2012.

20. Joshua McMahon, "Helstoski may 'reconsider' governor's race," *Star-Ledger*, April 17, 1973.

21. Kenneth D. McPherson, interview for Rutgers-Eagleton Byrne Archive, September 22, 2006.

22. Brendan T. Byrne, interview with author, August 6, 2013.

23. Article VIII, New Jersey Constitution of 1947; *Robinson v. Cahill*, 62 N.J. 473, 303 A.2d 273 (1973).

24. Ronald Sullivan, "Jordan, a Reformer, Ends Jersey City Machine Rule," *New York Times.* November 3, 1971.

25. Rodgers had first been elected mayor in 1946 and would serve for forty-eight years, at one time the longest mayoral tenure in U.S. history. Fitzpatrick's election in 1951 as the county freeholder director had been opposed by the bosses, but they soon regrouped to defeat him, only to see Fitzpatrick later elected as Bayonne's mayor in 1962. Evelyn Nieves, "24 Terms Are Enough, Harrison Mayor Decides," *New York Times*, March 29, 1994.

26. Kenneth D. McPherson, interview for Rutgers-Eagleton Byrne Archive, September 22, 2006.

27. The continuing resentment toward Meyner among Hudson Democrats was also reflected in the 1969 gubernatorial election in which Republican William Cahill defeated Meyner's attempt to return to the office he had left some eight years before, when Hudson's returns demonstrated an unusual level of Hudson support for the Republican.

28. Brendan T. Byrne, interview with Andrew Szanton.

29. Ibid.

30. Brendan T. Byrne, interview with author, September 28, 2012.

31. Pierre Salinger, Kennedy's press secretary during the campaign and later in the White House, subsequently wrote: "As the voting got under way, Bob Kennedy placed a call to one of our floor men: 'Go tell Bob Meyner [the governor of New Jersey] that we're going to win this thing on the first ballot, and this is his last chance. He either switches his votes to us or he's going to be rolled over.' The word came back in moments. 'Meyner's going to stand pat on the first ballot. He doesn't think we can make it on the first time around and will take the votes for himself as a favorite son.' It was a classical political error." Pierre Salinger, *With Kennedy*, Garden City, NY: Doubleday & Co. 1966, 43.

32. Brendan T. Byrne, interview with Andrew Szanton. Others have suggested that Meyner's motive was to keep the Convention from nominating Kennedy in the hope of an eventual deadlock that would result in a draft of Adlai Stevenson, the Party's presidential nominee in the 1952 and 1956 elections. Meyner's wife Helen was a cousin of Stevenson, and some analysts speculated that Meyner believed he might be selected as the nominee for vice president on a ticket headed by Stevenson. See Michael S. Mayer, "Robert B. Meyner," in *The Eisenhower Years,* New York: Facts on File, 2010, 510.

33. Brendan T. Byrne, interview with author, October 5, 2012.

34. Sources for background and quotes relating to the Byrne-Fitzpatrick meeting are Brendan T. Byrne, interview with author, September 28, 2012; Kenneth D. McPherson, interview for Rutgers-Eagleton Byrne Archive, September 22, 2006.

35. Brendan T. Byrne, interview with author, October 5, 2012.

36. Dugan and McPherson quotes are from, respectively, James P. Dugan, telephone conversation with author, April 7, 2014; Kenneth D. McPherson, interview for Rutgers-Eagleton Byrne Archive, September 22, 2006.

37. Brendan T. Byrne, interview with author, October 5, 2012.

38. Jeffrey Kanige, "Brendan Byrne on Brendan Byrne," *New Jersey Reporter*, June 1988, 9.

39. Ibid. August T. Lembo, "Judge Byrne in Morris County," e-mail to author, January 12, 2013.

40. Byrne and Pollock had first met the summer before when they both attended a continuing legal education program at Harvard Law School. On the morning of the day he submitted his resignation, Byrne had his law clerk, August Lembo, call Pollock and the other attorney in the case to ask if they wanted to have him make a decision before final arguments, or to retry the case before a new judge. Pollock and the opposing lawyer agreed to have Byrne decide the case. Stewart Pollock, interview for Rutgers-Eagleton Byrne Archive, October 25, 2010.

41. Joseph Katz, interview for Rutgers World War II Oral History Archives, November 8, 1995. Accessed December 23, 2012 at http://oralhistory.rutgers.edu/donors/30-interviewees/interview-html-text/487-katz-joseph-part-2

42. Brendan T. Byrne, interview for Rutgers-Eagleton Byrne Archive, April 4, 2006.

43. Harvey Fisher, interview for Rutgers-Eagleton Byrne Archive, September 25, 2007.

44. Fred Hillman, "Byrne quits court for governor race," *Star-Ledger*, April 25, 1973.

45. Ronald Sullivan, "Byrne Quits Court to Run for Jersey Governorship," *New York Times*, April 25, 1973.

46. Martin L. Greenberg, telephone conversation with author, April 8, 2014.

47. Joseph Carragher, "Coffee quits race and backs Byrne," *Star-Ledger*, April 27, 1973.

48. Brendan T. Byrne, interview with author, October 5, 2012; see also; Ronald Sullivan, "Crabiel Drops Out of Race, Throws Support to Byrne," *New York Times*, May 3, 1973.

49. Martin L. Greenberg, telephone conversation with author, April 8, 2014.

50. To some extent, the Coffee organization inherited the legacy of the former Mercer and State Democratic chairman Thorn Lord, who had been a major figure in the political careers of both Governors Meyner and Hughes and himself had been the 1960 Democratic nominee in an unsuccessful challenge to the incumbent U.S. Senator Clifford Case. Lord had hosted an informal group in Princeton that would be the source of Democratic policy ideas for several years, and later would become more formally organized with the founding of the nonprofit Center for Analysis of Public Issues, which published policy papers and subsequently *New Jersey Reporter* magazine.

51. Orin Kramer later would become a leading national Democratic activist and fundraiser, serving in the Carter and Clinton administrations and as one of President Obama's top fundraisers. He also was named as chair of the New Jersey Investment Council by his close friend, Governor Jon Corzine. Orin S. Kramer, interview for Rutgers-Eagleton Byrne Archive, May 16, 2006.

52. Ibid.

53. Brendan T. Byrne, interview for Rutgers-Eagleton Byrne Archive, August 7, 2006.

54. Brendan T. Byrne, interview with author, October 5, 2012.

55. Brendan T. Byrne, interview for Rutgers-Eagleton Byrne Archive, September 13, 2006.

56. Steven P. Perskie, "A Political History," February 22, 2009 (unpublished manuscript).

57. Richard C. Leone, interview for Rutgers-Eagleton Byrne Archive, April 5, 2006.

58. Ronald Sullivan, "Campaign Funds: Differing Views," *New York Times*, May 29, 1973.

59. Alan Sagner previously had been active in the effort to draft Adlai Stevenson for the 1960 Democratic presidential nomination and had chaired, at the request of Governor Hughes, the 1968 Hubert Humphrey presidential campaign in New Jersey. Within the state, he had been one of several Essex County Democrats seeking to reform the county organization then controlled by Democratic county chairman Dennis Carey. Alan Sagner, interview for Rutgers-Eagleton Byrne Archive, May 16, 2006.

60. Brendan T. Byrne, interview with Andrew Szanton.

61. Dale Mezzacappa, "Was Brendan Byrne Too Good for New Jersey," *Today: The Inquirer Magazine*, January 1982.

62. Jerry F. English, interview for Rutgers-Eagleton Byrne Archive, December 13, 2006.

63. James J. Florio, interview for Rutgers-Eagleton Byrne Archive, October 8, 2008.

64. Richard C. Leone, interview for Rutgers-Eagleton Byrne Archive, April 5, 2006; Daniel J. O'Hern, interview for Rutgers-Eagleton Byrne Archive, January 4, 2006.

65. Brendan T. Byrne, interview for Rutgers-Eagleton Byrne Archive, April 4, 2006.

66. Brendan T. Byrne, interview with author, December 16, 2013.

67. Orin S. Kramer, interview for Rutgers-Eagleton Byrne Archive, May 16, 2006.

68. Richard C. Leone, interview for Rutgers-Eagleton Byrne Archive, April 5, 2006.

69. Fariborz Fatemi, interview with author, June 22, 2012.

70. Jerry F. English, interview for Rutgers-Eagleton Byrne Archive, December 13, 2006.

71. Brendan T. Byrne, interview with author, September 28, 2012; Fariborz Fatemi, interview with author, June 22, 2012.

72. Ibid.

73. Richard Phalon, "Byrne is Man of Caution," *New York Times*, November 7, 2013.

74. Alan Sagner, interview for Rutgers-Eagleton Byrne Archive, May 16, 2006.

75. Fred Hillman, "Mrs. Klein claims she's closing the gap on Byrne," *Star-Ledger*, June 1, 1973.

76. Dan Weissman, "Dem hopefuls stage chaotic TV debate," *Star-Ledger*, June 4, 1973.

77. Brendan T. Byrne, interview for Rutgers-Eagleton Byrne Archive, April 4, 2006.

78. Joseph Carragher, "Tuesday's vote will gauge the power of the organization," *Star-Ledger*, June 3, 1973.

79. Fred Ferretti, "Byrne Learning to Doff Habits with Robes," *New York Times*, May 18, 1973; "The Jersey Primaries," *New York Times*, June 1, 1973.

80. Brendan T. Byrne, interview with author, September 28, 2012.

81. Eagleton Institute Poll No. 7, May 1973.

82. Michael Kramer, "Is Something Rotten in the State of New Jersey?" *New York Magazine*, October 15, 1973, 75.

83. Joseph Carragher, "State indicts Colsey, Mahon in plot to gain bank favors," *Star-Ledger*, April 20, 1973; Leonard Fisher, "McCrane pleads the Fifth in Cahill campaign probe," *Star-Ledger*, April 28, 1973.

84. Raymond Bateman, interview for Rutgers-Eagleton Byrne Archive, January 11, 2007.

85. Eagleton Institute Poll No. 7, May 1973.

86. "Eagleton poll indicates Cahill would beat Dems," *Star-Ledger*, June 1, 1973.

87. Fred Hillman, "Sandman landslide over Cahill; Byrne trounces Democratic foes," *Star-Ledger*, June 6, 1973; Monica Moskue, Barbara Kukla, Tex Novellino, "Dems' man of hour," *Star-Ledger*, June 6, 1973.

88. Garth had become a leading strategic consultant and innovator in television campaigning. In addition to Lindsay's 1969 mayoral reelection victory, he would later work for the campaigns of, among others, New York Mayors Ed Koch; Rudolph Giuliani; Michael Bloomberg; New York Governor. Hugh Carey; Connecticut Governor Ella Grasso; Pennsylvania Senators Arlen Specter and John Heinz; and Los Angeles Mayor Tom Bradley.

89. "Mr. NYC, David Garth," June 2, 2010 (blog post). Accessed September 12, 2012 at http://mrnyc.blogspot.com/2010/06/david-garth-new-yorks-boss.html

90. Brendan T. Byrne, interview with author, September 28, 2012.

91. Michael Kramer, "Is Something Rotten in the State of New Jersey?" *New York Magazine*, October 15, 1973, 76.

92. Ibid., 79.

93. Frank X. McDermott, interview for Rutgers-Eagleton Byrne Archive, June 20, 2006.

94. James P. Dugan, interview for Rutgers-Eagleton Byrne Archive, April 20, 2009.

95. Michael Kramer, "Is Something Rotten in the State of New Jersey?" *New York Magazine*, October 15, 1973, 75.

96. Richard Leone, interview with author, October 2, 2012.

97. Brendan T. Byrne, interview for Rutgers-Eagleton Byrne Archive, April 4, 2006.

98. Richard C. Leone, interview with author, October 2, 2012.

99. Michael Kramer, "Is Something Rotten in the State of New Jersey?" *New York Magazine*, October 15, 1973, 76.

100. Ronald Sullivan, "G.O.P. Leaders Say Sandman is Facing a Major Defeat," *New York Times*, October 28, 1973.

101. Michael Kramer, "Is Something Rotten in the State of New Jersey?" *New York Magazine*, October 15, 1973, 76.

102. Brendan T. Byrne, interview for Rutgers-Eagleton Byrne Archive, April 4, 2006.

103. Michael Kramer, "Is Something Rotten in the State of New Jersey?" *New York Magazine*, October 15, 1973, 76.

104. Richard C. Leone, interview with author, October 2, 2012.

105. Brendan T. Byrne, interview for Rutgers-Eagleton Byrne Archive, April 4, 2006.

106. "Byrne Attacks Sandman on the Income-Tax Issue; Charges Exchanged," *New York Times*, October 16, 1973.

107. Michael Kramer, "Is Something Rotten in the State of New Jersey?" *New York Magazine*, October 15, 1973, 76.

108. Frank X. McDermott, interview for Rutgers-Eagleton Byrne Archive, June 20, 2006.

109. Michael Kramer, "Is Something Rotten in the State of New Jersey?" *New York Magazine*, October 15, 1973, 76.

110. *New York Times*, October 16, 1973.

111. *Trenton Times*, October 5, 1973.

112. Albert Burstein, interview for Rutgers-Eagleton Byrne Archive, May 15, 2006.

113. Richard C. Leone, interview for Rutgers-Eagleton Byrne Archive, April 5, 2006.

114. "Byrne, Sandman in a Clash on TV," *New York Times*, November 5, 1973.

115. Michael Kramer, "Is Something Rotten in the State of New Jersey?" 76.

116. Fred Hillman, "Sandman hammers at four issues," *Star-Ledger*, June 1, 1973.

117. Walter H. Waggoner, "Byrne Attacks Sandman on the Income Tax Issue," *New York Times*, October 16, 1973.

118. Victor R. Yanitelli, letter to Brendan T. Byrne, October 10, 1973.

119. Brendan T. Byrne, interview for Rutgers-Eagleton Byrne Archive, August 13, 2007.

120. Donald Janson, "Byrne Attacked by Abortion Foes," *New York Times*, November 3, 1973.

121. Joseph F. Sullivan, "Turnout Called Key to Vote on Tuesday," *New York Times*, November 4, 1973.

122. Ibid.

123. Eagleton Institute Poll No. 8.

124. The NBC poll showed Byrne ahead by 57 percent to 24 percent; CBS reported a 66 percent to 32 percent lead. Ronald Sullivan, "Jersey Republicans Fear a Major Defeat," *New York Times*, November 4, 1973.

125. "Byrne for New Jersey," *New York Times*, October 24, 1973.

126. Richard C. Leone, interview for Rutgers-Eagleton Byrne Archive, April 5, 2006.

127. Brendan T. Byrne, interview for Rutgers-Eagleton Byrne Archive, August 28, 2006.

128. Brendan T. Byrne, interview with author, September 28, 2012; Mark Funston, Roger Harris, "Cheers, Laughter: Revelers toast stunning Byrne victory," *Star-Ledger*, November 7, 1973.

129. Fred Hillman, "Byrne Landslide," *Star-Ledger*, November 7, 1973.

130. "Election Decimates the G.O.P.'s Ranks in Trenton," *New York Times*, November 8, 1973.

131. Raymond Bateman, interview for Rutgers-Eagleton Byrne Archive, January 11, 2007.

132. Joseph F. Sullivan, "Byrne Says Vote Reflects A Lack of Confidence in Nixon," *New York Times*, November 8, 1973.

133. Ronald Sullivan, "Sandman Routed: GOP Loses Control of Legislature 3rd Time in Century," *New York Times*, November 8, 1973.

134. Brendan T. Byrne, interview with author, September 13, 2013.

CHAPTER 6

1. Brendan T. Byrne, interview with author, October 25, 2012.

2. Herb Jaffe, "Cahill nominates Hughes as the new chief justice," *Star-Ledger*, November 8, 1973.

3. Brendan T. Byrne, remarks at "New Jersey Governors and the State Supreme Court," conference co-sponsored by NJ State Bar Association and Eagleton Institute of Politics, Rutgers University, New Brunswick, NJ, May 8, 2008.

4. N.J.S.A. 5:10-1 et seq. The legislation stipulated that a major league franchise in either baseball or football had to be secured before any bond issue could be sold by the Authority. Owing to league rules protecting territorial rights in both sports, the Authority targeted the Yankees and the Giants, who were both playing in aging Yankee Stadium, as the most promising candidates to relocate to the Meadowlands.

5. McCrane's father-in-law, Eugene Mori, also had real estate holdings in Secaucus in the Meadowlands, and in 1950 had unsuccessfully sought approval to build a flat and harness racing track on his property. In 1959, he had explored building a baseball stadium for the Philadelphia Phillies adjacent to Garden State Park in Cherry Hill. Bob Ford, "Path To The Vet Led Through N.J. In The '60s, The Phils Looked To Cherry Hill," *Philadelphia Inquirer*, July 26, 1989; Ann Marie T. Cammarota, *Pavements in the Garden: the Suburbanization of Southern New Jersey*, Cranbury, NJ: Fairleigh Dickinson University Press, 2001, 167–68.

6. Werblin began his career as an agent with the Music Corporation of America in the 1930s. See Robert McG. Thomas, Jr.,"Sonny Werblin, an Impresario of New York's Sports Extravaganza, Is Dead at 81," *New York Times*, November 23, 1981; Robert H. Boyle, "Show-biz Sonny And His Quest For Stars," *Sports Illustrated*, July 19, 1965.

7. Ray Kennedy, "Miracle In The Meadows," *Sports Illustrated*, September 12, 1977. Accessed October 27, 2012 at http://sportsillustrated.cnn.com/vault/article/magazine/MAG1092823/9/index.htm

8. Ibid.

9. Herb Jaffe, "Cahill condemns N.Y. bids to kill sports complex," *Star-Ledger*, November 6, 1973.

10. Ibid.

11. Dan Weissman, "Sports Complex: Byrne to decide soon on 'moral pledge'," *Star-Ledger*, November 8, 1973.

12. Brendan T. Byrne, interview with author, October 25, 2012.

13. Brendan T. Byrne, interview for Rutgers-Eagleton Byrne Archive, October 30, 2007.

14. Richard C. Leone, interview with author, September 28, 2012.

15. Alvin S. Felzenberg, *Governor Tom Kean: From the New Jersey Statehouse to the 9-11 Commission*, New Brunswick, NJ: Rutgers University Press, 2006, 129–30.

16. Brendan T. Byrne, interview with author, September 28, 2012.

17. Brendan T. Byrne, interview with Andrew Szanton.

18. Dan Weissman, "Byrne neutrality sidelines sports complex aid," *Star-Ledger*, November 13, 1973; Ronald Sullivan, "Byrne Stand Kills Bond-Pledge Bill," *New York Times*, November 13, 1973.

19. Goldman later recounted a meeting with McCrane and officials from the Giants and the Sports Authority relating to the original site they had selected for the stadium in which he asked: "Well, how are you going to get, you know, 20,000 cars in there?" And, they said 'Oh, we're going to build a bridge like the Ponte Vecchio over the Turnpike and it will have shopping.' And, I said 'Well, I don't think you can do it, I don't think you can have that kind of traffic with one exit and I said plus you've got the deepest bedrock in the whole Meadowlands there. You know, the piling costs would be astronomical.' And, you have liquefied natural gas tank on the site which you can't get rid of because the Federal government forced them down our throats.' We had contested that. McCrane turned to me and said 'Where should it go.' And, I said 'Right there' [the eventual site]." Clifford A. Goldman, interview for Rutgers-Eagleton Byrne Archive, January 11, 2007.

20. Brendan T. Byrne, interview for Rutgers-Eagleton Byrne Archive, September 13, 2006.

21. "A Governor's Diary," *Star-Ledger*, May 1–8, 2008.

22. James R. Zazzali, telephone conversation with author, May 18, 2013.

23. Herb Jaffe, "Byrne led way to Sportsplex's great success," *Star-Ledger*, March 29, 1977.

24. "A Governor's Diary," *Star-Ledger*, May 1–8, 2008. Brendan T. Byrne, interview for Rutgers-Eagleton Byrne Archive, September 13, 2006.

25. Herb Jaffe, "Byrne led way to Sportsplex's great success," *Star-Ledger*, March 29, 1977.

26. Brendan T. Byrne, interview for Rutgers-Eagleton Byrne Archive, September 13, 2006.

27. Jeffrey Laurenti, interview for Rutgers-Eagleton Byrne Archive, December 13, 2006.

28. Ray Kennedy, "Miracle In The Meadows," *Sports Illustrated*, September 12, 1977.

29. Ronald Sullivan, "Jersey Assembly Backs Bond Issue," *New York Times*, December 5, 1973.

30. "Two Stadiums Gain, With a Study Here And Cahill's Signing," *New York Times*, December 5, 1973.

31. Ray Kennedy, "Miracle In The Meadows," *Sports Illustrated*, September 12, 1977.

32. Brendan T. Byrne, interview with author, September 28, 2012.

33. "As Stadiums Vanish, Their Debt Lives On," *New York Times*, September 7, 2010.

34. "Alfred E. Driscoll Expressway," Eastern Roads. Accessed January 12, 2013 at http://www.nycroads.com/roads/ae-driscoll/

35. Walter H. Waggoner, "Turnpike Agency Contesting Byrne," *New York Times*, December 19, 1973.

36. "Turnpike Lets Driscoll Contract," *New York Times*, November 22, 1973.

37. Ronald Sullivan, "Byrne's Opposition Blocks Jersey Turnpike Extension," *New York Times*, December 17, 1973.

38. Walter H. Waggoner, "Byrne Says Plans to Add to Turnpike are Being Postponed," *New York Times*, December 28, 1973; Ronald Sullivan, "Byrne's Opposition Blocks Jersey Turnpike Extension," *New York Times*, December 17, 1973.

39. Ronald Sullivan, "Driscoll's Status on Panel in Doubt," *New York Times*, February 3, 1975.

40. Ronald Sullivan, "Funeral for Driscoll Held; Byrne Absent at Request," *New York Times*, March 13, 1975.

41. Brendan T. Byrne, interview with author, September 28, 2012.

42. "Alfred E. Driscoll Expressway," NYCRoads.com. Accessed December 4, 2012 at http://www.nycroads.com/roads/ae-driscoll/

43. "Highlights from Interview with Byrne," *New York Times*, December 31, 1973; Brendan T. Byrne, interview for Rutgers-Eagleton Byrne Archive, August 7, 2006.

44. Lewis B. Kaden, interview for Rutgers-Eagleton Byrne Archive, September 27, 2010.

45. Brendan T. Byrne, interview for Rutgers-Eagleton Byrne Archive, August 7, 2006.

46. Kaden would take and pass the New Jersey bar exam during Byrne's first year in office.

47. Lewis B. Kaden, interview for Rutgers-Eagleton Byrne Archive, September 27, 2010.

48. Brendan T. Byrne, interview for Rutgers-Eagleton Byrne Archive, August 7, 2006.

49. Ronald Sullivan, "Byrne's Advisers Credited with Ambitious Programs," *New York Times*, October 14, 1974.

50. Brendan T. Byrne, interview with author, October 28, 2012.

51. An editorial published by the *Trenton Times* in the fall of 1976 urging Byrne not to seek reelection ("The Governor Should Say it: 'I Choose Not to Run'") would provoke a letter to the editor from Mrs. Jean Byrne challenging the editorial and defending her husband's record in office. See p. 200.

52. Brendan T. Byrne, interview with author, October 25, 2012.

53. Harold Hodes, interview for Rutgers-Eagleton Byrne Archive, August 28, 2006.

54. Brendan T. Byrne, interview for Rutgers-Eagleton Byrne Archive, August 7, 2006.

55. Cabinet-level holdovers from the Cahill administration included Phillip Alampi, the secretary of agriculture, whose nomination by the State Board of Agriculture was subject to the governor's approval, and Ralph Dungan, the chancellor of the Department of Higher Education, whose appointment to a five-year term was made by the Board of Higher Education with the governor's approval. A Democrat and former aide to President Kennedy, Dungan had originally been appointed during the Hughes administration when the Department was created.

56. Ronald Sullivan, "Crabiel Chosen by Byrne to be Secretary of State," *New York Times*, December 5, 1973.

57. Lewis B. Kaden, interview for Rutgers-Eagleton Byrne Archive, September 27, 2010.

58. Ronald Sullivan, "Byrne Displays His Pre-Inauguration Power," *New York Times*, December 4, 1973.

59. John B. Wefing, *The Life and Times of Richard J. Hughes: The Politics of Civility*, New Brunswick, NJ: Rivergate Books/Rutgers University Press, 2009, 48; Ronald Sullivan, "Byrne's Advisers Credited with Ambitious Programs," *New York Times*, October 14, 1974. Hyland became a close friend of bandleader Benny Goodman after he filled in as a clarinetist at one of Goodman's New Jersey performances, and was named coexecutor of Goodman's estate upon his death in 1986.

60. Richard C. Leone, telephone conversation with author, May 2, 2013.

61. Brendan T. Byrne, interview with author, September 28, 2012.

62. Alan Sagner, interview for Rutgers-Eagleton Byrne Archive, May 16, 2006.

63. Timothy Carden, interview for Rutgers-Eagleton Byrne Archive, Rutgers University, October 30, 2007.

64. Lewis B. Kaden, interview for Rutgers-Eagleton Byrne Archive, September 27, 2010.

65. Brendan T. Byrne, interview for Rutgers-Eagleton Byrne Archive, August 7, 2006.

66. Ronald Sullivan, "Byrne Appoints Insurance and Labor-Industry Chiefs," *New York Times*, January 11, 1974.

67. An author gives this account of Sheeran's meeting with Jack Byrne (no relation to BTB), the chief executive of GEICO Insurance, on the company's rate increase request: "'I [Byrne] did all the arm-twisting I could, and Sheeran was intractable' Byrne pulled the license out of his pocket and threw it on Sheeran's desk. 'I have no choice but to turn in this license', or something to that effect but containing more four-letter words. He then drove back to the office with tires screeching, sent out telegrams to thirty thousand policyholders canceling their insurance and fired two thousand New Jersey employees in a single afternoon, before Sheeran could go to court to stop him." Alice Schroeder, *The Snowball: Warren Buffett and the Business of Life*, New York: Random House Digital, 2008, 436.

68. Brendan T. Byrne, interview with author, October 12, 2012.

69. Fred Ferretti, "Cahill's Record on Environment Is a Source of Pride and a Target," *New York Times*, June 2, 1973; Walter H. Waggoner, "Sullivan Reviews Record in Office," *New York Times*, January 23, 1974.

70. Dan Weissman, "Sullivan quits state environment post," *Star-Ledger*, January 19, 1974.

71. Betty Wilson, interview for Rutgers-Eagleton Byrne Archive, June 28, 2007.

72. See Chapter 12.

73. Brendan T. Byrne, interview for Rutgers-Eagleton Byrne Archive, August 7, 2006.

74. Richard C. Leone, interview with author, May 2, 2013.

75. Brendan T. Byrne, interview for Rutgers-Eagleton Byrne Archive, August 7, 2006.

76. Wally Edge, "How the Secretary of Agriculture gets his job," PolitickerNJ. com, December 2, 2008. Accessed January 12, 2012 at http://www.politickernj.com/wallye/25827/how-secretary-agriculture-gets-his-job#ixzz2m8z8SLSV

77. Ibid.

78. Donald H. Janson, "Jersey to Test a Program to Preserve Agriculture and Open Space in State Agriculture," *New York Times*, August 23, 2013. The pilot project to purchase development rights was followed by legislation enacted in the Kean Administration, the Farmland Retention and Development Act of 1983, L.1983, c. 32.

79. Brendan T. Byrne, interview for Rutgers-Eagleton Byrne Archive, August 7, 2006.

80. Brendan T. Byrne, interview with author, October 12, 2012; David Ramirez, "David B. Kelly, 79; Led New Jersey State Police," *New York Times*, September 25, 1997; "Byrne Nominates Capt. Pagano as Superintendent of State Police," *New York Times*, October 10, 1974.

81. Edward J. Mullin (ed.), *New Jersey Legislative Manual*, Edward J. Mullin: Trenton, NJ, 1974.

82. Richard C. Leone, interview for Rutgers-Eagleton Byrne Archive, April 5, 2006.

83. Ibid.

84. See p. 135.

85. Brendan T. Byrne, interview with author, October 4, 2012. Lew Kaden, who would become Byrne's counsel and accompanied Byrne to the session with Rockefeller, recalled that the meeting in Manhattan was held "in his personal townhouse which he used as the New York office and he had all these extraordinarily capable and well-known figures come in one at a time to brief Governor Byrne, the new governor elect, about transportation and law enforcement and education, and so it was quite impressive." Lewis B. Kaden, interview for Rutgers-Eagleton Byrne Archive, September 27, 2010.

86. At the beginning of the 1974 legislative session, the Senate had twenty-nine Democrats; nineteen Republicans; and one Independent; and the General Assembly had sixty-six Democrats and fourteen Republicans.

87. "Jersey Democrats Elect Leaders," *New York Times*, December 10, 1973.

88. See Wally Edge, "Part One: The Democrats who will decide Lonegan's fate," PolitickerNJ.com, March 5, 2009. Accessed January 12, 2012 at http://www.politickernj.com/wallye/27892/part-one-democrats-who-will-decide-lonegans-fate#ixzz2m9BpW1fq

89. Brendan T. Byrne, interview with author, September 12, 2013.

CHAPTER 7

1. Brendan T. Byrne, interview for Rutgers-Eagleton Byrne Archive, October 30, 2007.

2. The governor under the 1776 Constitution was given few duties to perform other than heading the militia and serving as president of the Legislative Council. NJ Constitution of 1776. Accessed January 12, 2013 at http://www.state.nj.us/njfacts/njdoc10a.htm

3. NJ Constitution of 1947, Article V. Accessed January 12, 2013 at http://www.njleg.state.nj.us/lawsconstitution/constitution.asp

4. See Richard J. Hughes, "Foreword," in Robert F. Williams (ed.), *The New Jersey State Constitution: A Reference Guide*, New Brunswick, NJ: Rutgers University Press, 1997, xvi; see also John E. Bebout and Joseph Harrison, "The Working of the New Jersey Constitution of 1947," *William & Mary Law Review* 337 (1968), 10.

5. See, e.g., Barbara G. Salmore and Stephen A. Salmore, *New Jersey Politics and Government: Suburban Politics Comes of Age*, Lincoln, NE: University of Nebraska Press, 1998, 45–47.

6. Brendan T. Byrne, interview with author, November 6, 2013.

7. *Trenton Times*, January 15, 1974.

8. Brendan T. Byrne, interview with author, October 4, 2012.

9. One seating issue arose when Maria Jeritza, a former featured performer at the Metropolitan Opera, Vienna State Opera and other leading opera companies, complained that the location of her assigned seat did not sufficiently indicate her prominence, declaring "I sit only behind kings!" Jeritza had become a close friend of both Brendan and Jean Byrne after a chance meeting with Byrne during his campaign, later becoming an active supporter of his candidacy and introducing him to

prominent figures she knew in Manhattan, including Cardinal Terence James Cooke, the Archbishop of New York. Brendan T. Byrne, interview with author, November 6, 2013.

10. Brendan T. Byrne, interview with author, October 4, 2012.

11. L.1974, c. 26, s. 2, eff. May 6, 1974.

12. Brendan T. Byrne, Inaugural Address, January 14, 1974.

13. Executive Order No. 1, February 5, 1974. Accessed March 12, 2011 at http:// njlegallib.rutgers.edu/eo/docs/byrne/order001-/index.pdf. Richard DeKorte, Cahill's outgoing counsel, also agreed to head a new energy office for Byrne created by the executive order.

14. Brendan T. Byrne, interview with author, October 4, 2012.

15. Rutgers Eagleton Poll No. 10, March–April 1974.

16. James J. Hughes and Joseph Seneca, "This Then and Now: Sixty Years of Economic Change in New Jersey," Rutgers Regional Report, January 2004, Edward J. Bloustein School of Planning and Public Policy, Rutgers University. Accessed January 10, 2013 at http://policy.rutgers.edu/reports/rrr/rrrjan04.pdf

17. The share of total state employment represented by manufacturing had already fallen from 55 percent in 1943 to 33 percent by 1970. U.S. Bureau of Labor Statistics; New Jersey Department of Labor and Workforce Development.

18. Lewis B. Kaden, interview for Rutgers-Eagleton Byrne Archive, Rutgers University, September 27, 2010.

19. Brendan T. Byrne, interview with author, September 9, 2013.

20. L. 1975, c. 231; N.J.S.A. 10:4–6, et seq.

21. Executive Order No. 15, January 7, 1975. Accessed October 12, 2012 at http:// njlegallib.rutgers.edu/eo/docs/byrne/order015-/index.pdf

22. Ibid.

23. The name Morven is "big mountain" in Gaelic from a poem describing a mythical Gaelic kingdom. For the history of Morven, see generally Alfred Hoyt Bill, *A House Called Morven*, Princeton: Princeton University Press, 1978.

24. In August 1776, after New Jersey had declared its independence, Stockton and William Livingston tied in the initial vote by the new legislature to elect the first state governor; on the second vote, Livingston was elected by single vote over Stockton. Bill, *A House Called Morven*, 38.

25. Brendan T. Byrne, interview with author, October 4, 2012.

26. Jean Featherly Byrne, interview for Rutgers-Eagleton Byrne Archive, Rutgers University, January 30, 2013.

27. Brendan T. Byrne, interview with author, October 5, 2012.

28. Michael Fedorko, interview with author, September 7, 2013.

29. Joan Cook, "Small Touches at Morven Change Mansion into Home for Byrnes," *New York Times*, March 20, 1974.

30. Ibid.

31. Brendan T. Byrne, interview with author, September 9, 2013.

32. "Good neighbor Brendan," *Star-Ledger*, May 16, 2001.

33. Joan Cook, "Small Touches at Morven Change Mansion into Home for Byrnes," *New York Times*, March 20, 1974.

34. Brendan T. Byrne, interview for Rutgers-Eagleton Byrne Archive, January 25, 2011.

35. Brendan T. Byrne, interview with author, October 4, 2012.

36. Ibid.

37. Ibid.

38. Ibid.

39. Like the federal legislation funding presidential elections enacted the year before in response to the Watergate scandal, the state plan for financing gubernatorial campaigns gave money directly to candidate committees rather than party organizations. N.J.S.A. 19:44A-1 et seq.

40. Salmore et al., *New Jersey Politics and Government: The Suburbs Come of Age*, 49; see also Ronald Sullivan, "Campaign Controls Voted in Jersey and Connecticut," *New York Times*, April 25, 1974.

41. Kanige, "Brendan Byrne on Brendan Byrne," *New Jersey Reporter*, 10.

42. Ralph Nader, "Government Under Glass," *The Public Interest*, August 5, 1974. Accessed September 4, 2012 at http://nader.org/1974/08/05/government-under-glass/

43. Brendan T. Byrne, interview with author, October 4, 2012.

44. Kanige, "Brendan Byrne on Brendan Byrne," *New Jersey Reporter*, 10.

45. Recollection of the author.

46. Dennis Hevesi, "Stanley Van Ness, State Public Advocate, Dies at 73," *New York Times*, September 27, 2007.

47. Assembly Bill 1875 proposed to impose an income tax at the rate of 1.5 percent to 8 percent on taxable income. See generally Richard Van Wagner, "The New Jersey Gross Income Tax: An Analysis from Background to Enactment," *Seton Hall Legislative Journal*, 2 (Summer 1977), 100.

48. In 1974, the Senate had twenty-nine Democrats, ten Republicans and one Independent. The Assembly had sixty-six Democrats and fourteen Republicans.

49. Joseph F. Sullivan, "Jersey Secretary of State Indicted for Bid-Rigging," *New York Times*, August 1, 1974.

50. After the charges against Crabiel were dismissed in April 1975, he returned to the cabinet, with Byrne quoted, "Ed Crabiel has been through a tremendous ordeal, and has a right to return to fill out his term as he has expressed his intention of doing." Walter H. Waggoner, "Crabiel Cleared on All Counts; Plans Return to Byrne Cabinet," *New York Times*, April 24, 1975. Reflecting years later on the Crabiel prosecution, Byrne said that he was concerned that the indictment was brought when there were serious questions surrounding the case: "when I was a prosecutor, I wouldn't have indicted someone in that situation without being sure I could get a conviction." Brendan T. Byrne, interview with author, September 9, 2013. To a degree, Byrne and Crabiel repaired their relationship after Crabiel returned to the cabinet; when Crabiel announced his resignation as secretary of state in March 1977, the month before Byrne announced he would seek reelection, Byrne praised Crabiel as a "valued counselor." *New York Times*, February 2, 1977.

51. Brendan T. Byrne, interview with author, September 9, 2013. After rejecting Byrne's demand that he resign, Crabiel took a leave of absence to fight the charges against him.

52. The Tocks Island project had been proposed by the Army Corps of Engineers to dam the Delaware River to create a 37-mile-long lake with a surrounding 60,000-acre recreation area to be administered by the National Park Service. Congressman Frank Thompson, whose district included Trenton and other affected municipalities, led efforts which resulted in Congressional approval in 1962 for construction of the dam, along with a companion plan authorized in 1965 to acquire land for the recreation area. Richard C. Albert, *Damming the Delaware*, 149–51. See also Ronald Sullivan, "Byrne Says He Opposes Tocks Construction Now; Construction Blocked Earlier," *New York Times*, June 30, 1974. In the next year, at a meeting of the governors of the four-state Delaware River Basin Commission on July 31, 1975, Byrne voted against building the dam, joining New York and Delaware in outvoting Pennsylvania, which under Governor Milton Shapp had strongly argued for the dam's water supply and flood control benefits. Recognizing that without the dam, the state needed to expand its water supply capacity, the Governor later directed the state DEP to develop a long-term water supply plan that ultimately led to construction of several smaller reservoirs and pipelines throughout the State. Donald Janson, "3 Governors Vote to Kill Tocks Dam," *New York Times*, August 31, 1975.

53. Ibid.; Matt Friedman, "Organizers: Weekend rally against N.J. Gov. Chris Christie's budget cuts could draw 30K," NorthJersey.com, May 21, 2010. Accessed January 12, 2013 at http://www.northjersey.com/news/NJ_rally_against_Gov_Chris_Christies_budget_cuts_could_draw_30K_organizers_say.html?c=y&page=2

54. Brendan T. Byrne, interview with author, August 14, 2013.

55. Ibid. Marciante also had led the AFL-CIO's opposition to Governor Cahill's proposal in 1972 of an income tax and statewide property tax. "Cahill Sees His Tax Reform Program Doomed Unless Labor Reverses Its Course," *New York Times*, June 2, 1972.

56. Ronald Sullivan, "Deep Trouble for Byrne," *New York Times*, August 2, 1974.

57. Eagleton Poll No. 13, November 1974; Eagleton Poll No. 11, May 1974.

58. Lewis B. Kaden, interview for Rutgers-Eagleton Byrne Archive, Rutgers University, September 27, 2010.

59. Ken Auletta, "It Has All Been Downhill for Brendan Byrne of New Jersey," *New York Times*, June 8, 1975.

60. Ibid.

61. Ibid.

62. James Florio, interview for Rutgers-Eagleton Byrne Archive, October 8, 2008 (video).

63. Brendan T. Byrne, interview with author, September 3, 2013.

64. "Dugan Wins Byrne's Vote," *New York Times*, July 20, 1975.

65. Thomas H. Kean, interview with author, October 1, 2013.

66. Allan F. Yoder, "Jersey's $64 question: When will the governor govern?," *The Record*, November 24, 1974.

67. L.1974, c.80 (N.J.S.A. 34:1B-4). Byrne's key advisers, notably Dick Leone, Cliff Goldman, and Robert Powell, each of whom held doctorates from the Woodrow Wilson School at Princeton, developed the idea, and Powell was appointed by Byrne as the Authority's first executive director.

68. Carl E. Van Horn, "Economic Development Policy," in Gerald M. Pomper (ed.), *The Political State of New Jersey,* New Brunswick, NJ: Rutgers University Press, 1986, 228–32.

69. Brendan T. Byrne, interview with author, October 4, 2012.

70. Executive Order No. 37, April 9, 1976. Accessed November 3, 2012 at http://njlegallib.rutgers.edu/eo/docs/byrne/order037-/index.pdf

71. Ray Kennedy, "Miracle In The Meadows," *Sports Illustrated*, September 12, 1977. Accessed October 27, 2012 at http://sportsillustrated.cnn.com/vault/article/magazine/MAG1092823/9/index.htm

72. Kanige, "Brendan Byrne on Brendan Byrne," *New Jersey Reporter*, 13.

73. Brendan T. Byrne, interview with author, October 5, 2012. The MacNaughton Commission was officially the "Governor's Commission to Evaluate the Capital Needs of New Jersey."

74. "Panel Urges a Five-Year Plan of Capital Investment," *New York Times*, April 25, 1975. Gerald Miller (ed.), *Handbook of Debt Management.* London: CRC Press, 1996, 238.

75. Brendan T. Byrne, interview with author, September 9, 2013.

76. Byrne once quipped: "When I made a campaign speech at a sewage facility, I started off by saying, 'This is the first time I've been able to campaign on my opponent's platform.'" Brendan T. Byrne, interview with author, October 4, 2012.

77. Brendan T. Byrne, interview for Rutgers-Eagleton Byrne Archive, August 14, 2007.

78. NJAC 7:1C-1.1 et seq.

79. Van Horn, "Economic Development Policy," in Pomper (ed.), *The Political State of New Jersey*, 234.

80. Executive Order No. 43, September 27, 1976. Accessed October 10, 2012 at http://njlegallib.rutgers.edu/eo/docs/byrne/order043-/index.pdf

81. N.J.S.A. 40A:3-1 et seq.

82. The internationally known architect I. M. Pei, retained by J&J to design its headquarters, described the completion of Route 18 as "vital to the future of New Brunswick." Quoted in Eric Schkrutz, "Urban Development in the City of the Traveler: The Story of New Brunswick and Why It May Never Resolve Its Identity Crisis" (honors thesis submitted to the Department of History, Rutgers University), April 2011. Accessed October 12, 2012 at http://history.rutgers.edu/component/docman/cat_view/82-undergraduate/108-honors-papers-2011?start=20

83. Brendan T. Byrne, interview with author, September 9, 2013.

84. Walter H. Waggoner, "2 Long-Disputed Projects to Begin," *New York Times*, July 9, 1977.

85. Joseph Hoffman, the commissioner of Labor & Industry, declared that the proposed route "is vital to the economic revitalization of the New Brunswick area and, in the last analysis, is essential to the economic development of our state." See also Eric Schkrutz, "Urban Development in the City of the Traveler: The Story of New Brunswick and Why It May Never Resolve Its Identity Crisis" (honors thesis submitted to the Department of History, Rutgers University), April

2011. Accessed October 12, 2012 at http://history.rutgers.edu/component/docman/ cat_view/82-undergraduate/108-honors-papers-2011?start=20

86. Bardin aggressively took charge of commissioning a prominent architectural firm to draft a master plan, and then designated Jerome "Jerry" McCabe, a highly-decorated World War II combat pilot, to oversee the reclamation and cleanup of the waterfront, the construction of a walkway and other visitor amenities, and the renovation of the badly deteriorated terminal building. See "Oral History Interview with Jerome J. McCabe," December 21, 2001, World War II oral history interview, New Jersey Department of Military and Veterans Affairs. Accessed May 3, 2012 at http://www.state.nj.us/military/museum/mccabe.html

87. See "History of Liberty State Park," Liberty State Park. Accessed May 3, 2012 at http://www.libertystatepark.com/history.htm

88. Brendan T. Byrne, interview with author, August 14, 2013.

89. On January 7, 1975, addressing a conference in Princeton attended by representatives of fifteen states, Byrne called for consideration of the states forming their own consortium to compete against major energy companies for the leases to be auctioned off by the US Department of the Interior. "What is good for big oil," he was quoted as saying during his remarks, "is not necessarily good for the people of the United States," *New York Times*, January 8, 1975.

90. Brendan T. Byrne, interview with author, August 14, 2013.

91. Brendan T. Byrne, interview with author, September 9, 2013.

92. Spill Compensation and Control Act, N.J.S.A. 58:10–23.11.

93. The Comprehensive Environmental Response, Compensation, and Liability Act (CERCLA), 42 USC 9601.

94. Thomas Belton, *Protecting New Jersey's Environment: From Cancer Alley to the New Garden State*, New Brunswick, NJ: Rutgers University Press, 2010, 7–9.

95. "Cancer Alley no more? Incidence declining in most of New Jersey," Heartbeats, MyCentralJersey.com April 12, 2010. Accessed October 10, 2012 at http://blogs.mycentraljersey.com/heartbeats/2010/04/12/cancer-alley-no-more-incidence-declining-in-most-of-new-jersey/

96. Local environmental issues included pollution of the Raritan River by the Kin-Buc landfill in Edison in Middlesex County; asbestos exposure to students in school buildings leading to the closing of schools in Howell Township in Monmouth County; and the contamination of drinking water in wells and the Toms River in Ocean County by discharges from the dye and chemical plant operated by the Ciba-Geigy Corp. See, e.g., "State Orders Edison Landfill Shut," *New York Times*, June 28, 1977. After testing of asbestos exposure in Howell Township, Byrne notified all 607 school districts to ask that they remove asbestos from all of the state's 2,500 public schools. Martin Waldron, "State Tells All Schools to Remove Asbestos Fibers as a Health Step," *New York Times*, January 7, 1977.

97. New Jersey Worker and Community Right to Know Act, N.J.S.A.34:5A et seq.; Environmental Rights Act, L. 1974, c. 169; N.J.S.A. 2A:35A et seq.

98. During Byrne's first year in office, the cozy relationship between state regulators and the hospitals was attacked in a policy paper, written by Robert Powell, who would

join the administration as the head of the newly established EDA, and published by a think tank closely associated with some of Byrne's key advisers, including his campaign manager and State Treasurer Richard Leone. See generally Siegel, Bruce, M.D., Anne Weiss, Jane Lynch, "Setting New Jersey Hospital Rates: A Regulatory System Under Stress", *University of Puget Sound Law Review*, vol. 14:601 (1991). Accessed March 3, 2011 at http://lawpublications.seattleu.edu/cgi/viewcontent.cgi?article=1333 &context=sulr&sei-redir=1#search=%22nj%20rate%20setting%20hospital%22

99. Ibid.

100. Brendan T. Byrne, interview with author, August 14, 2013.

101. Ibid.

102. *In Re Quinlan*, 70 N.J.10, 355 (1976). In his closing argument at the trial, Hyland noted that the case, which had attracted wide public attention, "has greater potential for affecting the lives of people on into the future than almost anything else that could be happening." Quoted in Michael S. Lief and H. Mitchell Caldwell (eds.), *And the Walls Came Tumbling Down: Greatest Closing Arguments Protecting*, Civil Liberties, New York: Simon and Schuster, 2006, 29. Quinlan was taken off a respirator in 1976, but contrary to the expectations of her physicians, lived for ten more years. In January 1977, the state announced guidelines to implement the *Quinlan* decision by providing for hospitals to create committees to review requests for ending life-support. Alfonso A. Narvaez, "Jersey Adopts Plan on Patients in Coma," *New York Times*, January 26, 1977.

103. Dylan later performed at Trenton State Prison where Carter was held, as well as at later benefit concerts for the Carter defense fund.

104. Brendan T. Byrne, interview with author. August 14, 2013; Eldridge Hawkins, "The Rubin 'Hurricane' Carter and John Artis Investigation." GraphicWitness.com. Accessed July 2, 2011 at http://www.graphicwitness.com/carter/hawkins/pages/Hawkins_01.htm

105. *State v. Carter*, 69 N.J. 420 (1976). At their second trial in 1976, both Carter and Artis were again convicted. Artis was paroled from prison in 1981, and Carter was released in 1985 after a federal court granted his habeas corpus petition on the ground that the evidence suppressed by the prosecution was a significant factor contributing to his conviction. *Carter v. Rafferty*, 826 F.2d 1299 (3rd Cir. 1987), cert. denied 484 U.S. 1011 (1988); Selwyn Raab, "Jersey Ends Move to Retry Rubin Carter," *New York Times*, February 20, 1988.

106. Brendan T. Byrne, interview with author, October 5, 2012.

107. Robert E. Mulcahy, III, interview for Rutgers-Eagleton Byrne Archive, September 13, 2006.

108. Brendan T. Byrne, interview with author, September 3, 2013.

109. Robert E. Mulcahy, III, interview for Rutgers-Eagleton Byrne Archive, September 13, 2006.

110. For a few months prior to his appointment as corrections commissioner, Mulcahy also had worked closely with Byrne and his staff in implementing a federally funded program for capital projects and infrastructure. Ibid.

111. Ibid.

112. Brendan T. Byrne, interview with author, October 5, 2012.

CHAPTER 8

1. Paul A. Stellhorn, "Harold Hoffman," in Michael J. Birkner, Donald Linky, and Peter Mickulas (eds.), *The Governors of New Jersey: Biographical Essays,* New Brunswick, NJ: Rutgers University Press, 2014, 268.

2. Brendan T. Byrne, interview with author, October 3, 2012.

3. Summary Report of New Jersey Tax Policy Committee. The proposed income tax had rates graduated from 1.5 to 14 percent and a statewide property tax of $1 per $100 of assessed valuation. Accessed October 12, 2012 at http://www.state.nj.us/dca/affiliates/luarcc/meetings/2008/05-29-2008cahill_commissumry.pdf; see also Richard J Connors, "William Thomas Cahill," in Michael J. Birkner, Donald Linky, and Peter Mickulas, (eds.), *The Governors of New Jersey: Biographical Essays 1664–1974,* East Brunswick, NJ: Rutgers University Press, 2014, 300.

4. Ronald Sullivan, "Jersey Assembly Rejects Proposal for an Income Tax," *New York Times,* July 18, 1972.

5. *Robinson v. Cahill,* 62 N.J. 473 (1973). The "T&E" language was first included in an amendment approved in 1875 to the then state constitution of 1844 and was subsequently incorporated without significant change in the 1947 constitution. The language in the current constitution of 1947 reads: "The Legislature shall provide for the maintenance and support of a thorough and efficient system of free public schools for the instruction of all the children in the State between the ages of five and eighteen years." Article VIII, section IV, paragraph 1.

6. The California Supreme Court issued the most prominent decision accepting the equal protection argument in *Serrano v. Priest,* 5 Cal.3d 584 (1971). At the oral argument in January 1973 of the appeal of Judge Botter's decision in *Robinson,* Weintraub and other justices had expressed reservations over the use of the equal protection clause in a challenge to financing public education. But less than two weeks before the *Robinson* decision was released, the United States Supreme Court, in a 5 to 4 decision in *San Antonio Independent School District v. Rodriguez,* 411 U.S. 1 (1973), rejected a challenge based on equal protection to the Texas school financing system based on widely varying revenues derived from local property taxes.

7. Paul L Tractenberg, "Robinson v. Cahill: The 'Thorough and Efficient' Clause," *Law and Contemporary Problems* 38 (Winter 1974), 312–32. In 1966, the State Aid to School Districts Study Commission was established and after nearly two years of work, issued a report in late 1968, which became the basis for the Bateman-Tanzman Act adopted in October 1970. The Bateman Report observed that "Basic in any State support plan is the concept that education is a State and not a local responsibility. . . . This means that the State has a responsibility not only to provide financial assistance to the local district but also to delineate the broad terms of operation of the local district, both financially and educationally." *Robinson v. Cahill,* 62 N.J. at 519.

8. The Court retained jurisdiction so that "[a]ny party may move for appropriate relief before or after December 31, 1974, if new circumstances so warrant." 63 N.J. at 196 (1973).

9. Richard Lehne, *The Quest for Justice: the Politics of School Finance Reform*, New York: Longman, 1978, 159.

10. The New Jersey Education Association, primarily representing teachers, and the New Jersey School Boards Association, the statutorily created organization representing local school boards, both saw Robinson as a vehicle for directing more state resources to education—a mutually shared goal. Other organizations, such as the League of Women Voters and the National Association for the Advancement of Colored People, endorsed the decision for its promotion of tax reform and expanded educational opportunity. Business groups also were generally supportive, viewing education reform as insuring the quality of their future workforce, and tax reform as potentially easing the burden that private employers had borne under the prevailing system of heavy reliance on property taxes and special business levies. See generally Lehne, *The Quest for Justice,* 82–83.

11. Ibid., 85.

12. "Byrne Attacks Sandman On the Income-Tax Issue; Charges Exchanged," *New York Times*, October 16, 1973.

13. *Trenton Times*, October 5, 1973.

14. Robert Schwanenberg, "Property tax task forces: long history, few results," *Star-Ledger*, May 9, 2004. Accessed January 23, 2013 at http://www.nj.com/news/stories/0509proptx.html

15. Brendan T. Byrne, interview with author, August 16, 2013.

16. Clifford Goldman, e-mail to author, April 1, 2013.

17. Ronald Sullivan, "Cahill Restates Income Tax Plea," *New York Times*, January 9, 1974.

18. Brendan T. Byrne, First Inaugural Address, January 14, 1974.

19. See Tractenberg, 317.

20. Albert Burstein Memoir, 47.

21. Richard C. Leone, "The Politics of Gubernatorial Leadership: Tax and Education Reform in New Jersey," Ph.D. dissertation, Princeton University, 1969.

22. Clifford A. Goldman, interview for Rutgers-Eagleton Byrne Archive, January 11, 2007.

23. Brendan T. Byrne, interview with author, January 23, 2013.

24. Clifford A. Goldman, e-mail to author, March 25, 2013.

25. Steven P. Perskie, "A Political History," February 22, 2009 (unpublished manuscript).

26. John J. Degnan, telephone conversation with author, January 22, 2014.

27. Jeffrey Laurenti, e-mail to author, May 12, 2013.

28. The proposal for a statewide property tax was developed primarily with the backing of Democratic legislators from shore districts in Monmouth and Ocean counties, including Senators Eugene Bedell and John Russo and Assemblymen Richard Van Wagner and Daniel Newman. See Richard Van Wagner, "The New Jersey Gross Income Tax: An Analysis from Background to Enactment," *Seton Hall Legislative Journal* 100 (Summer 1977), 115–17.

29. See Deborah Yaffe, *Other People's Children: The Battle for Justice and Equality in New Jersey's Schools*, New Brunswick, NJ: Rutgers University Press, 2007.

30. Richard Leone, telephone conversation with author, October 3, 2013; see also Carl Zeitz, "Leone says two issues point to an income tax," *Star-Ledger*, April 1, 1974.

31. Brendan T. Byrne, interview with author, October 12, 2012.

32. Lewis B. Kaden, interview for Rutgers-Eagleton Byrne Archive, September 27, 2010.

33. "Byrne Administration Task Force, Proposed Education Reform—Property Tax Relief Program," Part II, May 1974, 2. Quoted in Lehne, *The Quest for Justice*, 115.

34. Of the new revenue, $550 million in state school aid was to be used to replace local property tax revenues; $200 million was allocated for homestead property tax rebates; $200 million was designated for the state to assume certain judicial and social services costs then being borne by local governments; and $300 million supported state budget items that could not be funded through existing state revenue sources. The personal income tax was proposed to have rates graduated from 1.8 percent on federal taxable incomes below $1,000 to an 8 percent rate on incomes above $25,000, with a minimum tax of 3 percent on incomes over $50,000 (in order to capture revenue from those with high levels of deductions under the federal tax code). Lehne, *The Quest for Justice*, 114–15.

35. Fred Hillman, "Byrne hands legislators 'must' tax reform plan," *Star-Ledger*, June 14, 1974; Linda Lamendola, "A chilly reception in the chamber," *Star-Ledger*, June 14, 1974.

36. Ronald Sullivan, "Byrne Tax Proposal Appears in Trouble; G.O.P. is Opposed," *New York Times*, June 14, 1974.

37. In June, State Senator Eugene Bedell and Assemblyman Richard Van Wagner from Monmouth County introduced legislation for a statewide property tax, with rates higher for commercial property than for residences, with the state assuming the full cost of operating public schools by replacing the existing portion of local school taxes without resort to an income tax. A somewhat similar plan was introduced by the Ocean County Democratic delegation of Senator John Russo and Assemblymen John Paul Doyle and Daniel Newman, but with even higher property tax rates for commercial properties, as well as increases in the existing corporation income and business personal property taxes. Still another proposal came from Jersey City Mayor Paul Jordan, who recommended combining a state income tax with a statewide property tax. Treasurer Leone criticized the statewide property tax proposal as requiring "a relentless succession of yearly rate increases" to keep pace with increasing costs and inflation. John McLaughlin, "Dodd Stalls Byrne Tax Bill," *New York Daily News*, June 25, 1974.

38. Leone's two quotes are, respectively, both from articles by Ronald Sullivan, "Foes of Byrne's Proposal Put Forth an Alternative," *New York Times*, June 19, 1974, and "Legislators Get Rival Tax Plans," *New York Times*, June 16, 1974.

39. Brendan T. Byrne, interview with author, October 12, 2012.

40. Ibid.

41. Lewis B. Kaden, interview for Rutgers-Eagleton Byrne Archive, September 27, 2010.

42. Brendan T. Byrne, interview for Rutgers-Eagleton Byrne Archive, October 30, 2007.

43. Betty Wilson, interview for Rutgers-Eagleton Byrne Archive, Rutgers University, June 28, 2007.

44. Walter Waggoner, "State Aide Assails Property Tax Plans," *New York Times*, June 25, 1974; John McLaughlin, "Dodd Stalls Byrne Tax Bill," *New York Daily News*, June 25, 1974.

45. Vincent Zarate, "One Thing Perfectly Clear in Passage of Income Tax," *Somerset Gazette*, July 18, 1974.

46. Raymond Garramone, mimeographed statement quoted in Lehne, *The Quest for Justice*, 120. Garramone gave up his seat to challenge Byrne in the 1977 Democratic primary, finishing sixth in a field of eleven candidates with 6,602 votes, 1.1 percent of the total vote.

47. Brendan T. Byrne, interview with author, January 23, 2013.

48. Jeffrey Laurenti, e-mail to author, May 12, 2013.

49. James P. Dugan, telephone conversation with author, April 7, 2014.

50. Lehne, *The Quest for Justice*, 122.

51. Byrne did speak to Anthony Imperiale, the controversial senator who was elected in 1973 as an independent after gaining notoriety as a leader of antidesegregation forces in Newark's Italian North Ward neighborhood, recalling that he "came close" to persuading Imperiale since the tax would bring significant new aid for Newark schools, but ultimately was unable to get Imperiale to vote for the income tax. Brendan T. Byrne, interview with author, January 23, 2013.

52. Ronald Sullivan, "Foes of Byrne's Proposal Put Forth an Alternative," *New York Times*, June 19, 1974.

53. Brendan T. Byrne, transcript of Governor Byrne press conference.

54. "Byrne Presses Late Drive for a Jersey School Tax," *New York Times*, December 24, 1974.

55. Brendan T. Byrne, interview with author, January 23, 2013.

56. Ronald Sullivan, "Jersey Democrats Draft Tax Proposal To Net $700 Million," *New York Times*, December 24, 1974.

57. Jeffrey Laurenti, e-mail to author, May 12, 2013.

58. Clifford Goldman, e-mail to author, March 25, 2013.

59. Ronald Sullivan, "Jersey's Legislature Quits Without Acting on Tax," *New York Times*, December 20, 1974.

60. Raymond Bateman, letter to Chief Justice Richard Hughes, December 20, 1974.

61. A-1875 as amended. N.J. Senate Journal 334–35.

62. Albert Burstein Memoir, New Jersey State Legislature Oral History Project, recorded May–June 2000, 38.

63. Albert Burstein Memoir, 39.

64. *Robinson v. Cahill*, 67 NJ 35 (1975), at 37.

65. 67 N.J. at 356.

66. Lehne, *The Quest for Justice*, 135.

67. Ronald Sullivan, "$2.8 Billion asked in Jersey Budget; Byrne Calls for New Taxes and 'Sacrifices' to Meet $487-Million Deficit," *New York Times*, February 4, 1975.

68. Ibid.

69. Minutes of Governor Byrne Cabinet Meeting, May 27, 1975.

70. Jeffrey M. Stonecash and Mary P. McGuire, *The Emergence of State Government: Parties and New Jersey Politics, 1950–2000*, Madison, NJ: Fairleigh Dickinson University Press, 2001, 120.

71. In his budget address, Byrne also dealt with another issue underlying widespread skepticism that any added revenue from new taxes would be put to good use; in response to a report released the month before disclosing rampant waste in the Newark school system, he named a respected former state budget director to review the report's findings and make recommendations on reforms. Walter H. Waggoner, "Budget Expert to Head School Reform," *New York Times*, February 6, 1975.

72. Ronald Sullivan, "$2.8 Billion Asked in Jersey Budget," *New York Times*, February 6, 1975.

73. Another issue which also became a frequent complaint of the demonstrators and other Byrne opponents was the Governor's intention to allow the scheduled raise of his salary from $60,000 to $65,000 to take effect as of January 1976. Ronald Sullivan, "Jersey Employees Denounce Byrne," *New York Times*, February 6, 1975.

74. Ronald Sullivan, "Byrne Now Expects to Get Income Tax Passed," *New York Times*, March 9, 1975.

75. "Byrne Asks July 1 Deadline for School-Aid Legislation," *New York Times*, February 26, 1975.

76. "Senate Warns Court on School-Aid Issue," *New York Times*, March 5, 1975; "Byrne Asks July 1 Deadline for School-Aid Legislation," *New York Times*, February 26, 1975.

77. Brendan T. Byrne, interview with author, January 30, 2013.

78. Walter H. Waggoner, "High Court Hears Byrne on School Financing Issue," *New York Times*, March 19, 1975.

79. Brendan T. Byrne, interview with author, January 30, 2013; Walter H. Waggoner, "High Court Hears Byrne on School Financing Issue," *New York Times*, March 19, 1975.

80. 69 N.J. 133 (1975).

81. Brendan T. Byrne, Address to Special Session of the Legislature, June 18, 1975. Rutgers-Eagleton Byrne Archive.

82. Ronald Sullivan, "Jersey Tax Vote is Tomorrow," *New York Times*, June 24, 1975.

83. Dan Weissman, "Income tax defeated," *Star-Ledger*, June 17, 1975; Ronald Sullivan, "Jersey's Senate Bars Income Tax by a 21-to-17 Vote," *New York Times*, June 28, 1975.

84. Linda Lamendola, "Budget cuts will affect vital services," *Star-Ledger*, June 29, 1975; Ronald Sullivan, "All called Losers in Jersey Tax Battle," *New York Times*, July 2, 1975.

85. Ibid.

86. The tax package included extension of the sales tax to some business and professional services, a capital gains tax, an unincorporated business tax, increased rates for the corporation business tax, and an increase in motor vehicle fees. Harriet Heyman and Milton Leebaw, "N.J.'s Answer is the Nuisance Tax," *New York Times*, July 27, 1975.

87. Dan Weissman, "2% tax plan rejected; Assembly still at work," *Star-Ledger*, July 1, 1976.

88. Chapter 212, Laws of 1975; N.J.S.A. 18A:7A et seq.

89. Subsequently, after the "thorough and efficient" law was enacted, the Department's implementation of the law through the adoption of regulations mandating student testing and monitoring, annual evaluations for tenured teachers, and annual school reviews provoked objections from administrators and teachers over the time and paperwork needed to meet the requirements. See Yaffe, *Other People's Children*, 45.

90. Ibid.

91. *Robinson v. Cahill V*, 69 N.J. 449 (1976).

92. Ibid.

93. Yaffe, *Other People's Children*, 47.

94. See generally Van Wagner, "The New Jersey Gross Income Tax," 115–17.

95. Brendan T. Byrne, interview with author, January 30, 2013.

96. See generally Van Wagner, "The New Jersey Gross Income Tax," 115–17.

97. Richard Leone, memo to Clifford A. Goldman, February 18, 1975. Rutgers-Eagleton Byrne Archive.

98. Yaffe, *Other People's Children*, 48; see also James McQueeny, "A Scenario finally Played out to Conclusion," *Star-Ledger*, June 18, 1976.

99. Clifford A. Goldman, e-mail to author, March 25, 2013.

100. Van Wagner, "The New Jersey Gross Income Tax," 117.

101. Yaffe, *Other Peoples Children*, 48.

102. Bob Cunningham and Allan F. Yoder, "A Tax Bill Nobody Liked," *Record*, June, 18 1976.

103. Jim Goodman and Michael J. Hall, "Jersey schools closed," *Trenton Times*, July 2, 1976.

104. Joseph Sullivan, "Suits Seek to Halt Shutdown of Public Schools Thursday," *New York Times*, June 29, 1976.

105. Whipple's decision to convene the entire court may have been designed to avoid potential criticism of the court in the event that the case was assigned to Judge Frederick Lacey, who, two years earlier, had been the subject of press reports that, in light of Governor Byrne's declining popularity, he was considering a potential candidacy for the 1977 Republican gubernatorial nomination. See "Lacey Considered as '77 Candidate," *New York Times*, August 28, 1975.

106. Lewis B. Kaden, interview for Rutgers-Eagleton Byrne Archive, September 27, 2010.

107. Dan Weissman, "2% Tax Plan Rejected, Assembly Still at Work," *Star-Ledger*, July 1, 1976.

108. Jim Goodman and Michael J. Hall, "Jersey schools closed," *Trenton Times*, July 2, 1976.

109. Raymond Bateman, interview for Rutgers-Eagleton Byrne Archive, January 11, 2007.

110. Jim Goodman and Michael J. Hall, "Jersey schools closed," *Trenton Times*, July 2, 1976.

111. Van Wagner, "The New Jersey Gross Income Tax," 117–18.

112. Robert Cohen, "Order for school closings stands," *Star-Ledger*, July 1, 1976; Jim Goodman, "'The Zoo' in chaos," *Trenton Times,* July 2, 1976.

113. Alfonso Navarez, "Jersey Assembly, Defers Tax Issue," *New York Times*, July 3, 1976.

114. Assembly Republican Leader Thomas Kean later recounted that on the day before the final Assembly vote on the income tax, he asked Democrat Kenneth Gewertz how he intended to vote, and Gewertz replied that he would vote against the tax "until hell freezes over." After Gewertz in fact voted for the tax on the following day, Kean asked him why he had changed his mind; Gewertz replied, "funny thing, the devil was at my door that morning all caked in ice." Thomas H. Kean, interview with author, October 1, 2013.

115. Jim Goodman, "Grateful governor extends plaudits," *Trenton Times*, July 8, 1976.

116. Alfonso Navarez, "Jersey Assembly, Ending Deadlock, Votes Income Tax," *New York Times*, July 8, 1976.

117. Byrne later quipped that the pen that he had used to sign the income tax was subsequently encased in lucite, "thankfully making it too large to use it for the purpose that my critics had suggested."

118. Dan Weissman and Philip Lentz, "Byrne signs tax bill," *Star-Ledger*, July 9, 1976; Steven Ford, "Jersey gets an income tax," *Trenton Times*, July 9, 1976; Alfonso Navarez, "New Jersey Votes State Income Tax; Byrne Signs Bill," *New York Times*, July 8, 1976. As soon as the income tax was enacted, the Treasury proceeded to put the complex program into place, which generated a significant increase in the administrative workload of its staff, through purchasing and renovating a building, acquiring mail processing and computer equipment, hiring and training hundreds of workers, and designing and mailing a variety of new forms, including homestead rebate applications. In September, the first tax forms were mailed; in April 1977, state income tax refunds were received before the federal refunds, followed shortly by the homestead rebate checks with an accompanying letter from Governor Byrne. Perhaps with the aid of careful planning, applications for the next year's rebates arrived on the Monday before election day in November. Clifford Goldman, e-mail to author, March 26, 2013; see also "Leone declares state will process income tax," *Star-Ledger*, November 6, 1976.

119. Rutgers-Eagleton Byrne Archive.

120. *Robinson v. Cahill*, 70 N.J. 465 (1976).

121. Lehne, *The Quest for Justice*, 160.

122. Alvin Maurer, "Jersey's Tax Fight Took Place in a Power Vacuum," *New York Times*, July 11, 1976.

123. Yaffe, *Other People's Children*, 47.
124. Brendan T. Byrne, annual message to the legislature, January 11, 1977.

CHAPTER 9

1. Byrne was not the only one to report on the sorry condition of the City and its visitor facilities. After checking into his hotel room, George Meany, the powerful president of the American Federation of Labor and Congress of Industrial Organizations, had the faucet of his bathroom sink break off while trying to turn on the water; with faucet in hand, he reportedly stormed back to the lobby to berate the front desk clerk, "I'm a plumber by trade, but this is not what I came for!" Quoted in Amy S. Rosenberg, "1964 Democratic Convention Exposed Atlantic City, N.J. as Faded, Dirty Resort," *Philadelphia Inquirer*, June 5, 2000.

2. Buckley wrote a withering assessment of the City: "Queen Elizabeth could walk through Atlantic City and be untouched by its tawdriness. Uncle Cornpone [President Johnson] can't: the salt-water taffy, instead of curtseying, tends to stick to him; Sally Rand, who would-you-believe-it, is still disrobing for the boys, does an extra can-can in his honor, and the perennial flagpole sitter (he is trying to break his own record of 77 days and has now reached 62) will add another day to his silly ordeal—but all of this is not in the spirit in which the juggler juggled for Our Lady. Atlantic City is not paying homage to LBJ. It is simply cashing in on a $600,000 misunderstanding. The City might wish it hadn't lured the big show down this way. Too much copy is being written about the place. . . . The people of Atlantic City are not responsible for the ineffable vulgarity of the place, which even the healing sea cannot cleanse. . . . The customer gets what he wants, and what the customer evidently wants is Atlantic City the way it is, with only a single memorable restaurant, no attractive outdoor cafés, an architectural chaos which, to the extent it favors any single style at all, seems to favor a sort of crypto-Byzantine. . . ." William F. Buckley, Jr., *National Review*, September 8, 1964. Accessed September 11, 2010 at http://old.nationalreview.com/flashback/flashback200407260119.asp

3. John B. Wefing, *The Life and Times of Richard Hughes*, New Brunswick, NJ: Rutgers University Press 2009, 88.

4. "1964 Democratic Convention Exposed Atlantic City, N.J. as Faded, Dirty Resort," *Philadelphia Inquirer*, June 5, 2000. Accessed August 6, 2012 at http://www.accessmylibrary.com/article-1G1-122061673/1964-democratic-convention-exposed.html

5. See generally for the history of Atlantic City, Nelson Johnson, *Boardwalk Empire*, Medford, NJ: Plexus Publishing, 2002; Barbara Kozek, "History of Atlantic City," City of Atlantic City. Accessed August 3, 2012 at http://www.cityofatlanticcity.org/about.aspx#history

6. As early as 1801, Cape May hotels began advertising for summer visitors from Philadelphia and soon began running their own daily stage coaches to bring their

guests back and forth. With the introduction of commercial steam boats in the 1820s, travelers from Philadelphia could take regularly scheduled boats on the Delaware River without dependence on the tide, making the planning of trips more practical and convenient. From the south, ships from Baltimore and other ports brought many others, including Washington officials and politicians along with wealthy southern plantation owners, seeking relief from the summer heat. hotels began advertising for summer visitors from Philadelphia and soon began running their own daily stage coaches to bring their guests back and forth. With the introduction of commercial steam boats in the 1820s, travelers from Philadelphia could take regularly scheduled boats on the Delaware River without dependence on the tide, making the planning of trips more practical and convenient.

7. Subsequent boasts, with little evidence, were that the ocean air was rich in ozone, which could ". . . cure consumption, rheumatism, laryngitis, digestive disorders and insanity." Liz Eisenberg and Vicki Gold Levy, "Atlantic City," in Maxine N. Lurie and Marc Mappen (eds.), *Encyclopedia of New Jersey*, New Brunswick, NJ: Rutgers University Press, 2004, 43.

8. Charles E. Funnell, *By the Beautiful Sea: The Rise and High Times of that Great American Resort: Atlantic City*, New York: Alfred A. Knopf, 1975.

9. Victorian-era religious leaders often decried the moral laxity of Atlantic City and other resorts. "To many Protestant clerics," as one scholar points out: "commercial resorts, even in their most innocent aspects, presented a continual public spectacle of sin and social disorder. This could be true of any day in Atlantic City where such things as mixed bathing and drinking and dancing to the strains of popular music excited the worst fears of evangelicals. But it was especially true of resort Sundays, when the crowds were largest, and the seeming indifference of the people to the sanctity of the Sabbath and the laws of the state confirmed the evangelical view that commercial recreation had legitimized the worst manifestations of industrial society." See Martin Paulsson, *The Social Anxieties of Progressive Reform: Atlantic City, 1854–1920*, New York: New York University Press, 1996, 5–6.

10. The boardwalk was named after Alexander Boardman, a conductor on the Camden and Amboy Railroad, who with Jacob Keim, a hotel owner, conceived the idea of constructing a boardwalk as a means of keeping beach visitors from tracking sand into railroad cars and hotels. The City used its tax revenues to build an eight-foot-wide temporary wooden walkway from the beach into town that could be dismantled during the winter, which was later replaced by a more permanent walkway. See "Today in History: June 26, American Memory," Library of Congress. Accessed July 19, 2010 at http://memory.loc.gov/ammem/today/jun26.html

11. Quoted in Paulsson, *Social Anxieties*, 2.

12. In assessing whether Governor Wilson's motives in targeting Atlantic City were political or puritanical, the *New York Times* reported: "When inquiring into political conditions, Mr. Wilson found that for its population of 45,000 its vote was grossly disproportionate. There were more Lewis votes than there should have been voters." The article went on to point out that nearly 50 percent of the City's registered voters were African Americans, most of whom worked in the hotels during the summer months, with many leaving the City at the end of the season, but that they were

recorded as voting in the November election. See "More Arrests Stir Atlantic City Talk," *New York Times*, July 29, 1911, 4.

13. Johnson, *Boardwalk Empire*, 76–77; "Prison Term for Atlantic City Boss; Court Imposes Year's Sentence on Republican Leader Kuehnle for Grafting," *New York Times*, January 15, 1912, 20. Kuehnle served six months of his sentence. After his release, he was elected as a City commissioner and was viewed as a reformer opposed to the new political machine run by Johnson, but never regained the power he held prior to his imprisonment. See "L.N. Kuehnle Dead, Political Leader," *New York Times*, August 6, 1934.

14. Johnson's father, Smith Johnson, was a member of the three-man group that dominated Atlantic County and City governments prior to the rise of Kuehnle, and had been elected in 1886 as the County sheriff for a three-year term. In 1905, Sheriff Johnson selected his 22-year-old son Nucky as his undersheriff, and in 1908 Nucky was elected himself as sheriff when his father's term expired, a position he would hold only until 1911, when he was removed by order of a state judge for his role in helping Kuehnle pack the grand jury that declined to pursue the allegations of election fraud in the 1910 election. Subsequently, Johnson would rule from his appointed post as County treasurer and leader of the county Republican Party, disdaining elected office as beneath his stature, but still controlling the selection of grand juries through the new sheriff, his brother Alfred. After Atlantic County's Walter Edge was elected in 1916 as New Jersey governor, Edge also appointed Johnson as clerk of the state Supreme Court, a largely titular position which nonetheless allowed Johnson to forge new alliances in Trenton. Johnson, *Boardwalk Empire*, 85.

15. Quoted in *Johnson, Boardwalk Empire*, 87; see also Jon Blackwell, *Notorious New Jersey*, New Brunswick, NJ: Rutgers University Press, 2007, 186; "Enoch L. Johnson, Ex-Boss in Jersey – Prohibition-Era Ruler of Atlantic City, 85, Dies," *New York Times*, December 10, 1968, 47.

16. Prohibition was implemented under the Volstead Act (officially the National Prohibition Act) authorized by the 18th Amendment to the U.S Constitution. The Act went into effect when Congress overrode Wilson's veto, a veto based largely on technical grounds. Johnson, *Boardwalk Empire*, 84–87.

17. Johnson*, Boardwalk Empire*, 90.

18. See Derek Harper, "80 years ago, the Mob came to Atlantic City for a little strategic planning," *Atlantic City Press*, May 13, 2009. In 1972, Meyer Lansky was indicted on charges that he and others had skimmed millions of dollars from the Flamingo Hotel Casino in Las Vegas that they owned; the indictment of Lansky was later dismissed since he was considered too ill to face trial. "Meyer Lansky," FBI Records: The Vault. Accessed October 4, 2012 at http://vault.fbi.gov/meyer-lansky

19. Ovid Demaris, *The Boardwalk Jungle*, New York: Bantam Books, 1986, 27–28.

20. "Abner Zwillman," FBI Records: The Vault. Accessed October 15, 2012 at http://vault.fbi.gov/Abner%20Zwillman/Abner%20Zwillman%20Part%202%20 of%207/view

21. The Convention Hall was intended to extend Atlantic City's visitor season beyond the peak summer months by attracting conventions, exhibitions, and trade shows, allowing conventioneers to use the excuse of a business event to enjoy a visit

to the City throughout the year. James D. Ristine, *Atlantic City*, Mount Pleasant, SC: Arcadia Publishing, 2008, 54.

22. See Vicki Gold Levi and Lee Eisenberg, *Atlantic City: 125 Years of Ocean Madness*, Berkeley, CA: Ten Speed Press, 1979, 154.

23. Johnson, *Boardwalk Empire*, 104.

24. According to some accounts, Hearst, who "was every bit the lady's man Nucky was" and made frequent visits to Atlantic City, had targeted Johnson because the two men had competed for the affections of a showgirl at the City's Silver Slipper Saloon. Ibid.

25. See generally Johnson, *Boardwalk Empire,* see also Michael Clark and Dan Good, "Nucky Johnson: The Man who Ran Atlantic City for 30 Years," *Atlantic City Press*, August 15, 2010. Accessed August 20, 2010 at http://www.pressofatlanticcity.com/blogs/boardwalk_empire/article_4277415c-a815-11df-be3f-001cc4c002e0.html

26. Jimmy Boyd, clerk of the County freeholder board, worked closely with both Johnson and Farley to enforce discipline within the county organization and dispense patronage and contracts to loyalists in return for kickbacks.

27. Paulsson, "Farley, Frank Sherman," in *Encyclopedia of New Jersey*, 266.

28. Johnson, *Boardwalk Empire*, xviii.

29. Brendan T. Byrne, interview with author, August 14, 2012.

30. Ibid.

31. See p. 34.

32. Convention Hall was closed to public events and taken over by the Army Air Forces as a headquarters and training facility. The federal presence, however, also brought with it the price of closing the City's illicit gambling dens in bars and night clubs. According to one observer, "There were a very large number of soldiers in town, and the Army flat-out said, 'We're not gonna have our guys losing their *money in your gambling joints.'*" Ibid.

33. Final Report of the Special Senate Committee to Investigate Organized Crime in Interstate Commerce, August 27, 1951, 39. Accessed August 4, 2010 at http://www.nevadaobserver.com/Reading%20Room%20Documents/Kefauver%20Final%20Report.htm

34. Farley was president of the "21 Club" composed of New Jersey's county Republican chairmen, and which provided a platform for his statewide political influence. In 1968, he was a key player at the Republican National Convention in swinging the New Jersey delegation from its support of favorite son, U.S. Senator Clifford Case, to back the eventual nominee, Richard Nixon. Even after Farley left office, he successfully intervened in 1972, at the request of community leaders, with President Nixon to block the plan by the Federal Aviation Administration to close the National Aviation Facilities Experimental Center, one of the largest employers in Atlantic County Nixon also repaid Farley's endorsement by coming to New Jersey for a fundraiser hosted by Farley and also overruled federal officials who had recommended the closure of the Federal Aviation Administration's test center in Atlantic County. See Paulsson, "Farley, Frank Sherman," *Encyclopedia of New Jersey*, 266.

35. The 500 Club seated a thousand people and included a plush casino in the back of the house which was kept operating by regular payoffs to the City's police

and municipal officials. D'Amato had become particularly close to Bruno (after whom he named his only son "Angelo") and to Sinatra and Chicago Mafia leader Sam Giancana, for whom he had briefly worked as manager of their jointly owned Cal-Neva Lodge in Lake Tahoe. Sinatra's gratitude to D'Amato, who kept hiring him after his career faded in the 1940s, was reflected in his appearing without pay when he again had become a top draw, sometimes joined by fellow members of his "Rat Pack" like Dean Martin and Sammy Davis, Jr. Other headliners who made regular appearances at the Club included Sophie Tucker, Patti Page, Jimmy Durante and Jerry Lewis and Dean Martin, who first teamed up as a comedy act at the Club in 1946. See Archie Black, Atlantic City Newsletter, March 2000. Accessed July 10, 2012 at http://www.ratpack.biz/rat-pack-archive/skinny-damato-atlantic-city-newsletter.htm

36. Fox's suggestion of legalizing gambling provoked anonymous death threats, apparently from those profiting from the status quo, and her children were escorted to school by the FBI for some six months. Michael Pollock, *Hostage to Fortune: Atlantic City and Casino Gambling*, Princeton: Center for Analysis of Public Issues, 1987, 13.

37. Jeffrey Kanige, "Brendan Byrne on Brendan Byrne," *New Jersey Reporter*, June 1988, 18.

38. Brendan T. Byrne, quoted in Casinoconnection.com, Vol. 5, No. 5, May 2008. Accessed August 2, 2012 at http://casinoconnectionac.com/issue-printer/may_2008

39. Others attending included Mike Segal, the mayor of Ventnor; Mario Floriani, the Atlantic City police chief; two City commissioners; Mack Latz, the owner of the City's popular Knife and Fork restaurant; as well as a state judge and the owner of a Philadelphia sausage company.

40. Jonathan Van Meter, *The Last Good Time: Skinny D'Amato, the Notorious 500 Club and the Rise and Fall of Atlantic City*, New York: Crown Publishers, 2003, 231.

41. Dena Kleiman, "Frank S. Farley, 75, Ex-Legislator and G.O. Leader in Jersey, Dies," *New York Times*, op cit.

42. Along with other New Jersey political figures, Farley was mentioned in transcripts released in 1970 of wiretaps recorded in 1963 by the FBI of conversations among prominent Mafia figures. Farley was allegedly cited as being able to fix criminal cases and protect rackets in Atlantic County. See "F.B.I.-Taped Conversation Sheds Light on 1962 Gangland Slaying of Strollo; Jersey Figures Mentioned in Underworld Talks Recorded by the F.B.I.," *New York Times*, January 8, 1970.

43. Sternlieb and Hughes, *The Atlantic City Gamble*, 38; see also Richard Lehne, *Casino Policy*, New Brunswick, NJ: Rutgers University Press, 1986, 28–29.

44. See Lehne, *Casino Policy*, 28–29. In January 1971, the *Trenton Times* and the *Atlantic City Press* published articles on Atlantic City's options written by Herb Wolfe, who later would become Governor Byrne's press secretary and, after leaving government, the president of the Showboat Hotel and Casino. Wolfe's reports were the first to focus on the move toward legalization, as well as pointing to D'Amato as "the man to be reckoned with" if casinos were to come to the City. Van Meter, *The Last Good Time*, 231.

45. Cahill did oversee implementation, however, of the New Jersey lottery, which was overwhelmingly approved by New Jersey voters in November 1969, the same

election in which Cahill was elected Governor. New Jersey was the third state after New Hampshire and New York to approve a lottery. "History of the New Jersey Lottery," New Jersey Lottery Commission. Accessed August 3, 2012 at http://www. state.nj.us/lottery/general/6-2-2_history.htm

46. After the legislature enacted enabling legislation authorizing the third state lottery after New Hampshire and New York, Governor Cahill himself ceremoniously purchased the first lottery ticket on December 16, 1970. The new lottery program implemented under the Cahill Administration also quickly became much more successful than its predecessors in other states, primarily by offering tickets at low prices, establishing hundreds of agent locations and launching an aggressive marketing campaign.

47. See generally Wally Edge, "Legislators were 'entirely too comfortable with organized crime'," PolitickerNJ.com, 29 January 2009. Accessed August 4, 2012 at http://www.politickernj.com/wallye/26961/legislators-were-entirely-too-comfortable-organized-crime

48. Ibid.

49. Republican Assemblyman Robert Littell of Sussex County introduced Assembly Concurrent Resolution 51 in 1969 and Senator Frank McDermott of Union County introduced Senate Concurrent Resolutions 39 and 74 in 1970 to authorize referenda on casino gambling; while public hearings were held on the proposals, none were reported out of committee. See Lehne, *Casino Policy*, 28–29; see also "New Owner Raises Hope for Ski Area's Turnaround," *New York Times*, March 2, 1998. Accessed August 6, 2010 at http://www.nytimes.com/1998/03/02/nyregion/new-owner-raises-hope-for-ski-area-s-turnaround.html

50. McGahn was the brother of attorney Patrick "Paddy" McGahn, who had represented the local NAACP in lawsuits charging that the Farley machine had engaged in practices to deny minorities the right to vote. See Nelson Johnson, *Boardwalk Empire*, 37. Perskie was the son of former Atlantic County Judge David M. Perskie, who sat on the bench from 1966 to 1969, and the grandson of former New Jersey Supreme Court Justice Joseph B. Perskie, who served from 1933 to 1947. His grandmother Beatrice Perskie was the president of the Atlantic City Board of Education and his uncle, Marvin Perskie, was a Democratic assemblyman from Cape May County from 1966 to 1968. His cousin Leon Perskie was the photographer for Franklin D. Roosevelt's 1932 and 1936 presidential campaigns. See "Happy Birthday to Steve Perskie, 21 years younger than Frank Lautenberg," PolitickerNJ. com, January 10, 2008. Accessed August 3, 2012, at http://www.politickernj.com/happy-birthday-steve-perskie-21-years-younger-frank-lautenberg-15290

51. Steven P. Perskie, "A Political History," February 22, 2009 (unpublished manuscript).

52. See "Democratic Gains Posted in Jersey; G.O. Control of Assembly Imperiled and Senate Edge Is Cut—Farley Beaten Jersey Democrats Score Gains in the Legislature," *New York Times*, November 3, 1971.

53. Perskie, "A Political History." Farley was never indicted, but the grand jury brought charges that led to the convictions of two former Atlantic City mayors and other officials for bribery, extortion, and conspiracy. Paulsson, "Frank Sherman Farley," *Encyclopedia of New Jersey*, 266. Coming at the beginning of the

1969 election campaign, Brennan's charge sparked a political uproar, with Senator McDermott, who had been elected to serve as Senate president for the 1969 session, calling for an investigation. Farley was one of those suspected of being the subject of Brennan's comments, but ultimately he was not one of those identified by the legislative committee as prompting Brennan's accusation. At the same time, the federal government launched an anti-Mafia strike force consisting of officials from seven federal agencies. Based in Newark, the team conducted raids and gathered intelligence on Mafia families believed to be raking in $1 billion a year in the state as U.S. Attorney Frederick Lacey indicted 122 state and local officials in the early 1970s. A dozen high-ranking mobsters went to jail rather than break "omerta," the Mafia's code of silence, and Lacey most notably won a conviction against Newark Mayor Hugh Addonizio for extortion and conspiracy. See generally "Legislators were 'entirely too comfortable with organized crime'," PolitickerNJ. com, January 29, 2009. Accessed August 4, 2010 at http://www.politickernj.com/wallye/26961/legislators-were-entirely-too-comfortable-organized-crime

54. Sternlieb and Hughes, *The Atlantic City Gamble*, 38–41.

55. See Public hearing on Senate Concurrent Resolution no. 74, February 10, 1971, Trenton, New Jersey, Senate Judiciary Committee, New Jersey Legislature, Print; see also "12 New Democratic Assembly Members Take Oaths", PolitckerNJ.com, January 8, 2008. Accessed August 2, 2012 at http://www.politickernj.com/assembly-democrats-12-new-democratic-assembly-members-take-oaths-office-15192

56. Benjamin "Bugsy" Siegel, who had begun his criminal career as a bootlegger in New York, New Jersey, and Philadelphia, oversaw the construction and opening of the Las Vegas' Flamingo in 1947 financed by Lucky Luciano and Meyer Lansky and other Eastern mobsters, gaining a Nevada gaming license despite his extensive and violent criminal record. Some of the casinos that followed the Flamingo in the 1950s also were allegedly financed by mobsters, including the Desert Inn backed by Cleveland's boss Moe Dalitz, another participant at the 1929 Atlantic City conference hosted by Nucky Johnson. The Desert Inn, Las Vegas's fourth casino resort, opened on April 24, 1950. Seven more casinos, all allegedly backed by mob money, included the Sands and Sahara opened in 1952, the Riviera and Dunes in 1955, the Hacienda in 1956, the Tropicana in 1957, and the Stardust in 1958. During that same time period the population of the Las Vegas Valley grew from 45,000 to 124,000. The Teamsters-financed Circus Circus opened in 1968. See Dennis Griffin, *The Battle for Las Vegas: The Law vs. The Mob*, Las Vegas: Huntington Press, 2006.

57. Brendan T. Byrne, interview with author, September 28, 2012.

58. Steven P. Perskie, remarks at "Atlantic City: Looking Back and Ahead," forum sponsored by Eagleton Institute of Politics, Rutgers University, May 10, 2007.

59. Steven P. Perskie, interview for Rutgers-Eagleton Byrne Archive, May 10, 2007.

60. Brendan T. Byrne, remarks at "Atlantic City: Looking Back and Ahead," forum sponsored by Eagleton Institute of Politics, Rutgers University, May 10, 2007.

61. Brendan T. Byrne, interview for Rutgers-Eagleton Byrne Archive, September 13, 2006.

62. Quoted in Thomas Kean and Brendan T. Byrne, "A dicey experiment, a mixed success," *Newark Star-Ledger*, May 25, 2003.

63. Steven P. Perskie, remarks at "Atlantic City: Looking Back and Ahead," forum sponsored by Eagleton Institute of Politics, Rutgers University, May 10, 2007.

64. See Lehne, *Casino Policy*, 34.

65. Brendan T. Byrne, interview with author, October 4, 2012.

66. Assembly Concurrent Resolution 128 (1974).

67. *Star-Ledger*, April 30, 1974. Quoted in Felzenberg, *Governor Tom Kean*, 133.

68. See generally Lehne, *Casino Policy*, 32–35.

69. Jonathan Goldstein, quoted in Sternlieb and Hughes, *Atlantic City Gamble*, 44.

70. Sternlieb and Hughes, *Atlantic City Gamble*, 45.

71. Lacy McCrary, "Byrne Pleased His Casino Vote Was Wasted," *Philadelphia Inquirer*, November 11, 1974.

72. Brendan T. Byrne, interview with author, October 5, 2012.

73. *New York Times*, November 10, 1974.

74. Resorts International was the largest contributor to CRAC, providing $300,000 of the total raised of $1.3 million.

75. Source for Perskie quote and description of Farley invitation to Assembly is Steven P. Perskie, "A Political History," February 22, 2009 (unpublished manuscript). Sanford Weiner, the consultant hired by the pro-casino forces, believed that the referendum's support by Sheriff Job was crucial. "I would go so far as to say that we would not have won without his help. . . . [U]ntil Job came aboard, we totally lacked not only a Bergen County spokesman but a spokesman for North Jersey, and he proved to be the one person who had the credibility and popularity that would help us prove we were alive and well up north." Quoted in Sternlieb and Hughes, *Atlantic City Gamble*, 55. See also Bryant Simon, *Boardwalk of Dreams*, New York: Oxford University Press, 2004.

76. Some 700,000 more voters turned out in 1976 than in 1974. Carl Zeitz, remarks at "Atlantic City: Looking Back and Ahead," forum sponsored by Eagleton Institute of Politics, Rutgers University, May 10, 2007.

77. Stewart Pollock, interview for Rutgers-Eagleton Byrne Archive, Rutgers University, October 25, 2010.

78. Brendan T. Byrne, interview with author, October 10, 2012.

79. See Lehne, *Casino Policy*, 44. One of the Nevada officials Byrne met with was Attorney General Harry Reid, later Democratic Majority Leader of the U.S. Senate.

80. Richard J. Codey, interview for Rutgers-Eagleton Byrne Archive, March 23, 2010.

81. While holding a scheduled retreat for his cabinet and staff at the nearby Seaview Country Club in Absecon, the governor adjourned the session so that he and the others at the retreat could go to the facility's top floor to view the dynamiting of the Chalfonte-Haddon Hall.

82. Brendan T. Byrne, interview with author, October 10, 2012.

83. Ibid.

84. Steven P. Perskie, telephone conversation with author, October 3, 2013.

85. Steven P. Perskie, "A Political History," February 22, 2009 (unpublished manuscript).

86. Fariborz S. Fatemi, interview with author, August 21, 2012.

87. After speaking with Byrne, the mayor, according to Fatemi, "could not have been more cooperative. He went all-out, all city departments were put to work to provide the necessary permits, security for traffic and crowd control and even a red carpet in front of Convention Hall. The mayor even declared a holiday for all city workers and Atlantic City schools so that they could participate and view the parade." Ibid.

88. Ibid.

89. See generally for the scene at the signing of the casino legislation and Farley and Byrne quotes, Demaris, *The Boardwalk Jungle*, 4–10. "Gambling in American History: New Jersey and Atlantic City Casinos". Accessed August 23, 2012 at http://gamblinginamerica.name/new-jersey-and-atlantic-city-casinos-gambling-in-america/

90. Lehne, *Casino Policy*, 44–48.

91. Brendan T. Byrne, remarks at "Atlantic City: Looking Back and Ahead," Brendan T. Byrne Archive, forum sponsored by Eagleton Institute of Politics, Rutgers University, May 10, 2007.

92. Ibid.

93. McGahn, known as a maverick, also had secured the 1971 Democratic nomination without the backing of the Democratic organization in his successful campaign against Senator Farley.

94. Steven P. Perskie, remarks at "Atlantic City: Looking Back and Ahead," forum sponsored by Eagleton Institute of Politics, Rutgers University, May 10, 2007.

95. A master plan developed for the City by Angelos C. Demetriou, an internationally known architect, city planner, and urban designer who worked on projects to revitalize the Georgetown waterfront in Washington as well as designs for the capital of Pakistan, also was the focus of debate, with some local interests and Governor Byrne questioning the plan's recommendations as impractical and ridiculing its recommendations to preserve several of the City's dilapidated buildings as "historic," preferring a course that would favor widescale demolition and new construction as a quicker path to renewal. See March 14, 1979 Cabinet meeting agenda and letter from Cabinet Committee to City Planning Board.

96. Roger Gros, "Thirty Years of Gaming," Casinoconnection.com, May 5, 2008. Accessed August 2, 2010 at http://casinoconnectionac.com/issue-printer/may_2008

97. Executives of Resorts had visited the City prior to the November 1976 gaming referendum and the firm had become a major contributor to the successful campaign. Even before the vote, Resorts purchased an option for 55 acres of land on the Boardwalk from the City's Housing and Re-Development Authority, paying $2.5 million to purchase the historic Chalfonte-Haddon Hall Hotel, which had been combined from two adjacent hotels originally built in the nineteenth century.

98. Lehne, *Casino Policy*, 90.

99. William Gormley, quoted in Roger Gros, "Thirty Years of Gaming," Casinoconnection.com, Vol. 5, May 2008. Accessed August 2, 2010 at http://casinoconnectionac.com/issue-printer/may_2008

100. Lehne, *Casino Policy*, 89–93. John J. Degnan, interview for Rutgers-Eagleton Byrne Archive, June 20, 2011.

101. Ibid.

102. Robert S. Strauss, "When casinos came to town: 30 facts about gambling's start in Atlantic City," *Philadelphia Daily News*, May 23, 2008. Accessed June 23, 2012 at http://articles.philly.com/2008-05-23/entertainment/25262329_1_casino-gambling-first-casino-second-casino

103. "Resorts International, Inc. History," www.fundinguniverse.com. Accessed December 22, 2012 at http://www.fundinguniverse.com/company-histories/resorts-international-inc-history/

104. Robert E. Mulcahy, III, memo dated January 2, 1979 re phone conversation of December 20, 1978 with Joel Sterns.

105. Lehne, *Casino Policy*, 91–93.

106. Clifford and Stuart Perlman had past business dealings with Alvin Malnik, a Miami Beach lawyer who had previously been indicted for income tax evasion and fraud. Malnik's partner, Samuel Cohen, had earlier been convicted for taking part in a $36 million profit-skimming scheme at Bugsy Siegel's Flamingo Hotel in Las Vegas. Martin Waldron, "Degnan Charges Caesars Had Mob Ties in Las Vegas," *New York Times*, February 8, 1980. See also "Caesar's World, Inc. Company History." Accessed August 12, 2010 at http://www.answers.com/topic/caesars-world-inc

107. Donald Janson, "Caesars' 2 Top Officers Must Quit If Jersey Casino Is to Get a License," *New York Times*, October 24, 1980.

108. Donald Janson, "Bally to Get Casino License If It Cuts Ties With Its Chief," *New York Times*, December 24, 1980.

109. John J. Degnan, interview for Rutgers-Eagleton Byrne Archive, June 20, 2011.

110. Brendan T. Byrne, interview with author, September 12, 2012.

111. Ibid.

112. See generally Lehne, *Casino Policy*, 73–78. MacDonald resigned from the Commission in February 1980.

113. Brendan T. Byrne, interview with author, September 12, 2012.

114. Mike Kelly, "'American Hustle' renews old questions about Abscam," December 25, 2013, NorthJersey.com. Accessed December 26, 2013 at http://www.northjersey.com/columnists/kelly/Kelly_American_Hustle_renews_old_questions_about_Abscam.html?page=all#sthash.uSgwUieW.dpuf

115. Others convicted were Congressmen Raymond Lederer and Michael "Ozzie" Myers (both of Pennsylvania), John Jenrette (South Carolina), and Richard Kelly (Florida). Despite being solicited by the FBI agents, New Jersey Congressmen William Hughes, James Florio and James Howard not only rejected the offers, but reported them to the FBI. Ibid. See also Demaris, *Boardwalk Jungle*, 152–65.

116. Pollock, *Hostage to Fortune: Atlantic City and Casino* Gaming, 75. Lordi's comments relating to the restructuring of the Casino Control Commission are quoted in Demaris, *Boardwalk Jungle*, 178.

117. John Galloway, chief executive of Atlantic City Tropicana Hotel Casino, conversation with author at indeterminate date.

118. Thomas Carver, former president of Casino Association of New Jersey, remarks at "Atlantic City: Looking Back and Ahead," forum sponsored by Eagleton Institute of Politics, May 10, 2007.

119. Wynn would use the premium price he received from Bally's to build The Mirage on the Las Vegas strip, which opened in 1989 featuring an indoor rain forest, an outdoor volcano, a dolphin pool and, somewhat later, the highly popular Siegfried and Roy white tiger act. Wynn's imagination and flair for marketing would later be evident on even larger themed properties in Las Vegas and Asia.

120. Martin Greenberg, interview for Rutgers-Eagleton Byrne Archive, July 5, 2006.

121. David Schwartz, "Wynn, Lose or Draw," *Casino Connection*, Vol. 5, No. 12, December 2008. Accessed July 16, 2012 at http://casinoconnectionac.com/issue/december__2008/article/wynn__lose_or_draw

122. Taking office in January 1982 as Byrne's successor, Governor Kean long had opposed bringing casinos to New Jersey, twice allowing his name to be used by groups seeking to defeat the casino referenda in 1974 and 1976. The new Kean Administration gave its priority attention to the development of the Hudson waterfront, creating a task force to focus on attracting investment to the region. In 1988, the *New York Times* ran a series of articles outlining the continuing problems and poverty found in many Atlantic City neighborhoods, taking Governor Kean to task: "It is among the more notable shadows on the burnished reputation of Governor Kean, the keynote speaker at the Republican National Convention this month and a patrician who, since his election in 1981, has carefully kept his distance from the infighting, the gaming and the squalor here." The article went on to quote Steven Perskie, who was then a Superior Court judge after serving previously as Governor Florio's chief of staff and subsequently as chairman of the Casino Control Commission: "'The casinos' only responsibility was to come in, obey the laws and churn out the money. I don't fault them; it's not their job to make public policy. It's government's job to do what needs to be done." Steven Erlanger, "Atlantic City: Failure Behind the Façade," *New York Times*, August 29, 1988.

123. Democrat Michael Matthews, the first mayor of the City to be directly elected, was accused of having close ties with Philadelphia Mafia boss Angelo Bruno. Matthews also allegedly tried to extort money during a FBI sting operation in return for the below-market sale of City-owned property for a proposed casino. Some two years after taking office, Matthews was deposed as mayor as a result of a recall election, only days before his federal indictment which subsequently would lead to his guilty plea and a sentence of fifteen years in prison. Matthews's successor, James Usry, a Republican and the first African American to become mayor, also was indicted for allegedly accepting $6,000 in exchange for allowing a motor-cart franchise to operate on the City's boardwalk and, after he was defeated for reelection in 1990, pled guilty to a reduced charge of not reporting the money as a campaign contribution.

124. As part of the original Casino Control Act enacted in 1977, each casino licensee had been required to reinvest 2 percent of its gross gaming revenue in non-gaming projects. By the beginning of 1984, however, no casino licensee had yet made any of its required reinvestments.

125. Brendan T. Byrne, interview with author, September 12, 2012.

126. In February 1992, a development which received little notice at the time but which in later years would pose threats to the viability of the Atlantic City domination of East Coast casino gaming occurred when the Mashantucket Pequot Tribal Nation in Connecticut added table games, followed shortly by slot machines, to the high-stakes bingo hall it had opened in 1986. By 1998, Foxwoods had grown to become the world's largest casino complex, and had been joined by the nearby Mohegan Sun opened by the Mohegan Pequot Tribe in 1996.

127. Kevin C. Shelly, "Special report: Small gambling sites win big as A.C. loses out," *Courier-Post*, June 10, 2013. Accessed June 23, 2013 at http://www.courierpostonline.com/article/20130610/NEWS01/306100029/Special-report-Small-gambling-sites-win-big-C-loses-out

128. See Wayne Parry, "Casino closures brings mass unemployment filing," *Associated Press*, September 3, 2014; Suzette Parmley, "If 4 A.C. casinos close, then what?," *Philadelphia Inquirer*, July 22, 2014.

129. Steven P. Perskie, telephone conversation with author, October 3, 2013.

CHAPTER 10

1. William F. Hyland, letter to Senator John Fay, January 10, 1976.

2. John O. Davies, "Brendan says one term may be enough," *Courier-News*, April 24, 1976.

3. Brendan T. Byrne, interview with Andrew Szanton.

4. Brendan T. Byrne, interview with author, September 28, 2013.

5. John O. Davies, "Dugan Calls Byrne Feud 'Civilized'," April 22, 1976, *Courier-Post*.

6. Brendan T. Byrne, interview for Rutgers-Eagleton Byrne Archive, September 13, 2006.

7. John J. Degnan, interview for Rutgers-Eagleton Byrne Archive, August 7, 2006.

8. Jean Featherly Byrne, quoted in Linda Lamendola, "Jersey's First Lady: 'It takes courage to stand up for what you believe is right,'" *Star-Ledger,* May 10, 1977.

9. Jean Featherly Byrne, quoted in Linda Lamendola, "First Lady advises governor: 'You've got to get tough'," *Star-Ledger*, November 13, 1977.

10. President Gerald Ford, transcript of remarks at October 13, 1976 campaign reception in Union, The American Presidency Project; University of California at Santa Barbara. Accessed December 23, 2012 at http://www.presidency.ucsb.edu/ws/index.php?pid=6459&st=byrne&st1=brendan

11. Joseph F. Sullivan, "Carter Cancels a Visit to Jersey; Fear of Tax Protest Seen in Move," *New York Times*, October 27, 1976.

12. Eagleton Poll No. 23, October 1976. Six percent of respondents said they had no opinion or did not know enough about the tax.

13. "Governor should say it: "I do not choose to run," *Trenton Times*, November 30, 1976. Wolfe would later become an executive in Atlantic City casino-hotels, including serving as president of the Showboat and the Sands. See Bill Kent, "Captain of the Showboat," *New York Times*, February 18, 1996.

14. Jean Featherly Byrne, interview for Rutgers-Eagleton Byrne Archive, January 30, 2013.

15. Jean Featherly Byrne, letter to the editor, *Trenton Times*, December 7, 1976.

16. Brendan T. Byrne, interview with author, July 25, 2012.

17. John J. Degnan, interview for Rutgers-Eagleton Byrne Archive, August 7, 2006.

18. Eagleton Poll No. 23, October 1976.

19. Joseph F. Sullivan, "The Race to Be No. 1 Heats Up," *New York Times*, January 2, 1977.

20. Ibid.

21. "Preliminary Conclusions from the Recent Survey of New Jersey Democrats," memo from Paul Lutzker, Vice President, William R. Hamilton & Staff, to Jim Florio, February 3, 1977.

22. Ibid.

23. James Florio, interview for Rutgers-Eagleton Byrne Archive, August 6, 2012.

24. James Florio, interview for Rutgers-Eagleton Byrne Archive, October 8, 2008 (video).

25. James Florio, interview for Rutgers-Eagleton Byrne Archive, August 6, 2012.

26. Barry H. Evenchick, interview for Rutgers-Eagleton Byrne Archive, October 31, 2007.

27. Brendan Byrne, interview with author, January 22, 2013.

28. Joseph F. Sullivan, "Kean Opens Drive for Governor, Says He'd Let Income Tax Expire," *New York Times*, January 14, 1977.

29. Ibid.

30. Raymond Bateman, interview for Rutgers-Eagleton Byrne Archive, January 11, 2007.

31. Lewis B. Kaden, interview, Rutgers. September 27, 2010.

32. Jeffrey Kanige, "Brendan Byrne on Brendan Byrne," *New Jersey Reporter*, June 1988, 14.

33. Brendan T. Byrne, interview with author, September 28, 2012.

34. John J. Degnan, interview for Rutgers-Eagleton Byrne Archive, April 5, 2006.

35. Richard Leone, telephone conversation with author, April 23, 2013.

36. Brendan T. Byrne, interview for Rutgers-Eagleton Byrne Archive, August 28, 2006.

37. Kanige, "Brendan Byrne on Brendan Byrne," 14.

38. B. Thomas Byrne, Jr., interview for Rutgers-Eagleton Byrne Archive, September 18, 2012.

39. Brendan T. Byrne, interview with author, September 28, 2012.

40. Kanige, "Brendan Byrne on Brendan Byrne," 14.

41. John J. Degnan, interview for Rutgers-Eagleton Byrne Archive, August 7, 2006.

42. "Byrne in Fighting Speech at Headquarters Opening," *Asbury Park Press*, April 26, 1977.

43. Brendan T. Byrne, interview for Rutgers-Eagleton Byrne Archive, August 7, 2006.

44. Fariborz S. Fatemi, phone conversation with author, August 8, 2013.

45. Harold Hodes, interview for Rutgers-Eagleton Byrne Archive, August 28, 2006.

46. Kanige, "Brendan Byrne on Brendan Byrne," 15.

47. Jeffrey Laurenti, e-mail to author, May 12, 2013.

48. Robert E. Mulcahy, III, interview for Rutgers-Eagleton Byrne Archive, January 31, 2007.

49. Joseph F. Sullivan, "Jordan Cancels Gubernatorial Bid, Will Support Byrne for Re-election," *New York Times*, May 17, 1977.

50. Harold Hodes, interview for Rutgers-Eagleton Byrne Archive, August 28, 2006.

51. "A Governor's Diary," *Star-Ledger*, May 1–8, 2001.

52. James Florio, interview for Rutgers-Eagleton Byrne Archive, August 6, 2012.

53. Brendan T. Byrne, interview with author, September 3, 2013.

54. In 2006, Alaska Governor Frank Murkowski lost his bid for a second term when he received just 19 percent of the vote in finishing third in the Republican primary. Wally Edge, "Frank Murkowski breaks Brendan Byrne's record," PolitickerNJ.com, August 23, 2006. Accessed December 10, 2012 at http://www.politickernj.com/frank-murkowski-breaks-brendan-byrnes-record?quicktabs_mostx=commented

55. Brendan T. Byrne, interview with author, September 3, 2013.

56. Raymond Bateman, interview for Rutgers-Eagleton Byrne Archive, January 11, 2007.

57. John J. Degnan, interview for Rutgers-Eagleton Byrne Archive, August 7, 2006.

58. Bateman and Hughes had forged a close friendship when they both happened to be patients in a Philadelphia hospital together when Hughes was governor. When Hughes learned that Bateman was in a room on a lower floor, "every afternoon at four o'clock," Bateman recalled later, "Betty Hughes would come down with a wheelchair and take me up to the seventh floor and we'd drink martinis to six, and that's how Dick Hughes and I became very fast friends." Raymond Bateman, interview for Rutgers-Eagleton. Byrne Archive, January 11, 2007.

59. Brendan T. Byrne, interview with author, July 25, 2012.

60. Fariborz S. Fatemi, interview with author, August 18, 2012.

61. Raymond Bateman, interview for Rutgers-Eagleton Byrne Archive, January 11, 2007.

62. "A Governor's Diary," *Star-Ledger*, May 1–8, 2001.

63. Brendan T. Byrne, interview with author, July 25, 2012.

64. See Chapter 10.

65. Yaffe, *Other People's Children*, 51.

66. Clifford Goldman, e-mail to author, April 1, 2013.

67. Brendan T. Byrne, interview for Rutgers-Eagleton Byrne Archive, August 28, 2006; see also Philip Lentz, "Governor Criticizes Bateman Tax Plan," *Star-Ledger*, September 27, 1977.

68. Raymond Bateman, interview for Rutgers-Eagleton Byrne Archive, January 11, 2007.

69. Richard Leone, telephone conversation with author, April 23, 2013.

70. Jeffrey Laurenti, email to author, May 12, 2013.

71. John J. Degnan, interview for Rutgers-Eagleton Byrne Archive, April 5, 2006.

72. Brendan T. Byrne, interview with author, July 25, 2012.

73. Raymond Bateman, interview for Rutgers-Eagleton Byrne Archive, January 11, 2007.

74. Clifford Goldman, e-mail to author, April 1, 2013.

75. Fariborz S. Fatemi, interview with author, August 18, 2012.

76. Jeffrey Laurenti, e-mail to author, May 12, 2013.

77. Clifford Goldman, e-mail to author, April 1, 2013. In the first year of the program, property taxes declined in over half of the state's municipalities, with a total reduction, including homestead rebates, of some $350 million. Richard Van Wagner, "The New Jersey Gross Income Tax: An Analysis from Background to Enactment," *Seton Hall Legislative Journal*, vol. 2, Summer 1977, 100, 121.

78. Kanige, "Brendan Byrne On Brendan Byrne," 12.

79. Brendan T. Byrne, interview for Rutgers-Eagleton Byrne Archive, September 13, 2006.

80. Alfonso A. Narvaez, "Byrne Fails to Win Endorsement Of A.F.L.-C.I.O. Convention," *New York Times*, September 16, 1973.

81. Joseph F. Sullivan, "Trenton Suspends Two Officers in Leak of Report on Lordi," *New York Times*, June 16, 1978.

82. John J. Degnan, interview for Rutgers-Eagleton Byrne Archive, April 5, 2006.

83. Brendan T. Byrne, interview with author, July 25 2012; Fariborz Fatemi, telephone conversation with author, July 15, 2013.

84. Richard Leone, telephone conversation with author, April 23, 2013.

85. Robert E. Mulcahy, III, interview for Rutgers-Eagleton Byrne Archive, September 13, 2006.

86. Brendan T. Byrne interview with author, September 28, 2012.

87. Raymond Bateman, interview for Rutgers-Eagleton Byrne Archive, January 11, 2007.

88. Brendan T. Byrne, interview with author, July 25 2012.

89. John J. Degnan, interview for Rutgers-Eagleton Byrne Archive, August 7, 2006.

90. Raymond Bateman, interview for Rutgers-Eagleton Byrne Archive, January 11, 2007.

91. Robert E. Mulcahy, III, interview for Rutgers-Eagleton Byrne Archive. September 13, 2006.

92. Source for Byrne quotes at victory celebration from Robert L. King, *Courier-Post*, "Two-term Byrne," November 6, 1977; Jean Byrne quotes from Linda

Lamendola, "First Lady advises governor: 'You've got to get tough'," *Star-Ledger*, November 13, 1977.

93. Brendan T. Byrne, interview with author, July 25, 2012.

CHAPTER 11

1. Brendan T. Byrne, Second Inaugural Address, January 18, 1978.
2. Brendan T. Byrne, interview with author, September 28, 2012.
3. "Governor Brendan T. Byrne's Job Approval," Eagleton Institute of Politics, Rutgers University. Accessed January 12, 2014 at http://governors.rutgers.edu/on-governors/nj-governors/governor-brendan-t-byrnes-job-approval.
4. Cliff Zukin, "Political Culture and Public Opinion," in Gerald M. Pomper (ed.), *The Political State of New Jersey*, New Brunswick, NJ: Rutgers University Press, 1986, 21.
5. Linda Lamendola, "First Lady advises governor: 'You've got to get tough'," *Star-Ledger*, November 13, 1977.
6. Alan Rosenthal, telephone conversation with author, January 4, 2013.
7. Brendan T. Byrne, interview with author, September 28, 2012.
8. Thomas H. Kean, interview with author, October 8, 2013.
9. Brendan T. Byrne, interview with author, September 28, 2012.
10. Mulcahy quotes from telephone conversation with author, April 1, 2014. Pollock previously had been appointed by Byrne in his first term as commissioner on the Board of Public Utilities, the restructured agency of the former PUC.
11. Harold Hodes, telephone conversation with author, May 2, 2013.
12. Robert E. Mulcahy III, telephone conversation with author, April 1, 2014. Administrative Procedure Act, N.J.S.A.
13. Ibid.
14. Martin Waldron, "Gov. Byrne Now Enjoys Both Perks and Power," *New York Times*, July 15, 1979.
15. Thomas H. Kean, interview with author, October 8, 2013.
16. Brendan T. Byrne, interview with author, September 28, 2012.
17. Van Wagner, "New Jersey Gross Income Tax: An Analysis from Background to Enactment," *Seton Hall Legislative Journal*, 121.
18. Martin Waldron, "The Region: An Urban Policy Begins To Take Shape in N.J.," *New York Times*, January 1, 1978.
19. Degnan became convinced that the Governor was likely to appoint a more senior lawyer, such as Senator Steven Wiley, who had taken a key role in the school reform and income tax battle in the first term, or Justice Alan Handler, whom Byrne had named to the state Supreme Court after Handler had served as his counsel in the first term. John J. Degnan, interview for Rutgers-Eagleton Byrne Archive, June 20, 2011.
20. Jean Featherly Byrne, interview for Rutgers-Eagleton Byrne Archive, January 30, 2013.
21. On the day before Byrne's scheduled announcement, Degnan was convinced he would not be selected since Byrne avoided him at the State House during the

day. That evening, Degnan recalled, he told his wife Mary, "It's not me. I don't know who it's going to be tomorrow. But he hasn't even told me." John J. Degnan, interview for Rutgers-Eagleton Byrne Archive, June 20, 2011.

22. Ibid.

23. At the press conference later that day, the first question to Byrne was, "what credentials does John Degnan have to be attorney general?" to which Byrne replied, "He's a quick learner." Ibid.

24. *Heir v. Degnan*, 82 N.J. 109 (1980).

25. John J. Degnan, interview for Rutgers-Eagleton Byrne Archive, June 20, 2011.

26. At Byrne's suggestion, Degnan also allowed New Jersey law firms to compete for representing government, school boards, and other public authorities and agencies seeking to issue bonds, legal work that was previously exclusively the province of a few Manhattan law firms based on their purported expertise. Ibid.

27. Brendan T. Byrne, interview with author, September 28, 2012.

28. In 1977, Byrne had suggested that he might back off on his opposition to signing a bill restoring the death penalty if the legislature also passed the penal code reform. His position was criticized by some of his usual supporters, including Assemblyman Charles Yates, who suggested it was a departure by Byrne from his usual unyielding stands on issues of principle. When the penal reform was not passed, the Governor vetoed the death penalty bill, and in his second term he vetoed two subsequent death penalty bills.

29. Martin Waldron, "New Jersey Law Changes Reflect the New Morality," *New York Times*, August 10, 1979.

30. Brendan T. Byrne, Office of Governor Press release, August 29, 1979. See Richard J. Codey, *Me Governor? My Life in the Rough-and-Tumble World of New Jersey Politics*, New Brunswick, NJ: Rutgers University Press, 2011, 63–64.

31. Gregory L. Acquaviva, Jonathan L. Marshfield and David M. Stauss, "A Tribute to Chief Justice James R. Zazzali; More than a Caretaker," *Rutgers Law Review*, Summer 2007, 667, 672–73.

32. David B. Sachsman, Warren Sloat, *The Press and the Suburbs: the Daily Newspapers of New Jersey*, Piscataway, NJ: Transaction Publishers, 1985, 39.

33. Robert McFadden, "Fred G. Burke, 79, Official Who Promoted Changes in Public School Financing, Dies," *New York Times*, March 13, 2005.

34. Brendan T. Byrne, Annual Message to the Legislature, January 9, 1979.

35. "Conciliatory Statement by Dr. Burke Expected to Kill Plan to Censure Him," *New York Times*, December 6, 1975.

36. Brendan T. Byrne, interview with author, September 28, 2012.

37. For the history of New Jersey's hospital rate-setting system, see generally Mindy Widman and Donald W. Light, *Regulating Prospective Payment: An Analysis of the New Jersey Hospital Rate-Setting Commission*, Ann Arbor, MI: Health Administration Press, 1988, 13–18.

38. Brendan T. Byrne, interview with author, September 28, 2012.

39. As adapted by Finley for New Jersey, the concept also allowed the cost of uncompensated care to be a factor in setting rates, a reform that garnered the support of urban hospitals saddled with heavy indigent case loads, and, more reluctantly, of

the New Jersey Hospital Association, which was concerned that the issue might lead to a split in its membership, resulting in urban hospitals withdrawing to form their own organization.

40. In 1978, the state also enacted legislation to establish a commission to set hospital rates so that the burden of treating indigent patients would no longer be borne solely by hospitals in the older cities but shared statewide through imposing higher premiums on health care plans. Martin Waldron, "Hospital Rate-Setting Law is Signed by Byrne," *New York Times*, July 21, 1978; see generally Bruce Siegel, M.D., Anne Weiss, Jane Lynch, "Setting New Jersey Hospital Rates: A Regulatory System Under Stress," University of Puget Sound Law Review, Vol. 14:601, 1991. Accessed March 3, 2012 at http://lawpublications.seattleu.edu/cgi/viewcontent.cgi ?article=1333&context=sulr&sei-redir=1#search=%22nj%20rate%20setting%20 hospital%22

41. See Chapter 13.

42. Brendan T. Byrne, interview with author, September 19, 2013.

43. "Chemical Control Indicted for Pollution," *New York Times*, March 10, 1981; Robert Hanley, "New Jersey Struggles To Tame Toxic Monster," *New York Times*, April 19, 1981.

44. In 1987, when Hollander was confirmed for his third term as chancellor, one reporter wrote that under Hollander "the state has become nationally prominent for its imaginative approach to financing colleges, a generous financial-aid program for students and its recognition of the importance of recruiting and retaining minority students." Priscilla Van Tassel "Higher Education: Ongoing Challenge," *New York Times*, February 22, 1987.

45. Brendan T. Byrne, interview with author, September 19, 2013.

46. John J. Degnan, interview for Rutgers-Eagleton Byrne Archive, June 20, 2011.

47. Congressman Andrew Maguire withdrew from the race due to lack of funds and Leone launched an early advertising effort that boosted his name recognition over state Senator Alex Menza, making Menza a marginal candidate to Bradley and Leone for the remainder of the race. Menza received 8.8 percent of the vote. See generally for the Leone-Bradley primary campaign, Richard F. Fenno, Jr., *Senators on the Campaign Trail: The Politics of Representation*, Norman, OK: University of Oklahoma Press, 1996, 87, 173.

48. Bill Bradley, *Time Present, Time Past: A Memoir*, New York: Alfred A. Knopf, 1997, 148, 173.

49. Ibid.

50. Richard Leone, telephone conversation with author, April 5, 2013.

51. Brendan T. Byrne, interview with author, September 19, 2013.

52. Dave Anderson, "The Once and Always Champ," *New York Times*, July 1, 1979; Brendan T. Byrne, interview with author, October 4, 2012.

53. Brendan T. Byrne, interview with author, September 19, 2013.

54. The Office of Civil Defense was transferred to the Department of Law and Public Safety by a Reorganization Plan submitted by the Governor to the legislature on July 22, 1976. In 1980, following President Carter's consolidation of federal civil defense and other emergency services under the Federal Emergency Management

Agency, Byrne created by executive order the state Office of Emergency Management within the Division of the State Police and designated its director as the state's emergency services coordinator. Executive Order No. 101 December 17, 1980.

55. During Byrne's second year in office, on August 31, 1975, water supplies were cut off to some 200,000 homeowners and businesses in Trenton and three surrounding municipalities by an equipment failure at Trenton's water filtration plant on the Delaware River. Pursuant to an executive order issued by Byrne, an emergency pipeline system was quickly built to connect the Elizabethtown Water Company system at Princeton with Trenton. The crisis gradually eased, with water completely restored after nine days. See Executive Order No. 26, September 2, 1975. Accessed October 4, 2012 at http://njlegallib.rutgers.edu/eo/docs/byrne/order026-/index.pdf; Executive Order No. 27, September 2, 1975. Accessed October 4, 2012 at http://njlegallib.rutgers.edu/eo/docs/byrne/order027-/index.pdf; Alfonso A. Narvaez, "Report Lays Blame for '75 Trenton Water Crisis," *New York Times*, June 2, 1976.

56. Cass Peterson, "A Decade Later, TMI's Legacy is Distrust," *Washington Post*, March 28, 1989.

57. Brendan T. Byrne, interview with author, October 4, 2012.

58. Timothy Carden, interview for Rutgers-Eagleton Byrne Archive, October 30, 2007.

59. Clinton Pagano, interview for Rutgers-Eagleton Byrne Archive, October 25, 2010.

60. Brendan T. Byrne, handwritten notes of meeting, March 31, 1979.

61. Brendan T. Byrne, interview with author, September 28, 2012; see also Byrne handwritten notes of March 31, 1979 meeting.

62. Ibid.

63. Martin Waldron, "Capital Report," *New York Times*, August 31, 1980.

64. Brendan T. Byrne, interview with author, October 11, 2013.

65. Robert E. Mulcahy III, telephone conversation with author, April 1, 2014.

66. Terence Smith, "President Summons Aides to Camp David for a Broad Review," *New York Times*, July 7, 1979.

67. Brendan T. Byrne, interview with author, October 11, 2013.

68. See Kevin Mattson, "A Politics of National Sacrifice," *The American Prospect*, March 23, 2009. Accessed October 22, 2012 at http://prospect.org/article/politics-national-sacrifice; "Carter's 'Crisis of Confidence' Speech, American Experience, PBS.org, http://www.pbs.org/wgbh/americanexperience/features/general-article/carter-crisis-speech/. Byrne was more successful in having several photos he took while at Camp David published by *Newsweek* magazine in return for a contribution the magazine made at Byrne's request to Seton Hall University. Brendan T. Byrne, interview with author, October 4, 2012; "Governor Byrne, Snapshot Artist, Has Photos Published," *New York Times*, July 21, 1979.

69. Crude Oil Windfall Profit Tax Act, P.L. 96-223.

70. Frank Thompson (ed.), *Public Papers of the Presidents of the United States, Jimmy Carter, 1979*, Washington, DC: Government Printing Office 1981. Byrne later recounted the story of how he expressed his displeasure at Carter

for using the "five fingers' remark without attribution: "After Jimmy Carter left office, I had to take him to my house for dinner. And that evening, people came in with his book contract. He had me witness his signature. I said to him, 'Mr. President, if you use my line about the five fingers, and don't credit me, there will be hell to pay.' So the book comes out, the line is there, and he credits me." Quoted in John Schoonejongen, "9 Quotes from Brendan Byrne on his 90th Birthday," Asbury Park Press, April 1, 2014. Accessed April 3, 2014 at http://blogs. app.com/capitolquickies/2014/04/01/9-quotes-from-brendan-byrne-on-his-90th-birthday/#sthash.LdWlnoIw.dpuf

71. Comprehensive Environmental Response, Compensation, and Liability Act of 1980, 42 U.S.C. 9601; Spill Compensation and Control Act, N.J.S. 58:10-23.11.

72. See Chapter 12.

73. Brendan T. Byrne, interview with author, September 19, 2013.

74. Ibid.

75. Indirectly, Byrne's impact on the Court was continued when James Zazzali, Byrne's former Attorney General and member of his Essex County Prosecutor's Office staff, was appointed in 2000 by Governor Christine Todd Whitman as an associate justice and was subsequently nominated as chief justice by Governor Jon Corzine and confirmed in October 2006, serving until he reached the mandatory retirement age of 70 on June 17, 2007.

76. Pollock had previously been appointed by Byrne to serve on the PUC and the State Commission on Investigation. "When he [Byrne] first asked me to work for him, I thought he might have forgotten that I was a Republican, so I reminded him," Pollock was later quoted upon his retirement from the Court in 1999. "He paused for a moment and said, 'I can stand it if you can.'" David Kocieniewski, "Judge Leaving High Court After 20 Years as Unifier," *New York Times*, February 26, 1999.

77. See Chapter 12.

78. N.J.S.A. 58:10-23.11.

79. Brendan T. Byrne, interview with author, October 4, 2012; see also Robert Cohen, "Wilentz Choice May Usher in New Court Era," *Star-Ledger*, March 18, 1979.

80. Jerry F. English, interview for Rutgers-Eagleton Byrne Archive, December 13, 2006.

81. Brendan T. Byrne, interview with author, October 4, 2012.

82. See e.g. *Abbott v. Burke*, 100 N.J. 269 (1985); *Abbott v. Burke*, 119 N.J. 287 (1990); *Abbott v. Burke*, 136 N.J. 444 (1994). For the subsequent history of the *Abbott* litigation, see "The History of Abbott," Education Law Center. Accessed October 12, 2012 at http://www.edlawcenter.org/cases/abbott-v-burke/abbott-history.html

CHAPTER 12

1. See generally "Pinelands Final Environmental Impact Statement," Northeast Regional Office, Heritage Conservation and Recreation Service, US Department of the Interior, 1981. New Jersey's cranberry production is carried out almost exclusively

in the center of the Pinelands. Cranberry farming is directly tied to the water supply, depending on bogs that must be periodically flooded for cultivation and harvest. The large, cultivated blueberry was first developed in the Pinelands by Elizabeth White and Frederick Coville in 1916.

2. During the Revolutionary War, cannon balls for George Washington's Continental Army were made from Pinelands bog iron—created from the interaction of decaying vegetation and iron-rich clays found in the streams and bogs. Between 1765 and the end of the Civil War, some thirty iron furnaces operated in the forests. Robert J. Mason, *Contested Lands: Conflict and Compromise in New Jersey's Pine*, Barrens, PA: Temple University Press, 1992, 56. In the 1870s, the pure water of the aquifer provoked the interest of businessman Joseph Wharton, who bought large tracts of land for his plan to build a pipeline to ship the water to Philadelphia, but the project was blocked when legislation was enacted in Trenton barring the export of the water outside the state. Martin Waldron, "Land-Lust Bedevils the Pine Barrens," *New York Times*, July 30, 1978. Wharton's property would later be acquired by the state and incorporated in Wharton State Forest.

3. "Southern New Jersey and the Delaware Bay: Historic Themes and Resources within the New Jersey Coastal Heritage Trail," National Park Service. Accessed January 12, 2013 at http://www.cr.nps.gov/history/online_books/nj2/chap5.htm

4. Brendan T. Byrne, interview with author, February 12, 2013.

5. John McPhee, *The Pine Barrens*, New York: Farrar, Straus & Giroux, 1968.

6. A McPhee cousin also later was a receiver on the Princeton football team led by the All-American Dick Kazmaier. "I can still hear the announcer," Byrne recalled, "saying, Kazmaier to McPhee for the Princeton touchdown!" Brendan T. Byrne, interview with author, February 12, 2013.

7. McPhee, *The Pine Barrens*, 156. Brendan T. Byrne, interview with author, February 12, 2013.

8. John McPhee, "The Pine Barrens," *The New Yorker*, November 25, December 2, 1967. McPhee discussed the process of researching and writing his articles and *The Pine Barrens* in John McPhee, "The Writing Life: Structure," *The New Yorker*, January 14, 2013. An excerpt from *The Pine Barrens* would be published in the *New York Times* on July 4, 1976, the nation's bicentennial.

9. See generally James F. McCloy and Ray Miller, *The Jersey Devil*, Wallingford, PA: Middle Atlantic Press, 1976. See also Stephen Winick, "Tales of the Jersey Devil," Benjamin Botkin Lecture Series, American Folklife Center, Library of Congress, August 23, 2005. Accessed October 4, 2012 at http://www.loc.gov/folklife/events/BotkinArchives/2004thru2005PDFandVideo/WinickFlyer.html

10. Elizabeth Kite, a researcher at the Vineland Training School for Feeble-Minded Girls and Boys, published a paper titled "The Pineys," from which newspapers within and outside New Jersey published excerpts emphasizing her most sensational findings of mental and physical disabilities. Joseph G. Bilby, Harry F. Ziegler and James Martin Madden, *Hidden History of New Jersey*, Charleston, SC: The History Press, 2011, 85. Some of Kite's research was used by Henry H. Goddard, the Vineland Training School's research director, in writing his own book advancing his theory that nearly all piney families were descended from one man, whom he claimed fathered

an illegitimate son with an imbecile barmaid, producing subsequent generations of imbeciles, prostitutes, epileptics, and drunks. *The Kallikak Family: A Study in the Heredity of Feeble-Mindedness*, New York: MacMillan, 1912.

11. *New York Sun*, June 29, 1913, 44. Quoted in Mason, 63; McPhee, *The Pine Barrens*, 52–53.

12. Brendan T. Byrne, interview with author, October 12, 2012.

13. McPhee, *The Pine Barrens*, 11. The excerpt is from a poem written by Annie Johnson Flint (1866–1932), a resident of Vineland who from an early age was afflicted with crippling arthritis. See Rowland V. Bingham, "The Triumphant Story of Annie Johnson Flint." Accessed January 12, 2014 at http://www.preceptaustin.org/annie_johnson_flint%27s_biography.htm

14. Brendan T. Byrne, interview with author, October 12, 2012.

15. The testing was done by the Army's new Chemical Warfare Service established in May 1918. Charles E. Heller, "Chemical Warfare in World War I: The American Experience, 1917–1918," Combat Studies Institute, US Army Command and General Staff College, Fort Leavenworth, KS, September 1984. Accessed December 4, 2012 at http://www.cgsc.edu/carl/resources/csi/heller/heller.asp

16. In 1928, the pines briefly were the focus of attention when "the Mexican Lindbergh," Emilio Carranza, was killed when his plane crashed in the forest as he was returning home to Mexico, just one month after completing the third-longest solo flight at the time—a goodwill journey from Mexico City to New York City. Matt Chiappardi, "Remembering Mexican aviator Emilio Carranza," PhillyBurbs. com, July 10, 2011. Accessed January 22, 2013 at http://www.phillyburbs.com/news/local/burlington_county_times_news/remembering-mexican-aviator-emilio-carranza/article_356fdda4-319b-5a5f-b6ad-c33a5a9401a6.html

17. Barbara G. Salmore and Stephen A. Salmore, *New Jersey Politics and Government: the Suburbs Come of Age*, New Brunswick, NJ: Rivergate Books, 2008, 355–56.

18. Jay Romano, "Growth Transforms A 'Sleepy' County," *New York Times*, May 5, 1991.

19. Beryl Robichaud Collins and Emily W. B. Russell (eds.), *Protecting the New Jersey Pinelands*, New Brunswick, NJ: Rutgers University Press, 1988, 47.

20. Mason, *Contested Lands*, 76; "Pine Barrens," *The Record*, February 25, 1979.

21. Ibid., 76–77.

22. William Burrows, "Time Runs Out at JFK," *New York Magazine*, July 29, 1968, 14.

23. "Pinelands Jetport to Get U.S. Review," *New York Times*, June 7, 1967.

24. Ibid.

25. The military also opposed the jetport on the ground that it might conflict with current or future operations at its existing installations at Lakehurst, Fort Dix, and McGuire Air Force Base. Beryl Robichaud Collins and Emily W. B. Russell (eds.), *Protecting the New Jersey Pinelands*, New Brunswick, NJ: Rutgers University Press, 1988, 40–44.

26. "Mr. Meyner Turns Left," *New York Times*, August 30, 1969. Mason, *Contested Lands*, 79.

27. By the time Cahill left office in 1974, declining airport profits and the opening for civilian use of Stewart Air Force Base in New York undercut the past interest by the Port Authority and leading airlines in building a new airport. Gary Shenfield, "Jetport in Barrens Called Dead Issue," *New York Times*, October 27, 1974.

28. "In a few instances, projects were withdrawn or even rejected on PEC advice, but most often PEC findings were ignored." Robichaud, *Protecting the New Jersey Pinelands*, 50. "Plan for Saving Pine Barrens," *New York Times*, July 16, 1972.

29. Robichaud, Ibid., 45–47. Ironically, DeMarco later benefited from selling development rights for 3,600 acres for $3 million in the transfer of development rights program and subsequently sold his land for preservation to the New Jersey Conservation Foundation. See Robert Mason, "The Pinelands," in Mark B. Lapping and Owen J. Furuseth, *Big Places, Big Plans*, Burlington, VT: Ashgate, 2004, 46.

30. See Chapter 11.

31. The Authority had argued that since it had previously issued bonds for financing the construction of the Expressway, it "no legal recourse" except to proceed to comply with the covenants issued to buyers of the bonds Walter H. Waggoner, "Turnpike Agency Contesting Byrne," *New York Times*, December 19, 1973.

32. *Plan for the Pinelands*, Pinelands Environmental Council, Browns Mills, NJ, 1975.

33. David Bardin, letter to Garfield DeMarco, August 22, 1975. Quoted in Mark B. Lapping and Owen J. Furuseth, *Big Places, Big Plans*, 52; Beryl Robichaud Collins and Emily W.B. Russell (eds.), *Protecting the New Jersey Pinelands*, 46; Terry Connelly, "Bardin attacks Pinelands plan for development," *Star-Ledger*, August 27, 1975.

34. Collins and Russell, *Protecting the New Jersey Pinelands*, 47. The PEC's image also would be tarnished by the indictment of its executive director, Joseph Portash, for corruption in his position as mayor of Manchester Township. Garfield DeMarco resigned as chairman in 1979.

35. Ibid., 50.

36. Ibid., 50–51.

37. Ibid., 52.

38. John J. Degnan, "The Pinelands Protection Act: A Discussion by Participants in the Process," Eagleton Institute of Politics, Rutgers University, October 15, 1987, 19.

39. Mason, "The Pinelands," in Lapping and Furuseth (eds.), *Big Places, Big Plans*, 35.

40. Donald Janson, "Damage to Pine Barrens Feared from Cities, Casinos and the Sea," *New York Times*, December 17, 1976.

41. "Chairman of Pinelands Council says GOP Victories helped council," *The Beacon*, November 11, 1976.

42. Special Counsel Alan Handler and Assistant Counsel Donald Linky, memo to Governor Byrne, November 18, 1976. See also notes of Governor Byrne, November 19, 1976. Floyd West was one of the few local officials to advocate for a strong preservation program and would later be appointed as a member of the Pinelands Commission.

43. Donald Janson, "Gains are Seen in Efforts to Preserve the Pine Barrens," *New York Times*, May 7, 1977.

44. Collins and Russell, *Protecting the New Jersey Pinelands*, 53.

45. Executive Order No. 56, 28 May 1977. Accessed January 12, 2013 at http://njlegallib.rutgers.edu/eo/docs/byrne/order056-/index.pdf

46. Ibid.

47. Brendan T. Byrne, interview for Rutgers-Eagleton Byrne Archive, August 11, 2009.

48. Brendan T. Byrne, interview with Andrewc Szanton.

49. Florio would later say that his initial interest in the Pinelands had been sparked by the Nixon Administration's plans to allow offshore drilling for oil and gas off the New Jersey coast, with the prospect that any discovery would lead to the construction of pipelines through the forests to refineries in Philadelphia. James Florio, interview for Rutgers-Eagleton Byrne Archive, October 8, 2008. Accessed December 10, 2012 at http://www.youtube.com/watch?v=1le3EdOZmQ8. Greenline parks were a new conservation approach intended for areas where there was mixed private and public ownership (contrasting with past federal programs in which land was acquired for establishing national parks, forests and wildlife preserves and where the federal government owned all of the property). Florio's bill required states to create "land management commissions" that would regulate land use and control development in the designated area according to a master plan. Once this plan was in place, federal aid would be available for the area. Edward C. Burks, "Congress Heeds Pine Barrens' Plight," *New York Times*, March 20, 1977. Edward C. Burks, "Florio Opposed on Plan to Save Barrens," *New York Times*, October 9, 1977.

50. "Lawmakers differ on Pinelands," *Star-Ledger*, November 29, 1977; The Forsythe-Hughes alternative called for the creation of a central federal wildlife refuge in the core of the Pinelands. In the remainder of the region, separate Pinelands agencies would be created in each of forty-one municipalities affected by the legislation. By May 1978, the three Congressmen reached a compromise that built on common elements of their proposals, but no bill made it out of the House committee. Edward C. Burks, "A Ray of Hope for Pine Barrens," *New York Times*, May 14, 1978.

51. Secretary of the Interior Cecil Andrus, letter to Governor Byrne, December 10, 1978.

52. The bill authorized $26 million for the Pinelands, $3 million for planning and $23 million for land acquisition.

53. Donald Linky, "The Pinelands Protection Act A Discussion by Participants in the Process," Eagleton Institute of Politics, Rutgers University, October 15, 1987, 19.

54. Executive Order No. 71, February 8, 1979. Accessed January 12, 2013 at http://njlegallib.rutgers.edu/eo/docs/byrne/order072-/index.pdf

55. Dan Weissman, "Byrne puts 'core' of Pinelands into a development moratorium," *Star-Ledger*, February 9, 1979.

56. "A Plan for a Pinelands National Preserve," Rutgers Center for Coastal and Environmental Studies.

57. Mason, *Contested Lands*, 87.

58. Donald Janson, "Pine Barrens Construction Ban Stirs Up an Emotional Debate," *New York Times*, March 25, 1979.

59. Ibid.

60. As a member of the Assembly in 1974, Merlino had introduced legislation to give the state stronger controls over land use along state highways, arguing that vast shopping malls—like ones then under construction along U.S. 1 in Mercer County—inevitably degraded the utility of the highway and also drew retail and commercial enterprises out of the cities. Jeffrey Laurenti, e-mail to author, July 2, 2013. Merlino had written to Byrne on July 8, 1977, requesting that "your office get a strong Pinelands protection bill prepared for introduction this summer." Joseph P. Merlino, letter to Governor Byrne, July 8, 1977.

61. Donald Janson, "Pine Barrens Construction Ban Stirs Up an Emotional Debate," *New York Times*, March 25, 1979. Merlino's interest in the Pinelands also may have had a trace of ethnic nostalgia. "The Pinelands were, for Trenton Italians of a certain generation," as Merlino's legislative aide Jeff Laurenti reflected years later, "a place where members of sportsmen's clubs went hunting. I could never get Joe out on a canoe on the Batsto, which for the safety of others on the river was probably just as well, but he felt strongly about the environment and believed he had the power to do something about it. He surely wanted to be remembered for more than pushing the income tax through the Senate and for urban issues—and the Pinelands would be a crowning environmental achievement." Jeffrey Laurenti, e-mail to author, July 2, 2013.

62. Participants included Jeffrey Laurenti, Merlino's legislative aide and staff director of the Senate Democrats; Kathryn Crotty, aide to Senator Pat Dodd, chairman of the Senate Environment Committee; Donald Linky, director of the Governor's Office of Policy and Planning; Jeffrey Light, assistant counsel to the governor; Steven Picco, Glenn Paulson and Sean Reilly from the Department of Environmental Protection; and Richard Ginman and Richard Binetsky from the Department of Community Affairs.

63. Ibid., 94.

64. Donald Linky, "The Pinelands Protection Act A Discussion by Participants in the Process," Eagleton Institute of Politics, Rutgers University October 15, 1987, 19.

65. N.J.S.A.13:18A-9 specifies the goals of the Comprehensive Management Plan.

66. Ibid.; "Crowd rips Pinelands building ban," *Trenton Times*, February 18, 1979. The colorful Gewertz sometimes would dress in yellow plaid suits, a full-length fur coat or colonial costumes while attending legislative sessions. Perhaps his best-known incident occurred during a visit to Atlantic City, when he filed a police report that his $8,000 watch had been stolen from his hotel room by a prostitute. See "Kenneth Gewertz, 72, 'Mr. Deptford,'" *Philadelphia Inquirer*, December 14, 2006. Accessed January 12, 2013 at http://articles.philly.com/2006-12-14/news/25398931_1_partisan-politics-dark-ages-big-friends/2

67. Albert Burstein, interview for Rutgers-Eagleton Byrne Archive, May 15, 2006.

68. For editorials, see "Pinelands Moratorium," *Trenton Times*, February, 11, 1979; "Preserving the Pinelands," *Star-Ledger*, February 26, 1979; "Pine Barrens," *The Record*, February 25, 1979; "Pinelands Moratorium," *Asbury Park Press*, February 18, 1979; "The Pinelands Plan," *The Press of Atlantic City*, February 14, 1979.

69. Donald Janson, "Pine Barrens Construction Ban Stirs Up an Emotional Debate," *New York Times*, March 25, 1979.

70. Brendan T. Byrne, interview with Andrew Szanton.

71. Brendan T. Byrne, interview with author, September 28, 2012. The New Jersey Supreme Court later upheld the Pinelands Commission's regulations restricting development on agricultural property in *Gardner v. New Jersey Pinelands Comm'n*, 125 NJ 193 (1991).

72. "Byrne bans construction in Pinelands," *Trenton Times*, February 9, 1979. Perskie would later be credited—inaccurately, as it turned out—to have been the driving force behind excluding sections of the coast that were regulated under the Coastal Area Facilities Review Act from the more stringent provisions of the bill. And to this day, this myth persists, with this excluded area still known as "Perskie's thumb and forefinger." The area in question was also not included in the Rutgers report boundary map. Michael Catania, e-mail to author, April 29, 2013.

73. "Many Jerseyans never heard of Pines," *Trenton Times*, February 14, 1979.

74. The only southern legislator to openly back the moratorium was Senator Charles Yates. Citing a 1977 poll that showed 90 percent of Burlington County Democrats favored preservation, Yates concluded that there was broad public support of the interim ban on building. Dan Weissman, "Builders and Realtors will sue on Byrne's Pinelands moratorium," *Star-Ledger*, February 14, 1979.

75. John J. Degnan, "The Pinelands Protection Act A Discussion by Participants in the Process," Eagleton Institute of Politics, Rutgers University, October 15, 1987, 19.

76. Brendan T. Byrne, "The Pinelands Protection Act A Discussion by Participants in the Process," Eagleton Institute of Politics, Rutgers University, October 15, 1987, 19.

77. John J. Degnan, "The Pinelands Protection Act A Discussion by Participants in the Process," Eagleton Institute of Politics, Rutgers University, October 15, 1987, 19.

78. Ibid.

79. Ibid. Support for the Merlino-Yates bill in the Senate came largely from Central and North Jersey. The Chairman of the Senate Energy and Environment Committee, Essex County Democrat Frank "Pat" Dodd, who while senate president during Byrne's first term had clashed sharply with the Governor on the income tax, stated that his committee would pass the bill "essentially as is" and would not limit the scope of the bill to the inner core of the Pinelands. He also refused to insert in the bill exemptions to the moratorium for individual projects. Dan Weissman, "Builders and Realtors will sue on Byrne's Pinelands moratorium," *Star-Ledger*, February 14, 1979.

80. Dan Weissman, "Senate clears broad controls over Pinelands development," *Star Ledger*, May 22, 1979.

81. Robert E. Mulcahy III, telephone conversation with author, April 1, 2014.

82. Brendan T. Byrne, interview with author, October 22, 2012.

83. Robert E. Mulcahy III, telephone conversation with author, April 1, 2014.

84. Harold Hodes, "The Pinelands Protection Act: A Discussion by Participants in the Process," Eagleton Institute of Politics, Rutgers University, October 15, 1987, 30.

85. Ibid.

86. Harold Hodes, telephone conversation with author, May 9, 2013.

87. Michael Catania, "The Pinelands Protection Act: A Discussion by Participants in the Process," Eagleton Institute of Politics, Rutgers University, October 15, 1987, 30.

88. Brendan T. Byrne, interview with author, October 22, 2012.

89. A motion to block discussion failed 38-27, and another to open the bill to amendments was narrowly defeated by a 35-31 vote.

90. Ironically, in his role as the neutral staffer to the legislature, Michael Catania was forced to help both sides of the debate on the bill he had largely written, "I was kept very busy writing questions for Assemblyman Stewart to ask Stockman," Catania recalled years later, "and then sitting on the floor with Stockman helping him to answer those same questions." Michael Catania, e-mail to author, April 29, 2013.

91. Robert E. Mulcahy III, interview with author, November 1, 2013.

92. Robert Schwanenberg, "Debate holds up Pinelands Bill," *Star-Ledger*, June 22, 1979.

93. Harold Hodes, "The Pinelands Protection Act: A Discussion by Participants in the Process," Eagleton Institute of Politics, Rutgers University, October 15, 1987, 30.

94. L.1979, c. 1ll, s. 1, N.J.S.A.

95. Dan Weissman, "Byrne signs Pinelands control bill in 'emotional' Trenton ceremony,'" *Star-Ledger*, June 29, 1979; see also "Remarks of Governor Brendan Byrne, Signing of Pinelands Protection Bill," June 28, 1979.

96. Harold Hodes, telephone conversation with author, May 9, 2013.

97. *New Jersey Builders Ass'n v. Byrne*, 80 N.J. 469 (1979). A decision released after Byrne left office, *Orleans Builders & Developers v. Byrne*, 186 N.J. Super. 432 (App. Div. 1982) certification denied 91 N.J. 528 (1982) dismissed the plaintiff's claim that the Byrne executive order was unconstitutional, emphasizing that it was for a limited period and purpose: "The Governor's proclamation did not restrict development in the Pinelands pursuant to local permits and other approvals. It prohibited the issuance of permits and other approvals only by agencies subject to the Governor's authority within the Executive Branch of State Government, pending enactment of state legislation regulating development in the Pinelands in accordance with the federal act establishing the Pinelands National Reserve. The interim moratorium under the Pinelands Protection Act was likewise of limited duration until adoption of the comprehensive management plan."

98. Brendan T. Byrne, interview with author, October 22, 2012.

99. Brendan T. Byrne, interview with Andrew Szanton.

100. Moore, then the executive director of the Newark Watershed Conservation and Development Corporation, had previously worked closely with Harold Hodes when Hodes was an aide to Newark Mayor Kenneth Gibson, and Hodes persuaded the Governor to go ahead to announce that he was naming Moore to fill the post. "Frank Parker learned from Byrne in the Governor's office just before they came out for the signing that Byrne was going to announce my appointment," Moore later recounted. "I had to run out in the hall after the signing to call Ken Gibson so he would not be surprised by the announcement." Terrence Moore, e-mail to the author, June 9, 2013.

101. Candace Ashmun, "The Pinelands Protection Act: A Discussion by Participants in the Process," Eagleton Institute of Politics, Rutgers University, October 15, 1987, 46.

102. Deborah Poritz, then a deputy attorney general and later chief justice of the state Supreme Court, quickly wrote an opinion that $500,000 in state Green acres bond funds could be used since the plan being drafted by the Commission would lead to acquisition of land. The Geraldine Dodge Foundation also awarded a grant for $200,000 to fund staff for the interim development review process, and U.S Secretary of the Interior Cecil Andrus provided $800,000 in discretionary Land and Water Conservation Fund money for the remainder of the planning costs. Terrence Moore, e-mail to author, June 9, 2013.

103. The plan also recommended property tax relief for municipalities, projected that it would cost an estimated 80 million dollars to acquire land for preservation by the federal and state governments and conservation groups, and proposed a system of "development credits" that would allow landowners of highly restricted property to sell rights they received for agreeing to forego development of their property to those owning property in other areas where higher density development was permitted. The property tax relief recommendation later resulted in legislation enacted during the Kean administration, the Pinelands Municipal Property Stabilization Act, P.L. 1983, c. 551. The development credit program was largely based on prior work and publications by commission member Budd Chavooshian, a Rutgers professor who had advocated the system as a means to alleviate public costs of land acquisition. The Commission also looked closely at the existing TDR program in Montgomery County, Maryland. Terrence Moore, e-mail to author, June 9, 2013.

104. Shayna Panzer, "Safeguards for the Pinelands," *New York Times*, July 13, 1980.

105. Assembly Majority Leader Doyle sponsored a bill to give the Legislature the power to veto the master plan and mandate a five-month delay in its implementation which passed the Assembly by 64 to 5, but did not receive a vote in the Senate. Dan Weissman, "Assembly votes to uproot Byrne's power on Pinelands," *Star-Ledger*, June 17, 1980.

106. Approval of the protection area plan came after compromises were struck to soften opposition from local officials and landowners, including allowing those owning an acre or more of land prior to the moratorium imposed by Byrne's executive order to build a single-family home without Commission approval and increasing the overall density permitted in certain sections. See Mason, *Contested Lands*, 105. In the vote on the final plan on November 21, 1980, the commissioners appointed by Atlantic, Ocean, and Cape May voted against approval; the Burlington, Camden, and Gloucester representatives joined the majority in voting to adopt the plan. The Cumberland County appointee, Brian McFadden, abstained, according to Terry Moore, "in order to be able to work with his communities more effectively on compliance." Terrence Moore, e-mail to author, June 24, 2013.

107. N.J.S.A. 13:18A-10 (b).

108. The boundaries of the Pinelands National Reserve and the Pinelands Area, as defined by the state legislation, differ somewhat. The Reserve, totaling 1.1 million

acres, includes land east of the Garden State Parkway and to the south bordering Delaware Bay, which is omitted from the 927,000 acre state Pinelands Area. The two jurisdictions together cover all or parts of 56 municipalities spread across seven counties—Atlantic, Burlington, Camden, Cape May, Cumberland, Gloucester, and Ocean. "Final Environmental Impact Statement: Proposed comprehensive management plan for the Pinelands National Reserve," U.S. Heritage Conservation and Recreation Service. Northeast Regional Office, U.S. Dept. of the Interior.

109. In response to the Department of Defense's objections to the authority given to the Commission to review military installation plans that threatened to delay the plan's approval, Terry Moore submitted a letter of interpretation during the federal review of the plan confirming that the plan could not impact national security interests. Robert McIntosh later became the federal representative to the commission in the Clinton Administration under Secretary of the Interior Bruce Babbitt. Terrence Moore, e-mail to author, June 9, 2013.

110. Following the approval by Andrus, the Comprehensive Management Plan was submitted to Congress, which had ninety days to act to request a formal review, but despite concerns that Congressmen Hughes and Forsythe would seek to delay the plan's implementation, the ninety-day period lapsed without Congressional action. See Mason, *Contested Lands*, 105. Byrne also attempted another late move to forestall any attempt by the Reagan Administration to undermine the preservation program when he persuaded his Republican 1977 reelection opponent, former Senator Raymond Bateman, to accept appointment by outgoing Secretary Andrus as the federal representative to the Pinelands Commission. Byrne hoped that Bateman, with whom he continued to have a warm relationship even after their partisan exchanges in the 1977 campaign, would be difficult, as a prominent Republican, for Reagan to replace with a more pro-development appointee. The clever scheme failed, however, when Reagan's new Secretary of the Interior named his own appointee to succeed Bateman at the urging of Congressman Edwin Forsythe, who opposed the regulation of land for preservation without the payment of compensation. Skip Wollenberg, "Battle within state jeopardizes funds for Pines," *Courier-Post*, June 12, 1981.

111. *Orleans Builders & Developers v. Byrne*, 186 N.J. Super. 432 (App. Div. 1982) certification denied 91 N.J. 528 (1982).

112. Skip Wollenberg, "Battle within state jeopardizes funds for Pines," *Courier-Post*, June 12, 1981.

113. Joseph Donohue, "Environmental Groups Rap Perskie's Pines Bill," *Atlantic City Press*, June 24, 1981.

114. Dan Weissman, "'Compromise' emerges on Pines development," *Star-Ledger*, June 23, 1981. Just three days after the Perskie bill was introduced, Perskie said he had received a pledge from Governor Byrne's chief counsel, Daniel O'Hern, that he would strongly recommend the Perskie bill to the Governor. O'Hern's nomination to the Supreme Court was then pending before the Senate Judiciary committee chaired by Perskie. O'Hern had been a somewhat reluctant supporter of the Byrne Pinelands initiative. Michael Catania, who participated in the discussions between Perskie and O'Hern, recalls warning Perskie that the Governor was unlikely to support the bill. "But the Senator thought his control over the O'Hern nomination,"

Catania stated, "gave him a winning hand, and he refused to heed that warning." Michael Catania, e-mail to author, April 29, 2013. Despite his pedigree as a Harvard Law graduate who had clerked for Justice William Brennan on the United States Supreme Court, O'Hern had spent most of his career practicing law in Red Bank representing many clients of modest means; during staff meetings on the Pinelands bill, he expressed his concerns over the financial impact of the strict development constraints on the "little old ladies" who may have invested in real estate in the region in planning their retirement.

115. Carol Barrett, quoted in Joseph Donohue, "Environmental Groups Rap Perskie's Pines Bill," *The Press of Atlantic City*, June 24, 1981; New York Times quote is from "The Pinelands, Still Not Rescued," *New York Times*, July 7, 1981; *The Press of Atlantic City* is from "Perskie, Pines, People," July 2, 1981.

116. Donald Linky, the Governor's policy director, sent the Governor a memorandum on July 1 that stated "a successful effort by Perskie this year to weaken the Act with you as Governor would appear only to encourage further attempts to weaken the Act in future years with a governor who has less of a personal stake and commitment to this initiative." Donald Linky, memo to Governor Byrne, July 1, 1981.

117. Joseph Donohue, "Gov. Byrne Stuns Perskie, Rejects Pinelands 'Compromise' Bill," *The Press of Atlantic City*, July 9, 1981.

118. Franklin Parker, "The Pinelands Protection Act: A Discussion by Participants in the Process," Eagleton Institute of Politics, Rutgers University, October 15, 1987, 11.

119. Thomas H. Kean, remarks at "Environmental Policy in the Kean Administration," Eagleton Institute of Politics, Rutgers University, May 14, 2013.

120. Joseph F. Sullivan, "New Jersey Pinelands Preservation Works so Well it Hurts," *New York Times*, May 27, 1983; see generally Charles Siemon, "Legal and Legislative Challenges," in Robichaud and Collins, *Protecting the New Jersey Pinelands*, 261.

121. Terrence Moore, "The Pinelands Protection Act: A Discussion by Participants in the Process," Eagleton Institute of Politics, Rutgers University, October 15, 1987, 47, 48.

122. Candace Ashmun, "The Pinelands Protection Act: A Discussion by Participants in the Process," Eagleton Institute of Politics, Rutgers University, October 15, 1987, 47.

123. Mason, *Contested Lands*, 187.

124. John Hasse, Rowan University and Richard Lathrop, Grant R. Walton, Center for Remote Sensing and Spatial Analysis, Rutgers University, "Tracking New Jersey's Dynamic Landscape: Conflict and Compromise in New Jersey's Pine Barrens," 46–48. The study also found that the overall development allowed within the Pinelands growth areas compared well with that of the state as a whole, suggesting that the initial fears that the plan would stifle development were misplaced. Accessed March 12, 2013 at http://crssa.rutgers.edu/projects/lc/download/urbangrowth86_95_02/HasseLathrop_njluc_final_report_07_14_08.pdf

125. Ibid., 8.

126. Terrence Moore, e-mail to author, June 10, 2013.

127. Brendan T. Byrne, interview with Andrew Szanton.

CHAPTER 13

1. "In the 1920s, the intersection of Broad Street and Market Street in Newark was known as the busiest intersection at rush hour in the country, busier even than Times Square," according to a recent account by Adam Zipkin, deputy mayor for economic development in Newark. Quoted in Nancy Solomon, "A Walking Tour: Newark Broad Street," WNYC.org. Accessed December 17, 2012 at http://www.wnyc.org/articles/wnyc-news/2011/dec/15/newark-broad-street/

2. The first electric trolley in New Jersey was introduced in the 1880s on the Orange Crosstown Line, which eventually ran from Orange to Bloomfield. See City of Orange Township Historical Overview, City of Orange Township. Accessed September 12, 2012 at http://www.ci.orange.nj.us/history_main.html

3. The bus operations were previously named Public Service Transportation and then Public Service Coordinated Transport.

4. Alan J. Karcher, *New Jersey's Multiple Municipal Madness*, New Brunswick, NJ: Rutgers University Press, 1998, 64.

5. The influence of the Camden and Amboy in the state government is reviewed in Lawrence E. Mitchell, *The Speculation Economy: How Finance Triumphed Over Industry*, San Francisco: Berrett-Koehler Publishers, 2008, 36.

6. Brendan T. Byrne, interview with author, December 13, 2012.

7. Karcher, *New Jersey's Multiple Municipal Madness*, 63.

8. Jerome G. Rose, *Legal Foundations of Land Use Planning*, New Brunswick, NJ: Rutgers University Press, 1979, 19.

9. John B. Wefing, *The Life and Times of Richard J. Hughes: The Politics of Civility*, New Brunswick, NJ: Rutgers University Press, 2007, 113.

10. In its early months of operating in bankruptcy reorganization, the intercity passenger operations of Penn Central and other bankrupt railroads were transferred to Amtrak, a newly created private corporation established under authority of the federal Rail Passenger Service Act and which relied on substantial federal subsidies to meet its deficits. The Penn Central continued to operate in bankruptcy as it reduced its network and pared its services until the remaining passenger and freight system was transferred, pursuant to federal legislation enacted in 1976, to the Consolidated Rail Corporation (commonly known as "Conrail"), another new corporation created by federal legislation.

11. The other board members of the COA were the state treasurer, and the commissioner and assistant commissioner of the Department of Transportation. N.J.S.A. 27:25–24.

12. Joseph Carragher, "PUC chief calls for state to run commuter rails," *Star-Ledger*, September 22, 1968.

13. Lewis Kaden, Byrne's campaign policy adviser who later became his special counsel, had been a partner in the Manhattan law firm of Theodore Kheel, who since the 1950s had served as New York City's transit arbitrator and had become the Port Authority's most prominent critic; at one point, Kheel contended that the Authority "has taken a copout on mass transportation." See "Kheel Says That Port Authority Hoards Profits," *New York Times*, April 17, 1970.

14. Ibid.

15. Ibid.

16. Joseph F. Sullivan, "Jersey Will Cut Rail-Bus Subsidies," *New York Times*, July 9, 1975; see also memo from Manuel Carballo to Clifford Goldman, June 23, 1975.

17. Donald Janson, "Jersey Proposes Bus and Rail Rises," *New York Times*, August 13, 1975.

18. Martin E. Robins, telephone conversation with author, June 5, 2013.

19. Edward C. Burks, "Fare-Raise Plan for PATH Dropped," *New York Times*, February 15, 1974.

20. Ronald Sullivan, "Byrne Moves for Repeal of Covenant Curbing Port Authority Transit Aid," *New York Times*, February 14, 1974.

21. Ronald Sullivan, "A PATH Extension Ordered by Byrne," *New York Times*, February 14, 1974.

22. *United States Trust Co. of New York v. New Jersey*, 431 U.S. 1 (1977).

23. Brendan T. Byrne, interview with author, September 3, 2013.

24. Louis J. Gambaccini, interview for Rutgers-Eagleton Byrne Archive, February 7, 2006.

25. Ibid.

26. Martin Waldron, "Jersey Bus Service Declining Despite Big Subsidies," *New York Times*, April 19, 1979.

27. Louis J. Gambaccini, interview for Rutgers-Eagleton Byrne Archive, February 7, 2006.

28. Ibid.

29. The federal Employee Retirement Income Security Act (ERISA), P.L. 93-206, 29 U.S.C. Ch. 18, enacted in 1974 imposed new minimum funding requirements on employers to insure that adequate reserves were available to meet outstanding and future pension liabilities.

30. Martin E. Robins, telephone conversation with author, May 8, 2013.

31. Louis J. Gambaccini, interview for Rutgers-Eagleton Byrne Archive, February 7, 2006.

32. Martin E. Robins, "How the New Jersey Transit Corporation Was Born," New Jersey Transport Heritage Center Symposium, Alan M. Voorhees Transportation Center, Rutgers University, March 31, 2007; Telephone conversation with Martin E. Robins, June 5, 2013.

33. Mark Magyar, "Gambaccini Aims at Bus Takeover," *Red Bank Register*, January 26, 1979.

34. Brendan T. Byrne, interview with author, September 3, 2013.

35. Senate Bill No. 3137.

36. Louis J. Gambaccini, interview for Rutgers-Eagleton Byrne Archive, February 7, 2006.

37. W. Cary Edwards, interview for Rutgers-Eagleton Byrne Archive, December 22, 2008.

38. Ibid.

39. Louis J. Gambaccini, interview for Rutgers-Eagleton Byrne Archive, February 7, 2006.

40. Robert E. Mulcahy, III, telephone conversation with author, April 1, 2014.

41. Public Transit Act of 1979, P.L.1979, c.150. The state was represented in the negotiations by Allen Lowenstein, founder of Lowenstein Sandler, one of the state's most prominent law firms. Ibid.

42. Ibid.

43. Ibid.

44. Alan V. Lowenstein, *Alan V. Lowenstein: New Jersey Lawyer & Community Leader*, New Brunswick, NJ: Institute for Continuing Legal Education, 2001, 280.

45. Ibid., 288.

46. Ibid., 288–90.

47. Martin Waldron, "Jersey Acquires 2 Key Bus Lines for $32 million," *New York Times*, September 18, 1980.

48. "History and Structure," New Jersey Transit. Accessed January 22, 2013 at http://www.njtransit.com/tm/tm_servlet.srv?hdnPageAction=CorpInfoTo

49. Alfonso A. Narvaez, "Transport Bond issue at Stake," *New York Times*, September 9, 1979.

50. Louis J. Gambaccini, interview for Rutgers-Eagleton Byrne Archive, February 7, 2006.

51. New Jersey Department of Transportation, *People: The Transportation Connection*, October 2001. Accessed January 12, 2013 at http://www.state.nj.us/transportation/publicat/people.pdf

52. Alfonso A. Narvaez, "Transport Bond issue at Stake," *New York Times*, September 9, 1979.

53. The only other bond issue on the ballot, authorizing $95 million for higher education facilities, was rejected by a vote of 748,737 against to 611,639 for approval. Edward J. Mullin (ed.), *Manual of the Legislature of New Jersey: 1982*, Trenton, NJ: Edward J. Mullin, 1982.

54. Brendan T. Byrne, interview with author, September 3, 2013.

55. Louis J. Gambaccini, interview for Rutgers-Eagleton Byrne Archive, February 7, 2006; see also Louis J. Gambaccini, "Soapbox: Confessions of a Gas Tax Advocate," *New York Times*, March 7, 2004.

56. Brendan T. Byrne, interview with author, September 3, 2013.

CHAPTER 14

1. Dale Mezzacappa, "Was Brendan Byrne Too Good for New Jersey?" *Today: The Inquirer Magazine*, January 17, 1982.

2. Ibid.

3. John J. Degnan, interview for Center on the American Governor, Eagleton Institute of Politics, Rutgers University, Brendan T. Byrne Archive (hereafter cited as Rutgers-Eagleton Byrne Archive), June 6, 2011.

4. Robert E. Mulcahy III, interview with author, November 1, 2013.

5. Brendan T. Byrne, interview with author, October 23, 2012.

6. Before Byrne left office, the legislature passed a resolution placing a referendum on the ballot seeking voter approval of the Community Development Bond Act

(P.L. 1981, c. 486), which was approved at the November 1982 election. See "New Jersey Future to Honor Brendan Byrne," New Jersey Future, November 14, 2011. Accessed October 23, 2012 at http://www.njfuture.org/news/news-releases/2011-news-releases/brendan-byrne-event/

7. Clifford Goldman, e-mail to author, May 21, 2013.

8. Michael Breslin, interview by Barry H. Evenchick, September 28, 2005.

9. Richard Meislin, "What's In A Name? It Depends," *New York Times*, October 25, 1981; see also "Jersey Court to Decide On Arena-Name Vote," *New York Times*, October 11, 1981.

10. Lewis Thurston, then the executive director of the Senate Republican staff, later expanded: "The petition drive to change the name of the arena was headed by Senator Garrett Hagedorn with assistance from the Republican Senate office. At one point an intern in the office gathered 400 signatures to the petition at a Giants' football game and reported that he had approached a woman who gladly signed the petition but said 'young man I only want to change one letter in the name.' He looked at her signature: 'Brenda Byrne.'" Lewis Thurston, e-mail to author, August 17, 2013; see also Joseph Sullivan, "An Issue Emerges: The Byrne Arena," *New York Times*, October 4, 1981.

11. Mezzacappa, "Was Brendan Byrne Too Good for New Jersey?" *Today: The Inquirer Magazine.*

12. *New York Times*, December 6, 1981.

13. Richard J. Codey, "Let's Be Good Sports About The Arena's Name," *New York Times*, August 9, 1981.

14. S. J. Horner, "First Family Gets Ready to Move," *New York Times,* December 13, 1981.

15. Brendan T. Byrne, interview with author, September 3, 2013.

16. Brendan T. Byrne, interview with author, September 28, 2012; James Tuite, "Hambletonian Race: Money vs. Tradition," *New York Times*, September 30, 1979. With Byrne in attendance, the race on August 8, 1981, was won, perhaps appropriately, by a trotter named Shiaway St. Pat. Mike DelNagro, "When A Country Horse Trots A City Course," *Sports Illustrated*, August 17, 1981.

17. Mezzacappa, "Was Brendan Byrne Too Good for New Jersey?" *Today: The Inquirer Magazine.*

18. Primary election candidates were required to raise only $50,000 to qualify for state matching funds, with a candidate raising $350,000 receiving $600,000, the maximum amount of public support. Byrne unsuccessfully proposed increasing the minimum qualifying level from $50,000 to $150,000, but the bill died in the Assembly. Joseph F. Sullivan, "Turning Off Party Machines Turned On the Candidates" *New York Times*, March 8, 1981.

19. Joseph F. Sullivan, "Jersey Primary Ballot Bill Signed," *New York Times*, March 24, 1981.

20. John J. Degnan, interview for Rutgers-Eagleton Byrne Archive, June 20, 2011.

21. Brendan T. Byrne, interview with author, September 28, 2012.

22. Joseph F. Sullivan, "Lan quits governor race; Byrne makes Degnan ad," *New York Times*, April 30, 1981.

23. John J. Degnan, interview for Rutgers-Eagleton Byrne Archive, June 20, 2011.

24. Ibid.

25. Alfonso A. Narvaez, "Byrne Urges 3 To Give Up Their Gubernatorial Quest," *New York Times,* May 29, 1981.

26. Byrne, interview with author, September 28, 2012.

27. Eagleton Poll, No. 43, September 1981.

28. Alvin S. Felzenberg, *Governor Tom Kean: From the Jersey Statehouse to the 9-11 Commission,* New Brunswick, NJ: Rutgers University Press 2006, 173.

29. Ibid., 179.

30. Michael Specter, "Florio and Kean Making A Heavy Pitch On TV," *New York Times,* October 4, 1981.

31. Felzenberg, *Governor Tom Kean,* 168.

32. Ibid., 168.

33. President Reagan's own popularity had fallen from 75 percent in May to 49 percent in September. Ibid., 175.

34. Trish G. Graber, "Election night 1981, when the N.J. governor's race was too close to call," *Star-Ledger,* November 3, 2009. Accessed January 23, 2013 at http://www.nj.com/news/index.ssf/2009/11/election_night_1981_when_the_n.html

35. Brendan T. Byrne, interview with author, September 28, 2012.

36. Graber. "Election night 1981, when the N.J. governor's race was too close to call," *Star-Ledger.*

37. Felzenberg, *Governor Tom Kean,* 352–53.

38. Graber, "Election night 1981, when the N.J. governor's race was too close to call," *Star-Ledger.*

39. David Wald, "Florio Concedes Race to Kean," *Star-Ledger,* December 1, 1981; Joseph F. Sullivan, "Florio concedes governor's race to Kean in Jersey," *New York Times,* December 1, 1981.

40. Brendan T. Byrne, interview with author, September 28, 2012.

41. Ibid.

42. Richard Leone, interview with author, May 10, 2013. Leone also had begun appearing with Kean as an analyst on state affairs on New Jersey Network, the state government's public television station.

43. Felzenberg, *Governor Tom Kean,* 193.

44. Brendan T. Byrne, interview with author, September 28, 2012.

45. Jim Goodman, "Bills, vetoes cram Byrne's last days," *Trenton Times,* January 13, 1982.

46. Brendan T. Byrne, interview with author, October 30, 2013.

47. The state Senate's confirmation of Jacobson's nomination had been blocked by Republican State Senator James Wallwork from Essex County through the exercise of senatorial courtesy on the ground that none of the five casino commissioners resided in South Jersey. An Essex County resident, Jacobson then moved his official residence to his shore home in Long Beach Township; Democratic Senator John Russo then agreed to allow the nomination to proceed, but a majority of Democrats on the Senate Judiciary Committee refused to vote for the nomination to be released for a vote by the full Senate. Outgoing Senate President Merlino, however, replaced one of the

anti-Jacobson Democrats on the committee with another senator who voted for release of the nomination and the full Senate confirmed the nomination. Wally Edge, "In an emergency, Rabner can use the Jacobson plan," PolitickerNJ.com, June 14, 2007. Accessed September 29, 2013 at http://www.politickernj.com/emergency-rabner-can-use-jacobson-plan-9472

48. Matthew Purdy, "Byrne bids state an eloquent farewell," *Trenton Times*, January 12, 1982.

49. "Misjudgment in the Senate," *New York Times*, December 3, 1981.

50. Brendan T. Byrne, interview with author, October 30, 2013.

51. Wally Edge, "If Case beat Bell, Kean would have appointed two U.S. Senators in one week," PolitickerNJ.com, March 5, 2010. Accessed July 12, 2012 at http://www.politickernj.com/wallye/37430/if-case-beat-bell-kean-would-have-appointed-two-us-senators-one-week#ixzz2UsqoM0Wu

52. Brendan T. Byrne, interview with author, October 30. 2013.

53. "In the Best of Hands," *The Record*, January 15, 1982.

54. Ibid.

55. Matthew Purdy, "The Byrne Years: A Study in Paradox," *Trenton Times*, January 17, 1982.

56. Robert Comstock and John Framer quotes from Mezzacappa, "Was Brendan Byrne Too Good for New Jersey?"

57. Brendan T. Byrne, interview with author, October 22, 2012.

CHAPTER 15

1. S. J. Horner, "First Family Gets Ready to Move," *New York Times*, December 13, 1981.

2. Brendan T. Byrne, interview with author, January 16, 2013.

3. Thomas H. Kean, interview with author, October 1, 2013.

4. Ibid.

5. Thomas H. Kean, quoted in Barbara Fitzgerald, "The Odd Couple," *New York Times*, May 12, 2002.

6. Thomas H. Kean, Executive Order No. 175, June 8, 1987; Tom Johnson, "Kean signs wetlands bill, lifts building moratorium," *Star-Ledger*, July 2, 1987; Alvin S. Felzenberg, *Governor Tom Kean: From the New Jersey Statehouse to the 9-11 Commission*, New Brunswick, NJ: Rutgers University Press, 2006, 285–88.

7. Freshwater Wetlands Protection Act, P.L.1987, c. 156; N.J.S.A.13:9B-1 et seq.

8. Brendan T. Byrne, interview with author, January 16, 2013.

9. Ibid.

10. Ibid.

11. Pals Cabin closed in 2013. Peter Genovese, "Pals Cabin, a Jersey food landmark, closes for good today," *Star-Ledger*, May 30, 2013.

12. Brendan T. Byrne, interview with author, September 3, 2013.

13. Ibid.

14. Brendan T. Byrne, interview with author, August 23, 2013; see *Lightning Lube, Inc. v. Witco Corp.*, 802 F. Supp. 1180 (US District Court N.J. 1992), affirmed 4 F.3d 1153 (US Court of Appeals, 3rd Circuit 1993).

15. Brendan T. Byrne, interview with author, August 29, 2013.

16. Ibid.

17. Ibid.

18. Matthew Creamer, "Rewind: Carvel's Slightly Creepy But Super Memorable Ads From the Eighties," *Advertising Age*, October 26, 2012. Accessed August 30, 2013 at http://adage.com/article/rewind/carvel-s-slightly-creepy-memorable -ads-80s/237958/

19. Brendan T. Byrne, interview with author, August 23, 2013.

20. Ibid.

21. Ibid.

22. State Capital Group. Accessed August 30, 2013 at http://www.statecapital-group.org/

23. Brendan T. Byrne, interview with author, January 16, 2013.

24. Byrne's appointment as a director of Prudential was made by New Jersey Chief Justice Robert Wilentz pursuant to a statute that authorized the chief justice to name six of the twenty-three board members to protect the public interest when Prudential was a company owned by its policy holders. Former Governors Meyner, Hughes, and Cahill preceded Byrne on the board. The practice of the New Jersey chief justice appointing directors ended when Prudential restructured as a public company in 2000. See Wefing, *The Life and Times of Richard Hughes*, 264.

25. Brendan T. Byrne, interview with author, August 23, 2013.

26. Brendan T. Byrne, interview for Rutgers-Eagleton Brendan T. Byrne Archive, January 25, 2011.

27. The case study was developed for Dukakis by Charles Kireker, a special assistant to Byrne during his first term who later became a teaching assistant to Dukakis at the Kennedy School. Michael Dukakis and Charles Kireker, "New Jersey Growth Policy," John F. Kennedy School of Government, Harvard University.

28. "John McMullen," *Bill Shannon Biographical Directory of New York Sports*, New-York Historical Society Museum & Library. Accessed January 12, 2013 at http://sports.nyhistory.org/john-mcmullen/

29. Brendan T. Byrne, interview with author, August 23, 2013. After Byrne left office in January 1982, Bob Mulcahy, the chief executive of the Sports Authority and Byrne's former chief of staff, had continued to work with Governor Kean to recruit a hockey franchise to fill out the dates when the Nets, who had moved to the Arena in the previous year, were not scheduled to play at home. Before Byrne left office, the Sports Authority had begun exploring bringing an NHL team to the Byrne Arena to join the New Jersey Nets of the National Basketball Association, which had relocated to the Arena in 1981. See also Rich Chere, "As Devils celebrate 30th anniversary, John McMullen remains most important person in team history," *Star-Ledger*, March 11, 2012.

30. When Byrne was governor, McMullen had been a limited partner in the Yankees under George Steinbrenner until he sold his interest in the Yankees and

purchased the Houston Astros major league baseball team in 1979. Ibid.; Lawrie Mifflin and Michael Katz, "Defending a Name," *New York Times*, July 6, 1982.

31. The Rockies were previously purchased by New Jersey trucking and real estate millionaire Arthur Imperatore, who hoped to relocate the team to the Meadowlands, but was frustrated by the high indemnification costs demanded by the New York Rangers, New York Islanders, and Philadelphia Flyers for entering the regional market.
Brendan T. Byrne, interview with author, January 16, 2013.

32. "Baseball owners oust Bowie Kuhn," *Associated Press*, November 2, 1982.

33. Brendan T. Byrne, interview with author, January 16, 2013.

34. Ibid.

35. Joseph F. Sullivan, "Sports Authority Facing Scrutiny," *New York Times*, November 15, 1987.

36. Brendan T. Byrne, interview with author, January 16, 2013.

37. Ibid.

38. Robert E. Mulcahy, III, conversation with author, December 30, 2013.

39. Brendan. T. Byrne, Jr., quoted in Neil MacFarquhar, "The Meadowlands, by Any Other Name, Will Still Be the Meadowlands," *New York Times*, December 31, 1995.

40. Brendan T. Byrne, interview with author, October 4, 2012.

41. Under the state constitution, judges appointed to the Supreme and Superior courts are appointed for an initial seven-year term, and, if reappointed and confirmed by the Senate to a second term, have tenure until reaching the mandatory retirement age of 70. Joseph F. Sullivan, "A Close Victory for Chief Jersey Judge," *New York Times*, August 1, 1986. After Wilentz's death, Pollock described Wilentz on the court: "He was courageous. He was intelligent and he was dedicated. To me, his most striking characteristic was his intensity. You would not want to steal his bicycle." Stewart Pollock, interview for Rutgers-Eagleton Byrne Archive, October 25, 2010.

42. Brendan T. Byrne, interview with Andrew Szanton.

43. Ibid.

44. Ruthi Zinn Byrne, e-mail to author, December 4, 2013.

45. Ruthi Zinn Byrne, e-mail to author, December 26, 2013.

46. Ruthi Zinn Byrne, interview with author, February 6, 2013.

47. Brendan T. Byrne, interview with author, January 16, 2013; Ruthi Zinn Byrne, interview with author, February 6, 2013.

48. Ruthi Zinn Byrne, interview with author, August 29, 2013.

49. Thomas H. Kean, interview with author, October 1, 2013.

50. *The Washington Monthly*, Vol. 29, No. 7, July 1997.

51. Brendan T. Byrne, interview with author, August 23, 2013.

52. Ibid.

53. Barbara Fitzgerald, "The Odd Couple," *New York Times*, May 12, 2002.

54. Ibid.

55. Brendan T. Byrne, interview with author, August 23, 2013; Brendan T. Byrne, interview for Rutgers-Eagleton Byrne Archive, January 25, 2011.

56. Brendan T. Byrne, interview with author, September 3, 2013.

57. After the fire, Byrne recalled being introduced at an event marking the start of the theater's rebuilding by Angelo Del Rossi, the long-time executive director of the Playhouse. In welcoming Byrne, Del Rossi noted to the audience that Byrne had brought his future wife Jean to the Playhouse on dates during their courtship and may have even proposed to her there. In his own remarks, Byrne said he had not proposed at the Playhouse, and that "if I had, Jean may have burned the place down herself." Brendan T. Byrne, interview with author, August 29, 2013.

58. Joseph Catinella, "Paper Mill Playhouse on the Road to Revival," *New York Times*, November 29, 1981; Campbell Robertson, "Financial Emergency for Celebrated Nonprofit Theater in New Jersey," *New York Times*, April 4, 2007.

59. Brendan T. Byrne, interview with author, November 6, 2013.

60. Laura Griffin, "Diabetes Foundation Honors Former Governor's Family," *Millburn-Short Hills Patch*, February 26, 2012.

61. Ruthi Zinn Byrne, e-mail to author, December 8, 2013.

62. Brendan T. Byrne, interview with Andrew Szanton.

63. Ryan Hutchins, "Four former N.J. governors oppose Pinelands gas project," *Star-Ledger*, December 18, 2013.

64. Ibid.

65. McGreevey's executive order renaming the forest cited, in part, Byrne's "bold steps . . . to protect and preserve the vast pine-oak forests, cedar swamps, and the extensive surface and ground water resources of New Jersey's Pinelands." James E. McGreevey, Executive Order No. 22, July 24, 2002.

66. Brendan T. Byrne, interview with Andrew Szanton. In an ironic twist, shortly after the renaming of the forest, Byrne's old antagonist Garfield DeMarco announced that he had agreed to sell nearly all of his property holdings of over 9,000 acres of cranberry bogs, blueberry fields and unspoiled land for permanent preservation by the New Jersey Conservation Foundation, which agreed to raise $12 million for the property, about half its appraised value, with the remaining value considered a gift. The DeMarco property linked the newly named Brendan Byrne State Forest with Wharton State Forest, Bass River State Forest, Greenwood Wildlife Management Area, and Penn State Forest. DeMarco previously had sold development rights to the state for a portion of his holdings for $7 million, taking advantage of a state program created by the commission to encourage farmers and others to preserve property. "People will learn about my family's contribution to the state," DeMarco said, "and what my family has done here." Jill P. Capuzzo, "Leaving a Legacy After a Lifetime In the Bogs," *New York Times*, November 17, 2002.

67. Brendan T. Byrne, quoted in "John Travolta, Queen Latifah Among Inductees Into NJ Hall Of Fame," *Associated Press*, June 5, 2011. Accessed November 29, 2013 at http://newyork.cbslocal.com/2011/06/05/john-travolta-queen-latifah-among-inductees-into-nj-hall-of-fame/

68. Ted Sherman, "Former N.J. Gov. Brendan Byrne is mugged, punched in face while in London," *Star-Ledger*, February 16, 2010. Accessed January 25, 2013 at http://www.nj.com/news/index.ssf/2010/02/former_gov_brendan_byrne_is_mu.html

69. Brendan T. Byrne, interview with author, August 29, 2013; see also The Auditor, "Brendan Byrne wanted Chris Daggett for governor," *Star-Ledger*, January 31, 2010.

70. Ruthi Zinn Byrne, e-mail to author, December 4, 2013.

71. Fran Wood, "Former governor: Buono should consider dropping out of race," *Star-Ledger*, May 19, 2013.

72. Eunice Lee, "Former Gov. Brendan Byrne quips at unveiling of sculpture: 'I didn't need a statue as a reward'," *Star-Ledger*, October 3, 2013.

73. Peggy McGlone, "Byrne notice: Former Gov. Brendan Byrne 'roasted' for charity," *Star-Ledger*, April 2, 2014. A few days after the "roast," Ray Bateman, Byrne's 1977 Republican opponent wrote of his own long friendship with Byrne that had withstood their hotly contested election: "At the Byrne 'roast,' the bipartisan respect jumped off the head table for everyone to see and understand. . . . There is no question that politics and government, then, were fun, friendly and competitive. Democrats and Republicans ran against each other, fought on issues in the legislature and in the public— but retained a respect for each other that is seldom seen in today's political arenas." Raymond P. Bateman, "Byrne roast recalls better political times," mycentraljersey. com. Accessed April 7, 2014 at http://www.mycentraljersey.com/article/20140408/ NJOPINION03/304080005/Byrne-roast-recalls-better-political-times

74. Brendan T. Byrne, interview with author, April 4, 2014.

Bibliography

BOOKS AND REPORTS

Austin, John. *More of Hollywood's Unsolved Mysteries*, New York: Shapolsky Publishers, 1992.

Belton, Thomas. *Protecting New Jersey's Environment: From Cancer Alley to the New Garden State*, New Brunswick, NJ: Rutgers University Press, 2010.

Bilby Joseph G., Harry F. Ziegler and James Martin Madden. *Hidden History of New Jersey*, Charleston, SC: The History Press, 2011.

Bill, Alfred Hoyt. *A House Called Morven*, Princeton: Princeton University Press, 1978.

Blackwell, Joe. *Notorious New Jersey: 100 True Tales of Murders and Mobsters*, New Brunswick, NJ: Rutgers University Press, 2007.

Burton, Hal. *The Morro Castle: Tragedy at Sea*, New York: Viking Press, 1973.

Caldwell, Donald L. and Richard Muller. *The Luftwaffe Over Germany: Defense of the Reich*, London: Greenhill, 2007.

Cammarota, Ann Marie T. *Pavements in the Garden: the Suburbanization of Southern New Jersey*, Cranbury, NJ: Fairleigh Dickinson University Press, 2001.

Codey, Richard J. *Me Governor? My Life in the Rough-and-Tumble World of New Jersey Politics*, New Brunswick, NJ: Rutgers University Press, 2011.

Collins, Beryl Robichaud and Emily W. B. Russell (eds.), *Protecting the New Jersey Pinelands*, New Brunswick, NJ: Rutgers University Press, 1988.

Commager, Henry Steele and Donald L. Miller. *The Story of World War II*, New York: Simon & Schuster, rev. ed. 2002.

Connors, Richard J. "William Thomas Cahill," in Michael J. Birkner, Donald Linky and Peter Mickulas (eds.), *The Governors of New Jersey: Biographical Essays*, New Brunswick, NJ: Rutgers University Press, 2014, 300.

Cressey, Donald Ray. *Theft of a Nation: the Structure and Operations of Organized Crime in America*, New Brunswick, NJ: Transaction Publishing, 2008.

Demaris, Ovid. *The Boardwalk Jungle*, New York: Bantam Books, 1986.

Dente, Marcia A. *Great Falls of Paterson*, Charleston, SC: Arcadia Publishing, 2010.

Dukakis, Michael and Charles Kireker. "New Jersey Growth Policy," John F. Kennedy School of Government, Harvard University, 1980.

Eisenberg, Lee and Vicki Gold Levi. "Atlantic City," in Maxine N. Lurie and Marc Mappen (eds.), *Encyclopedia of New Jersey*, New Brunswick, NJ: Rutgers University Press, 2004, 42.

Felzenberg, Alvin S. *Governor Tom Kean: From the New Jersey Statehouse to the 9-11 Commission*, New Brunswick, NJ: Rutgers University Press, 2006.

Fenno, Richard F. Jr. *Senators on the Campaign Trail: The Politics of Representation*, Norman, OK: University of Oklahoma Press, 1996.

Fleming, Thomas J. *New Jersey: A History*, New York: W.W. Norton & Co., 1984.

Fremont-Barnes. Gregory. *American Bomber Crewman: 1941–45*, Oxford: Osprey, 2008.

Funnell, Charles E. *By the Beautiful Sea: The Rise and High Times of that Great American Resort: Atlantic City*, New York: Alfred A. Knopf, 1975.

Goddard. Henry H. *The Kallikak Family: A Study in the Heredity of Feeble-Mindedness*, New York: MacMillan, 1912.

Gray, Peter. *The Irish Famine*, New York: Henry N. Abrams, 1995.

Griffin, Dennis. *The Battle for Las Vegas: The Law vs. The Mob*, Las Vegas: Huntington Press, 2006.

Harris, Leslie M. *In the Shadow of Slavery: African Americans in New York City, 1626–1863*, Chicago: University of Chicago Press, 2003.

Heidenry, John. *The Gashouse Gang: How Dizzy Dean, Leo Durocher, Branch Rickey, Pepper Martin, and Their Colorful, Come-from-Behind Ball Club Won the World Series—and America's Heart—During the Great Depression*, New York: Public Affairs, 2007.

Hoffman, Paul. *Tiger In The Court*, Chicago: Playboy Press, 1974.

Hook, Sidney. *Common Sense and the Fifth Amendment*, New York: Criterion Books, 1957.

Hughes, Richard J. "Foreword," in Robert F. Williams (ed.), *The New Jersey State Constitution: A Reference Guide*, New Brunswick, NJ: Rutgers University Press, 1997.

Johnsen, Frederick A. Walter J. Boyne. *B-17 Flying Fortress: The Symbol of Second World War*, New York: McGraw-Hill, 2000.

Johnson, James P. *New Jersey History of Ingenuity and Industry*, Northridge, CA: Windsor Publications, 1987.

Johnson, Nelson. *Boardwalk Empire*, Medford, NJ: Plexus Publishing, 2002.

Karcher, Alan. *New Jersey's Multiple Municipal Madness*, New Brunswick, NJ: Rutgers University Press, 1998.

Lehne, Richard. *The Quest for Justice: the Politics of School Finance Reform*, New York: Longman, 1978.

———. *Casino Policy*, New Brunswick, NJ: Rutgers University Press, 1986.

Lemmey, William. "Robert Baumle Meyner," in Michael J. Birkner, Donald Linky and Peter Mickulas (eds.), *The Governors of New Jersey: Biographical Essays*, New Brunswick, NJ: Rutgers University Press, 2014.

Lender, Edward. "The Cockpit Reconsidered: Revolutionary New Jersey as a Military Theater," in Maxine Lurie (ed.), *A New Jersey Anthology*, New Brunswick, NJ: Rutgers University Press, 2010.

Levi, Vicki Gold and Lee Eisenberg. *Atlantic City: 125 Years of Ocean Madness*, Berkeley, CA: Ten Speed Press, 1979.

Levine, Alan J. *The Strategic Bombing of Germany, 1940–1945*, Westport, CT: Praeger, 1992.

Lief, Michael S. and H. Mitchell Caldwell (eds.), *And the Walls Came Tumbling Down: Greatest Closing Arguments Protecting Civil Liberties*, New York: Simon and Schuster, 2006.

Linnett, Richard. *In the Godfather Garden: The Long Life and Times of Richie "the Boot" Boiardo*, New Brunswick, NJ: Rutgers University Press, 2013.

Lowenstein, Alan V. *Alan V. Lowenstein: New Jersey Lawyer & Community Leader*, New Brunswick, NJ: Institute for Continuing Legal Education, 2001.

Mappen, Marc. *Prohibition Gangsters: The Rise and Fall of a Bad Generation*, New Brunswick, NJ: Rutgers University Press, 2013.

Mason, Robert J. *Contested Lands: Conflict and Compromise in New Jersey's Pine Barrens*, Philadelphia: Temple University Press, 1992.

———. "The Pinelands," in Mark B. Lapping and Owen J. Furuseth (eds.), *Big Places, Big Plans*, Burlington, VT: Ashgate, 2004.

Mayer, Michael S. "Robert B. Meyner," in *The Eisenhower Years*, New York: Facts on File, 2010.

McCloy, James F. and Ray Miller. *The Jersey Devil*, Wallingford, PA: Middle Atlantic Press, 1976.

Miller, Donald L. *Masters of the Air*, New York: Simon & Schuster, 2006.

Moakley, Maureen. "Political Parties," in Gerald M. Pomper (ed.), *The Political State of New Jersey*. New Brunswick, NJ: Rutgers University Press, 1986.

Mullin, Edward J. (ed.), *New Jersey Legislative Manual*, Trenton, NJ: Edward J. Mullin, 1974.

Paulsson, Martin. *The Social Anxieties of Progressive Reform: Atlantic City, 1854–1920*, New York: New York University Press, 1996.

———. "Frank Sherman Farley," in *Encyclopedia of New Jersey*, New Brunswick, NJ: Rutgers University Press, 2004, 266.

Perskie, Steven P. "A Political History" (unpublished manuscript), February 22, 2009.

Pollock, Michael. *Hostage to Fortune: Atlantic City and Casino Gambling*, Princeton: Center for Analysis of Public Issues, 1987.

Quinn, Dermot. *The Irish in New Jersey: Four Centuries of American Life*, New Brunswick, NJ: Rutgers University Press, 2004.

Raichle, Donald R. *New Jersey's Union College: A History, 1933–1983*, Madison, NJ: Fairleigh Dickinson University Press, 1983.

Reavill, Gil. *Mafia Summit: J. Edgar Hoover, the Kennedy Brothers, and the Meeting That Unmasked the Mob*, New York: St. Martin's Press/Thomas Dunne Books, 2013.

Ristine, James D. *Atlantic City*, Mount Pleasant, SC: Arcadia Publishing, 2008.

Rockaway, Robert A. *But He was Good to His Mother: The Lives and Crimes of Jewish Gangsters*, Jerusalem: Gefen Publishing House, 2000.

Rose Jerome G. *Legal Foundations of Land Use Planning*, New Brunswick, NJ: Rutgers University Press, 1979.

Rudolph, Robert. *The Boys from New Jersey: How the Mob Beat the Feds*, New Brunswick, NJ: Rutgers University Press, 1995.

Sachsman, David B. and Warren Sloat, *The Press and the Suburbs: the Daily Newspapers of New Jersey*, Piscataway, NJ: Transaction Publishers, 1985.

Salinger, Pierre. *With Kennedy*, Garden City, NY: Doubleday & Co., 1966.

Salmore, Barbara G. and Stephen A. Salmore. *New Jersey Politics and Government: the Suburbs Come of Age*, New Brunswick, NJ: Rivergate Books, 2008.

Schroeder, Alice. *The Snowball: Warren Buffett and the Business of Life*, New York: Random House Digital, 2008.

Sheeran, James. *No Surrender: A World War II Memoir*, New York: Berkley Caliber, 2011.

Stellhorn, Paul A. "Harold Hoffman," in Michael J. Birkner, Donald Linky and Peter Mickulas (eds.), *The Governors of New Jersey: Biographical Essays*, New Brunswick, NJ: Rutgers University Press, 2014.

Sternlieb, George and James W. Hughes. *The Atlantic City Gamble: A Twentieth Century Fund Report*, New York: Twentieth Century Fund, 1983.

Stonecash, Jeffrey M. and Mary P. McGuire. *The Emergence of State Government: Parties and New Jersey Politics, 1950-2000*, Madison, NJ: Fairleigh Dickinson University Press, 2002.

Troeger, Virginia B. *Berkeley Heights Revisited*, Charleston, SC: Arcadia Publishing, 2005.

Tuttle, Brad R. *How Newark Became Newark: The Rise, Fall, and Rebirth of an American City*, New Brunswick, NJ: Rutgers University Press, 2009.

United States Department of the Interior, National Park Service. "Southern New Jersey and the Delaware Bay: Historic Themes and Resources within the New Jersey Coastal Heritage Trail," Accessed January 12, 2013 at http://www.cr.nps.gov/history/online_books/nj2/chap5.htm.

United States Department of the Interior, Heritage Conservation and Recreation Service. Northeast Regional Office. "Final Environmental Impact Statement: Proposed comprehensive management plan for the Pinelands National Reserve."

———. "Proposed comprehensive management plan for the Pinelands National Reserve," October 1981. Simon, Bryant. *Boardwalk of Dreams: Atlantic City and the Fate of Urban America*, New York: Oxford University Press, 2004.

Van Horn, Carl E. "Economic Development Policy," in Gerald M. Pomper (ed.), *The Political State of New Jersey*, New Brunswick, NJ: Rutgers University Press, 1986.

Van Meter, Jonathan. *The Last Good Time: Skinny D'Amato, the Notorious 500 Club and the Rise and Fall of Atlantic City*, New York: Crown Publishers, 2003.

Wefing, John B. *The Life and Times of Richard Hughes: The Politics of Civility*, New Brunswick, NJ: Rutgers University Press, 2009.

Widman, Mindy and Donald W. Light. *Regulating Prospective Payment: An Analysis of the New Jersey Hospital Rate-Setting Commission*, Ann Arbor: Health Administration Press, 1988.

Wik, Reynold M. *Henry Ford and Grass-Roots America*, Ann Arbor: University of Michigan Press, 1972.

Yaffe, Deborah. *Other People's Children: The Battle for Justice and Equality in New Jersey's Schools*, New Brunswick, NJ: Rutgers University Press, 2007.

Zukin, Cliff. "Political Culture and Public Opinion," in Gerald M. Pomper (ed.), *The Political State of New Jersey*, New Brunswick, NJ: Rutgers University Press, 1986, 21.

JOURNALS AND PERIODICALS

Acquaviva, Gregory L., Jonathan L. Marshfield and David M. Stauss. "A Tribute to Chief Justice James R. Zazzali; More than a Caretaker," *Rutgers Law Review* 59 (Summer 2007), 667.

Anderson, Dave. "The Once and Always Champ," *New York Times*, July 1, 1979.

Asbury Park Press. "Byrne in Fighting Speech at Headquarters Opening," April 26, 1977.

———. "Pinelands Moratorium," February 18, 1979.

Ascolese, Mike. "Cahill approves Pike extension," *Star-Ledger*, April 25, 1973.

Associated Press. "Bitter Session Ends with Bigelow OK'd for Rutgers Board," August 11, 1956.

———. "Baseball owners oust Bowie Kuhn," November 2, 1982.

———. "John Travolta, Queen Latifah Among Inductees Into NJ Hall Of Fame," June 5, 2011. Accessed November 29, 2013 at http://newyork.cbslocal.com/2011/06/05/john-travolta-queen-latifah-among-inductees-into-nj-hall-of-fame/.

Auletta, Ken. "It Has All Been Downhill for Brendan Byrne of New Jersey," *New York Times*, June 8, 1975.

Atlantic City Press [*Press of Atlantic City*]. "The Pinelands Plan," *Press of Atlantic City*, February 14, 1979.

———. "Perskie, Pines, People," *Press of Atlantic City*, July 2, 1981.

Beacon. "Chairman of Pinelands Council says GOP Victories helped council," November 11, 1976.

Bebout, John E. and Joseph Harrison. "The Working of the New Jersey Constitution of 1947," *William & Mary Law Review* 10 (1968), 337. Accessed November 29, 2013 at http://scholarship.law.wm.edu/wmlr/vol10/iss2/4.

Becker, Peter, Ph.D. "The Role of Synthetic Fuel In World War II Germany," *Air University Review*, July–August 1981. Accessed December 10, 2012 at http://www.airpower.maxwell.af.mil/airchronicles/aureview/1981/jul-aug/becker.htm.

Bigart, Homer. "Newark Riot Deaths at 21 as Negro Sniping Widens; Hughes May Seek U.S. Aid," *New York Times*, July 17, 1967.

Buckley, William F., Jr. "Atlantic City without the Girls," *National Review*, September 8, 1964.

Burks, Edward C. "Fare-Raise Plan for PATH Dropped," *New York Times*, February 15, 1974.

———. "Congress Heeds Pine Barrens' Plight," *New York Times*, March 20, 1977.

———. "Florio Opposed on Plan to Save Barrens," *New York Times*, October 9, 1977.

———. "A Ray of Hope for Pine Barrens," *New York Times*, May 14, 1978.

Burrows, William. "Time Runs Out at JFK," *New York Magazine*, July 29, 1968.

Callas, Toni. "Longtime Pinelands advocate tapped to lead commission," *Philadelphia Inquirer*, June 10, 2005.

Capuzzo, Jill P. "Leaving a Legacy After a Lifetime In the Bogs," *New York Times*, November 17, 2002.

Carragher, Joseph. "PUC chief calls for state to run commuter rails," *Star-Ledger*, September 22, 1968.

———. "Coffee quits race and backs Byrne," *Star-Ledger*, April 27, 1973.

———. "Tuesday's vote will gauge the power of the organization," *Star-Ledger*, June 3, 1973.

———. "Independent pollster puts Byrne ahead by landslide 400,000," *Star-Ledger*, November 7, 1973.

Catinella, Joseph. "Paper Mill Playhouse on the Road to Revival," *New York Times*, November 29, 1981.

Cedrone, Connie. "Byrne and Lordi win confirmation by lame-ducks," *Star-Ledger*, January 10, 1968.

Chere, Rich. "As Devils celebrate 30th anniversary, John McMullen remains most important person in team history," *Star-Ledger*, March 11, 2012.

Chiappardi, Matt. "Remembering Mexican aviator Emilio Carranza," PhillyBurbs. com, July 10, 2011. Accessed January 22, 2013 at http://www.phillyburbs.com/ news/local/burlington_county_times_news/remembering-mexican-aviator-emilio-carranza/article_356fdda4-319b-5a5f-b6ad-c33a5a9401a6.html.

Clark, Michael and Dan Good. "Nucky Johnson: The Man who Ran Atlantic City for 30 Years," *Atlantic City Press*, August 15, 2010. Accessed August 20, 2010 at http://www.pressofatlanticcity.com/blogs/boardwalk_empire/article_4277415c-a815-11df-be3f-001cc4c002e0.html.

Codey, Richard J. "Let's Be Good Sports About The Arena's Name," *New York Times*, August 9, 1981.

Cohen, Robert. "Order for school closings stands," *Star-Ledger*, July 1, 1976.

———. "Wilentz Choice May Usher in New Court Era," *Star-Ledger*, March 18, 1979.

Connelly, Terry. "Bardin attacks Pinelands plan for development," *Star-Ledger*, August 27, 1975.

Cook, Joan. "Small Touches at Morven Change Mansion into Home for Byrnes," *New York Times*, March 20, 1974.

Creamer, Matthew. "Rewind: Carvel's Slightly Creepy But Super Memorable Ads From the Eighties," *Advertising Age*, October 26, 2012. Accessed August 30, 2013 at http:// adage.com/article/rewind/carvel-s-slightly-creepy-memorable-ads-80s/237958/.

Cunningham, Bob and Allan F. Yoder. "A Tax Bill Nobody Liked," *The Record*, June 18, 1976.

Davies, John O. "Brendan says one term may be enough," *Courier-News*, April 24, 1976.

———. "Dugan Calls Byrne Feud 'Civilized'," *Courier-Post*, April 22, 1976.

DelNagro, Mike. "When A Country Horse Trots A City Course," *Sports Illustrated*, August 17, 1981.

Donohue, Joseph. "Environmental Groups Rap Perskie's Pines Bill," *Atlantic City Press*, June 24, 1981.

———. "Gov. Byrne Stuns Perskie, Rejects Pinelands 'Compromise' Bill," *Atlantic City Press*, July 9, 1981.

Edge, Wally. "Frank Murkowski breaks Brendan Byrne's record," PolitickerNJ.com, August 23, 2006. Accessed December 10, 2012 at http://www.politickernj.com/frank-murkowski-breaks-brendan-byrnes-record?quicktabs_mostx=commented.

———. "If Case beat Bell, Kean would have appointed two U.S. Senators in one week," PolitickerNJ.com, March 5, 2010. Accessed July 12, 2012 at http://www.politickernj.com/wallye/37430/if-case-beat-bell-kean-would-have-appointed-two-us-senators-one-week#ixzz2UsqoM0Wu.

———. "In an emergency, Rabner can use the Jacobson plan," PolitickerNJ.com, June 14, 2007. Accessed September 29, 2013 at http://www.politickernj.com/emergency-rabner-can-use-jacobson-plan-9472.

———. "Part One: The Democrats who will decide Lonegan's fate," PolitickerNJ.com, March 5, 2009. Accessed January 12, 2012 at http://www.politickernj.com/wallye/27892/part-one-democrats-who-will-decide-lonegans-fate#ixzz2m9BpW1fq.

———. "How the Secretary of Agriculture gets his job," PolitickerNJ.com, December 2, 2008. Accessed January 12, 2012 at http://www.politickernj.com/wallye/25827/how-secretary-agriculture-gets-his-job#ixzz2m8z8SLSV.

Erlanger, Steven. "Atlantic City: Failure Behind the Façade," *New York Times*, August 29, 1988.

EyeWitness to History, Ibis Communications. "Life and Death Aboard a B-17, 1944," www.eyewitnesstohistory.com (2005). *New Yorker*, August 12, 1944. Accessed January 13, 2013 at http://www.eyewitnesstohistory.com/b17.htm.

Fecht, Audrey A. "Brendan T. Byrne: Name in The News," *Newark Evening News*, January 9, 1970.

Ferretti, Fred. "Cahill's Record on Environment Is a Source of Pride and a Target," *New York Times*, June 2, 1973.

———. "Byrne Learning to Doff Habits with Robes," *New York Times*, May 18, 1973.

Fitzgerald, Barbara. "The Odd Couple," *New York Times*, May 12, 2002.

Ford, Bob. "Path To The Vet Led Through N.J. In The '60s, The Phils Looked To Cherry Hill," *Philadelphia Inquirer*, July 26, 1989.

Ford, Steven. "Jersey gets an income tax," *Trenton Times*, July 9, 1976.

Funston, Mark and Roger Harris. "Cheers, Laughter: Revelers toast stunning Byrne victory," *Star-Ledger*, November 7, 1973.

Friedman, Matt. "Organizers: Weekend rally against N.J. Gov. Chris Christie's budget cuts could draw 30K," NorthJersey.com, May 21, 2010. Accessed January 12, 2013 at http://www.northjersey.com/news/NJ_rally_against_Gov_Chris_Christies_budget_cuts_could_draw_30K_organizers_say.html?c=y&page=2.

Gambaccini, Louis J. "Soapbox: Confessions of a Gas Tax Advocate," *New York Times*, March 7, 2004.

Genovese, Peter. "Pals Cabin, a Jersey food landmark, closes for good today," *Star-Ledger*, May 30, 2013.

Goodman, Jim. "'The Zoo' in chaos," *Trenton Times*, July 2, 1976.

———. "Grateful governor extends plaudits," *Trenton Times*, July 8, 1976.

———. "Bills, vetoes cram Byrne's last days," *Trenton Times*, January 13, 1982.

Goodman, Jim and Michael J. Hall. "Jersey schools closed," *Trenton Times*, July 2, 1976.

Graber, Trish. "Election night 1981, when the N.J. governor's race was too close to call," *Star-Ledger*, November 3, 2009. Accessed January 23, 2013 at http://www.nj.com/news/index.ssf/2009/11/election_night_1981_when_the_n.html.

Gribbins, J. Joseph. "Under the State House Dome," *Independent-Leader*, November 14, 1946. Accessed January 12, 2013 at http://archive.woodbridgelibrary.org/Archive/IndependentLeader/1946/1946-11-14/pg_0007.pdf.

Griffin, Laura. "Diabetes Foundation Honors Former Governor's Family," *Millburn-Short Hills Patch*, February 26, 2012.

Gros, Roger. "Thirty Years of Gaming," Casinoconnection.com, May 5, 2008. Accessed August 2, 2010 at http://casinoconnectionac.com/issue-printer/may_2008.

Grutzner, Charles. "Mafia Obtained Secret U.S. Data," *New York Times*, January 20, 1970.

Halbfinger, David M. "Ex-Rep. Helen S. Meyner, 69; Born Into Democratic Politics," (obituary) *New York Times*, November 3, 1997.

Hanley, Robert. "New Jersey Struggles To Tame Toxic Monster," *New York Times*, April 19, 1981.

Harper, Derek. "80 years ago, the Mob came to Atlantic City for a little strategic planning," *Atlantic City Press*, May 13, 2009.

Hevesi, Dennis. "Stanley Van Ness, State Public Advocate, Dies at 73," *New York Times*, September 27, 2007.

Heyman, Harriet and Milton Leebaw. "N.J.'s Answer is the Nuisance Tax," *New York Times*, July 27, 1975.

Hillman, Fred. "Byrne quits court for governor race," *Star-Ledger*, April 25, 1973.

———. "Mrs. Klein claims she's closing the gap on Byrne," *Star-Ledger*, June 1, 1973.

———. 'Sandman hammers at four issues," *Star-Ledger*, June 1, 1973.

———. "Sandman landslide over Cahill; Byrne trounces Democratic foes," *Star-Ledger*, June 6, 1973.

———. "Byrne, Sandman spar in final confrontation," *Star-Ledger*, November 5, 1973.

———. "Byrne Landslide," *Star-Ledger*, November 7, 1973.

———. "Byrne hands legislators 'must' tax reform plan," *Star-Ledger*, June 14, 1974.

Horner, S. J. "First Family Gets Ready to Move," *New York Times*, December 13, 1981.

Hutchins, Ryan. "Four former N.J. governors oppose Pinelands gas project," *Star-Ledger*, December 18, 2013.

Jaffe, Herb. "Cahill condemns N.Y. bids to kill sports complex," *Star-Ledger*, November 6, 1973

———. "Cahill nominates Hughes as the new chief justice," *Star-Ledger*, November 8, 1973.

————. "State banks and insurers fill sports complex funding gap," *Star-Ledger*, January 18, 1974.

————. "Byrne led way to Sportsplex's great success," *Star-Ledger*, March 29, 1977.

Janson, Donald. "Byrne Attacked by Abortion Foes," *New York Times*, November 3, 1973.

————. "Jersey Proposes Bus and Rail Rises," *New York Times*, August 13, 1975.

————. "3 Governors Vote to Kill Tocks Dam," *New York Times*, August 31, 1975.

————. "Damage to Pine Barrens Feared from Cities, Casinos and the Sea," *New York Times*, December 17, 1976.

————. "Gains are Seen in Efforts to Preserve the Pine Barrens," *New York Times*, May 7, 1977.

————. "Pine Barrens Construction Ban Stirs Up an Emotional Debate," *New York Times*, March 25, 1979.

————. "Caesars' 2 Top Officers Must Quit If Jersey Casino Is to Get a License," *New York Times*, October 24, 1980.

————. "Bally to Get Casino License If It Cuts Ties With Its Chief," *New York Times*, December 24, 1980.

————. "Jersey to Test a Program to Preserve Agriculture and Open Space in State Agriculture," *New York Times*, August 23, 2013.

Johnson, Tom. "Kean signs wetlands bill, lifts building moratorium," *Star-Ledger*, July 2, 1987.

Kanige, Jeffrey. "Brendan Byrne on Brendan Byrne," *New Jersey Reporter*, June 1988.

Katz, Joseph W. "Byrne Named for Essex Post," *Newark Evening News*, May 26, 1959.

Kean, Thomas H. and Brendan T. Byrne. "A dicey experiment, a mixed success," *Star-Ledger*, May 25, 2003.

Kelly, Mike. "'American Hustle' renews old questions about Abscam," December 25, 2013, NorthJersey.com. Accessed December 26, 2013 at http://www.northjersey.com/columnists/kelly/Kelly_American_Hustle_renews_old_questions_about_Abscam.html?page=all#sthash.uSgwUieW.dpuf.

Kennedy, Ray. "Miracle In The Meadows," *Sports Illustrated*, September 12, 1977. Accessed September 27, 2012 at http://sportsillustrated.cnn.com/vault/article/magazine/MAG1092823/9/index.htm.

Kent, Bill. "Captain of the Showboat," *New York Times*, February 18, 1996.

Kenworthy, E. W. "Byrne Threatens He Will Sue if U.S. Spurs Ocean Drilling," *New York Times*, February 11, 2014.

King, Robert L. "Two-term Byrne," *Courier-Post*, November 6, 1977.

King, Wayne. "Robert B. Meyner Is Dead at 81; Flamboyant New Jersey Governor," *New York Times*, May 29, 1990.

Kleiman, Dena. "Frank S. Farley, 75, Ex-Legislator and G.O.P. Leader in Jersey, Dies," *New York Times*, May 29, 1990.

Kocieniewski, David. "Judge Leaving High Court After 20 Years as Unifier," *New York Times*, February 26, 1999.

Kramer, Michael. "Byrne Is Ahead, But . . .," *New York Magazine*, October 15, 1973.

———. "Is Something Rotten in the State of New Jersey?" *New York Magazine*, October 15, 1973.

"A Governor's Diary," *Star-Ledger*, May 1–8, 2001.

Lamendola, Linda. "A chilly reception in the chamber," *Star-Ledger*, June 14, 1974.

———. "Jersey's First Lady: 'It takes courage to stand up for what you believe is right,'" *Star-Ledger*, May 10, 1977.

———. "Budget cuts will affect vital services," *Star-Ledger*, June 29, 1975.

———. "First Lady advises governor: 'You've got to get tough'," *Star-Ledger*, November 13, 1977.

Lee, Eunice. "Former Gov. Brendan Byrne quips at unveiling of sculpture: 'I didn't need a statue as a reward'," *Star-Ledger*, October 3, 2013.

Lentz, Philip. "Governor Criticizes Bateman Tax Plan," *Star-Ledger*, September 27, 1977.

MacFarquhar, Neil. "The Meadowlands, by Any Other Name, Will Still Be the Meadowlands," *New York Times*, December 31, 1995.

Madden, William. "The PUC sees the train film . . . and shudders," *Star-Ledger*, June 27, 1968.

Magyar, Mark. "Gambaccini Aims at Bus Takeover," *Red Bank Register*, January 26, 1979.

Martin, Antoinette. "Hat Factory Is a Focus of Redevelopment in Orange," *New York Times*, May 9, 2004.

Mattson, Kevin. "A Politics of National Sacrifice," *The American Prospect*, March 23, 2009. Accessed October 22, 2012 at http://prospect.org/article/politics-national-sacrifice.

Maurer, Alvin. "Jersey's Tax Fight Took Place in a Power Vacuum," *New York Times,* July 11, 1976.

McCleery, William. "A Visit with New Jersey's 'Born-Again' Governor," *Princeton Alumni Weekly*, June 28, 1978.

McCrary, Lacy. "Byrne Pleased His Casino Vote Was Wasted," *Philadelphia Inquirer*, November 11, 1974.

McFadden, Robert D. "New York and Jersey Report No Excess Radioactivity Despite Pattern of Winds," *New York Times*, April 2, 1979.

———. "Fred G. Burke, 79, Official Who Promoted Changes in Public School Financing, Dies," *New York Times*, March 13, 2005.

McGlone, Peggy. "Byrne notice: Former Gov. Brendan Byrne 'roasted' for charity," *Star-Ledger*, April 2, 2014.

McKenna, John F. "Famous Ring Wars: Joe Louis vs. 'Two Ton' Tony Galento," BoxingNews.com, January 29, 2012. Accessed January 12, 2013 at http://www.boxingnews24.com/2012/01/famous-ring-wars-joe-louis-vs-%e2%80%9ctwo-ton%e2%80%9d-tony-galento/#D2PHGjTV14Vz8BZF.99.

McLaughlin, John. "Dodd Stalls Byrne Tax Bill," *New York Daily News*, June 25, 1974.

McMahon, Joshua. "Helstoski may 'reconsider' governor's race," *Star-Ledger*, April 17, 1973.

McPhee, John. "The Pine Barrens," *The New Yorker*, November 25, December 2, 1967.

————. "The Writing Life: Structure," *The New Yorker*, January 14, 2013. http://lawpublications.seattleu.edu/cgi/viewcontent.cgi?article=1333&context=sulr&sei-redir=1#search=%22nj%20rate%20setting%20hospital%22.

McQueeny. James. "A Scenario finally Played out to Conclusion," *Star-Ledger*, June 18, 1976.

Meislin, Richard. "What's In A Name? It Depends," *New York Times*, October 25, 1981.

Mezzacappa, Dale. "Was Brendan Byrne Too Good for New Jersey," *Today: The Inquirer Magazine*, January 1982.

Mifflin, Lawrie and Michael Katz. "Defending a Name," *New York Times*, July 6, 1982.

Moskue, Monica, Barbara Kukla and Tex Novellino. "Dems' man of hour," *Star-Ledger*, June 6, 1973.

Nader, Ralph. "Government Under Glass," *The Public Interest*, August 5, 1974. Accessed September 4, 2012 at http://nader.org/1974/08/05/government-under-glass/.

Narvaez, Alfonso A. "Byrne Fails to Win Endorsement of A.F.L.-C.I.O. Convention," *New York Times*, September 16, 1973.

————. "Jersey Assembly, Defers Tax Issue," *New York Times*, July 3, 1976.

————. "Jersey Assembly, Ending Deadlock, Votes Income Tax," *New York Times*, July 8, 1976.

————. "New Jersey Votes State Income Tax; Byrne Signs Bill," *New York Times*, July 8, 1976.

————. "Jersey Adopts Plan on Patients in Coma," *New York Times*, January 26, 1977.

————. "Transport Bond issue at Stake," *New York Times*, September 9, 1979.

————. "Byrne Urges 3 To Give Up Their Gubernatorial Quest," *New York Times*, May 29, 1981.

New Jerseyans for an Alternative to the Death Penalty. "Commentary." Accessed May 24, 2012 at http://www.njadorg/comment.

Newark Evening News. "Giuliano Charges Canceled," February 5, 1970.

New York Times. "Llewellyn Park," April 23, 1865. Accessed July 21, 2012 at http://www.nytimes.com/1865/04/23/news/llewellyn-park.html.

————. "More Arrests Stir Atlantic City Talk," July 29, 1911.

————. "Prison Term for Atlantic City Boss; Court Imposes Year's Sentence on Republican Leader Kuehnle for Grafting," January 15, 1912.

————. "L.N. Kuehnle Dead, Political Leader," August 6, 1934.

————. "Pinelands Jetport to Get U.S. Review," June 7, 1967.

————. "Enoch L. Johnson, Ex-Boss in Jersey – Prohibition-Era Ruler of Atlantic City, 85, Dies," December 10, 1968.

————. "Mr. Meyner Turns Left," August 30, 1969.

————. "Excerpts From FBI Transcripts of Tapes Released at the De Carlo Trial," January 7, 1970.

————. "F.B.I.-Taped Conversation Sheds Light on 1962 Gangland Slaying of Strollo; Jersey Figures Mentioned in Underworld Talks Recorded by the F.B.I.," January 8, 1970.

————. "Kheel Says That Port Authority Hoards Profits," April 17, 1970.

———. "Jersey Judge Bars Penalty of Death," October 13, 1971.

———. "Cahill Sees His Tax Reform Program Doomed Unless Labor Reverses Its Course," June 2, 1972.

———. "Plan for Saving Pine Barrens," July 16, 1972.

———. "Fight Over Marburger Poses a Threat to Cahill," November 5, 1972.

———. "Insurgent Democrats Reported Urging Byrne to Enter Primary," January 31, 1973.

———. "The Jersey Primaries," June 1, 1973.

———. "Byrne Attacks Sandman On the Income-Tax Issue; Charges Exchanged," October 16, 1973.

———. "Byrne for New Jersey," October 24, 1973.

———. "Byrne, Sandman in a Clash on TV," November 5, 1973.

———. "Election Decimates the G.O.P.'s Ranks in Trenton," November 8, 1973.

———. "Turnpike Lets Driscoll Contract," November 22, 1973.

———. "Two Stadiums Gain, With a Study Here and Cahill's Signing," December 5, 1973.

———. "Jersey Democrats Elect Leaders," December 10, 1973.

———. "Highlights from Interview with Byrne," December 31, 1973.

———. "Byrne Nominates Capt. Pagano as State Police Superintendent," October 10, 1974.

———. "Byrne Presses Late Drive for a Jersey School Tax," December 24, 1974.

———. "Byrne Asks July 1 Deadline for School-Aid Legislation," February 26, 1975.

———. "Senate Warns Court on School-Aid Issue," March 5, 1975.

———. "Panel Urges a Five-Year Plan of Capital Investment," April 25. 1975.

———. "Dugan Wins Byrne's Vote," July 20, 1975.

———. "Laccy Considered as '77 Candidate," August 28, 1975.

———. "Conciliatory Statement by Dr. Burke Expected to Kill Plan to Censure Him," December 6, 1975.

———. "State Orders Edison Landfill Shut," June 28, 1977.

———. "Governor Byrne, Snapshot Artist, Has Photos Published," July 21, 1979.

———. "Chemical Control Indicted for Pollution," March 10, 1981.

———. "The Pinelands, Still Not Rescued," July 7, 1981.

———. "Jersey Court to Decide on Arena-Name Vote," October 11, 1981.

———. "Misjudgment in the Senate," December 3, 1981.

———. "New Owner Raises Hope for Ski Area's Turnaround," March 2, 1998.

———. "As Stadiums Vanish, Their Debt Lives On," September 7, 2010.

Nieves, Evelyn. "24 Terms Are Enough, Harrison Mayor Decides," *New York Times*, March 29, 1994.

O'Hern, Daniel J. "Brennan and Weintraub: Two Stars to Guide Us," *Rutgers Law Review* 45, 3 (Spring 1994), 1049. Accessed July 21, 2012 at http://njlegallib.rutgers.edu/weintraub/PDF/weintraub.1994.pdf.

Panzer, Shayna. "Safeguards for the Pinelands," *New York Times*, July 13, 1980.

Passaic Herald-News. "Bucanis Escapes Death Sentence," June 25, 1955.

Pearce, Jeremy. "Trouble in Paradise," *New York Times*, June 23, 2002.

Peterson, Cass. "A Decade Later, TMI's Legacy is Distrust," *Washington Post*, March 28, 1989.

Phalon, Richard. "Byrne is Man of Caution," *New York Times*, November 7, 2013.

Philadelphia Inquirer. "Kenneth Gewertz, 72, 'Mr. Deptford,'" (obituary) December 14, 2006. Accessed January 12, 2013 at http://articles.philly.com/2006-12-14/news/25398931_1_partisan-politics-dark-ages-big-friends/2.

PolitickerNJ.com. "12 New Democratic Assembly Members Take Oaths," PolitckerNJ.com, January 8, 2008. Accessed August 2, 2012 at http://www.politickernj.com/assembly-democrats-12-new-democratic-assembly-members-take-oaths-office-15192.

———. "Happy Birthday to Steve Perskie, 21 years younger than Frank Lautenberg," PolitickerNJ.com, January 10, 2008. Accessed August 3, 2012, at http://www.politickernj.com/happy-birthday-steve-perskie-21-years-younger-frank-lautenberg-15290.

———. "Legislators were 'entirely too comfortable with organized crime'," PolitickerNJ.com, January 29, 2009. Accessed August 4, 2012 at http://www.politickernj.com/wallye/26961/legislators-were-entirely-too-comfortable-organized-crime.

———. "Paul Sherwin," PolitickerNJ.com, February 19, 2009. Accessed October 25, 2012 at http://www.politickernj.com/tags/paul-sherwin#ixzz2AK7ayypa.

———. "Frank Guarini," PolitickerNJ.com, May 19, 2010. Accessed October 25, 2012 at http://www.politickernj.com/tags/frank-guarini#ixzz2AKNApIZ5.

Polster, Sandor M. "The Man the Mob Couldn't Bribe," *New York Post*, January 8, 1970.

Purdy, Matthew. "Byrne bids state an eloquent farewell," *Trenton Times*, January 12, 1982.

———. "The Byrne Years: A Study in Paradox," *Trenton Times*, January 17, 1982.

Raab, Selwyn. "Jersey Ends Move to Retry Rubin Carter," *New York Times*, February 20, 1988.

Ramirez, David. "David B. Kelly, 79; Led New Jersey State Police," *New York Times*, September 25, 1997.

The Record. "Pine Barrens," February 25, 1979.

———. "In the Best of Hands," January 15, 1982.

Robertson, Campbell. "Financial Emergency for Celebrated Nonprofit Theater in New Jersey," *New York Times*, April 4, 2007.

Robins, Martin E. "How the New Jersey Transit Corporation Was Born," New Jersey Transport Heritage Center Symposium, Alan M. Voorhees Transportation Center, Rutgers University, March 31, 2007.

Romano, Jay. "Growth Transforms A 'Sleepy' County," *New York Times*, May 5, 1991.

Rosenberg, Amy S. "1964 Democratic Convention Exposed Atlantic City, N.J. as Faded, Dirty Resort," *Philadelphia Inquirer*, June 5, 2000.

Ryan, Pat. "'Mad as a Hatter': The History of a Simile," *New York Times*, March 6, 2010.

Saxon, Wolfgang. "Robert J. Burkhardt, 83, Leader Of New Jersey Democrats in 60's," (obituary), *New York Times*, January 5, 2000.

Schwanenberg Robert. "Debate holds up Pinelands Bill," *Star-Ledger*, June 22, 1979.

————. "Property tax task forces: long history, few results." *Star-Ledger*, May 9, 2004.

Schwartz, David. "Wynn, Lose or Draw," *Casino Connection* 5, 12 (December 2008). Accessed July 16, 2012 at http://casinoconnectionac.com/issue/december__2008/article/wynn__lose_or_draw.

Shear, Jeffrey. "Radiation Unit Keeps on Alert," *New York Times*, March 30, 1980.

Shelly, Kevin C. "Special report: Small gambling sites win big as A.C. loses out," *Courier-Post*, June 10, 2013. Accessed June 23, 2013 at http://www.courierpostonline.com/article/20130610/NEWS01/306100029/Special-report-Small-gambling-sites-win-big-C-loses-out.

Shenfield, Gary. "Jetport in Barrens Called Dead Issue," *New York Times*, October 27, 1974.

Sherman, Ted. "Former N.J. Gov. Brendan Byrne is mugged, punched in face while in London," *Star-Ledger*, February 16, 2010. Accessed January 25, 2013 at http://www.nj.com/news/index.ssf/2010/02/former_gov_brendan_byrne_is_mu.html.

Siegel, Bruce M.D., Anne Weiss and Jane Lynch. "Setting New Jersey Hospital Rates: A Regulatory System Under Stress," *University of Puget Sound Law Review* 14 (1991), 601. Accessed March 3, 2011 at http://lawpublications.seattleu.edu/cgi/viewcontent.cgi?article=1333&context=sulr&sei-redir=1#search=%22nj%20rate%20setting%20hospital%22.

Smith, Sandy. "The Crime Cartel," *Life Magazine* 63, 9 (September 1, 1967).

Smith, Terence. "President Summons Aides to Camp David for a Broad Review," *New York Times*, July 7, 1979.

Specter, Michael. "Florio and Kean Making A Heavy Pitch On TV," *New York Times*, October 4, 1981.

Star-Ledger. "Byrne reveals state sent wrong man to prison," February 11, 1965.

————. "Mob put up cash for favored candidates," *Star-Ledger*, January 7, 1970.

————. "Newark election in 1962: A discussion on the mob's help to Addonizio," January 7, 1970.

————. "Eagleton poll indicates Cahill would beat Dems," June 1, 1973.

————. "The People's Choice," November 7, 1973.

————. "Leone declares state will process income tax," November 6, 1976.

————. "Lawmakers differ on Pinelands," *Star-Ledger*, November 29, 1977.

————. "Preserving the Pinelands," Star-Ledger, February 26, 1979.

————. "Good neighbor Brendan," May 16, 2001.

————. "Brendan Byrne wanted Chris Daggett for governor," (The Auditor), January 31, 2010.

————. "Hon. June Strelecki," (obituary), March 12, 2013.

Sullivan, Joseph F. "Jordan, a Reformer, Ends Jersey City Machine Rule," *New York Times*, November 3, 1971.

————. "Jersey Rejects Education Chief," *New York Times*, November 17, 1972.

————. "Byrne Quits Court to Run for Jersey Governorship," *New York Times*, April 25, 1973.

————. "Crabiel Drops Out of Race, Throws Support to Byrne," *New York Times*, May 3, 1973.

———. "Turnout Called Key to Vote on Tuesday," *New York Times*, November 4, 1973.

———. "Byrne Says Vote Reflects A Lack of Confidence in Nixon," *New York Times*, November 8, 1973.

———. "Jersey Secretary of State Indicted for Bid-Rigging," *New York Times*, August 1, 1974.

———. "Jersey Will Cut Rail-Bus Subsidies," *New York Times*, July 9, 1975.

———. "Suits Seek to Halt Shutdown of Public Schools Thursday," *New York Times*, June 29, 1976.

———. "Carter Cancels a Visit to Jersey; Fear of Tax Protest Seen in Move," *New York Times*, October 27, 1976.

———. "The Race to Be No. 1 Heats Up," *New York Times*, January 2, 1977.

———. "Kean Opens Drive for Governor, Says He'd Let Income Tax Expire," *New York Times*, January 14, 1977.

———. "Jordan Cancels Gubernatorial Bid, Will Support Byrne for Re-election," *New York Times*, May 17, 1977.

———. "Trenton Suspends Two Officers in Leak Of Report on Lordi," *New York Times*, June 16, 1978.

———. "Turning Off Party Machines Turned On the Candidates," *New York Times*, March 8, 1981.

———. "Jersey Primary Ballot Bill Signed," *New York Times*, March 24, 1981.

———. "Lan quits governor race; Byrne makes Degnan ad," *New York Times*, April 30, 1981.

———. "An Issue Emerges: The Byrne Arena," *New York Times*, October 4, 1981.

———. "Florio concedes governor's race to Kean in Jersey," *New York Times*, December 1, 1981.

———. "New Jersey Pinelands Preservation Works so Well it Hurts," *New York Times*, May 27, 1983.

———. "Sports Authority Facing Scrutiny," *New York Times*, November 15, 1987.

Sullivan, Ronald. "Jersey Assembly Rejects Proposal for an Income Tax," *New York Times*, July 18, 1972.

———. "Campaign Funds: Differing Views," *New York Times*, May 29, 1973.

———. "G.O.P. Leaders Say Sandman is Facing a Major Defeat," *New York Times*, October 28, 1973.

———. "Jersey Republicans Fear a Major Defeat," *New York Times*, November 4, 1973.

———. "Sandman Routed: GOP Loses Control of Legislature 3rd Time in Century," *New York Times*, November 8, 1973.

———. "Byrne Stand Kills Bond-Pledge Bill," *New York Times*, November 13, 1973.

———. "Byrne Displays His Pre-Inauguration Power," *New York Times*, December 4, 1973.

———. "Crabiel Chosen by Byrne to be Secretary of State," *New York Times*, December 5, 1973.

———. "Jersey Assembly Backs Bond Issue," *New York Times*, December 5, 1973.

———. "Byrne's Opposition Blocks Jersey Turnpike Extension," *New York Times*, December 17, 1973.

———. "Cahill Restates Income Tax Plea," *New York Times*, January 9, 1974.

———. "Byrne Appoints Insurance and Labor-Industry Chiefs," *New York Times*, January 11, 1974.

———. "Byrne Moves for Repeal of Covenant Curbing Port Authority Transit Aid," *New York Times*, February 14, 1974.

———. "A PATH Extension Ordered by Byrne," *New York Times*, February 14, 1974.

———. "Campaign Controls Voted in Jersey and Connecticut," *New York Times*, April 25, 1974.

———. "Byrne Tax Proposal Appears in Trouble; G.O.P. is Opposed," *New York Times*, June 14, 1974.

———. "Legislators Get Rival Tax Plans," *New York Times*, June 16, 1974.

———. "Foes of Byrne's Proposal Put Forth an Alternative," *New York Times*, June 19, 1974.

———. "Deep Trouble for Byrne," *New York Times*, August 2, 1974.

———. "Byrne's Advisers Credited with Ambitious Programs," *New York Times*, October 14, 1974.

———. "Jersey's Legislature Quits Without Acting on Tax," *New York Times*, December 20, 1974.

———. "Jersey Democrats Draft Tax Proposal To Net $700 Million," *New York Times*, December 24, 1974.

———. "Driscoll's Status on Panel in Doubt," *New York Times*, February 3, 1975.

———. "$2.8 Billion asked in Jersey Budget; Byrne Calls for New Taxes and 'Sacrifices' to Meet $487-Million Deficit," *New York Times*, February 4, 1975.

———. "$2.8 Billion Asked in Jersey Budget," *New York Times*, February 6, 1975.

———. "Jersey Employees Denounce Byrne," *New York Times*, February 6, 1975.

———. "Byrne Asks July 1 Deadline for School-Aid Legislation," *New York Times*, February 26, 1975.

———. "Byrne Now Expects to Get Income Tax Passed," *New York Times*, March 9, 1975.

———. "Funeral for Driscoll Held; Byrne Absent at Request," *New York Times*, March 13, 1975.

———. "Jersey Tax Vote is Tomorrow," *New York Times*, June 24, 1975.

———. "Jersey's Senate Bars Income Tax by a 21-to-17 Vote," *New York Times*, June 28, 1975.

———. "All called Losers in Jersey Tax Battle," *New York Times*, July 2, 1975.

Stile, Charles. "Seeds for liberal era take root from a defeat," *The Record*, July 26, 2009. Accessed January 22, 2013 at http://www.northjersey.com/news/politics/political_stile/Stile_Seeds_for_liberal_era_take_root_from_a_defeat.html?page=all.

Strauss, Robert S. "When casinos came to town: 30 facts about gambling's start in Atlantic City," *Philadelphia Daily News*, May 23, 2008. Accessed June 23, 2012 at http://articles.philly.com/2008-05-23/entertainment/25262329_1_casino-gambling-first-casino-second-casino.

Thomas, Robert McG, Jr. "Sonny Werblin, an Impresario of New York's Sports Extravaganza, Is Dead at 81," *New York Times*, November 23, 1981.

Tillman, Barrett. "The Forgotten Fifteenth," *Air Force Magazine*, September 2012. Accessed January 22, 2013 at http://www.airforcemag.com/MagazineArchive/Pages/2012/September%202012/0912fifteenth.aspx.

Time Magazine. "Democratic Hopefuls," November 24, 1958.

Tractenberg, Paul L. "Robinson v. Cahill: The 'Thorough and Efficient' Clause," *Law and Contemporary Problems* 38 (Winter 1974), 312. Accessed January 15, 2013 at http://scholarship.law.duke.edu/cgi/viewcontent.cgi?article=3413&context=lcp.

Trenton Times. "Governor should say it: 'I do not choose to run'," November 30, 1976.

———. "Byrne bans construction in Pinelands," February 9, 1979.

———. "Pinelands Moratorium," February 11, 1979.

———. "Many Jerseyans never heard of Pines," February 14, 1979.

———. "Crowd rips Pinelands building ban," February 18, 1979.

———. "James J. Sheeran," (obituary), July 17, 2007.

Tuite, James. "Hambletonian Race: Money vs. Tradition," *New York Times*, September 30, 1979.

Van Tassel, Priscilla. "Higher Education: Ongoing Challenge," *New York Times*, February 22, 1987.

Van Wagner, Richard. "The New Jersey Gross Income Tax: An Analysis from Background to Enactment," *Seton Hall Legislative Journal* 2 (Summer 1977), 100.

Waggoner, Walter H. "Courtrooms Calm as Trials Start for 27 Indicted in Newark Riots," *New York Times*, September 26, 1967.

———. "Byrne Attacks Sandman on the Income Tax Issue," *New York Times*, October 16, 1973.

———. "Turnpike Agency Contesting Byrne," *New York Times*, December 19, 1973.

———. "Byrne Says Plans to Add to Turnpike are Being Postponed," *New York Times*, December 28, 1973.

———. "Sullivan Reviews Record in Office," *New York Times*, January 23, 1974.

———. "State Aide Assails Property Tax Plans," *New York Times*, June 25, 1974.

———. "Budget Expert to Head School Reform," *New York Times*, February 6, 1975.

———. "High Court Hears Byrne on School Financing Issue," *New York Times*, March 19, 1975.

———. "2 Long-Disputed Projects to Begin," *New York Times*, July 9, 1977.

Wald, David. "Florio Concedes Race to Kean," *Star-Ledger*, December 1, 1981.

Waldron, Martin. "State Tells All Schools to Remove Asbestos Fibers as a Health Step," *New York Times*, January 7, 1977.

———. "The Region: An Urban Policy Begins To Take Shape in N.J.," *New York Times*, January 1, 1978.

———. "Hospital Rate-Setting Law is Signed by Byrne," *New York Times*, July 21, 1978.

———. "Land-Lust Bedevils the Pine Barrens," *New York Times*, July 30, 1978.

———. "Jersey Bus Service Declining Despite Big Subsidies," *New York Times*, April 19, 1979.

———. "Gov. Byrne Now Enjoys Both Perks and Power," *New York Times*, July 15, 1979.

———. "New Jersey Law Changes Reflect the New Morality," *New York Times*, August 10, 1979.

———. "Degnan Charges Caesars Had Mob Ties in Las Vegas," *New York Times*, February 8, 1980.

———. "Capital Report," *New York Times*, August 31, 1980.

———. "Jersey Acquires 2 Key Bus Lines for $32 million," *New York Times*, September 18, 1980.

Wefing, John B. "Search and Seizure-New Jersey Supreme Court v. United States Supreme Court," *Seton Hall Law Review* 7 (1975–1976), 771.

Weissman, Dan. "Dem hopefuls stage chaotic TV debate," *Star-Ledger*, June 4, 1973.

———. "Sports Complex: Byrne to decide soon on 'moral pledge'," *Star-Ledger*, November 8, 1973.

———. "Byrne neutrality sidelines sports complex aid," *Star-Ledger*, November 13, 1973.

———. "Sullivan quits state environment post," *Star-Ledger*, January 19, 1974.

———. "Income tax defeated," *Star-Ledger*, June 17, 1975.

———. "2% tax plan rejected, Assembly still at work," *Star-Ledger*, July 1, 1976.

———. "Assembly will vote on 2 to 2.5 pct. tax," *Star-Ledger*, July 3, 1976.

———. "Byrne puts 'core' of Pinelands into a development moratorium," *Star-Ledger*, February 9, 1979.

———. "Builders and Realtors will sue on Byrne's Pinelands moratorium," *Star-Ledger*, February 14, 1979.

———. "Senate clears broad controls over Pinelands development," *Star Ledger*, May 22, 1979.

———. "Byrne signs Pinelands control bill in 'emotional' Trenton ceremony," *Star-Ledger*, June 29, 1979.

———. "Assembly votes to uproot Byrne's power on Pinelands," *Star-Ledger*, June 17, 1980.

———. "'Compromise' emerges on Pines development," *Star-Ledger*, June 23, 1981.

Weissman, Dan and Philip Lentz. "Byrne signs tax bill," *Star-Ledger*, July 9, 1976.

Wollenberg, Skip. "Battle within state jeopardizes funds for Pines," *Courier-Post*, June 12, 1981.

Wood, Fran. "Former governor: Buono should consider dropping out of race," *Star-Ledger*, May 19, 2013.

Yoder, Allan F. "Jersey's $64 question: When will the governor govern?" *The Record*, November 24, 1974.

Zarate, Vincent. "One Thing Perfectly Clear in Passage of Income Tax," *Somerset Gazette*, July 18, 1974.

Zeitz, Carl. "Leone says two issues point to an income tax," *Star-Ledger*, April 1, 1974.

INTERNET RESOURCES AND PUBLICATIONS

American Presidency Project, University of California at Santa Barbara. Gerald Ford, transcript of remarks at October 13, 1976 campaign reception in Union, NJ. Accessed December 23, 2012 at http://www.presidency.ucsb.edu/ws/index.php?pid=6459&st=byrne&st1=brendan.

Answers Corp. "Caesar's World, Inc. Company History." Accessed August 12, 2012 at http://www.answers.com/topic/caesars-world-inc.

Bateman, Raymond P. "Byrne roast recalls better political times," mycentraljersey.com. Accessed April 7, 2014 at http://www.mycentraljersey.com/article/20140408/NJOPINION03/304080005/Byrne-roast-recalls-better-political-times.

Black, Archie. "Skinny D'Amato," *Atlantic City Newsletter*, Rat Pack Archive, March 2000. Accessed July 10, 2012 at http://www.ratpack.biz/rat-pack-archive/skinny-damato-atlantic-city-newsletter.htm.

Bergius, Friedrich. "Chemical reactions under high pressure," Nobel Lecture, May 21, 1932. Accessed January 2, 2013 at http://www.nobelprize.org/nobel_prizes/chemistry/laureates/1931/bergius-lecture.pdf.

Bohnstedt, Duane L. "Blechhammer," 15th Air Force. Accessed February 12, 2013 at http://www.15thaf.org/55th_BW/460th_BG/Stories/PDFs/Blechhammer.pdf.

Eastern Roads. nycroads.com. "Alfred E. Driscoll Expressway." Accessed January 12, 2013 at http://www.nycroads.com/roads/ae-driscoll/.

Education Law Center. "The History of Abbott." Accessed October 12, 2012 at http://www.edlawcenter.org/cases/abbott-v-burke/abbott-history.html.

Fagan, Joseph. "Fertile Farmland that Became the Pleasant Valley," WestOrangeHistory.com. Accessed May 26, 2012 at http://www.westorangehistory.com/id94.html.

Federal Bureau of Investigation. "Meyer Lansky," FBI Records: The Vault. Accessed October 4, 2012 at http://vault.fbi.gov/meyer-lansky.

———. "Abner Zwillman," FBI Records, The Vault. Accessed October 5, 2012 at http://vault.fbi.gov/Abner%20Zwillman.

Forrester, Wade. "May 27, 1982: The Colorado Rockies Hockey Franchise Is Sold," On this Day in Sports. Accessed January 12, 2013 at http://onthisdayinsports.blogspot.com/2013/05/may-27-1982-colorado-rockies-hockey.html.

Gambling in American History. "Gambling in American History: New Jersey and Atlantic City Casinos." Accessed August 23, 2012 at http://gamblinginamerica.name/new-jersey-and-atlantic-city-casinos-gambling-in-america/.

Gladwell, Malcolm. "The strange tale of the Norden bombsight," (video) TED Conferences July 2011. Accessed April 4, 2013 at http://www.ted.com/talks/malcolm_gladwell.html.

Hawkins, Eldridge. "The Rubin 'Hurricane' Carter and John Artis Investigation," GraphicWitness.com. Accessed July 2, 2011 at http://www.graphicwitness.com/carter/hawkins/pages/Hawkins_01%207/view.

Heller, Charles E. "Chemical Warfare in World War I: The American Experience, 1917–1918," Combat Studies Institute, US Army Command and General Staff College, Fort Leavenworth, KS, September 1984. Accessed December 4, 2012 at http://www.cgsc.edu/carl/resources/csi/heller/heller.asp.

History Learning Site. "B17 Flying Fortress," Accessed January 13, 2013 at http://www.historylearningsite.co.uk/b17_flying_fortress.htm.

Hughes, James J. and Joseph Seneca. "This Then and Now: Sixty Years of Economic Change in New Jersey," Rutgers Regional Report, January 2004, Edward J. Bloustein School of Planning and Public Policy, Rutgers University. Accessed January 10, 2013 at http://policy.rutgers.edu/reports/rrr/rrrjan04.pdf.

IMDb.com. "Pierre Norman." Accessed November 3, 2012 at http://www.imdb.com/name/nm0635604/bio.

Kozek, Barbara. "History of Atlantic City," City of Atlantic City. Accessed August 3, 2012 at http://www.cityofatlanticcity.org/about.aspx#history.

Lendio (www.fundinguniverse.com). "Resorts International, Inc. History." Accessed December 22, 2012 at http://www.fundinguniverse.com/company-histories/resorts-international-inc-history/.

Llewellyn Park Historical Society. "Llewellyn Park." Accessed July 25, 2012 at http://www.llewellynpark.com/History-of-Llewellyn-Park~101499~13266.htm.

Library of Congress. "Today in History: June 26, American Memory." Accessed July 19, 2010 at http://memory.loc.gov/ammem/today/jun26.html.

———. "Immigration." Accessed May 26, 2012 at http://www.loc.gov/teachers/classroommaterials/presentationsandactivities/presentations/immigration/irish4.html.

LyricsFreak.com. "On a Wing and a Prayer" (song lyrics by Harold Adamson). Accessed February 22, 2013 at http://www.lyricsfreak.com/r/ry+cooder/comin+in+on+a+wing+and+a+prayer_20171102.html.

National Baseball Hall of Fame and Museum. "Larry Doby." Accessed May 26, 2012 at http://baseballhall.org/hof/doby-larry.

New Jersey Future. "New Jersey Future to Honor Brendan Byrne." November 14, 2011. Accessed October 23, 2012 at http://www.njfuture.org/news/news-releases/2011-news-releases/brendan-byrne-event/.

New Jersey, (State of). Department of Military and Veterans Affairs. World War II oral history interview. "Oral History Interview with Jerome J. McCabe," December 21, 2001. Accessed May 3, 2012 at http://www.state.nj.us/military/museum/mccabe.html.

———. Department of Transportation. "People: The Transportation Connection," October 2001. Accessed January 12, 2013 at http://www.state.nj.us/transportation/publicat/people.pdf.

———. Governor's Select Commission on Civil Disorder. "Report for Action," February 1968. Accessed May 26, 2012 at http://blog.nj.com/ledgernewark/2007/06/report_for_action.html.

———. Liberty State Park. "History of Liberty State Park." Accessed May 3, 2012 at http://www.libertystatepark.com/history.htm.

———. Lottery Commission. "History of the New Jersey Lottery." Accessed August 3, 2012 at http://www.state.nj.us/lottery/general/6-2-2_history.htm.

———. New Jersey Transit. "History and Structure." Accessed January 22, 2013 at http://www.njtransit.com/tm/tm_servlet.srv?hdnPageAction=CorpInfoTo.

————. Tax Policy Committee, Summary Report. Accessed October 12, 2012 at http://www.state.nj.us/dca/affiliates/luarcc/meetings/2008/05-29-2008cahill_commissumry.pdf.

New York Botanical Garden. Mertz Library. Thomas Alva Edison Papers. Accessed September 12, 2013 at http://sciweb.nybg.org/science2/libr/finding_guide/edison2.asp.html Orange Township, City of. Township Historical Overview. Accessed September 12, 2012 at http://www.ci.orange.nj.us/history_main.html.

PBS.org. American Experience, "Carter's 'Crisis of Confidence' Speech," http://www.pbs.org/wgbh/americanexperience/features/general-article/carter-crisis-speech/.

Princeton University Library. Department of Rare Books and Special Collections. Dwight D. Eisenhower, White House Press Releases 1952–1961, "Henry Roemer McPhee, Jr." Accessed January 12, 2013 at http://findingaids.princeton.edu/collections/MC053.

Project Gutenberg. *Select Speeches of Daniel Webster, 1817–1845.* Accessed January 3, 2013 at http://infomotions.com/etexts/gutenberg/dirs/etext05/7sweb10.htm.

Rutgers University, Department of Sociology and Anthropology, University College-Newark. "The Newark and Detroit Riots of 1967." Accessed June 2, 2012 at http://www.67riots.rutgers.edu/index.htm.

Schkrutz, Eric. "Urban Development in the City of the Traveler: The Story of New Brunswick and Why It May Never Resolve Its Identity Crisis" (honors thesis submitted to the Department of History, Rutgers University), April 2011. Accessed October 12, 2012 at http://history.rutgers.edu/component/docman/cat_view/82-undergraduate/108-honors-papers-2011?start=20.

Simpson, Albert F. "Sicily and Southern Italy," in Wesley Frank Craven et al. (eds.), *The Army Air Forces in World War II.* Accessed January 12, 2013 at http://www.ibiblio.org/hyperwar/AAF/II/AAF-II-16.html.

Solomon, Nancy. "A Walking Tour: Newark Broad Street," WNYC.org. Accessed December 17, 2012 at http://www.wnyc.org/articles/wnyc-news/2011/dec/15/newark-broad-street/.

Thompson, George A. "Look to your right, look to your left—one of them won't be here next year," (blog entry) at "The Bug Apple," BarryPopik.com. Accessed July 22, 2013 at http://www.barrypopik.com/index.php/new_york_city/entry/look_to_your_right_look_to_your_left_one_of_them_wont_be_here_next_year/.

United States Senate, Special Senate Committee to Investigate Organized Crime in Interstate Commerce. Final Report, August 27, 1951. Accessed August 4, 2010 at http://www.nevadaobserver.com/Reading%20Room%20Documents/Kefauver%20Final%20Report.htm.

————. "Permanent Subcommittee on Investigations Historical Background," December 1, 2000. Accessed October 22, 2012 at http://www.hsgac.senate.gov/subcommittees/investigations/media/permanent-subcommittee-on-investigations-historical-background.

————. U.S. Senate Historical Office Oral History Project. Interview with Stewart McClure, May 3, 1983. Accessed September 11, 2012 at http://www.senate.gov/artandhistory/history/resources/pdf/McClure8.pdf.

Weiner, Robert. "To 'land' a date, Jewish kids found the 'Dunams'," *New Jersey Jewish News*, December 16, 2009. Accessed May 26, 2012 at http://njjewishnews. com/article/546/to-land-a-date-jewish-kids-found-the-dunams.

Winick, Stephen. "Tales of the Jersey Devil," Benjamin Botkin Lecture Series, American Folklife Center, Library of Congress, August 23, 2005. Accessed October 4, 2012 at http://www.loc.gov/folklife/events/BotkinArchives/2004thru2005PDFand Video/WinickFlyer.html.

JUDICIAL DECISIONS

Abbott v. Burke, 100 N.J. 269 (1985).

Abbott v. Burke, 119 N.J. 287 (1990).

Brennan v. Byrne, 31 N.J. 333 (1960).

Carter v. Rafferty, 826 F.2d 1299, U.S. Court of Appeals, 3rd Circuit (1987), *certiorari* denied 484 U.S. 1011 (1988).

Gardner v. New Jersey Pinelands Comm'n, 125 N.J. 193 (1991).

Escobedo v. Illinois, 378 U.S. 478 (1964).

Funicello v. New Jersey, 403 U.S. 948 (1971).

Heir v. Degnan, 82 N.J. 109 (1980).

In Re Quinlan, 70 N.J. 10, 355 (1976).

Lightning Lube, Inc. v. Witco Corp., 802 F.Supp. 1180 (US District Court N.J. 1992), affirmed 4 F.3d 1153 (US Court of Appeals, 3rd Circuit 1993).

Miranda v. Arizona, 384 U.S. 436 (1966).

Mapp v. Ohio, 367 U.S. 643 (1961).

New Jersey Builders Ass'n v. Byrne, 80 N.J. 469 (1979).

Orleans Builders & Developers v. Byrne, 186 N.J. Super. 432 (App. Div. 1982) certification denied 91 N.J. 528 (1982).

Robinson v. Cahill, 62 N.J. 473 (1973).

Robinson v. Cahill, 67 N.J. 35 (1975).

Robinson v. Cahill, 69 N.J. 449 (1976).

Robinson v. Cahill, 70 N.J. 465 (1976).

Serrano v. Priest, 5 Cal.3d 584 (1971).

State v. Bucanis, 26 N.J. 47 (1958).

State v. Carter, 69 N.J. 420 (1976).

State v. Cerce, 22 N.J. 236 (1956).

State v. Davis, 50 N.J. 16 (1967), *certiorari* denied, 389 U.S. 1054 (1968).

State v. Funicello, 49 N.J. 553 (1967).

State v. Funicello, 60 N.J. 60 (1972).

State v. Macri, 72 N.J. Super. 511, Law Div. (1962) affirmed 39 N.J. 250 (1963).

State v. White, 116 N.J. Super. 416 (Law Div. 1971).

United States v. Addonizio et al., 313 F.Supp. 486 (U.S. District Court N.J. 1970) affirmed U.S. Court of Appeals, 3rd Circuit (1987), 451 F.2d 49 (1971), *certiorari* denied 405 U.S. 936 (1972).

United States v. Jackson, 390 U.S. 570 (1968).

United States Trust Co. of New York v. New Jersey, 431 U.S. 1 (1977).

ARCHIVES

State of New Jersey, Department of State, New Jersey State Archives, http://www. nj.gov/state/archives/index.html.

Byrne, Brendan T. (filings) http://www.nj.gov/state/archives/catgovernors.html.

Rutgers University, Eagleton Institute of Politics, Center on the American Governor, Brendan T. Byrne Archive. Accessed April 15, 2014 at http://governors.rutgers. edu/on-governors/nj-governors/governor-brendan-t-byrne-administration.

Rutgers University, Rutgers Oral History Archives-World War II, Korean War, Vietnam War, Cold War. Accessed December 12, 2013 at http://oralhistory.rutgers. edu/military-history/29-conflict-index/164-world-war-ii-european-theater-index.

Rutgers University, Special Collections and University Archives, Rutgers University Libraries, Brendan T. Byrne Papers. Accessed December 12, 2013 at http://www2. scc.rutgers.edu/ead/manuscripts/brendanbyrnef.html.

Seton Hall University, Monsignor Field Archives & Special Collection Center, Brendan Byrne Papers. Accessed January 2, 2013 at http://academic.shu.edu/find-ingaids/mss0007.html#N10000.

State of New Jersey, Executive Orders of Governor Brendan T. Byrne, 1974–1982. Accessed January 2, 2013 at http://www.state.nj.us/infobank/circular/eoindex. htm#byrne.

CONFERENCES AND FORUMS

Rutgers University, Eagleton Institute of Politics, Center on the American Governor, Eagleton Institute of Politics, Brendan T. Byrne Archive. "Governor Brendan T. Byrne Colloquium," September 6, 2006. Accessed April 12, 2014 at http://governors.rutgers.edu/video-library/cag-forums/governor-brendan-t-byrne-opening-colloquium.

Rutgers University, Eagleton Institute of Politics, "The Pinelands Protection Act: A Discussion by Participants in the Process," October 15, 1987. Accessed January 2, 2014 at http://governors.rutgers.edu/testing/wp-content/uploads/2013/10/BTB-10-15-87Pinelandscolloquium.pdf.

Rutgers University, Eagleton Institute of Politics, Center on the American Governor, Eagleton Institute of Politics, Brendan T. Byrne Archive." Atlantic City: Looking Back and Ahead." Accessed January 2, 2014 at http://governors.rutgers.edu/test-ing/wp-content/uploads/2014/01/AtlanticCityRoundtable_transcript_5-10-07.pdf.

Rutgers University, Eagleton Institute of Politics, Center on the American Governor, Eagleton Institute of Politics, Brendan T. Byrne Archive and New Jersey State Bar Association. "New Jersey Governors and the State Supreme Court," transcript of conference May 8, 2008. Accessed April 12, 2014 at http://governors.rutgers.edu/ video-library/cag-forums/nj-governors-and-the-state-supreme-court.

Rutgers University, Eagleton Institute of Politics, Center on the American Governor, Eagleton Institute of Politics, Brendan T. Byrne Archive. "The Meadowlands and the Sports Complex: Looking Back and Ahead," September 24, 2009. Accessed April 12, 2014 at http://governors.rutgers.edu/testing/wp-content/uploads/2013/10/ TR-Meadowlands-forum.pdf

Index

abortion, BTB 1973 campaign position and concern over impact on Catholic vote, 102–3

Abbott v. Burke, 165, 234–35

Abscam scandal, 192–93, 284

Absecon Island, history of, 174; as site for bootlegging, 175

Addonizio, Hugh, meeting with Prosecutor BTB; election as Newark mayor in 1962, 58; pressure on Governor Hughes to remove BTB as Essex County Prosecutor, 60–61; conviction on federal extortion and conspiracy charges, 62, 319n72, 354n53; subject of mobster conversations recorded by FBI, 63; role in July 1967 Newark riots, 63–64

Adubato, Stephen, as leader of North Ward Educational and Cultural Center in Newark encouraging BTB to run in gubernatorial election, 78; view of BTB that support would help cut into DeRose vote in Essex County in 1973 primary election, 95

AFL-CIO (American Federation of Labor and Congress of Industrial Organizations), 212

Agee, James K., 111, 113, 200–3

Agency for Public Transit, 266

Ahr, George, 126

Alampi , Philip, as secretary of agriculture, 121, 333n55; role in Pinelands legislation, 250

alcoholic beverages, deregulation of price controls, 223

Alcoholic Beverage Commission, Governor Hughes offer to appoint Prosecutor BTB as director, 61

Alfred E. Driscoll Expressway, 111–12, 120, 242

Alexander, Archibald, as encouraging BTB to run for elected office, 77, 78

Ali, Muhammad, and Rubin "Hurricane" Carter case, 143; as BTB opponent in exhibition boxing match, 228; BTB comment on London assault compared to Ali match, 301

Alitalia Airlines, as BTB client, 290

AMTRAK, 273, 379n10

Anastasia, Albert, 59, 176

Andrus, Cecil, approval of Pinelands Comprehensive Management Plan, 232, 256; request to BTB for creation of Pinelands planning commission, 246; funding for Pinelands Commission, 375n102

413

About the Author

Donald Linky served as counsel to the governor and director of the Governor's office of policy and planning in the administration of Governor Brendan T. Byrne. He has previously practiced law with major firms in New Jersey and as general counsel to the New Jersey Business & Industry Association.

He is a co-editor of *the Governors of New Jersey: Biographical Essays* published by Rutgers University Press in 2014, and has been editor of the reference books *The New Jersey Directory: The Insider Guide to New Jersey Leaders* and *The New Jersey Almanac*. He also has been a monthly columnist for *New Jersey Reporter* and *New Jersey Business* magazines.

A former visiting professor and senior policy fellow at the Eagleton Institute of Politics of Rutgers University, he developed and coordinated the program at the Institute now known as the Center on the American Governor. A graduate of Dartmouth College and the Harvard Law School, he served as a law secretary to the Supreme Court of New Jersey.